THE BLACK HANDBOOK

THE BLACK HANDBOOK

THE PEOPLE, HISTORY AND POLITICS OF AFRICA AND THE AFRICAN DIASPORA

E.L. Bute and H.J.P. Harmer

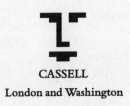

CASSELL

London and Washington

Cassell
Wellington House
125 Strand
London WC2R 0BB

PO Box 605
Herndon, VA 20172

First published 1997

British Library Cataloguing-in-Publication Data
Bute, E. L.
   The black handbook : the people, history and politics of
   Africa and the African diaspora
   1. African diaspora
   I. Title   II. Harmer, H. J. P.
   304.8'096

ISBN 0-304-33542-8 (hardback)
         0-304-33543-6 (paperback)

Designed and typeset by Ben Cracknell Studios
Printed and bound in Great Britain by Biddles Ltd,
Guildford and King's Lynn

CONTENTS

CONTENTS

≡ PREFACE ≡

The primary aim of *The Black Handbook* has been to assemble, in a single volume, the key events, personalities, ideas, facts and figures of historical and contemporary Africa and the African Diaspora. As the story is one of wide-ranging achievement and tragedy it is inevitable that much has to be left out. The authors ask readers to help remedy this by making suggestions for inclusion in a future edition.

It would have been impossible to produce *The Black Handbook* without access to institutional and public libraries and the help of the peple who work in them. The authors want to thank particularly the Library of the School of Oriental and African Studies in London, the National Army Museum Library in Chelsea, the Public Record Office in Kew, the United Nations Information Centre in London and the Information Service Reference Center at the US Embassy in London. Despite constant cuts in their budgets, public libraries continue to provide a valuable service. We want to thank the Islington, Haringey, Hackney, Westminster and Lambeth library services.

On a more personal level, the authors wish to mention a number of people who have helped with suggestions or in other ways. Chris Cook and James Robinson were constantly encouraging, as was Erif Rison (who will remind us what is missing). Among others who made this book possible were Paul Yates, Charlotte Helliwell, Martin Tupper, Caroline Hall, Mircea Campeanu, Alex Louis, Ruth Bush, Emelda Bute, Annie Shaw, and Jon and Karen Hayon (who diverted us by getting married). Helen Brown made us start it and Chelsey Fox made it possible for us to do so. Finally, to Anna Harmer, Tom Harmer and Rosie Tattersall, who were particularly neglected while we were preoccupied with producing *The Black Handbook*, we hope you think it was worth it.

For
Iona Lotina Bute, Gerald Kitchener Bute,
Ruby Lavinia Harmer, Harry Thomas Harmer
and Alice Lavinia Rockett

PEOPLE

ABACHA, Sani (born 1943)
Nigerian military ruler

Educated Nigerian, British, US military academies. Leading member of coup which overthrew civilian government, 1983. Chief of Army Staff, 1985. Leading participant in military coup, 1985. Minister of Defence, 1985–93. Seized power in military coup, 1993. Convened National Constitutional Conference (NCC), 1994. NCC announced Abacha would have open-ended term of office, 1995. Survived attempted coup, March 1995.

ABBOTT, Diane Julie (born 1953)
British politician

Born in London of Jamaican parents. Educated Harrow County Girls' Grammar School and Newnham College, Cambridge University. Home Office administrative trainee; National Council for Civil Liberties race relations officer; television researcher and reporter; press officer for Greater London Council and London Borough of Lambeth. Joined Labour Party, 1971; active in party Black Sections movement. Member of Westminster City Council, 1982–6. Elected as first black woman Member of Parliament for Hackney and Stoke Newington, 1987. Secretary, Parliamentary Black Caucus.

ABBOTT, Robert Sengstacke (1870–1940)
US publisher

Born St Simon Island, Georgia. Studied law at Kent College, Chicago; graduated 1898. Practised law until 1905. Founded the influential black newspaper *Chicago Defender*, 1905. Appointed member of State Race Relations Commission following the 1919 Chicago race riots. His newspaper campaigned against segregation and discrimination and encouraged black migration to the northern states. Prominent in the National Urban League.

ABERNATHY, Ralph David (born 1926)
US clergyman and civil rights leader

Born Linden, Alabama. Baptist minister; rose to prominence with Martin Luther King, Jr, during the Montgomery bus boycott, 1955; co-founder with King of the Southern Christian Leadership Conference (SCLC), 1957, acting as secretary-treasurer. Appointed pastor in Atlanta, 1961. SCLC President, 1968–77. Organized the Poor People's Campaign and Resurrection City, USA in Washington, DC, 1968, and imprisoned for 20 days; organized SCLC's Operation Breadbasket in Atlanta, 1967–71.

ACHEAMPONG, Ignatius Kutu (1931–79)
Ghanaian military ruler

Born in Asante. A teacher, he joined the army, 1953; commissioned in 1959. Trained in Britain and the USA. Served in United Nations peacekeeping force in the Congo (now Zaïre), 1959, 1962–3. Led military coup in 1972, appointing himself Chairman of the National Redemption Council and of the Supreme Military Council, Minister of Defence and of Sport. Suspended the 1969 constitution. Attempted to encourage self-sufficiency in Operation Feed Yourself, 1972. Proposal for military–civilian Union Government approved in an allegedly rigged referendum, 1978. Growing unpopularity forced his ousting by fellow officers in 1978. Executed following trial by Armed Forces Revolutionary Council, 1979.

ADAMS, Grantley Herbert (1898–1971)
Barbados politician

Born at Government Hill, Barbados; educated Barbados and Oxford University; practised as a lawyer. Elected to House of

Assembly, 1934; president of the Barbados Workers' Union, 1941. A founder of the Barbados Labour Party (BLP), 1938; elected president of the Caribbean Labour Congress, 1947. Chief Minister of Barbados, 1948–58; Premier, 1954–8. First and only prime minister of the West Indies Federation, 1958–62. Following collapse of the federation in 1962, he withdrew from politics until becoming Barbados House of Assembly opposition leader, 1966–70.

ADAMS, Tom (1931–85)
Barbados politician

Barrister and journalist trained in Britain. Returned to Barbados, 1962. Assistant general-secretary of the Barbados Labour Party (BLP) led by his father Grantley Adams, 1965; elected to the House of Assembly in 1966. He became opposition leader in 1971 after the defeat of the BLP and the death of his father. In 1973 he became BLP leader and was elected prime minister in 1976 when the BLP won the elections. He supported the US invasion of Grenada in 1983.

AFONSO I (died c.1543)
Ruler of the Kongo kingdom (in what is now Angola, Congo and Zaïre)

A Christian; seized the throne in 1506. Obtained Portuguese technical and military support in return for granting trading concessions, including slavery. Unsuccessfully attempted to curb slave trade by decree, 1526. His son was consecrated as a bishop in Rome. Survived Portuguese assassination attempt, 1540. Enlarged kingdom through conquest but failed to reduce growing Portuguese influence.

AFRIFA, Akwasi (1936–79)
Ghanaian military ruler

Born in Asante; joined the army in 1957; trained in Britain and served with United Nations peacekeeping force in the Congo (now Zaïre), 1962. A leader of the coup that ousted Nkrumah, 1966. Member of the National Liberation Council (NLC), 1966–9. Chair of the NLC and Head of State, 1969. Restored civilian rule. Chair of the Presidential Commission, member of the Council of State, 1969–72. Supporter of the failed Busia coup in 1972, he was imprisoned until 1973. Elected to the National Assembly, 1979. Charged with corruption and executed by the Armed Forces Revolutionary Council, 1979.

AGUIYI-IRONSI, Johnson Thomas Umunankwe (1924–66)
Nigerian military ruler

Joined the army, 1942. Lieutenant-colonel on independence, 1960. Served with United Nations peacekeeping force in the Congo (now Zaïre), 1961. General Officer Commanding, 1965. Participated in Nigeria's first military coup which overthrew the civilian government, 1966. Became Head of the Federal Military Government and Armed Forces Supreme Commander. Abolished Nigeria's federal structure, May 1966. An Ibo, other groups in Nigeria feared that his group would become dominant. Assassinated in Nigeria's second military coup, July 1966.

AHIDJO, Ahmadou (1924–89)
Cameroon politician

Post-office radio-operator. Member of Territorial Assembly, 1947–58; member of the French National Assembly, 1953–6; Vice-president and Interior Minister, 1957–8. Prime Minister of Autonomous French Cameroon, 1958–60. First president on independence in 1960, amalgamating the country with British Cameroons in 1961. Re-elected five times (with 99 per cent of the vote in 1975); retired through ill-health, 1982. Retired to France; remained president of the Union Nationale Camerounaise (UNC). Attempted to regain power through a coup in 1984. Sentenced to death in absence, he remained in exile in France.

AKANG'O, Odera (c.1878–1919)
Luo chief in Kenya
Appointed a sub-chief by the British colonial authorities, 1901. Encouraged agriculture and instituted compulsory labour. Appointed full chief, 1915. Following tour of Uganda, introduced compulsory primary education, construction schemes and afforestation. Moved by the British to Teso area, 1916. Deposed and detained by the British because of his unpopularity. Died in mysterious circumstances the day before his release.

AKUFFO, Frederick W. K. (1937–79)
Ghanaian military ruler
Civil servant, 1955–7. Joined army; served with United Nations peacekeeping force in the Congo (now Zaïre). Member of Supreme Military Council (SMC), 1975–9. Chief of Defence Staff, 1976–8. Chairman of the SMC and Head of State, 1978. Lifted ban on political parties, 1979. Ousted by Armed Forces Revolutionary Council and executed, June 1979.

AMATHILA, Libertine (born 1940)
Namibian politician
Trained as a doctor in Poland, Britain, Mali, Tanzania and Sweden. Director of the South West Africa People's Organisation (SWAPO); member of the SWAPO Politburo, 1991. Deputy Minister for Health and Welfare, 1991–3; Minister of Local Government and Housing, 1993.

AMIN DADA, Idi Oumee (born 1924)
Ugandan military ruler
A member of the Kakwa tribe. Joined the King's African Rifles in 1943; served in Burma and Kenya. An officer on independence in 1962. Commander of the armed forces, 1966–70. Following his dismissal by President Obote, Amin overthrew the government in January 1971. Abolished the constitution, declaring himself Life President. Purged the security forces of thousands of Acholi and Langi tribe members. Instituted martial law under which 300,000 Ugandans died. Ordered mass expulsion of Asians, 1972. Chairman of the Organization of African Unity (OAU), 1975–6; invaded Tanzania in 1978. Overthrown by Tanzanian forces and Ugandan dissidents, April 1979. Went into exile in Libya and Saudi Arabia. Unsuccessfully attempted to return to Uganda via Zaïre in 1989; renewed exile in Saudi Arabia.

ANKRAH, Joseph Arthur (born 1915)
Ghanaian military ruler
Teacher. Joined the army, 1942; commissioned, 1947. Served with United Nations peacekeeping force in the Congo (now Zaïre), 1960–1. Decorated for saving the life of Patrice Lumumba. Deputy Chief of Defence Staff, 1961–5. Forced to resign by Nkrumah. Chairman of the National Liberation Council (NLC) following February 1966 military coup. Head of State, 1966–9. Resigned following corruption allegations by NLC, 1969.

ARCHER, John Robert (1863–1932)
British political and Pan-Africanist activist
Born in Liverpool; moved to London, 1890. Worked as a photographer in Battersea. Elected to Battersea Borough Council, 1906; Mayor of Battersea, 1913. Founding president of the African Progress Union, 1918;

British delegate to the Pan-African Conference, 1919. Held position of deputy Labour Party leader on Battersea Council on his death.

ARISTIDE, Jean-Bertrand (born 1952)
Haitian priest and politician
Born in Port-au-Prince; educated by the Salesian Order of Missionaries. Priest in Port-au-Prince; anti-Duvalier activist; supporter of radical liberation theology; survived assassination attempt, 1986. Expelled from the Salesian Order for political activities, 1988. Formed and led the National Front for Change and Democracy; elected President, 1990. Instituted an anti-corruption campaign; purged the military of Duvalier supporters. Ousted in military coup, September 1991; in exile in Venezuela and the USA. Restored to office, 1994.

ATTUCKS, Crispus (1723–70)
American revolutionary
Son of an African and a native American. Escaped from slavery to become a sailor. Attended meetings attacking British taxation of the American colonies; wrote a protest letter to the provincial governor. First to die in a clash with British soldiers in Dock Square, Boston, on 5 March 1770.

AWOLOWO, Obafemi (1908–87)
Nigerian politician
A Yoruba. Journalist and trade union leader. Studied law in London, 1944–6; called to the Bar. Returned to Nigeria to establish the Action Group to promote Yoruba culture. Chief Minister of Nigeria's Western Region, 1954. Built the Action Group into a national party. Federal opposition leader, 1959. Imprisoned 1962–6 for alleged conspiracy to overthrow the federal government. Founded United Party of Nigeria (UNP), 1978. Stood unsuccessfully for the federal presidency in 1979 and 1983.

AZIKIWE, Benjamin Nnamdi (1904–96)
Nigerian politician
An Ibo. Educated at mission schools and Universities of Pennsylvania and Columbia. Taught at Lincoln University; newspaper owner and editor and a banker in Nigeria and the Gold Coast (now Ghana). Founded Nigerian Youth Movement, 1944; president of the National Council of Nigeria and the Cameroons, 1946–60. Member of the Western House of Assembly, 1952–4; Premier of Eastern Nigeria, 1954–9. First Governor-General of independent Nigeria, 1960. Elected president when Nigeria became a republic, 1963; deposed in a military coup, 1966. Adviser to the secessionist Biafran government, 1967. Chancellor of Lagos University, 1972. Became leader of Nigeria People's Party and ran unsuccessfully for the federal presidency in 1979 and 1983. Among his writings are *My Odyssey* (1971), *Military Revolution in Nigeria* (1972), *Democracy with Military Vigilance* (1974).

BABANGIDA, Ibrahim (born 1941)
Nigerian military ruler
Joined Nigerian army, 1963; fought in Biafran Civil War, 1967–70. Chief of Staff following 1973 military coup. President and Armed Forces Commander-in-Chief following bloodless coup, 1985. Austerity measures provoked serious rioting, 1989. Promised return to civilian rule by 1992. Banned political parties but formed two officially backed parties, 1989. Survived attempted coup, 1990. Refused to allow results of June 1993 presidential elections to be released. Resigned, August 1993.

BAGAZA, Jean-Baptiste (born 1946)
Burundi politician
A Tutsi; educated in Belgium; joined the Burundi army; rose to position of Deputy

Chief of Staff. Seized power from President Micombero in bloodless coup, 1976. President, 1976–87. Ousted in military coup, September 1987; exiled to Belgium.

BAKER, Ella (1903–86)
US civil rights activist
Born in North Carolina; moved to New York City. Worked for *American West Indian News* and *Negro National News*. National director, Young Negroes' Co-operative League, 1932. National Association for the Advancement of Colored People (NAACP) field secretary and branch director in southern states, 1940–46. Appointed Southern Christian Leadership Conference (SCLC) executive director, 1958. Broke with SCLC; Student Non-Violent Co-ordinating Committee (SNCC) activist from 1960. Co-ordinator, Mississippi Freedom Democratic Party. Worked for Southern Conference Educational Fund and active in campaigns for African independence struggles.

BALEWA, Alhaji (Sir) Abubakar Tafawa (1912–66)
Nigerian politician
A Hausa. Trained as a teacher; became an education officer. Elected to the Northern Region House of Assembly in 1946; member of Central Legislative Council, 1947–52. Deputy president-general, Northern People's Congress (NPC). Minister of Works, 1952–4; Federal Minister of Transport, 1954–7. First prime minister of the Federation of Nigeria, 1957, remaining in office on independence in 1960. Government discredited by corruption. Assassinated in a military coup, 1966.

BANANA, Canaan Sodindo (born 1936)
Zimbabwean politician
Teacher; church minister. Founder member of the African National Council, 1971. Lived in USA, 1973–5. Imprisoned on return to Rhodesia, 1975–6. Joined Zimbabwe African National Union; arrested and detained 1978–9. First post-independence president of Zimbabwe, a ceremonial post, 1980–87.

BANDA, Hastings Kamuzu (born 1905)
Malawian politician
Clerk in South Africa. Studied political science at Chicago University, medicine at Mecheray Medical School, Nashville, Tennessee and Edinburgh University. Doctor in England and the Gold Coast (now Ghana); President-General of the African National Congress, Nyasaland, 1958. Campaigned against the Central African Federation; arrested by British during state of emergency imposed following riots, 1959; released in 1960 to become leader of Malawi Congress Party (MCP) and to negotiate independence. Became prime minister on independence, 1964; president on declaration of a republic, 1966. Established relations with apartheid South Africa, 1970. President for life, 1971. Defeated in referendum on introduction of multi-party democracy, 1993. Lost presidential election, 1994. Acquitted of charge of a 1983 conspiracy to murder three ministers, 1995.

BARRE, Mohamed Siad (born c.1919)
Somali politician
Educated in military academy, Italy. Police officer under Italian and then British colonial authorities, 1941–50. Joined Somali army, 1960. Led bloodless coup, 1969; formed Supreme Military Council and the country's sole legal party, the Somali Revolutionary Socialist Party (SRSP). SRSP confirmed him as national president for a further seven years, 1986. Deposed following a long period of inter-clan warfare, 1991.

BARROW, Errol Walton (1920–87)
Barbados politician

Educated in Barbados; went to England in 1940 and served throughout World War II in the Royal Air Force, reaching rank of flight-lieutenant. Qualified as a lawyer, 1949. Elected as Barbados Labour Party (BLP) member of the House of Assembly, 1951. Founder member of the Democratic Labour Party, 1955. Premier of Barbados, 1961–6; prime minister, 1966–76, 1985–7.

BELL, Rudolph Douala Mango
(1873–1914)
Cameroon resistance leader

Educated in Germany; succeeded father as chief, 1908. Accused German colonial authorities of breaking treaty by annexing land, 1910; Germans removed his title, 1913. Organized resistance force with Martin-Paul Samba. Executed by German authorities for encouraging rebellion at the outbreak of World War I, 1914.

BELLO, (Sir) Ahmadu (1906–66)
Nigerian politician

Educated in Nigeria and England. Holder of the traditional military title of Sardauna of Sokoto; founder and leader of the Northern People's Congress 1951. First elected minister in Northern Nigeria, 1952. Prime Minister of the Northern Region on the formation of the Federation of Nigeria, 1954. On independence in 1960, his party united with the National Council of Nigeria and the Cameroons (NCNC) to control the federal parliament. Assassinated in a military coup in 1966.

BERRY, Abner Winston (Baba Sufu)
(1902–87)
US radical political activist

Packing plant worker in Chicago; reporter on black magazine in Houston. Joined Communist Party (CP), 1929. Organized black and white Unemployed Council in Kansas City, 1931. Elected to CP Central Committee, 1934. Party organizer in Upper Harlem, 1934–40. *Daily Worker* reporter, 1940–42. Served in Europe with army. Returned to newspaper reporting. Resigned from the CP, 1957. Worked as a journalist. Taught Marxism to black activists; joined the African People's Party. Organized African Liberation Day in Washington, DC, 1974. Involved in formation of Black Workers for Justice in North Carolina.

BETHUNE, Mary McLeod (1875–1955)
US educationalist

Born Maysville, South Carolina. Educated at Scotia College, North Carolina, 1888–95; Moody Bible Institute in Chicago, 1895–7. In 1904 founded Daytona Normal and Industrial Institute for Negro Girls, Florida, which became Bethune–Cookman College in 1927; president until 1947. President of the National Association of Colored Women's Clubs, 1924–8; founder of the National Association of Colored Women, 1926; founder and president of the National Council of Negro Women, 1935–49. Appointed administrator of the Office of Minority Affairs by President Franklin D. Roosevelt, 1935; a director of the Division of Negro Affairs; the National Business League, the National Urban League, and the Commission of Inter-racial Co-operation. Director of the National Youth Administration Division of Negro Affairs. The first black American woman to head a federal office.

BIKO, Steve (1947–77)
South African black consciousness leader

Born in Kingwilliamstown, Natal. Studied medicine at the University of Natal Medical School; co-founder of the South African Students Organisation (SASO), 1969.

Became honorary president of the black consciousness movement, the Black People's Convention (BPC), 1972. The BPC was banned in 1973. Organized the Black Community Programme in opposition to apartheid. Subject to a government Banning Order, 1972; arrested frequently between 1973–6. Murdered in custody by South African police, September 1977.

BINAISA, Godfrey Luskwongwa
(born 1920)
Ugandan politician
Educated Makerere College; called to the Bar in England. Lawyer in Uganda, 1956–62; joined Ugandan People's Congress. Attorney-General, 1962–7; resigned over imposition of new constitution by Obote. Lived in USA during the regime of Amin. Returned to Uganda following Amin's overthrow in 1979, becoming president. Deposed in military coup, 1980, following tribal divisions and economic problems.

BIRD, Vere Cornwall   (born 1903)
Antiguan politician
Founder member of the Antigua Trade and Labour Union, 1939; became union president, 1941. Elected to the Legislative Council, 1940. Negotiated successful end to the 1951 sugar workers' strike. Chief Minister of Antigua, 1960–7; Premier 1967–71. Re-elected in 1976; became first prime minister of independent Antigua and Barbuda, 1981. Re-elected 1985, 1989.

BISHOP, Maurice Rupert   (1944–83)
Grenadian politician
Born in Aruba of Grenadian parents. Educated in Grenada and USA; qualified as a barrister in England, 1969. Returned to Grenada, 1970, and formed an organization which became the New Jewel Movement in 1972. Imprisoned, 1973–4, for accusing the Gairy government of corruption and autocracy. Elected to the House of Representatives in 1976, becoming leader of the opposition. Led the coup which overthrew Gairy, March 1979. Suspended constitution and formed a People's Revolutionary Government (PRG); nationalized assets and attempted reforms in the face of external opposition. Deposed and killed by fellow PRG members, 1983.

BLAIZE, Herbert Augustus   (1918–89)
Grenadian politician
Born on the island of Carriacou; worked as a civil servant. Elected to the Legislative Council, 1957; the first chief minister, 1960. Premier for six months when Grenada became an Associated State in 1967. Opposed both the Gairy government and the People's Revolutionary Government of Maurice Bishop. Returned to office, 1984.

BLYDEN, Edward Wilmot   (1832–1912)
Liberian emigrationist and politician
Born St Thomas, West Indies. Emigrated to USA, 1850. Emigrated to Liberia under New York Colonization Society sponsorship, 1850. Monrovia high school principal, 1857. Professor of Classics and Liberia College president. Secretary of State, 1864–6; Minister of the Interior, 1880–82; Ambassador to Britain, 1877–8, 1892. Director of Education, 1901–6. Encouraged black American migration to Liberia; a forerunner of *négritude*. Wrote, among many other works, *Christianity, Islam and the Negro Race*.

BOATENG, Paul Yaw   (born 1951)
British politician
Born Gold Coast (now Ghana); educated Ghana International School, Accra Academy, Apsley Grammar School, and Bristol University. Moved to Britain, 1966. Joined Labour Party, 1966. Qualified as a solicitor, 1976; called to the Bar, 1989. Labour Party

member of the Greater London Council, 1981–6; chairman of Police Committee. Elected as Member of Parliament for Brent South, 1987; severed links with Labour Party Black Sections movement, 1988. Opposition spokesman on Treasury and economic affairs, 1989–92; spokesman on legal affairs from 1992.

BOGLE, Paul (c.1825–65)
Jamaican leader
Born a slave, he lived at Stony Gut in the south-east of the island. Appointed deacon of Stony Gut Baptist Church in the 1860s, he concentrated his activity on improving the conditions of the poor. Led two demonstrations in Morant Bay in 1865, the second of which became the Morant Bay Uprising. Arrested, tried summarily and hanged.

BOKASSA, Jean-Bédel (1921–96)
Central African Republic military ruler
Member of the French Colonial Army, 1939–60. Commissioned, 1956. Chief of Staff, 1962. Overthrew his cousin President Dacko, appointing himself president, 1966. Declared and crowned himself emperor, 1977. Ousted and replaced by Dacko when French withdrew support, 1979. Retired to the Côte d'Ivoire and then to France. Returned to the Central African Republic in 1986; tried for embezzlement, cannibalism and murder. Sentenced to hard labour for life, 1988; released 1994.

BONGO, Omar (Albert-Bernard) (born 1935)
Gabonese politician
Educated Brazzaville. Joined French civil service, 1957; head of Ministry of Information and Tourism, 1963. Minister of National Defence, 1964–5; appointed vice-president, 1966. Became president on death of M'Ba, 1967. Declared a one-party state, with his Parti Démocratique Gabonais (PDG) the sole legal party, 1968. Survived a series of attempted military coups and popular protests. Converted to Islam, 1973. Forced to legalize opposition parties, 1990. PDG won elections amid allegations of fraud. Re-elected in 1993.

BOUKMAN (dates unknown)
Haitian slave leader
Led black slaves in the Haiti Revolution, 1791. A decree had given political rights to people born of free parents, discriminating against mulattos. Black slaves under Boukman joined the mulatto uprising in which plantations were destroyed, 10,000 slaves and mulattos were killed and 2000 whites died.

BRADSHAW, Robert (1916–78)
St Kitts and Nevis politician
Sugar factory worker; founder member of St Kitts' first trade union, 1940, becoming president in 1944. Founder member of the St Kitts and Nevis Labour Party, 1946. Elected to the Legislative Council, 1946; deputy president, 1956. Trade and Production Minister, 1956–8. West Indies Federation Minister of Finance, 1958–62. St Kitts Chief Minister, 1966; Premier, 1967–78.

BRAITHWAITE, Nicholas (born 1925)
Grenadian politician
Teacher. Chief Education Officer, 1969–74. Worked in Guyana, 1975–83. Chairman of Advisory Council which governed Grenada following 1983 US invasion. Elected leader of opposition National Democratic Congress, 1989. Prime Minister, Minister for External Affairs, Finance, and National Security following election victory, 1990.

BRAMBLE, William Henry (1902–88)
Montserrat politician

A farmer and carpenter, he joined a trade union in 1951 and became its president in 1954. Served as member of the Legislative Council, 1952–8, and as Montserrat representative in the West Indies Federation Parliament, 1958–61. Chief Minister of Montserrat from 1961; he retired from politics on his election defeat in 1970.

BRAUN, Carol Moseley (born 1947)
US politician

Born in Chicago; educated at University of Illinois and University of Chicago Law School. Assistant US Attorney, 1973–7. Elected to Illinois State Legislature, 1979. Cook County Recorder of Deeds, 1986. Elected first black woman member of US Senate, 1992.

BRIGGS, Cyril (1887–1966)
US radical political activist

Born in the Caribbean; emigrated to New York, 1905. Reporter and editor, *Amsterdam News*. Founded and edited monthly magazine, *The Crusader*, 1918. A Pan-Africanist and a socialist; advocated communism for the US and an independent black state, 1921. Initially sympathetic to the Universal Negro Improvement Association; turned against the support of Garvey for capitalism. Formed the Crusader News Service, 1922. Edited the newspaper of the American Negro Labor Congress. Contributed from 1936 to *Negro Worker*, the organ of the International Trade Union Committee of Negro Workers. Expelled from the Communist Party (CP) for continuing to advocate black nationalism, 1939. Rejoined the CP in the late 1940s, working as an official in Los Angeles.

BROWN, H. Rap (Jamil Abdullah Al-Amin) (born 1943)
US civil rights activist

Chairman of the Student Non-Violent Co-ordinating Committee (SNCC), 1967. Underwent a number of trials; accused of inciting a riot in Louisiana. Disappeared following death of two colleagues in a car explosion, 1970. Wounded in gun battle with police following a bar robbery in New York, 1971. Arrested and imprisoned, 1973. Converted to Islam while in prison; leader of the Community Mosque, Atlanta, Georgia, following release. *Die Nigger Die* published in 1969.

BROWN, Ronald Harmon (1941–96)
US politician and businessman

Born in Washington, DC; grew up in New York. Qualified as a lawyer; worked with the Urban League and the Senate Judiciary Committee. Active in Edward Kennedy's Presidential nomination campaign, 1980. Lobbyist for the Sugar Growers of Guatemala and Jean Claude Duvalier. Elected Democratic Party chairman, 1989; organized Clinton presidential campaign, 1992. Killed in aircraft crash leading a mission to gain contracts for American business in the reconstruction of Bosnia and Croatia.

BRUCE, Blanche Kelso (1841–98)
US politician

Born a slave in Farmville, Virginia. Escaped and set up black school, 1861; became a planter in Mississippi; sheriff, revenue collector, school superintendent. Elected to the US Senate; the first black American to serve a full term, 1875–81. US Treasury registrar, 1871–89, 1895–8; District of Columbia recorder of deeds, 1889–93.

BRUCE, John Edward (1856–1924)
US journalist and activist

Born Piscataway, Maryland, to slave parents. Educated in Washington, DC. Joined *New York Times*, 1874, and contributed to the *Progressive American* and other newspapers. Founded *The Argus*, 1875, and the *Sunday Item*, the first black Sunday newspaper, in 1879. Adopted lifelong pen name 'Bruce Grit' in 1884. Opposed inter-racial marriage and supported defensive violence. Co-founder of the Negro Society for Historical Research, 1911. Joined Universal Negro Improvement Association, 1918; known as the 'Duke of Uganda'.

BUHARI, Muhammadu (born 1942)
Nigerian military ruler

Joined the army, 1962; served in United Nations peacekeeping force in the Congo (now Zaïre). Appointed a Military State Governor, 1975. Federal Commissioner for Petroleum and Energy, 1976. Returned to the army on restoration of civilian rule, 1979. Head of State and Commander-in-Chief of the Armed Forces following military coup, 1983. Ousted by Babangida, 1985; under arrest until 1988.

BUNCHE, Ralph Johnson (1904–71)
US diplomat and academic

Born in Detroit; educated University of California, Harvard and London School of Economics. Taught at Howard University; contributed to influential book on race relations, *An American Dilemma*, 1944. Lifelong supporter of the National Association for the Advancement of Colored People (NAACP). Served in World War II with the US Joint Chiefs of Staff and the State Department. Joined Secretariat of the United Nations (UN), 1946. As a member of the Palestine Peace Commission, 1947, negotiated a truce between Arabs and Jews and became the first black American to be awarded the Nobel Peace Prize. Director of the UN Trusteeship Division, 1948–54. As UN Under-Secretary for Political Affairs, responsible for peacekeeping operations in Suez (1956), Congo (1960) and Cyprus (1964). Awarded Presidential Medal of Freedom, 1963.

BUSIA, Kofi Abrefa (1913–78)
Ghanaian politician

Member of an Asante royal family. Sociologist and writer. Elected to the Legislative Council, 1954. Opponent of independence under Nkrumah in 1957; forced into exile, 1959. Prime Minister, following election victory after restoration of civilian rule, 1969. Imposed austerity measures, expelled Nigerians, repressed trade unions. Overthrown in military coup, 1972. Died in exile in England.

BUTHELEZI, Gatsha Mangosuthu (born 1928)
South African politician

Educated at Fort Hare University College, 1948–50. Zulu hereditary chief of the Buthelezi clan, 1953. Joined the African National Congress (ANC) as a student, but was expelled in 1950. Chief Executive Officer, KwaZulu territorial authority, 1970–72. Chief Executive Councillor, KwaZulu Legislative Assembly, 1972. Chief Minister of KwaZulu, 1976. Revived Inkatha (founded by his grandfather King Dinizulu), 1974; opposed sanctions and use of violence to remove apartheid regime. Home Affairs Minister in post-apartheid Government of National Unity, 1994.

BUTLER, Tubal Uriah ('Buzz')
(1891–1977)
Trinidadian politician

Born in Grenada; served in the British West Indies Regiment in World War I. Founded Grenada Union of Returned Soldiers. Emigrated to Trinidad, 1921. Worked as a pipe fitter; invalided out of oil industry following injury, 1929. Chief pastor of the Butlerite Moravian Baptist Church, 1931. Joined Trinidad Workingmen's Association (TWA); led a hunger march from the oil fields to Port of Spain in 1935. Formed British Empire Workers' and Citizens' Home Rule Party, 1936. British authorities' attempt to arrest him led to Caribbean-wide riots. Imprisoned for sedition, 1937–9; detained without trial, 1939–45. Expelled from the Oilfield Workers' Trade Union for advocating a general strike, 1946. Formed British Empire Workers', Peasants' and Ratepayers' Union, 1946. Won majority of seats in 1950 elections but denied power by British governor of island. Lived in England, 1951–6.

CABRAL, Amilcar Lopes (1924–73)
Guinea nationalist leader

Born in Cape Verde islands; educated in Portugal where he was active in anti-fascist protests; graduated from the Lisbon Institute of Agronomy, 1952. Returned to Guinea-Bissau to work as an engineer agronomist, 1953, but was exiled for anti-colonial activity in 1955. Working in Angola, he was involved in founding the Popular Movement for the Liberation of Angola (MPLA). In 1956 he founded and became leader of the African Party for the Independence and Union of the Peoples of Guinea and Cape Verde (PAI), renamed the African Party for the Independence of Guinea and Cape Verde (PAIGC) in 1960. Led guerrilla struggle from 1963. Assassinated January 1973, a year before the country achieved independence.

CABRAL, Luis de Almeida (born 1931)
Guinea-Bissau nationalist leader

Educated in Portuguese Guinea. Trained as an accountant; worked as a clerk and trade-union organizer (1953–60). Fled the country in 1960 to escape capture and became a leader in the guerrilla war against Portuguese rule. PAIGC member; elected secretary of the PAIGC on the assassination of his brother Amilcar Cabral in 1973. President of Guinea-Bissau on independence, 1974. Deposed in a coup led by João Vieira in 1980; held under house arrest; released in 1982 and exiled to Cape Verde.

CARMICHAEL, Stokely (born 1941)
US political activist

Born in Trinidad; educated at Howard University, Washington, DC. Joined Student Non-Violent Co-ordinating Committee (SNCC); graduated 1964 and became full-time SNCC worker; chairman, 1966. Participated in James Meredith March through Mississippi during which he used the expression 'Black Power', 1966. Expelled from the SNCC in 1968, he aligned himself with the Black Panther Party, advocating an armed revolution. Resigned from the BPP, 1969. Became a Ugandan citizen, taking the name Kwame Touré, 1973. Later returned to the USA. Wrote *Black Power: the Politics of Black Liberation*; co-authored *Black Power: The Political Liberation of America*.

CATO, Milton (born 1915)
St Vincent politician

Barrister. Founded St Vincent Labour Party (SVLP), 1955. Member of West Indies Federation Parliament, 1958–62. Elected to St Vincent House of Assembly, 1961. Chief Minister, 1967; Premier, 1969. Leader of the Opposition, 1972–4. Premier in coalition government with People's Political Party, 1974. Prime Minister on independence, 1979. Defeated in 1984 general election following repressive policies and political scandals. Retired from politics.

CÉSAIRE, Aimé (born 1913)
Martinican writer and politician
Teacher. Co-founder of magazine *L'Etudiant Noir*, advocating négritude, 1934. Elected Mayor of Fort-de-France, 1945. Member of French Constituent Assembly, 1945. Elected as Communist Party (CP) member of French National Assembly, 1946. Left CP in protest against invasion of Hungary and party's lack of interest in French Caribbean colonies, 1956. Founded Martinican Progressive Party, 1958. President of Martinique regional council, 1983–8. Rejected offer of office in French Socialist government, 1988. Among his writings are *Return to My Native Land* (1939), *Discourse on Colonialism* (1950), *Toussaint* (1961), *Tragedy of King Christophe* (1963) and *A Season in the Congo* (1966).

CETEWAYO (c.1832–84)
Zulu king
Defeated rival for the throne, Mbulazi, at the battle of Tugela River, 1856; became Zulu ruler, 1872. Made alliance with the British to prevent Boer advances. Rebuilt Zulu military power; rejected British demands to disband army, 1878. Defeated British at battle of Isandhlwana; defeated by the British at battle of Ulundi, 1879; captured, deposed and imprisoned. Travelled to Britain, met Queen Victoria, restored to throne, 1883. Deposed in civil war following weakening of authority through Zulu faction fighting; possibly assassinated.

CHARLES, Mary Eugenia (born 1919)
Dominican politician
Took law degree in Canada, called to the Bar in England; practised law in Dominica from 1949–70. President of the Dominica Employers' Federation. Co-founder of Dominica Freedom Party (DFP), 1968. Elected to House of Assembly, 1975, becoming Leader of the Opposition. Member of the Committee for National Salvation which mounted a 'constitutional coup' to restore order, 1979. First Caribbean woman prime minister on election victory, 1980. Survived two coup attempts, 1981. Chair of Organisation of Eastern Caribbean States; supported US invasion of Grenada, 1983. Re-elected, 1985 and 1990.

CHATOYER, Joseph (died 1796)
St Vincent Black Carib leader
Led revolt of the Black Caribs against the British, 1796. Killed in single combat by a British officer. Honoured as St Vincent's first national hero, 1988.

CHAVIS, Benjamin Franklin (born 1948)
US civil rights activist
Born in Oxford, North Carolina; educated at University of North Carolina, Duke University Divinity School and Howard University. High school chemistry teacher; trade union organizer, 1969. Organizer for the South Christian Leadership Council, 1967–9; United Church of Christ civil rights organizer. Sentenced to up to 34 years imprisonment for alleged fire-bomb attack on grocery store, 1971; released on parole and conviction reversed, 1980. Appointed Commission for Racial Justice executive director, 1985. Elected National Association for the Advancement of Colored People (NAACP) executive director, 1993; dismissed for allegedly misusing NAACP funds, 1994. Established National African American Leadership Conference, 1995; Million Man March executive director, 1995. Among his works is *Let My People Go: Psalms from Prison* (1977).

CHIBESAKUNDA, Lombe Phyllis
(born 1944)
Zambian lawyer and diplomat
Educated at National Institute of Public Administration and Gray's Inn, London, 1966–9. State Advocate, 1969–73; Solicitor-General, 1973–4. Joined diplomatic service, 1975. Ambassador to Japan, 1975–7; High Commissioner to the UK, 1978; ambassador to The Netherlands and the Holy See.

CHIEPE, Gaositwe Keadakwa Tibe
(born 1926)
Botswana politician and diplomat
Born Serowe, Bechuanaland (now Botswana). Educated Fort Hare University College, 1944–7; Bristol University, 1955–7. Education officer; Director of Education, 1968–9. High Commissioner to the UK and Nigeria, 1970–4. Minister of Commerce, 1974–7; Minister of Mineral Resources, 1977–84; appointed Minister of External Affairs, 1984.

CHILEMBWE, John (c.1870–1915)
Nyasaland (now Malawi) nationalist activist
Joined Baptist Church, 1892. Visited Britain and USA, 1897. Educated at black American Baptist seminary, 1898–1900. Founded Providence Industrial Mission in Nyasaland, 1900. Led protests against white settlers' treatment of Africans; agitated against forced African recruitment into army for World War I, 1914. His church destroyed by a European opposed to African education, 1915. Organized a violent rising in which white settlers were killed, 1915. Shot trying to escape into Mozambique.

CHIPEMBERE, Henry Blasius Masauko (1930–75)
Malawian politician
Educated at Fort Hare University College. District Officer in Nyasaland (now Malawi).

Elected to Legislative Council, 1956. Member of Nyasaland African Congress. Opposed British formation of Central African Federation. Imprisoned by British authorities for independence agitation, 1958; released 1961. Minister of Local Government, 1962; Minister of Education before and after independence, 1964. Resigned when Hastings Banda dismissed ministers calling for more radical Africanization, 1964. Led an abortive anti-Banda rising, 1964. Escaped to exile in Tanzania and then to the USA in 1965 where he taught until he died.

CHIRWA, Orton Edgar Ching'oli
(1919–92)
Malawian politician
Qualified as a lawyer in England. Founded Malawi Congress Party (MCP), 1959; acting MCP president, 1960. Minister of Justice before and after independence, 1962–4. Dismissed by Banda after calling for more radical Africanization, 1964. Escaped to Tanzania; lawyer in Dar es Salaam. Founded opposition Malawi Freedom Movement, 1977. Kidnapped in Zambia with his wife, 1981. Both sentenced to death for treason, 1983. Sentence commuted to life imprisonment following international protests.

CHISHOLM, Shirley (born 1924)
US politician
Born in Brooklyn, New York; educated at Brookley College and Columbia University. Nursery school teacher, 1946–53; and organizer. Elected to New York State legislature, 1964. Elected as first black congresswoman, 1968; re-elected for successive terms until 1982. Attempted to win Democratic presidential nomination, 1972, gaining support of 150 party convention delegates. Returned to teaching after retirement from politics; co-founder of the National Political Congress of Black Women. Wrote *Unbossed and Unbought* (1970), *The Good Fight* (1975).

CHISSANO, Joaquim Alberto
(born 1939)

Mozambique politician

Educated in Portugal. Founder member of the Front for the Liberation of Mozambique (FRELIMO), 1962; secretary to FRELIMO leader Mondlane, 1966–9. FRELIMO representative in Tanzania, 1969–74. Politburo member. Prime Minister of Mozambique transitional government, 1974–5. President of Mozambique on the death of Machel, 1986. Abandoned FRELIMO's Marxist-Leninist ideology, 1989. Introduced multi-party democracy, 1990.

CHITEPO, Herbert Wiltshire Tfumaindini (1923–75)

Zimbabwean nationalist leader

First black barrister in Southern Rhodesia (now Zimbabwe). Joined National Democratic Party, 1960; Zimbabwe African People's Union, 1961. Director of Public Prosecutions in Tanzania. Joined Zimbabwe African National Union, becoming national chairman in 1963. Planned and organized armed struggle against white Rhodesian regime from Zambia. Chairman, Zimbabwe Revolutionary Council. Assassinated in Zambia by Rhodesian agents, 1975.

CHRISTOPHE, Henri (1767–1820)

Haitian revolutionary

Born in Grenada, became a sailor and by 1780 was working in Saint Domingue (now Haiti). Joined rising against the French led by Toussaint, 1794, becoming a general. Following independence, divided the country with Pétion, becoming president of the northern half, the State of Haiti, 1807. Proclaimed a monarchy with himself as King Henri I, 1811. Following a mutiny by royal troops encouraged by the neighbouring Republic of Haiti, committed suicide in 1820.

CLARK, Septima Poinsette (1898–1987)

US educationalist and civil rights activist

Born Charleston, South Carolina. School principal; dismissed for refusing to leave the National Association for the Advancement of Colored People (NAACP), 1956. Director of Education, Highlander Folk School, Tennessee. Organized Freedom Schools in the southern states to help black Americans pass literacy tests for voting. Member of the Southern Christian Leadership Conference (SCLC).

CLEAVER, Leroy Eldridge (born 1935)

US politician and activist

Born Wabaseka, Arkansas. Imprisoned twice for drug dealing and assault. Senior editor *Ramparts* magazine, 1966. Minister of Information, Black Panther Party, 1967. Guest lecturer, University of California, 1968; Peace and Freedom Party presidential candidate, 1968. Attacked by police, arrested for parole violation, 1968; fled to Cuba, Algeria, France. Returned to USA from exile, 1976. Became a born-again Christian and a Republican Party supporter. His main works include *Soul on Ice* (1968), *Post Prison Writings and Speeches* (1976).

COFFY (died 1763)

African slave leader

Born in West Africa. Led a rebellion of slaves in Berbice (now part of Guyana). Divisions arose between slaves born in the colony and those born in Africa. Coffy gave up leadership after three months and committed suicide. Honoured as the first national hero of Guyana.

COMPTON, John George Melvin
(born 1926)

St Lucian politician

Oil refinery worker in Curaçao. Qualified as barrister; studied at London School of

Economics. Elected to House of Assembly as an Independent, 1954. Joined St Lucia Labour Party, 1956. Minister of Trade and Industry, 1958–61. Founded National Labour Movement; amalgamated with People's Progressive Party to form United Workers' Party under his leadership, 1964. Chief Minister, 1964; Premier, 1967. Led St Lucia to independence, 1979. Defeated in 1979 general election. Returned to power, 1982; won the 1987 and 1992 general elections.

CRAFT, Ellen (1826–97)

Escaped US slave

Born in Georgia; escaped to Philadelphia through the Underground Railroad with husband William; moved with abolitionist help to England, where the couple learned to read and write and had three children; William wrote a description of their escape, *Running a Thousand Miles for Freedom* (1868); returned to Georgia and bought a farm, 1868.

CRUMMELL, Alexander (1819–97)

US clergyman and writer

Born in New York, the son of free parents. Educated New York and Cambridge University, England. Ordained a Protestant Episcopal Church minister, 1844; obtained a degree at Cambridge University, 1853. Missionary and teacher in Liberia, 1853–73. Worked with American Colonisation Society to promote black emigration to Liberia. Returned to the USA; participant in the Pan-African Chicago Congress of Africa, 1893. Founded the American Negro Academy, 1897. Used the expression 'the talented tenth' at his opening address to the Academy. Wrote, among many other works, *Future of Africa* (1862), *Africa and America* (1892).

CUDJOE (dates unknown)

Jamaican slave leader

Born in West Africa; taken as a slave to Jamaica. Escaped to central Jamaican mountains in 1690, becoming the most prominent of the Maroon leaders. Settled in Cockpit County; mounted attacks on plantations with his two brothers which led to the First Maroon War. His followers were offered land and guaranteed liberty by the British, 1738. Appointed commander of Trelawny Town, west Cockpit County. The first Monday in January is celebrated by Maroons in Jamaica as Cudjoe Day.

CUFFAY, William (1788–1870)

British radical activist

Born in Chatham, Kent; worked as a tailor. Joined the radical Chartist movement, 1839; President of the Chartist Metropolitan Delegate Conference, 1842. Chaired the committee elected to present the Chartists' petition to the House of Commons, 1848. Arrested for allegedly planning an uprising; exiled to penal colony in Tasmania for life.

CUFFE, Paul (1759–1817)

US emigrationist

Born Massachusetts of a West African father and Native American mother. Became sailor; master of own ship at 25; traded with Sierra Leone. A Quaker; involved in setting up missionary activity in Sierra Leone from 1800. Believed setting up colonies in Africa would contribute towards ending slavery in the USA. Petitioned the president and congress for money for black repatriation, 1814. Organized emigration of 40 black Americans to Sierra Leone, 1815; funded settlement at his own expense.

DACKO, David (born 1930)
Central African Republic politician

Leader of teachers' union; elected to Territorial Assembly, 1957. Minister of Agriculture, 1957; Minister of Administrative Affairs, 1958; Minister of Interior, 1958–9. Became leader of the Mouvement d'Évolution Sociale de l'Afrique Noire (MESAN) and Premier, 1959. President on independence, 1960; banned opposition parties, 1962. Overthrown following a general strike, 1966, and imprisoned for ten years. Overthrew Bokassa with French support, 1979. President until deposed in a bloodless coup, 1981. Lived in exile in France.

DANQUAH, Joseph Kwame Kyereti Boakye (1895–1965)
Ghanaian politician

Legal clerk; became secretary to his brother, a paramount chief. Educated at University College, London, returning to the Gold Coast (now Ghana) to practise law, 1927. Established influential *Times of West Africa*, 1931. Founded Gold Coast Youth Congress, 1937. Formed United Gold Coast Convention with Kwame Nkrumah, 1947, but later broke with him. Imprisoned for anti-colonial agitation, 1948. Following independence, joined the United Party, 1957; ran unsuccessfully as president against Nkrumah, 1960. Imprisoned for attacks on Nkrumah's policies, 1961–2 and 1964–5. Died in prison.

DAVIDSON, William (1786–1820)
British radical activist

Born in Kingston, Jamaica. Son of a black mother and the white Attorney-General. Educated in Jamaica and Scotland. Apprentice lawyer, seaman, apprentice cabinet-maker. Member of the radical socialist Society of Spencean Philanthropists; secretary of a shoemakers' trade union. Davidson was responsible for buying and storing arms for the group who organized the Cato Street Conspiracy to assassinate the Tory Cabinet and provoke revolution. The plot was organized by a police provocateur and the conspirators were arrested. Davidson and four others were convicted of high treason, 1820. They were the last men to be beheaded in Britain.

DAVIS, Angela Yvonne (born 1944)
US academic and radical activist

Born Birmingham, Alabama. Educated at Brandeis University, University of California at San Diego and Frankfurt University, Germany. Joined Student Non-Violent Co-ordinating Committee (SNCC), Black Panther Party and the Communist Party (CP), 1968. Dismissed from teaching post at University of California, Los Angeles, for CP membership, 1969. Accused of involvement in escape attempt of George Jackson, 1970; acquitted 1972. Renamed her defence committee the National Alliance Against Racist and Political Repression. Travelled in Soviet Union and Eastern Europe; lectured in USA; worked with Black Women's Health Project. CP Vice-presidential candidate, 1980 and 1984. Works include *If They Come in the Morning: Voices of Resistance* (1971), *Lectures on Liberation* (1972), *Angela Davis: With My Mind on Freedom, An Autobiography* (1974).

DAVIS, Benjamin Oliver, Senior (1877–1970)
US Army officer

Enlisted as private, 1899; served in the Philippines. Commissioned as cavalry second-lieutenant, 1901. Military attaché in Liberia. Promoted to major in World War I; colonel, 1930. Taught military science at Wilberforce University and Tusgekee

Institute. Promoted to Brigadier-General, 1940, becoming the first black American to reach this rank. Retired, 1940; recalled as special adviser to US forces in Europe in World War II; assistant to the Inspector-General, Washington, DC. Retired, 1948.

DAVIS, Benjamin Oliver, Junior
(born 1912)
US Air Force officer
Born Washington DC. Son of Benjamin Oliver Davis, Senior. Graduated from West Point Military Academy, 1936. Transferred to the Army Air Corps; commanded the black 99th Fighter Squadron which flew its first combat mission in 1943. Led combat units in Europe, North Africa and Korea. Awarded the Silver Star and Distinguished Flying Cross. First black American to be promoted to Air Force Brigadier-General, 1954 . Retired 1970. Appointed Assistant-Secretary, Department of Transportation.

DAVIS, Bernard (1903-64)
US radical political activist and lawyer
Born Atlanta, Georgia. Educated Amherst College and Harvard Law School. Defence lawyer in Herndon case. Joined Communist Party (CP), 1932. Forced to leave Atlanta; moved to New York City. Appointed editor of the *Daily Worker* and the *Harlem Liberator*. Elected as CP New York City councillor, 1943 and 1945; lost seat in 1947. Imprisoned for membership of Communist Party, 1948. Returned to Harlem on release.

DELARGE, Robert Carlos (1842-74)
US politician
Born Aiken, South Carolina; a farmer. Elected to South Carolina House of Representatives, 1868. One of the first black Americans to be elected to the US House of Representatives, 1870. Retired from national politics, 1873; became a magistrate in South Carolina.

DESSALINES, Jean-Jacques
(c.1758–1806)
Haitian ruler
Born in Guinea; taken as a slave to Haiti. Joined revolt against the French led by Toussaint, 1791; by 1794 a leading figure in the army. Forced French invasion force from Haiti, 1803. Created governor; proclaimed himself Emperor Jacques I of Haiti, 1804. Assassinated by officers in Port-au-Prince, 1806.

DIA, Mamadou (born 1910)
Senegalese politician
Educated in Paris; worked as a teacher and journalist. Councillor for Senegal in French Assembly, 1946–52; Grand Councillor for French West Africa and Deputy in the French National Assembly, 1952–8. President of the Autonomous Republic of Senegal, 1959–60; Vice-President of the Mali Federation, 1960. Prime Minister of independent Senegal, 1960. Involved in unsuccessful attempt to overthrow President Senghor, 1962. Imprisoned until 1974; remained politically active.

DINGAAN (c.1795–1840)
Second Zulu king, 1828–40
Killed half-brother Shaka and seized throne, 1828. Attempted to gain popular support by ending wars of conquest. Mounted unsuccessful attacks on the Portuguese, 1833; and the Ndebele in the Transvaal, 1832 and 1837. Granted increased concessions to British traders; allowed Afrikaaner farmers to settle in Natal from 1837. Fought against Boers, 1838; peace treaty negotiated by the British. Unsuccessfully attempted to conquer Swazi territory. Half-brother Mpande seized crown with Afrikaaner support, 1840. Following civil war, Dingaan died a fugitive.

DINGISWAYO (c.1770–c.1816)
Nguni leader, forerunner of Zulu kingdom (in what is now South Africa)
Exiled from Zululand after dispute with father. Impressed by Portuguese military methods; returned to kill and succeed his brother as a Mthethwa chief, 1805. Built Nguni army; expanded confederation of Nguni kingdoms through diplomacy rather than war. Killed by a rival Nguni leader.

DIORI, Hamani (1916–87)
Niger politician
Educated in Dahomey and Dakar; language teacher, 1938–46. Founder member of Niger branch of Rassemblement Démocratique Africaine, 1946. French National Assembly Deputy, 1946–51, 1956–7. Founded Niger Progressive Party, 1957. Head of Niger Government Council, 1958. Prime Minister, 1956–60. First president of independent Niger, 1960; re-elected 1965, 1970. Deputy Chairman of the West African Economic Community, 1973. Deposed in a military coup, 1974; under house arrest until allowed to go into exile in Morocco where he died, 1987.

DIXON, Sharon Pratt (born 1944)
US politician
Born Washington, DC; educated at Howard University. Joint Centre for Political Studies counsel, 1970–1. Private law practice and teacher at Antioch Law School, 1971–6. Worked for Potomac Electric Power Co, 1976–90. Democratic Party treasurer, 1985–9. Elected Mayor of Washington, DC, 1990, the first black woman to become mayor of a major city.

DOE, Samuel Kenyon (1950–90)
Liberian soldier and politician
Joined army, 1969; promoted to Master Sergeant, 1979. Led non-commissioned officers' coup against President Tolbert, 1980. Promoted himself to general and army Commander-in-Chief, 1981. Chairman of the ruling People's Redemption Council, 1980–5. Ordered public execution of former state officials. Formed National Democratic Party of Liberia, 1984; elected president, 1985. Survived an estimated nine coup attempts. Faced major rebellion in Nimba province, 1989. Captured and killed by forces of Prince Johnson, 1990.

DOMBO (died c.1696)
Founder of the Changamire dynasty
Cattle owner who built the Changamire empire (now Zimbabwe). Captured Shona-speaking territories in the 1680s and attacked northern Transvaal. Aided Munhu Mutapa kingdom in driving Portuguese out, 1693–5; then made the area a province of his empire.

DOMINGO, Wilfred A. (1889–1968)
Jamaican nationalist activist
Member of Socialist Party in Harlem. First editor of the *Negro World*, organ of the Universal Negro Improvement Association (UNIA). Broke with UNIA following dispute with Garvey over socialism, 1919. Socialist Party speaker and teacher at party school. African Blood Brotherhood activist, 1920s. Formed Jamaica Progressive League, 1936. Returned to Jamaica to become vice-chair of the Trades Union Advisory Council and contributor to *Labour Weekly*. Returned to New York City, 1947.

DOUGLASS, Frederick (c.1817–95)
US abolitionist
Born a slave in Talbot County, Maryland. Taught at Sunday school. Escaped from slavery following a number of unsuccessful attempts, 1838. Worked in New York City as a labourer. Emerged as an activist in the Massachusetts anti-slavery movement, 1841. Travelled in England and Ireland speaking

on slavery and women's rights, 1845; raised money to purchase freedom. Founder and editor of abolitionist journal *North Star*, 1847. Fled to Canada to escape attempted arrest by the government of Virginia. Encouraged recruitment to the 54th and 55th Massachusetts Negro regiments during 1861–5 Civil War. Civil rights activist following the war. Police commissioner for the District of Columbia; marshal, 1871; Recorder of deeds, 1881. Minister-resident and consul-general to the Republic of Haiti. Resigned in protest against American business activities in Haiti, 1891.

DU BOIS, William Edward Burghardt (1868–1963)

US Pan-African, academic and writer

Born Great Barrington, Massachusetts. Graduated from Fisk University, Tennessee, 1888; Harvard PhD, 1895. Professor at Atlanta University, 1897–1914, becoming an acknowledged race relations specialist. Organized Pan-African Conference in London, 1900. *The Souls of Black Folk*, published 1902. Established the Niagara movement, 1905. Founded National Association for the Advancement of Colored People (NAACP), 1909, and was actively involved in its work until 1934. Joined the Socialist Party, 1911. Returned to Atlanta University and wrote *An Essay towards an Autobiography of a Race Concept*. An organizer of the post-World War II Pan-African Conference in Manchester, England, working with Kwame Nkrumah. Ran for the Senate as an American Labor Party candidate in New York, 1950. Accused, and acquitted, of being a communist, 1951. Advocated socialism for Africa, 1958. Joined the Communist Party of the USA, 1961, and awarded the Lenin Peace Prize by the Soviet Union. Moved to Ghana, becoming a citizen. Died in Ghana. Among his many works are *The Suppression of the African Slave Trade in the United States of America 1638–1870* (1896), *The Philadelphia Negro* (1899), *The Gift of Black Form* (1924), *Black Reconstruction* (1935), *Dusk of Dawn* (1940), *Color and Democracy* (1945), and *The World and Africa* (1946).

DUVALIER, François ('Papa Doc') (1907–71)

Haitian politician

Trained as a doctor. Joined the Griots as a supporter of *noirisme*, 1930s. Secretary-General, Worker-Peasant Party, 1946. Minister of Health and Labour, 1949. Went underground following overthrow of the government, 1950. Elected president, 1957. Formed Tontons Macoutes to counter opposition violence, opening a reign of terror, 1958. Survived US attempt at overthrow, 1963. Declared himself president for life, 1964.

DUVALIER, Jean Claude ('Baby Doc') (born 1951)

Haitian politician

Survived assassination attempt, 1963. Named as successor by his father; approved in a referendum by 2,391,916 votes to one, 1971. Initially relatively liberal. Undermined his father's ideology of *noirisme* by marrying a rich mulatto's daughter, 1980. Economic decline and growing repression provoked a national uprising. Flown into exile in France by US government, 1986.

ELLIOTT, Robert B. (1842–84)

US politician

Born Boston, Massachusetts. Educated Boston, Jamaica, England. Practised law in England and South Carolina; editor of *Charleston Leader*. Member of South Carolina state legislature, 1868–70; South Carolina assistant Adjutant-General, 1969–71. One of the first black Americans to be elected to the House of Representatives,

1871; resigned 1874. Returned to law practice in New Orleans.

EQUIANO, Olaudah (1745–?)
Anti-slavery activist; also known as Gustavus Vassa

Born in Essaka, Benin (now Nigeria); taken as a slave to work on a Virginia plantation, 1756. Taken to Britain, 1757; sold and moved to Montserrat where he purchased his freedom and returned to Britain. Appointed Commissary of stores and provision to the Sierra Leone resettlement scheme, 1786. Active campaigner against slavery and the slave trade; involved in campaign to bring the perpetrators of the *Zong* incident to justice. Joined the radical working-class London Corresponding Society, 1792. Wrote two-volume autobiography, *The Interesting Narrative of the Life of Olaudah Equiano, or Gustavas Vassa, the African: by Himself* (1790).

ESTEVANICO (Little Stephen)
(c.1500–?)
Reputedly the first African in the New World

Taken by his Spanish owner on an expedition to Mexico, 1527. Landed in Florida; Estevanico negotiated with Native Americans. Only four survived of the 500 who attempted to reach Narváez settlement in Mexico, 1536. Sold to the Viceroy of Spain. Sent as scout on expedition to the 'Seven Cities of Gold'. Disappeared; believed killed in Native American attack.

EVERS, James Charles (born 1922)
US civil rights activist

Born Decatur, Mississippi. Served in US army in Korean War; ran family business. Moved to Chicago; returned to Mississippi following the assassination of his brother Medgar, 1963. Took over his brother's post as National Association for the Advancement of Colored People (NAACP) Mississippi field director. Elected first black mayor of a racially mixed southern town, Fayette, Mississippi, 1969 and 1973. Unsuccessful candidate for state governor, 1972.

EVERS, Medgar Wiley (1925–63)
US civil rights activist

Born Decatur, Mississippi. Studied law, University of Mississippi. Active in civil rights movement from 1954; National Association for the Advancement of Colored People Mississippi field director. Assassinated, 1963.

EYADÉMA, Gnassingbe (formerly Etienne) (born 1937)
Togo politician

Joined French army, 1953. Fought in Indo-China and Algeria. Transferred to Togo army on independence, 1960. Shot President Olympio outside US Embassy, 1963. Promoted to general and chief of staff, 1965. Overthrew President Grunitzky and appointed himself head of state, 1967. Formed Rassemblement du Peuple Togolais; declared it the only legal political party and dissolved trade unions, 1969. Elected president with 99 per cent of vote, 1972. Survived several assassination attempts. Re-elected, 1979. Riots forced agreement to multi-party democracy, 1991. Stripped of powers, but retained office with army support.

FANON, Frantz Omar (1925–61)
Martinique writer and political activist

Born in Martinique, educated in France where he qualified as a psychiatrist. *Black Skins, White Masks* was published in 1952. Worked in Algeria, 1953–6, where he became an active supporter of the liberation movement. *Studies in a Dying Colonialism*, a result of this experience, was published in 1956; *The Wretched of the Earth*, advocating an armed socialist revolution, in 1961; and *Towards the African Revolution*, in 1964.

FARMER, James (born 1920)
US civil rights activist

Born Marshall, Texas; educated at Wiley College and Howard University. Vice-President, National Council of Methodist Youth and Christian Youth Council of America. Race relations secretary, Fellowship of Reconciliation, 1941. Founder and first National Director of the Congress of Racial Equality (CORE), 1942. Organized sit-ins and Freedom Riders. Left CORE, 1966. Assistant-Secretary of Health, Education and Welfare in President Nixon's government, 1969. Severed connections with CORE, 1976. Unsuccessful attempt to establish another civil rights organization, 1980. Among his works are *Freedom When?* and *Lay Bare the Heart*.

FARRAKHAN, Louis (Louis Eugene Walcott) (born 1933)
US religious leader

Born New York City. Musician and singer. Joined Nation of Islam, 1950s; became minister of the Boston Mosque. Opposed Malcolm X when he left the Nation of Islam, 1963; became leader of the Harlem Mosque. Left the World Community of Al-Islam when it admitted white members, 1975. Established rival Nation of Islam. Supported presidential candidacy of Jesse Jackson, 1984. Appeared to be emerging as *de facto* black leader in the US by organizing the Million Man March on Washington, 1995. World Friendship Tour, 1996; asked President Mandela for land in Africa to resettle a million black Americans; criticized by US Congress for accepting $1 million from President Gaddafy of Libya. There were suggestions in 1996 that he planned to launch a black American political party.

FAUSET, Jessie Redmon (1886–1961)
US writer and Pan-Africanist

Born Philadelphia, Pennsylvania. Educated at Cornell University and University of Pennsylvania. Delegate to Pan-African Congress, 1921. Literary editor of the National Association for the Advancement of Colored People (NAACP) journal, *The Crisis*. Returned to teaching.

FLIPPER, Henry Ossian (1856–1940)
US soldier and engineer

Born a slave in Thomasville, Georgia; his father purchased the family's freedom. Educated at Atlanta University. First black graduate from West Point Military Academy, 1877. Assigned to the black Tenth Cavalry regiment. Accused of embezzlement of public funds and conduct unbecoming in an officer; found guilty on second charge and dishonourably discharged, 1881. Worked as a civil and mining engineer in Mexico; conducted missions for Senate Committee on Foreign Relations and the Secretary of the Interior. Given posthumous honourable discharge, 1976.

FOREMAN, James (born 1929)
US civil rights activist

Born Chicago, Illinois. Educated at Roosevelt University; a teacher. Executive-Secretary, Student Non-Violent Co-ordinating Committee (SNCC). Joined League of Revolutionary Black Workers, 1969. Wrote *The Black Manifesto*, 1969, demanding $500 million from religious institutions as reparations for black suffering under slavery and capitalism. His Black Economic Development Conference successfully raised $1 million to distribute to black groups. Other works include *The Making of Black Revolutionaries: a Personal Account* (1972).

FORTUNE, Timothy Thomas
(1856–1928)
US journalist and Pan-African activist

Born a slave; freed 1865. Printer; educated at Howard University. Founded newspaper *New York Age*, 1879; founder New York *Freeman*, 1884. Contributed to Boston *Transcript* and New York *Sun*. Formed National Afro-American League (forerunner of National Association for the Advancement of Colored People) to promote African nationalism, 1890; co-organizer of the National Afro-American Press Association. Wrote, among other works, *Black and White: Land, Labor and Politics in the United States* (1884), *The Negro in Politics* (1886). Died in obscurity.

GAIRY, (Sir) Eric Matthew (born 1922)
Grenadian politician

Teacher, trade union organizer. Founded Grenada Manual and Mental Workers' Union, 1949; led a national strike, 1950. Formed Grenada United Labour Party (GULP), 1951. Elected to Legislative Council, 1951; suspended from membership 1952; re-elected, 1954; suspended 1955. Minister of Trade and Production, 1956–7. Disenfranchised for five years for wasting public money, 1957. Chief Minister following 1961 general election victory. Dismissed by British authorities for alleged corruption, 1962. Premier following election victory, 1967. Led Grenada to independence, 1974, becoming prime minister in midst of demonstrations against his authoritarian style. Overthrown by New Jewel Movement, 1979. Returned to Grenada from the USA, 1983. Failed to be elected to House of Representatives, 1990.

GARVEY, Marcus Mosiah (1887–1940)
Jamaican Pan-Africanist

Worked as a printer in Jamaica, 1901–10; wrote political pamphlets and published a newspaper. Travelled in Central America, working as a journalist in Costa Rica and Panama, 1910–12. Lived in England, 1912–14. Founded Universal Negro Improvement Association (UNIA) in Kingston, Jamaica, with Amy Ashwood, 1914, initially as a self-help and cultural organization. Moved to USA, 1916. Radicalized UNIA aims, 1917–18; stressed equal rights, economic independence, black unity, anti-imperialism, a unified independent Africa. Organized international Black Convention, 1920; founded *The Negro World*. Met hostility from white authorities and black leaders. Operated the Black Star Shipping Line between New York and the Caribbean, 1919–23. Met Ku-Klux-Klan leaders, declaring they had similar aims as separatist organizations, 1922. Attempted to purchase land in Liberia for black settlement. Convicted on spurious mail fraud charge, 1923; imprisoned from 1925–7; deported to Panama. Returned to Jamaica, revived UNIA, and formed the People's Political Party. Won a seat on Kingston Parish Council, 1929; unable to take seat while in prison for contempt of court. Moved to England, 1935; died in obscurity. His remains were returned to Jamaica, 1964. A national hero of Jamaica.

GBAGHO, Laurent (born 1944)
Côte d'Ivoire politician

History teacher; exiled by government, 1981–7. Returned to found Ivorian Popular Front, the first recognized opposition group, 1988.

GIBBS, Mifflin Wister (1828–1903)
US lawyer, businessman and civil rights activist

Born in Philadelphia, a free black; moved to San Francisco, 1850. Established a clothing store. Campaigned against an 1852 law prohibiting black testimony in court.

Established *Mirror of the Times*, California's first black newspaper, 1855. Left California to settle in British Columbia; elected to local council for a white district, 1866. Studied law; admitted to Arkansas bar, 1870. First elected black judge, Little Rock, Arkansas, 1873. US Consul in Madagascar, 1901–10.

GOWON, Yakubu (Jack) (born 1934)
Nigerian military ruler
Educated Nigeria, Eton College and Sandhurst. Joined army, 1954; served in United Nations peacekeeping force in the Congo (now Zaïre), 1960–1, 1963. Chief of Staff and member of military government following January 1966 coup. Head of Federal Military Government and Army Commander-in-Chief following July 1966 coup. Led federal troops in civil war against secessionist Biafra, 1967–70. Delayed promised return to civilian rule, 1974. Overthrown in coup while at an Organization of African Unity meeting in Uganda, 1975. Studied at University of Warwick, England. Dismissed from army for alleged complicity in attempted coup, 1976. Pardoned, 1981. Settled in Togo, 1981.

GRANT, Bernard Alexander Montgomery (born 1944)
British politician
Born in British Guiana (now Guyana); educated at St Stanislaus College, Tottenham Technical College. Technical analyst in Guyana, 1961–3. Member of the Socialist Labour League, 1963–74; joined Labour Party, 1975. British Railways clerk, 1963–5; telephonist, 1969–78; National Union of Public Employees area officer, 1978–83. Development worker, Black Trade Unionists Solidarity Movement, 1983–4; race relations adviser, London Borough of Newham, 1985–7. Elected to London Borough of Haringey council, 1978; deputy leader, 1982–3; leader 1985–7. Elected as Member of Parliament for Tottenham, 1987. Chairman of Parliamentary Black Caucus, 1987. National executive committee member, Anti-Apartheid, 1989–91. Chairman, Parliamentary Standing Committee on Race Equality in Europe, 1990.

GRAVELY, Samuel Lee (born 1922)
US naval officer
Born Richmond, Virginia; enlisted in US navy. One of the Golden Thirteen selected for officer training; became first black naval officer, 1944. Demobilized in 1948; returned to service, 1949. The first black commander of a US navy ship, USS *Falgout*, 1962; first black rear admiral, 1971. Commanded a 30-strong flotilla, 1973. Retired from the navy, 1978. Director of Defense Communications Agency, 1978–80.

GRUNITZKY, Nicolas (1913–69)
Togo politician
Born central Togoland of African family with Polish connections. Trained as an engineer in France; returned to Togo, 1937. Formed pro-French Party of Togolese Unity (PUT), 1946; stood unsuccessfully for Territorial Assembly. Elected to French Chamber of Deputies, 1951; his party won control of the Territorial Assembly, 1955. Prime Minister, 1955–8. Returned to power on assassination of Sylvanus Olympio, 1963; overthrown in a military coup, 1967. Went into exile in Côte d'Ivoire; died in automobile accident.

GUMBS, Emile (born 1928)
Anguillan politician
Sailor; elected to the island council as sole opposition member, 1972. Minister of Works, Communications and Trade. Chief Minister, 1977. Leader of Anguilla National Alliance (ANA). Defeated at 1980 general election. Won general elections in 1984 and 1989 (with independent support).

HABYARIMANA, Juvénal (1937–1994)
Rwandan military ruler

A Hutu; educated in Zaïre. Army Chief of Staff, 1963–5; Minister for the National Guard and Chief of Staff of Police, 1965–73. Overthrew President Kayibanda in bloodless coup, 1973, appointing himself President and Minister of National Defence; added office of prime minister, 1974. Formed economic community with Zaïre and Burundi, 1974. Founded and became president of the National Revolutionary Movement for Development (MRND), 1975. Joined Burundi, Tanzania and Uganda in Kagera River basin project, 1977. Survived Rwandan Patriotic Front invasion, 1990. Died in air crash with the President of Burundi, 1994.

HAILE SELASSIE I ('Might of the Trinity', Tafari Makonnen) (1892–1975)
Ethiopian ruler

Cousin of Emperor Menelik II. Governor of Harar province, 1910. Led successful revolt of barons against Emperor Iyasu V, 1916. Regent, head of government and heir apparent with title Ras, 1916–28. Gained admission to League of Nations by promising to abolish slavery, 1923. Overthrew Empress Zauditu in a palace coup, 1928. Crowned Negus Nagast ('king of kings', or Emperor) with dynastic name Haile Selassie ('Lion of Judah'), 1930. Introduced the country's first parliament, 1931. Left Ethiopia following Italian invasion, 1936, remaining in exile until restored to throne in 1941. Attempted to modernize the country; leading figure in the Organization of African Unity (OAU). Introduced a new constitution allowing elections to parliament, 1955. Acted as mediator in the Sudanese and Nigerian civil wars. Survived coup attempt, 1960. Deposed by the Dergue, 1974. Died under house arrest, 1975.

HALL, Prince (c.1735–1807)
Founder of Black Freemasonry

Born in Barbados; moved to America in 1771; leather worker. Fought in the War of Independence. Joined a British Army Freemasons' Lodge. After independence, unable to find a Lodge that would accept him, he formed the first African Lodge of Masons in Boston, 1784. Travelled to England; granted a charter as Grand Master of Africa Lodge No 459, Boston, 1787. Organized lodges in Philadelphia and Providence. Black Freemasonry is now known as 'Prince Hall Masonry' and is not recognized by the official movement. Petitioned Massachusetts Legislature for assistance to poor blacks wanting to return to Africa, 1787.

HARPER, Frances Ellen Watkins (1825–1911)
US poet and equal rights activist

The most popular of nineteenth-century black poets. Born of free parents, Baltimore, Maryland. Lectured against slavery and for equal rights for black people and women. Among her works are *Forest Leaves* (1845), *Poems on Miscellaneous Subjects* (1857) and *Sketches of Southern Life* (1872).

HARRIS, Patricia Roberts (1924–85)
US politician

Born Mattoon, Illinois. Educated Howard University, George Washington University Law School. Practised as lawyer. Co-chair of the National Women's Committee on Civil Rights, 1961. Ambassador to Luxembourg, 1965–7. Professor of Law at Howard University, 1969; active civil rights campaigner. Member of the Democratic Party National Committee, 1973. Appointed Secretary of Housing and Urban Development, 1977. Unsuccessfully contested election for Mayor of Washington, DC, 1982;

law professor, George Washington University, 1983–5.

HARRISON, Hubert (1883–1927)
US radical political activist and writer
Born in Virgin Islands. Postal worker; joined Harlem branch of Socialist Party, 1909. Party organizer, 1911. Established the Colored Socialist Club in Harlem, 1912. Writer for the *Call*; assistant editor of the *Masses*. Left Socialist Party following his criticism of racism of some party leaders, 1914. Formed Liberty League of Negro-Americans to encourage self-defence against racist attacks, 1917, and its journal *The Voice*. Editor of Universal Negro Improvement Association (UNIA) journal, *Negro World*, 1920–22. Advocated a separate black state in USA; founded International Colored Unity League and its journal *Voice of the Negro*, 1925. Among his books are *The Negro and the Nation* (1917) and *When Africa Awakes: The Inside Story of the Stirrings of the New Negro in the Western World* (1920). Died in poverty.

HAYWOOD, Harry (1898–1985)
US radical political activist
Joined Communist Party (CP) in Chicago, 1925. Studied in Moscow, meeting anti-colonialist activists, 1926. Advocated self-determination in the American south 'black belt'; expelled from the CP, 1959. Commentator on civil rights campaign and black power movements throughout 1960s. Main works include *Negro Liberation* (1948) and his autobiography *Black Bolshevik* (1978).

HEALY, James (1830–1900)
US clergyman
Born in Georgia; ordained as Roman Catholic priest in Paris, France, 1854. Assistant parish priest in Boston, Massachusetts; Bishop of Portland, Maine, 1875; the first black American Roman Catholic Bishop. Appointed assistant to the papal throne, 1900.

HENSON, Josiah (1789–1883)
US abolitionist
Born a slave in Charles County, Maryland. Methodist Episcopal Church preacher, 1828. Escaped from slavery into Canada, 1830; active in the Underground Railroad. Unsuccessful attempt to establish a British–American Labour Institute, 1842. Met Harriet Beecher Stowe who reputedly used his story as the basis for *Uncle Tom's Cabin*. Travelled to England to receive an award from abolitionists. Autobiography published, 1849. Died in Canada.

HENSON, Matthew (1866–1955)
US explorer
Stevedore, coachman, clerk. Accompanied Robert Peary on expedition to Nicaragua, 1887; joined first expedition to the North Pole, 1909. Worked in obscurity on return as a parking attendant. Elected member of the Explorers Club, 1937; awarded medal by the US Congress, 1944. Wrote autobiography, *A Negro Explorer at the North Pole* (1912).

HORTON, James Africanus Beale (1835–82)
West African physician and political theorist
Born in Sierra Leone, son of a freed Ibo slave. Educated at mission schools and Fourah Bay Institute; sent to study medicine in London and Edinburgh, 1853; qualified, 1859. Served as a military physician in West Africa; retired as lieutenant-colonel, 1872. Wrote articles and books, including *West African Countries and Peoples* (1868). As a political theorist, advocated African development on the European model; based his thinking on his belief in African cultural inferiority. Influenced the establishment of

a short-lived Fante Confederation in what is now Ghana, 1871.

HOUPHOUËT-BOIGNY, Félix (1900–93)
Côte d'Ivoire politician

Born Yamoussoukro. Medical training in Dakar; qualified 1925. Worked as physician and planter. President of the Syndicat Agricole Africaine, 1944; transformed this into the Parti Démocratique de la Côte d'Ivoire, a radical party affiliated with the French Communist Party, 1945. Deputy in French National Assembly, 1945–59. Founding president of the Rassemblement Démocratique Africain (RDA). Minister in French colonial government and president of the Grand Council of French West Africa, 1956–9. Côte d'Ivoire prime minister, 1959; president, 1960. Survived coup attempts, 1980 and 1985. Victory in first contested presidential election, 1990. Died in office.

HUDSON, Hosea (born 1898)
US political and union activist

Born in Georgia; moved to Birmingham, Alabama, to work as iron moulder, 1924. Joined Communist Party , 1931. Organized Right to Vote Club to encourage black voting, 1938. Union of Steel Workers activist, 1940–7. Dismissed from work, lost union office, for being a communist, 1947. Underground party organizer in southern states, 1950–4. Honoured by city of Birmingham as a civil rights pioneer, 1980.

HUNTE, Julian (born 1940)
St Lucian politician

Insurance agent; joined United Workers' Party. Mayor of Castries, 1971–2. Resigned to join St Lucia Action Movement and then St Lucia Labour Party. Labour Party deputy chairman, 1982; leader, 1984. Elected to House of Assembly as Leader of the Opposition, 1987.

IGHODARO, Irene Elizabeth Beatrice (1916–95)
Nigerian doctor, social reformer and women's rights activist

Educated at University of Durham Medical School; graduated 1945. First African woman to qualify as a doctor in Britain; first woman doctor in Sierra Leone. Moved to Nigeria, 1952. Founder member National Council of Women's Societies, 1959; President, Nigerian Association of University Women; World Vice-President, Young Women's Christian Association, 1967. Founded University of Benin teaching hospital, 1968.

ILENDELA (dates unknown)
A Namwanga headman in the north-east of Northern Rhodesia (now Zambia) in the 1890s

Led armed resistance to an attempt by the British South Africa Company to capture Africans for forced labour, 1896. The British burnt down his village and killed one African. A white missionary attempted to claim compensation from the authorities for the death and damage.

JABAVU, John Tengo (1859–1921)
South African political activist

Educated in Methodist mission. Teacher, journalist. Founded the first South African black newspaper, *Imvo Zabantsundu* (Views of the Bantu People), Cape Town, 1883. Advocated Xhosa voters' support for white Liberal candidates; lost popular support as Liberal policies became increasingly anti-black. Member of delegation to London protesting at loss of black franchise on formation of the Union of South Africa, 1909. Leading figure in founding Fort Hare College, 1916.

JACKSON, George (1941-71)
US radical activist

Imprisoned at age of 15 for stealing $70; remained in prison for remainder of life. Educated himself in radical politics in prison and wrote on his analysis of the roots of crime and racism. Killed a white guard in Soledad Prison, 1970. Shot dead in unsuccessful escape attempt, 1971. Among his writings are *Soledad Brother: The Prison Letters of George Jackson* (1970) and *Blood in My Eye* (1972).

JACKSON, Jesse (born 1941)
US politician and civil rights activist

Born Greenville, South Carolina. Educated in Carolina and at Chicago Theological Seminary; ordained as Baptist minister, 1968. Joined Southern Christian Leadership Conference (SCLC), 1965. SCLC Operation Breadbasket national executive director, 1967–71; led Poor People's Campaign, 1968. Led Active Black Coalition for United Community Action, 1969. Founded Operation PUSH (People United to Save Humanity), 1971; formed PUSH–EXCEL to encourage black educational achievement. Campaigned for Democratic presidential nomination with National Rainbow Coalition, 1984 and 1988. Continued Rainbow Coalition campaigns on economic, social and civil rights issues.

JAJA (c.1821-91)
King of Opobo (in what is now Nigeria)

A former slave of Ibo origin. Head of the house of Opobo, a powerful trading dynasty in the Kingdom of Bonny, 1862. Seceded from Bonny and established independent state following defeat in war with rival Manilla Pepple dynasty, 1869; crowned as king, 1870. Controlled trade on the Oil Rivers; began direct exports to Europe, 1873. Sent troops to assist British in war against Asante, 1875. Kidnapped by British following their failure to break African trading monopoly by force, 1887. Deported to Accra and then to the Caribbean. Died at Tenerife while returning to Opobo.

JAMES, Cyril Lionel Richard (1901-89)
Trinidadian writer and political activist

Educated in Trinidad; teacher and journalist in the 1920s. Co-producer of two magazines encouraging indigenous Caribbean writing, *Trinidad* and *The Beacon*, 1929–32. Moved to England in 1932; cricket correspondent for the *Manchester Guardian* and Glasgow *Herald* until 1938; joined the Independent Labour Party, involved in formation of the Revolutionary Socialist League and with African independence movements. Moved to the USA, 1938; active in the Socialist Workers' Party. Expelled from the USA for political activity, 1953. Returned to England, and then to Trinidad, where he worked with the People's National Movement (PNM), editing its journal *The Nation*. Involved in formation of the West Indies Federation. Secretary of the Federal Labour Party; expelled from PNM for alleged embezzlement, 1961. Returned to England, 1962. Travelled in Africa, Europe, the Caribbean and the USA from 1966 onwards. His writings include a novel *Minty Alley*, a play *Toussaint L'Ouverture*, and a book on cricket *Beyond the Boundary* (all in 1936); *World Revolution 1917–36*, (1937); *The Black Jacobins* (1938), *Party Politics in the West Indies* and *Marxism and the Intellectuals* (both in1962), *Nkrumah and the Ghana Revolution* (1977), *Spheres of Influence: Selected Writings* (1980).

Jamil Abdullah Al-Amin See BROWN, H. Rap.

JAWARA, (Sir) Dawda Kairaba
(born 1924)

Gambian politician

Educated The Gambia, Gold Coast and Britain. Chief veterinary officer, 1958. Reorganized the Protectorate People's Society into, and became leader of, the People's Progressive Party, 1960. Elected to the House of Representatives; Minister of Education, 1960–1; Chief Minister, 1962–5. Prime Minister of independent Gambia, 1965–70. First president of the Republic of The Gambia, 1970. Survived military coup attempt, 1981. Vice-President of the Confederation of Senegambia, 1982–9. Re-elected as president of The Gambia, 1992.

JOHN, Patrick (born 1937)

Dominican politician

Teacher; founded Seamen and Waterfront Workers' Union, 1964. Elected to House of Assembly, 1970; appointed Minister of Communications and Works. Home Affairs Minister, Deputy Premier and Finance Minister, 1973. Premier, 1974. Increasingly repressive anti-trade union and press policies; instituted Dread Act, 1974. Led Dominica to independence, 1978. Forced to resign following general strike, 1979. Imprisoned for twelve years for attempting overthrow of Prime Minister Eugenia Charles, 1985. Released from prison, 1990.

JONES, Claudia
(née Cumberbatch) (1915–64)

US and British radical political activist

Born Port-of-Spain, Trinidad; moved with family to Harlem, 1923. Joined Young Communist League (YCL) and Communist Party (CP); editor of YCL *Weekly Review* and *Spotlight*. Active in anti-racism, anti-imperialism and black working-class women's struggles. Leader of National Negro Congress youth council in Harlem.

Secretary, CP Women's Commission, 1945. Imprisoned one year for CP membership, 1951. Deported to England, 1955. Founded and edited monthly *West Indian Gazette and Afro-Asian Caribbean News*, Britain's first campaigning black newspaper, 1958–64; co-organizer of London's first Caribbean Carnival, 1959.

JORDAN, Barbara (1936–96)

US politician

Born Houston, Texas. Educated Texas Southern University, Boston University Law School; practised law. First black American elected to the Texas Senate since 1883, in 1966; President of the Texas Senate, 1972. Elected to the US House of Representatives, 1972; served three terms. Professor at University of Texas, 1979–82. Co-author of *Barbara Jordan: A Self-Portrait* (1979) and *The Great Society: A Twenty Year Critique* (1986).

JORDAN, Edward (1800–69)

Jamaican civil rights activist, politician and journalist

Born free in Jamaica, active in the 1820s in campaign for citizenship and civil rights for free blacks which succeeded in 1830. Founded an abolitionist newspaper, *The Watchman*, 1829. Arrested for sedition and imprisoned for six months, 1832. After emancipation, became a member of the House of Assembly; advocated extension of the franchise. Mayor of Kingston for 14 years, he was also Speaker of the House of Assembly from 1861–4.

JOSHUA, Ebenezer (born 1908)

St Vincent politician

Teacher and official in the Oil Workers' Trade Union, Trinidad, 1920s. Returned to St Vincent after failure to be elected to Trinidad legislature. Formed People's Political Party (PPP), 1950. Elected to St

Vincent Legislative Council, 1951. Minister of Trade and Production, 1958; Chief Minister, 1961 and 1966. Dismissed by British authorities and defeated in general election, 1967. Deputy premier in coalition government, 1972–4. Minister of Trade and Agriculture, 1974–8. Retired from politics, 1980.

KABAREGA (c.1850–1923)
African resistance leader
Ruler of the Nyoro kingdom (now Uganda), 1866–99; led resistance to the British. Succeeded brother as King of Bunyoro following civil war. Rebuilt army and administration; successfully resisted British-controlled Egyptian-Sudanese invasion. War with Buganda in the 1880s; defeated Bugandan invasion, 1886. Led long guerrilla campaign against Imperial British East Africa Company, 1894–8. Captured by British, 1899; exiled to Seychelles. Died on return to Uganda.

KADALIE, Clements (c.1896–1951)
South African trade union activist
Born in Nyasaland (now Malawi). Educated at mission school; became a teacher. Worked in Southern Rhodesia (now Zimbabwe) and South Africa. Organized black and coloured South Africans into the Industrial and Commercial Union (ICU). National Convention of Labour leader, 1920. National Secretary of reorganized ICU, 1921. Resigned following dispute over the Pass laws, 1929. Remained an active trade unionist in East London.

KAGAME, Paul (born 1957)
Rwandan politician
A Tutsi; taken by parents into exile in Uganda, 1959. Educated at Makarere University, Kampala. Joined the National Resistance Army of Yoweri Museveni, 1981. Following the capture of Kampala became head of military intelligence, 1986. Military training in USA, 1990. Returned to command Tutsi Rwandan Popular Front (FPR) invasion force in Rwanda, 1990. Led FPR conquest of the country, 1993–4. Appointed Rwandan Vice–President, 1994.

KAMWANA, Elliott Kenan
(c.1872–1956)
Nyasaland (now Malawi) independence activist; founder of the Watch Tower movement in Central Africa
Led Presbyterian revival in Nyasaland, 1899–1903. Joined Jehovah's Witnesses in South Africa. Returned to Nyasaland, 1909; forecast millennium in 1914, when all Europeans would leave Africa. Exiled to South Africa by British colonial authorities; expelled from Mozambique by Portuguese for preaching. Returned to Nyasaland; exiled to Seychelles for discouraging African recruitment in World War I. Returned to Nyasaland, 1937; continued to lead the movement.

KAPEPWE, Simon (1922–80)
Zambian politician
Teacher; helped form Northern Rhodesia African National Congress, 1958. Elected to National Assembly, 1962. Minister of Home Affairs, 1964; Minister of Foreign Affairs, 1967–70; Minister of Local Government, 1970–1. Resigned from the ruling United National Independence Party (UNIP), accusing President Kaunda of unfair treatment of the Bemba people; formed the United Progressive Party which was banned. Arrested and detained, 1972–3. Rejoined UNIP, 1978.

KARIUKI, Josiah Mwangi (1929–75)
Kenyan politician
Detained by the British authorities during the Mau Mau emergency. Private secretary to Kenyatta, 1961. Increasingly radical,

condemning government corruption and Kikuyu dominance. Returned to Parliament with an increased majority as 'The People's Friend,' 1974. Detained by security forces; later found murdered, 1975.

KASAVUBU, Joseph Ileo (1910–69)
Congo Republic (now Zaïre) politician
Trained as a priest, 1928–39; teacher, civil servant. Member of Kongo cultural organizations advocating renewal of the Kongo kingdom. President Kongo association, Abako, 1955; transformed into a major political party. Mayor of Léopoldville (now Kinshasa), 1957. Participant in independence negotiations with Belgium, 1960. President on independence, 1960. In dispute with Prime Minister Lumumba over form the state should take; both dismissed by the army, 1960; Kasavubu restored to power following assassination of Lumumba. Replaced following Mobutu coup, 1965.

KATILUNGU, Lawrence (1914–61)
Northern Rhodesia (now Zambia) trade union leader and politician
Teacher; worked in copper mines from 1936. Led strike for higher wages, 1940. Worked in the Congo, 1940–7. President of the Mineworkers' Union when it was recognized by the British, 1949. Active in the Northern Rhodesia African Congress (later African National Congress). Founding president of the Northern Rhodesia Trade Union Congress, 1950. Member of African Representative Council (ARC), 1950. Active in campaign against the Central African Federation. Led strikes, 1952, 1955. Defeated as ANC candidate for the African Representative Council, 1959. ANC Deputy National President, 1961. Died in automobile accident.

KAUNDA, Kenneth (born 1924)
Zambian politician
Born Northern Rhodesia (now Zambia). Teacher in Tanganyika (now Tanzania), 1940s. Returned to Northern Rhodesia; organized farmers' association; African National Congress (ANC) general-secretary, 1953. Left ANC to form the Northern Rhodesia National Congress; imprisoned by British, released in 1960; became leader of the United National Independence Party. Chief Minister in coalition government, 1962. Prime Minister, 1964. President on independence, 1964; one-party state on grounds of need to prevent tribal fragmentation, 1972; adoption of new constitution and subsequent election in 1973 ratified power; played part in independence negotiations for Zimbabwe and Mozambique. Resigned following defeat in 1991 elections. Renewed involvement in politics, 1995.

KAWAWA, Radhidi Mfaume
(born 1929)
Tanzanian politician
Trade unionist; Prime Minister when Tanzania became independent in 1962. Vice-President, 1962–72; Prime Minister, 1972–7; Minister of Defence, 1977–80; Minister without Portfolio, 1980. Chama Cha Mapinduzi Secretary-General, 1982. Failed unexpectedly to succeed to the presidency, 1985.

KAYIBANDA, Grégoire (1924–76)
Rwanda politician
Journalist; school inspector. Hutu campaigner against Tutsi dominance. Founded and led Hutu Social Movement, 1957; transformed this into Hutu Democratic Republican Movement (PARMEHUTU), 1959. Prime Minister on winning the first national elections, 1960. President following a referendum abolishing the monarchy,

1962. Massacre of Tutsis, 1963. Re-elected 1965, 1969. Allowed Tutsi participation in administration; overthrown in bloodless coup by Defence Minister Habyarimana, 1973. Died under house arrest.

KEITA, Modibo (1915–77)
Mali politician
Educated in Dakar and France. Director of Les Ballets Africains. Helped form Rassemblement Démocratique Africain, 1946. Elected to Territorial Assembly, 1948; Deputy for Mali in the French National Assembly, 1956–9. Prime Minister of the Mali Federation with Senegal. Following federation's collapse, declared independent Mali Republic, becoming president, 1960. Radical supporter of Ghanaian President Kwame Nkrumah. Dissolved National Assembly, 1968. Deposed in military coup, November 1968. Imprisoned; died after unsuccessful attempt to restore him to power.

KENYATTA, Jomo (Kamau Wa Ngengi) (c.1889–1978)
Kenyan politician
Educated at a Church of Scotland mission school; government clerk. Member of the East African Association, 1922; general-secretary of the Kikuyu Central Association (KCA). Agitated for restoration of white-owned land in the Kenyan Highlands to the Kikuyu; sent to Europe by KCA to campaign. Studied anthropology in Britain from 1931–44; published *Facing Mount Kenya* in 1938. Founder member of the Pan-African Federation, 1945. Returned to Kenya and established nationalist Kenya African Union (KAU), 1946. Teacher training college principal, 1946–7. Accused of being leader of the anti-British Mau Mau; sentenced to hard labour in 1952; released into internal exile, 1958. Leader of Kenya African National Union (KANU) on its

formation, 1960. Prime Minister, 1963; President on independence, 1964. Remained in office until his death.

KÉRÉKOU, Mathieu (born 1933)
Benin politician
Born Atakora, Dahomey (now Benin); educated in Senegal and France. Joined French army, 1960; commission into Benin army on independence. Participated in military coup, 1967; Vice-President of the Military Revolutionary Council, 1967–8; Deputy Chief of Staff, 1970. Led military council, becoming president, 1972. Declared Benin a Marxist–Leninist state and People's Republic, 1974; one-party state, 1975. Survived French-backed coups, 1975 and 1977. Re-elected as sole candidate, 1980, 1984, 1988. Abandoned Marxism–Leninism, 1980. Defeated in presidential elections by Nicéphore Soglo, 1991; returned to office, 1996.

KHAMA, Seretse (1921–80)
Botswana politician
Ngwato chief, 1925, but did not take office. Graduated Fort Hare University College, 1944. Studied law in England; marriage to a white woman aroused black and white criticism. Banned from return to Bechuanaland (now Botswana) by British for refusing to renounce hereditary rights, 1950–6. Returned, entered politics, forming the Botswana Democratic Party; elected prime minister, 1965. President on independence, 1966.

KIMBANGU, Simon (1889–1951)
Messianic religious leader in the Belgian Congo (now Zaïre)
Born in N'Kamba; educated at a Baptist mission. Preacher and teacher; migrant labourer in Léopoldville (now Kinshasa). Returned to N'Kamba, 1915; established mass revivalist movement, Kimbanguism,

drawing on anti-European sentiment, and declaring himself a prophet, 1921. Arrested for sedition by Belgian authorities; death sentence commuted to life imprisonment. Died in prison. His movement survived as an underground church.

KING, Coretta Scott (born 1927)
US civil rights activist and singer

Born Marion, Atlanta; educated Antioch College, New England Conservatory of Music. Performed as a singer in USA and India. Women's Strike for Peace delegate at the Geneva Disarmament Conference, 1962. Following the assassination of Martin Luther King Jr, president of the Martin Luther King Center for Non-Violent Social Change, 1969. Anti-apartheid activist; arrested in 1985; visited South Africa, 1986.

KING, Martin (Michael) Luther, Jr (1929–68)
US civil rights activist

Born in Atlanta, Georgia; educated Morehouse College, Crozier Theological College, Boston University School of Theology; PhD, 1955. Ordained at his father's Ebenezer Baptist Church, 1947. Pastor at Dexter Avenue Baptist Church, Montgomery, Alabama; involved in organization of Montgomery bus boycott, 1955–6. Founder member and president of the Southern Christian Leadership Conference (SCLC), 1957. Survived stabbing attempt, 1958. Imprisoned during Birmingham, Alabama, non-violent protests, 1963. Delivered 'I have a dream' speech at March on Washington, 1963. Awarded Nobel Peace Prize, 1964. Attempted to build coalition on civil rights and anti-Vietnam War movements. His assassination in April 1968 led to a wave of violent protest throughout the USA. After his death the extent of harassment by the Federal Bureau of Investigation (FBI) was revealed. His

widow established the Martin Luther King Center for Non-Violent Social Change in Atlanta, 1969.

KINJIKITILE NWAGLE (died 1905)
Religious and resistance leader in German East Africa (now Tanzania)

Nothing is known about his life until his arrival in Ngarambe in 1902. He became a preacher, building on local beliefs and taking the name of a local god, Bokero; credited with a number of miracles. Called for a rising to evict Germans; gave sacred water (maji) to his followers. The Maji-Maji rising took place in 1905 before he gave the order and continued until 1907. Arrested and hanged by the German authorities, the first African to die in the rising.

KUTAKO, Hosea (1870–1970)
Namibian independence leader

Participated in Herero revolt against German occupation of South West Africa (now Namibia), 1904; captured by Germans. Became a teacher; appointed Herero paramount chief by South African government, 1917. Rejected South African plans to resettle Hereros and absorb territory into South Africa, 1933. Petitioned United Nations for independence, 1946. Advocated Namibian independence until it became an international issue.

LAMIZANA, Sangoulé (born 1916)
Upper Volta (later Burkina Faso) military ruler

Born in Dianra. Joined French army in 1936, serving in Morocco, Algeria and Indo-China; promoted to lieutenant. Chief of Staff of the Upper Volta army on independence, 1961. Seized power when President Yaméogo was ousted in a popular uprising, 1966. Introduced new military–civilian government, 1970; dismissed civilian prime minister, 1974. Elected president, 1978.

Overthrown in a bloodless military coup, 1980. Acquitted on charges of misusing public funds, 1984.

LANGALIBALELE (c.1818–89)
African resistance leader
Hereditary chief of the Hlubi people of Zululand; driven out of Zululand by King Mpangazitha, 1849. Established a settlement in Natal in the foothills of the Drakensberg mountains. British attempted to force Hlubis to register weapons fearing a threat to whites, 1873; Langalibalele refused. Invasion forced the Hlubis to flee to Lesotho. British pursued; Langalibalele captured and tried for rebellion and murder. Imprisoned on Robben Island; returned to Zululand after 13 years.

LAWS, Courtney Alexandre Henriques (1931–96)
British community activist
Born in Jamaica; educated Rollington School and Lincoln College. Moved to England, 1952; worked in biscuit factory in South London. Co-organizer of the Somerleyton and Geneva Roads Association to protect tenants' interests in Brixton; emerged as a leading community activist and organizer. Diploma of Social Studies, University of Leicester, 1967; formed Brixton Neighbourhood Community Association, an advice centre and the West Indian Senior Citizens Association. Awarded Order of Distinction, Jamaica; Order of the British Empire.

LE BLANC, Edward Oliver (born 1923)
Dominican politician
A civil servant; joined the Dominican Labour Party, 1957. Elected to the West Indies Federation Parliament, 1958; resigned to run in the Dominican general election, 1961.

Appointed chief minister; became premier, 1964. An autocratic leader, he was forced to resign in 1974 following a period of mounting disorder.

LENSHINA, Alice (1924–78)
Zambian religious leader
Educated in a Church of Scotland mission. Following a vision, organized an anti-witchcraft movement in Northern Rhodesia (now Zambia), 1953; claimed 100,000 supporters by 1961. Organized Lumpa Church, 1963. Opposed Kaunda government on independence; refused to pay taxes. Government forces killed over 700 followers and banned church. Arrested and imprisoned until 1975.

LIBERIA PETERS, Maria (born 1941)
Netherlands Antilles politician.
Teacher; elected to Curaçao council, 1974. Health commissioner, 1977–8. Acting Lieutenant-Governor of Curaçao, 1982. Leader of the National People's Party, 1983. Minister of Economic Affairs; became first woman premier, 1984. Returned to office in 1988 and 1990 general elections.

LIMANN, Hilla (born 1934)
Ghanaian politician
Educated at Universities of London and Paris. Member of constitutional committee preparing for restoration of civilian rule, 1969; then held various diplomatic posts abroad. Returned to Ghana to lead the People's National Party (PNP) in elections, 1979; became president, September 1979. Government collapsed following economic problems and increasing PNP ethnic divisions, 1981. Detained 1982–3 but cleared of criminal charges.

LITTLE, Malcolm See Malcolm X.

LOBENGULA (c.1836–94)

Last King of the Ndebele in what is now Zimbabwe

Born in the western Transvaal; nominated to succeed his father Mzilikazi as king, 1868. Granted mining concessions to the British. Survived attempts to overthrow him by rival claimant to throne, 1870 and 1872. Organized attacks on neighbouring Shona and into what is now Zambia and Botswana; increasingly inefficient army defeated by the Tswana, 1883, 1885. Under pressure from British, Germans, Portuguese and Afrikaaners; granted exclusive mining rights to British South Africa Company, 1888; interpreted by British as right to annex land. British invaded and conquered territory, 1893. Lobengula fled but died of smallpox.

LONG, Jefferson (1836–1900)

US politician

Born Knoxville, Georgia; worked in a shop, then became a tailor. Campaigned for enforcement of the 15th Amendment to the constitution which promised the right to vote. One of the first black Americans to be elected to the House of Representatives, 1870; the only black legislator elected in Georgia in the nineteenth century. Returned to tailoring business, 1871.

LOUISON, George (born 1951)

Grenadian politician

Teacher and farmer. Minister of Education in New Jewel Movement government, 1979; Minister of Agriculture, 1981. Resigned following arrest and murder of Maurice Bishop, 1983. Imprisoned; released following US invasion of Grenada. Co-founder, Maurice Bishop Patriotic Movement.

LOVE, Nat (1854–1921)

American cowboy

Left Tennessee in 1869 to work in Kansas, Texas and Arizona. Fought bandits and Native Americans. Won Deadwood, South Dakota, marksmanship competition, 1876; known thereafter as 'Deadwood Dick' Became a Pullman porter on Denver and Rio Grande Railroad, 1889. Wrote autobiography, *The Life and Adventures of Nat Love, Better Known in Cattle Country as Deadwood Dick* (1907).

LUMUMBA, Patrice (1925–61)

Congo (now Zaïre) politician

Assistant-postmaster and union activist; founder of the country's first national party, the Congolese National Movement (MNC), 1958. Imprisoned for anti-Belgian agitation, 1959; released to attend independence negotiations. Led MNC to victory in pre-independence elections, becoming prime minister on independence, June 1960. Faced immediate army rebellion and secession of Katanga province; United Nations peace-keeping force failed to end secession. Increasingly radicalized, Lumumba sought advice from Nkrumah of Ghana and Soviet aid. Deposed in army coup by Mobutu, September 1960; attempting to re-establish his government he was captured and murdered by soldiers, January 1961.

LUTHULI, Albert Muvumbi (1898–1967)

South African nationalist leader

Born in Southern Rhodesia (now Zimbabwe). Educated in mission schools, Natal. Inherited Zulu chieftainship, 1935. Joined African National Congress (ANC), 1946, becoming Natal branch president. Advocated passive resistance during Defiance Campaign, 1952. ANC President-General, 1952–60. Subject to persistent banning orders. Detained for anti-apartheid activity, 1956–7; defendant in Rivonia Trials. Placed under permanent banning order, 1959. Awarded Nobel Peace Prize for his moderating influence, 1960. Autobiography *Let My People Go* (1962) banned in South Africa. Killed by train in suspicious circumstances.

MACHEL, Samora Moises (1932–86)
Mozambique politician

Nurse; joined Front for the Liberation of Mozambique (FRELIMO) in Tanzania, 1962. Trained in Algeria; led first guerrilla attack, 1964. Secretary for Defence, 1966; Commander-in-Chief, 1968. Following the death of Mondlane, elected FRELIMO president, 1969. Instituted collectivization and socialist education in occupied zones. On independence, proclaimed People's Republic and became president, 1975; supported Zimbabwe liberation struggle. Signed Nkomati Accord with South Africa, 1984. Died in unexplained aircraft crash, 1986.

MACIAS NGUEMA, Francisco (1922–79)
Equatorial Guinea politician

Colonial civil servant; appointed mayor of Mongomo. Joined left-wing anti-Spanish party, 1963, becoming its leader. Vice-president of the Government Council, 1964–8. Elected first president of independent Equatorial Guinea, 1968. Instituted a reign of terror, killing opponents and members of own party. Banned all parties; declared himself president for life, 1972. Ordered replacement of Christian names by African names, 1976; banned Roman Catholic Church, 1978. Overthrown in military coup, July 1979. Tried for murder and treason; executed September 1979.

MAHERERO, Samuel (c.1854–1923)
Namibian resistance leader

Son of an Herero chief. Recognized as paramount chief by German colonial authorities in return for land. Led Herero revolt to regain land, January 1904; suffered decisive defeat by Germans, August 1904. Led Herero retreat across the desert to British Bechuanaland (now Botswana) where he settled.

MALCOLM X (El-Hajj Malik El-Shabazz) (1925–65)
US black nationalist activist

Born Malcolm Little in Omaha, Nebraska, the son of a radical Baptist minister; his father was possibly killed by the Ku-Klux-Klan; placed in a foster home. Moved to New York City, 1940; waiter, drug dealer, burglar. Imprisoned for ten years, 1946; converted to Nation of Islam. Released on parole and became a Nation of Islam activist, 1952. Assumed name Malcolm X; established a mosque in Philadelphia; founded the newspaper *Muhammad Speaks*; appointed minister of Harlem Temple No 7, 1954. Advocated black separatism and use of violence in self-defence. Suspended for saying President Kennedy's assassination was 'chickens coming home to roost', 1963. Formed Muslim Mosque Inc and the Organisation of Afro-American Unity, combining Islam, African socialism, anti-colonialism and racial solidarity. Pilgrimage to Mecca, 1964; moderated anti-white stance. Assassinated by Black Muslim enemies in Harlem following the fire-bombing of his home, 1965. Among his works, or collections after his death, are the *Autobiography of Malcolm X* (1965), *Malcolm X Speaks* (1965), *The Speeches of Malcolm X at Harvard* (1968), *By Any Means Necessary: Speeches, Interviews, and a Letter by Malcolm*

X (1970), and *The End of White Supremacy: Four Speeches by Malcolm X* (1971).

MALLOUM, Felix (born 1932)
Chad soldier and politician

Attended military schools in Brazzaville and France. Served in French army in Indo-China and Algeria. Joined Chad national army on independence, 1960; Commander-in-Chief, 1972. Imprisoned by President Tombalbaye in 1973; released during military coup, 1975. President of the Supreme Military Council and head of provisional government, 1975. Faced continual resistance from the Chad National Liberation Front (FROLINAT). Under French pressure, formed government of national unity with himself as president and former FROLINAT leader Hissène Habré as prime minister, 1977. FROLINAT refused to accept the agreement; Malloum resigned and went into exile, 1979.

MANDELA, Nelson Rolihlahla
(born 1918)
South African politician

Born Umtata (now Transkei). Heir to a Thembu chiefdom which he renounced. Educated Headtown School, Fort Hare University College, 1938–40; expelled from Fort Hare for political activity. Articled to solicitors in Johannesburg; enrolled for law degree at University of the Witwatersrand, 1942. Joined African National Congress (ANC); founded ANC Youth League with Walter Sisulu, 1944. Elected as ANC deputy president, 1952; suspended prison sentence for organizing Defiance Campaign. Established first black South African law firm with Oliver Tambo, 1953. Charged with treason, 1956; under a banning order until acquitted, 1961. Went underground to organize ANC armed wing Umkhonto we Sizwe, 1961. Left South Africa illegally; travelled to Ethiopia, Algeria and Britain, 1962.

Sentenced to five years' imprisonment for incitement to strike, 1962. Life sentence on Robben Island following the Rivonia Trial, 1964. Rejected offer of release if he renounced political violence, 1985. Released, 1990; ANC national organizer and vice-president, 1990–1; ANC president, 1991. Awarded Nobel Peace Prize, 1993. Led ANC to victory in first multi-racial elections; President of South Africa in a Government of National Unity, 1994. Among his writings are *No Easy Walk to Freedom* (1965) and his autobiography *Long Walk to Freedom* (1993).

MANDELA, Winnie (née Nkosikazi Nobandle Nomzano Madikizela)
(born 1936)
South African politician and anti-apartheid activist

Born Pondoland, Transkei. Qualified as the first black South African social worker, 1956; married Nelson Mandela, 1958; after his sentencing to life imprisonment in 1964 began a 27-year campaign to secure his release and defeat apartheid. Arrested and imprisoned in solitary confinement, 1969–70; placed under a banning order, 1976; banished to Brandfort, 1977. Appointed head of African National Congress (ANC) social welfare department, 1990. Given two-year suspended prison sentence for involvement in kidnapping and assault of four youths by her bodyguards, 1991. Resigned from ANC post following accusations of misappropriation of funds, 1992. Appointed deputy Minister of Arts and Culture, 1994; forced to resign from government post following housing corruption enquiry. Divorced 1997.

MANIGAT, Leslie (born 1930)
Haitian academic and politician

Joined Foreign Ministry, 1953. Founded international studies institute with support of President Duvalier, 1958. Imprisoned by Duvalier, 1961; went into exile, 1963. Taught in USA, Trinidad, Venezuela and Europe. Sentenced to death in absence by Duvalier, 1968. Founded Rally of National Progressive Democracy, 1979. Returned to Haiti, 1986. Elected as president with armed forces backing, February 1988. Overthrown by the army, June 1988. Returned to exile.

MANLEY, Michael Norman (1924–97)
Jamaican politician
Served with Royal Canadian Air Force in World War II. Educated London School of Economics, 1945–9; economist and journalist. Returned to Jamaica, 1951. Organizer of the National Workers' Union (NWU), 1953; NWU Vice-President, 1955; President, 1984. President, Caribbean Bauxite, Mine and Metal Workers' Federation, 1964–74. Appointed as a Senator, 1962. Elected to the House of Representatives, 1967. Succeeded his father as leader of the People's National Party (PNP), 1969. Prime Minister following PNP election victory, 1972; re-elected 1976. Vice-President of the Socialist International, 1979. Defeated in 1980 general election following pressure from the USA because of democratic socialist policies. Abandoned left-wing stance; re-elected 1989. Among his works are *The Politics of Change* (1975), *Up the Down Escalator* (1988).

MANLEY, Norman Washington
(1893–1969)
Jamaican politician
Educated in Jamaica; won a Rhodes Scholarship to Oxford University, 1914. Served in the British Army in World War I, returning to Oxford in 1919. Qualified as a barrister, 1921; practised as a lawyer in Jamaica, 1922–38. Formed People's National Party, 1938. Elected to the legis-

lature, 1947. Jamaica's first chief minister, 1955–7; Prime Minister 1957–62. Refused offer of leadership of the West Indies Federation, 1958. Declared National Hero of Jamaica.

MARGAI, (Sir) Albert (1910–80)
Sierra Leone politician
Qualified as lawyer in England; returned to Sierra Leone to practise, 1947. Founded Sierra Leone People's Party (SLPP) with his half-brother Milton Margai, 1951. Elected to Legislative Council, 1951. Left the SLPP after dispute with half-brother. Rejoined party on independence, 1961; Minister of Finance, 1962; Prime Minister on half-brother's death, 1964. Proposal to create a one-party state caused a crisis, 1966. Defeated in 1967 general election by Siaka Stevens; refused to leave office. Went into exile in England following military coup. Unsuccessfully attempted to regain power following military coup, 1968; died in USA.

MARGAI, (Sir) Milton Augustus Striery (1895–1964)
Sierra Leone politician
First Sierra Leonian to qualify as a doctor, 1926. Worked in Sierra Leone Medical Service, 1928–50. Formed a Protectorate Party to work for independence, 1946. Formed Sierra Leone People's Party (SLPP), with his half-brother Albert, 1951. Chief Minister, 1954; Prime Minister, 1956. Led Sierra Leone to independence, 1961.

MARRYSHOW, Terry (born 1952)
Grenadian politician
Teacher. Commander in People's Revolutionary Army following the New Jewel Movement takeover, 1979. Medical student in Cuba, 1979–86. Elected leader of the Maurice Bishop Patriotic Movement, 1988. Grandson of T. Albert Marryshow.

MARRYSHOW, Theophilus Albert
(1887–1958)
Grenadian anti-colonialist activist and politician
Edited *St. George's Chronicle*; founded *The West Indian*, advocating independence and a West Indies federation, 1915. Elected to Legislative Council, 1925. Co-founder, Grenada Workingmen's Association, 1931. Campaigned for self-rule in Caribbean and Britain. Elected first president of the Caribbean Labour Congress, 1945. Described as the 'Father of the Federation', he became a member of the Upper House of the Federation of the West Indies Parliament in 1958 but died before taking his seat.

MARSHALL, Thurgood (born 1908)
US lawyer and civil rights activist
Born Baltimore, Maryland. Educated Lincoln University, Howard University Law School. Practised as civil rights lawyer; appointed National Association for the Advancement of Colored People (NAACP) chief legal officer, 1938; director-general, NAACP Legal Defense Fund. Awarded NAACP Springarn Medal, 1946. Led NAACP legal team in seminal US Supreme Court case *Brown v Board of Education*, 1954. Appointed Appeals Court judge, 1961; first black US Solicitor-General, 1965; first black Supreme Court justice, 1967. Publicly attacked President Reagan's civil rights record, 1987. Retired, 1991.

MARTINA, Don (born 1935)
Netherlands Antilles politician
Civil engineer. Elected to Curaçao council, 1971. Founded New Antilles Movement, 1971. Justice commissioner, 1972–6. Premier of coalition government, 1979–84; coalition reformed 1985 and returned to office in 1988.

MASIRE, Quett Ketumile (born 1925)
Botswana politician
Journalist; entered politics through the Bangwaketse Tribal Council, 1962. Founded the Botswana Democratic Party with Seretse Khama. Deputy Prime Minister, 1965; Vice-President on independence, 1966. Became president, 1980; re-elected 1984, 1989 and 1994.

MAYNARD, Clement (born 1928)
Bahamas politician
Medical technician. Leader of the Senate and Minister without Portfolio, 1967. Elected to House of Assembly, 1968. Minister of Works, 1968–9; Minister of Tourism, 1969–79; Minister of Labour and Home Affairs, 1979–84; Minister of Foreign Affairs and Tourism, 1985–9. Deputy Prime Minister, 1989–92.

M'BA, Léon (1902–67)
Gabon politician
Accountant and journalist. Exiled from Gabon by French colonial authorities for political activities, 1933–46. Elected to Gabon Territorial Assembly, 1952; founded Bloc Démocratique Gabonais (BDG) in 1953; Mayor of Libreville, 1956. Prime Minister, 1957; led the country to independence, 1960. Elected president in 1961, forming a coalition government. Deposed in a military coup, 1964; restored to office by French troops; transformed Gabon into a one-party state. Died in office.

MBEKI, Govan Archibald Mvuyelwa (born 1910)
South African nationalist activist
Studied at Fort Hare University College; joined African National Congress (ANC), 1935. Teacher until dismissed for political activities. ANC National Chairman, 1956. Joined South African Communist Party,

1961. Detained in 1960–1 and then under house arrest; went underground to join Umkhonto we Sizwe. Arrested; sentenced to life imprisonment at the Rivonia Trials, 1964. Served sentence on Robben Island, where he wrote *South Africa: The Peasants' Revolt*. Released 1987.

MBEKI, Thabo Mvuyelwa (born 1942)
South African politician
Born in Eastern Cape. African National Congress (ANC) activist and Communist Party member; sent abroad by ANC leadership, 1962. Studied at University of Sussex; master's degree in economics, 1966. Military and political training in the Soviet Union. Represented ANC internationally. Assistant-secretary of ANC revolutionary council, 1971. Member of ANC National Executive, 1975. ANC representative in Nigeria, 1976–8. ANC President's Political Secretary, 1978; member of the Communist Party politburo, 1979–81, 1984–90. ANC Director for Information, 1985; Director of International Affairs, 1987. Member of ANC delegation which met President de Klerk, 1990. First deputy president of South Africa following 1994 elections; declared by President Nelson Mandela as his likely successor, 1996.

MBOYA, Thomas Joseph (1930–69)
Kenyan politician
A Luo. Educated Catholic mission school. Sanitary inspector and trade unionist. Active in trade union activity following banning of Kenya African Union, 1952. General-Secretary of the Kenya Federation of Labour, 1953–62. Studied at Oxford University. Opposition leader on Legislative Council, 1957. Kenya African National Union (KANU) Secretary-General, 1960. Minister of Justice, 1963–4; Minister of Economic Planning and Development, 1964–9. Seen as natural successor to President Kenyatta. Assassination in the capital Nairobi triggered rioting between members of Luo and Kikuyu groups.

McKAY, Claude (1890–1948)
Jamaican socialist activist and writer
Published poetry in Jamaica; moved to USA, 1912. Joined radical socialist Industrial Workers of the World, 1919. Member of editorial board of socialist newspaper, *The Liberator*, 1919; joined the African Blood Brotherhood. Travelled in Europe, 1919–23; contributed to British revolutionary socialist newspaper *Workers' Dreadnought*, 1919–21. Became important figure in the Harlem Renaissance. Left the USA to live in Europe until 1934; converted to Roman Catholicism 1944. Among his works are *Literary Shadows*, *Home to Harlem*, *Banjo*, *Banana Bottom*.

MENELIK II (Sahlé Mariam) (1844–1913)
Emperor of Ethiopia
Heir to the throne of the independent Shoa kingdom; taken prisoner by Emperor Tewodoros II, 1855; escaped and proclaimed King Menelik of Shoa, 1865. Built Shoa into a powerful kingdom during Ethiopian civil war; expanded territory and imported European arms and technology. Remained neutral in Ethiopian war with Italy; proclaimed Emperor on death of Yohannes IV. Established capital at Addis Ababa, 1886. Signed Treaty of Ucciali with Italy; decisively defeated Italian army at Adowa, 1896. Began Ethiopian modernization, building roads, bridges, schools, hospitals; founded national bank, 1905. Secured British, French and Italian recognition of independence by treaty, 1906. Died following many years of illness.

MENGISTU, Haile Mariam (born 1937)
Ethiopian military ruler

Member of staff of Emperor Haile Selassie. Vice-Chairman of the Provisional Military Administrative Committee (the Dergue) on overthrow of Haile Selassie, September 1974; involved in the killing of the Dergue's chairman, November 1974. Advocated a socialist state, 1976. Proclaimed head of state, 1977; purged opposition and sought aid from the Soviet Union. Fought Somalia and Eritrean and Tigre rebels with Cuban and Soviet military support. Abolished the Dergue, 1980. Formed and became secretary-general of the Workers' Party of Ethiopia, 1984. Proclaimed Democratic People's Republic, 1986; became president, 1987. Fled to Zimbabwe following military defeat by Tigre and Eritrean rebels, 1991.

MITCHELL, James Fitzallen (born 1931)
St Vincent politician

Born in Bequia; educated in St Vincent, Trinidad and University of British Columbia. St Vincent Chief Agricultural Officer, 1958–60; worked for British Ministry of Overseas Development, 1960–6. Joined St Vincent Labour Party, 1966; elected to the House of Assembly, 1966; Minister of Trade, Agriculture and Tourism, 1967. Resigned from Labour Party; re-elected as an Independent, 1972. Premier in coalition with the People's Political Party; defeated in 1974 general election. Founded New Democratic Party (NDP), 1975. Re-elected for the Grenadines, 1980; Leader of the Opposition, 1983. Prime Minister following NDP election victories, 1984, 1989.

MITCHELL, Keith (born 1946)
Grenadian politician

Academic in the USA. Elected to the Grenada House of Representatives for the New National Party (NNP), 1984.

Appointed Minister of Communications, Works and Utilities. NNP general-secretary, 1986; elected NNP leader, replacing Herbert Blaize, 1989; dismissed from government by Blaize.

MOBUTU, Sese Seko Kuku Ngbendu Wa Za Banga (formerly Joseph-Désiré) (born 1930)
Zaïrean soldier and politician

Born in Lisala; a Bengala. Conscripted into Belgian colonial army; rose to rank of sergeant. Journalist; joined Lumumba's Congolese National Movement (MNC), 1958. Worked in Belgium; attended independence negotiations. Appointed Army Chief of Staff as colonel on independence, June 1960; Commander-in-Chief, September 1960. Mounted temporary coup; his troops killed Lumumba, 1961. Second military coup, 1965; appointed himself president. Introduced new constitution and founded Popular Movement of the Revolution as sole legal party, 1967. Renamed Congo, Zaïre, in sweeping 'African authenticity' programme, 1970. Accepted multi-party democracy, 1991, but placed obstacles to its progress.

MOI, Daniel Torotitch arap (born 1924)
Kenyan politician

Teacher, 1945–57. Elected to the Legislative Council, 1957. Assistant treasurer of the Kenya African National Union (KANU), 1960, but left objecting to Kikuyu and Luo domination. Joined Kenya African Democratic Union (KADU). Member of pre-independence coalition government as Minister of Education, 1961–2, and Minister of Local Government, 1962–3. When KANU absorbed KADU under President Kenyatta, served as Minister of Home Affairs, 1964–7; Vice-President, 1967–78. Became president on Kenyatta's death, 1978. Appointment confirmed by election,

1979. Survived attempted coup and banned all parties but KANU, 1982; re-elected president, 1983. Introduced multi-party democracy following demonstrations, 1991; re-elected against divided opposition, 1993.

MOMOH, Joseph Saidu (born 1937)
Sierra Leone politician
Civil servant, 1955–8. Joined West African Frontier Force, 1959. Trained in Ghana, Nigeria and Britain. Promoted colonel, 1970; Brigadier, 1973. Nominated for parliament by President Stevens, 1974; appointed a cabinet minister, 1978. Promoted to major-general, 1983. President, 1985. Faced attempted coups and anti-government riots. Declared economic state of emergency, 1987. Instituted multi-party democracy, 1991. Overthrown in military coup after allegations of corruption, 1992.

MONDLANE, Eduardo Chivambo (1920–69)
Mozambique liberation leader
Educated mission school; expelled from University of the Witwatersrand for political activities; post-graduate research in USA. Amalgamated three nationalist movements into the Front for the Liberation of Mozambique in Tanzania (FRELIMO), 1962; elected president. Organized headquarters and guerrilla force. Re-elected FRELIMO president despite ideological disputes over his alleged pro-Westernism, 1968. Killed by letter bomb.

MOODY, Harold Arundel (1882–1947)
Jamaican doctor and activist
Studied medicine in London; qualified in 1910. Unable to find hospital appointment because of racism; set up as general practitioner in South London, 1913. Active in black community in London. Founded the League of Coloured Peoples as a pressure group and welfare organization for black settlers in Britain, 1931.

MOORE, Audley ('Queen Mother') (born 1898)
US radical political activist
Born Louisiana; joined Universal Negro Improvement Association (UNIA), 1919. Organized armed defence of Garvey meeting in New Orleans, 1919. Moved to New York City; joined Communist Party (CP), 1936. Secretary, New York State branch, 1942. Left CP in 1950, objecting to its opposition to black self-determination. Founded Universal Association of Ethiopian Women to campaign against lynchings. Established a Reparations Committee to agitate for compensation for descendants of slaves, 1963. Associated with Republic of New Africa declaration of independence, 1968.

MOORE, Lee (born 1939)
St Kitts-Nevis politician
Lawyer; aide to Premier Bradshaw, 1967. Vice-president of the St Kitts-Nevis Trades and Labour Union. Appointed Attorney-General, 1971. Premier from 1979 until the Labour Party's defeat in the 1980 general election. Leader of the Opposition; lost seat at the 1984 general election. Resigned the party leadership, 1989.

MORRIS, William (Bill) (born 1938)
British trade union leader
Born and educated, Jamaica; emigrated to Britain, 1954. Transport and General Workers' Union (TGWU) National Secretary (Passenger Services), 1979–85. Trades Union Congress (TUC) General Council member from 1988. Member of Commission for Racial Equality (CRE), 1977–87. TGWU Deputy general-secretary, 1986–90; general-secretary, 1990; re-elected 1995.

MOSHOESHOE II (Constantine Bering Seeiso) (1938–96)

Lesotho monarch

Educated Basutoland (now Lesotho), England and Oxford University. Crowned king, 1960; remained monarch on independence, 1966. Placed under house arrest for alleged political involvement; released after signing pledge to remain a constitutional monarch, 1967. Placed under house arrest, replaced by Queen Mamohato and exiled to Holland, 1970; allowed to return when he agreed to cease political involvement. Deposed and replaced by his son Letsi III, 1990. Restored to the throne, 1995. Died in automobile accident.

MUGABE, Robert Gabriel (born 1924)

Zimbabwean politician

Graduated from Fort Hare University College, 1951. Teacher in Zambia and Ghana. Publicity secretary for National Democratic Party (NDP), 1961–2; deputy secretary-general of the Zimbabwe African People's Union (ZAPU), 1962–3. Arrested by white Rhodesian authorities; escaped to Tanzania. Founded Zimbabwe African National Union (ZANU) with Ndabaningi Sithole, 1963. Returned to detention in Rhodesia, 1964–74. Escaped to Mozambique, 1975, becoming President of ZANU (PF) and Commander-in-Chief of guerrilla Zimbabwe African National Liberation Army (ZANLA). Joint leader with Joshua Nkomo of ZAPU–ZANU delegation at independence negotiations, 1979. Independent Zimbabwe's first prime minister, 1980; Executive President, 1987; re-elected 1990, 1996.

MUHAMMAD, Elijah (Robert Poole) (1886–1975)

US religious leader

Born Sandersville, Georgia; son of former slaves. Left home at 16, working in various jobs; automobile worker in Detroit, 1923. Met Wallace D. Fard (Wali Farad, Master Farah Muhammad) and joined his Moorish Science Temple; led a breakaway group in 1930 which became the Nation of Islam (NOI); adopted the name Elijah Muhammad and the titles Messenger of Allah and Supreme Minister of the Nation of Islam. Modified strict racial separatism but advocated black self-reliance and economic self-sufficiency. Imprisoned for draft evasion in World War II. NOI spread from Detroit to Chicago under his leadership; by 1960 there were 80 Islamic temples and over 15,000 members; expelled Malcolm X for political radicalism, 1963.

MUNROE, Trevor (born 1944)

Jamaican academic and political activist

Lecturer, University of the West Indies. Founder and general-secretary of the Workers' Liberation League (later the Worker's Party of Jamaica), 1974. Founder and president of the University and Allied Workers' Union. Following inner-party divisions, refused to abandon the WPA's Marxist–Leninist stance in 1988.

MUSEVENI, Yoweri Kaguta (born 1944)

Ugandan politician

Educated at Dar es Salaam University. Worked with President Obote; exiled when Amin took power, 1972. Fought with the Front for the Liberation of Mozambique before forming the Front for National Salvation guerrilla movement. Leading figure in the Ugandan National Liberation

Front when Amin was overthrown, 1979. Appointed Minister of Defence; demoted to Minister for Regional Co-operation. Vice-President of the Military Commission which overthrew President Binaisa, 1980. Led Uganda People's Movement in December 1980 elections, winning only one seat. Went underground to lead National Resistance Army struggle against President Obote, 1981. Sworn in as president at head of broadly based National Resistance Council, 1986; elected as president, 1996.

MUZOREWA, Abel Tendekayi
(born 1925)
Zimbabwean politician and church leader
Ordained as a Methodist minister, 1953; consecrated as the first black bishop of the United Methodist Church in Southern Rhodesia (now Zimbabwe), 1968. Founded African National Council to campaign against British settlement with white rebel regime, 1971. Signed 'internal settlement' with white regime; joined transitional government, 1978. Prime Minister of Zimbabwe-Rhodesia, 1979. As guerrilla war continued, handed power to Britain as preliminary to independence negotiations. His party won only three seats in the 1980 elections, none in 1985. Returned to church affairs, 1986. Presidential candidate, 1996; withdrew after complaining about the electoral system.

MWINYI, Ndunga Ali Hassan
(born 1925)
Tanzanian politician
Born in Zanzibar; trained in Zanzibar and Britain as a teacher. Worked as a teacher before becoming Minister of Education under President Nyerere. Succeeded Nyerere as president of Tanzania, 1985; re-elected 1990. Amended the Constitution to institute multi-party democracy, 1992.

NAMPHY, Henri **(born 1932)**
Haitian general
Joined the army, 1952. Deputy Commander-in-Chief, 1981; Commander-in-Chief, 1984. Became President when Jean Claude Duvalier fled Haiti, 1986. Replaced by President Manigat in February 1988 following elections; restored to office by a junior officers' coup, June 1988; ousted in a further coup, September 1988. Went into exile in the Dominican Republic.

NANNY **(dates unknown)**
Jamaican resistance leader
One of the Maroon leaders in Jamaica in the early eighteenth century. Led a stronghold in the Blue Mountains during the First Maroon War known as Nannytown. It was captured and destroyed by the British in 1734. Declared a National Hero of Jamaica in the 1970s.

NETO, Antonio Agostinho **(1922–79)**
Angolan politician
Studied medicine in Portugal; graduated, 1958; practised in Luanda. Helped form Popular Movement for the Liberation of Angola (MPLA) while in prison for political activity, 1956; exiled to Cape Verde; placed under house arrest in Portugal, 1962. Escaped to Zaïre; appointed MPLA president. Organized guerrilla operations against Portuguese colonial authorities with Soviet aid. Formed transitional government in Angola with Holden and Savimbi, 1975. Proclaimed People's Republic of Angola with himself as president on independence, 1975. Died undergoing surgery in Moscow, 1979.

NEWTON, Huey P. **(1942–89)**
US political activist
Born Monroe, Louisiana; educated Oakland City College, San Francisco Law School.

Formed an Afro-American Society in Oakland. Founded Black Panther Party with Bobby Seale, 1966. Convicted of killing a police officer, 1967; conviction later overturned. PhD thesis on the Black Panthers, 1980. Charged with illegal possession of weapons, 1987. Murdered by a drugs dealer, 1989.

NGENGI, Kamau *See* KENYATTA, Jomo.

NGOUABI, Marien (1939–77)
Congolese politician
Born in the north of the country. Military training in France; paratroop officer, 1963. A Marxist; armed forces representative in the National Movement of the Revolution (MNR). Led military coup, 1968; took office as president; formed the Parti Congolais du Travail (PCT) as sole legal party; renamed the country the People's Republic of the Congo. Purged opposition; faced increasing clashes between northerners and southerners, guerrilla warfare and a general strike. Assassinated in an unsuccessful military coup, 1977.

NGOYI, Lilian (1911–80)
South African anti-apartheid activist
Educated in the Transvaal. Joined African National Congress (ANC) Women's League, 1952; spoke and organized anti-apartheid activity. Elected president of the Women's League, 1953; elected president of the Federation of South African Women, 1956. Charged with treason, 1956; in solitary confinement until acquitted, 1961. Subjected to a banning order and confined to Orlando township.

NJONJO, Charles (born 1920)
Kenyan politician
A Kikuyu; studied at Fort Hare University College and London University. First Attorney-General of independent Kenya, 1963–80. Adviser to President Moi, 1978. Elected to parliament, becoming Minister for Home and Constitutional Affairs, 1980. Accused of plotting overthrow by President Moi, dismissed and forced from parliament, 1983. Pardoned by Moi on twenty-first anniversary of independence.

NKOBI, Thomas (1922–94)
South African political activist
Born Matabeleland, Southern Rhodesia (now Zimbabwe); moved to Alexandra township, South Africa, 1932. Abandoned education to organize a bus boycott in Alexandra; joined African National Congress (ANC) Youth League. Active in 1952 Defiance Campaign and 1957 potato boycott. Appointed ANC organizing secretary; helped formulate the ANC underground network, 'M Plan'. Exile in Tanzania from 1963 until the ANC was legalized in 1990. ANC treasurer-general, 1973–94.

NKOMO, Joshua Mqabuko Nyongolo (born 1917)
Zimbabwean politician
Educated South Africa; returned to Southern Rhodesia (now Zimbabwe) as a social worker, 1945. General-Secretary, Rhodesian Railway African Employees' Association, 1951. Joined Rhodesian African National Congress (ANC), 1951; elected ANC National President, 1957. President of the National Democratic Party (NDP), formed on banning of ANC, 1960. Active in opposition to the Central African Federation. President on foundation of Zimbabwe African People's Union (ZAPU). Imprisoned for ten years after calling on Britain to overthrow the illegal white Rhodesian regime, 1964. Minister of Home Affairs following independence, 1980. Dismissed for alleged involvement in coup attempt, 1982. Party Vice-President on amalgamation

of ZAPU and the Zimbabwe African National Union (ZANU), 1987.

NKRUMAH, Kwame (Francis Nwia Kofie) (1909–72)
Ghanaian politician and Pan-Africanist
Born Ankroful, Gold Coast (now Ghana). Educated Catholic mission schools, Achimota College; became a teacher. Went to USA, 1935; studied at Lincoln University, University of Pennsylvania; taught Lincoln University. Went to London, 1945; studied at London School of Economics. Organized Fifth Pan-African Conference with W. E. B. Du Bois. Returned to Gold Coast to lead United Gold Coast Convention (UGCC), 1947. Arrested and deported to north of the country by colonial authorities following anti-British demonstrations. Forced to resign from UGCC following organization of civil disobedience campaign; formed and led Convention People's Party (CPP), 1949. Freed from prison to become Leader of Government Business in the National Assembly, 1951. Led Ghana to independence, 1957; President, 1960. Survived first of a number of assassination attempts, 1962. Declared himself president for life and banned opposition parties, 1964. Ousted in military coup, 1966. Moved to Guinea where he was appointed joint head of state; developed theory of neo-colonialism. Died in Romania. Among his most important works are *Towards Colonial Freedom* (1946), *Africa Must Unite* (1963), *Neo-Colonialism* (1965), and *Dark Days in Ghana* (1968).

NKUMBULA, Harry (1916–83)
Zambian politician
Founder and president of African National Congress II, 1951. Led agitation against Central African Federation; imprisoned, 1955. Decision to run in federal elections split the party in 1958; dissidents left to form the United National Independence Party (UNIP). Minister of African Education in coalition government, 1962–4. Opposition leader after independence until Zambia became a one-party state in 1972. Joined UNIP, 1973.

NUJOMA, Sam Daniel (born 1929)
Namibian politician
Born Ondangua, Ovamboland. Office messenger; dismissed for political activity. Helped form Ovamboland People's Organisation (OPO), 1959. Founding President of the South West Africa People's Organisation (SWAPO), 1960. Arrested by South African authorities; exiled to Dar es Salaam, 1960; established SWAPO provisional headquarters. Led petitioning of United Nations to end South African control of Namibia. Returned to South West Africa but expelled, 1966. Established SWAPO military wing, the Peoples' Liberation Army of Namibia (PLAN), 1966. Led guerrilla war against South African forces from Angolan bases. Led boycott of South African organized elections in Namibia, 1975. Elected president of independent Namibia, 1990. Re-elected, 1995.

NURSE, Malcolm See PADMORE, George.

NYAGUMBO, Maurice (1924–89)
Zimbabwean politician
Member of the African National Congress (ANC), Zimbabwe African People's Union (ZAPU) and Zimbabwe African National Union (ZANU); imprisoned for 20 years for nationalist activity. Released to attend independence negotiations at Lancaster House Conference, 1979. Elected to House of Assembly in 1980 elections; appointed Minister of Mines and Energy Resources in post-independence government. Leading member of the ZANU (PF) central com-

mittee. Accused of corruption in 1989, he committed suicide. Buried in Heroes' Acre as a national hero.

NYERERE, Julius Kambarage

(born 1922)

Tanzanian politician

Educated at Makerere College, 1943–5; University of Edinburgh, 1949–52. The country's first black graduate. Resigned from post as a teacher in Tanganyika (now Tanzania) to help form Tanganyika African National Union (TANU), 1954, becoming president. Led a non-violent, non-racial campaign for independence from Britain. Chief minister, 1960; prime minister on independence, 1961. Resigned to reorganize TANU. President on declaration of a Republic, 1962. Advocated an East African Federation. Merged Tanganyika with Zanzibar to form the United Republic of Tanzania, 1964. Instituted one-party state, 1965. Issued Arusha Declaration, 1967. Merged TANU with Zanzibar's Afro-Shirazi Party to form Chama Cha Mapinduzi, 1977. Invaded Uganda to oust Amin, 1979. Retired from politics, 1985. Among his works are *Freedom and Unity – Uhuru na Umoja* (1967), *Freedom and Socialism – Uhuru na Ujamaa* (1968), and *Ujamaa: Essays on Socialism* (1969).

NYUNGU YA MAIVE (?–1884)

Ruler of an empire in Manyoru (part of modern Tanzania), 1870s

A member of the Nyamwezi people; built a powerful army of 'ruga-rugus', soldiers driven out by Nguni invasions. Established an effective administration which ensured Manyoru survived his death but it fell to German colonialists in the 1890s.

NZINGA MBANDE (Ann Zingha)

(c.1582–1663)

Ndongo and Matamba monarch (in what is now Angola)

Sister of the King of Ndongo; sent to negotiate recognition of independence by Portuguese governor, she was converted to Christianity and baptized Dona Ana de Souza, 1622. Queen of the Mbundu people, 1624; driven out by Portuguese, 1626. Renounced Christianity and built an anti-Portuguese army; conquered Matamba kingdom. Developed slave trade; allied with the Dutch against Portugal. Resumed relations with Portuguese following their defeat of the Dutch, 1656. Resumed belief in Christianity before her death.

OBASANJO, Olusegun (born 1937)

Nigerian military ruler

Attended military academy in England. Joined Nigerian army, 1958; served with United Nations peacekeeping forces in the Congo (now Zaïre), 1960. Fought in Biafran Civil War and took Biafran surrender, 1970. Army Chief of Staff on overthrow of Gowon government, 1975. Appointed head of military government on death of General Muhammed, 1976. Introduced new constitution, 1978; restored civilian government, 1979. Retired to become a farmer. Strong advocate of return to civilian rule under the government of Abacha; detained for allegedly plotting a coup against Abacha, 1995.

OBOTE, Apollo Milton (born 1924)

Ugandan politician

Educated Makerere College; a teacher. Elected to the Legislative Council, 1958. Merged radical nationalist wing of the Uganda National Congress and the Uganda People's Union to form Uganda People's Congress (UPC), 1960. Prime Minister on independence of UPC–Kabaka Yekka coalition government, 1962. Mounted a coup against head of state, King Mutasa II of Buganda, declared a Republic, became executive president, 1966. Deposed by Idi Amin, 1971. Restored to office following Amin's overthrow, 1980. Deposed in military coup, 1985; lives in exile in Zambia.

ODINGA, Ajuma Oginga (1911–94)
Kenyan politician
Educated Makerere College; a teacher. Joined Kenya African Union, 1946. Elected to Legislative Council, 1957; elected to National Assembly, 1961. Vice-President of the Kenya African National Union (KANU), 1960–6. Minister for Home Affairs, 1963–6; Vice-President of Kenya, 1964–6. Left government in protest against the shift towards capitalism by President Kenyatta, 1966. Formed opposition Kenya People's Union (KPU) with 29 MPs; KPU banned 1969. Detained until 1971; rejoined KANU; arrested and expelled from KANU, 1977. Rejoined KANU as a supporter of President Moi, 1978; appointed head of Cotton Marketing Board. Expelled from KANU for criticizing Moi, 1982. Formed National Democratic Party (NDP), later the Forum for the Restoration of Democracy (FORD), to end one-party state, 1991. Leader of the opposition following elections, 1992.

ODLUM, George (born 1934)
St Lucia politician
Economist; Executive-Secretary of the West Indies Associated States Council of Ministers, 1967. Co-founded St Lucia Action Movement (SLAM), 1973; merged SLAM with the St Lucia Labour Party (SLP), 1973. President, St Lucia Farmers' and Farm Workers' Union. SLP deputy leader, 1977. Deputy Prime Minister and Foreign Minister, 1979. Dismissed, 1980; founded Progressive Labour Party, 1981. Lost seat in election, 1982.

OJUKWU, Chuckwuemeka Odumegwu (born 1933)
Biafran military ruler
An Ibo; born in northern Nigeria; educated in Nigeria and at Oxford University. Nigerian Public Service, 1955–7. Joined the army, 1957; served in United Nations peace-keeping force in the Congo (now Zaïre), 1960. Appointed Military Governor of the Eastern Region following the January 1966 coup. President of the Republic of Biafra when the region seceded from Nigeria 1967. Following defeat in the 1967–70 civil war, in exile in the Côte d'Ivoire. Returned to Nigeria following amnesty, 1982. Joined the National Party of Nigeria and unsuccessfully contested 1983 senate elections. Detained following 1983 military coup; released 1984.

OKELLO, Tito Lutwa (1914–96)
Ugandan soldier and military ruler
Born in northern Uganda; member of the Acheli people. Worked as sales clerk; joined King's African Rifles, 1940; served in Somalia, Burma and Kenya. Lieutenant in Ugandan army on independence, 1962; appointed chief of staff, 1970. Fled to Tanzania following coup by Amin, 1971; helped organize exile resistance. Appointed Ugandan army commander, 1980; led repression of National Resistance Army. Overthrew President Obote, 1985; chairman of the ruling military council. Exile in Sudan and Tanzania following victory of Museveni in 1986. Returned to Uganda under amnesty, 1994.

O'LEARY, Hazel (born 1937)
US politician
Born Virginia; educated Fisk College and Rutgers University Law School. Member of New Jersey and Washington, DC bars; lobbyist for Northern States Power Co. Appointed Secretary of Energy by President

Clinton, 1993; the first black woman member of an American cabinet.

OLYMPIO, Sylvanus (1902–63)
Togo politician

Born in Lomé, educated in France and England. United Africa Company district manager, 1946. Active in the Comité de l'Unité Togolaise (CUT); appointed president of the Territorial Assembly when the CUT won elections, 1946. Led party's boycott of the Territorial Assembly elections, 1955. Prime Minister, 1958; agitated for independence from France. On independence in 1960 became Togo's first president. Instituted one-party state, 1961; survived three assassination attempts. Shot outside the US Embassy in a military coup, 1963.

OSBORNE, Bertrand (born 1935)
Montserrat politician

Businessman and building contractor. Formed National Development Party, 1984. Founded the island's sole newspaper, the *Montserrat Reporter*. Elected to Legislative Council, 1987, becoming leader of the opposition.

OSBORNE, John (born 1936)
Montserrat politician

Farmer and property developer; elected to Legislative Council for the Montserrat Workers' Progressive Party, 1966. Founder-member of the Progressive Democratic Party, 1970. Minister of Agriculture, Trade, Lands and Housing, 1979. Formed People's Liberation Movement (PLM), 1976. Chief Minister on PLM electoral victory, 1978. Re-elected to office in 1983 and 1987 elections.

OSBORNE, Larry (1922–96)
Trinidadian navigator and air traffic controller

Born Port of Spain; member of the customs service. Joined Royal Air Force (RAF), 1939; trained in Canada as a navigator. Member of Coastal Command, flying from Iceland and Northern Ireland; served on escort duty on Murmansk convoys to Soviet Union. Became an air-traffic controller; the first black Group Captain in the RAF. Helped create the West German Air Force; appointed RAF deputy head of procurement. Retired from RAF, 1977; worked for Crown Agents.

PADMORE, George (born Malcolm Nurse) (1902–59)
Trinidadian political activist and writer

Emigrated to the USA, 1924; studied law. Joined the Communist Party of the USA, 1927, changing his name. Lived in USSR from 1930 to 1933, when he was expelled from the Communist Party and moved to England. Active in African affairs and the movement for colonial independence; moved to independent Ghana in 1957; personal adviser on African affairs to President Nkrumah. Among his works are *How Britain Rules Africa* (1936), *The Gold Coast Revolution* (1953), and *Pan-Africanism or Communism?* (1956).

PAPA DOC See DUVALIER, François.

PARKS, Rosa Lee (born 1913)
US civil rights activist

Born Tuskegee, Alabama. Seamstress. Refused to sit in seats reserved for blacks on a bus and ejected, 1943. Member of the National Association for the Advancement of Colored People (NAACP); secretary of Montgomery NAACP. Arrested after refusing to give up her seat on a bus to a white passenger, 1955. Led to the 361-day Montgomery bus boycott. Dismissed from her job following the bus boycott. Moved to Detroit; became administrative assistant to Representative John Conyers of Michigan.

Her autobiography, *Rosa Parks*, was published in 1992.

PARSONS, Lucy (1853–1942)
US radical political activist
Born a slave in Texas. Moved to Chicago, 1873. Began writing for the *Socialist*, 1978. Joined anarchist International Working People's Association (IWPA), 1883; Knights of Labor, 1884. Editor of IWPA journal *Alarm*, 1884, advocating 'propaganda by deed'. Published *Freedom*, attacking treatment of black people, 1892. Founder member of Industrial Workers of the World, 1905. Active in Communist-led International Labor Defense; member of executive committee, 1927. Joined Communist Party, 1939.

PASCALL-TROUILLOT, Ertha (born 1943)
Haitian politician
The country's first woman lawyer, 1971. Appointed as a judge, 1980; Supreme Court, 1988. Appointed interim president, governing with a Council of State, in March 1990 to organize elections in December 1990.

PATTERSON, Louise Thompson (born 1901)
US radical political activist
Educated University of California, Berkeley. Taught in Arkansas and Virginia; forced to resign after supporting students' strike. Moved to New York City, 1930; active in black cultural movement. Formed Harlem branch of Friends of the Soviet Union; assistant national secretary, National Committee for the Defense of Political Prisoners; joined Communist Party, 1933. Founder member, Civil Rights Congress (CRC), 1946. Co-founder, Sojourners for Truth and Justice, black women's auxiliary of CRC.

PATTERSON, William L. (1891–1980)
US radical political activist
Law degree, Hastings College, 1919. Active in defence of anarchists Sacco and Vanzetti, 1920s. Joined Communist Party of the USA, 1927. Frequent visits to the Soviet Union, early 1930s. CP organizer in Pittsburgh and Harlem; executive-secretary, International Labor Defense; active in Scottsboro Case. CP organizer, Chicago South Side, 1938. National executive-secretary, Civil Rights Congress, 1946. Led delegation to United Nations charging US government with sanctioning genocide against black Americans. Editor, *Sunday Worker*, 1958.

PAYNE, Clement Osbourne (1904–47)
Barbadian radical activist
Born in Trinidad of Barbadian parents. Leading figure in the Trinidad National Unemployed Movement (NUM),1934–5; Negro Welfare Cultural and Social Association (NWC&SA), 1935–7. Founder and leader of the Federated Workers' Trade Union, 1937. Secretary of the radical Workers' United Front Committee, 1938. Returned to Barbados in 1937; his deportation by the British colonial authorities triggered off the Barbados riots, 1938. Collapsed and died speaking at a public meeting, 1947.

PEREIRA, Aristides Maria (born 1923)
Cape Verde politician
Born on Boa Vista island; educated in Senegal; radio-telegraphist. Co-founder with Amilcar Cabral of the African party for the Independence of Portuguese Guinea and Cape Verde (PAIGC), 1956. Exiled to Guinea by the Portuguese authorities, 1960. Leader of the PAIGC council, 1965–74. President of independent Cape Verde, 1975; re-elected in 1981 and 1986 general elections; defeated in 1991.

PETERS, Thomas (c.1738–92)
American emigrationist organizer

A slave; escaped to join British army during the American War of Independence; promoted to sergeant. Fled to Nova Scotia with British loyalists, 1784. Went to London to protest about the failure of black settlers to receive promised land; joined Sierra Leone settlement scheme. Nova Scotia representative of the Sierra Leone Company; organized sailing of 1198 black settlers from Nova Scotia to Sierra Leone, 1792.

PÉTION, Alexandre (1770–1818)
Haitian ruler

Participant in the 1791 slave revolt led by Toussaint; joined Christophe and Dessalines in 1794 to force the French from Sainte Domingue. President of the Republic of Haiti, 1807–18.

PINDLING, Lynden (born 1930)
Bahamas politician

Lawyer; elected to House of Assembly as a Progressive Liberal Party (PLP) member, 1956, becoming party leader. Leader of the Opposition, 1964. Premier with the support of independents, 1967. Declared a 'Bahamaianization' programme; led the country to independence, 1973. Elected as prime minister, 1977, 1982. Denied accusations in the US media of involvement in drug smuggling, 1983; won the 1987 general election; defeated in 1992.

PITT, David Thomas (Lord Pitt of Hampstead) (born 1913)
British civil rights activist and politician

Born in Grenada; educated Grenada Boys' Secondary School and Edinburgh University Medical School. Medical officer in St Vincent, 1938–9; general practitioner in Trinidad, 1941–7. Co-founder of West Indian National Party, 1941; party president, 1943–7. Member of San Fernando Borough Council, 1941–7. Moved to London as general practitioner, 1947. Member of London County Council, 1961–4; member of Greater London Council, 1964–77. Member of the League of Coloured People. Appointed chairman of the Campaign Against Racial Discrimination (CARD), 1965. Deputy chairman, Community Relations Commission, 1968–77; chairman, 1977. Chairman of Shelter, 1979–90. Created a life peer, 1975.

POWELL, Adam Clayton, Jr (1908–72)
US politician

Succeeded father as minister of the Abyssinian Baptist Church, Harlem, 1937; organized anti-discrimination campaigns. Elected to New York City Council, 1941. Founded weekly *People's Voice*, 1944. Elected to House of Representatives for Harlem, 1944; re-elected eleven successive times. Chair of the House Committee on Education and Labour, 1960; steered anti-poverty and education legislation through Congress. Lost seat following censure motion, 1957; re-elected, 1961. Retired from politics, 1970.

POWELL, Colin L. (born 1937)
US army officer

Commissioned, 1958. Military adviser in Vietnam, 1962. Promoted to brigade commander, 1976; assistant divisional commander, 1981. Military assistant to the Secretary of Defense, 1983. Head of the National Security Council, 1987. Chairman of the Joint Chiefs of Staff, 1989–93. Leading figure in the Gulf War, 1991. Resisted calls to become presidential candidate, 1995–6.

PROSSER, Gabriel (c.1775–1800)
Slave resistance leader

Led a rising of 1000 slaves in Virginia, August 1800; betrayed by a fellow slave.

Captured in September; tried and hanged, October.

RADIX, Kendrick (born 1941)
Grenadian politician
Founded Movement for the Assemblies of the People with Maurice Bishop, 1972; enlarged to form the New Jewel Movement (NJM), 1973. Minister of Legal Affairs when NJM took power, 1979. Forced to resign and removed from NJM executive committee during leadership crisis, 1983. Imprisoned, he was freed following the US invasion. Founded Maurice Bishop Patriotic Movement; president of the movement, 1988.

RAINEY, Joseph Hayne (1832–87)
US politician
Born a slave in Georgetown, South Carolina. A barber; escaped to the British West Indies, 1862. Elected to the South Carolina Senate, 1869. One of the first black Americans to be elected to the US House of Representatives, 1870; served five terms. Appointed US Treasury revenue agent, 1879. Resigned and became a banker, 1881.

RAMAPHOSA, Cyril (born 1953)
South African politician and lawyer
Built the National Union of Mineworkers as secretary-general. Leading figure in the United Democratic Front (UDF), 1980s. Appointed African National Congress (ANC) secretary-general, 1991. Chief ANC negotiator in constitutional discussions with the white National Party. Disappointed in hope of becoming Deputy Vice-President following the 1994 elections; appointed chairman of the Constitutional Assembly. Left politics for business, 1996.

RANDOLPH, Asa Philip (1889–1979)
US trade union and civil rights leader
Born Crescent City, Florida. Moved to Harlem, 1911; studied at City College of New York while working in a series of manual jobs. Co-founded socialist weekly *The Messenger*, 1917; taught at Rand School of Social Science, New York. Street orator and active strike supporter; arrested for anti-war activity. Ran unsuccessfully as Socialist Party candidate for New York state comptroller, 1920. Left Socialist Party because of its attitude towards the black struggle. Organized Brotherhood of Sleeping Car Porters (BSCP), 1925. Involved in composing New Deal labour legislation; leader of National Negro Congress, 1935–40. His threat to mount a 100,000 strong black march on Washington, DC, persuaded President Franklin D. Roosevelt to form the Fair Employment Practices Committee, 1941. Appointed to the New York Housing Authority, 1942; founded League for Non-Violent Civil Disobedience in the Armed Forces, 1947. Threat of civil disobedience campaign forced President Truman to issue Executive Order No. 9981, 1948. Executive council member of the American Federation of Labor-Congress of Industrial Organizations, 1955; founded Negro American Labor Council, 1960, serving as president until 1966. Proposal for a civil rights march on Washington, DC, criticized by President Kennedy and black leaders, 1963; supported by 250,000 people.

RAWLINGS, Jerry (born 1947)
Ghanaian politician
Air Force officer, 1969. Led junior officers in military coup, 1979. Chairman of the Armed Forces Revolutionary Council, June–September 1979, during which period eight former military leaders were executed, People's Courts established and assets of

corrupt officials were confiscated. Returned power to civilians and retired from the Air Force, November 1979. Seized power, 1981, becoming head of state and Chairman of the Provisional Defence Council. Restored political activity, 1992; elected president, November 1992.

RAY, Charlotte (1850–1911)
US civil rights activist
Born New York; educated Institution for the Education of Colored Youth, Washington, DC. Teacher at Howard University, 1869; studied law at night. Admitted to the Bar in Washington, DC as the first black woman lawyer, 1872. Unable to practise because of insufficient clients. Teacher in Brooklyn, 1879. Attended Annual Convention of the National Women's Suffrage Association, 1876; active in National Association of Colored Women.

REINETTE, Luc (born 1950)
Guadeloupe independence activist
Housing officer. Formed Armed Liberation Group, 1979; imprisoned for bomb attacks, 1981. Helped found Popular Movement for an Independent Guadeloupe, 1982. Leader of the Caribbean Revolutionary Alliance, 1983. Sentenced to 23 years imprisonment for bombings, 1985. He escaped, was recaptured in 1987, and was released under amnesty in 1989.

REVELS, Hiram Rhoades (1822–1901)
US politician and civil rights activist
Born free in North Carolina. American Methodist Episcopal pastor in Illinois, Missouri and Indiana. Army chaplain and recruiter of black troops for the Union during the Civil War. First black American to be elected to the US Senate (for Missouri), 1870; served for one year. Editor of the *South Western Christian Advocate*, 1876. President of Alcorn State University, Mississippi.

ROBERTS, Joseph Jenkins (1809–76)
Liberian politician
Born in Virginia, USA. Emigrated to Monrovia, 1829. Trader and militia officer. Elected lieutenant-governor, 1839; first black governor, 1841. Visited Europe to secure recognition of Liberia's status. Unsuccessful in attempts to develop relations with people in the interior. First president of independent Liberia, 1848–56; incorporated black autonomous colonies. Represented the lighter-skinned element and heightened tension with darker skinned. First president of Liberia College, 1857. Invited to resume the presidency, 1872.

ROBESON, Paul Leroy (1898–1976)
US actor, singer and radical political activist
Lived in Britain, 1927–39; sang at trade-union benefit concerts and became socialist activist. Visited USSR, 1934. Spoke and performed in Spain in support of the Republican government, 1938. Returned to USA, 1939. Active in civil rights and left-wing campaigns. First major artist to refuse to perform before segregated audiences. Attacked President Truman's refusal to legislate effectively against lynching; threatened black armed self-defence, 1946. Passport withdrawn by government, 1950–8; persistently harassed by CIA and FBI; prevented from working. Income fell from $100,000 in 1947 to $6000 in 1952. Travelled abroad, rebuilding career, 1958–63. Co-author of *Here I Stand* (1958).

ROBINSON, Arthur Napoleon Raymond ('Ray') (born 1926)
Trinidad and Tobago politician
Educated in Trinidad and Oxford University; a barrister. Helped found the People's National Movement (PNM), 1956. Member of the West Indies Federation Parliament, 1958–60; elected to the Trinidad

and Tobago House of Representatives, 1961. Minister of Finance, 1961–7; Minister for External Affairs, 1967–70. PNM deputy leader, 1967. Resigned from government and party after allegedly attempting to depose Prime Minister Eric Williams during the Trinidad uprising, 1970. Formed Action Committee for Dedicated Citizens, renamed the Democratic Action Congress (DAC). Chairman of the Tobago House of Assembly, 1980–6. Founder leader of four-party National Alliance for Reconstruction (NAR), 1985. Elected prime minister, 1986.

ROBINSON, Roscoe, Jr (born 1928)
US army officer
Born St Louis, Missouri. Educated US Military Academy, West Point; University of Pittsburgh. Army personnel management officer, 1965–7; commanding officer 2nd Brigade of the 82nd Airborne Division, 1968. Promoted to general, 1973. Executive chief of staff, Pacific Command. Commander of 7th Army and first black American four-star general, 1978. US representative to NATO, 1982–3.

ROMNEY, Cyril (born 1931)
British Virgin Islands politician
Educated in the USA; economist, teacher and senior civil servant. Elected to the Legislative Council as an Independent, 1960; Chief Minister, 1983. Faced allegations of drugs money laundering; called an election, re-elected but replaced as chief minister, 1986.

ROYE, Edward James (1815–71)
Liberian politician
Born and educated in Ohio, USA. Emigrated to Liberia as a businessman. Elected to Supreme Court, 1865; appointed Chief Justice, 1867. Successful True Whig candidate for presidency, 1870, with dark-skinned support against the light-skinned Republican Party elite. Negotiated an unpopular British loan, 1871. Deposed for attempting to extend presidential term of office from two to four years. Died in mysterious circumstances immediately after.

RUSSWURM, John Brown (1799-1851)
Liberian administrator
Born in Jamaica. Educated in the USA; the first black graduate of an American college, Bowdoin College, Maine, 1826. Co-founded the first black newspaper in the USA, *Freedom's Journal*, in 1827. Moved to Liberia in 1830, becoming superintendent of schools. Publisher of the *Liberia Herald*, 1830–50. Governor of Maryland, an independent state which later amalgamated with Liberia, from 1836 until his death.

SABLE, Jean Baptiste Pointe du (1745 –1818)
Founder of the city of Chicago
Son of an African slave mother and a French father. Educated in Paris; became a seaman. Shipwrecked off New Orleans; settled in the territory of the Illinois Indians, 1799. Married a member of the Potowatomi tribe; built a settlement on the St Charles River which became Chicago.

SALEM, Peter (c.1750–1816)
American War of Independence soldier
Born a slave in Massachusetts; freed on joining the American colonial army. Fought on first day of the Revolutionary War in Concord, April 1775. In action at Battle of Bunker Hill, June 1775; thought to have killed the first British soldier. Served through the remainder of the war; died in obscurity.

SAMBA, Martin-Paul (c.1870–1914)
Cameroon resistance leader
Educated in American mission and Germany. Commissioned into German army; resigned after participating in military

action against Africans in German Kamerun (now Cameroon). Organized resistance force among Boulou people with Rudolph Bell; offered to support France against German forces on outbreak of World War I. Captured and executed by Germans, 1914.

SAMOEI, Koitatel Arap (died 1906)

Nandi traditional leader in the British colony of Kenya

Led Nandi resistance against British forces, 1890–1906. Killed in action.

SANDIFORD, Erskine (born 1937)

Barbados politician

Teacher; elected to House of Assembly for the Democratic Labour Party (DLP), 1967. Minister of Education 1967–75; Minister of Health, 1975–6. Elected to House of Assembly, 1971. DLP general secretary, 1967–71. DLP President, 1976. Supported US invasion of Grenada, 1983. Deputy Prime Minister and Education Minister, 1986. Elected prime minister, 1987 and 1991.

SANKARA, Thomas (1949–87)

Burkina Faso politician

Born in Yago, educated at mission schools and military academy in France. An army officer when Burkina Faso gained independence, he became Secretary for Information. Nominated as prime minister on the overthrow of President Saye Zerbo, 1982; arrested but freed by army supporters. Seized power, declaring himself president, 1983. Adopted World Bank economic policies, encouraging small farmers at expense of town dwellers, curbing trade unions and the civil service. Assassinated, 1987.

SANTOS, José Eduardo dos (born 1942)

Angolan politician

Joined Popular Movement for the Liberation of Angola (MPLA), 1962. Studied engineering and telecommunications in Soviet Union, 1963–70. Appointed Foreign Minister on independence, 1975; Vice Prime Minister; Minister of Public Planning, 1978. President on the death of Neto, 1979. Signed Nkomati Accord with South Africa closing South West African People's Organization bases, 1984. Abandoned MPLA's Marxist–Leninist ideology, 1991. Fought continuing civil war against opposition UNITA forces. Elected president, 1992.

SARO-WIWA, Kenyule Beeson (1941–95)

Nigerian writer and political activist

Born Bori, Ogoniland. Founder member, the Movement for the Survival of the Ogoni People (MOSOP), 1990. President of MOSOP, 1993. Organized boycott of Nigerian presidential election, 1993; threatened secession of Ogoniland from Nigeria. Accused of complicity in murder of four Ogoni leaders; executed, 1995.

SASSOU-NGUESSO, Denis (born 1943)

Congo army officer and politician

Military education in France; commissioned, 1962. Member of the Council of State, 1976–7. Vice-President of the Military Committee of the Parti Congolais du Travail (PCT). Led coup against President Yhombi-Opango; became president of the People's Republic of Congo, 1979. Improved relations with the West and neighbouring states; liberalized the economy. Re-elected president and PCT central committee member, 1984. Abandoned Marxism–Leninism, 1990. Stripped of powers by the Higher Council of the Republic, 1991.

SAUNDERS, Norman (born 1943)

Turks and Caicos Islands politician

Businessman; elected to Parliament, 1967. Co-founder of the Progressive National Organisation, 1976. Formed Progressive

National Party and went on to win 1980 general election. Chief Minister, 1980; re-elected in 1984. Resigned following arrest in Miami, 1985; imprisoned for bribery and drug smuggling. Released and returned to Turks and Caicos Islands, 1987.

SCOTT, Dred (c.1795–1858)
US slave; participated in seminal Supreme Court case, Scott v Sandford

Born Southampton County, Virginia; moved with owner to Missouri, 1827. Travelled with new owner in Illinois and Wisconsin territories, 1833–8. Son of former owner brought a case to the Missouri state court that Scott was a free man because he had lived in a free territory, 1846; court ruled against Scott, 1852. Supreme Court confirmed the decision and ruled that Scott was not a citizen and ineligible to sue in a Federal court, 1857. Freed with his family by new owner, 1857. Worked as a hotel porter in St Louis where he died of tuberculosis.

SEACOLE, Mary Jane (née Grant)
(1805–81)
Jamaican businesswoman and nurse

Daughter of a Jamaican 'doctress' and a Scottish army officer; best known as a nurse in the Crimean War, 1854–6, she was also a traveller and gold prospector; relief worker in Jamaican cholera epidemic, 1850; opened a store in Panama goldfields and treated cholera victims, 1850. Her offer of nursing services in the Crimean War was rejected by the British War Office; went at her own expense and nursed British soldiers, often on the battlefield (unlike her white contemporary Florence Nightingale); wrote autobiography *Wonderful Adventures of Mrs Seacole in Many Lands* (1856).

SEAGA, Edward Phillio George
(born 1930)
Jamaican politician

Educated in Jamaica and Harvard University. Elected leader of the Jamaican Labour Party (JLP), 1974. Defeated in 1976 general election; became prime minister following defeat of Michael Manley, 1980. Conservative, pro-Western policies encouraged US aid. Re-elected, 1983; defeated 1989.

SEALE, Bobby (Robert George)
(born 1936)
US political activist

Born Dallas, Texas; worked as sheet-metal worker. Attended Merritt College, joined Afro-American Society, 1960. Formed Black Panther Party with Huey Newton, 1966. Acquitted of murdering a suspected informer, 1971. Defeated in election for mayor of Oakland, 1973. Left the Black Panthers, 1974; lecturer and writer. Among his works are *Seize the Time: The Story of the Black Panther Party* (1970) and *A Lonely Rage: The Autobiography of Bobby Seale* (1978).

SENGHOR, Léopold Sédar (born 1906)
Senegalese politician

Educated in Dakar and Paris; taught in France, 1935–9. Joined the French army; German prisoner-of-war, 1940–2. Active in the French Resistance, 1942–4. Founded négritude magazine in Paris, *Présence Africaine*, 1947. Helped form the Bloc Africain, the political union of French African countries, 1945. Deputy in the French National Assembly, 1946–58. Formed the Bloc Démocratique Sénégalais in 1948; amalgamated with another group to create the Union Progressiste Sénégalais, 1958. President of the Federal Assembly of the united Senegal and Mali, 1959. President of Senegal on its secession and independence, 1960. An authoritarian ruler, he introduced limited democracy, 1970. Retired as president, 1981. Elected to the French Academy, 1983.

SHAKA (c.1787–1828)

Zulu military leader

Founder of the Zulu kingdom. Born into Mhlongo people; soldier in the Mthethwa army of Dingiswayo. Seized Zulu throne, 1815; formed a sub-empire under Dingiswayo. Developed new military tactics; absorbed or destroyed conquered peoples. Rebuilt collapsed Mthethwa confederation under Zulu rule, controlling most of what is now Natal. Defeated Ndwande attacks, 1818 and 1826. Established relations with Britain, 1824. A campaign he waged in Mozambique in 1828 aroused resentment; assassinated by half-brothers Dingaan and Mhlangane.

SHEARER, Hugh (born 1923)

Jamaican politician

Trade-union official. Appointed Legislative Council member and Minister without Portfolio, 1951. Elected to House of Representatives for Jamaican Labour Party (JLP), 1955; lost seat, 1959. Appointed senator on independence, 1962; Jamaica's deputy representative at the United Nations. Re-elected to House of Representatives; Foreign Minister, Prime Minister, 1967. Defeated in 1972 general election; lost JLP leadership, 1974. Deputy Prime Minister and Foreign Minister, 1980–9.

SIMMONDS, Kennedy (born 1936)

St Kitts-Nevis politician

Medical training in Jamaica. Co-founder and Vice-President of People's Action Movement, 1965. Practised medicine in Bahamas, 1966–8; studied in USA, 1968–9. Elected to St Kitts-Nevis National Assembly, 1989; prevented from taking seat by dissolution.

Premier in coalition government with Nevis Reformation Party following general elections, 1980. Prime Minister following independence, 1983. Re-elected, 1984, 1989.

SISULU, Nontsikelelo Albertina (born 1918)

South African anti-apartheid and women's rights activist

Joined the African National Congress Women's League, 1948. Suffered detention, the imposition of banning orders and ten years house arrest for her anti-apartheid activities in the 1950s and 1960s. One of the three presidents of the United Democratic Front, 1983. Charged with treason in 1985 but the trial collapsed.

SISULU, Walter Max (born 1912)

South African nationalist leader

Joined the African National Congress (ANC), 1940; Treasurer of the ANC Youth League, 1944. ANC Secretary-General, 1949; organized the Defiance Campaign, 1952. Arrested and subject to banning orders. Charged with high treason at Rivonia Trial and acquitted, 1956–61. Imprisoned for violation of house arrest, 1962. Escaped to Botswana; recaptured and given life sentence on Robben Island. Released, 1989.

SITHOLE, Ndabaningi (born 1920)

Zimbabwean politician

US divinity college, 1953–6. Ordained a Methodist minister, 1959. Helped form Zimbabwe African People's Union (ZAPU), 1962. Founder and first leader of the Zimbabwe African National Union (ZANU) 1963. The party was banned and Sithole was detained until 1974. Lost ZANU leadership to Robert Mugabe and formed his own party, 1977; member of the transitional government, 1978–9. Unsuccessfully contested the pre-independence 1980 elections; moved to the USA. Returned to Zimbabwe to lead

ZANU-Ndonga, a right-wing opposition party which won two of the 150 parliamentary seats in the 1995 elections. Arrested on charges of plotting the assassination of President Mugabe in 1995. Presidential candidate, 1996; withdrew after alleging persistent harassment by state security forces.

SKIPPINGS, Oswald (born 1953)
Turks and Caicos Islands politician
Teacher; co-founder of the People's Democratic Movement (PDM), 1975. Chief Minister, 1980 until PDM lost general elections in that year. Lost PDM leadership, becoming deputy leader, 1984. Returned to party leadership, 1987; led PDM to victory in 1988 general elections, returning to office of chief minister.

SMALLS, Robert (1839–1915)
US politician
Born a slave; escaped enforced service in the Confederate forces during the *Planter* incident, 1862. Served in US navy until 1866, reaching rank of captain. Elected to South Carolina House of Representatives, 1868; member of South Carolina Senate, 1870–4. Elected to first of five terms in the House of Representatives, 1875. Major-General in South Carolina militia. Convicted, and pardoned, for accepting a bribe while a state senator. Retired from politics, 1887. Appointed to official position in Beaufort, South Carolina, 1889.

SOBUKWE, Robert Mangaliso
(1927–78)
South African nationalist leader
Studied at Fort Hare University College. Joined the African National Congress (ANC) Youth Wing; dismissed as a teacher for participation in the 1952 Defiance Campaign. Left the ANC because of disagreement with its moderation, 1958; helped form the Pan-Africanist Congress (PAC); elected first president, 1959. Organized anti-pass law demonstrations which culminated in the Sharpeville massacre, 1960. The PAC was banned, Sobukwe was arrested and jailed for three years, later being transferred to Robben Island. Subject to a banning order in 1969, he practised as a lawyer.

SOGLO, Nicéphore (born 1934)
Benin (formerly Dahomey) politician
Born Lomé, Togo. Educated University of Paris. Inspector of Finances; Minister of Finance and Commerce, 1965–6. Taught National University of Benin; attached to World Bank, Washington, DC, 1979–86. Returned to post of Inspector of Finances, 1987–90. Prime Minister, 1990–1. President of Benin, 1991–6.

SOKOINE, Edward Moringe (1938–84)
Tanzanian politician
Elected to parliament, 1965. Held a variety of ministerial posts until becoming prime minister, 1977. Resigned because of ill health, 1980. Reappointed prime minister in 1983; resumed trade and diplomatic relations with Kenya and Uganda. Seen increasingly as the natural successor to President Nyerere, he died in a road accident.

SSEMOGERERE, Paul (born 1932)
Ugandan politician
A schoolteacher. Active in the Democratic Party in the 1960s; leader and presidential candidate, 1980. Defeated in widely disputed elections, he became leader of the opposition. Minister of Internal Affairs in the military government which ousted President Obote. Appointed one of Uganda's three deputy prime ministers, 1988.

STEVENS, Siaka Probyn (1905–88)
Sierra Leone politician
Police officer, 1923–30; founded United Mineworkers Union, 1943. Studied

industrial relations at Oxford University, 1945. Helped form Sierra Leone People's Party (SLPP), 1951. Left SLPP following 1957 elections. Member of delegation negotiating independence, 1960. Formed All People's Congress (APC), 1960; opposition leader on independence, 1961. APC won election by narrow margin, 1967; prevented from taking office by military coup until 1968. Declared Sierra Leone a Republic and became president, 1971. Survived coup and assassination attempts. Instituted a one-party state, 1978. Retired from office, 1985.

STOKES, Carl Burton (1927–96)
US politician

Dropped out of school to support his family; returned to higher education in his early twenties, supporting himself as a pool player. Attended Marshall School of Law; qualified as a lawyer, 1956. Probation officer; lawyer. First black Democrat elected to Ohio state legislature, 1962; defeated as Independent candidate for mayor, 1965. Elected Mayor of Cleveland as a Democrat, 1967, the first black mayor of a major US city; re-elected 1969. Attempted to reform police department and attract industry. Television news anchorman, 1971–9. Municipal court judge, 1983. Appointed US Ambassador to the Seychelles, 1994.

SWAN, John (born 1935)
Bermudan politician

Real estate operator. Elected to House of Assembly as United Bermuda Party (UBP) member, 1972. Minister of Marine and Air Services, 1976; Minister of Labour and Immigration. Premier, 1982; re-elected 1989.

TAMBO, Oliver Reginald (1917–93)
South African nationalist leader

Educated at Fort Hare University College. Formed law firm with Nelson Mandela, 1952. Joined the African National Congress (ANC), 1944, helping to establish the ANC Youth League. Member of the ANC executive, 1949; ANC Secretary-General, 1955; deputy president, 1958; acting president, 1967; president, 1978–91. Subject to banning order, 1954–6; arrested for treason, 1956; released, 1957. Left South Africa to form an ANC exile wing following the Sharpeville massacre, 1960. Established ANC headquarters in Tanzania, 1965. Travelled widely seeking international support for the anti-apartheid campaign. Died in office as ANC chairman.

TAYLOR, Charles (dates unknown)
Liberian civil war leader

Born of mixed Americo-Liberian and Gola descent. Trained as an economist in the USA; president of the Association of Liberians in the USA. Returned to Liberia, 1980; became director of government procurement agency under President Doe. Fled to the USA to avoid embezzlement charges, 1983; escaped from prison while awaiting extradition to Liberia. Moved to Ghana; raised and trained National Patriotic Front of Liberia (NPFL) guerrillas in Libya. Led NPFL invasion of Liberia, 1989.

TEKERE, Edgar (born 1937)
Zimbabwe politician

Member of the African National Congress; founder member of the National Democratic Party (1960), the Zimbabwe African People's Union (1961), and the Zimbabwe African National Union (1963). Imprisoned for nationalist activities, 1964–74. Joined Robert Mugabe in Mozambique, 1975. As ZANU Secretary-General, involved in the 1979 independence conference. Won a seat in the 1980 elections and served as minister until charged (and acquitted) of murdering a white farmer, 1981. Dismissed as ZANU (PF) chairman in Matabele Province, 1987;

expelled from the party after alleging government corruption, 1988. Formed opposition Zimbabwe Unity Movement (ZUM), 1989. Won 16 per cent of the vote in presidential elections, 1990. Merged ZUM with the United African National Council of Bishop Abel Muzowera, 1994.

TEMBO, John Zenas Ungapake
(born 1932)

Malawian politician
Teacher; elected to the Legislative Council, 1961, and to the National Assembly in 1963. Minister of Finance and Trade, 1964–70; governor of the Reserve Bank of Malawi, 1974–80. Member of the Malawi Congress Party Central Committee; treasurer-general, 1987. Presidential Minister of State, 1992.

TERRELL, Mary Eliza Church
(1863–1954)

US teacher and civil rights activist
Born in Memphis, Tennessee; daughter of a former slave. Educated Oberlin College, 1884–8; in Europe, 1888–90. Taught at Wilberforce University; appointed first black woman school board member, 1895. First president of the National Association of Colored Women, 1896–1901. Led successful campaign against segregation in the District of Columbia, 1953. Among her writings are *What Role is the Educated Negro Woman to play in the Uplifting of Her Race*, and an autobiography *A Colored Woman in a White World* (1940).

THUKU, Harry (1895–1970)

Kenyan nationalist activist
Moved to Nairobi, 1911. Worked as printer and telephone operator. Following campaign against African wage reductions became founding president of the East African Association, 1921. Imprisoned, 1922–30, after advocating civil disobedience. Elected president of the Kikuyu Central Association,

1932. Increasingly moderate; formed the Kikuyu Provincial Association, 1935. Supported Kikuyu participation alongside Britain in World War II; opposed Mau Mau. Left politics for farming.

TOIVO ja TOIVA, Herman (later Andimba) (born 1924)

Namibian politician and trade-union organizer
Forced to return to South West Africa (now Namibia) by the South African authorities in 1957 after forming the Ovamboland People's Congress. Co-founder of the South West Africa People's Organisation (SWAPO), 1960. Sentenced to life imprisonment for nationalist activities, 1968. Released in 1984, he was elected SWAPO Secretary-General.

TOLBERT, William Richard (1913–80)

Liberian politician
Graduated from Liberia College, 1934; worked in government supply department. Member of the House of Representatives, 1943–51; vice president, 1953–71. President of the Baptist World Alliance for Africa, 1965–70. Liberian president, 1971–80; established Mano River Union with Sierra Leone, 1973. Criticized for inviting apartheid South African leader to Liberia, 1975. Attempted to make Liberia self-sufficient in food but rising rice prices led to violent protests in 1980. Killed in a military coup, April 1980.

TOMBALBAYE, Ngarta (formerly François) (1918–75)

Chad politician
Teacher and trade-union organizer; a founder of the Chad branch of the Rassemblement Démocratique Africain, 1947. Member of the Territorial Assembly, 1952; member of the General Council of West Africa, 1957. Overthrew government

of Gabriel Lisette, 1959; President of independent Chad, 1960. Increasingly authoritarian, his Parti Progressiste Tchadien (PPT) became the sole party. Saved by French troops from being overthrown by the Chad National Liberation Front (FROLINAT), 1968. Instituted 'cultural revolution', outlawing Christian names and substituting Chad for French place names. Assassinated in a military coup, 1975.

TOURÉ, Ahmad Sekou (1922–84)
Guinean politician
Trade-union organizer, involved in the formation of the Union Cégétiste des Syndicats de Guinée, 1947. Imprisoned by the French authorities for subversion, he was released in 1952. Secretary of the Guinea branch of Rassemblement Démocratique Africain (RDA); organized a general strike against French colonial power, 1953. Member of the Territorial Assembly, 1953; mayor of Conakry, 1955; deputy in French National Assembly, 1957. Founded Union Générale des Travailleurs d'Afrique Noir, 1957. Vice-President of the Governor's Council, 1957. Organized the defeat of a French referendum on Guinea joining the French-African community. President of independent Guinea, 1958; continuously elected, weakening the opposition by the constant discovery of conspiracies. Died while undergoing surgery, 1984.

TOUSSAINT, François Dominique
(1746–1803)
Haitian revolutionary leader
Born to African slave parents; freed, 1777. Joined slave rebellion in Sainte Domingue, 1791; appointed commander, October 1791. Organized and trained an effective guerrilla army. Expelled French commissioner from the colony, 1797. Defeated a British invasion force, 1798; defeated a mulatto army, 1799.

Promulgated a constitution and proclaimed himself governor, 1801. Led resistance to renewed French invasion; captured by French by trickery, 1802. Died in the French prison of Fort-du-Joux, 1803.

TOUSSAINT L'OUVERTURE See TOUSSAINT, François Dominique.

TRAORÉ, Moussa (born 1936)
Mali politician
Joined the French army, becoming a member of the Mali army on independence, 1960. Participated in an officers' coup which overthrew President Keita, 1968; became head of state and promoted himself to general. Secretary-General of the Democratic Union of the Malian People (UDPM), 1974. Following two attempted coups in 1979 and 1981, amended constitution to allow only the UDPM to nominate presidential candidates. Won presidential election with 99.94 per cent of the vote, 1985. Overthrown in military coup, 1991.

TROTTER, William Monroe (1872–1934)
US publisher and civil rights activist
Born Springfield, Ohio; educated Harvard University. Left insurance career to found and edit the campaigning newspaper, the *Boston Guardian*, 1901. Opposed moderate policy of Booker T. Washington. Founded the National Equal Rights League to agitate for integration and voting rights; active in the Niagara Movement; refused leading position in the National Association for the Advancement of Colored People (NAACP) because of his suspicion of white motives. Imprisoned for leading protests against the film *Birth of a Nation* in Massachusetts, 1915. Represented the National Equal Rights League at the Paris Peace Conference, 1919.

TRUTH, Sojourner (1797–1883)
US anti-slavery activist

Born Isabel Baumfree, a slave, in Ulster County, New York. Escaped with the youngest of her children, 1826. Freed by New York State Emancipation Act, 1827. Following a religious vision in 1843, left New York and changed name. Took up anti-slavery and women's rights agitation. First black woman to speak out publicly against slavery. Delegate at the first National Women's Rights Convention, 1850. Delegate to second National Woman's Suffrage Convention, 1852; made famous 'Ain't I a Woman' speech. Nurse during 1861–5 Civil War; met Abraham Lincoln, 1864. After the Civil War, an advocate of women's rights and equal education. Published autobiography *The Narrative of Sojourner Truth* (1850).

TSHOMBE, Moïse Kapenda (1919–69)
Congo Republic (now Zaïre) politician

Director of family business, 1951. Formed the Confédération des Associations Tribales du Katanga (CONAKAT), 1958. Represented CONAKAT in independence negotiations, advocating a federal system, 1960. Won elections on independence, becoming Katanga provincial president, 1960. President of the secessionist Katanga province, 1960–3. In exile following United Nations overthrow of his regime, 1963–4. Congo Republic prime minister, 1964. Formed National Congolese Convention; won elections, 1965. In exile following the Mobutu coup, 1965. Kidnapped in 1967; died in prison in Algeria.

TUBMAN, Harriet (1823–1913)
US anti-slavery activist, known as 'Black Moses'

Born a slave in Maryland; escaped to Philadelphia, 1849. 'Conductor' on the Underground Railroad, taking over 300 slaves, including her brother and sister, to freedom. A bounty for her capture was placed at $40,000. Cook, scout and spy for the Union Army during the 1861–5 Civil War. Founded home for aged black Americans after the war.

TURNER, Henry McNeal (1834–1915)
US clergyman and Pan-African activist

Born free in South Carolina; worked as a messenger and handyman; ordained a minister in the African Methodist Episcopal Church, 1853; Bishop, 1880. Chaplain with the 54th Massachusetts Negro Regiment in the 1861–5 Civil War; worked with Freedman's Bureau. Founded and edited *Voice of Missions* and *Voice of the People*. Elected to the Georgia State Legislature. Described the US constitution as 'a dirty rag, a cheat'; advocated black emigration to Africa from 1876 until his death; sponsored an expedition to Liberia, 1878. Participated in the Pan-African Chicago Congress of Africa, 1893.

TURNER, Nat (1800–31)
American anti-slavery activist

Born a slave in Virginia. A religious enthusiast. Led the best-known American slave revolt in 1831. Escaped following its failure; captured in October 1831; executed in November.

TUTU, Desmond Mpilo (born 1931)
South African cleric and anti-apartheid activist

A teacher from 1955–8, he was ordained in 1961. Studied in Britain, 1962–6; taught in South Africa, 1966–72. Worked in Britain for the World Council of Churches, 1972–5. Dean of Johannesburg, 1975–6; Bishop of Lesotho, 1976–8; Secretary-General of the actively anti-apartheid South African Council of Churches, 1978–84. Bishop of

Johannesburg, 1985–6; the first non-white Anglican Archbishop of Cape Town, 1986–96. Awarded the Athinai Prize, 1980; Nobel Peace Prize, 1984. A patron of the United Democratic Front, supported negotiations with the white government from 1990. Chairman of the Truth Commission to encourage black–white reconciliation, 1996.

WAIYAKI, Wa Hinga (?–1892)
Kikuyu resistance leader in the British colony of Kenya
Ordered destruction of Dagoretti Fort in response to raids by Imperial British East African Company, 1891. Wounded in protests at the rebuilding of the fort; captured by British and died at Kibwezi.

WALKER, ('Madame') C. J. (née Sarah Breedlove) (1867–1919)
Businesswoman, first woman black American millionaire
Born Delta, Louisiana. Washerwoman who developed a hair product which she sold from door to door, going on to produce the pressing comb and a chemical formula for hair-straightening; built a hair preparations factory in Indianapolis which eventually employed 5000 black women, 1910. Involved in charity work and the National Association for the Advancement of Colored People (NAACP); died leaving an estate valued at two million dollars.

WALKER, David (1785–1830)
US pamphleteer
Born in North Carolina, son of a slave father and free mother; lived as a free black in Boston. Owned an old clothes store. *An Appeal to the Coloured Citizens of the World*, published 1829, called for an end to slavery by any means, including violence, in America and the Caribbean. A slave owner offered a reward for his death; refused to flee to Canada and died in mysterious circumstances.

WALKER, Maggie Lena (1867–1934)
US teacher and businesswoman
First woman American bank president. Born Richmond, Virginia. Secretary and treasurer of the charitable Independent Order of St Luke's Society, 1899; established the St Luke Penny Savings Bank, 1903; later chairman of the board of the St Luke Bank and Trust Company; founded an insurance company, the *St Luke Herald* black newspaper, and a girls' home and school; a street, theatre and high school were named after her in Richmond.

WALTER, George (born 1928)
Antigua-Barbudan politician
General-Secretary of Antigua Trades and Labour Union; expelled following power struggle with Vere Bird, 1967. Formed Antigua Workers' Union. Founded Progressive Labour movement 1968; won 1971 elections, becoming Premier. Defeated in 1976 elections; imprisoned for corruption in 1979, but released on appeal in 1980. Founded United People's Movement, 1982. Defeated in elections, 1984. Retired from politics, 1986.

WASHINGTON, Booker Taliaferro (1856–1915)
US activist and educationalist
Born a slave in Franklin County, Virginia; worked in coal mines, salt furnaces and as a houseboy. Began education at Hampton Institute, 1871; worked as janitor to pay fees; graduated, 1875. Returned to Virginia as a teacher; appointed head of Tuskegee Normal and Industrial Institute, 1891. Delivered Atlanta Compromise speech at Cotton States Exposition, 1895; argued for black economic and educational advance rather than agitation. Helped establish National Negro

Business League; confidant of Presidents Theodore Roosevelt and William Howard Taft. Met with increasing opposition from other black activists, culminating in the establishment of the National Association for the Advancement of Colored People (NAACP), 1909.

WEBSTER, Ronald (born 1936)
Anguilla politician
Farmworker; led Anguillan revolt against rule from St Kitts, 1967. Declared Anguilla an independent republic, 1969. Appointed chief minister after Britain agreed to renew its administration of the island, 1971. Founded People's Progressive Party (PPP), 1972; won 1972 and 1976 general elections. Dismissed by the PPP, returned as chief minister in 1980 elections as leader of the Anguilla United Party. Defeated in 1984 and 1989 elections.

WEDDERBURN, Robert (c.1762–?)
British radical and anti-slavery activist
Born in Jamaica; son of a slave and a plantation owner. Travelled to England, 1778; worked as seaman, tailor. Became a Unitarian preacher and publisher of radical pamphlets and journals. Charged with sedition (changed to blasphemous libel), 1819; sentenced to two years' imprisonment. Continued publishing and working class activities; received a further prison sentence, 1831.

WELLS, Ida Barnett (1862–1931)
US civil rights activist
Born a slave in Holly Springs, Mississippi; began work as a teacher at 14. Moved to Memphis, Tennessee, to study at Fisk University, 1884. Dismissed from teaching after losing a case following her refusal to give up a 'whites only' seat on a train. Wrote for a Memphis black weekly, *Living Word*; co-owner and editor of the weekly, *Free Speech*, 1891. Left for New York following destruction of offices by a white mob, 1892. Anti-lynching lecturer in the USA and Britain; led anti-lynching delegation to President McKinley, 1898. Secretary, Afro-American Council, 1898; founded Negro Fellowship League, 1908. Became probation officer in Chicago, 1913. Vice-President, Equal Rights League, 1915. Her writings include *Southern Horrors* (1892), *A Red Record* (1895), and an autobiography (edited by Alfred Duster) *Crusade for Justice* (1970).

WHEATLEY, Willard (born 1915)
British Virgin Islands politician
Teacher; elected to Legislative Council as an Independent. Held various junior ministerial posts. Chief Minister of a coalition government, 1971–9. After losing position became leader of the United Party, becoming chief minister again in 1983. Resigned 1986; lost seat and ensuing general election and lost leadership of the United Party.

WHITE, Walter Francis (1893–1955)
US civil rights activist
Born Atlanta, Georgia; graduated Atlanta University, 1916. National Association for the Advancement of Colored People (NAACP) official, 1918. Journalist investigating race riots and lynchings. Appointed NAACP national secretary, 1930; led campaigns against lynching and discrimination. Adviser to Presidents Roosevelt and Truman; influential in establishment of World War II Committee on Fair Employment Practice. Consultant to US delegations to the United Nations, 1945 and 1948. Among his most important writings are *Rope and Faggot: A Biography of Judge Lynch* (1929), *A Rising Wind: A Report of the Negro Soldier in the European Theatre of War* (1945), *A Man Called White* (1948) and *How Far the Promised Land?* (1955).

WILKINS, Roy (1908–81)
US civil rights activist

Born St. Louis, Missouri; educated University of Minnesota. Journalist on black Kansas City *Call*. Appointed assistant-executive of the National Association for the Advancement of Colored People (NAACP), 1931. Succeeded Du Bois as the editor of *Crisis*, 1934. NAACP acting executive-secretary, 1934; executive-secretary, 1955. Chairman of the Leadership Conference on Civil Rights; member of the Board of Directors, Peace and Freedom.

WILLIAMS, Eric Eustace (1911–81)
Trinidad and Tobago politician and historian

Born in Port of Spain, Trinidad; PhD, Oxford University; Fellow of All Souls. Taught at Howard University, USA. Worked for Anglo-American Caribbean Commission, 1943–55. Founded Trinidad's first effective political party, the People's National Movement (PNM), 1956; Chief Minister of Trinidad and Tobago, 1956–9; Premier, 1959–62. Led Trinidad and Tobago to independence, Prime Minister 1962–81. Declared state of emergency following Trinidad uprising, 1970. Among his many works are *Capitalism and Slavery*; *History of the People of Trinidad and Tobago* (1962), *British Historians and the West Indies* (1964), *Documents of West Indian History* (1965), an autobiography, *Inward Hunger* (1969), *From Columbus to Castro: The History of the Caribbean 1492–1969* (1970).

WILLIAMS, Henry Sylvester
(1869–1911)
Trinidadian Pan-African activist

Born Arouca, Trinidad; worked as a teacher. Moved to the USA, 1881; entered the University of Dalhousie, Canada, 1893. Moved to London, registered at King's College and studied for the Bar, 1897.

Founded the African Association, 1897. Leading organizer of the Pan-African Conference, 1900. Secretary of the Pan-African Association, 1900. Published and edited *The Pan-African*, 1901–2. Elected to Marylebone Borough Council as a Progressive. Moved to South Africa to practise as a lawyer, 1903; acted as adviser to Kings Lerotholi and Lewanika. Left South Africa following death threats, 1904. Returned to Trinidad, where he died.

WOODSON, Carter Godwin
(1875–1950)
US historian

'Father of Negro history'. Born New Canton, Virginia; son of former slaves. Self-educated until attended college at age of 20; graduated 1903. School supervisor in the Philippines, 1903–7. Studied University of Chicago, Europe and Asia. Teacher in Washington, DC, 1908–12; PhD, 1912. Leading founder of the Association for the Study of Negro Life and History, 1915; first editor of *Journal of Negro History*, 1916. Among his works are *The Education of the Negro Prior to 1861* (1915), *A Century of Negro Migration* (1918), *The Negro in Our History* (1922).

YAMÉOGO, Maurice (born 1921)
Burkina Faso (formerly Upper Volta) politician

A member of the Mossi tribe. A civil servant; elected to the Territorial Assembly in 1946, and to the Grand Council of French West Africa, 1948. Founded the Union Démocratique Voltaique, 1957. Minister of Agriculture, 1957–8; Minister of the Interior, 1958–60. First president on independence, 1960; banned opposition parties; re-elected with 91 per cent of the vote, 1965. Overthrown in 1966; imprisoned for embezzling public funds and exiled to the Côte d'Ivoire. Returned to Burkina Faso, 1970; continued to exert political influence behind the scenes during the 1980s.

YOHANNES (John) IV (1831–89)
Emperor of Ethiopia
Succeeded Emperor Theodore, 1868. Position threatened in the 1880s by Italy in Eritrea, Mahdist forces in the Sudan, and King Menelik of Shoa in the south. Designated Menelik as successor, 1882. Died fighting Mahdist invasion, 1889.

YOKO, Madame (c. 1850–1905)
Leader of the Mende people in Sierra Leone
Widow of the former leader, Senehun, she developed her authority through the women's society, the Bundu, and also as one of the rare female members of the male secret society, the Poro, which dominated social and political life. Allied with the British against the rival Tenne people and did not resist Britain's establishment of a protectorate in Sierra Leone in 1898. Committed suicide, 1905.

YOULOU, Fulbert (1917–72)
Congo politician
Educated in Cameroon and Gabon; Roman Catholic priest. Entered politics as an independent; suspended by the Church, 1956. Mayor of Brazzaville, 1956. Formed the Union Démocratique pour la Défense des Intéréts Africains; won half the seats in the Territorial Assembly elections, 1957. Congo Republic prime minister, 1957–60; first president following independence, 1960–3. Attempted to institute a one party state, 1963. Forced to resign following demonstrations; imprisoned for two years; fled to Europe, 1965.

ZAUDITU (1876–1930)
Ethiopian empress
Daughter of Emperor Menelik II. Married Ras Gugsa Wolie, 1902. Succeeded to the throne on condition she renounced Gugsa Wolie, 1916; crowned in Addis Ababa, 1917. Her authority was gradually undermined by Ras Tafari Makonnen (Haile Selassie); overthrown in a palace coup by Ras Tafari Makonnen, 1928. Gugsa Wolie led a revolt in the northern provinces to restore her to power. Zauditu collapsed and died on hearing he had been captured and executed.

PLACES AND EVENTS

Aba women's riot

Rising which occurred in Nigeria in 1929 following rumours that the British colonial government was planning to extend payment of the poll tax to women. The fears began after a chief near Aba counted women and children when assessing how much tax to levy on families in his area. The effect of levying the tax on men had been that many were forced to borrow the money from chiefs to pay the tax and then to work for nothing to pay off the debt. Women feared that they would be put in the same position if they had to pay the tax. Ibo women in Aba and Owerri attacked chiefs and Europeans, looting and destroying property. As the disturbances spread, police opened fire on a crowd, killing 55 people and wounding many more. An official Commission of Enquiry exonerated the police. But a second investigation, which included two Nigerian barristers, criticized the way in which the incidents had been handled by the administration. The British Secretary of State for the Colonies accepted the second report.

ABC Islands

Name formerly given to the three Caribbean islands of Aruba, Bonaire and Curaçao in the Netherlands Antilles. Aruba left the Antilles to become a separate territory within the Kingdom of the Netherlands in 1986.

Aburi Conference

Attempt by the Ghanaian head of state, General Ankrah, between 4 and 5 January 1967 to prevent a civil war in Nigeria by resolving the conflict between the federal government under General Gowon and Lieutenant-Colonel Ojukwu of the Eastern Region. Although agreement was reached on a number of constitutional matters, a severing of relations was followed by the secession of Biafra from Nigeria in May 1967 and a civil war from July 1967 to January 1970 in which Biafra was defeated.

Accra, battle of

The first battle of Accra (now in Ghana) was fought in 1824 during the First Asante War when the Asante attempted to remove British occupiers from the coastal region. Ten thousand Asante soldiers surrounded 1000 British troops, defeating them and killing their commander. The British sent for reinforcements, leading to the second battle of Accra in 1825. Fifteen thousand Asante marching on Gold Coast Castle were defeated by a British force consisting of 400 white soldiers and 4600 Africans. The defeat opened the way for the eventual British annexation of the whole of the Gold Coast (now Ghana).

Addis Ababa, Treaty of

Signed by Italy and Abyssinia (now Ethiopia) on 26 October 1896. Following its defeat by the Ethiopian army at the battle of Adowa, Italy was forced to acknowledge Ethiopia's independence under the treaty. Italy's invasion and occupation of Ethiopia in 1935–6 was in revenge for this humiliation.

Adowa, battle of

The most decisive military defeat inflicted on a European colonial power by an African army in the nineteenth century. Ethiopia's ruler, Menelik II, refused to acknowledge Italian attempts to force his country into becoming a protectorate. A 20,000-strong Italian army commanded by General Oreste Baratieri was attacked and destroyed by an Ethiopian army of 80,000 on 1 March 1896 and the Italians were forced to sign the Treaty of Addis Ababa in October.

Ahiara Declaration

Pronouncement of a Biafran Revolution on 1 June 1969 by Lieutenant-Colonel Chuckwuemeka Odumegwu Ojukwu, the leader of secessionist Biafra, in the village of Ahiara. The declaration proposed the establishment of an egalitarian state with the slogan 'all property belongs to the community' together with the encouragement of private economic enterprise. Biafra had seceded from Nigeria in 1967 and was defeated in 1970 following a three-year civil war.

Akwamu

An African kingdom established in the early seventeenth century by the Abrade people, members of the Akan group on the Gold Coast (now Ghana). The kingdom's strength was built on its command of trade routes and its influence spread along the coast as far as the kingdom of Dahomey. Akwamu collapsed in 1730 when it was conquered by its western neighbour, Akim.

Amistad revolt

The successful seizure of a slave ship in May 1836 by 49 slaves from the Mende people led by Joseph Cinque (c.1811–78). The *Amistad* was sailing from Havana where the slaves had been sold. Following the seizure, Cinque and his fellow slaves ordered the crew to sail to Africa but during the night the ship was turned north and was taken into custody by a US naval vessel. After landing at Montauk Point, Long Island Sound, the slaves were charged with mutiny and piracy. Abolitionists and black American societies rallied to their cause and raised funds for their defence, securing the services of prominent lawyers. Judge A. T. Judson ruled that they had been smuggled illegally into Cuba, were not legitimate slave property and ordered their freedom. The slave-traders, who had brought the case, appealed and in January 1841 the Supreme Court finally upheld Judge Judson's decision. The freed slaves returned to Africa, 32 of them going to Sierra Leone. Following his return, Cinque was reputed to have become involved in the slave trade. Among other successful revolts on board ship were those that took place on the *Jolly Bachelor* (1740) and the *Little George* (1730).

Amoaful, battle of

Fought in the Second Asante War in what is now Ghana between the British under General Sir Garnet Wolseley (with 5000 men) and 20,000 Asante. The British were defeated, losing almost 200 dead, but went on to attack Kumasi, where they were more successful.

Anguillan secession

The Caribbean island of Anguilla seceded from St Christopher on 30 May 1967, objecting to control by the St Christopher–Nevis–Anguilla premier Robert Bradshaw. Some 250 armed Anguillans expelled the police, and the islanders voted for independence in June. Following abortive talks with Britain, Ronald Webster declared Anguilla an independent republic on 6 February 1969, after a referendum. British troops and police mounted Operation Sheepskin and occupied the island. An enquiry in 1970 recommended Anguillan autonomy under St Christopher but this was rejected by the islanders and British authority was formally restored in 1972. Anguilla was granted autonomy under a British governor in 1980.

Asante (Ashanti)

The African kingdom established in the late seventeenth century under the military leader Osei Tutu, the head of the Oyoko clan. Asante spread from the trading centre of Kumasi and expanded through conquest of the surrounding Akan kingdoms, initially as a loose federation. Osei Tutu took the title Asantehene. By 1700, Asante controlled forest goldfields which were operated with slave labour. Under Opoku Ware (1717–50), Asante expanded until it covered most of present-day Ghana, an area of almost 400,000 square miles, with a population of four million. Further wars of conquest throughout the eighteenth century encouraged a greater administrative centralisation. In the nineteenth century, Asante came into conflict with advancing British colonialism. In 1896, British troops burnt the capital Kumasi, and stole the Golden Stool, the Asante symbol. The Asantehene was forced from the throne and the kingdom divided into a number of separate colonies as a British Protectorate.

Atlanta riots

Following a campaign to exclude black voters from the electoral roll, white mobs attacked black areas in Atlanta, Georgia, on 1 September 1906. Black people armed to defend themselves and, in several days of fighting which brought ordinary life in the city to a halt, inflicted more casualties on the whites than they suffered themselves. The riots were followed by the introduction of legislation preventing black people from voting. Black activists and white liberals organized the Atlanta Civil League in an attempt to prevent future violence.

Baltimore riots

Rioting broke out in Baltimore, Maryland, on 6 April 1968, two days after the assassination of Martin Luther King Jr. Five people were killed and 258 injured in clashes during which 5000 Federal troops and 6000 National Guards were deployed.

Bandung Conference

Held in the Indonesian city of Bandung on 17–22 April 1955 and attended by 29 African and Asian countries, together with black American representatives and delegates from the African National Congress (ANC). Agreement was reached on the need for closer cultural, economic and political links and the development of a neutral position between the communist and capitalist states in the Cold War. Five principles were adopted by the conference: non-aggression; respect for sovereignty; non-interference in internal affairs; equality; and peaceful co-existence. The conference led to the establishment of the Movement of Non-Aligned Countries in 1961.

Baptist War

Rising by slaves in the British Caribbean colony of Jamaica in 1831, so-called because many of those who took part were staunch Baptist converts. The rising, which is also sometimes described as the Emancipation rising, was led by Sam Sharpe (a deacon at the Baptist Chapel in Montego Bay), and was concentrated in the Great River Valley in western Jamaica. Over 200 estates were affected and 60,000 slaves were involved. The events were triggered by rumours that the British government had abolished slavery but that the white-controlled Jamaican Assembly had withheld emancipation. Many of those involved intended only to refuse to work, but others expected confrontation with the colonial authorities and prepared to fight. For over a week, one-fifth of the island came under control of the slaves, 200 of whom were killed in clashes with troops and the militia. A dozen whites were killed. There were no major battles, but rebels abandoned a stockade at Greenwich Hill when government troops advanced. The rising ended when the authorities offered an amnesty on 3 February 1832 to all slaves who returned to their estates within ten days. However, in the aftermath, 344 slaves were executed. Over 200 properties were destroyed or damaged, at an estimated cost of £1 million. Slave-owners were paid compensation for their loss of slaves. The rising encouraged the British government to speed moves towards emancipation.

Barbados riots 1876

Clashes which erupted on the British-controlled Caribbean island of Barbados on

17 April 1876. The riots derived from long-standing grievances at treatment since the end of slavery. In the period immediately before the riots, 16,000 people had had to leave the island to seek work. Against the background of divisions among the white population over constitutional issues, black rioters attacked police, destroyed plantation property and looted shops and warehouses. On 20 April the island's governor mobilized troops to assist the police but rioting continued until 26 April. During the events, eight black people were killed and hundreds injured. Police casualties were eight wounded.

Barbados riots 1937

Riots broke out in the main town of Bridgetown in 1937 when the authorities deported radical activist, Clement Payne, a Trinidadian with a large following in Barbados. The protesters fought police, burnt and looted stores and pushed cars into the sea. After a reading of the Riot Act, police opened fire, killing 14 demonstrators and wounding 47.

Benin

The African empire which developed from the city state of Benin in the eleventh century. By the fifteenth century Benin had expanded into a walled city covering a substantial area under a ruler known as the Oba. Benin's mid-fifteenth-century Oba, Ewuare, recruited a standing army and developed the empire through conquest. By 1500 Benin occupied territories from the Niger delta in the east to the Lagos coastal region in the west and was selling war captives as slaves to the Portuguese. Expansion ended by the end of the sixteenth century and the sale of slaves was largely replaced by trade in ivory, pepper and cotton cloth. Protracted civil war in the eighteenth century led to a decline in power and in 1897 British troops sacked and looted the city of Benin. The empire had no connection with the present-day state of Benin.

Berbice rising

On the eve of the rising in the Dutch colony of Berbice, the population consisted of 3833 slaves and 346 Europeans. In July 1762, 30 slaves burnt their owners' house and fled to the forest but most were recaptured. In February 1763 slaves rose on two plantations, killing whites, moving along the Corentyne river to establish a base from which they made further attacks. As whites began to flee the colony, the governor sent to Suriname for troops. On 8 March the rising's leaders – Coffy, Atta and Akkara – wrote to the governor proposing the division of the colony into a Dutch section and a section for freed slaves. This was rejected as more troops arrived. On 13 May the rebels were driven back with heavy casualties after attacking the Dagerad plantation. Internal disputes now weakened the rebels and, following Coffy's suicide, they offered little resistance to an attack by Dutch troops. Almost 3000 surrendered and, of these, many were executed. A third of the white population had died or fled in the rising and a significant proportion of the colony's plantations had been destroyed. The colonial authorities declared a general amnesty for the rebels in late 1763.

Berea, battle of

Fought during what the British describe as the Kaffir Wars (the war against the Basuto people) on 20 December 1852. The Basuto people were resisting British attempts to weaken their leaders' powers and attempted to drive the British from the area (now Lesotho). Thousands of Basutos under King Moshoeshoe attacked a British force of 2500 led by General Cathcart, forcing it to retreat after a day's fighting. The British were, however, eventually successful.

Berlin Conference

Convened by German Chancellor Otto von Bismarck and held from 15 November 1884 to 26 February 1885. The conference agreed on a final carve-up between the European powers of those parts of Africa which remained uncolonized and marked the beginning of the 'Scramble for Africa'. The conference was attended by Austria-Hungary, Belgium, Denmark, France, Germany, Italy, Luxembourg, the Netherlands, Norway, Portugal, Russia, Spain, Sweden, Turkey, the UK, and the USA. The delegates recognized the King of Belgium's control over the Congo Free State (later the Belgian Congo, now Zaïre) and the borders of the colonies of Britain, France, Germany, Portugal and Spain. Within 25 years only Liberia and Ethiopia remained independent states. Following independence, the Organization of African Unity (OAU) agreed that the national frontiers drawn by the European powers should remain largely unchanged.

Biafra

The Eastern Region of Nigeria which seceded from the Federal Republic in May 1967 under Lieutenant-Colonel Chuckwuemeka Odumegwu Ojukwu. Biafra was defeated in a bloody civil war which ended with the country's surrender in January 1970.

Birmingham bombing

Four girls were killed when a bomb exploded at the 16th Street Baptist Church in Birmingham, Alabama, on 15 September 1963. The bombing took place three weeks after the 250,000 strong march on Washington, DC, demanding civil rights and anti-poverty legislation.

Bisho massacre

South African troops fired on 70,000 African National Congress (ANC) supporters demonstrating in the Ciskei 'homeland' on 7 September 1992, killing at least 28 people and wounding 190. The incident temporarily delayed the South African peace process as the ANC and the government accused each other of responsibility for events leading to the shootings.

Blood River, battle of

Fought between the Zulus led by Dingaan and Boers under Andries Pretorius in what is now Natal, South Africa, on 16 December 1838. Boers moving north had earlier clashed with Zulus and 600 had been killed. The Zulu army went on to destroy the town of Durban. Five hundred Boers (together with over 300 African servants) made a stand at Blood River and were attacked by 10,000 Zulus. The Boers inflicted almost 3000 casualties on the Zulu forces and drove off the attack. After their victory, the Boers founded the Republic of Natal.

Boipatong massacre

Over 40 men, women and children were killed in this South African township on 17 June 1992, allegedly by 200 Inkatha supporters with the connivance of the South African security forces.

Bondelswart rising

A rebellion in May 1922 by the Khoi people (called Bondelswarts by the South African authorities) of South West Africa (now Namibia) against a 40 per cent increase in taxation levied on the owners of dogs. The Khoi, denied access to the most fertile land, depended on dogs for hunting to supplement their farm produce. The tax had originally been imposed by the German colonial authorities before 1914, to force the farmers to work for whites. Under the leadership of Arthur Morris, the Khoi people refused to pay the increased tax and then refused to hand Morris over to the South African authorities. The rising was crushed by

South African troops in five days using aircraft and machine guns. Over 100 Khoi were killed and 150 were imprisoned for their part in the rebellion.

Bophuthatswana

A South African homeland which was declared 'independent' by the apartheid government in December 1977. Its 1.3 million Tswana population was scattered across seven dispersed areas. Another 1.2 million people remained in South Africa and were allowed South African citizenship in 1986. In March 1990 protesters in Bophuthatswana demanded reincorporation into the new South Africa.

Boston anti-emigration declaration

The declaration, made at a public meeting in Boston, Massachusetts, on 28 April 1862, was the response of black American leaders to proposals for US government-sponsored emigration of the black population to Central America. The main points of the declaration were: 'That when we wish to leave the United States we can find and pay for that territory which shall suit us best . . . That when we are ready to leave, we shall be able to pay our own expenses of travel . . . That we don't want to go now . . . That if anybody else wants us to go, they must compel us.'

Brixton riot 1981

The events followed increasing tension in this area of South London during three weeks of a police anti-street-crime operation. Thousands of black youths had been stopped and searched and a hundred arrested. Rioting broke out on 10 April 1981 when police questioning a black youth suffering from a stab wound were attacked. As rioting spread over the next two days, 20 buildings and 30 cars were destroyed. Four ambulances and 118 police vehicles were damaged. Fifty civilians were injured and 401 police. In total, there was almost £5

million damage. A total of 257 people were arrested, of whom 172 were later convicted. Of the hundreds involved in the rioting, over two-thirds were black. The riot was followed by police raids on black homes, ostensibly in searches for looted goods. The government appointed the Scarman Commission to investigate the causes of this and other riots which occurred throughout Britain during the summer.

Brixton riot 1985

Armed police raided the home of Cherry Groce on 29 September 1985, searching for her son. Mrs Groce was accidentally shot by police and left paralysed. Protests outside Brixton police station led to clashes with police in which over half the participants were black. During the rioting shops were looted, cars were burnt and eleven buildings were damaged. Two people died, 31 civilians and 93 police were injured.

Brixton riot 1995

Clashes between police and mainly black youths broke out on 14 December following a protest rally outside Brixton Police Station against the death in police custody of Wayne Douglas. Protesters alleged Douglas's death had been caused by police batons although a post-mortem examination reported he was suffering from a heart condition. Rioters looted and burnt 50 shops and three public houses and destroyed ten cars and a coach. Over 20 people were arrested and twelve, including three police, injured.

Broadwater Farm riot

Broadwater Farm is a local authority housing estate in Tottenham, North London. On 5 October 1985 police raided the home of Cynthia Jarrett searching for her son. Mrs Jarrett suffered a fatal heart attack. On 6 October youths on the estate clashed with police. Over 70 per cent of those involved in the riot were black. One building was destroyed, 16 damaged and £243,000 worth of damage was caused. Seventeen civilians were injured and 163 police, one of whom died in a machete attack. There were 319 arrests. Three youths, wrongly imprisoned for the murder of the police officer, were later released. Haringey Council leader, Bernie Grant (later elected as a Member of Parliament for the area), said after the events that the rioters had given the police a 'bloody good hiding'. He later withdrew this remark.

Brownsville incident

On 13 August 1906 shots were fired in the town of Brownsville, Texas, killing one white man and wounding two others, including a policeman. Soldiers from the all-black 25th Infantry stationed outside the town were immediately accused of being involved, despite evidence from their officers that the men were in their quarters at the time of the incident. There had been a history of complaints by soldiers of discrimination in restaurants and stores in Brownsville and about the behaviour of police officers and the men were accused of seeking revenge. The dishonourable discharge of 170 members of the regiment was confirmed by President Theodore Roosevelt. The incident attracted widespread publicity in both the black and white press. The report of a Senate Committee upheld the discharge but in 1909 a court of enquiry reported that there was no evidence to link the soldiers with the incident and 14 were reinstated. In 1973, when only one of the original company remained alive, the government reversed the punishment and awarded the men honourable discharges.

Bulawayo, battle of

Fought on 23 October 1893 during the British conquest of Matabeleland (now Zimbabwe). Whites had moved into Mashonaland following the discovery of gold and the Matabele king Lobengula granted concessions to the British South Africa Company. His decision to withdraw these provoked a British attack near the Matabele capital of Bulawayo. The British, equipped with machine guns, defeated Lobengula's army and occupied Bulawayo. Resistance ceased with Lobengula's death in January 1894.

Bulawayo riots

In April 1948, African workers in Bulawayo – the second largest city in Southern Rhodesia (now Zimbabwe) – mounted a general strike in protest against wage reductions. The city, with an African population of 30,000, lay in the heart of the mineral-rich 'copper belt'. Strikers attacked Africans who attempted to continue working and demonstrated their hostility towards Europeans. The riots were the first significant show of violence against colonialism since the defeats at the hands of the British in Mashonaland and Matabeleland 50 years before. The armed struggle against white domination began in 1966 and in 1980 Zimbabwe regained its independence.

Bulhoek massacre

In May 1921, South African police and soldiers fired on the congregation of the Israelite Movement, killing 163 people and wounding 120. The congregation had tried to resist with spears and swords when attempts were made to evict them from their settlement at Bulhoek Common, Cape Province.

Bussa's rebellion

Slaves in the parish of St Philip in the British Caribbean colony of Barbados rose on 14 April 1816 under the leadership of an African-born slave-driver named Bussa. Among other leaders whose names survive were Dick Bailey, Jackey Davis, King Wiltshire and Nanny Grigg. The revolt, which gained the support of free blacks, spread rapidly across the centre and south of the island and took four days for troops and militia to suppress. The survivors of the attack were hunted down in May and June and 214 were executed following their capture. Others were transported to Sierra Leone. One white member of the militia was killed during the rising and an estimated £175,000 damage caused to property.

Cacos War

See Corvée revolt.

Caprivi Strip

Narrow corridor of land between German South West Africa (now Namibia) and British Bechuanaland (now Botswana), named after the German Chancellor Count von Caprivi. The Strip also borders on modern Angola and Zambia. In 1890 ownership of the Strip was transferred from Britain to Germany to allow the German colonial authorities access to the River Zambezi. In return, Britain received the island of Zanzibar (now part of Tanzania).

Cardiff race riot

On 10 June 1919, members of the long-standing black community in Cardiff, South Wales (many of them seamen), were subjected to an attack by whites in which a gun was fired. As crowds of whites attacked homes and shops in Bute Street, one man was killed and 14 people injured. There were further attacks on 11 June, led by two armed soldiers. Black men being attacked defended themselves with razors and other weapons. The police took black people into protective custody and attempted to put down sporadic rioting which followed with the aid of armed troops. On 13 June a column of black seamen left the city accompanied by police. Official estimates put the cost of damage at £4000. The attacks, together with growing unemployment, prompted some of the black community to appeal to the British government to pay for their repatriation.

Carib Wars

Three wars fought between the Black Caribs of the Caribbean island of St Vincent, descendants of escaped African slaves and the indigenous population, and European occupiers. In the First Carib War of 1772–3, the British carried out a successful invasion of the island (following a failed attempt in 1723) but were held off by Black Caribs under the leadership of Chatoyer for five months. Under the terms of a subsequent peace treaty, the Black Caribs acknowledged British control over St Vincent but were allowed an area of their own in return for delivering escaped slaves to the British authorities. A Second Carib War against the British under Chatoyer's leadership began, with French support, in 1779. The French occupied the island but were driven out by the British in 1783 and the Black Caribs were restored to their former status. In the Third Carib War of 1805, Chatoyer was killed in fighting against British troops and militia and the Black Caribs were deported to Central America.

Central African Empire

The name of the Central African Republic from 1976–9 under Emperor (formerly President) Bokassa.

Chicago Congress of Africa

Held in 1893, the Congress was attended by representatives of the African diaspora. Participants included Bishop Henry McNeal Turner, a leading advocate of the Back to Africa movement, and Bishop Alexander Crummell. The Congress discussed the European partition of Africa which followed the 1884 Congress of Berlin, French threats to the independence of Liberia and Abyssinia (Ethiopia), and the possibility of Africa as a future homeland for the diaspora.

Chicago riots

1. The first broke out in July 1919 following the drowning of a black youth in the section of Lake Michigan which was restricted to white swimmers. During 13 days of rioting, 38 people were killed and over 500 injured. 2. The second took place after the assassination of Martin Luther King, Jr, in April 1968. Police were overwhelmed by the intensity of the rioting and 6000 National Guard and 5000 federal troops were deployed. Seven black people and four whites died and over 350 were arrested during the clashes.

Christianborg riot

Nii Kwabena Bonne III organized a boycott in the British colony of the Gold Coast (now Ghana) in 1948 of European goods which had risen in price after the imposition of increased duties. The colonial government responded by reducing prices for three months and the boycott was lifted. The Ex-Servicemen's Union (many of whose members had served in Burma) followed up the boycott by organizing a 2000-strong march in Accra demanding an end to the appointment of European colonial governors. The demonstrators gathered at the governor's residence, Christianborg Castle, and a 22-strong contingent of police opened fire. Two protesters were killed and five wounded. In the rioting this provoked, 15 Africans were killed and 115 injured. Eighteen months after this incident, 90,000 people attended the Ghana Constituent Assembly organized by Kwame Nkrumah at Accra.

Christina disaster

The ferry *Christina* capsized and sank in 60 feet of water during a sea passage between the Caribbean islands of St Christopher and Nevis on 1 August 1970. Of the 300 passengers, 240 drowned, most of the victims coming from Nevis. The ferry was found to have been overloaded and unseaworthy.

Ciskei

A former South African homeland, the second established by the apartheid regime for the Xhosa people. When Ciskei was declared nominally 'independent' in December 1981, the territory had a population of 600,000. But a further 1.4 million of its 'citizens' lived and worked in South Africa, and in 1986 the white government allowed them to retain South African citizenship. Ciskei's head of state, Lennox Sebe, declared himself president for life in 1983 but was overthrown in a military coup in March 1990. Ciskei rejoined the new South Africa when apartheid ended.

Cleveland battle

Rioting in Cleveland, Ohio, on 5 July 1968 developed into five days of clashes during which black snipers fired on police. Of the 22 casualties from shooting, 15 were police. An estimated $2 million worth of damage was caused and 63 businesses were either destroyed or damaged in the events. The battle took place in the first major city to have elected a black mayor, Carl B. Stokes.

Congo–Kasai rebellion

An armed rising in the Belgian Congo (present-day Zaire) in May 1931. The rising, which had the support of followers of Kimbanguism and members of the Watchtower Movement, began among workers on palm plantations and followed earlier protests against the imposition of taxes and forced labour by the colonial government. The workers killed government officials and plantation company agents and burnt 'cheques' with which they were paid instead of cash. The cheques could only be used to pay taxes. The rebels were able to retain control of Congo–Kasai province for several months before being defeated by Belgian troops. After the rising, troops confiscated 4000 rifles. A further rising in December 1931 spread to nine other provinces in the Belgian Congo. The colonial authorities deployed 9000 troops in the area from 1932 to 1933 to prevent further resistance.

Congress of the People
Organized by the African National Congress (ANC), Coloured People's Congress, South African Congress of Trade Unions, and the white Congress of Democrats at Kliptown, Transvaal, on 26 June 1955. The Congress formed a Congress Alliance to co-ordinate agitation against the apartheid regime and issued a Freedom Charter setting out the programme for a non-racial South Africa.

Corvée revolt
A rising, also known as the Cacos War, by Haitians in 1918 against US occupation forces instituting forced labour to construct roads. The Americans revived a law of 1864 which required peasants to work on road construction for three days a year, known as the *corvée*. The American-controlled gendarmerie were used to compel Haitians to carry out the work for months, often away from their own areas. The rebels in northern Haiti, led by Charlemagne Péralte and Benoit Batraville, overwhelmed the local gendarmerie, took control of territory in the Central Plateau and threatened to take the capital, Port-au-Prince. The USA deployed marines to crush the revolt from March 1919 to November 1920, using aircraft to support ground attacks. US official figures put American deaths at 13 and Haitian at 3071.

Dahomey
The African kingdom founded in the early seventeenth century by Aja people moving north from the coast under pressure from encroaching Europeans, overrunning the rural villages of the Fon people. Dahomey, which covered the area of present-day Benin, was organized as a centralized state with its capital in Abomey by Wegbaja. Declaring all land to be owned by the king, Wegbaja instituted taxation and reduced the power of traditional chiefs through a formal succession. In the 1720s Dahomey was weakened by attacks from the Yoruba Oyo kingdom but with the latter's collapse in the nineteenth century, Dahomey rose to prominence again. Dahomey boasted the largest army in West Africa, consolidated its control over the coast and attacked Asante and Oyo. Dahomey initially conducted a trade in slaves with Europeans but in the nineteenth century exported palm products. From 1890 to 1894 the kingdom came into conflict with advancing French colonialism. The French authorities exiled King Béhanzin to the Caribbean colony of Martinique and installed Agoli Agbo as a puppet ruler. He was deposed and exiled in 1900, ending the Dahomean dynasty. The area became independent as Benin in 1960.

Demerara rebellion
In the British colony of Guyana, thousands of slaves on the east coast of Demerara refused to work in 1823. They demanded an improvement in their conditions and more time to work on their gardens. The produce of the gardens was used to supplement the inadequate food provided by the slave-owners and to earn money by selling the surplus in local markets. The authorities killed 250 slaves in putting down the rebellion.

Detroit riots
Clashes with police on 23 July 1967 followed police raids on gambling clubs used by black people. The police withdrew but returned the following morning to confront 3000 people who had gathered in the streets. Following stoning and burning of cars, the police withdrew once more but raids on homes of black residents provoked further

violence in which the National Guard was deployed. In clashes which continued until 30 July, 43 people were killed, at least 30 of them by the police. There were 7200 arrests and an estimated $22 million damage to property.

Dogali, battle of
A defeat inflicted by Ethiopia on the Italian army in January 1887, second in significance only to the battle of Adowa, nine years later. Italy had acquired the Red Sea port of Massawa in 1885 and penetrated inland into the villages of Sahati and Wia. Following Ethiopian complaints, the Italians fortified the villages and despatched a further 500 troops. These were ambushed and killed by an Ethiopian force led by Ras Alula at Dogali. The Italians evacuated Sahati and Wia and blockaded Ethiopia. Emperor Yohannes (John) IV rejected British mediation which sought to allow Italy to reimpose its occupation of the villages. Italy renewed its advance following Yohannes's death in 1889.

Don't Buy Where You Can't Work campaign
Organized in the USA in the 1920s by black professionals and businessmen with support from the wider black community. The purpose of the campaign was to persuade white-owned businesses in black areas to employ black workers. The campaign proved effective in some areas. In Chicago in 1929, for example, a series of boycotts and pickets under the slogan Spend Your Money Where You Can Work secured an estimated 2000 jobs for black workers in white businesses.

East St Louis riot
The most violent race riot of a series which took place in 1917 in the USA. The East St Louis, Illinois, riot broke out in July over the employment of black workers in a factory in which the white workers were on strike.

White mobs, helped by police, burnt black homes and killed black men, women and children. Estimates of the numbers killed in the rioting varied. A congressional investigation said at least 39 black people and eight whites died but the National Association for the Advancement of Colored People (NAACP) estimated that up to 175 black people may have been killed. Nine of the attackers died.

Elizabethan repatriation policy
First recorded formulation of a policy of repatriating black people from England. On 1 July 1596 Queen Elizabeth I published an open letter authorizing town officials throughout the country to deport black people. A further proclamation in 1601 declared that black people were in England 'to the great annoyance of my own liege people' and were a 'drain on the public purse'.

Emancipation
The abolition of slavery in the Caribbean. The process of emancipation took over 40 years through legislation in six European parliaments. Slavery was abolished in the British West Indies in 1834, in the Swedish possession of St Barthélmy in 1846, in the French and Danish West Indies in 1848, in the Dutch West Indies in 1863, and in the Spanish territories of Puerto Rico and Cuba in 1873 and 1878 respectively.

Emancipation rising
See Baptist War.

Enugu Colliery strike
The Enugu Colliery was owned and controlled by the British colonial administration in Nigeria before independence. In November 1949 the miners, believing wages were being withheld, began a go-slow strike. On 19 November, 900 armed police attempting to remove explosives from the colliery were confronted by 1500 miners,

supported by their families. The police opened fire, killing 21 miners and wounding 51. The shootings were followed by clashes in Aba, Port Harcourt, Onitsha and Calabar in which there were further shootings by the security forces. The Fitzgerald Commission, which was appointed to investigate the events, criticized the authorities for misinterpreting the strike as political rather than purely industrial.

Ethiopian famine
Ethiopia has suffered serious famines throughout the country's recorded history, most notably in 1540, 1543, 1567, the late 1770s, 1888–92, 1913–14, 1921, 1953, 1958–9, 1961, 1964 and 1970. Corruption and inefficiency in the distribution of grain supplies sent by Europe and the USA during the 1973 famine contributed to the overthrow of Emperor Haile Selassie in the following year. During a further famine in 1984, the ruling Co-ordinating Committee of the Armed Forces (the Dergue), attempted to cover up the extent of the devastation during celebrations of the tenth anniversary of the revolution that brought it to power. Hundreds of thousands of people died in Eritrea, Tigray, Wello and Gojoom. Ethiopia was stricken with famine again in the north of the country in 1987 and 1990, during a civil war. The collapse of the government of Haile Mariam Mengistu in 1991 eased the flow of relief supplies. In 1992 the leaders of Djibouti, Ethiopia, Eritrea, Sudan and Kenya met to agree on concerted regional action against a recurrence.

Exodus of 1879
The mass migration of freed slaves from the southern states to Kansas and the West led by Henry Adams and Benjamin 'Pap' Singleton. The participants, who numbered over 20,000, were known as the Exodusters.

Fair Helen of the West Indies
Term used for St Lucia. This strategically important island changed hands between the French and British fourteen times between 1605 and 1796.

Federation riots
In 1876 the British governor of the Caribbean colony of Barbados, John Pope Hennessy, attempted to force the white Assembly to accept his proposal to become a member of a Windward Islands federation. When the plantation owners rejected this, Hennessy threatened to 'raise up the blacks'. In March, as rumours were spread by Hennessy that the plantation owners were preventing land reform and denying wage increases, there were riots in which eight people were killed by troops from British Guiana (now Guyana) and Jamaica. Hennessy was recalled to Britain.

Fédon's rebellion
A slave rising led by a mulatto plantation-owner, Julien Fédon, on the Caribbean island of Grenada in 1795, using the slogan 'Liberty, Equality, or Death'. During the rising, the British governor of the island, Sir Ninian Home, was taken prisoner and held on Fédon's estate with 50 other hostages. Home was killed when British forces advanced on the rebels. Fédon was never captured but the majority of his fellow leaders were executed or exiled to Honduras.

First Maroon War
A conflict in Jamaica between the Maroons (escaped slaves) and the British colonial authorities. In the First Maroon War, two groups – the Leeward (or western) Maroons under Cudjoe and the Windward (or eastern) Maroons under Nanny – allied to fight a guerrilla war against the British. The Maroons carried out attacks on plantations and colonial settlements from bases in the hills, most notably Nannytown, which the

British captured in 1734. In March 1738 the Leeward Maroons made a peace treaty with the British, followed by the Windward Maroons in June 1739. Under the Articles of Pacification, the freedom of the Maroons was recognized by the British and they were granted 1500 acres of land to cultivate (although they were not allowed to grow sugar) and allowed to trade. In return the Maroons agreed to return fugitive slaves and to support the British in any conflict with rebels. The Maroons were not satisfied with the land allocated to them and a Second Maroon War was fought in 1795.

Fort Hare University College

An institution which provided education for many prominent southern Africans, including Nelson Mandela, Inkatha leader Mangosuthu Buthelezi, Botswana politician Seretse Khama, South African activist Govan Mbeki, Zimbabwean independence leader Robert Mugabe, Robert Sobukwe (founder of the Pan-Africanist Congress) and African National Congress leader Oliver Tambo. Founded in 1916 for post-primary education for Africans, Fort Hare became an institute of higher education in 1923, conferring University of South Africa degrees. Control was transferred to the Ministry of Bantu Education in 1960 when the apartheid regime divided education racially and Fort Hare became an institution specifically for Xhosa-speaking students and was given autonomous status in 1970.

Fort Pillow massacre

During the 1861–5 American Civil War, Confederate troops commanded by General Nathan Bedford Forrest killed 300 unarmed black soldiers who had been captured while serving with the Union Army at Fort Pillow, Tennessee. Forrest went on to establish the virulently racist Ku-Klux-Klan in Pulaski, Tennessee, in 1866.

Ghana

An African empire, located south of the Sahara and north-west of present-day Ghana, which began its development in the fifth and sixth centuries and which reached the height of its influence in the eleventh century. The empire's name is believed to derive from the title of its ruler. In 1063, under its ruler Tunka Manin, Ghana had an army of 200,000. Much of Ghana's power came from its Soninke rulers' command of the Saharan salt and gold trade. Ghana's power gradually waned following the destruction of its capital, Kumbi, at the end of the eleventh century. The disintegrating empire was incorporated into the rising Mali empire. There is no connection between the kingdom and the modern state of Ghana.

Great Migration

Movement of large numbers of the black population of the USA from the southern states to the industrial north-east in the early twentieth century. The migration was prompted by exploitation and discrimination and by growing economic depression in the southern states. It was encouraged by northern employers and by black newspapers, such as the *Chicago Defender*, which promised greater opportunity and regularly compared northern and southern wage rates. Between 1910 and 1930 the black population of Chicago, as a result of the migration, rose from 44,000 to 234,000. Those who moved were, however, forced into ghettos by racial violence and faced continuing discrimination. The Niagara Movement, the National Urban League and the National Association for the Advancement of Colored People (NAACP) were formed to assist in adjustment to new conditions and to combat discrimination. A further migration took place after World War II, this time towards California.

Grebo Revolution

In 1875 the Grebo people of Liberia declared war on the government which had historically been under the control of the Americo-Liberian elite. Over 30,000 people participated in the rising against the control exercised over the country's indigenous Africans. US forces were landed from a warship to suppress the rising following an appeal for aid from the Liberian government.

Guadeloupe rising

Slaves from Angola in the French Caribbean colony of Guadeloupe rose in 1656, with the aim of killing all whites on the island and taking power under two African kings. The rising was crushed after two weeks, partly because of the reluctance of slaves from other parts of Africa to participate. The two men designated as kings were hung and quartered while the other rebels were executed or flogged.

Harlem riot

Following rumours that a black youth had been killed by a shopkeeper who accused him of stealing in March 1935, the people of the New York Harlem ghetto launched attacks on property which symbolized white economic domination. Individual whites were left unmolested. There was widespread looting and 200 stores were destroyed. Following charges that the rioters had been incited by communists, the *New York Post* declared that, 'it would have been impossible to inflame Harlem residents if there had not been discrimination in employment and on relief, and justifiable complaints of high rents and evil living conditions.' A commission which reported on the events said they were caused by, 'resentments against racial discrimination and poverty in the midst of plenty.'

Herero compensation demonstration

Protests by over 300 members of the Herero ethnic group at the German embassy in Windhoek, Namibia, demanding compensation for atrocities carried out by German colonial troops between 1896 and 1905, including the Omaheke Desert massacre. The German government refused on the grounds that it had provided large amounts of financial aid to Namibia since independence in 1990.

Herndon case

One of the most significant criminal cases in black American history, comparable with the Scottsboro case. In 1932 Angelo Herndon, a 19-year-old Communist Party member, was arrested in Atlanta, Georgia, after organizing an inter-racial hunger march and charged with 'incitement to insurrection' under a state law dating back to slavery. His defence lawyer, Bernard Davis, Jr, denounced the selection of an all-white jury and the use of the insurrection law as unconstitutional and attacked the judge's racist language. Herndon was found guilty and sentenced to 20 years with hard labour. In 1937, following protracted appeals, the US Supreme Court voted 5 against 4 that the Georgia insurrection law was unconstitutional and released Herndon. The case informed a generation of northerners and liberals about the racism of the legal system in the southern states.

Heroes' Acre

Memorial garden opened in 1980 to commemorate the dead in Zimbabwe's independence struggle. People designated as Zimbabwean national heroes are buried there.

Hispaniola rising

The first recorded slave rising in the Americas began on 27 December 1522 on an estate belonging to Don Diego, the son of Christopher Columbus, on the island of Hispaniola (now Haiti). Twenty slaves from Diego's estate were joined by an equal number from a neighbouring estate and rose under the leadership of Enrique. The rebels went into the mountains and conducted guerrilla war against the Spanish occupiers of the island. The rebels were attacked by a force deployed by Diego and were hunted down, captured and hanged. A further rising took place on the island in 1547.

Houston riots

Members of the black 24th Infantry Regiment stationed in Houston, Texas, were disarmed by their officers who feared that they would respond to constant racial abuse and police violence. On 26 August 1917, two white police arrested a black woman and beat a black soldier who asked for an explanation. Rumours spread that he had died and black troops seized weapons, attacked the town and killed 17 white soldiers and wounded 64. Thirteen black soldiers were accused of murder and sentenced to death or life imprisonment after a one-day trial.

Hurricane André

This hurricane struck the Caribbean in August 1992, killing four people in the Bahamas, making 1700 homeless and causing B $20 million damage.

Hurricane Bertha

This hurricane struck the Caribbean between 9 and 12 July 1996, killing six people in the Bahamas, the Turks and Caicos Islands, the Virgin Islands and Puerto Rico. The hurricane then moved on to threaten the south-eastern USA.

Hurricane Charlie

This hurricane struck Jamaica between 15 and 20 August 1951, killing 152 people, injuring over 2000 and making 25,000 of the island's inhabitants homeless.

Hurricane Cleo

This hurricane struck the Caribbean between 22 and 26 August 1964, causing $70 million damage and killing 200 people in Cuba, Guadeloupe, Haiti and the southern USA.

Hurricane David

This hurricane struck the Caribbean between 29 August and 1 September 1979. It was responsible for the deaths of 2000 people in the Dominican Republic and 20,000 were made homeless. Fifty-six died in Dominica and 60,000 people were driven from their homes. Seven people were killed in Puerto Rico.

Hurricane Flora

This hurricane struck the Caribbean between 30 September and 8 October 1953, killing 8000 people in Cuba, Haiti and Tobago and causing damage estimated at over $500 million.

Hurricane Gilbert

This hurricane struck the Caribbean between 9 and 14 September 1988, devastating Jamaica where 45 people were killed and a fifth of the population made homeless by the destruction of 100,000 homes. The government declared a month-long state of emergency and imposed a curfew in Kingston and Spanish Town to prevent looting.

Hurricane Hazel

This hurricane struck the Caribbean between 5 and 13 October 1954. Haiti was the worst affected, with over 1000 people killed.

Hurricane Hugo

This hurricane, the most devastating in the eastern Caribbean for 25 years, struck between 16 and 18 September 1989. Over 40 people were killed and an estimated $4 billion damage was inflicted on Guadeloupe, Montserrat, Puerto Rico, St Christopher and Nevis, the Virgin Islands and the southern USA.

Hurricane Inez

This hurricane struck the Caribbean between 27 September and 1 October 1979, affecting Cuba, the Dominican Republic, Guadeloupe and Haiti. Over 900 people were killed and the area suffered $200 million damage.

Hurricane Luis

This hurricane struck the Caribbean between 5 and 7 September 1995, affecting the Leeward group of the Lesser Antilles and then spreading west towards Dominica, Cuba and Puerto Rico. Its most drastic impact was in Guadeloupe where ten people died. One person was killed in Dominica and 90 per cent of agriculture destroyed. In Antigua and Barbuda the hurricane seriously damaged 80 per cent of the buildings and damage was estimated at $300 million.

Hurricane Marilyn

This hurricane struck the Caribbean between 15 and 22 September 1995, causing damage in Bermuda and killing five people in the US Virgin Islands.

Inhlobane Mountain, battle of

Fought between Zulus and the British in what is now Natal, South Africa, on 28 March 1879. A British force of 1,500 soldiers attempted to dislodge 15,000 Zulus from a strongly defended area but were pushed back with heavy casualties.

Isandhlwana, battle of

The most decisive military defeat inflicted on the British by an African army during the nineteenth century. Britain had recognized Cetewayo as the Zulu king in 1872 but became concerned that he was raising an army to invade neighbouring colonies. The British sent a force of over 800 Europeans and 430 Africans under Colonel Durnford to disarm the Zulus. Fifteen thousand Zulus, armed mainly with assegais and led by Matyana, overwhelmed the British at Isandhlwana in what is now Natal, South Africa, on 22 January 1879, killing over half of the force.

Jamaica rebellion

A wave of strikes and riots which spread through Jamaica from April to June 1938. Workers at the Frome estate, owned by Tate and Lyle, were threatened with revolvers by officials after protesting at being paid slowly. The protest then developed into a strike for $1 a day wages. On 2 May four strikers were killed by armed police and 96 arrested. When news reached the island's capital, Kingston, 3000 people demonstrated in support of the Frome strikers. On 21 May the Kingston dockworkers struck and were joined the following day by street-cleaners and transport workers. Strikers paraded through Kingston persuading other workers to join them, building barricades and stoning the police. British troops were deployed to assist the police and a destroyer landed marines. On 24 May two women and a child were killed by police. Strikes and clashes then spread throughout the island and on 25 May the British governor declared a State of Emergency but offered concessions. The Kingston dockworkers refused to return to work until Alexander Bustamante, a labour leader, was released from prison on 28 May. Negotiations then opened on pay increases. But the revolt continued outside Kingston until the colonial authorities offered a £500,000 land-settlement scheme to alleviate unemployment. During the revolt 12 civilians were killed, 32 suffered gunshot wounds and 139 other injuries. Almost 500 people were tried and sentenced, many of them to terms of imprisonment. The events ensured the rise of Bustamante to prominence as a labour leader.

Jolly Bachelor revolt

A slave-ship sailing on the Sierra Leone River in Africa in 1740 which was attacked by Africans who freed the slaves and destroyed the ship's sails and rigging before returning to land. Among other successful slave revolts on board ship were those that took place on the *Amistad* (1839) and the *Little George* (1730).

Kambula, battle of
Fought between the Zulus and the British in what is now Natal, South Africa, on 29 March 1879. A Zulu army of 20,000 attempted to drive a British force of 2000 (which included many Africans) from a strongly defended position but was beaten off and forced to retreat. The defeat weakened the authority of Cetewayo as Zulu leader.

Kassinga massacre
South African security forces bombed and attacked a camp in Angola housing 5000 refugees from South West Africa (now Namibia) on 4 May 1978. South Africa claimed that the camp was a base for the military wing of the South West Africa People's Organisation (SWAPO). The troops killed 600 people, wounded 1000 and took over a hundred women as hostages. Many of those who died were children. The massacre is commemorated annually in Namibia as a symbol of the independence struggle.

Kongo
The African kingdom south of the River Congo which spread from the fourteenth century into the area of present-day Angola, the Congo and Zaïre. By the late-fifteenth century the kingdom extended 150 miles along the coast and 250 miles inland and traded in ivory, copper and slaves. In the late-fifteenth century its king was baptized as a Christian by Portuguese missionaries. King Afonso I negotiated with the Portuguese in the sixteenth century for military and technical assistance. Portugal, in return, expected rights to exploit the kingdom's natural resources. In 1665 Portuguese forces invaded the kingdom and King Antonio I was killed. Although Portugal withdrew from the area, the Kongo kingdom was unable to regain its former strength.

Kromatine
Principal English fort on the West African Gold Coast (now Ghana) where slaves were collected before transportation to America. The fort was established in 1631 and was a central point for the export of slaves for 30 years. The slaves transported from the fort became known as Coramantes.

Kumasi, battle of
Fought between the British and the Asante in what is now Ghana, on 4 February 1874 during the Second Asante War of 1873–4. Kumasi is 115 miles north-west of Accra in what is now Ghana. The Asante forces were led by Kofi Karikari and the British (with their Fante allies) by General Sir Garnet Wolseley. After defeating the Asante, the British set fire to Kumasi and then retreated to the coast. When a second British force returned to the now-deserted town, Kofi offered peace and withdrew his claims to the territory occupied by the British. He was then deposed by his brother Mensa.

KwaMakutha massacre
Killings of a priest, five women and seven children at the home of an anti-apartheid activist in KwaZulu-Natal, South Africa, on 21 January 1987. The massacre was believed to be the work of the so-called 'Third Force', a conspiracy of security force members with powerful political backing. The massacre was intended to provoke destabilization when South Africa appeared to be entering an era of change. In November 1995, former Defence Minister General Magnus Malan, and other former senior officers were charged with participation in a conspiracy to murder. Evidence revealed the possible involvement

of the Inkatha Freedom Party in the 'Third Force' conspiracy.

Lancaster House Agreement

The final terms agreed upon at the Lancaster House Conference on the future of 'Zimbabwe-Rhodesia' (now Zimbabwe), held in London from 10 September to 15 December 1979. The conference was attended by nationalist leaders Robert Mugabe and Joshua Nkomo, together with representatives of the 'Zimbabwe-Rhodesia' government of Bishop Muzowera and the white minority. Agreement was reached on a cease-fire, multi-racial elections, the formation of a new government, and independence on 18 April 1980.

Lari massacre

The killing in Kenya of 100 Kikuyu by supporters of the Mau Mau movement on 26 March 1953. The massacre suggested that the Mau Mau struggle was as much a Kikuyu civil war as a fight against British colonialism. Many Kikuyu who had backed the movement withdrew their support, weakening its effectiveness.

Lesotho

The African kingdom which originated in the 1820s under Moshoeshoe, the chief of the Mokotedi branch of the Sotho people. Britain annexed Lesotho in 1869, renaming it the Basutoland Protectorate. Lesotho became an independent kingdom in 1966.

Lincoln repatriation conference

On 14 August 1862, President Lincoln held the first conference between a US president and black Americans at the White House. The object was to persuade them that it was their duty, because the two races could not live in harmony, to leave America. Lincoln proposed a settlement in Central America and five black representatives were asked to recruit slaves and free blacks for resettlement. The representatives declined the request. The representatives of free black Americans had already made their attitude clear with the Boston anti-emigration declaration of April 1862.

Little George revolt

Ninety-six slaves, being transported from Africa on the *Little George* in 1730, freed themselves from their shackles, overwhelmed and imprisoned the crew, sailed the ship up the Sierra Leone River and regained their freedom. Among other successful revolts on slave-ships were those that took place on the *Amistad* (1839) and the *Jolly Bachelor* (1740).

Lozi

The African kingdom in the area which is now western Zambia. The origins of the Lozi kingdom, which was ruled by an aristocracy known as the Luyi, are obscure. Its territory was known as Bulozi or Barotseland. Civil war followed the death of Mulambwa in the mid-1830s and continued until the restoration of Luyi rule under Lwanika Lumbosi in 1885. In 1890 the kingdom signed a treaty with the British South Africa Company which led eventually to Lozi becoming a Protectorate and then the British colony of Northern Rhodesia (now Zambia).

Luluaborg mutiny

The garrison of Luluaborg in the Congo Free State (now Zaïre), consisting of African troops recruited by the Belgian authorities to fight anti-colonialist rebels, mutinied in 1895 in protest against the continual abuses they suffered from the European commander. He was killed. The mutineers controlled a large part of Kasai Province for six months until overwhelmed by superior forces loyal to the Belgians.

Lumumba Institute

Founded in Kenya by Jomo Kenyatta and Oginga Odinga on 14 December 1964, two days after the country became a republic. The institute was founded at the insistence of radicals in the ruling Kenya African National Union (KANU) and was established to define, teach and popularize African socialism. It was named after the Congo politician Patrice Lumumba who was murdered in 1961. The institute developed into a centre for instruction in scientific socialism and became an embarrassment to an increasingly conservative President Kenyatta, and was closed down.

Magdala, battle of

Fought on 13 April 1868 following the British invasion of Ethiopia. Emperor Theodore (Ras Kassa) had seized the throne in 1855. In 1865 and 1866 he arrested British representatives in the capital. A punitive expedition despatched under General Sir Robert Napier gathered support from anti-Theodore dissidents. The British forced the Ethiopian army to retreat from Magdala. Following the defeat, Theodore committed suicide with a pistol presented to him by the British Queen Victoria.

Makerere University

Opened as a technical school in 1921, the institution became the Makerere University College of the University of East Africa in 1963 and Uganda's national university in 1970. Many prominent Africans have been educated at Makerere including Milton Obote, Ugandan president in 1966–71 and 1980–5; Godfrey Binaisa, Ugandan president in 1979–80; and the Kenyan politician Oginga Odinga. Students demonstrating at the university against President Amin were violently repressed in 1976.

Mali

The African empire which began a process of expansion in the early thirteenth century following the defeat of the Sossa state under whose control the area had been. The Mali empire expanded rapidly, with its capital at Niani in the upper Niger valley, close to the Bure goldfields. At its period of greatest influence in the fourteenth century, Mali extended from the Atlantic (south of modern Senegal) to the Niger in the east, from the forest in the south to the Sahara in the north. Although the majority of rulers were Moslems, the people retained their traditional beliefs. Mali, which was based on agriculture and the gold trade, evolved a highly developed administrative system together with a large standing army. The empire was weakened by dynastic struggles. In the late fourteenth century these were renewed as the outer province of Songhay broke away. By 1500 the Mali empire had fallen back to its Malinke origins.

Mangrove demonstration

Black march in the Notting Hill area of west London on 9 August 1970. The march was organized by Black Power supporters to protest at attempts by the local authority and police to force the closure of the black-owned Mangrove Club. There were clashes between demonstrators and police in which 17 police were injured and 19 people arrested.

Mangrove Nine trial

A celebrated trial in Britain in 1971 which followed arrests during the Mangrove demonstration. The nine black defendants faced charges of riot, affray, possession of an offensive weapon, and actual and grievous bodily harm. The accused were Anthony Carlisle Innis, Rothwell Kentish, Rhodan Gordon, Frank Critchlow, Rupert Glasgow Boyce, Radford (Darcus) Howe, Althea Jones-Lecointe, Barbara Beese and Godfrey Millette. During the eleven-week trial at the Old Bailey in which several defendants conducted their own defence, the issue of persistent police harassment and brutality against the black community was consistently raised. The jury brought in not guilty verdicts in 25 of the 32 charges against the defendants. Seven guilty verdicts were brought in with suspended sentences of between nine and 15 months. The trial ended on 16 December 1971. On 17 December Rhodan Gordon was assaulted by police and arrested for alleged obstruction and assault.

March against Fear
A civil rights demonstration in the USA in 1966 mounted following the shooting of James Meredith. Meredith began a lone march to cover the 225 miles from Memphis, Tennessee, to Jackson, Mississippi, on 5 June 1966 but was shot and seriously wounded by whites, ten miles into Mississippi. The Southern Christian Leadership Conference (SCLC), Student Non-violent Co-ordinating Committee (SNCC) and the Congress on Racial Equality (CORE) agreed to continue Meredith's project. The march itself was dominated by young activists, symbolized by the substitution of the slogan, 'We shall overrun' for the by-now-traditional 'We shall overcome.' It was on this march that the expression 'Black power' first came into public prominence when used by Stokely Carmichael.

Mbwilla, battle of
Fought in what is now northern Angola in 1665 between the army of King Antonio of the Kongo and the Portuguese. The Kongo kingdom had remained independent of Portuguese domination, although Portugal controlled the coastal region. Antonio's defeat marked the effective destruction of the kingdom. Both armies were made up of Africans and Portuguese. The Portuguese included 100 African musketeers and 3000 African bowmen in their army, while Antonio was supported by 200 Portuguese traders and settlers.

Memphis riots
During celebrations of their discharge from the army on 30 April 1866, several troops from a black regiment were arrested. Police fired on fellow soldiers who attempted to prevent the arrests, provoking three days of rioting in which large parts of the black section of Memphis, Tennessee, were destroyed by fire. Forty-nine black people and two white sympathizers were killed, and five black women were raped. Ninety homes, twelve schools and two churches were burnt down.

Miami riots
Two days of rioting which began in the black 'Liberty City' district of Miami, Florida, on 18 May 1980 following the acquittal by a white jury of four white deputy-sheriffs accused of beating to death Arthur McDuffie, a black businessman. There had also been growing anger in the black community over alleged preferential treatment given to Cuban refugees arriving in the area. After attacks on whites, looting and sniping at the police, the National Guard was deployed. Among eleven demands made by a black community organization were work and promotion for blacks, an amnesty for looters and the dismissal of the State Attorney. Over 200 people were injured in the riots and 18 died. Damage to property was estimated at hundreds of millions of dollars.

Million Man March
A rally of black American men in Washington, DC, on 16 October 1995, the largest black demonstration since the 1963 march on Washington, organized by the Nation of Islam. Louis Farrakhan called for 'one million disciplined, committed and dedicated black men . . . showing the world a vastly different picture of the black male.' The event was also described as a Day of Atonement reflecting what Farrakhan described as the failure of black men in their duty towards black women and children. The date was chosen because of the message of atonement in Leviticus 16. Those not

participating were asked not to work or to spend money, to demonstrate black economic power. Farrakhan estimated that over a million congregated on the steps of the Capitol building, while police claimed 400,000 attended. A survey suggested the majority were middle-class professional men. Farrakhan's speech, in which he denounced white society and condemned Washington, Jefferson and Lincoln as racists, was shown live on national television. He said, 'There are still two Americas, black and white, separate and unequal.' In London 500 people attended a Black Unity conference held at Broadwater Farm estate in North London to show solidarity with the Washington march.

Montego Bay Conference

Meeting attended by the representatives of all British-controlled islands in the Caribbean (with the exception of the Bahamas) which culminated in the formation of the Federation of the West Indies in 1958.

Montgomery bus boycott

Following the refusal of Rosa Parks to give her seat up to a white man on a bus in Montgomery, Alabama, on 1 December 1955, other women proposed a boycott of the transport system. Although local black ministers were initially reluctant to give support to the proposal in public, a Montgomery Improvement Association was formed under the presidency of Martin Luther King, Jr. The boycott, which began on Monday 5 December, was originally intended only to last for a day but, in the event, continued for over a year. A number of the 50,000 boycotters, the majority of whom walked rather than use buses, were attacked by whites. On 20 December 1956 the US Supreme Court ordered the desegregation of the buses.

Morant Bay rising

A rebellion in Jamaica in 1865, in protest against an unpopular decision made by a local magistrate and the imposition of new taxes. Four hundred people from the hills around Morant Bay in the parish of St Thomas-in-the-East stormed the courthouse on 11 October attempting to rescue a prisoner and were confronted by the militia. A volley of stones from the demonstrators was met with gunfire and the militia retreated into the courthouse. The demonstrators set fire to the building and killed 15 of them, including magistrates, as they tried to escape. Over the next four days, groups went through the parish, looting plantation houses and killing three unpopular whites. The rising was harshly repressed by Edward Eyre, the British governor. Among the forces used to repress the rising were Maroons and the West India Regiment. A thousand black homes were burnt down, 439 people killed and 600 flogged. The leader of the original demonstration, George Gordon – one of only ten black members in the 47-seat Assembly – was tried by court martial in Morant Bay and hanged in front of the courthouse. Governor Eyre was recalled to England and prosecuted for his repressive methods. A jury rejected the charge.

Mount Pelée volcano

The volcano erupted on 8 May 1906 killing the 6000 inhabitants of St Pierre, the capital of the French Caribbean colony of Martinique. The sole survivor, who was discovered three days after the disaster, was a prisoner who had been condemned to death. There were allegations that the extent of the deaths could have been avoided had the population been warned that the eruption was imminent. However, elections were due and politicians did not want the electorate to leave the area.

Muflira miners' strike

The first organized mass black working-class strike in Northern Rhodesia (now Zambia), which broke out at the Muflira mine on 22 May 1935. The strikers demanded higher wages, a reduction in taxes, an improvement in working conditions and an end of systematic racial discrimination. On 26 May the strike spread to the Nkana mine and by 28 May workers at the Luansa mine had become involved. Troops deployed to break the strike killed or wounded 28 miners and carried out mass arrests of strikers.

Nairobi riots

Demonstrators protesting against the arrest of Harry Thuku, leader of the Young Kikuyu Association in Nairobi, the main city in Kenya, were fired on by police on 16 March 1922 and 25 were killed. The protests took place against the background of an attempt by European employers to reduce the wages of African workers by a third. Thuku was placed in detention for nine years, symbolizing fears that his attempts to link African urban and rural grievances against the colonial authorities might prove successful.

Namibia general strike

Thirteen thousand migrant workers struck from December 1971 to January 1972 in protest against the contract labour system operated in South West Africa (now Namibia). Gathering wide support from the African population, the strikers brought the mining industry to a standstill. The authorities declared a State of Emergency and attempted to intimidate strikers by firing on their meetings. South African police arrested thousands of miners after surrounding their compound at Katutura. The strike ended when troops from the South African Defence Force were deployed in January 1972.

Nannytown

Maroon settlement believed to have been first established by escaped slaves in the Blue Mountains of the British Caribbean colony of Jamaica in the early eighteenth century. It was named after the resistance leader, Nanny, who become a national hero of Jamaica in the 1970s. The earliest mention of Nannytown was by a Maroon spy named Sarra who was captured by the British in 1773. He claimed that as many as 300 men and their families lived in the town. Nannytown was captured by the British, following a number of unsuccessful attempts, during the First Maroon War on 16 December 1734. The majority of the Maroons escaped capture after burning much of the settlement. British forces were garrisoned in the town for a year following its capture. The ruins of Nannytown were rediscovered in 1968.

Natal poll-tax revolt

A rebellion in the South African province of Natal against a tax of £1 levied on every African living in the area. The tax was introduced after heavy fines had failed to force peasant farmers to abandon their farms to work for private employers in the gold mines. Government troops killed 5000 people in repressing the rising and deported a further 3000. The paramount chief, Dinizulu, was arrested for the part he played in the rebellion and remained in prison until 1910.

National Emigration Convention

Sessions of the Convention were held in the USA in 1854, 1856 and 1858. The Convention was organized in Cleveland, Ohio, by Martin R. Delany, an anti-slavery activist who favoured black emigration to Haiti, Central America and to the Niger Valley in Africa. As an 'emigrationist' rather than an 'assimilationist', Delany saw no future for black people in the USA. Many black Americans who shared his view had already made their own way to Canada. Following the 1858 Convention, James Theodore Holly (1828–1911) was despatched to Haiti and Delany to West Africa to seek out suitable sites for black colonization. With the outbreak of the Civil War in 1860 and the hopes raised by emancipation, little emerged from their expeditions. When these hopes were disappointed the idea was renewed.

Ncome, battle of
The Zulu King Dingaan, had reached an agreement with the white Boers moving into Natal in the 1830s, but in 1838 attacked their settlements, killing most of the inhabitants. Five hundred Boers returned the same year with superior weapons. Circling their wagons into a laager at Ncome, the Boers killed 3000 of the elite of the Zulu army, going on to establish a white 'republic of Natalia'.

Ndebele
The African kingdom, also known as Matabele, which ruled over what is now south-west Zimbabwe and northern South Africa. The kingdom went through a process of growth and decline in the nineteenth century, following its foundation by Mzilikazi and a few hundred members of the Khumalo people who refused to accept the authority of the Zulu king, Shaka. The Khumalo, organized in fighting regiments, moved to the high veldt in 1821, raided northern and central Sotho, and settled in the Marico river basin in the 1830s. They were described by the Sotho-Tswana people – who they absorbed – as Matabele but described themselves as Ndebele or Amandebele. The Ndebele formed regimental villages and raided neighbouring kingdoms. In 1838–40, threatened both by the Zulus and the Boers, they migrated north of the Limpopo river, overrunning the Shona Rozvi state in present-day Zimbabwe. The kingdom was conquered by the British in 1893–6, but the Ndebele language and culture retained its strength despite colonial occupation.

Netherlands Antilles
A federation of islands in the Caribbean off the north coast of South America. They include Curaçao, Bonaire, Saint Maarten, Saint Eustatius (Statia) and Saba. The Antilles are the last colonial territories which remain under Dutch rule.

New York draft riots
Against a background of economic competition between Irish emigrants and black workers, some Irish objected to the introduction of military conscription to expand the Union Army in the American Civil War. In four days of violence which erupted on 11 July 1863, 2000 blacks and 1000 whites were killed. What began as a protest against the draft turned into race riots as white mobs attacked black areas, burning down the Colored Orphan Asylum.

New York race riots
Following a fight in Harlem in August 1900 between a black man and a white police officer, in which the officer died, white mobs from neighbouring areas attacked black people while police stood by. In two days of rioting no whites were arrested and black people suffered the highest casualties.

Nigerian general strike
A 37-day strike organized in July 1945 to demand wage increases to keep up with the rise in prices through World War II. The British colonial government had approved a cost of living allowance which the Nigerian workers rejected as unsatisfactory. They demanded a 50 per cent increase and a minimum wage of two shillings and sixpence (12 and a half pence). The union leaders' call for a general strike, with the support of nationalist politicians, was backed by railway,

postal and telegraph workers and government technicians. The strike ended when a government-appointed Commission of Enquiry recommended an increased cost of living allowance and guaranteed basic wages. The strike took place after the presentation of a new constitution to the Legislative Council that failed to meet the demands of Nigerian nationalists. The strikers' victory strengthened the nationalist position in arguments with the British colonial authorities.

Nottingham race riots

Following a series of assaults against black people in Nottingham in the north of England in 1958, racial tensions led to outbreaks of violence. On 23 August a fight between a black and a white man escalated and a hostile crowd of 1500 gathered. The violence continued for ninety minutes resulting in many casualties, including several stabbings, before police dispersed the crowd. Further incidents occurred on the following two weekends. In one incident, a mob of up to 4000 white youths and men roamed the streets attacking any black people they found. The majority of the black residents remained indoors, many of them defending their homes, against bricks and bottles. The crowds then fought among themselves and attacked the police. Following the arrest of more than 50 people, charges were brought against 24 white rioters under the Public Order Act.

Notting Hill race riots

Attacks on black people in West London which spread over several days in the summer of 1958. The events covered a wide area in which there was a significant black community, including Shepherd's Bush, Paddington, Notting Dale and Maida Vale. Systematic attacks on black people followed a prolonged spate of 'nigger hunting' by white youths in the area. In July a black-owned café was attacked twice, causing serious damage. The events were marked by an increase in activity in the area by white extremist parties. On 23 August white youths damaged black homes, while a group roamed the streets attacking individual black people. Five men were taken to hospital, three of them with serious injuries. Four weeks later the white youths were sentenced to four years imprisonment. Serious violence erupted once more in Notting Dale on 30 August when 200 white youths attacked black homes and fought the police. The climax of the events came on 1 and 2 September when 55 whites were arrested following attacks on black homes. Most members of the black community obeyed police requests to stay indoors but there were some examples of militant self-defence. The events were used by the right to assert that there was an 'immigrant problem'.

Nyasaland rising

Rebellion in the British colony (now Malawi) in January 1915 led by John Chilembwe. Chilembwe had organized a campaign against white settler treatment of African labour and led protests in 1914 against British enforced recruitment of black soldiers for service in World War I. The rising was planned in November–December 1914 and at the end of January Chilembwe led several hundred followers in attacks on white farms, killing a number of settlers. Many of his followers in the rebellion were escaped slaves of the Anguru people. In white retaliation, marked by its violence, Chilembwe was captured by police and killed as he attempted to escape into Mozambique. The movement was crushed by the British authorities using black soldiers of the King's African Rifles.

Nyoro

Also known as Bunyoro, a Bantu-speaking agricultural people living in what is now western Uganda. The Bunyoro–Kitara kingdom was established in the fourteenth and fifteenth centuries. Two kings of the Chwezi dynasty built an empire larger in extent than the modern state of Uganda. The kingdom declined in the eighteenth century and, following a brief revival in power in the nineteenth century, was conquered by advancing British colonialism in 1899. The kingdom was absorbed into the Uganda Protectorate. Following independence, the Bunyoro kingdom was abolished with other Ugandan kingdoms in 1967.

Omaheke Desert massacre

The massacre followed an uprising by 7000 Hereros against the German occupation of South West Africa (now Namibia) in January 1904. German forces drove poorly armed Hereros into the Omaheke Desert in August 1904 and massacred thousands. The German commander then made the Extermination Proclamation.

Operation Perejil

The massacre over three days in October 1937 of 20,000 Haitian migrants on the border with the Dominican Republic ordered by Dominican dictator General Rafael Trujillo. The killings began in the town of Dajabon. The Haitians were cane cutters and the motivation for the massacre was racism – black Dominicans represented only 11 per cent of the population. Dominican soldiers identified Haitians by asking them to say the word *perejil* (parsley). As predominantly Creole speakers, Haitians pronounced *r* as *w*. General Trujillo agreed to pay $750,000 compensation to the victims' families in 1938 but little more than half was ever received.

Operation Sheepskin

The invasion of Anguilla on 19 March 1969 by 300 British troops and 50 police at the request of St Kitts premier Robert Bradshaw following the Anguillan secession.

Oyo

The African kingdom in much of what is now Nigeria, established by Oranyan. By the end of the fourteenth century, Oyo was the dominant power in northern Yorubaland and continued expanding through wars of conquest with neighbouring kingdoms. A powerful force of cavalry was central to the kingdom's military success. At the end of the sixteenth century the kingdom wielded regional power over all of its Yoruba and non-Yoruba neighbours, with the exception of Benin. The kingdom's wealth was based on its dominance of the salt trade and trading routes which connected with European slavers on the coast. After waging a successful war from 1726–30, the Oyo kingdom dominated the kingdom of Dahomey, going on to defeat Asante in 1764. Internal schisms and Islamic holy wars in the early nineteenth century fragmented the kingdom into competing states in almost perpetual conflict.

Pan-African Conference on Refugees

Held in Arusha, Tanzania, in May 1979. Most independent African states were represented, together with liberation movements, United Nations and intergovernmental organizations and major aid donors. Resolutions passed at the conference called upon African states to respect the human rights not only of refugees but of their own citizens and condemned the forced expulsion of refugees. Nevertheless, in 1982 Uganda expelled thousands of Rwandans and in 1990 Kenya expelled Somalis, including many who were Kenyan citizens. Congo and Burundi had also expelled refugees from Zaïre. The conference represented concern that a greater proportion of Africa's population had become refugees from war and war-induced famine than any other continent since 1960. By 1980 there were an estimated five million refugees and in 1990 this figure had hardly declined, despite the return of many to Zimbabwe, Namibia, South Africa, Angola and Ethiopia. By the end of 1991 a million Mozambicans had been forced, by continuing civil war, to seek refuge in neighbouring Malawi. Refugees were forced to flee by events in Rwanda in 1994, in Burundi in 1995, and in the Liberian civil war from 1990. Attempts to seek refuge outside Africa were met, in western Europe in particular, by increasingly strong barriers in the 1990s.

Pan-African Conference

The 'First Congress of Persons of Black African Descent' was held in London in July 1900 and attempted to co-ordinate the political objectives of Africans and the African diaspora. Of the 33 participants, the majority came from the USA, although a few representatives were able to travel from Africa. W. E. B. Du Bois wrote an Address to the Nations of the World for the conference. The Address included the declaration, 'The problem of the Twentieth Century is the problem of the colour-line.' Bishop Alexander Walters (1858–1917) of the American Methodist Episcopal Zion Church (a founder member of the National Association for the Advancement of Colored People) was elected president. The participants demanded rights for Africans in the European colonies and presented a petition to Queen Victoria specifically criticizing British conduct. The conference called on the colonial powers to prepare to grant independence. The Pan-African Association emerged from the conference, but plans to publish a journal and to meet every two years failed. The 1900 Pan-African Conference did, however, encourage the development of the Pan-African Congress.

Pan-African Congress

Six Pan-African Congresses were held between 1919 and 1974, the first four of which were dominated by the presence of

W. E. B. Du Bois. The First Congress was held in Paris in 1919 to coincide with the Peace Conference which followed World War I. Delegates unsuccessfully called for the victorious Allied powers to accept that President Wilson's principle of national self-determination should apply to Africa. The Second Congress held in London and Brussels in 1921 made more radical criticisms of European colonialism in Africa and white racism in the USA and denounced imperialism in a 'Declaration to the World'. The Third and Fourth Congresses, held in London and Lisbon (1923) and in New York City (1927), continued the criticism of colonialism and racism and were the last at which Du Bois was an effective force. An attempt to mount a Congress in Africa in 1929 was prevented by the French colonial authorities. The Fifth Congress, held in 1945, attempted to involve labour representatives from Africa and the Caribbean. Among its leading organizers were George Padmore (Trinidad), Kwame Nkrumah (Gold Coast, now Ghana), and Jomo Kenyatta (Kenya). The Congress was the first at which there was significant representation from the African continent. There were demands for independence for African colonies and support for the right of all colonized nations to self-determination. By the Sixth Congress, held in Dar es Salaam, Tanzania, in 1974, the majority of African states had achieved independence. Among the 500 delegates were representatives of liberation movements in countries which remained under white domination – the African National Congress (ANC), the South West Africa People's Organisation (SWAPO), and the Front for the Liberation of Mozambique (FRELIMO). But the Congress met against the background of disappointment in Africa over what had been achieved since independence.

Pende rising

A rebellion by peasants and workers of the Pende people living in Kwilu in the Belgian Congo (now Zaïre) in 1931. The rebels were protesting against the combination of a massive increase in taxation, a reduction in the price paid for commodities produced by the peasantry for sale, and a cut in wages on plantations owned by Unilever. The rising was ruthlessly suppressed by the colonial authorities. Four hundred Pende people were killed but only one European died.

Plessy v Ferguson

The US Supreme Court decision in 1896 which legalized systematic race discrimination by using the concept of 'separate but equal'. The court ruled that the object of the Fourteenth Amendment to the Constitution was 'undoubtedly to enforce the absolute equality of the two races before the law, but, in the nature of things, it could not have been intended to abolish distinctions based upon color, or to enforce social, as distinguished from political, equality, or a commingling of the two races upon terms unsatisfactory to either. Laws permitting, and even requiring, their separation . . . do not necessarily imply the inferiority of either race to the other . . .' The ruling governed the conduct of race relations in the USA for over half a century.

Port-au-Prince Church Massacre

Fifty armed men attacked a church during a mass conducted by Father Jean-Bertrand Aristide on 11 September 1988. They killed 13 members of the congregation and wounded 70 others using guns and machetes before setting fire to the building. Father Aristide, a leading opponent of the government and political corruption, was elected president of Haiti in 1990, ousted in a military coup in 1991 and restored to office in 1994.

Potgietersrus Primary

A landmark civil rights incident in post-apartheid South Africa. In February 1996 parents at the predominantly white Potgietersrus Primary School in Northern Province blockaded the entrance to prevent 22 black pupils from attending. They claimed their culture would be 'swamped' if the children were educated at the 600-place school and were supported by the white extremist Afrikaner Volksfront. The South African Supreme Court ordered the school to allow entry to the children on 17 February on the grounds that no school could 'unfairly on the grounds of race, ethnic or social origin, culture, colour or language, refuse to admit any child'. Sixteen black pupils entered the school on 22 February, escorted by 20 police. The majority of the white children were kept away from school by their parents.

Province of Freedom

Territory established by the British authorities on the Sierra Leone peninsula in West Africa in 1789. The area was settled by free blacks and slaves escaping from Jamaica and the USA.

Rat Island

An island off St Lucia where New Left representatives from eight Caribbean countries met in 1970 following the February – April 1970 Trinidad revolt. The meeting resulted in the formation of 'Forum' groups in Dominica, Grenada, St Lucia and St Vincent to encourage the development of radical socialist politics. Among those present was Maurice Bishop, leader of the People's Revolutionary Government in Grenada from 1979 to 1983.

Reconstruction

The period of rebuilding the southern USA from 1865–77 following the 1861–5 Civil War. Reconstruction was intended to rebuild the economy in the southern states and to transform them politically. In addition, it set out to integrate the freed slaves and protect them from re-enslavement and exploitation. Initially, the prospects for black people were hopeful. Legislation promised emancipation (Thirteenth Amendment to the Constitution), recognition as citizens (Fourteenth Amendment) and the right to vote (Fifteenth Amendment). A Freedman's Bureau was established to protect black interests. Two black Americans were elected to the Senate and 20 to the House of Representatives. Although they were unable to have a significant national political impact, representatives in the states gained important reforms in education and the judicial system. The hopes that Reconstruction had raised were already fading when federal troops were withdrawn from the former slave states in 1877, leaving black people unprotected in the face of racist state governments and white terrorist organizations.

Red Summer

Description by James Weldon Johnson of the National Association for the Advancement of Colored People (NAACP) of the period from April – October 1917 when there were race riots in 25 towns and cities in the USA. In Chicago, 23 blacks and 13 whites died. In Phillips County, Arkansas, over 20 black tenants and sharecroppers were killed after trying to form a union. During this period lynch mobs murdered 79 black people, ten of them army veterans in uniform. A further eleven black men were burned alive.

Rivonia Trial

Show trial mounted against opponents of the South African apartheid regime called after the area in which eight Umkhonto we Sizwe activists were captured by the security forces in July 1963. The eight (together with Nelson Mandela, who had been captured earlier) were charged with sabotage and conspiracy to overthrow the state. In 1964, eight of the nine (including Mandela, Mbeki and Sisulu) were sentenced to life imprisonment.

Robben Island

Prison on an island near Cape Town, first used by the British to detain opponents in South Africa, among them the nineteenth-century Hlubi resistance leader, Langalibalele. The prison was then used to detain political opponents of the apartheid regime. Among the prisoners sent there to serve terms of hard labour were the prominent African National Congress (ANC) activists Nelson Mandela, Govan Mbeki, and Walter Sisulu; Pan-Africanist Congress (PAC) leader Robert Sobukwe and the South West Africa People's Organisation (SWAPO) activist Herman Toivo ja Toiva.

Rorke's Drift, battle of

Fought between the Zulus and the British in what is now Natal, South Africa, on 22 January 1879. Having inflicted a massive defeat on the British at Isandhlwana, 4000 of the Zulu army led by Dabulamanzi went on the same day to attack 139 British at Rorke's Drift on the Tugela River. The British killed 400 Zulu troops for the loss of 25 of their own forces.

Sahel

One-million-square-mile area reaching from Senegal in the west to the Horn of Africa in the east which contains Burkina Faso, Chad, Mali, Mauritania, Niger and Senegal. The area has few natural resources, is largely semi-desert and has a poor climate, making it one of the least-developed areas of the world, with falling Gross Domestic Product in each country together with declining per capita income. Droughts in 1969–71, 1982–4 and 1987–8 triggered food crises.

St Christopher (St Kitts) general strike

On 29 January 1935, plantation workers on the Shadwell Estate in the British Caribbean colony of St Christopher refused to agree to their employer's wage offer of 8d (3p) a ton. The dispute turned into a general strike when they were joined by plantation and sugar-factory workers across the island. Demonstrators were confronted by armed police who killed two labourers and a factory watchman when they refused to disperse after a reading of the Riot Act. The strike was broken by marines who were landed from a British warship. Thirty-nine strikers were arrested, six of whom were imprisoned for up to five years.

St John rising

A slave rebellion in the Danish Caribbean colony of St John, an island with a population of 1087 black slaves and 208 whites, in November 1733. In January 1733, in response to frequent slave escapes, the Danish Royal Council ordered increased punishment for fleeing, including mutilation, torture and hanging. The slave revolt began on 13 November with an attack on the fort at Coral Bay. The rebels killed the small garrison, capturing 25 muskets and two cannon. The firing of a cannon signalled a general uprising across the island. A Danish force from the neighbouring island of St Thomas was forced to leave with a small number of rescued plantation owners. The remaining whites, with the exception of a doctor, were killed by the rebels. The slaves held the island for six months before being confronted by a force of Danish troops assisted by 400 soldiers from the French colony of Martinique. Three hundred of the rebels killed themselves rather than be captured. Two were executed on St John and a further 26 on St Thomas.

St Landry Massacre

A massacre carried out in September 1868 with the intention of preventing black voters exercising their right to vote for the Republican candidate, Ulysses S. Grant, in the US presidential elections. In St Landry, the Republican majority in a previous election had been 1071. White racists killed over 200 black men in the massacre and not one vote was cast for Grant. In nearby Bossier, where the Republicans had previously won a 1938 majority, 200 people were killed. Grant received one vote. Similarly, in Caddo, 40 people were killed, and only one person voted for Grant. The Fifteenth Amendment to the Constitution in March 1870 and the Civil Rights Act of May 1870 attempted to provide greater protection for black voters' rights.

St Vincent riots

In 1935 the governor of the British Caribbean colony of St Vincent proposed to increase customs duties, which had the effect of raising prices of food and clothing. No corresponding wage increases were offered. Protesters attempted to persuade a member of the town council to present their grievances to the governor. The governor initially agreed to receive a deputation but when it became clear he was preparing to leave the island, demonstrators forced their way into the government buildings and attacked him and the Attorney-General. They also released ten prisoners from the gaol. Police opened fire on the demonstrators after a reading of the Riot Act, killing one. Disturbances spread throughout the island, with bridges being destroyed and telephone wires cut. The authorities landed troops from a British warship and declared a State of Emergency for three weeks. A leading figure in the protests, Sheriff Lewis, was sentenced to 21 years imprisonment, of which he served five.

Scottsboro case

One of the most significant criminal cases in black American history, equalled only by the Herndon case. On 21 March 1931, the nine Scottsboro boys, youths aged from 13 to 21, were charged with the rape of two white women on a train in Paint Box, Alabama. At a rushed trial before an all-white jury, with inadequate representation and at which little real evidence was presented, the nine were convicted and eight were sentenced to death. The Communist Party's International Legal Defense (ILD) initiated a legal and agitational campaign to secure their release, revealing the weakness of the National Association for the Advancement of Colored People (NAACP). The ILD ensured the case became internationally known and succeeded in forcing a second trial in March 1933 after one of the women withdrew the complaint of rape. An all-white jury convicted them once more. Following a joint ILD–NAACP campaign, a third trial took place in 1936. The nine were once again convicted but in 1937 four were released. The remaining five served long prison sentences, the last of the defendants not being released until 1950. But, as part of the litigation, the US Supreme Court ruled in 1932 in Powell *v* Alabama that the Fourteenth Amendment had been violated because of the state's failure to ensure adequate representation for the defendants. In Norris *v* Alabama in 1936 the Supreme Court found there had been systematic exclusion of blacks from the jury, encouraging a campaign asserting the right of black Americans to sit on juries. The mass inter-racial agitation around the case prefigured the civil rights campaigns of the 1960s. Later studies concluded that the Scottsboro boys were the innocent victims of racist justice.

Scramble for Africa

The final division of Africa between the European colonial powers in the late-nineteenth century, the majority of which took place after the Berlin Conference. Between 1876 and 1900 the proportion of African territory held by Europeans was enlarged from one-tenth to nine-tenths. Britain acquired a further 4,754,000 square miles and 88 million people between 1870 and 1890. France acquired 3,583,580 square miles and 36,553,000 people between 1884 and 1900. Germany, which was late in the race, acquired 1,026,220 square miles and 16,687,100 people between 1884 and 1900.

Second Maroon War

A war in Jamaica between the Maroons (escaped slaves) and the British colonial authorities which broke out because of Maroon dissatisfaction with agreements reached after the First Maroon War. In 1795, Maroons in Trelawny Town protested about the adequacy of 1500 acres of land allotted to them, their treatment by whites and the appointment of a Superintendent-General, who they drove out in July. The British colonial authorities declared martial law and ordered the Maroons to surrender their weapons. A small number who did were ill-treated, provoking the remaining Maroons under the leadership of Johnson to set fire to Trelawny Town and attack Schaw Castle. Allied with 200 escaping slaves, 300 Maroons then retreated to the mountains, inflicting heavy casualties on their pursuers. However, the British then imported a hundred Cuban dogs to hunt down the rebels. In an agreement reached with the British commander, General Walpole, on 21 December, the Maroons agreed to apologize, to settle wherever the colonial authorities decided and to return fugitive slaves. In return Walpole pledged that they would not be removed from Jamaica. However, against

Walpole's protests, many were deported to Nova Scotia and then to Sierra Leone.

Senegambia

Confederation of Senegal and The Gambia formed on 1 February 1982, a year after President Jawara of The Gambia had called in Senegalese troops to assist him against an attempted military coup. The Senegambian government consisted of a Council of Ministers of five representatives from Senegal and four from The Gambia, together with a Confederal Assembly with 40 Senegalese and 20 Gambian members. The confederation was intended to create an economic and military union but relations collapsed as The Gambia increasingly resisted losing its sovereignty. Senegambia was dissolved in September 1989.

Shangani River, battle of

Fought between the Matabele and the British in what is now Zimbabwe on 3 December 1893. A small British force was attacked by a Matabele army led by King Lobengula and completely destroyed.

Sharpeville massacre

A peaceful protest against the Pass laws under the South African apartheid regime held on 21 March 1960 in the black township of Sharpeville, near Johannesburg, was attacked by police who killed 69 unarmed demonstrators. The government declared a State of Emergency and banned the African National Congress (ANC) and the Pan-Africanist Congress (PAC). The PAC leader Robert Sobukwe was arrested for organizing the protest and many ANC leaders went into exile or underground. The ANC armed wing, Umkhonto we Sizwe, was formed shortly afterwards. The massacre brought South Africa close to civil war, and led to an international outcry and a largely symbolic withdrawal of overseas investment.

Shashemane

Town in southern Ethiopia in which Haile Selassie granted land to followers of Rastafarianism which now houses the headquarters of the Ethiopian World Federation. The land was intended to provide a home for people of African descent, particularly from the Caribbean. Rastafarians from across the world hold an annual festival in the town to celebrate Haile Selassie's birthday.

Shell House Massacre

The shooting of 55 people in Johannesburg, South Africa, on 28 March 1994 during an anti-African National Congress (ANC) demonstration by Inkatha Freedom Party members. The shootings took place outside the ANC headquarters at Shell House. President Mandela admitted on 1 June 1995 that he had personally ordered guards at Shell House to shoot to kill if the building was attacked.

Somerset Case

A decision in the British courts in 1772 which reversed the Yorke-Talbot decision of 1729 and slightly extended the rights of black slaves in Britain. Somerset, a fugitive slave, brought a case against his owner who was attempting to force him to return to the West Indies. Lord Justice Mansfield ruled that it would be illegal to remove Somerset from the country against his wishes. However, there continued to be no legal protection for free blacks in Britain.

Songhay

The African empire in the area which now comprises Niger and Mali. Songhay was able to expand as the Mali empire declined, through a combination of astute leadership and its strategic position on trade routes. It was ruled by a Muslim-backed dynasty from 1493 but fell to Moroccan conquest in 1591.

Soweto (South West Township)

A black South African city near Johannesburg developed in the 1950s to house people evicted from townships and squatter camps nearer the city. By the 1980s it was the largest black settlement in the southern hemisphere. The population, housed in primitive conditions, commuted to Johannesburg to work. The scene in 1976 of the Soweto rising (see below).

Soweto rising

Protests in the South West Township, near Johannesburg in South Africa against the apartheid government's attempted imposition of Afrikaans as the language to be used in the education system. The protests, which began on 16 June 1976, developed into three days of riots in which 236 black South Africans were killed by the police and two whites were killed by rioters. The government withdrew the proposal on 6 July but the area remained a centre of anti-government agitation. In the aftermath of the rising large numbers of young blacks left South Africa to train with the resistance Umkhonto we Sizwe in Angola, Mozambique and Tanzania.

Springfield riots

Following tension caused by the use of black miners as strike-breakers, a black man was wrongly accused of raping a white woman in Springfield, Illinois. During 14 and 15 August 1908, white mobs destroyed black areas, killing eight black people (two of whom were lynched) and forcing over 2000 to flee. Four whites were killed. No whites were charged and an economic boycott was instituted to force the remaining black people from the city. Black and white liberals met in Springfield, the following year, to develop what became the National Association for the Advancement of Colored People (NAACP).

Tacky's rising

A slave-rising in the British Caribbean colony of Jamaica which began in April 1760. There had been minor revolts on the island in 1742 and 1745 which were quickly suppressed. Up to a hundred Coromantes led by an Asante chief named Tacky rose at Port Maria in the north of the island on 8 April, captured Fort Haldane and seized weapons, then marched south killing whites and gathering support. The initial failure of troops and the militia to crush the rebels triggered further risings across Jamaica, with up to a thousand involved in the western area of Westmoreland. The rebels killed 60 whites and two British regiments and the militia were deployed to end the rising. Tacky and 25 of the rebels fled to the hills but were hunted down by the Maroons, one of whom killed Tacky in October 1761. Tacky's head was displayed on a pole on the road to the capital, Spanishtown. In the aftermath of the rising, 400 slaves were killed and 600 deported to Honduras where they were sold. New laws were passed restricting the movements and worsening the conditions of slaves.

Takrur Kingdom

The African kingdom believed to have been in existence in the eighth and ninth centuries. The kingdom was established by the Tukolor people in West Africa and covered the valley of the Senegal River, stretching north towards the desert and south towards the Gambia. It rose to prominence in the ninth century under the Dya'ogo dynasty and prospered through trade in gold, salt and slaves. Islam was introduced to the kingdom in the eleventh century by War-Jabi, a Takrur ruler who died in 1040. Takrur declined into a number of smaller states when it lost control of the gold trade routes east of the Senegal River and lost territory to newer developing states.

Taranto mutiny
A revolt by men of the 9th Battalion of the British West Indies Regiment which began in Taranto, Italy, after World War I. On 6 December 1918, men of the battalion refused to work and attacked their officers. A group of sergeants sent a petition to the British Secretary of State for the Colonies protesting at the persistent racial discrimination soldiers in the regiment suffered. A number of the mutineers also formed an underground Caribbean League with wider objectives. At the end of the mutiny, one soldier was shot by a firing squad and others were sentenced to up to 20 years imprisonment. Shortly afterwards the entire regiment was disbanded and the men were returned to the Caribbean. The colonial authorities were warned that many ex-soldiers were likely to become involved in agitation when they returned home.

Toxteth riots
Following rising tension in this decaying area of Liverpool, England, clashes began after police had chased a black youth, forced him from his motorcycle and accused him of stealing it. His father was already suing the police for persistent harassment. Large parts of Toxteth were burnt in rioting which spread over 3 to 7 July 1981 and there was mass looting of supermarkets by both black and white members of the community. An estimated £4.7 million worth of damage was caused and 132 civilians and 128 police were injured. Of the 244 people arrested, 172 were convicted.

Transkei
The first pre-liberation South African homeland for 1,500,000 Ngoni Xhosa people, created by the apartheid regime in 1963. Transkei was declared independent with its own National Assembly under Paramount Chief Ndamase in October 1976. Transkei remained unrecognized outside South Africa. Major-General Bantu Holomisa, Chief of the Defence Force, mounted a bloodless coup in 1988, suspended the constitution and declared martial law. In February 1990, he promised a referendum on reintegration with South Africa. Transkei was reincorporated into the new South Africa following the collapse of apartheid.

Transvaal miners' strike
In February 1920, 71,000 black workers at 22 mines in the Transvaal, undertook the largest strike in South African history until 1946. The strike was broken by the use of a heavy force of police and troops.

Treason trial
The trial in South Africa of 156 campaigners against apartheid which began in December 1956. The accused were charged with membership of an 'international Communist conspiracy' – the African National Congress (ANC) – and of plotting to overthrow the South African government. The trial lasted until March 1961, when the remaining defendants were acquitted. The ANC had by then become a banned organization.

Trinidad coup
An attempted overthrow of the government of Arthur Robinson and the establishment of an Islamic state by the 2000-strong militant black Muslim group, Jamaat al Muslimeen. The coup began on 27 July 1990 and took place against a background of prolonged economic recession, culminating in the imposition of taxes which drastically increased food prices. Under the leadership of Imam Yasin Abu Bakr (Lennox Phillips, a former policeman), the rebels destroyed police headquarters and seized Trinidad's legislative building, the Red House, and the state television station. Robinson was shot in the legs on the first day of the coup. He and several cabinet ministers

were held hostage by 120 rebels in the Red House and wired with explosives. The group demanded Robinson's resignation, the establishment of a coalition government (including Imam Yasin) and elections within 90 days. The events were accompanied by rioting and looting by crowds in the capital, Port of Spain. Police and troops surrounded the occupied buildings, leading to Robinson's release, following his agreement to the rebels' demands on 31 July. The rebels surrendered on 1 August and the bringing to trial of its leadership was delayed for the decision of the Privy Council in Britain. On 5 December 1995, the Trinidad prime minister, Basdeo Panday, met Imam Yasin to discuss the group's demands for land and compensation for damages.

Trinidad general strike

A strike of dockworkers in the capital, Port of Spain, in 1919–20 which developed into a wider agitation. Following the refusal of the employers to negotiate with the Trinidad Workingmen's Association (TWA), the dockworkers began a strike for higher wages, overtime pay and an eight-hour day on 15 November 1919. The employers immediately recruited scab labour in an attempt to break the strike. The strikers had wide public support and were joined by city council workers and coal carriers. On 1 December, a march through Port of Spain brought the city to a standstill. Strikers attacked warehouses and expelled strike-breakers from the area. The employers immediately began negotiations with the TWA and on 3 December agreed to a 25 per cent pay increase. This success encouraged a wave of strikes throughout Trinidad and Tobago including plantation and oilfields workers. The authorities then turned to repression. One estate worker was killed and seven wounded by British marines. A white vigilante force was formed when the authorities

feared that black police would prove unreliable and mass arrests of strikers began. A Seditious Publications Order banned the *Negro World*, *The Crusader* and other black newspapers. A Strikes and Lockout Ordinance in 1920 made all strikes illegal.

Trinidad revolt

Disturbances in Trinidad from 26 February to 21 April 1970 led by the National Joint Action Committee (NJAC), a predominantly middle-class black power movement, supported by students and urban employed and unemployed youth. The NJAC expressed a widespread disappointment with what had been achieved since independence, denounced the Trinidad elite as 'Afro-Saxons' who were over concerned with the interests of foreign investors, and – although anti-Marxist – called for public ownership of land and the sugar industry. There were also criticisms of unemployment and proposed anti-trade union legislation. On 26 February, the NJAC mounted protests against Canadian imperialism and racism on the first anniversary of a demonstration over the arrest of black students in Canada. Nine NJAC leaders were arrested but were greeted by 10,000 supporters who paralysed the capital, Port of Spain, on their release on 4 March and marched to Shanty Town. As the situation developed – with burning of businesses, looting and clashes with police – it became clear that NJAC had no coherent programme that could encourage a revolution. In addition, it proved impossible to build an alliance with the Indian population. On 23 March, Prime Minister Eric Williams offered concessions and praised the concept of black power. On 9 April over 50,000 people attended the funeral of an NJAC member shot by police. As a number of unions expressed support and proposed a general strike on 21 to 22 April, the government declared a State of

Emergency and imposed a dawn-to-dusk curfew. A section of the 750-man Defence Force mutinied on 21 April, leading to fears of a military coup. The mutiny was quelled by the Coast Guard. The arrest of the mutiny's leaders, combined with the State of Emergency, effectively ended the revolt. Opposition parties boycotted elections held in 1971 and a guerrilla group, the National Union of Freedom Fighters, was formed.

Trinidad riots

Strikers in oil fields owned by Trinidad Leaseholds (a South African-controlled company) protesting against their employers' racism, occupied the fields in 1937 under the leadership of Uriah 'Buzz' Butler. Two oil fields were set on fire by the strikers and two police officers were killed when they attempted to arrest Butler. The strikes spread to the sugar estates and business premises were burnt down in San Fernando and Port of Spain. Fourteen people were killed and 59 wounded in clashes with sailors and marines who were deployed by the British colonial authorities.

Trinidad water riots

The result in 1903 of an attempt by the government to meter water consumption in the Trinidadian capital, Port of Spain. The Legislative Council was mobbed at the first attempt to pass a Water Ordinance and the proceedings were abandoned. At the second attempt the authorities restricted admission to ticket holders only. Over 5000 people gathered to protest outside the government offices. The leaders of the demonstration were refused admission and the crowd attacked and set fire to the building. The riot was put down using sailors from two British warships anchored in the harbour.

Trois Glorieuses

The 'three glorious days' of 13 to 15 August 1963 which led to the resignation of President Fulbert Youlou of the Congo Republic. The issuing of draft proposals to establish a one-party state and to weaken trade unions by President Youlou triggered mass demonstrations of students and the unemployed in the capital, Brazzaville, on 13 August. The arrest of trade-union leaders accused of organizing the demonstrations provoked a general strike. The government declared a State of Emergency but President Youlou was forced to resign and flee the country on 15 August. He was sentenced to death in his absence in September 1963. The three days were celebrated each year as a national festival.

Tulsa race riots

Following the arrest of a black man for the alleged rape of a white woman, 75 black people marched to the prison in Tulsa, Oklahoma, on 31 May 1921 to prevent what they feared would be a lynching. When the protesters were dispersing after discussions with the sheriff, a white man attempted to disarm one of them and a shot was fired. In exchanges that followed, ten whites and two blacks died. Several thousand armed whites invaded the black area, 'Little Africa', setting fire to and destroying a large number of houses. The estimated total fatalities were up to 200 blacks and 50 whites.

Tuskegee Institute

Established in Alabama in 1881 by Booker T. Washington, as the Tuskegee Normal and Industrial Institute. Washington became the first principal. The institute was founded to provide a practical education in the humanities and was intended to lay the basis for an economically independent black American population. In 1882, Washington bought 100 acres of land on a former plantation to enlarge the institute. Washington's political influence was exercised through what was described as the 'Tuskegee Machine'.

Ulundi, battle of

Decisive battle fought between Zulu and British forces on 4 July 1879, in what is now Natal, South Africa. Following their defeat at Isandhlwana, the British under Lord Chelmsford mounted a counter-offensive with 5000 troops (over a thousand of whom were Africans), against a 20,000-man army led by Cetewayo. The British attacked Cetewayo's headquarters at Ulundi, 115 miles north-east of Durban, and killed 1500 Zulus for the loss of 15 men. The war between the Zulus and the British ended with the capture of Cetewayo on 28 August. Following the Zulu defeat, their land was divided into 13 chiefdoms but, after a period of disorder, Cetewayo was restored to his throne by the British in 1883.

Union Island uprising

A predominantly youth rebellion in December 1979, on the Grenadine island of Union (population 4000), led by a Rastafarian, Charles Lennox. The rising protested at the neglect of the island by St Vincent, demanded autonomy for Union, and criticized the toleration of drug smuggling and the increasing exploitation of the island by foreign tourism. Lennox and his supporters were put down by police from St Vincent and troops from Barbados, one civilian dying in the process. The government declared a State of Emergency for six months. Lennox escaped to Carriacou Island but was returned to St Vincent where he was tried and sentenced to eight years hard labour in 1980.

Venda

A South African homeland for the Venda people under the apartheid regime. Declared 'independent' in September 1979, Venda was not recognized outside South Africa.

Wal Wal well

The scene of a clash between Italian and Ethiopian troops in November 1934 which was used as a pretext for the Italian invasion in October 1935. Italy demanded an apology, Ethiopian acknowledgement of Italian control over Wal Wal and payment of compensation. Emperor Haile Selassie refused and went to the League of Nations for support. While the League was considering the issue, Italian forces invaded Ethiopia on 3 October 1935 without declaring war.

Watts riots

Six days of riots in the predominantly black and Hispanic area of Los Angeles which began on 11 August 1965 following a police officer's attempt to arrest a black youth. They were a protest against economic deprivation, social injustice, racism and increasing military conscription of young black men to fight the war in Vietnam. An estimated 30,000 people (15 per cent of the black population) participated in the riots. Thirty-four people were killed, over a thousand injured and 3927 arrested. Of those arrested, 556 were under 18, 2111 over 25, and 602 over 40. Property worth $175 million was damaged. The events allegedly contributed to the white backlash against the civil rights movement and government legislation.

West Indies

The name in the colonial period for the English-speaking Caribbean, replaced after independence by the term Caribbean. However, the expression continues to be used, for example, in referring to the West Indies cricket team and the University of the West Indies.

Westmoreland rising

A slave-rising in the south-west of the British Caribbean colony of Jamaica, which broke out on 2 June 1760, immediately after Tacky's rising. Three companies of British infantry, the militia and a force of marines took five months to capture the last of the 600 slaves who rose. A further rising took place in the same area in 1777.

Wilmington riots

Following a campaign to disenfranchise black voters and the election of white supremacists, over 400 whites attacked the black area of Wilmington, Carolina, in November 1898, in an attempt to drive the black population from the town, killing at least 30 people, and burning down the offices of the *Wilmington Record*, a newspaper under black editorship.

Windhoek massacre

Police fired on demonstrators against the enforced removal of the population from the town of Windhoek, South West Africa (now Namibia) on 10 December 1959. Eleven people were killed and over 50 wounded. The massacre was followed by the arrests of nationalist leaders by the South African authorities.

Xhosa

The largest southern Nguni branch of the Bantu-speaking peoples. In the fifteenth century the Xhosa were living in the area of modern Natal in South Africa. Until the late eighteenth century they were ruled by a paramount chief but had not developed a centralized administrative and political system. Some smaller groups broke away to form separate kingdoms, but in the late-eighteenth century there was a major division into two kingdoms, the Gcaleka and the Rarabe. As Europeans encroached from the Cape Colony, the Xhosa lost land in wars fought from the 1770s to the 1870s. In 1886 all Xhosa territory was annexed by the Cape Colony.

Yorke–Talbot decision

A legal opinion delivered by Solicitor-General Yorke and Attorney-General Talbot in 1729 which clarified the legal status of slaves in Britain. Yorke and Talbot ruled that holding slaves in Britain was legal and confirmed the right of slave-owners to forcibly return slaves to the Caribbean plantations. Until their decision the position had been confused. Under common law, slavery in Britain appeared to be illegal and judges had made a number of contradictory rulings. Among these were that Africans were heathens and so not subject to Christian laws, and that baptism or simply landing on British soil automatically conferred freedom. The Yorke–Talbot decision was reversed in the 1772 Somerset Case.

Zong incident

A British slave-ship, the *Zong*, was sailing to Jamaica in 1783 when it was struck by an epidemic. As insurance only covered slaves who were lost at sea and not those who died from sickness brought on by bad conditions, the commander of the *Zong*, Captain Collingwood ordered 133 slaves to be thrown overboard. Thirty-six who resisted were shackled together before being cast into the sea. A further ten jumped over themselves. Olaudah Equiano brought the incident to the attention of the white abolitionist activist Granville Sharpe. Sharpe's campaign to bring the murderers to trial failed but the incident affected British public opinion to the extent that there were attempts in 1788 to legislate for greater regulation in the slave trade.

Zulu kingdom

The African kingdom in the area occupied in part of present-day South Africa, formed in the early nineteenth century as a clan of a number of small northern Nguni groups. Shaka (*c.* 1816–28) led the occupation of northern Natal (modern Zululand) and developed a strongly centralized state. The Zulu kingdom collapsed on the death of Cetewayo in 1884 and was divided up under British administration.

TERMS, MOVEMENTS AND IDEAS

AALC

See African–American Labour Centre.

ABB

See African Blood Brotherhood.

ACMHR

See Alabama Christian Movement for Human Rights.

ACP Countries

African, Caribbean and Pacific Countries, the 70 signatory states to the Lomé Convention and successive agreements with what is now known as the European Union. The first Lomé Convention, signed on 28 February 1975, guaranteed tariff-free entry of ACP products into the European Economic Community and promised increased aid and investment. Lomé II was signed on 31 October 1979 and promised a further $7 billion aid. A third Convention was signed in 1984 and a fourth in 1989.

Affirmative action

Attempt to redress the imbalance of opportunities against minorities, particularly in employment. In 1943 President Franklin D. Roosevelt established a Fair Employment Practices Commission to prevent discrimination against black Americans seeking work in industry. Under the 1964 Civil Rights Act, an Office of Federal Contract Compliance was established to encourage institutions and businesses which received federal contracts or funding to develop affirmative action programmes. An Equal Employment Opportunities Commission (EOC) was established at the same time. This was followed by legislation in 1972 extending protection to federal employees and giving the EOC authorization to prosecute private employers where conciliation had failed. US Supreme Court decisions in 1978 and 1979 supported 'positive discrimination' in education and the establishment of special training programmes by employers and trade unions to enhance job opportunities for minority employees. By the mid-1980s, much affirmative action had been weakened in the USA under President Reagan because of its allegedly economically restrictive effects. Supreme Court decisions in the 1990s further undermined affirmative action in education.

African–American

Descriptive term used by some Americans of African descent in the USA during the 1980s. A report by the Joint Center for Political and Economic Studies in January 1991 said, however, that most black Americans preferred to describe themselves as 'black'.

African–American Labour Centre (AALC)

Based in Lomé, Togo, the AALC is financed by unions in the USA to encourage the development of labour organizations in Africa and produces African trade union journals.

African Association

Formed in London on 24 September 1897, with the Trinidadian, Henry Sylvester Williams, as its leading figure. The association emerged in response to the European partition of Africa which followed the 1884–5 Congress of Berlin. Its formation marked an early stage in the development of the anti-colonialist movement. The association was established to encourage the unity of Africans and people of African descent, particularly in territories of the British empire. The association issued a circular in March 1898 calling for a Pan-African Conference. Following the conference in London in July 1900, the association merged into a wider Pan-African Association.

African Blood Brotherhood (ABB)

Organization formed in New York City in October 1919 by Cyril Briggs, a supporter of the 1917 Russian Revolution, editor of the *Amsterdam News* and founder of *The Crusader*. The ABB, which later affiliated to the Communist Party, was a revolutionary Pan-Africanist organization which advocated black self-defence against racial attacks and lynchings. Central administration was in New York, although the ABB organized throughout the USA. At its peak in the early 1920s, membership was an estimated 50,000, with 50 branches in the USA, the Caribbean and Latin America. Initially sympathetic to the Universal Negro Improvement Association (UNIA), Briggs criticized the view of Marcus Garvey that black liberation could be achieved through capitalism. Among the ABB's objectives was to, 'bring home to the Negro worker his class interests as a worker and to show him the real source of his exploitation and oppression'. ABB members were expelled from UNIA at its 1921 convention. As the ABB waned in effectiveness, many of its active members moved to the American Negro Labor Congress.

African Carrier Corps
British military unit in World War I made up of 160,000 African volunteers from the East African Protectorate (later named Kenya). The corps carried equipment and supplies in the campaign against German forces in Tanganyika (now Tanzania). An estimated 50,000 members of the corps died, largely from disease brought on by malnutrition and inadequate health care.

African Economic Community
The creation of a continent-wide economic community was agreed on at a meeting of the Organization of African Unity (OAU) heads of state in June 1991. The agreement proposed the formation of a common market by the year 2025, beginning with a five-year programme to strengthen existing economic groupings in Africa. Before it could come into effect, the agreement required ratification by two-thirds of OAU members.

African Emigration Association
Formed in the US in 1881, the association advocated the return of black Americans to Africa and was the first organisation to advance the Pan-Africanist aim of building a 'United States of Africa'.

African Independent Churches
Christian churches in Africa that sought independence from foreign control. They were also referred to as African Indigenous Churches. The first was the Settlers' Meeting in Sierra Leone which split from the Wesleyan Mission in Freetown in 1819. The independent churches replaced the European style of worship with an African style, incorporating elements of traditional religion, but continued to stress the centrality of the Bible in their beliefs. Independent churches continued to be established in the twentieth century. These include the African National Church in Tanganyika (now Tanzania), formed in the 1930s for Africans who had been expelled from missionary churches for retaining polygamy; the Dini yo Roho (Holy Ghost Church), formed among the Abaluyia people as a breakaway from the Friends' African Mission in Kenya in 1927 and, also in Kenya, the Joroho (Holy Ghost) Church among the Luo people in 1932. Among those that are still active are the Apostolowa Fe Dedefia Habobo (Apostolic Revelation Society) in Ghana, Calici ca Makolo (Church of the Ancestors) in Malawi, and the Church of the White Bird in Zimbabwe.

African Indigenous Churches
See African Independent Churches; Ethiopianism.

African Methodist Episcopal Church
The oldest autonomous black organization in the USA, founded in 1787 in Philadelphia

under the leadership of Richard Allen. The Baltimore African Church had been formed in 1787 when white Methodists refused to allow fellow black believers to occupy pews or receive Holy Communion. This, together with the Bethel Church (an off-shoot of the Free African Society), united with a number of small Methodist bodies to escape increasing racial discrimination. The AME was not officially recognized until 1816.

African Reparations Movement (ARM)

Organization formed in Britain in 1993 to campaign for symbolic reparations for slavery. ARM's leading figure is Bernie Grant, the Labour Member of Parliament for Tottenham. In November 1993, he set out demands for Britain to make good the damage caused to Africa by slavery and colonialism, calling on the government and Queen Elizabeth as Head of State to apologize. He also called for the return of jewellery and artefacts stolen from Africa during the colonial period.

African Research and Information Bureau

Umbrella organization of African refugees and immigrants in Britain. The bureau researches and publishes information on Africa, offers advice and assistance to Africans in Britain and acts as a forum for discussion. In 1991 the bureau established a journal, *Africa World Review* and called upon Africans to, 'challenge this New World Order and build upon African people's traditions of resistance for the past 200 years'.

African Social and Technical Society

Formed in September 1952 by skilled black workers in Liverpool, England, to attempt to find employment in large-scale development projects being undertaken in Africa, for example, the Gold Coast River Project.

The society also organized a wide range of cultural and social activities. It collapsed following internal disputes among its leading figures.

African Students' Association of the United States and Canada

Organized in 1941 among African students to agitate for the independence of Britain's African colonies. The association published a monthly newspaper, *The African Interpreter*. Among its leading figures was Kwame Nkrumah, who became leader of Ghana on independence in 1957.

African Union Society

Formed for free Africans in Newport, Rhode Island, 1780. The society was established to assist widows and children, to preserve records of manumission (the official notification of a slave's freedom) and birth, marriage and death certificates. The society also provided a discussion forum for planning and organizing the return to Africa. In 1796 agreement was secured with the British authorities for twelve families to move to Freetown, Sierra Leone, but, unable to obtain the required endorsement of a white clergyman, the society abandoned the project. Similar societies were formed in Boston, Philadelphia and Province.

Agbadjigbeto

Intelligence gathering and propaganda organization established by Agaja of Dahomey, during his reign from 1708–32. The Agbadjigbeto collected information on activities in neighbouring states and disseminated propaganda favourable to Dahomey within and outside the kingdom.

Akina Mama Wá Afrika (AMWA)

Solidarity among African women, an organization established in March 1985 to address issues affecting African women in Britain; to raise funds to assist and support women in Africa; to undertake research; and to promote and organize conferences. AMWA acts as a link between its members and other black and statutory organizations and publishes a journal, *African Women*. In November 1992, AMWA organized a conference in London on the role of women in the movement for democracy in Africa.

Alabama Christian Movement for Human Rights (ACMHR)

Movement active in the civil rights campaign from 1956 to 1962, founded by Baptist ministers Revd Fred L. Shuttlesworth and Revd Vernon Johns. The ACMHR was formed following the banning in Alabama of the National Association for the Advancement of Colored People (NAACP). The movement organized demonstrations and filed law suits to gain civil rights. It was succeeded by the Montgomery Improvement Association (MIA).

Aldeamentos

Villages set up by the Portuguese in their African colony of Angola during the 1961–74 war of independence. Ostensibly intended to protect the resettled population from the dangers of war, they were an attempt to deprive the anti-Portuguese guerrilla forces of rural support.

Alvor Agreement

Treaty signed between Portugal and the main Angolan nationalist movements, the Popular Movement for the Liberation of Angola (MPLA), the National Front for the Liberation of Angola (FNLA) and the National Union for the Total Independence of Angola (UNITA), in the Portuguese city of Alvor in January 1975. Under the terms of the treaty there was to be a cease-fire as a preliminary to the granting of independence on 11 November 1975. A transitional government formed in Angola following the agreement collapsed as fighting erupted between the competing movements.

Amaro

Term used in Dahomey and Nigeria to describe former slaves who had returned to the area from Latin America.

American Colonisation Society

The American Society for Colonising the Free People of Color in the USA was formed in Washington, DC, in 1816. The society, which included slave-owners among its leading members, was formed to encourage the repatriation of free blacks to Africa and did not support the abolition of slavery. The US government provided funds to the society and assisted in negotiations with African rulers to obtain land for settlement. In 1821 the Society's representatives purchased land for $300 from King Peter, in what became Liberia, after threatening to have him shot if he refused. King Peter attempted to prevent colonists landing but was overcome by their superior weapons. In 1838 the Commonwealth of Liberia was formed under the governorship of a society nominee. The society was dissolved in 1912.

American Negro Academy

Founded in March 1897 by the cleric and academic Alexander Crummell. The purpose of the academy was to encourage intellectual excellence in all fields among black Americans and to counter white racist propaganda. In his opening address, Crummell spoke of a 'talented tenth' who would become the black American intellectual elite.

American Negro Labor Congress (ANLC)

Formed by the Communist Party of the USA in Chicago in October 1925 as a successor to the African Blood Brotherhood. The congress was intended to organize black workers and farmers against discrimination and exploitation and to encourage unionization. It urged the establishment of 'local councils' of black and white workers and 'inter-racial labor committees' to combat union racism. The congress was relatively weak outside Chicago but was able to form a branch in Jamaica. It was dissolved in 1930 and was succeeded by the League of Struggle for Negro Rights.

Americo-Liberians

The elite – descended from free-born black Americans and former slaves who settled in Liberia in the nineteenth century – which dominated the country until the military coup led by Samuel Doe in 1980. The Americo-Liberians, who by 1980 comprised 3 per cent of the country's two million population, controlled the bulk of Liberia's wealth, monopolized political life through the True Whig Party, and dominated the military officer corps and the higher ranks of the state bureaucracy.

Amsterdam News

A weekly newspaper founded in New York City in 1909 by James Henry Anderson. The *News* originally comprised four pages and sold for two cents. In 1935, following a six-week strike, the *News* went into receivership and was bought by two black physicians. It was sold again in 1971 to a consortium of black businessmen and politicians. Among those who wrote for the *News* were the radical activist Cyril Briggs and the Pan-Africanist Timothy Thomas Fortune.

Anake wa 40 (40 Age Group)

Kikuyu organization operating in Nairobi in the 1940s and 50s at the time of the nationalist struggle. The organization found its support among the working class, particularly the unemployed, petty traders, thieves and prostitutes. These groups regarded nationalism as a means of improving their economic condition and were involved in boycotts, assassinations and

strikes. However, they opposed trade unions which they saw as only benefiting skilled and semi-skilled workers. The group played a significant role in organizing and financing the Mau Mau.

An Appeal to the Coloured Citizens of the World

Title of a pamphlet published in 1829 by David Walker, a free black American. The *Appeal*, which called on slaves to rise against their owners, was denounced and banned in a number of southern states. Walker wrote, 'We must and shall be free I say, in spite of you. You may do your best to keep us in wretchedness and misery, to enrich you and your children; but God will deliver us from under you.' Although a slave-owner offered a reward for his death, Walker refused the opportunity to leave for safety in Canada and died in mysterious circumstances.

Anatam Bumu

'Mothers of the King', a council of Lozi women in the area of Africa which is now Zambia, from the fifteenth to the nineteenth centuries. Women were chosen for their intelligence to join the council and participated in the conduct of government affairs under the supervision of the Maposhi, the 'Queen Mother'.

Anglophone

A term meaning 'English-speaking', sometimes used to describe former British colonies. It ignored the fact, however, that the majority of the inhabitants of the former African and Caribbean colonies have languages of their own.

ANLC

See American Negro Labor Congress.

Apartheid

Afrikaans word meaning 'apartness', the system of institutionalized racial discrimination introduced by the National Party government in South Africa after its 1948 election victory. In its election manifesto, the National Party said, 'The choice before us is one of two divergent causes: either that of integration, which would in the long run amount to national suicide on the part of the Whites; or that of apartheid . . .' The main legislation, building on pre-existing practice and consolidating the system, was the Group Areas Act 1950 (providing for separate housing areas), the Reservation of Separate Amenities Act 1953 (separate transport and other public facilities), the Bantu Education Act 1953 (separate education for children), the Extension of University Education Act 1959 (separate higher education), the Native Labour (Settlement of Disputes) Act 1953 (denying black workers the right to strike), the Native Building Workers' Act 1951 and the Industrial Conciliation Act 1956 (restricting skilled jobs to whites), the Prohibition of Mixed Marriages Act 1949 (outlawing inter-racial marriage), the Immorality Act 1957 (outlawing inter-racial sexual relations), the Population Registration Act 1950 (registering the entire population on a racial basis), the Natives (Abolition of Passes and Co-ordination of Documents) Act 1952 (extending and refining pre-existing Pass Laws). Apartheid's nominal objective of separating the races by forcing the black population to take the citizenship of spuriously independent Homelands or Bantustans began with the Bantu Homelands Constitution Act 1971. The Prohibition of Mixed Marriages Act and the Immorality Act were repealed in 1985 and on 1 February 1991, President de Klerk announced the end of the apartheid era. The remaining legislative pillars of apartheid were repealed in the summer. There were, however, complaints that despite this and the coming to power of President Mandela in April 1994, discrimination continued.

Apprenticeship

System instituted in the British Caribbean colonies to protect the interests of estate owners following the abolition of slavery in 1834. Of the 750,000 slaves in the area, only those under the age of six were granted outright liberty. Under the terms of apprenticeship, the remainder were to work for their former owners for 53 hours a week, 40 of which were to be without pay. Workers could obtain their release from apprenticeship if they were able to save enough from their wages to compensate their former owner. Apprenticeship was intended to last for six years following emancipation for field workers and four years for domestic workers. Stipendiary magistrates were appointed to supervise the system. Slaves in Jamaica and British Guiana (now Guyana) avoided apprenticeship by leaving the plantations and establishing free villages. Only the colony of Antigua refused to impose the scheme and granted unconditional freedom on 1 August 1834. Apprenticeship proved difficult to enforce and was abandoned on 1 August 1838.

ARM

See African Reparations Movement.

Army of Victory Church

Protestant church in Zaïre led by Pastor Fernando Kuthino which grew in influence following the beginning of the transition to democracy in 1990. Pastor Kuthino's teaching that the poor should not accept their condition but should resist exploitation and oppression under the slogan, 'We use all ways and means possible', alarmed the government. In February 1996, Pastor Kuthino was arrested for allegedly stockpiling weapons, despite his advocacy of non-violence.

Arusha Declaration

President Nyerere of Tanzania's declaration in 1967 of socialist principles and plans which were written into the country's constitution. The declaration set out provisions for the protection of human rights, proposed state intervention in the economy, and called for self-reliance and hard work by the people and their leaders. The Tanganyika African National Union (TANU), as the ruling party, was intended to develop a socialist programme based on the collective ownership of the means of production by farmers and workers rather than the East European model of the centralized state. *Ujamaa,* as Tanzanian socialism was known, produced some notable successes in education and health care. There were, however, charges that the role played by the state encouraged bureaucracy and corruption. As production fell, the policy set out in the declaration was modified from the early 1980s and largely abandoned by 1987.

Askari

Africans who served as police under British colonial rule in Northern Rhodesia (now Zambia). The expression was sometimes used to describe African soldiers who fought for the British in, for example, the King's African Rifles, although they objected to being described in this way.

Assimilados

Africans in the Portuguese colonies of Angola, Mozambique and Guinea who, unlike the indigenous majority, had abandoned their traditions, spoke Portuguese and were said by the authorities to have assimilated Portuguese culture. Assimilados were granted similar political rights to the white inhabitants of the colonies. By the late 1950s only 0.75 per cent of the black population in Angola, 0.5 per cent in Mozambique and 0.3 per cent in Guinea-Bissau had assimilated status.

Assimilation

French system of administration in its African colonies. In return for rejecting their own culture, heritage and language, Africans were granted full legal and political rights as French citizens. However, the educational qualifications required to realize these rights guaranteed that only a minority qualified. By the 1930s, throughout the French African colonies, 50,000 Africans were deemed to be 'assimilated' while another 500 were 'selectively assimilated'. The remaining 15 million 'subjects' continued to be denied all rights and could be imprisoned without charge or trial by the colonial administration.

Atlanta Compromise

The message of the 20-minute speech delivered by the educationalist and activist, Booker T. Washington to the Cotton States Exposition in Atlanta, Georgia, in 1895. Washington set out the moderate path for black advance in the USA. He urged black people to achieve their rights by concentrating on economic and educational advance and self-help, the acquisition of property and the development of 'high character'. He criticized political action, migration from the southern to northern states, and agitation for equality. The economic achievements of black people, he argued, would end racial animosity. Washington's activities, until his death in 1915, were a development of the views expressed in the speech. He was, however, accused by other black activists as being the white choice as leader of black Americans, and opposition to his views led to the establishment of the National Association for the Advancement of Colored People (NAACP) in 1909.

Atlanta World

The first black daily newspaper in the USA, founded in 1932. The *Atlanta World* had been established as a weekly by Cornelius Adolphus Scott in 1928.

Azania

The name used for South Africa by supporters of the black consciousness movement. Derived from the Greek form of Zanj-bar, the Persian expression for 'land of the blacks', Azania was used from the first century AD to describe the east coast of Africa. Azania was adopted as the title for South Africa by the Pan-Africanist Congress on its foundation in 1959.

Bakadogo

Name given to child soldiers in the guerrilla National Resistance Army (NRA) in Uganda, which fought against the Obote government under Yoweri Museveni from 1980–6. Estimates of their numbers, some as young as ten in age, varied from under a thousand to 5000. Museveni claimed they were orphans who had joined for protection but there were reports that many were involved in fighting against the Uganda National Liberation Army. Following the NRA victory in 1986, the bakadogo were ordered to return their weapons and uniforms and resume their education. Many, however, remained as adult members of the armed forces. In other parts of Africa, children were also recruited – either as volunteers or forcibly – as in Ethiopia (from 1987–91), and as members of the competing factions in Somalia in the 1990s. Many were members of RENAMO in the civil war that followed independence in Mozambique in 1974. Children were also used as soldiers in ZANLA in the war against the white regime in Rhodesia and in the UNITA guerrilla forces in Angola. Following the renewal of civil war in Liberia in 1992, the National Patriotic Front of Liberia (NPFL) had a specific 'Small Boy's Unit', with soldiers as young as nine. The rival rebel United Liberation Front for Democracy for Liberia also recruited children.

Banning order

A form of house arrest introduced in 1950 by the white South African regime, under the Suppression of Communism Act, as a means of silencing the opponents of apartheid. People on whom the order was served were forbidden to change their place of residence, to attend meetings, join organizations, visit educational institutions, newspaper offices, airports and seaports. The media was banned from quoting any statement made by people subject to an order.

Bantu

The related group of languages which predominates in south and central Africa. The word itself means 'people'. Over 500 culturally related groups of people are Bantu speakers. The four major groups are the Nguni (including Zulu, Ndebele, Swazi and Xhosa), Sotho, Tsonga and Venda. Under the South African apartheid regime, the areas allocated to Africans were known originally as Bantustans.

Bantustans

Areas set aside by whites for cultivation by black South Africans under the Land Acts of 1913 and 1936. The whites, who accounted for only 19 per cent of the population, allocated 87 per cent of the land to themselves. The land allocated to Africans was widely dispersed throughout the country and was generally the least productive agriculturally. In 1968 the Bantustans were renamed homelands and given a spurious 'independence' by the South African government as part of its policy of apartheid. Following the end of the white regime, the territories were reabsorbed into South Africa.

Beach Control Law (BCL)

Legislation introduced in the British colony of Jamaica by Norman Manley to counter the detrimental effects of tourism during the late 1950s and early 1960s. The growing acquisition of the best land by foreign hoteliers restricted access to the population and denied fishermen use of their traditional fishing sites. Manley's Beach Control Law was based on Crown ownership of the foreshore. Hoteliers whose development plans involved denying public access to beaches were refused a licence by a department set up under the Act. The Act also protected the traditional rights of fishermen to use specific sites to launch their boats from.

BITU

See Bustamente Industrial Trade Union.

Black Caribs

Term used to describe the descendants of the indigenous 'yellow' or 'red' Caribs who had intermarried with escaped African slaves on the Caribbean island of St Vincent. Africans first arrived on the island when a slave-ship was wrecked off it in 1685. St Vincent then became a haven for escaped slaves. In 1719 a force of 400 French troops who attempted to occupy the island were driven off by Black Caribs. A British invasion attempt was similarly beaten off in 1723. However, a further invasion proved successful and the Caribs were defeated in the First Carib War of 1772–3. A Second Carib War was fought against the British with French aid in 1779 and a final Third Carib War in 1805.

Black Consciousness Movement

A loosely structured organization formed in South Africa by Steve Biko in 1969 after he led African students out of the multi-racial National Union of South African Students and formed the South African Students Organization. A Black People's Convention emerged from this in 1972 with the aim of encouraging cultural and social co-operation. The Convention was banned by the apartheid government in 1976. Many of its leaders were arrested in 1977, Biko was killed while in police custody.

Black European Community Development Federation

Established in Britain in 1993, formerly the National Federation of Self-Help Organizations which was set up in 1975. The federation co-ordinates and assists in the work of self-help and community groups in various fields including education, health, housing, the arts and youth work. The federation operates in Britain and the states of the European Union.

Black Leadership Forum

National coalition of black civil rights groups and leaders formed in the USA in 1977. The forum intended to concentrate on economic and social issues that concerned black Americans and to influence government action through lobbying the government and by public statements by black members of the US Congress.

Black Liaison Group

A body of 50 black organizations in Britain formed in 1991. The group includes the National Black Caucus, the Society of Black Lawyers, the Association of Black Probation Officers, the National Convention of Black Teachers and the Standing Conference of West Indian Organisations. The group undertakes work, and attempts to provide a unified voice on, issues of specific concern to the black community.

Black Lions

Tequr Ambesa, a resistance group formed by young intellectuals following the occupation of Ethiopia by Italian forces in May 1936. The group was led by a second cousin of Emperor Haile Selassie, Leul-Ras Emru Haile Selassie (known as the 'red Ras' because of his liberal views). The Lions carried out a number of successful attacks on Italian forces but were surrounded during a mission in December 1936. Ras Emru was captured and imprisoned in Italy until 1943, but most of the group escaped to join other resistance groups, for example, the Patriots, that carried on guerrilla warfare against the occupiers until Ethiopia was liberated in 1941.

Black Manifesto

Presented at the National Black Economic Development Conference in the USA in 1969. The manifesto called for $500 million to be paid in reparations to black people by white Christian churches and Jewish synagogues to compensate for their role in slavery.

Black Moses

Harriet Tubman (1823–1913) was known as the Black Moses because of her role as a participant in the Underground Railroad, the escape route for many slaves from the southern USA to the north before the abolition of slavery in 1865. Tubman helped lead 300 people to freedom, including members of her own family, in the course of 19 missions.

Black Panther Collective

The Black Panther Collective was formed in New York City in 1994 by former members of the Black Panther Party. Its members declared that their aim was 'to continue the revolutionary legacy of the Black Panther Party, put forth a vision of a new and just society, build a revolutionary infrastructure and carry on a protracted revolutionary struggle'. The BPC has a ruling Central Committee of eleven.

Black Panther Party

The Black Panther and Self-Defense Party was formed in Oakland, California, in October 1966 by Huey Newton and Bobby Seale (joined by Eldridge Cleaver in 1967) and represented a shift from the non-violent stance adopted by most other contemporary black American organizations. The party set out its demands in a ten-point platform. These were: '1) We want freedom. We want power to determine the destiny of our Black Community . . . 2) We want full employment for our people . . . 3) We want an end to the robbery by the white man of our Black Community . . . 4) We want decent housing, fit for shelter of human beings . . . 5) We want education for our people that exposes the true nature of this decadent American society. We want education that teaches us our true history and our role in the present day society . . . 6) We want all black men to be exempt from military service . . . 7) We want an immediate end to police brutality and murder of black people . . . 8) We want freedom for all black men held in federal, state, county and city prisons and jails . . . 9) We want all black people when brought to trial to be tried in court by a jury of their peer group or people from their black communities, as defined by the Constitution of the United States . . . 10) We want land, bread, housing, education, clothing, justice and peace. And as our major political objective, a United Nations supervised plebiscite to be held throughout the black colony in which only black colonial subjects will be allowed to participate, for the purpose of determining the will of black people as to their national destiny . . .' The Panthers initially mounted armed patrols to monitor police activity on the streets and advocated black community self-defence. The party became a target for the police and a number of its members were killed in gun battles. In 1968–9 the party reported that 28 of its members had been shot by police. The party later broadened its activity and accepted support from white radicals. It sought to encourage pride and self-reliance among black youth and by 1971 chapters throughout the USA were operating free health clinics, classes and a breakfast programme for ghetto youth. The party was, however, weakened by the arrests of Seale and Newton and Cleaver's self-imposed exile in Algeria and a clearly co-ordinated state campaign against it. A Black Panther Movement which was formed in Britain renamed itself the Black Workers' Movement in the 1970s. A Black Panther Collective (BPC) was formed in New York City in 1994 to emulate the original party's work.

Black People's Convention (BPC)

Organized in South Africa in 1972 by the South African Students Organisation (SASO) with the slogan, 'Black man – you are on your own.' The BPC included a number of former Pan-Africanist Congress (PAC) members and shared the PAC's opposition to the multi-racialism of the African National Congress (ANC). The convention was influenced by black power ideas from the USA and aimed to emancipate black people, 'from both psychological and physical oppression'. The BPC was banned by the white government in 1973 but played a major part in the June 1976 Soweto uprising. Steve Biko was BPC honorary president. Following his murder in 1978, the Azanian People's Organisation (AZAPO) became the leading representative of the black consciousness tradition in South Africa.

Black Pimpernel

Name given to the African National Congress (ANC) leader, Nelson Mandela, in 1962 because of his success in evading arrest by the South African security forces. He was finally arrested on 5 August and sentenced to five years imprisonment on 8 November.

Black power

A term that emerged among black radicals in the USA following disappointment at the results of the civil rights movement led by Martin Luther King, Jr, the 1964 Civil Rights Act, and the assassination of Malcolm X in 1965. Black power advocates, whose influence in the USA peaked in 1968, argued that the destruction of the economic and political system was a prerequisite for black liberation in America. Its most influential figure was Stokely Carmichael (later known as Kwame Touré). The expression, which had been used by author Richard Wright as the title of a book in 1954, was popularized by Carmichael during a march through northern Mississippi in 1966. Militant blacks such as Carmichael and Huey P. Newton, following development in the thinking of Malcolm X before his death, argued that attempting to work within the system was ineffective and that white power should be confronted by black power. The value of pursuing non-violent tactics was also questioned. In a period of rising expectations, Malcolm X had developed a revolutionary programme which included the use of violence as a tactic. This strand in black power thinking was adopted by Carmichael and H. Rap Brown and was central to the practice of the Black Panther Party. But black power itself was shortlived, symbolized by the Black Panther's move away in 1972 from the armed struggle to more conventional political activity. In the English-speaking Caribbean, successive movements had 'black power' as their aim. Starting in the 1920s with Marcus Garvey, the movement promoted self-government for the islands which was achieved in the 1950s and 1960s. The growth of Rastafarianism and the black power movement in the USA in the 1960s and 1970s provided the rhetoric and militancy of black nationalism which appeared to threaten the survival of governments in Jamaica and Bermuda in 1968, Curaçao in 1970 and Trinidad in 1970. The movement's influence declined in the Caribbean in the 1970s with the rise of parties of the New Left. Black power briefly surfaced in Britain, notably through the Racial Adjustment Action Society and the Universal Coloured People's Association, both of which sought to end dependence on white-dominated organizations.

Black Sections

Movement in British Labour Party formed in the 1980s in an attempt to increase participation and influence of black and Asian people in local and national party activity and policy. The Labour Party refused at its 1984 and 1986 conferences to officially allow Black Sections to be formed on the grounds that the party was 'colour blind'. A number were, nonetheless, set up. Paul Boateng and Bernie Grant severed their links with the movement after being elected to Parliament at the 1987 General Election. In 1993, the party formed a Labour Party Black Socialist Society and the majority of executive committee positions were taken by members of the Black Sections movement.

Black Seminoles

Escaped North American slaves who allied with native American Seminole people who had migrated to Florida after splitting from the Creek nation (Seminole is Creek for 'runaway'). Slaves escaping from South Carolina were reported to be seeking refuge with the Seminole as early as 1738. The alliance went as far as becoming an African-Indian nation, with Africans often taking a leading role. The escaped slaves brought skills as interpreters and negotiators with Europeans, their fighting qualities in war and their agricultural knowledge. Black Seminoles retained their African names but wore Seminole clothing. The purchase of Florida from Spain by the USA in 1819 was encouraged by slaveholders in the neighbouring state of Georgia who feared the strength and attraction of Black Seminole settlements would threaten the survival of slavery. A US general described a war with the Seminoles as an African rather than 'an Indian war which if not quickly put down would affect the enslaved African population.' Many Black Seminoles fled to Mexico after the USA took over Florida but a number of their descendants returned in 1870 to form the Seminole Negro Indian Scouts.

Black Shots

Companies of black soldiers recruited by the British in Jamaica to fight the Maroons from 1730 onwards and on the Mosquito Coast (now Guyana) in 1782. They were raised under special British legislation – the Voluntary Parties Act – which allowed for the recruitment of mercenaries. Black Shots were paid 40 shillings (£2) for every runaway slave they captured. They were usually accompanied by groups of white mercenaries.

Black Women for Wages for Housework (BWWFH)

A British-based movement of black women throughout the world, campaigning for recognition of, and compensation for, unwaged work carried out by women. The movement was founded in 1976. BWWFH say payment should come from government military budgets and campaigns for implementation of the 1985 United Nations' decision that women's unwaged work should be included in each country's Gross Domestic Product. In Britain, BWWFH campaigns on social issues affecting black women.

BPP

See Black People's Convention.

Brazzaville Bloc

African regional grouping for economic and political development which emerged with United Nations support following the

Brazzaville Conference in 1960. The original members were Benin, the Central African Republic, Chad, Congo, Côte d'Ivoire, Gabon, Madagascar, Mauritania, Niger, Senegal, Togo, Upper Volta (later Burkina Faso). The bloc was joined in 1961 by Ethiopia, Liberia, Libya, Nigeria, Sierra Leone, Somalia and Tunisia and developed into the Organisation of Co-operation of the African and Malagasy States. In 1963 this became the Organization of African Unity (OAU).

Brazzaville Declaration

Agreement reached in January 1944 between representatives of the French colonies and the Free French authorities under General Charles de Gaulle. Rather than independence, the colonies were offered instead the status of members of a 'French Union' with the promise of economic reforms, participation in French elections, and the creation of local assemblies.

British West Indies Regiment

Formed in 1915 of volunteers from every British possession in the Caribbean to fight in World War I. A total of 397 officers and 15,204 other ranks joined the 13 battalions of the regiment before it was disbanded in 1919. The largest contingent, 303 officers and 9977 other ranks, came from Jamaica. Among other Caribbean islands which contributed to the regiment were Trinidad and Tobago (40 officers, 1438 other ranks), Barbados (20 officers, 811 other ranks), Grenada (445 men), Bahamas (411), St Lucia (359), St Vincent (305), and the Leeward Islands (229). The British were unwilling to allow the regiment to fight Europeans. Two battalions fought against the Turks in Palestine and troops carried out garrison duties in Egypt, East Africa and Mesopotamia. The majority, against their wishes, were used to carry out heavy labour in France and Italy. During the war, 1256 men were killed, 1100 died from sickness, and 697 were wounded. Members were awarded five Distinguished Service Orders and 37 Military Medals. Anger at the racism they experienced led a number of soldiers in the regiment to mount the Taranto mutiny in Italy in 1918–19. Many men from the regiment took part in anti-British demonstrations and strikes in the Caribbean after World War I.

Bronzeville

Originally a black section of Chicago, the expression became popular among white American journalists from the 1930s to the 1960s to describe any black community in the USA.

Brotherhood of Sleeping Car Porters

Formed in 1925 by A. Philip Randolph to negotiate with the Pullman Company, which monopolized railway sleeping-car services in the USA. Railway portering had become a traditional black male occupation. The Brotherhood's requests for affiliation to the American Federation of Labor (AFL) were rejected in 1928 and 1934 and the Brotherhood began a systematic fight to counter union discrimination against black workers. In 1935 the National Mediation Board, created under President Roosevelt's New Deal, recognized the Brotherhood as a union and AFL affiliation followed in 1936.

Buffalo Soldiers

Black regiments in the US army raised following legislation in 1866. The regiments, which were led by white officers, were the 9th and 10th Cavalry and the 24th and 25th Infantry Regiments. Units were first stationed in Oklahoma and Kansas in 1867 to perform garrison duty. From then until 1891, 12,000 black Americans fought Native Americans in Arizona, Colorado, New Mexico, Oklahoma, Texas and in the

Dakotas. The name Buffalo Soldiers was given to the troops by Native Americans. Over a fifth of the US cavalry active on the frontier was made up of black soldiers. Black soldiers in what remained a segregated army until the late 1940s continued to refer to themselves as Buffalo Soldiers.

Bula matari

Kilongo term meaning 'he who breaks rocks', used to describe the appearance of overwhelming force wielded by the regime of King Leopold II of Belgium, in the Congo Free State following its seizure in July 1885. The expression was used to describe the regime in general and colonial officials in particular.

Bustamente Industrial Trade Union (BITU)

Jamaica's leading trade union founded in 1938 by Alexander Bustamente. BITU's political wing is the Jamaica Labour Party. The union's main rival is the National Workers' Union, linked with the People's National Party.

BWWFH

See Black Women for Wages for Housework

Caribbean Democratic Union (CDU)

An alliance of Anglo-Caribbean conservative parties which were in power in Anguilla, Belize, Dominica, Grenada, Jamaica, Nevis, St Kitts, St Lucia and St Vincent, formed in 1986. The CDU had the backing of the US government and was connected to the right-wing International Democratic Union. It was led on its establishment by Jamaican prime minister, Edward Seaga.

Caribbean Labour Congress (CLC)

Formed in 1945, the congress was an early attempt to unite Caribbean trade unions and political groups active in the struggle for independence from British colonialism. The CLC advocated a federation of the English-speaking Caribbean islands. T. Albert Marryshow was elected the first president of the congress. The CLC was affiliated to the World Federation of Trade Unions and its continued affiliation during the Cold War led to accusations that it was a communist-front organization. Immigrant workers to Britain formed an influential London branch which functioned until the early 1960s. The London branch co-operated with the League of Coloured People to open a West Indian Cultural Centre and published *Caribbean News* from 1952 to 1956. The CLC in Britain was active in campaigning against the 1962 Commonwealth Immigration Act.

Caribbean League

Secret organization founded by 50 members of the British West Indies Regiment in Italy on 17 December 1918 during the Taranto mutiny. Angered by the racial discrimination they consistently experienced at the hands of the British authorities, the league's members met to discuss their grievances and to formulate demands. Among these were the replacement of white senior non-commissioned officers by blacks and self-government for the Caribbean islands. The league's existence was betrayed to officers and it was forced to disband.

Caribbean Regiment

A British army regiment formed in 1944 from volunteer units in the British West Indies. It was made up of members of the North Caribbean Force (with contingents from the Bahamas, British Honduras, Jamaica, and the Leeward Islands) and of the South Caribbean Force (from Barbados, British Guiana, Trinidad and Tobago, and the Windward Islands). The regiment was moved to Europe via the USA and then to Egypt but was still undergoing training when the war ended in 1945. The force was disbanded in 1946.

Caribbean News

The newspaper of the Caribbean Labour Congress (CLC), published in London from November 1952 until June 1956, the first post-war black paper in Britain. The *News* was founded by Billy Strachan, a Jamaican communist who had served in the Royal Air Force in World War II, reaching the rank of flight-lieutenant, and went on to train as a barrister. The newspaper, which began as a monthly and then appeared bi-monthly, covered black and international issues from a socialist angle and was banned in most Caribbean islands for its alleged subversiveness. The *News* encouraged black workers to become active trade unionists and argued for black and white working-class unity. It was succeeded in 1958 by the more broadly based *West Indian Gazette*.

Casablanca bloc

Grouping of African socialist states working for mutual co-operation from 1958–63. In 1958 Ghana and Guinea (later joined by Mali) produced draft proposals for a union of all African states. In 1961 they were joined by the Algerian provisional government and met in Casablanca to plan a unified African military command and an African Common Market. The bloc was absorbed into the Organization of African Unity (OAU) in 1963.

CBTU

Coalition of Black Trade Unionists.

CDU

See Caribbean Democratic Union.

Central African Federation

Established by the British colonial authorities in September 1953 in an attempt to protect the privileged position of the white minority population by amalgamating the colonies of Nyasaland (later Malawi), Northern Rhodesia (Zambia) and Southern Rhodesia (Zimbabwe). The federation aimed to counterbalance the neighbouring power of South Africa and to encourage investment. The federal government had control over defence, currency, external affairs and taxation. The federation was unpopular with the majority black populations who, despite claims that it was intended to encourage multi-racial co-operation, saw it as an obstacle to independence. There was prolonged agitation against the proposal in 1960–1. Zambia and Malawi became independent states in 1963. Southern Rhodesia, known as Rhodesia, remained under an illegal white government from 1965 until becoming independent as Zimbabwe in 1980.

CFA franc

The Communauté Financière Africaine franc, a common currency established by the French colonial authorities. After independence, the CFA franc continued to be the currency of West African Monetary Union members Benin, Burkina Faso, Côte d'Ivoire, Mali, Niger, Senegal and Togo.

Cha-cha-cha campaign

A movement based on an expression which came to symbolize the rapid advance of anti-British political consciousness in Northern Rhodesia (now Zambia) in the early 1960s. The cha-cha was a popular dance of the period. During a speech by Kenneth Kaunda advocating non-violent protest in July 1961 there were continual cries of 'cha-cha-cha'. Despite Kaunda's urgings, United National Independence Party (UNIP) youth groups began a campaign against British colonialism which included burning schools and attacking communications links such as bridges. The force of the campaign persuaded the British of the inevitability of independence, which came three years later.

Chaguaramas, Treaty of

Signed in 1973 by the heads of government of Barbados, Guyana, Jamaica, Trinidad and Tobago as the founding members of the Caribbean Community and Common Market. The community was later joined by Antigua and Barbuda, the Bahamas (not a member of the Common Market), Belize, Dominica, Grenada, Montserrat, St Christopher and Nevis, St Lucia, and St Vincent and the Grenadines. The British Virgin Islands and the Turks and Caicos Islands have associate membership. The Dominican Republic, Haiti, Mexico, Puerto Rico, Suriname and Venezuela participate as observers.

Changamire

The dynastic title of the rulers of southern Zimbabwe from the fifteenth century to the eighteenth century. In 1480, a vassal ruler in the Monomotapa empire proclaimed himself an independent emir (Changa Amir). The resulting kingdom conquered much of northern Zimbabwe in the eighteenth century, forming an obstacle to Portuguese colonial expansion.

Chicago Defender

Black weekly newspaper first published by Robert S. Abbott on 6 May 1905, which encouraged black migration from the southern states. Abbott had capital of 25 cents when he founded the *Defender*. By 1916 its circulation was 33,000, rising to 130,000 in 1919. Distributed by a network of Pullman car porters, the *Defender* was regarded as subversive by southern whites because of the coverage it devoted to lynchings and murders of black people. During a wave of lynchings of black people in 1915, the *Defender* declared, 'If you must die, take one with you.' Its comparison of wages available to black workers in the northern and southern states also disturbed employers in the south. Among the slogans the *Defender* used to encourage migration during the 'Great Northern' drive of 1917 were 'The Flight out of Egypt' and 'Bound for the Promised Land'. Abbott refused to allow the use of the term *negro* in the newspaper because of its closeness to the pejorative *nigger*, preferring *race man*. The *Defender* became a daily newspaper in 1956.

Chikunda

A large group of slave-traders operating in what is now Zambia, in the latter half of the nineteenth century. Many of them were escapees from black slave armies raised on estates in the Portuguese African colonies.

Chimurenga

The Zimbabwean 'war of independence'. Chimurenga Day is celebrated on 28 April and commemorates two struggles: 1) the unsuccessful 1893–7 campaign by the Mashona and Ndebele peoples to prevent British colonial settlers stealing their land; 2) the successful 1966–79 campaign against the white minority Rhodesian regime in which an estimated 14,000 guerrillas and 1000 government troops died. As a result of this Zimbabwe became an independent state in 1980.

Chimwenje

An armed dissident group which opposes the government of President Mugabe of Zimbabwe. Chimwenje members received training in guerrilla warfare in the area of Mozambique controlled by the Mozambique National Resistance (RENAMO). On 8 October 1995 three of its members were arrested for allegedly plotting the assassination of President Mugabe. Opposition leader the Revd Ndabaningi Sithole, a candidate in the forthcoming presidential elections, was arrested in connection with the plot on 15 October. On 1 December, the alleged leader of Chimwenje and a supporter of Revd

Sithole, was imprisoned after being found guilty of undergoing illegal military training.

Chona Commission

A national commission on the establishment of a one-party participatory democracy established in Zambia by President Kenneth Kaunda in 1972. The commission was named after the country's Vice-President, Mainza Chona. It was made up of members representing the army, business, churches, the civil service, chiefs and the ruling United National Independence Party (UNIP) and was intended to act in an advisory capacity on a pre-determined decision to form a one-party state. The commission issued a report after four months of hearings. Although many of its recommendations were accepted, those advocating strengthening the National Assembly, limiting the powers of the president and reforming the UNIP were ignored by the government.

Christy Commission

Appointed by the League of Nations in 1930 under the chairmanship of a British dentist, Cuthbert Christy, to investigate accusations that the Americo-Liberian elite which ruled Liberia was subjecting indigenous Liberians to slavery on Spanish-owned plantations and condoning the slave trade. Britain and the USA severed diplomatic relations with Liberia for five years over the issue. Christy reported on 8 September that there was no organized slave-trading but that labour was being forcibly recruited for public and private labour by the Liberian Frontier Force with the knowledge of senior government officials. He called for Liberia to be placed under a 'capable and warm-hearted white adminis-tration'. True Whig President King resigned and was replaced by Edwin J. Hardy. He rejected a League of Nations proposal that Liberia should be placed under an International Governing Commission. The Liberian government did, however, accept a League report calling for an improvement in treatment of indigenous Liberians, including granting them the right to education and to ownership of land.

Church of Jesus Christ on Earth through the prophet Simon Kimbangu (EJCSK)

See Kimbanguism.

Civilisado

Part of the administrative system in the Portuguese colonial territories. A minority, many of them mixed race, which adopted the Portuguese language and culture was, in return, excused forced labour and the payment of taxes, although it was not granted voting or other rights of citizenship. The minority consisted largely of clerks, teachers and traders.

CLC

See Caribbean Labour Congress.

CMA

See Condensed Milk Association.

Coalition of Black Trade Unionists (CBTU)

Formed in the USA in 1972, initially to oppose the support given by the American Federation of Labor-Congress of Industrial Organizations to President Nixon. The CBTU grew into a broader movement against the systematic exclusion of black members from leadership positions in the unions, discrimination in the workplace and the failure of the unions to address the concerns of black members. The CBTU found support in over 40 unions, including steel, automobiles, teamsters and government employees.

Code Noir

The Black Code, an ordinance of King Louis XIV in March 1685, which established a framework for the institution of slavery in the French Caribbean colonies of Guadeloupe, Martinique and Saint Domingue. The code was based on Roman law provisions for the treatment of slaves and on Roman Catholic teaching. A slave, according to the code, should be baptized as a Christian and should not be required to work on Sundays and holy days. The slave could marry with her or his owner's permission and slave families were not to be separated. Sexual attacks on slaves by whites were an offence, as were sexual relations between the owner and slaves. The code prescribed minimum standards for the provision of food and clothing, with the right of complaint by slaves to the King's Agent. The owner was obliged to care for old and sick slaves and could free slaves after they had worked for 20 years. To balance these apparently liberal provisions, slaves were banned from owning property and carrying weapons of any kind and were subject to penalties for attempted escape that ranged from mutilation to death. Striking an owner was a capital offence.

Colored American
The first black newspaper in the southern USA, founded in Augusta, Georgia, by J. T. Strutten in 1865.

Colored National Labor Union
Founded in the USA in 1869 with Isaac Myers, a carpenter and caulker, as its first president. The union was formed because of the reluctance of the white National Labor Union (founded in 1866) to allow individual black membership. It argued that black workers should form their own organizations and then affiliate. Both unions had a brief existence. Myers also founded a shipyard which employed only black workers, the Chesapeake Marine Railway and Dry Dock Company.

Committee for Improving the Industrial Conditions of Negroes in New York
An organization formed in 1906 to meet the problems arising from increasing black migration from the southern USA to the north. The committee was formed to deal with the economic problems caused by racism and to encourage the development of industrial training. It merged with a number of other organizations into the National Urban League in 1911.

Committee for National Salvation
An organization formed in Dominica in 1979 by business, labour, religious and political leaders in an attempt to restore order following turmoil set off by the authoritarian government of Edward Le Blanc. The committee mounted a 'constitutional coup' and formed a coalition government until elections were held in 1980.

Committee for the Participation of Negroes in National Defense
An umbrella organization set up in the USA in May 1939, including the Committee on Negro Americans in Defense and Allied Councils for Defense, by historian and World War I veteran Rayford W. Logan (1887–1982). Logan and representatives of the National Association for the Advancement of Colored People (NAACP), appeared before the House of Representatives to argue for an increase in the numbers of black military personnel and an expansion in the areas of service available for black Americans. Although President Roosevelt offered some concessions, a general policy of segregation continued. However, as the USA entered World War II, black strength in the army rose from 97,725 in November 1941 to 467,883 in December 1942.

Committee for the Relief of the Black Poor

A committee set up in London in 1786 to help destitute blacks of the city. The need for the committee was a demonstration of how numerous the African diaspora population in London was in the eighteenth century.

Committee of 22

A body formed on the Caribbean island of Grenada in 1973–4 with representatives of workers' organizations, professional bodies, the churches and the Chamber of Commerce, to organize agitation against the increasingly unpopular government of Eric Gairy. The committee organized a three-week general strike in January 1974 and daily demonstrations demanding Gairy's resignation. The campaign was repressed by the government's use of the army and the Mongoose Squad on 21 January but prepared the ground for the revolution of 13 March 1979.

Committee on Urban Conditions Among Negroes

An organization established in the USA in 1910 to study the economic and social conditions of black people in cities, prompted by increasing migration from the southern states. The committee was formed to train black social workers and to develop agencies to address specific needs. It merged with a number of other organizations into the National Urban League in 1911.

Commonwealth Caribbean

The countries in the region that are members of the Commonwealth of Nations (formerly the British Commonwealth). They are Jamaica (joined 1962), Trinidad and Tobago (1962), Barbados (1966), Guyana (1966), the Bahamas (1973), Grenada (1974), Dominica (1978), St Lucia (1979), St Vincent and the Grenadines (1979), Antigua and Barbuda (1981), Belize (1981), St Christopher and Nevis (1983). The British Dependant Territories of Anguilla, the British Virgin Islands, Cayman Islands, Montserrat, and the Turks and Caicos Islands are also usually included in this term.

Conakry Declaration

Agreement between Ghana and Guinea reached on 1 May 1959 in the Guinea capital to unify the two countries as a preliminary to creating an African Union of States. Although the two were joined by Mali on 1 July 1961, the attempt at a wider unity failed.

Condensed Milk Association (CMA)

Formed in Trinidad in 1936 by the Negro Welfare Cultural and Social Association (NWC&SA). Condensed milk was an essential commodity to the poor and the CMA led agitation over its high price and attacked advertising which attempted to persuade women to buy more expensive brands. The CMA was formed as part of a wider campaign mounted by the NWC&SA over the cost of living, nutrition, and the need for school meals, health services and pensions.

Congress Alliance

An anti-apartheid coalition formed to achieve a non-racial South Africa on 26 June 1955 by the African National Congress (ANC), the Coloured People's Congress, the South African Congress of Trade Unions and the white Congress of Democrats. The alliance was established by 3000 multi-racial delegates at a conference held in Kliptown, Transvaal and adopted a Freedom Charter setting up its objectives.

Congress of Racial Equality (CORE)

US civil rights organization, founded by James Farmer in Chicago in 1942 as the Chicago Committee of Racial Equality. The organization mounted its first successful anti-segregation sit-in at a Chicago restaurant in June 1943. This was followed by widespread picketing of segregated public facilities. CORE came into greater prominence during the 1960s civil rights campaign, renewing its earlier sit-in tactics and introducing Freedom Rides in 1961. The Freedom Rides succeeded in forcing the US Supreme Court to declare segregated interstate transport illegal. CORE co-operated in organizing the 1963 march on Washington, DC. Originally an inter-racial movement, CORE adopted the slogan of Black Power in 1965 and whites played a less pronounced part in its activities. In 1967, under the leadership of Floyd McKissick, the word 'multi-racial' was removed from the organization's constitution. McKissick was replaced as leader by Roy Innis in 1968 and CORE's influence waned in ensuing controversy over the organization's direction. Many influential members left but Innis survived a challenge to his leadership led by Farmer. Among prominent past members of CORE were the writer James Baldwin, a national advisory board member, and Stokely Carmichael.

Congress of South African Trade Unions (COSATU)

Multi-racial umbrella organization for trade unions in the industrial and service sectors founded in December 1985. COSATU is predominantly black in membership and at its foundation the National Union of Miners made up a third of its affiliated strength. COSATU was connected to the South African Communist Party and co-operated with the United Democratic Front (UDF) and the African National Congress (ANC) in agitation against the apartheid regime in the late 1980s and early 1990s.

Conscientious Objectors against Jim Crow

Formed in 1941 in the USA to establish the right of black Americans to claim exemption from military service on the grounds that segregation existed in the armed forces. Ernest Calloway, a union official, was imprisoned after refusing service on these grounds and the movement collapsed. A number of other people continued to refuse individually and were sentenced to terms ranging from one to three years.

CORE

See Congress of Racial Equality.

COREMO

See Revolutionary Committee of Mozambique.

COSATU

See Congress of South African Trade Unions.

Creole

From the Portuguese *crioulo*, a slave brought up in the owner's household. This became *criollo* in Spanish and *creole* in French. In the Spanish American colonies the word criollo referred to a person born there but of European descent. In Louisiana following its purchase from France by the USA in 1803, whites of French and Spanish descent described themselves as creoles to distinguish themselves from Americans of English descent. Later, in New Orleans in particular, creole also came to be used to describe people of mixed race. In the Caribbean, the expression was first used to describe Europeans who were born and remained in the area, and then to distinguish slaves born in the Caribbean rather than in Africa. It is now used loosely to describe almost anything native to the Caribbean, including culture, language and cooking. In the USA the word describes a person with French ancestry. The term is also used for the official language of Haiti since 1969. The language is used by 90 per cent of the population and is a combination of West African grammar and French dialect.

The Crisis

The magazine of the National Association for the Advancement of Colored People (NAACP), first published in November 1910 under the editorship of W. E. B. Du Bois. Circulation grew rapidly until, in the wake of the violent events of the Red Summer of 1917, *The Crisis* was selling over 100,000 copies. In the 1920s and 1930s, *The Crisis* played a significant part in the cultural awakening of the Harlem Renaissance, publishing the works of young black writers. Du Bois also used its columns to advocate the creation of a black economy based on self-help, arousing criticism from other NAACP leaders for encouraging segregation.

Crossroads

A black shantytown near Cape Town in South Africa. The apartheid regime attempted to force its inhabitants into a homeland in February 1985. Eighteen people were killed resisting an attack by government security forces. Faction-fighting between radical 'comrades' and government-supported conservative 'fathers' led to a further 69 deaths. Crossroads became a symbol of black resistance to the white government.

Deacons for Defense

Group formed in Louisiana in 1964 to provide armed protection for the black community and its leaders against white racist attack. The Deacons encouraged the creation of similar groups in other black areas of the USA.

Déchoukage ('uprooting')

Creole term originally used by Toussaint L'Ouverture to describe the successful nineteenth-century rising against French rule in Haiti. It then became a general term in Haiti to describe the overthrow of any government. Following the fall of the Duvalier régime in 1986, the term was used to describe the purging of Duvalier sympathizers.

Declaration of St George's

Agreement in the capital of Grenada made in 1979 by the left-wing leaders of Dominica, Grenada and St Lucia allowing free movement between the three countries. The agreement never came into effect.

Dergue, the

From the Amharic word meaning 'shadow', this was the name taken by the Co-ordinating Committee of the Armed Forces formed in Ethiopia in 1973 which led the successful attack on Haile Selassie. He was overthrown on 12 September 1974. The Dergue originally had 120 members from the armed forces with ranks ranging from private to major, and changed its name to the Provisional Military Administrative Council in 1974. It declared its role to be 'the guide of the Ethiopian revolution' and attempted sweeping reforms of the country's feudal structure. The Dergue's first chairman, Lieutenant-General Aman Mikael Andom was killed in November 1974, allegedly with the involvement of Lieutenant-Colonel Mengistu. His replacement, Brigadier-General Teferi Banti was killed in 1977. As Mengistu consolidated his own power, the Dergue was dissolved in 1980.

Dread Act

Legislation enacted by the Dominican government in 1974 empowering all citizens to shoot members of the Rastafarian sect on sight and imposing a mandatory life sentence on anyone who appeared to be a Rastafarian. The Act followed outbreaks of local violence for which the government held Rastafarians responsible. It was repealed in 1981.

East African Association

Militant political association established on 1 July 1921 in Nairobi, Kenya, by Harry Thuku (a clerk employed in the Treasury),

Jesse Kariuki, Job Muchuchu and Abdullah Tarrara. The association was multi-ethnic in composition and represented an attempt at political organization on a territorial, rather than simply local, basis. It aimed to contest the influence of the Kikuyu Association, a movement dominated by conservative chiefs. Thuku, who wrote in 1921 that unless young people organized, Africans in Kenya would 'remain voiceless' attempted to ally the Kikuyu with the Kamba, Luo and Ganda peoples and formed links with the Young Kavirondo Association and the Young Buganda Association. He also corresponded with W. E. B. Du Bois and Marcus Garvey. The association passed resolutions against the practice of forced labour by the British colonial authorities, heavy taxation and the denial of educational opportunity. Thuku's arrest on 14 March 1922 provoked protest demonstrations two days later in which 21 people were killed. His deportation to Kismayu led to the collapse of the association. A new organization which emerged in 1924, the Kikuyu Central Association, was less inclined to co-operate with non-Kikuyu.

Emigrationism

A form of resistance by black people in the British colonies in North America and later the USA. Emigrationism took the view that black people would only find freedom by returning to Africa or moving to territories where Africans could lead an autonomous existence. In 1773 a group of slaves in Massachusetts petitioned the British colonial authorities for permission to work to earn money to return to Africa. In 1787, 80 members of the African Society in Boston petitioned the State Legislature for financial assistance to return to Africa and buy land. Among leading advocates of emigrationism were Paul Cuffe, Mark Delaney and Alexander Crummell. Emigrationist views

were put forward at the 1817 and 1854 Negro Conventions. Emigrationists opposed the white-dominated American Colonisation Society which was seen as attempting to strengthen the institution of slavery by forcing free blacks from the USA.

Empire Windrush

Troopship which docked at Tilbury on 22 June 1948, bringing the first post-war Jamaican immigrants to Britain. Among the 492 were ex-servicemen who had been stationed in Britain during World War II but faced unemployment on their return to the Caribbean. The London *Evening Standard* headed its description of their arrival 'Welcome Home' and jobs were found immediately for 202 skilled men, the remainder finding work soon after. The *Orbita* carried 180 Jamaicans to Liverpool in October 1948, followed shortly by 39 (including 15 women) on the *Reina del Pacifico*.

Ethiopianism

An early form of Pan-Africanism, based on the African response to discrimination and racism in white Christian churches. The term came from the word Ethiopia, the Greek expression for Africa. The founders of Ethiopian churches accepted the tenets of Christianity but attempted to defend African culture from being undermined by white missionaries. It followed logically from this that they opposed European colonial interference in African affairs. Examples of Ethiopian churches are the American Methodist Episcopal church, founded in the USA in 1797, the Ethiopian Baptist Church founded in Jamaica in 1784, the Settlers' Meeting in Sierra Leone which split from the Wesleyan Mission in 1819, a breakaway from the Wesleyan Church formed in South Africa in 1892 and churches formed in Central Africa by John Chilembwe in 1915 and Simon Kimbangu in 1920. In Africa the churches were also known as African Independent Churches.

Evolués

Term used to describe Africans who accepted the Belgian system of local administration in their African colonies. A mixture of indirect rule and assimilation.

Exodusters

Freed slaves who left the southern USA and migrated to Kansas and the west from 1879. Leading figures in the movement were Henry Adams and Benjamin 'Pap' Singleton. When slavery was abolished at the end of the 1861–5 Civil War, Adams organized 'the committee' to examine the condition of freed slaves in Louisiana. The results of this prompted the setting up in 1874 of a 'colonization council' to ask the federal government to provide a separate territory in the USA for freed slaves or to finance emigration to Liberia. The government ignored the request. With the withdrawal of federal troops from the south in 1877, the southern states imposed new laws to worsen black conditions. The response was mass emigration from the south. In 1879, 40,000 black people moved west and by 1880 the black population of Kansas had risen to 43,000. From 1883, further offers of land encouraged the establishment of black communities in other western territories and in Mexico.

Extermination Proclamation

Following the Omaheke Desert massacre of Hereros who had risen against the German occupation of South West Africa (now Namibia) in August 1904, the German General von Trotha ordered all Hereros to leave their lands. 'If the people do not want this,' he declared, 'then I will force them to do it with the great guns. Any Herero found within the German frontier, with or without a gun, will be shot. I shall no longer receive any women or children; I will drive them back to their people. I will shoot them. This is my decision for the Herero people.'

Falashas

Black Jews living in Ethiopia, the majority of whom were moved to Israel in 'Operation Moses' during the 1985 famine under an agreement between the Ethiopian government and Israel. The remaining 14,000 were airlifted to Israel shortly before the fall of the Ethiopian government in May 1991. Falasha derives from a Hebrew word meaning 'exile'.

Fifth Brigade

A unit of the Zimbabwean army set up following independence in 1980 and trained by North Korea. When the brigade was deployed by the government to restore order in Matabeleland in 1983–4 its members were accused of committing atrocities against civilians.

Firestone Republic

Expression used to describe Liberia from 1926 – when the Firestone Company began its activities in the country, establishing US dominance of the economy – and President Tubman's attempts to weaken American influence by encouraging investment from other countries following his election in 1944. The Firestone Company made rubber Liberia's main cash crop and under a loan agreement in 1927 placed the country under the financial supervision of the USA.

First Black Independent Brotherhood

Organization in the USA which proposed that Oklahoma should become an all-black state. The brotherhood's leading activist was Edwin P. McCabe, who moved into the state in 1879. Many former slaves had migrated to Oklahoma from the southern states and there was a black majority in a number of towns, including Boley and Langston. The suggestion was made again by W. E. B. Du Bois in the 1940s when he proposed the creation of a separate, black '49th state'.

First Zambian Republic

The Zambian form of government from independence in October 1964 until a one-party system came into operation in December 1972, bringing in the Second Republic.

FNLC

See National Front for the Liberation of the Congo.

Francophone

A term meaning 'French-speaking', sometimes used to describe former French colonies. It ignored the fact, however, that the majority of the inhabitants of the former African and Caribbean colonies had languages of their own.

'Free by '63'

Slogan used by the National Association for the Advancement of Colored People (NAACP) and other black civil rights groups in the early 1960s, used as the rallying call at the August 1963 March on Washington for Jobs and Freedom.

Freedmen's Bureau

Organization established by US government in 1865. The bureau was administered by the War Department and was established to provide assistance for newly freed slaves and refugees of the 1861–5 Civil War. The bureau was intended to function for a year but its existence was extended. Assistance was to take the form of establishing schools, providing legal and medical services, supervising labour contracts, managing, and leasing and selling confiscated and abandoned land to former slaves. The bureau provided 21 million weekly rations of food between 1865 and 1869, 15 million of them to former slaves, and spent $2 million dollars on medical treatment. The bureau settled 4000 families on government-owned land in Arkansas, Mississippi, Alabama, Louisiana and Florida. In the southern states, the bureau encouraged the establishment of over 2000 schools providing education for almost 250,000 students. However, the bureau was unable to combat deep-rooted racism and was never provided by an ambivalent federal government with the finance necessary to carry out its work effectively.

Freedom Charter

Declaration of political, economic and human rights adopted by a multi-racial 'Congress of the People' on 26 June 1955, at which a Congress Alliance was formed to agitate for the Charter. The Charter represented a multi-racial 'Declaration of Independence' from the apartheid regime. Its opening clause declared, 'We, the people of South Africa, declare for all our country and the world to know that South Africa belongs to all who live in it, black and white, and that no government can justly claim authority unless it is based on the will of all the people.' Other clauses dealt with adult suffrage, equality before the law, the right to work, security and education, the nationalization of mineral wealth and the banks, and guarantees of the freedom of movement, speech and religion.

Freedom's Journal

The first black newspaper in the USA, published from 1827–30. It was founded by a Samuel E. Cornish (*c*.1795–1859), a clergyman who had organized the first black Presbyterian church in New York City and was a leader of the first National Negro Convention in 1830, and John Brown Russwurm (1799–1851). Russwurm was a journalist who was born in Jamaica. He left the newspaper to settle in what became Liberia in 1829. The *Journal*, which campaigned against slavery and growing discrimination against free blacks, changed its name to *Rights for All* in 1830.

Free villages

Faced by the establishment of the apprenticeship system following the end of slavery in the British Caribbean colonies in 1834, freed slaves deserted their former owners' plantations and attempted to establish free villages in Jamaica. Land was available for between £5 and £10 an acre and could potentially yield £30 worth of crops a year. However, plantation owners found it more economic to sell their estates as a whole rather than in patches. Missionaries, particularly Baptists, bought the land and then sold it in separate plots. Between 1835 and 1851, 3000 former slaves settled in free villages in the west of the island. The first free village established in 1835 was named Sligoville. Among others were Clarkson Town and Sturge Town. It was also possible to rent land for £1 an acre.

Front-line states

The African states of Angola, Botswana, Mozambique, Tanzania and Zambia in the front line against white rebel Rhodesia. They agreed in 1977 to provide increased support for the guerrilla campaigns being fought by Robert Mugabe and Joshua Nkomo for an independent Zimbabwe. When Zimbabwe achieved independence in 1980 the Organisation of African Unity (OAU) recognized Angola, Botswana, Mozambique, Zambia and Zimbabwe as front-line states against the South African apartheid regime.

Fruit of Islam

The paramilitary wing of the Nation of Islam (NOI), disbanded by Wallace Muhammad when he succeeded his father, Elijah Muhammad, as leader of the NOI on the latter's death in 1975. The Fruit of Islam was revived as a security unit when a rival

Nation of Islam was formed by Louis Farrakhan. In 1996 the unit was offered federal funding to provide security in black inner-city housing estates. The contract was withdrawn when Farrakhan accepted $1 million from President Gaddafy of Libya.

Golden Thirteen

The first black officers to be commissioned into the US Navy in March 1944. Sixteen black enlisted men had been enrolled on the only officer training course set up specifically for black naval personnel at Great Lakes, Indiana. One of the thirteen, Samuel Lee Gravely (born 1922), became the first black American to command a US Navy ship in 1962 and the first black Rear-Admiral in 1971.

Greater Zimbabwe

An Iron-Age city in Zimbabwe constructed in the thirteenth to fifteenth centuries as an imperial capital with an estimated 15,000 inhabitants. Archaeological evidence shows it was constructed by the Shona people. Zimbabwe is Shona for 'houses of stone'.

Griots

Group of nationalist intellectuals in Haiti from the 1930s, supporters of *noirisme*. A prominent member was François 'Papa Doc' Duvalier, President of Haiti from 1957 until his death in 1971. The term was originally used by the French in Africa to describe African professional oral historians. They played a key role in maintaining the history and traditions of pre-colonial societies with no tradition of written history. Referred to as 'praise singers' they were sometimes itinerants but were more commonly attached to the households of hereditary dynasties. The griots recited and sang the myths, poems and history of the rulers at social and religious occasions and acted as social commentators. The most important function of the griot was to act as historian for the dynasty by memorizing and reciting the family history, particularly its traditional rights and duties. Griots would often accompany an employer to war to memorize his exploits. In addition they often acted as advisors and private secretaries.

Gumbo

Combination of French and a number of African languages spoken by black people in some parts of Louisiana in the USA and the former French colonies in the Caribbean. The word is thought to derive from *nkombo*, meaning 'runaway slave' in the Bantu language of the Kongo people of Zaire.

Habitual Idlers Ordinance

Legislation passed in the British Caribbean colony of Trinidad in 1918, intended to prevent black indentured labourers whose contracts had expired from leaving the plantation to seek other work. Any male plantation worker who was unable to provide proof that he had worked for four hours in the previous three days could be forced to work for private contractors or be sent to a government labour camp.

Haitian Emigration Society of Coloured People

Formed in New York City to encourage free blacks to emigrate to Haiti, where they were welcomed following the overthrow of the French colonial government in 1804. By 1824 societies existed in New York, Baltimore and Philadelphia. Over 20,000 free blacks went to Haiti from the USA in the 1820s. But by 1826 a third had returned, disillusioned by problems over language, religion and culture. The Haitian government provided grants of land to black immigrants but many preferred to remain in the cities.

Harambee

Slogan meaning 'let us pull together' adopted in Kenya on independence in 1963. The expression was incorporated into the national coat of arms. The slogan implied avoiding reliance on foreign aid at a national level and working towards self-reliance at a local level.

Hatch system

Discriminatory practice in the British colony of Northern Rhodesia (now Zambia) which barred Africans from using the main entrances to shops, particularly butchers, but forced them to use hatches at the back or side of buildings to buy goods. The practice was ended following a campaign of boycotts mounted by Africans in the 1950s.

Holy Spirit Movement

Christian fundamentalist movement led by Alice Lakwena. The movement was active in northern Uganda in the late 1980s. Lakwena claimed to be possessed by the spirit of a dead Italian soldier and urged her followers to overthrow President Museveni and replace his government with one committed to enforcing the Ten Commandments. Lakwena was imprisoned in Kenya for illegal entry when she fled from Uganda. Her followers formed a short-lived organization named 'Lakwena Part 2'. The movement was succeeded in the 1990s by the Lord's Resistance Army.

Homelands

The Bantustans in South Africa which were given a spurious 'independence' by the apartheid government under the Bantu Homelands Constitution Act of 1971. The status of independence was not recognized outside South Africa under international law. The homelands, with the people who lived in them and the year in which they were deemed to be independent, were Transkei (Xhosa, 1976), Bophuthatswana (Tswana,

1977), Venda (Vhavenda, 1979), and Ciskei (Xhosa), 1981. During the 1980s there were military coups and counter-coups in each of the homelands. With the collapse of apartheid, the homelands rejoined the new state of South Africa.

Homeward Bound Fund
Launched in December 1981 by Ashton Gibson, director-general of Westindian Concern Ltd, to repatriate between 40 and 50 families in the London Borough of Hackney to the Caribbean each year. Mr Gibson appealed for £1 million. Although over 1000 people sought assistance, the Fund was closed in March 1982, having raised only £3000 and repatriated three families.

IAFA
See International African Friends of Abyssinia.

IASB
See International African Service Bureau.

Ichitupa
Identification certificate that Africans were forced to carry in the British colony of Northern Rhodesia until the territory's independence as Zambia in 1964, under legislation similar to the South African Pass laws. There were mass burnings of the certificates throughout Northern Rhodesia during protest demonstrations in 1961.

ICU
See Industrial and Commercial Union.

Immorality Act
Part of the legislative framework of the apartheid system in South Africa. Under the 1957 Immorality Act inter-racial sexual relations could be punished with up to seven years' imprisonment. The Act was repealed in 1985.

Independent National Patriotic Front of Liberia (INPFL)
A breakaway group from the National Patriotic Front of Liberia (NPFL), led by Prince Yorami Johnson, a former Liberian army officer expelled from the NPFL for executing members of his own force. Johnson formed the INPFL in February 1990 and was allegedly supported by the US Central Intelligence Agency, which mistook him for another NPFL figure. President Samuel Doe attempted to reach agreement with the INPFL to strengthen his position in the civil war. On 10 September 1990 he met INPFL representatives at the headquarters of the Economic Community of West African States peacekeeping force. But INPFL soldiers shot 60 of Doe's troops, taking Doe to Johnson's headquarters where the president was tortured to death.

Indigena
Portuguese word for 'native', the legal status of the majority of Africans in the Portuguese colonies of Angola, Guinea and Mozambique until 1961. Unlike the assimilados, indigena were subject to forced labour and had no citizenship rights.

Indirect rule
British form of administration in colonial Africa. African 'traditional' leaders were appointed at the lower levels of the judiciary to collect taxes, recruit labour and control unrest caused by the unpopular colonial measures which they were required to implement. These appointments often led to the creation of chieftainships where they had not existed previously, for example, among the Ibo of Nigeria and the Kikuyu of Kenya. The advantage for the colonial authorities was that this form of administration required few white personnel and acted as a buffer between them and the population.

Industrial and Commercial Union (ICU)

Trade union formed among black and coloured workers in South Africa in 1919 by Clements Kadalie. The ICU affiliated with other organizations to create the Industrial and Commercial Union of Africa in 1920, with Kadalie as National Secretary. By 1927, with 100,000 members, the ICU was the leading mass movement in Africa. ICU attempts to work within the white power structure were rejected, as was a request to join the League of Nations' International Labour Organisation in 1927. Divisions appeared over the ICU attitude towards the Pass laws and in 1928 Kadalie was forced to take a more militant position than he favoured. His resignation from office in 1929 weakened the ICU as an organization, with splits between radical and moderate members. It did, however, remain a model for later black South African union activity in the 1950s.

INPFL

See Independent National Patriotic Front of Liberia.

International African Friends of Abyssinia (IAFA)

Organization founded in London in August 1935 by Africans and people of African descent when it became clear that Italy was provoking a crisis to enable it to invade Abyssinia (now Ethiopia). Pan-African and Marxist theoretician C. L. R. James became chairman and Jomo Kenyatta was appointed secretary. The organizing committee included Joseph Danquah, Albert Marryshow, George Padmore and Amy Ashwood Garvey. The Friends' objective was to assist Abyssinia retain its territorial integrity and political independence. The formation of the Friends was part of a world-wide reaction among Africans and people of African descent to the threat posed to one of the only two states in Africa which had remained free from European colonialism. In Trinidad, for example, dockworkers refused to unload Italian ships. The Friends disbanded after Italy's invasion but many supporters went on to form the International African Service Bureau.

International African Service Bureau (IASB)

Formed in 1936 by Pan-African supporters of the disbanded International African Friends of Abyssinia. The IASB appealed for Africans and people of the African diaspora to defend Abyssinia against the 1935 Italian invasion, and to establish a united international movement to defend black rights. In 1944 the IASB merged with twelve other political, student and welfare organizations to form the Pan-African Federation.

International Colored Unity League

Organization founded in 1924 by the radical political activist Hubert Harrison to campaign for the establishment of a separate black territory in the USA. The league's journal was the *Voice of the Negro*.

Inyenzi ('cockroaches')

Tutsi commandos who mounted raids on Rwanda from July 1962 to July 1966. The Tutsis had been deposed by the Hutu and forced into exile and into refugee camps in neighbouring countries. The effect of the incursions was to consolidate Hutu power and at least 10,000 Tutsis in Rwanda were massacred by Hutus in retaliation.

Israelite Movement

An African Independent Church in South Africa led by Enoch Mgijima. Mgijima preached resistance to European rule, in particular the payment of taxes. In 1920 the congregation settled at Bulhoek Common near Queenstown in the Cape to await the end of the world, and were attacked by police and troops at the Bulhoek massacre of May 1921.

Jamaica Progressive League (JPL)

Founded in New York in 1936 by Wilfred A. Domingo and other politically active Caribbean immigrants to the USA. The JPL advocated Jamaican self-government, universal suffrage, the development of trade unionism, and the organization of consumer co-operatives. Following the formation of a branch in Jamaica in 1938, the JPL merged with the People's National Party led by Norman Manley.

Jamaican Political Reform Association

The association was founded in 1921 and was one of the first political organizations in Jamaica. The association led the campaign on the island against the British colonial authorities for political change.

Jamaat al Muslimeen

A militant black Muslim group in Trinidad led by Imam Yasin Abu Bakr (Lennox Phillips, a former policeman) which attempted to overthrow the government of Arthur Robinson during the Trinidad coup of July 1990. The movement was estimated at the time of the coup to have 2000 members. Its members occupied the state television station and the legislative building, where the prime minister and cabinet members were held hostage. On 5 December 1995, the Trinidad prime minister, Basdeo Panday, met Imam Yasin to discuss the group's demands for land and compensation for damages.

Jim Crow

Colloquial term used when describing legislation enforcing social, political and educational segregation in the southern USA from 1875 onwards, following the end of Reconstruction. There are a number of possible derivations of the term 'Jim Crow'.

The most generally accepted is that it derived from a black dance routine called *Jump Jim Crow* which a white minstrel-show performer, Thomas D. Rice (1808–60), copied in the late 1820s and popularized throughout the USA and in Britain. 'Jim Crow' then became a generic name for black people. However, the phrase has been dated to 1730 when black people were first described as 'crows'. Another suggestion is that the expression may derive from an enslaved West African chieftain John Canoe (or Jim Kano).

Jim Crow laws

Segregation legislation in the southern USA, intended to withdraw the political, economic and social gains made by black people in the period of Reconstruction following the 1861–5 Civil War. Federal troops were withdrawn from the former slave states in 1877 with the implication that no further intervention was necessary to protect the interests of black Americans. The 1875 Civil Rights Act, for example, provided for equal access to all public facilities to all citizens. However, the Supreme Court ruled in 1883 that the provisions of the Act did not apply to 'personal acts of social discrimination'. This opened the way for the southern states to introduce legislation providing for racial segregation in education, transport, relations between the sexes, and entertainment. The validity of Jim Crow legislation was underlined by the 1896 Supreme Court decision in Plessy *v* Ferguson, which introduced the concept of 'separate but equal'. The institutionalization of racism was backed at an everyday level by the threats of the Ku-Klux-Klan and by lynching. The Supreme Court's declaration in 1954 in Brown *v* Board of Education of Topeka that educational segregation was unconstitutional opened a period in which Jim Crow legislation was gradually eradicated. This process came to a culmination with the 1964 Civil Rights Act.

JPL
See Jamaica Progressive League.

KAR
See King's African Rifles.

KCU
See Kikuyu Central Association.

Kenya Land Freedom Army (KLFA)
A movement formed in Kenya in 1958 by former Mau Mau activists led by Mbaria Kaniu. The KLFA aimed to unite Africans in a campaign for independence and to obtain land for the landless in the white-owned Kenya Highlands. KLFA recruits swore a Mau Mau oath and by 1959 KLFA was strongly supported in the Rift Valley Province. It backed the Kenya African Democratic Union (KADU) on its foundation in 1960. The KLFA was outlawed by the British colonial authorities in 1961.

Kenyan Highlands Settlement Scheme
A plan following the country's independence in 1963 to redistribute land in the previously white-dominated Kenyan Highlands. The government bought 500,000 hectares of land at market prices, resettled 35,000 new farmers on 12- to 20-hectare properties, provided loans and training and encouraged modern mixed-farming techniques. The scheme proved expensive to administer and develop but played an important part in encouraging the growth of a new agricultural sector.

Kenyan Squatter Settlement Scheme
A government scheme introduced following independence in 1963, to assist landless Africans who had been forced into urban unemployment or the illegal occupation of

land. Families were provided with small two-hectare farms on land cleared from forests near villages and towns. Although no loans or grants were available, the new farmers were encouraged to become self-sufficient and to produce a surplus for sale where possible.

Kenya People's Redemption Council
Organization of members of the Kenyan Air Force who attempted to overthrow the government of Daniel arap Moi in August 1982 with the support of Nairobi University students. The council alleged that President Moi's government was corrupt and mis-managing Kenya. The rising was suppressed by September, with the death of 160 rebels. Over 700 rebels were placed on trial for their part in the rising and eleven were sentenced to death. They were hanged on 9 July 1985.

Kikuyu Central Association (KCA)
An organization formed in Kenya following the collapse of the East African Association. The Kikuyu Central Association was launched at Kahuhia in 1924 by Joseph Kang'ethe and James Beauttah, and was established to express the grievances of the Kikuyu people against the British colonial administration. It called for the return of land stolen by the Europeans, an end to racial discrimination, the restoration of the right of Africans to grow cotton and coffee (removed to provide European settlers with an agricultural monopoly). The association also campaigned against attempts by European Christian missionaries to end the practice of female circumcision. The association's activity intensified with the appointment of Jomo Kenyatta, the future president of independent Kenya, as general-secretary in 1928. Kenyatta founded a newspaper, *Mwigwithania* and stressed the need for a Kikuyu cultural revival. He was despatched to England in 1928 and 1929 to present petitions protesting against the lack

of security of tenure on land reserved for Africans but held by the Crown. The association's protests at the report of the Kenya Land Commission in 1931 were ignored by the colonial authorities. The association was banned by the British colonial authorities in 1940. The 1950s Mau Mau rising represented a response to the British failure to acknowledge Kikuyu grievances.

Kimbanguism

An African Independent Church which led national resistance to colonial rule in the Belgian Congo (now Zaïre) during the 1920s and 1930s, encouraging non-payment of taxes and the refusal to grow export crops. The movement was founded by Simon Kimbangu, a Bakongo peasant and Baptist preacher, in April 1921 and grew into the largest religious movement in modern Africa. Kimbangu was imprisoned by the colonial authorities in the same year. The church combined Christianity with traditional African practices and beliefs. Its members were persecuted by the Belgian authorities and formed an underground movement which took on an increasingly anti-European attitude. Some followers established their own churches but emphasized Kimbangu's inspiration and proclaimed his vision of the unity of the Belgian Congo, the French Congo and Angola. Kimbangu died after 30 years in prison but by the 1950s his son, Joseph Diangienda (born in 1918) had reunited many groups of supporters in the Church of Jesus Christ on Earth through the Prophet Simon Kimbangu (EJCSK). The ban on the church was lifted at independence in 1960. In 1969, the EJCSK became the first independent African church to be recognized by the World Council of Churches. It came under renewed persecution by the Mobutu regime in the 1970s. At the beginning of the 1990s the EJCSK claimed over three million members.

King's African Rifles (KAR)

A British army regiment in central and eastern Africa formed on 1 January 1902 by the amalgamation of the Central Africa Regiment, the Uganda Rifles and the East African Regiment. The King's African Rifles (KAR) had white officers and was made up of black soldiers and a number of Indians. It played an important part in the consolidation of British rule in the region. The British authorities used the KAR in Somaliland from 1902–4 and on internal security duties in East Africa until the outbreak of World War I in 1914. The regiment was used to defend the Uganda Railway from German attack from August 1914 to February 1916; in the invasion and occupation of German East Africa from March 1916 to November 1917; and in the pursuit of German forces into Portuguese East Africa until November 1918. During World War I the numbers of Africans in the regiment rose from 2300 to over 20,000. Of these, over a thousand were killed, almost 4000 wounded and over 3000 died of disease. Between the World Wars the KAR reverted to internal security. In World War II the regiment was used in the defence of Kenya and Somaliland against Italian threats; in the liberation of Ethiopia from Italian control from January to April 1941 and against Vichy French forces in Madagascar in 1942. Over 50,000 were sent to South-East Asia to fight the Japanese in Burma from August 1944 until the end of the war. As the British territories gained independence, the KAR provided the basis for the armies of each country. The Kenya African Rifles, the Tanganyika Rifles and the Zambia Regiment were formed in 1963 and the Malawi Rifles in 1964.

KLFA
See Kenya Land Freedom Army.

Kwacha
A slogan meaning 'the dawn is coming' used by African nationalists in Northern Rhodesia (now Zambia) during the independence campaign of the 1950s. The British authorities made it an offence to use the expression. Kwacha became the name of the Zambian currency in 1968.

Kwazaa
African–American holiday based on African harvest celebrations. Established in 1966 in Los Angeles by Dr Maulana Karenya of the University of California, the festival is celebrated by the black communities in a number of American cities including Los Angeles, Chicago, New Orleans, New York, Philadelphia and Washington.

Lagos Plan
An agreement reached by heads of state of the Organization of African Unity (OAU) in April 1980 that Africa should work towards economic self-reliance through industrialization. The plan's aim was that Africa would account for 1 per cent of world industrial output by 1985 and 2 per cent by 2000 but this goal was abandoned at the 1985 OAU conference.

Lagos Weekly Record
The leading campaigning newspaper against white colonial rule in Nigeria, established by Liberian-born John Payne Jackson (1848–1915). The *Record* was taken over by his son Thomas Horatio Jackson in 1915 and continued publication until 1930.

League of Coloured Peoples
Founded 1931 at the Central YMCA in Tottenham Court Road, London, by Harold Arundel Moody, a Jamaican doctor. The league campaigned for equal rights for black people living in London, for improved relations between the races and to interest its members in the welfare of black people internationally. Moody was president of the league until his death in 1947. A devout Christian, he came into conflict with the more radical members for his cautious approach to campaigning and what was seen as his collaboration with white officials and organizations. The league published a journal, *The Keys*.

League of Revolutionary Black Workers
US group formed by the amalgamation of a number of smaller black groups in the Detroit automobile industry in 1969. The league intended to unite black workers, unemployed youth, students and intellectuals to form a revolutionary vanguard against capitalism, imperialism and racism. Industrial members were to form a revolutionary caucus within trade unions and to display the potential of shop-floor militancy for all workers. Its effectiveness was limited by political differences among the league's leaders and its inability to spread beyond Detroit.

League of Struggle for Negro Rights
US organization led by the Communist Party, formed in 1931 as a successor to the American Negro Labor Congress. The league's activists led effective unemployed organization and rent strikes, particularly in Chicago. However, it was largely unsuccessful in its aim of taking revolutionary politics to the black population. The league was dissolved in 1935 and succeeded by the National Negro Congress.

League of the Poor
Lekhotla la Bafo, formed in British-occupied Basutoland (now Lesotho) in the 1920s. The league found its support among peasants who also worked as seasonal miners in the

Transvaal, South Africa. As a radical movement, the league was closer to the Communist Party of South Africa than the more moderate African National Congress. Alarmed by the league's growing support, the British colonial authorities ordered chiefs to ban the movement's meetings in 1928. The league mounted a protest in Maseru against this attempt to curb its activities in August 1928 and several thousand attended the first mass anti-colonial demonstration ever held in Basutoland.

Leopard Society

Secret society whose African name was Ekpe or Egbo, meaning leopard, which existed until the nineteenth century among the Efik people in Calabar, one of the states of the Niger Delta in Nigeria. The society was hierarchical, organized in grades and regulated the religious, political, social and economic life of the community. Membership was open to any man who could afford the initiation fee which was shared between the members. During the nineteenth century the society operated a segregated system where the freeborn lived in Calabar and the slaves on the palm plantations outside the city.

LGC

See Liberia Grand Coalition.

Liberia Grand Coalition (LGC)

Coalition of Liberian opposition groups formed under the repressive regime of President Doe. The LGC's leader, Gabriel Kpolleh, and twelve members were charged with treason in June 1988. Kpolleh and nine of the alleged traitors were sentenced to life imprisonment in October 1988.

Liberian Exodus and Joint Stock Steamship Company

Formed by American former slaves in South Carolina in 1877, to organize a return to Africa. The company bought a ship, the

Azor, which sailed to Liberia the following year with 206 passengers. The company went bankrupt shortly after.

Little Eight, the

The then-British Caribbean colonies of Antigua, Barbados, Dominica, Grenada, Montserrat, St Kitts, St Lucia and St Vincent who attempted to preserve a federal structure following the collapse in 1962 of the Federation of the West Indies. Recurrent disagreement between governments of the islands forced the final abandonment of the attempt in 1965.

Lomé Convention

See ACP countries.

Lord's Resistance Army

A Christian fundamentalist movement in northern and eastern Uganda, traditionally areas of resistance to central government. The army carried out terrorist attacks in the 1990s as part of a campaign to overthrow President Yoweri Museveni and install a government committed to enforcing the Ten Commandments. The army, which is led by Joseph Kony (a former Roman Catholic preacher), is a successor to the Holy Spirit Movement and is estimated to have 1000 members. The hard core of the army consists of former soldiers of the Acholi people, supporters of former president, Milton Obote. In January 1994, an offer to surrender in return for the provision of resettlement funds was rejected by the Ugandan government. In April 1995, the LRA attacked the village of Atiak on the Uganda–Sudan border, killing 200 people. The army's activities intensified in the run-up to the May 1996 presidential elections (despite the announcement by the LRA of a truce) and over 250 people were killed in its attacks and hundreds abducted. The LRA appeared to concentrate its attacks on owners of bicycles and villagers who kept white chickens and white pigs. In the elections, the army called for support for the opposition candidate Paul Ssemogerere. Although it claims to be a Christian movement, the army is supported by the Islamic fundamentalist government in Sudan. This is in response to the Ugandan government's support for the Sudan People's Liberation Army. In July 1996, the LRA was accused of the massacre of over 90 Sudanese refugees at a camp in the Kitgum district of northern Uganda.

Lumpa Church

Formed in Northern Rhodesia (now Zambia) by Alice Lenshina in 1963 following her excommunication from the Church of Scotland. After claiming to have had a vision in 1953, Lenshina organized an anti-witchcraft campaign in the north-east of the country. Following independence in 1964, the Church opposed President Kaunda, refused to pay taxes and fortified villages against government attack. The government banned the Church, killing 700 members and driving many into Zaïre. Lenshina was arrested and imprisoned until 1975. The Church continued in existence underground after her death in 1978.

Lusophone

A term meaning 'Portuguese-speaking', from Lusitania, the Latin name for Portugal, sometimes used to describe former Portuguese colonies. It ignored the fact, however, that the majority of the inhabitants of the former African and Caribbean colonies had languages of their own.

Maroons

From the Spanish *cimarrón*, an expression used from the sixteenth century onwards to describe African slaves who escaped and lived in freedom. The expression is most commonly used of Jamaica, which was occupied by the Spanish until taken by Britain in 1655. Maroons were regularly in conflict with the British colonial authorities in Jamaica through the eighteenth century. The most significant clashes were during the First Maroon War and the Second Maroon War. A number of Maroon communities remain in existence, notably in Jamaica and in Suriname where they are known as Saramacca.

Mau Mau

Name given by the British colonial authorities in Kenya to the predominantly Kikuyu guerrilla campaign from 1947–55. The name, intended to undermine resistance against the British, was taken up with pride by anti-colonialist activists. The movement demanded the return of Kikuyu lands taken by Europeans, the expulsion of all Europeans and Asians, increased education, and a return to the traditional Kikuyu practices of polygamy and female circumcision. An oath sworn by Mau Mau members allegedly said, 'If I am called upon to do so, with four others, I will kill a European. If I am called upon to do so, I will kill a Kikuyu who is against the Mau Mau, even if it be my mother or my father or brother or sister or wife or child . . . I will never disobey the orders of the leaders of this society.' In October 1952 Jomo Kenyatta was imprisoned by the British colonial authorities for allegedly being the leader of Mau Mau, although in August he had publicly denounced the movement.

Mbaaku Black Women's Group

Organization founded in Britain in 1983 to address the specific needs of black and ethnic minority women. The group provides information, helps facilitate education and self-help schemes, and liaises with other voluntary bodies and the private sector in Britain and Europe.

MIA

See Montgomery Improvement Association.

Middle passage

The month-long voyage across the Atlantic by slaves from Africa to the New World. Between one in six and one in eight were estimated to have died during the journey in ships designed to maximize the human cargo. In the early period of slave-trading the main carriers were the Portuguese, Dutch and Spanish but in the later period the British became the leading slave power. The middle passage was at the centre of the triangular trade. European slavers carried manufactured goods to the West African coast which they bartered for slaves. The slaves were shipped across the Atlantic to the Caribbean and the Americas where they were exchanged for plantation crops, such as sugar and tobacco, which in turn were shipped to Europe for sale.

Million Acre Scheme

Attempt to resolve the landlessness problem in Kenya in 1962 under which the Ministry of Lands and Settlement would enable 34,000 African farmers to be settled on former European-owned land within five years.

MK

See Umkhonto we Sizwe.

Mongoose Squad

Violent group active in Grenada in the 1970s which supported the Prime Minister Eric Gairy and which was used to intimidate and attack his political opponents. The activities of the Squad encouraged support for the revolution which overthrew Gairy in 1979.

Monrovia Bloc

Representatives of 19 non-socialist African states who met in Monrovia (Liberia) in May 1961 and Lagos (Nigeria) in January 1962, in an attempt to act as a counterweight to the more radical Casablanca Bloc. The bloc formulated a charter and organized a secretariat but merged into the Organization of African Unity (OAU) in 1963.

Montgomery Improvement Association (MIA)

Formed by Martin Luther King, Jr in 1955 to organize a black boycott of public transport in Montgomery, Alabama, following the arrest of Rosa Parks for refusing to give up her seat on a bus to a white man. The successful 381-day boycott resulted in an end to racial segregation in the city bus system.

Moorish Science Temple

A black American movement founded in Newark, New Jersey, by Nobel Drew Ali (Timothy Drew) in 1913. Ali combined Islam, the teaching of Marcus Garvey, and elements of Christianity and oriental philosophy. The Temple's main tenets were that black Americans should recognize their national origin as Moors, that Islam was the key to black unity and progress, that the world was divided into dark and light people and that the white race faced destruction. Ali took a politically conservative position and advocated obedience to the law and the avoidance of radical action. The Temple spread rapidly in Chicago, Detroit, Harlem and into a number of towns in the southern states and had at its peak an estimated 25,000 members. A schism within the movement led to the establishment of the Nation of Islam.

MOSOP

See Movement for the Survival of the Ogoni People.

Movement for the Survival of the Ogoni People (MOSOP)

Organization formed in 1990 by traditional leaders and civil servants to lead the campaign of the 500,000 Ogoni people living in the oil-rich Niger Delta in Nigeria against the environmental devastation resulting from operations of oil companies in the area. The Ogoni people sought mineral rights and a share in petroleum revenue. In 1992, MOSOP presented an ultimatum to the Anglo-Dutch Shell Company demanding $1 billion reparation. Following clashes with MOSOP activists, Shell left the area. Under the presidency of writer Kenyule Saro-Wiwa, MOSOP militancy increased and a youth wing and women's association were formed. MOSOP threatened secession from Nigeria and over 2000 people were killed in attacks by the security forces. In November 1995, Saro-Wiwa was executed with eight other people, for alleged complicity in the killing of four moderate Ogoni leaders. MOSOP virtually disintegrated as an organization.

Mulungushi Declaration

A programme of economic reforms in Zambia announced by President Kenneth Kaunda in April 1968. This included increased government participation in foreign-owned companies and Zambian control of leading retail outlets. The declaration was aimed particularly at the dominance of trading and transport by Asians and was part of a widespread Africanization policy in East Africa which took on an increasingly anti-Asian tone in, for example, Kenya and Uganda.

Mwakenya

Kenyan underground movement which emerged in the early 1980s aiming at the overthrow of the government of President Moi and its replacement with a socialist state. There was sporadic rioting in some Kenyan towns in July 1990 following the distribution of Mwakenya leaflets calling for an armed rising.

Mwigwithania

The monthly newspaper of the Kikuyu Central Association (KCA) established by Jomo Kenyatta when he became the Association's general-secretary in 1928. Kenyatta attempted to broaden support for the KCA among Kikuyu people through the newspaper and to encourage pride in Kikuyu culture. *Mwigwithania* contained, as well as news items, traditional proverbs and riddles.

Mzee

'Grand old man', the title taken by Jomo Kenyatta, leader of Kenya's independence struggle against the British and president from 1964 until his death in 1978.

NAACP

See National Association for the Advancement of Colored People.

Nation of Islam (NOI)

The Nation of Islam (NOI) emerged in 1930 from a schism in the Moorish Science Temple, one section of which left under the leadership of Wallace D. Fard (Wali Farad, Master Farah Muhammad). On Fard's disappearance in 1933, his followers became founding members of the NOI under Elijah Muhammad. Muhammad taught that Islam was the religion of black people and Christianity that of whites. God is black and the devil white, which the historical evidence of the evil perpetrated by the white race proved. Black people were to avoid the corruption inherent in white civilization and construct a nation in their own interests through a black united front, going on to build international racial and Islamic solidarity. Through this they would find what Muhammad described as 'freedom from contempt'. He encouraged independence and self-help, advocating the development of, for example, separate hospitals, industries and educational institutions. Muhammad initially recruited among unemployed black men from the southern states. After World War II he turned to ex-convicts and ghetto youth. By 1958 there were an estimated 15,000 members. As the NOI grew into a multi-million dollar organization, divisions emerged in the 1960s, symbolized by the expulsion of Malcolm X in 1963 for his radicalism. Malcolm X was later assassinated. There were allegations that internal conflicts were exacerbated by Federal Bureau of Investigation (FBI) infiltration. Elijah Muhammad was succeeded by his son, Wallace, as NOI leader in 1975. The NOI's emphasis was changed from religious black nationalism to orthodox Islam and Americanism and the movement was renamed the World Community of al-Islam in the West. Louis Farrakhan, who had replaced Malcolm X as national spokesman in 1963, objected to the new direction. In 1981, he attempted to reconstruct the Nation of Islam in its former image. Farrakhan established a newspaper, *The Final Call*, as part of the process of returning to Elijah Muhammad's original message. Farrakhan's movement is now the more prominent of the two. In October 1995, Farrakhan organized a successful Million Man March on Washington, DC, effectively becoming the black leader in the USA. On a world tour in 1996, Farrakhan was allegedly given $1 million for his organization by President Gaddafy of Libya. In South Africa, Farrakhan asked for land to be provided in Africa to re-settle a million black Americans. In the run-up to the November 1996 US presidential elections, Farrakhan abandoned his movement's boycott of electoral politics and encouraged black voters to participate. There were suggestions that his long-term aim was to establish a black political party centred around the Nation of Islam.

National Association for the Advancement of Colored People (NAACP)

The NAACP, established and sponsored in 1909 by white liberals, was for many years the leading organization in the USA combating racial discrimination and working for integration and equality of opportunity for black people. The NAACP was formed as an inter-racial and non-violent organization to achieve change through the courts, voting and publicity rather than agitation. It emerged from a National Negro Conference convened on the anniversary of President Lincoln's birthday in February 1909. There were, initially, criticisms – notably from William Trotter and Ida B. Wells – of white dominance among NAACP leaders. The leading black figure at its foundation was W. E. B. Du Bois, director of research and publicity and editor of the magazine *The Crisis*. An early NAACP success came with the 1915 Supreme Court Guinn *v* US decision outlawing 'grandfather clauses' intended to prevent black people from voting. The NAACP led a series of struggles to extend the franchise, culminating in the 1965 Voting Rights Act. From 1919 the expanding movement came increasingly under black control. In the 1920s and 1930s the NAACP played a major part in the attempt to secure federal anti-lynching legislation and to eliminate segregation in the organized labour movement. The NAACP Legal Defense and Education Fund was established in 1939 and broke away from the parent organization in 1959. In 1954 the NAACP achieved a major victory in Brown *v* Board of Education of Topeka when the Supreme Court overthrew the doctrine of 'separate but equal'. NAACP membership rose rapidly to over 470,000 as the struggle for civil rights intensified in the 1960s. However, new groups such as the Congress of Racial Equality (CORE), the Southern

Christian Leadership Conference (SCLC), and the Student Non-violent Coordinating Committee (SNCC) took the lead in campaigning. But it was the NAACP slogan 'Free by 63' that dominated the August 1963 March on Washington for Jobs and Freedom. Against a background of disorder, and under criticism by younger activists, the NAACP reaffirmed its commitment to non-violent change.

National Black Caucus

A coalition of black organizations and activists formed in Britain in the early 1990s. The caucus takes a similar position to the South African Pan-Africanist Congress (PAC), advocating self-organisation among black people to achieve their goals in the struggle against racism in a capitalist society. Its leading figure is Lee Jasper. In August 1991 the caucus organized a march against racism in South London and demonstrations against the Asylum and Immigration Appeals Bill (in co-operation with the Anti-Racist Alliance) in January 1993. The caucus is a member of the Black Liaison Group and has carried out joint activity with the 1990 Trust.

National Black Political Convention

First held in the USA at Gary, Indiana, in March 1972, attended by 3000 delegates and 5000 observers. The convention produced a Black Political Agenda and agreed to hold regular assemblies. It criticized both the Democratic and Republican Parties but did not advocate the creation of an independent black party. However, 1300 delegates at the Fourth Assembly held in New Orleans in August 1980 called for a National Black Independent Political Party to be formed to provide an alternative to the two major parties.

National Black United Front

Movement formed in the USA in June 1980 with regional and local regional organizations throughout the country. The Front concentrated on the everyday struggles of black Americans, defending civil rights laws and social services, and combating racist violence. The Front was also involved in political education, organizing strikes and boycotts and supporting African and Third World liberation movements. It attempted, in the longer term, to formulate a collective black American political agenda encompassing a range of views from moderate conservatism to nationalism.

National Congress of British West Africa (NCBWA)

Founded in 1919 in the Gold Coast (now Ghana) by the lawyer J. B. Casely Hayford and Dr Akiwande Savage of Nigeria. Congress membership was primarily among lawyers, doctors and businessmen. At the first conference held in Accra between 11 and 29 March 1919, there were 40 delegates from the Gold Coast, six from Nigeria, three from Sierra Leone and one from The Gambia. Further conferences were held in 1923 and 1925. The NBCWA called for a reform of British colonial administration including half the seats on Legislative Councils to be taken by elected Africans, senior official positions not to be restricted to Europeans, and the establishment of a West African university. It attacked the post-World War I partition of the former German colony of Togoland between Britain and France (severing the Ewe people) and the ceding of the Cameroons to France without consulting the population. The NBCWA sent a delegation to London in 1920 seeking the establishment of representative government in the four British West African colonies. New constitutions were formulated by the British in Nigeria in 1923, in Sierra Leone in 1924 and in the Gold Coast in 1925. Although the NBCWA was a generally conservative organization, the British government denied its claim to speak for Africans, insisting that only the chiefs could do this. Internal divisions further weakened any impact the NBCWA might have had and it went into decline following Hayford's death in 1930.

National Convention of Namibia

Formed in 1972 to unite all anti-South African forces in Namibia. The dominant group in the convention, the South West Africa People's Organisation (SWAPO), left in 1975, accusing other leading convention figures of collaborating with the South African government's unsatisfactory constitutional proposals for the area.

National Emergency Committee

An organization formed in Lagos, capital of the British colony of Nigeria, during the November 1949 incidents which culminated in the Enugu Colliery strike and the killing by police of miners. The committee, which was made up of leading Nigerian political figures, passed a resolution of no confidence in the Nigerian government but agreed to the appointment of a Commission of Enquiry into the shootings. It opposed a call from trade union leaders in the New Council of Labour for a general strike to protest against the events. In its evidence to the Fitzgerald Commission, the committee declared that independence was the only solution to Nigeria's problems.

National Forum

South African organization formed in 1983, strongly influenced by the black consciousness ideas of Steve Biko. The forum functioned as an umbrella organization for over 200 black anti-apartheid bodies and agitated for a democratic and socialist Azania (the Forum's preferred name for South Africa). It opposed both capitalism and racism. Although the forum co-operated with coloureds and Indians, it opposed the

willingness of the African National Congress (ANC) and United Democratic Front (UDF) to work with white liberals. The forum's largest affiliated body was the Azanian People's Organisation (AZAPO).

National Front for the Liberation of the Congo (FNLC)

A group formed in opposition to President Mobutu, of what is now Zaïre, by Nathaniel Bumba in 1968. The FNLC participated in an unsuccessful invasion of eastern Zaïre, aimed at restoring former prime minister, Moïse Tshombe, to power. On 7 March 1977, 2000 FNLC members (allegedly with Cuban backing) invaded Shaba province (formerly Katanga) from Angola. They were repelled with Moroccan support in mid-April. The FNLC launched a second invasion when 3000 supporters crossed from Angola on 11 May 1978 and were repelled by French and Belgian paratroopers. The revelation of the incompetence of Mobutu's armed forces encouraged a slight liberalization of his policies. The FNLC reputedly fought for the Portuguese colonial forces in the war for the liberation of Angola. Following Angola's independence in 1975 they were recruited by the governing party, the People's Movement for the Liberation of Angola (MPLA), during the civil war against the National Front for the Liberation of Angola (FNLA) and the National Union for the Total Independence of Angola (UNITA).

National Joint Action Committee (NJAC)

A predominantly middle-class black power and nationalist movement, prominent in the 1970 Trinidad revolt. The NJAC argued that British colonialism had been replaced on independence by neo-colonialism through which the white power structure retained control over Trinidad's economy. Trinidad's political leaders were accused of being 'black whites' and 'Afro-Saxons'. The NJAC, although anti-Marxist, called for revolutionary change, with national economic self-reliance, public ownership of land and the sugar industry and an end to unemployment. The movement first came into prominence in 1969 when it mounted a demonstration against the Canadian governor-general following the arrest of anti-racist black students in Canada. The NJAC's call for 'black power' faced the problem that while 42 per cent of Trinidad's population were black, 37 per cent were of Indian descent. The February–April 1970 events revealed the limitations of the NJAC, above all its lack of a coherent revolutionary programme. NJAC candidates won 3.3 per cent of the vote in the 1981 general election and 1.5 per cent in 1986.

National League for the Protection of Colored Women

An organization formed in the USA in 1906 to assist black women migrating north from the southern states to find work and housing. The league merged with a number of other organizations to form the National Urban League in 1911.

National Liberation Council of Nigeria

A dissident pressure group in Britain and the USA, the European branch of which was launched in London in September 1995. The council's most prominent member is the Nobel-laureate writer, Wole Soyinka. The council claimed to have an underground resistance movement working to remove the regime of President Sani Abacha by any means necessary.

National Negro Convention

Regular conferences held in the USA to debate methods of improving the condition of black Americans, to combat oppression and to promote education. The first was held in Philadelphia, Pennsylvania, in 1830. Following the end of slavery, conventions concentrated on voting rights, fair wages, equal education opportunities and the repeal of discriminatory legislation.

National Negro Labor Council

Formed by black workers in the USA in 1951 to combat discrimination in employment and persistent racism in the American union movement. Appeals to the white union leadership for co-operation were rejected. The council organized strikes and campaigns against police brutality, discrimination in transportation and public facilities and for employment. The council was forced to dissolve itself in 1956 when it was accused by the Subversive Activities Control Board of being a Communist-front organization.

National Patriotic Front of Liberia (NPFL)

One of the competing factions in the Liberian civil war since 1989, led by Charles Taylor. The 100-strong nucleus of the NPFL moved into Nimba County in the north east of Liberia from the neighbouring Côte d'Ivoire on 24 December 1989. The force, which intended to overthrow the government of President Samuel Doe, had been trained in Libya and consisted mainly of Liberians, together with mercenaries and supporters from Burkina Faso and Sierra Leone. The NPFL rapidly developed into a mass movement because of the indiscriminate violence used against the population of Nimba County by government troops. This enabled the NPFL, which was originally ethnically mixed, to declare itself the protector of the local Mano and Gio peoples against ethnic violence. Following some military success, the NPFL refused to participate in an Interim Government of National Unity (IGNU) proposed at the First All Liberia Conference in December 1990. During a period of peace from March

1991 to October 1992, the NPFL consolidated its control in northern and central Liberia. On 15 October its forces launched an unsuccessful attack on the capital Monrovia, clashing with a peacekeeping force from the Economic Community of West African States in 1993. Taylor dropped his demand at peace negotiations, which began in Geneva in July 1993, that he should head an interim government. But, against a background of violence increasingly dominated by local warlords, NPFL influence weakened to the extent that in 1994 violence was renewed between the NPFL and breakaway groups.

National Rainbow Coalition

A movement formed by Jesse Jackson in 1983 to organize his attempt to win the 1984 Democratic Party presidential nomination. Jackson attempted to reach beyond a purely black constituency to encompass poor whites, Hispanics, Asians and Native Americans. Although he gained 3.3 million votes in primaries, won two states and had 412 delegates at the 1984 Democratic Convention, the majority of his support came from black voters. In 1988, Jackson had greater success, gaining 6.7 million votes, winning 12 states, and having 1157 delegates at the party convention. The coalition continued to operate as a base for Jackson's involvement in economic, social and civil rights issues.

National Security Volunteers

See Tontons Macoutes.

National Unemployed Movement (NUM)

Formed in the British Caribbean colony of Trinidad in 1934 to lead hunger marches and agitation against growing unemployment. Although it was not a Communist Party movement, the NUM followed the pattern of communist organization among the unemployed in, for example, Britain, the USA and Germany. A similar organization, the Unemployed League, was formed in Jamaica. Hunger marches and unemployed demonstrations had been growing in number since 1933 and the NUM was formed as a radical street movement to encourage radical action and unity between black urban workers and Indian sugar workers. The NUM's leading figures were Clement Payne, Elma Francois, Jim Barette and Jim Headley. Headley had previously been a Young Communist League activist in the USA. In 1935, when the Communist Party internationally shifted away from a concentration on unemployment, the NUM was transformed into a wider-ranging Negro Welfare Cultural and Social Association.

National Urban League

Originally the National League on Urban Conditions Among Negroes, an umbrella body formed in New York in 1911. It was set up to co-ordinate the activities of the Committee for Improving the Industrial Conditions of Negroes in New York, the National League for the Protection of Colored Women and the Committee on Urban Conditions Among Negroes. The need to form the league reflected the problems encountered by black people migrating from the southern USA to the north during the Great Migration. The league concentrated on the social welfare issues of employment, housing, recreation and health rather than taking the political and agitational stance of the National Association for the Advancement of Colored People (NAACP). It did, however, carry influence with government leaders in periods of crisis. It remains in existence as an interracial non-profit-making organization aiming to secure equal opportunities for all racial minorities in the USA.

National Workers' Union (NWU)

Jamaica's second largest trade union, formed in 1952 by the opposition People's National Party (PNP). The union played an important part in the PNP's victory in the 1955 general election. Michael Manley became NWU president in 1984.

NCBWA

See National Congress of British West Africa.

Négritude

A literary movement of the 1930s which originated among French-speaking African and Caribbean writers. The movement reasserted black cultural values and attempted to encourage black people to take pride in their heritage and to study African life and culture. This led logically to widespread protests against the continuation of French colonial rule and the policy of assimilation. The expression *négritude* was first used by the writer and political activist, Aimé Césaire, and was popularized by, among others, Léopold Senghor, later the president of Senegal. Senghor developed the movement's political aspects and characterized African culture as 'Ethiopian', with a conception of reality fundamentally different from that of white culture. *Négritude*, unlike the Universal Negro Improvement Association (UNIA) or Rastafarianism, did not advocate the return to Africa but attempted to encourage African consciousness in people of African descent outside the continent. The movement condemned Christianity as a white colonialist weapon intended to perpetuate the mental enslavement of black people.

Negro American Labor Council

Formed in the USA in May 1960 to work within the broader American union movement to campaign against racism. The council co-operated with a broad range of black organizations to mount the 1963 March on Washington, the main demands of which were jobs and an end to discrimination in industry and the unions.

Negro Political Union

Formed in the United States by Marcus Garvey, leader of the Universal Negro Improvement Association (UNIA), in 1924 to mobilize the black vote in elections held in that year. The union issued a list of approved candidates and mobilized teams of canvassers to encourage black support. The union's activity proved particularly effective in the black areas of Chicago and New York City.

Niagara Movement

A black political organization founded in 1905 in the USA by W. E. B. Du Bois and William Monroe Trotter, at Niagara Falls in Ontario. Based on its 'Declaration of Principles', the movement was formed to conduct a militant campaign for the right to justice, education, voting, the abolition of the Jim Crow laws, equal treatment in the armed forces and enforcement of the Amendments to the US Constitution which purported to guarantee black rights. Its supporters opposed the more conservative outlook of Booker T. Washington and were involved in militant protest against racial discrimination and, in particular, lynching. The movement maintained a small membership until it merged with the National Negro Conference to form the National Association for the Advancement of Colored People (NAACP) in 1909.

Nigerian Farm Settlement Scheme

A government attempt to provide work for school leavers in south-west Nigeria following independence in 1960. The young people were settled in groups of 50 on 10- to 30-hectare farms and encouraged to grow crops with modern agricultural methods and to produce a surplus for sale. The scheme proved expensive and the initial ideas were modified following administrative and technical difficulties.

Nigerian League of Bribe Scorners

Organization active in the British colony of Nigeria in the early 1950s with the object of combating widespread corruption and the practice of 'dashing' (giving a bribe or a tip) in almost every sphere of everyday life. The league's members pledged neither to take nor offer bribes and wore badges with the slogan 'Fight Bribery and Corruption'.

1990 Trust

An organization formed in Britain in 1990 to promote black community development and to encourage African and Asian unity. The trust aims to use black skills and knowledge to address issues affecting the black community, organizes workshops and seminars and disseminates information through a Black Information Link (BLINK). The trust has conducted research and produced briefing papers on multi-racial juries, the British criminal justice system, and a draft Racial Harassment Bill. It has undertaken joint work on specific issues with the National Black Caucus.

NJAC

See National Joint Action Committee.

Nkomati Accord

Non-aggression pact signed on the bordering River Nkomati between Mozambique and South African apartheid government in March 1984. Mozambique agreed to cease providing a haven for African National Congress (ANC) guerrillas attacking South Africa, while South Africa promised to withdraw support from National Resistance Movement (RENAMO) rebels in Mozambique. South Africa later admitted breaking the agreement.

NOI

See Nation of Islam.

Noirisme

A form of *négritude* in Haiti which developed from the 1930s onwards. It was a reaction to both the white racism experienced during the occupation of Haiti by the USA from 1915 to 1934 and the privileged position accorded to mulattos. *Noirisme* asserted the superiority of the African-ness of the black majority population. The movement's supporters opposed the Roman Catholic Church's denunciation of traditional voodoo practices. In 1946 they led protests which ousted the mulatto President Elie Lescot and replaced him with a black president, Dumarsais Estimé. President François Duvalier used *noirisme* to justify repression of his opponents while in power between 1957 and 1971. *Noirisme* as a state ideology was undermined when Duvalier's successor, his son Jean-Claude, married the daughter of a mulatto.

NPFL

See National Patriotic Front of Liberia.

NUM

See National Unemployed Movement.

NWU

See National Workers' Union.

OATUU

See Organisation of African Trade Union Unity.

Operation Black Vote

Campaign launched in Britain in July 1996 to encourage black and Asian citizens to register to vote in the forthcoming general election and in local authority elections. Operation Black Vote was established by the 1990 Trust in co-operation with other campaigning organizations and was supported by two Labour Members of Parliament, Diane Abbott and Bernie Grant.

Ogoniland

See Movement for the Survival of the Ogoni People (MOSOP)

Oil Rivers

Term used by the British from the late-nineteenth century to describe the waterways of the Niger Delta of Eastern Nigeria. The waterways were essential to the traditional trading system of the region, being used to transport produce from the interior markets to the coastal ports. At the start of the nineteenth century commercial trade began to replace the trade in slaves in the region and the British became involved in the lucrative palm-oil trade which had flourished since the 1790s. Until the arrival of the British colonialists the trade was regulated by the kings of the Delta states. The region was declared a British Protectorate in 1887 when the British kidnapped and deported the most powerful of the trader kings, King Jaja of Opobo.

Opendaal Plan

The division of South West Africa (now Namibia) by the South African authorities in 1964 into twelve population groups – Rehoboth Basters, Namas, Damaras, Hereros, Kaokovelders, Ovambos, Kavangos, Caprivians, Tswanas, Bushmen, Whites and Coloureds – each of whom, apart from the Coloureds, was to be allocated a homeland similar to those being imposed under the apartheid regime in South Africa.

Operation Feed the Nation

Programme introduced by the Nigerian military ruler, General Obasanjo, in May 1976 to end the country's dependence on food imports. He attempted to encourage agricultural self-sufficiency through the provision of artificial fertilizers and insecticides at subsidized prices. The attempt was largely unsuccessful and in February 1980, President Shagari replaced it with a National Council on Green Revolution with similar aims.

Order of Blood Men

Organization established by slaves on the Qua River in the city-state of Calabar in the eastern Niger Delta, West Africa in 1850. The society was a means of self-protection for slaves who lived and worked on the palm plantations against the oppression and cruelty of their owners. Through organized protests, the Blood Men brought an end to the ritual funeral sacrifice of slaves which traditionally took place when a king died. From 1852 thousands of slaves gathered in Calabar on the death of a king or prominent person to prevent the sacrifice and succeeded in ending the practice.

Organisation of African Trade Union Unity (OATUU)

Founded in 1973 to overcome divisions in the African labour movement. Within three years, 67 trade-union bodies from 52 countries were affiliated, with only white organizations remaining outside. OATUU has its headquarters in Accra, Ghana, and is the only African labour organization recognized by the Organization for African Unity (OAU).

Osagyefo

'He who is successful in war', an honorific title adopted in the early 1960s by Kwame Nkrumah, leader of the campaign against British colonialism and president of Ghana from 1960 to 1966.

The Pan African

The monthly journal of the Pan-African Association, published and edited in London by Henry Sylvester Williams. The first issue appeared in 1902 but, despite efforts to arouse interest in Africa, the Caribbean and the USA, *The Pan-African* ceased publication after six issues.

Pan-Africanism

A body of thought and action among African people and people of the African diaspora which has two main strands. The African strand is directed towards the liberation and unity of the African continent itself. An international strand looks to the liberation, unity and solidarity of African people throughout the world. There are two identifiable approaches within the second strand. The first confines itself to international black solidarity. The second seeks as its ultimate aim the return of the African diaspora to the continent of Africa. The earliest manifestation of Pan-Africanism came with Ethiopianism and the African Independent Churches, formed in response to the white racism in the Christian churches. A Pan-African Association was founded in London following the first Pan-African Conference of 1901, with Henry Sylvester Williams as its leading figure and the composer Samuel Coleridge-Taylor among its executive members. The ideology of Pan-Africanism was developed in the USA by, for example, Marcus Garvey in the Universal Negro Improvement Association (UNIA) and W. E. B. Du Bois. Further impetus was given by the six meetings of the Pan-African Congress held between 1919 and 1974. However, as the African nations achieved independence, Pan-Africanism lost much of its radicalism. Kwame Nkrumah argued for African unity, but the Organization of African Unity (OAU) appeared to place obstacles in the way of this.

Panther UK

Movement established in Britain in October 1991 by the Militant Tendency, a Trotskyist group which worked within the Labour Party until its expulsion. Panther UK continued in existence when Militant established a separate party, Militant Labour. Panther UK's founder, Colin de Freitas, claimed that the movement modelled itself on the American Black Panther Party. Black Panther co-founder, Bobby Seale, spoke at a meeting in London in October 1992 and urged young blacks to join the movement to combat police harassment and to fight for education, housing and jobs. By 1993 it had an estimated 500 members. There was, however, increasing tension between the membership with a specific black agenda and Militant Labour members attempting to direct Panther UK's activities. In October 1993, Militant Labour members were expelled from the movement.

Pass laws

Part of the framework of the South African apartheid system by which all black people over 16 had to identify themselves and to prove they were entitled to be in areas designated as white. A 'reference book' had to be carried at all times for inspection by the police on demand. Failure to produce a pass led to fines and imprisonment. The Natives' (Abolition of Passes and Co-ordination of Documents) Act of 1952 built on pre-existing legislation of 1895 and 1923. Protests against their imposition reached their peak at the Sharpeville massacre in 1960. In addition to the 'reference book' Africans might also be required to carry a 'poll-tax receipt', a 'lodgers' permit' providing authorization to live in a town, a 'night special pass' giving permission to be out after 9pm, a 'trek pass' giving farm labourers permission to move from one farm to another, and a 'travelling pass' to authorize a train journey. Africans who were otherwise exempt from having to carry these passes were required to obtain an 'exemption pass' to produce to the police on request. The laws were abolished in 1985, when passes were replaced with identity cards (which included racial classification) to be carried by all South Africans.

Passing

A term for the methods used by certain people of African descent to avoid, or at least to alleviate, the discriminatory effects of white racism. Where the characteristics which distinguish people of African descent in white eyes are less distinct, for example, through having light skin and European features, it is possible for an individual to 'cross over', to avoid discrimination in education, employment, housing and social activities. A novel, *The Autobiography of an Ex-Colored Man*, by the American civil rights activist James Weldon Johnson (1871–1938), describing how a light-skinned black passed himself off as a white, was published in 1912.

People's Revolutionary Government (PRG)

The radical regime led by Maurice Bishop on the Caribbean island of Grenada from 1979 to 1983 following the overthrow of the government of Eric Gairy. The PRG was initially a coalition of the New Jewel Movement (NJM) and the business community in which the NJM's Marxism was not immediately in evidence. The US government nevertheless attempted to isolate the PRG, objecting to its links with Cuba and the Soviet Union. In response, the PRG enlarged the newly-formed People's Revolutionary Army and raised a voluntary militia. This led to fears for the security of governments of other islands in the region. There was, however, sympathy for the PRG's attempts to solve the economic and social problems shared throughout the Caribbean. The PRG instituted a literacy programme and attempted to build a free health and education service. It also attempted to construct an infrastructure to shift from a narrowly based economy. The USA, however, claimed that the construction of an international airport (with European as well as Cuban assistance) posed a military threat. The PRG curbed opposition media and rejected parliamentary democracy in favour of grassroots democracy. But support for the PRG waned as it became increasingly ideologically centralized. An internal schism on October 1983, in which Bishop was arrested and murdered, opened the way for a US-backed invasion on 25 October.

People's Liberation Army of Namibia (PLAN)

The military wing of the South West Africa People's Organisation (SWAPO), the leading organization in the struggle for the independence of Namibia from South Africa. SWAPO began armed operations in 1966 with an attack on a military base. PLAN was formally established in 1969 and extensively reorganized in 1973. Bases were established in neighbouring southern Angola in 1975. Despite suffering heavy casualties, PLAN succeeded in a war of attrition against South African forces. A cease-fire in April 1989 led to independence for Namibia in 1990.

Petits blancs

Expression used in Côte d'Ivoire to describe working-class Europeans who undertake manual and other menial work. The expression is sometimes used with reference to all Europeans.

PLAN

See People's Liberation Army of Namibia

Plantocracy

A term coined in Britain to describe British West Indian plantation owners in the late-eighteenth century, reflecting the wealth derived from the high profits on sugar produced by slave labour. The expression survived to be used as a more general description of the British colonialism which survived in the Caribbean into the 1960s.

Poqo

The armed wing of the Pan-Africanist Congress (PAC) in South Africa, formed in 1962 to carry out attacks on the white apartheid regime. Poqo's first action was to organize a riot at Paarl on 22 November 1962 in which two whites were killed and three injured. It continued to mount attacks under the slogan 'One settler, one bullet'. Poqo activity was formally suspended on 16 January 1994 when the PAC agreed to participate in South Africa's first multi-racial elections.

PRG

See People's Revolutionary Government.

Progressive Alliance of Liberia

An opposition grouping which organized protest demonstrations against the raising of rice prices by President Tolbert in 1979. The protests were violently suppressed but the alliance was allowed to register as an official party known as the Progressive People's Party at the end of the year. The subsequent arrest of its leaders when they called for a national strike led to the military coup led by Master Sergeant Doe in 1980.

Protest migrations

An expression used to describe the method adopted in French African colonies to avoid conscription into the colonial armies during World War I. Often, entire villages emptied as the inhabitants left to evade recruitment teams sent out by the colonial authorities. An estimated 62,000 people migrated from Côte d'Ivoire, Guinea, Haut-Sénégal-Niger and Senegal to neighbouring British-controlled territories.

Rastafarianism

From the Amharic 'Ras', a title used by Ethiopian royalty, and 'Tafari', the family name of the king. Rastafarianism is a Christian sect which regards Ethiopia as its spiritual and cultural homeland. Ethiopia's significance is that it was the only African state to retain its independence from European colonialism. Rastafarianism has its roots in the Back-to-Africa movement founded by Marcus Garvey and developed in the 1930s in the poorest areas of Kingston, Jamaica, in the wake of the decline of the Universal Negro Improvement Association (UNIA). The coronation of Emperor Haile Selassie (Ras Tafari) of Ethiopia in 1930 was seen as fulfilment of a biblical prophecy and provided a focus for groups which followed Garvey. Selassie was seen as a living god, although Garvey later denounced him as a tyrant. The coronation was considered to herald the end of the 'exile' of black people and their return to Africa. The early movement adopted the red, green and black colours of the UNIA (derived from the Ethiopian flag). Many of the early adherents formed communes in the hills of central Jamaica. The movement was of little significance outside Jamaica until the 1960s when the rise of the civil rights movement in the USA together with the emergence of black power movements encouraged the assertion of a black identity. By the mid-1970s followers were to be found in Britain, France, Holland, the USA, Australia and New Zealand. The growth of Rastafarianism, and its spread outside Jamaica, was encouraged by the popularity of the singer Bob Marley (1945–81) and the benevolent attitude of the Jamaican politician Michael Manley from 1971 to 1980. Selassie visited Jamaica in 1966. The movement developed a greater ideological sophistication, with many of the former religious elements pushed into the background. There was increased emphasis on black consciousness and dignity. At the same time, Rastafarianism attracted spurious followers who adopted the outward trappings, for example 'dreadlocks', and took advantage of the movement's belief in the therapeutic value of ganja (cannabis). Haile Selassie donated land in Shashemane to the movement in Ethiopia as a settlement. Rastafarianism has experienced persecution, as in Dominica with the 1974 Dread Act and following the 1979 Union Island rising. The movement was also brought into disrepute by the involvement of some supporters in Caribbean drug trafficking.

Real Estate Association

Founded by Benjamin 'Pap' Singleton in Nashville, Tennessee, in 1868. The organization was founded to help black southerners, the Exodusters, migrate to the West following emancipation and the end of the 1861–5 American Civil War. In 1875 the first group led by Singleton founded a black community in Baxter Spring, Kansas. The town of Nicodemus, in Graham County, Kansas, was first settled in 1877 and by 1878 the population had grown to between six and seven hundred.

Recaptives

Captured Africans taken from slave-ships off the coast of West Africa by the Royal Navy patrolling the area following the British abolition of the slave trade in 1807. They were given their freedom and, between 1807 and 1850, 40,000 settled in Sierra Leone and established farming villages.

Representative Government Associations

A Representative Government Association was first formed by T. A. Marryshow in Grenada in 1914 to campaign through public meetings and petitions for elected representation on Legislative Councils and for a federation of the British colonies in the Caribbean. The movement spread through the Caribbean after 1918, led largely by returning ex-servicemen.

Republic of New Africa

Black separatist group founded in the USA when 200 black Americans signed a declaration of independence in Detroit on 31 March 1968. The declaration proclaimed black Americans to be 'forever free and independent of the jurisdiction of the United States'. It went on to demand that the territory of the USA should be divided into a black area and a white area. The National Territory of the Black Nation would be established in Alabama, Georgia, Louisiana, Mississippi and South Carolina. Blacks were also to be paid reparations for slavery. An 'African Community' was formed in Jackson, Mississippi, in 1970 with Imam Abubakan Obadele as president. The headquarters moved to a farm named El Malik (in honour of Malcolm X) in Bolton, Mississippi, in March 1971. A police raid in August culminated in the arrest of eleven members, including Obadele, for murder. Obadele was sentenced to life imprisonment but was released after 20 months. The movement went into decline.

Revolutionary Committee of Mozambique

The Comite Revolucionário de Moçambique (COREMO), formed in 1965 with the encouragement of the Zambian government in an attempt to overcome divisions between the opponents of Portuguese colonial rule. COREMO collapsed when the Front for the Liberation of Mozambique (FRELIMO) withdrew because of the refusal of other members to acknowledge its leadership.

Revolutionary Military Council (RMC)

Formed in Grenada on 19 October 1983, by opponents of the People's Revolutionary Government (PRG) leader Maurice Bishop, following his murder. The 15-strong RMC was nominally headed by General Hudson Austin but effectively controlled by Bishop's former deputy, Bernard Coard. The RMC attempted to improve relations with states in the Caribbean which had become concerned at the PRG's radicalism. Following the US-backed invasion of Grenada on 25 October, Austin, Coard and other RMC members were placed on trial for treason.

RMC
See Revolutionary Military Council.

Revolutionary United Front (RUF)
Libyan-trained guerrilla force led by Foday Sankoh, a former corporal in the Sierra Leone army, imprisoned in 1969 for alleged involvement in an attempted military coup against Siaka Stevens. An RUF force, led by Sierra Leonians who had fought with the National Patriotic Front of Liberia (NPFL) in the early stages of the Liberian civil war, and including mercenaries from Burkina Faso together with exiled dissidents, crossed into Sierra Leone on 23 March 1991. In a two-pronged attack, the RUF sought to win support against the Sierra Leone government from the population of the districts of Pujehan and Kailahun. The RUF executed local traders, government officials and chiefs but met with opposition to its practice of forcibly recruiting young people. RUF forces in the south were driven back by government troops, while, in the north, the RUF was unable to move far from its base. Following the ousting of the Sierra Leone government in a military coup on 27 April 1992, the RUF divided into factions but continued fighting. This was, allegedly, not to further its original political aims but to retain control over mineral wealth, including diamonds, in the Sierra Leone–Liberia border region.

Royal African Company
Company established under Royal Charter in 1673 and granted a monopoly in supplying slaves to Britain for use in its American and Caribbean colonies. Members of the company included the Royal family, the aristocracy, City of London notables and the liberal philosopher John Locke. The monopoly was withdrawn in 1698.

Royal Ethiopian Regiment
A regiment of 300 men raised in 1775 by Lord Dunmore, the Governor of Virginia, to fight on the British side in the American War of Independence. The majority were fugitive slaves who were promised freedom, although this only applied to adult males. Other British army commanders followed Dunmore's example and by the end of the war the number of black loyalist soldiers was approximately 20,000. After the British withdrew, many of these soldiers could not return to their old lives. Some were sent to the West Indies as virtual slaves, others to New York from where some emigrated to Nova Scotia and Canada. Several hundred followed the evacuated army to Britain.

Rozvi ('the destroyers')
Private army of Dombo, the ruler of the Changamire empire, which dominated the Zimbabwe plateau in the late seventeenth century. Dombo led the Rozvi in the conquest of Shona-speaking territories and into northern Transvaal. In a campaign from 1684 to 1696, the Rozvi ousted the Portuguese.

RUF
See Revolutionary United Front.

SACC
See South African Council of Churches.

Saniquellie Declaration
The principle of creating a Community of Independent African States agreed on in the Liberian village of Saniquellie by President Nkrumah of Ghana, President Touré of Guinea and President Tubman of Liberia on 19 July 1959.

Saros

Yoruba term used to describe Africans rescued by the British Anti-Slavery Squadron who settled in the Freetown area of Sierra Leone following the British abolition of the slave trade in 1807. The province was controlled by the Sierra Leone Company which exploited their labour.

SCLC

See Southern Christian Leadership Conference.

Scottsboro Boys

Nine black youths from Scottsboro, Alabama, accused of raping two white women on 25 March 1931. The Scottsboro case became, with the Herndon case, one of the most significant of criminal cases in black American history. The nine (Charlie Weems, Ozie Power, Clarence Norris, Olen Montgomery, Willie Roberson, Haywood Patterson, Andy and Roy Wright, and Eugene Williams) were aged from 13 to 21. Eight of the nine were sentenced to death following the first trial. All were convicted at two further trials but four were released in 1937. The remaining five served long sentences, the final defendant remaining in prison until 1950. Studies have since concluded that all nine were innocent victims of racist justice.

SCWO

See Standing Conference of West Indian Organisations in Great Britain.

Selective Service Act

US legislation in 1917 to raise forces to fight in World War I. The Act effectively restricted the duties black soldiers could undertake. Three million black Americans registered under the Act for military service. Of these 400,000 were drafted into the army, 380,000 of whom were assigned to supply regiments. The majority of those who joined were assigned to non-combatant duties as cooks, labourers, drivers and stevedores. By 1919 only 1200 were commissioned officers. Black Americans were ineligible for service in such elite units as the Marine Corps, the Coast Guard or the Army Aviation Corps.

Seminole Negro Indian Scouts

US military unit formed on 4 July 1870 and recruited from Black Seminoles who returned from self-exile in Mexico. The scouts were led by Chief John Horse and, in return for patrolling the Texas-Mexico border, were guaranteed that their families would be provided with land and food. Three scouts – Sergeant John Ward, Trumpeter Isaac Payne and Private Pompey Factor – were awarded the Congressional Medal of Honor, the highest US bravery award, in 1875. The scouts were formally dissolved in 1914.

Sharpeville Six

Five men and one woman sentenced to death in December 1985 for sharing the 'common purpose' of a crowd which killed a deputy mayor in the Sharpeville township in September 1984. The Six were reprieved by South African President P. W. Botha in November 1988 following international protests.

Sherman expropriation

US General Sherman expropriated over 30 miles of Confederate-owned land along the coastline near Savannah, Georgia, in 1865 as a settlement for freed slaves. Each family was allocated 40 acres and 40,000 people immediately moved into the area. A few months later President Andrew Johnson had the settlers evicted and returned the land to its former owners.

Ship revolts

Resistance to slavery by Africans being taken to America and the Caribbean began on the slave-ships themselves, despite their being guarded, shackled and often weakened by disease. In 1702, 40 slaves and two of the crew were killed when slaves attempted to seize the *Tiger* off the coast of Gambia. In 1753 the *Adventure* was taken over by slaves who ran the ship aground and destroyed it. In October 1776, a Dutch ship was seized by slaves as it was leaving the Gold Coast. In an ensuing battle, the ship exploded, killing 400 people. The best-known successful revolts are the *Little George* (1730), the *Jolly Bachelor* (1740) and the *Amistad* (1839).

Sia

The National Development Agency for the Black Voluntary Sector, established in Britain in 1985 to build an infrastructure for black voluntary organizations. Sia undertakes research, organizes seminars and conferences on issues relevant to the black voluntary sector, provides training and advice on organization and funding, and produces briefing papers and information bulletins.

Sierra Leone Creoles

Descendants of settlers and freed slaves in Sierra Leone. Over a thousand freed slaves settled in the area between 1789 and 1800, the first of whom came from England in 1789, to be joined by Maroons from Nova Scotia in 1792 and Jamaica in 1800. Through intermarriage, the Creoles had become a distinct group, 40,000 strong by 1850. They developed their own language known as Krio. The Sierra Leone Creole culture and values had become closer to Europeans than the indigenous African population and they were active as Christian missionaries, traders and members of the colonial civil service. Their influential position declined following the imposition of a protectorate by the British in 1896.

Slave narratives

Between 1700 and 1945 in the USA over 6000 accounts of the experience of slavery were produced by former slaves. Among the earliest was *The Interesting Narrative of the Life of Olaudah Equiano; or Gustavas Vassa, the African; by Himself* (1790). Important autobiographies written by former slaves in the nineteenth century, many of whom went on to become anti-slavery activists, include William Wells Brown, *Narrative of William W. Brown: a Fugitive Slave* (1842); Frederick Douglass, *My Bondage and My Freedom* (1855); Josiah Henson, *Truth Stranger than Fiction* (1850).

SNCC

See Student Non-violent Coordinating Committee.

Solidarity among African Women

See Akina Mama wá Afrika.

South African Black Alliance

Formed under the chairmanship of Inkatha leader Chief Gatsha Buthelezi, in 1978 between Inkatha, the Inyandza National Movement of KaNgwane, the Labour Party and the Reform Party of the coloured and Indian communities. The alliance was formed following the banning of black consciousness organizations in the wake of the 1976 Soweto uprising. The alliance's objective was to make preparations for drawing up a non-racial constitution for South Africa. But the fear of leaders in the homelands that it was proving too radical weakened the alliance. The Labour Party withdrew when it agreed in 1983 to run candidates for the 'coloured' chamber of a three-tiered parliament of whites, coloureds and Indians proposed by the apartheid regime. The Parliament would exclude black South Africans on the grounds that they were citizens of the homelands.

South African Council of Churches (SACC)

An organization which, when Desmond Tutu was the SACC's first black secretary-general from 1978 to 1984, became a leading movement for black protest against the white apartheid regime. The SACC represented 13 million Christians in South Africa, 80 per cent of whom were black. Tutu during his period in office advocated non-violent resistance against apartheid, racial harmony and warned of violent upheaval if the demands of the black population were not satisfied.

Southern Christian Leadership Conference (SCLC)

A major US civil rights organization led by Martin Luther King Jr. and Ralph Abernathy. The SCLC (known initially as the Southern Negro Leaders' Conference and then the Southern Leadership Conference) emerged in January 1957 from the Montgomery Improvement Association, the body which had led the successful Montgomery bus boycott. It was established in the southern states to campaign for full citizenship rights, equality and integration using non-violent tactics influenced by Gandhi.

South West Africa National Union (SWANU)

Formed in 1959 by Herero students and intellectuals in an attempt to unite the people of South African-controlled South West Africa (now Namibia) in a single national front. Although it was recognized by the Organization of African Unity (OAU) from 1963 to 1965, SWANU was unable to draw the leading liberation movement, the South West Africa People's Organization (SWAPO) into the organization because of SWAPO's advocacy of armed struggle.

Special Action Council

A nine-man group formed in Northern Rhodesia (now Zambia), by the Zambian African National Congress in 1952 to lead the struggle against the creation of the Central African Federation. Five of the group were members of the Trade Union Congress and the council selected strikes as the most effective weapon.

Special Restriction Coloured Alien Seamen Order

Legislation passed in Britain in 1925 to discourage black sailors from entering the country. The order required the compulsory registration of all black seamen with the police, regardless of their nationality.

Special Services Units

US-equipped and -trained counter-insurgency units set up on the eastern Caribbean islands of Dominica, Grenada, St Kitts-Nevis and St Lucia in 1982 under the Regional Security System. The SSUs are intended to defend elected governments against internal subversion but are criticized as a means of repressing popular protest. St Vincent prime minister James Mitchell, disbanded the island's unit in 1984 but in 1987 Grenada prime minister, Herbert Blaize, called in SSUs from other islands for assistance.

SRBs

People with a 'strong rural background', a pejorative expression used by young, Western-educated middle-class professionals in Zimbabwe in the 1990s to describe the leaders and members of the ruling Zimbabwe African National Union (ZANU). In the 1996 presidential election the combined age of the three candidates who originally put themselves forward was 219.

Standing Conference of West Indian Organisations in Great Britain (SCWO)

SCWO was founded in 1958 to act as a representative body for West Indians in Britain, to research into and make representations on issues of specific interest to the black community. The conference disseminates information to statutory and voluntary bodies on the needs of the West Indian community in Britain, campaigns against injustice against groups and individuals, and provides legal and counselling services. The SCWO has a youth section addressing particular issues affecting black youth in Britain.

Student Non-violent Coordinating Committee (SNCC)

US civil rights organization formed in Raleigh, North Carolina, in 1960 by black students to co-ordinate student direct action against racial segregation. The inter-racial but predominantly black SNCC aimed to undertake more militant action than the influential Southern Christian Leadership Conference (SCLC). The SNCC organized Freedom Rides to encourage the desegregation of transportation in 1961 and led voter registration drives in Alabama and Mississippi. In 1964 three SNCC activists (one black and two whites) were murdered in Mississippi. Having been involved in gaining successes in the fields of voting rights and desegregation, by 1966 under the leadership of Stokely Carmichael, the SNCC had taken an increasingly black militant position. In 1968 Carmichael left to join the Black Panther Party. The SNCC took an early involvement in draft resistance against the Vietnam War. Under a new leader, H. Rap Brown, the organization changed its name in 1969 to the Student National Coordinating Committee but the movement subsequently lost momentum.

Swahili

Also known as Kiswahili, from the Arabic 'of the coast'. A Bantu language, widely used in the East African coastal regions. Swahili is Tanzania's official language, the national language of Kenya, and is also used in Uganda and a large part of Zaïre.

SWANU

See South West Africa National Union.

Tacky's Rebellion

A chief of the Asante people, Tacky, and his followers killed 60 whites during a rising in Jamaica in 1760. The militia were called in and many of the rebels surrendered. Tacky and 25 others fled to the hills and were hunted down by the Maroons. In the aftermath of the rising, 400 slaves were killed and 600 deported to Honduras, where they were sold.

Talented tenth

An expression first used in the USA by the cleric and academic, Alexander Crummell, at his opening address to the American Negro Academy in 1897. He believed that the future of black people in the USA depended on an educated elite. The concept was developed by W. E. B. Du Bois in *Dusk of Dawn: An Essay Toward an Autobiography of a Race Concept*. He wrote, 'I believed in the higher education of the Talented tenth who through their knowledge of modern culture could guide the American Negro into a higher civilisation. I knew that without this the Negro would have to accept white leadership . . .'

TANZAM railway

Railway constructed with Chinese aid which runs 1680 kilometres from Zambia to the Tanzanian port of Dar es Salaam, completed in 1975. The link, which provided an outlet for Zambian minerals, was crucial to central and southern African states to avoid dependence for communications on the white rebel regime in Rhodesia (now Zimbabwe).

Tequr Ambesa

See Black Lions.

'To Hell with Paradise'

Speech made in 1972 by the St Vincent Premier, James Mitchell, in which he attacked the growing dominance in the Caribbean of foreign-owned package tourism. Mitchell, who had held the office of Minister of Tourism, advocated the encouragement of indigenous tourism.

Tontons Macoutes

National Security Volunteers (NSV), a paramilitary force formed by President Duvalier of Haiti in 1958 to protect him against a possible military coup and to terrorize his opponents. Tontons Macoutes, as NSV members were generally referred to, was an expression used for 'bogeymen'. Tonton is Creole for 'uncle'. The NSV's thousands of members were nominally under the command of Rosalie 'Madame Max' Adolphe and were responsible for widespread killing and extortion. The NSV was officially dissolved in 1986 following the fall of Jean Claude Duvalier and hundreds were killed by civilians.

TransAfrica

Organization formed in the USA by Randall Robinson in 1977 to influence government foreign policy on political and human rights in Africa and the Caribbean. TransAfrica's activity was largely devoted to opposing the South African apartheid regime and the organization mounted demonstrations in 1984 and 1985 calling for the imposition of economic sanctions. The TransAfrica Forum was set up in 1981 to produce and disseminate information on African and Caribbean issues. Following the end of apartheid, TransAfrica's attention turned to, for example, the human rights violations of the Abacha regime in Nigeria.

Trinidad Workingmen's Association (TWA)

The Trinidad Workingmen's Association (TWA) was formed in 1897 and was initially based on skilled workers, although it attempted to broaden its base by recruiting among the unskilled. Walter Mills became the TWA's first president and was succeeded in 1906 by Alfred Richards. As trade unions were illegal, the TWA concentrated on attempting to gain political reforms rather than on industrial activity. In 1906 it unsuccessfully sought affiliation to the British Labour Party. The TWA split in 1916 but was reunited in 1918 when James Braithwaite became secretary. Membership grew in the post-World War I labour unrest in Trinidad and by 1920 the TWA had an estimated 6000 members. Many of its leading figures were also members of the Universal Negro Improvement Association (UNIA). The TWA successfully negotiated wage increases for dockworkers in the 1919–20 Trinidad general strike and by 1921 was recognized by the British colonial authorities as the representative of the Trinidad workers. In 1921, Captain Arthur Cipriani, a white former officer in the British West Indies Regiment, became the TWA president. He discouraged industrial activity and when trade unions were legalized in 1934, refused to allow the TWA to register as a union. The organization's underlying interest in political activity was acknowledged when it was transformed into the Trinidad Labour Party in 1934.

Truth and Reconciliation Commission

Body established by South African Justice Minister, Dullah Omar, under the chairmanship of Archbishop Desmond Tutu, in 1996 to investigate and report on human rights violations under the white apartheid regime. The Commission had 16 commissioners and three special committees concentrating on 'human rights violations', 'amnesties', and 'reparations'. Although the commission was an attempt to encourage reconciliation in the new South Africa, the proposal to grant amnesties to violators of human rights who confessed their crimes aroused controversy. Some families, including that of black consciousness leader Steve Biko, took court action in May 1996 to prevent the commission granting an amnesty to those who had murdered their relatives.

TWA
See Trinidad Workingmen's Association.

UDF
See United Democratic Front.

UDFN
See United Democratic Front of Nigeria.

Ujamaa
A Swahili word which is translated as 'familyhood' or 'togetherness'. The form of socialism promoted by President Nyerere of Tanzania in 1962. *Ujamaa* derived from an idealistic vision of pre-colonial Africa, and proposed an African socialism based on communal farms and villages, with the emphasis on rural development and a simple lifestyle. The official policy was for land and natural resources to be placed in the hands of the people in village communities. Over eight million farmers were forced into improvised villages but their resistance led to a sharp fall in agricultural production. The policy was moderated in 1977 and in 1987 the failure of *ujamaa* was recognized and there was an official return to the encouragement of individual proprietorship.

Umkhonto we Sizwe (MK)
('Spear of the Nation' in Xhosa) The armed wing of the African National Congress (ANC) formed in 1963. MK activists carried out attacks on economic targets in South Africa. By the 1980s there were an estimated 1000 MK activists in South Africa, with a further 8–10,000 in training camps in Angola, Mozambique and Tanzania. Joe Slovo, the only white member of the ANC national executive, was MK chief of staff until March 1987 when he was replaced by Chris Hani. After the 1994 elections, MK was largely assimilated into the South African National Defence Force.

Understudy policy
(*La politique de double*) Policy of the ruling Haitian mulatto elite of putting a black general in power as a figurehead to win the support of the black population. This came to an end in 1944 when the mulatto president, Elie Lescot, was replaced by a black president, Dumarsais Estimé.

UNIA
See Universal Negro Improvement Association.

United Democratic Front (UDF)
A South African multi-racial anti-apartheid organization formed in August 1983 by a coalition of over 600 bodies, including trade unions, community associations, women's and students' groups, with a combined membership of over 1.5 million. The UDF was effectively the internal arm of the banned and exiled African National Congress (ANC) and Albertina Sisulu was among its most prominent figures. The UDF charter called for a democratic non-racial South Africa and made a number of transitional demands including an end to forced removals of black people to the 'Homelands', the release of all political prisoners, the lifting of all banning orders, the construction of more homes, no rent increases, and an expansion in black education. The UDF mounted a campaign against a new constitution setting up a parliament for

Indians and Coloureds which excluded Africans. There were violent clashes between UDF supporters and those of the Inkatha Freedom Party and the Azanian People's Organisation (AZAPO), the latter objecting to its multi-racial stance. The front's leaders were accused of treason by the white government in 1985 and, although the charges were later dropped, many supporters were arrested under a State of Emergency. The UDF was banned in February 1988 and its role was taken over by the Mass Democratic Movement. Following the lifting of the ban in 1990, the UDF supported the negotiations with the white government which led to the formation of the Government of National Unity in 1994.

United Democratic Front of Nigeria (UDFN)

A coalition of 13 Nigerian pro-democracy groups formed at simultaneous meetings in Oslo and Johannesburg in March 1996 to work for the peaceful restoration of democracy. The Oslo meeting was chaired by Wole Soyinka, winner of the Nobel prize for literature in 1986. The UDFN set out its platform in ten resolutions, among which were a call for the immediate release of all political prisoners by the Abacha government, the imposition of an oil embargo, and a halt to loans to Nigeria by governments and international financial institutions.

United Native African Church

Formed in the British colony of Nigeria in 1891 as a secessionary body from the Anglican Church. The United Native African Church, which followed a historical tradition of African Independent Churches, by insisting on the right to religious self-government, believed that Africans should be evangelized by Africans rather than by Europeans.

Universal Negro Improvement Association (UNIA)

A movement to develop black consciousness and Pan-Africanism founded by Marcus Garvey in Jamaica in 1914, originally as the Universal Negro Improvement and Conservation Association and African Communities League. Unlike his contemporary, W. E. B. Du Bois, Garvey attempted to take his message to the masses rather than the 'talented tenth'. UNIA argued that equality was only possible if black people separated from white society and developed their own states and governments. Its aims, as set out in the UNIA publication *Negro World*, were: '1) to champion Negro nationhood by redemption of Africa; 2) to make the Negro race conscious; 3) to breathe the ideals of manhood and womanhood into every Negro; 4) to advocate self-determination; 5) to make the Negro world conscious; 6) to print all the news that will be interesting and constructive to the Negro; 7) to instil self-help; 8) to inspire racial love and self-respect.' Garvey moved to the USA in 1916 and formed a UNIA branch in New York City which gathered growing support. He announced the formation of a 'Back to Africa' movement, with the slogan 'Africa for the Africans', at the 1920 UNIA convention. In 1922 the UNIA petitioned the League of Nations to place former German colonies in Africa under its control. As part of the programme for self-help, UNIA planned to build a chain of black grocers and restaurants throughout the USA and to form a corps of nurses. A Black Star Fleet was planned for trading between the USA and Africa. To encourage black pride and solidarity, Garvey organized ceremonials and parades and designed a red, black and green UNIA flag. An African Orthodox Church attached to the UNIA represented Christ as black rather than white. By the mid-1920s there were 1120 UNIA branches in over 40 countries, with 50 in Cuba, 30 in Trinidad and 11 in Jamaica. Eight UNIA conventions were held between 1920 and 1938. The first five were held in New York, those of 1929 and 1934 in Jamaica, and the final 1938 convention in Canada. The movement went into decline following Garvey's imprisonment on a mail fraud charge in 1925. However, many of Garvey's ideas were soon adopted within a few years in Jamaica in what became Rastafarianism.

Victoria Federation of Co-operative Unions

Founded in Tanganyika in 1955, the VFCU was the largest co-operative organization in Africa. The main objective was to limit the Asian-owned monopoly buying system.

War Against Indiscipline

Programme introduced by the Nigerian government in 1984 as part of a 'reordering of Nigerian society'. The programme consisted of three measures, introduced in stages and designed to bring a sense of discipline and order into Nigerian society. These were to encourage queuing in shops and at bus stops; instil the work ethic to improve performance in offices; and to inject a sense of nationalism and patriotism in the population.

Watchtower Movement

An African independent church which developed from an organization established in northern Nyasaland (now Malawi) by Elliott Kimwana in 1908, the Church of the Watchtower or Kitawala (Kingdom). The movement gained widespread support throughout Central Africa and encouraged anti-colonialist sentiment, rejecting the authority of chiefs, missionaries and colonial administrators. Many of its supporters set up new villages in an attempt to evade colonial authority. In Northern Rhodesia (now Zambia), Watchtower predicted the collapse of white colonialism and the end of the world. In 1923, 17 of its leaders in Tanganyika (now Tanzania), were imprisoned by the British. By 1926, the movement had become an overtly anti-colonialist organization under the leadership of Tomo Nyirenda in the Belgian Congo (now Zaïre), under the slogan 'Africa for the Africans'. Nyirenda called for the assassination of Europeans and their collaborators among the chiefs. Facing arrest, he fled to Northern Rhodesia (now Zambia) in 1926 but was captured and executed by the British authorities. His death strengthened support for the movement which organized demonstrations against taxation and the chiefs appointed by Europeans.

Wellington Movement

A political movement founded in Transkei, South Africa, by Wellington Butulezi in the early 1920s. Influenced by the Pan-Africanist teachings of Marcus Garvey, Butulezi announced that black Americans would come to South Africa in aircraft to help in the struggle against white domination. As the movement gained influence, Butulezi and his fellow leaders were arrested by the white authorities and deported from the Transkei area. Support for the movement continued into the 1930s and supporters built schools and churches to disseminate the message.

West Africa Regiment

A black British army regiment formed in 1898 for service in West Africa with its headquarters in Sierra Leone. The majority of recruits were from the Mende people of Sierra Leone, where the regiment had its headquarters. The regiment was used by the British to fight in the 1900 Asante Campaign and against German forces in the Cameroons in 1914–15.

West African Frontier Force

A black British military unit formed in 1898 under the control of the Colonial Office. The force was an amalgamation of a number of white-officered forces including the Sierra Leone Frontier Force, the Gold Coast Constabulary and the Lagos Hausas. The force was first used by the British against the Asante in what is now Nigeria in 1901. At the outbreak of World War I in 1914 the force comprised the Nigeria Regiment, the Gold Coast Regiment, the Sierra Leone Battalion and the Gambia Company and was made up of infantry and artillery. It was used by the British against German forces in the Cameroons. In 1928 Royal was added to the force's title. As the British territories gained independence, the force laid the basis for their armies. The Gold Coast Regiment was enlarged into the Ghana Regiment of Infantry in 1957 and the Sierra Leone Battalion became the Sierra Leone Military Force in 1961.

West Indian Gazette

Newspaper founded in London in March 1958 as the weekly *West Indian Gazette and Afro-Asian Caribbean News*, edited by Claudia Jones. The first issue of the *Gazette* said that black people in Britain 'form a community with its own special wants and problems which our own paper alone would allow us to meet'. It contained news about discrimination, race relations and black achievements in Britain as well as reports of developments in Africa, the Caribbean and the USA. Within two years of first appearing, the *Gazette* had a circulation of 15,000. The *Gazette* was instrumental in organizing the first 'Caribbean Carnival' in London in January 1959. The *Gazette* ceased publication following Jones's death in 1964.

West India Regiment

Regiment of the British army with black soldiers and white officers which was in continual existence from 1795 to 1927. The 1st Battalion was originally raised in British North America as the South Carolina Regiment (Blacks) in 1778 but later looked to Jamaica for recruits. The 2nd Battalion was originally formed as St Vincent's Black Rangers in 1792 and then recruited mainly in Barbados. By 1800 there were twelve battalions throughout the Caribbean. Until 1808 many of the recruits were slaves. The British government had the right to have first selection of slaves landing in the Caribbean. From 1795 to 1808, 13,500 men were purchased for army service at a cost of one million pounds. At the end of the Napoleonic Wars in 1815, the regiment reverted to the original two battalions which for much of the century were garrisoned in Jamaica and Sierra Leone. A third battalion was raised in 1840, disbanded in 1870, raised again in 1897 and disbanded in 1904. During World War I the 2nd battalion was in action against German forces in the East African campaign. The regiment was reduced to one battalion in 1920 and disbanded in 1927. Among the West India Regiment's battle honours were Martinique (1809), Guadeloupe (1810), New Orleans (1814), West Africa (1887), Sierra Leone (1898), Cameroons (1915), East Africa (1916). Two members were awarded Victoria Crosses for bravery in The Gambia. Pioneer Samuel Hodges, from the British Virgin Islands, won his in 1866 and Lance Corporal William Gordon, a Jamaican, was awarded the medal in 1892. The regiment was revived from 1959 to 1962 under the West Indies Federation.

World Community of Al-Islam in the West

See Nation of Islam (NOI).

Xuma-Dadoo-Naicker Pact

Signed in 1946 by the presidents of the African National Congress (ANC), the Transvaal Indian Congress and the Natal

Indian Congress to initiate co-operation between the ANC and the South African Indian Congress in activity against the white government. In 1952 the participants launched a Defiance of Unjust Law Campaign (the 'Defiance Campaign'). The organization was proscribed by the government in 1953.

YBA
See Young Baganda Association.

YKA
See Young Kavirondo Association.

Young Baganda Association (YBA)
The YBA was established in Uganda in 1919 among young Catholic and Muslim men who had been active in protests against chiefs appointed by the British colonial authorities under the Buganda Agreement of 1900. The chiefs were accused of acting as collaborators with the British. The YBA was formed by Z. K. Sentongo, a prolific writer of political pamphlets. The association's initial aims were to work for the improvement of Uganda, to campaign for the removal of restrictions imposed by the British on African economic activity and to encourage education. However, in 1921 the YBA accused local Asians of exploiting the Africans and in 1922 called for the establishment of a republic and the removal of the Kabaka of Buganda, the country's monarch. The association went into decline following the imprisonment of three of its members for their attacks on the Kabaka and the chiefs and the offer of official positions to other members.

Young Kavirondo Association (YKA)
Established in Kenya on 23 December 1921 following the change in the area's status from the British East African Protectorate into the Crown Colony of Kenya. This aroused fears that African land in west Kenya would be acquired by European settlers. The YKA was formed under the leadership of Jonathan Okwiri, Benjamin Owuor Gumba and Simeon Nyende. The association called for the abolition of the identity card (kipande) Africans were forced to carry, a reduction in hut and poll tax, an end to forced labour and the granting of land rights. The colonial authorities ignored their demands but, afraid of the political potential of the organization, persuaded the YKA to accept a white missionary, Archdeacon Owen, as president. He changed the YKA's title to the Kavirondo Taxpayers' Welfare Association and effectively depoliticized it. The association split into Luo and Abaluyia factions in 1931. The Luo wing, still under Owen's control, survived until 1944.

ZANLA
See Zimbabwe African National Liberation Army.

Zimbabwe African National Liberation Army (ZANLA)
The military wing of the Zimbabwe African National Union (ZANU). ZANLA was the leading guerrilla force during the struggle for the overthrow of the white separatist Rhodesian government and the independence of Zimbabwe. Supported and initially trained by China, ZANLA was based in neighbouring Zambia and began operating in April 1966. In 1972, ZANLA moved its base to Mozambique and co-operated with the Front for the Liberation of Mozambique (FRELIMO) guerrillas against the Portuguese colonial authorities. ZANLA received growing assistance following Mozambique's independence in 1975. ZANLA was amalgamated with the Zimbabwe People's Revolutionary Army (ZIPRA) and the Rhodesian army to form the Zimbabwe Army following independence in 1980.

Zimbabwe People's Revolutionary Army (ZIPRA)

Military wing of the Zimbabwe African People's Union (ZAPU) during the fight for Zimbabwe's liberation from white rule. Based in neighbouring Zambia, ZIPRA was supplied with weapons by the Soviet bloc. It began military operations in 1966 but was not as prominent as the force deployed by the Zimbabwe African National Liberation Army (ZANLA). Following independence in 1980, ZIPRA was amalgamated with ZANLA and the Rhodesian army to form the Zimbabwe army.

ZIPRA

See Zimbabwe People's Revolutionary Army.

COLONIALISM, LIBERATION AND WAR

Note: Each section is arranged in chronological order.

RESISTANCE TO COLONIALISM

Asante *1821–31*

BACKGROUND Attempting to assert a protectorate imposed on the Fanti people on the Gold Coast (now Ghana), a British force under the governor, Major-General Sir Charles McCarthy, entered Asante in 1821.

MAIN EVENTS The British force was surrounded and defeated at the battle of Accra in 1824 and McCarthy was killed. In a second battle of Accra in 1825, the British prevented an Asante advance on Gold Coast castle. In August 1826 the British defeated the Asante army at the battle of Dodowah.

RESULT In a peace treaty in 1831 the Asante king accepted the British protectorate in the area between the Pra River and the sea.

Basutoland *1851–2*

BACKGROUND Basutoland (now Lesotho) was surrounded by the British Cape Colony in the south, Natal in the east and the Boer Orange Free State in the north and west. In the 1820s the area had been occupied by refugees from Zulu wars who created a Basotho kingdom under King Moshoeshoe. The kingdom had initially no dispute with Boers moving into the area and signed a treaty with Britain preventing further Boer encroachments. But in 1850 there was a boundary dispute.

MAIN EVENTS A small force of British troops (assisted by the Baralong people) was defeated at the battle of Viervoet on 30 June 1851. The British then concentrated a force of soldiers and the Cape Mounted Rifles and at the end of November 1852 advanced on Moshoeshoe's stronghold at Thaba Bosiu. On 20 December the British fought the Basotho army at Berea Mountain.

RESULT Moshoeshoe claimed victory and offered the British peace. The British commander accepted and withdrew from Basotho territory. The British made no further move against Moshoeshoe for a number of years.

Basutoland *1858–68*

BACKGROUND Following frequent boundary disputes, the Basothos led by King Moshoeshoe attempted to resist further Boer advances into their territory from the Orange Free State in 1858.

MAIN EVENTS Following clashes with the Boers in 1858, the governor of the Cape Colony mediated a temporary peace settlement. But in 1865 the Boers mounted an attack on Basotho territory. This was again settled by treaty in April 1866 but the Boers renewed their aggression in 1867, forcing King Moshoeshoe to appeal to the British colonial authorities in South Africa for assistance.

RESULT In March 1868 Britain annexed Basutoland (now Lesotho) to prevent further Boer advances. However, this involved giving up some of the area's most fertile land to settlers.

Asante *1873–4*

BACKGROUND The southern and coastal states of the Gold Coast (now Ghana) had been under British protection (a colonial euphemism for control) since the 1821–31 war. Kofi Karihari attempted to reassert Asante control over the area.

MAIN EVENTS In January 1873 an Asante army under Kofi Karihari attacked and occupied almost all the southern and coastal states which had been under British protection since the 1821–31 war. A British expeditionary force under General Sir Garnet Wolseley drove the Asante forces across the Pra River, met with strong resistance at

Amoafo but captured and burnt the Asante capital, Kumasi, in February 1874.

RESULT By the Treaty of Fomena, the Asante recognized the independence of the vassal states south of the Pra River. This provoked the disintegration of the Asante Confederacy as northern vassal states broke away. Kofi Karihari was deposed as Asantehene.

Egyptian invasion of Ethiopia 1875–6

BACKGROUND Egypt was part of the Turkish empire and Khedive Ismail Pasha was ordered by the Turks in 1865 to expand Egyptian territory to the east.

MAIN EVENTS Egyptian forces occupied Suakin and Massawa, threatening Ethiopian access to the sea. When Egypt occupied the port of Harar in 1875, King John II of Ethiopia declared war. Egyptian armies were defeated at the battles of Gundet on 13 November 1875 and Gura on 25 March 1876.

RESULT Ethiopia retained its independence and at the end of the nineteenth century was one of only two countries in sub-Saharan Africa to remain uncolonized.

Basutoland 1879–81

BACKGROUND Following the British annexation of Basutoland (now Lesotho) at the request of Moshoeshoe in 1868, the British handed over administration of the area to the Cape Colony.

MAIN EVENTS In 1879 the Phuti clan resisted imposition of taxes but were defeated on 20 November. In 1880, the colonial administration ordered the Basotho to hand in their weapons under the 1879 Cape Peace Preservation Act. Some leaders complied but Moshoeshoe's son and grandson, Masopha and Lerothodi, refused, opening the 'Gun War'. The colonial forces mobilized in

September 1880. The Basotho responded by besieging Mafeking in September and Maseru in October. But on 22 October Lerothodi's village was captured and hostilities were ended when Masopha made an armistice in February 1881.

RESULT Britain assumed control over Basutoland and made it a Crown Colony in 1884, with joint government by a British commissioner and the paramount chief. A clause in the agreement said that no white should be able to acquire land in the area. The Basotho were allowed to retain their weapons.

Zulu resistance 1879–1906

BACKGROUND In December 1878 the governor of the British Cape Colony (now part of South Africa) issued an ultimatum to Cetewayo, the Zulu leader, demanding the dismantling of his army. Cetewayo refused.

MAIN EVENTS On 11 January 1879, a British force under Lord Chelmsford entered Zulu territory. Of the 16,000 strong army, 9000 were Africans. The Zulu army numbered 50,000. Chelmsford divided his forces into three and one section suffered the heaviest defeat inflicted on a British force in colonial warfare at Isandhlwana on 22 January. On the same day 4500 attacked the British at Rorke's Drift. Chelmsford launched a second invasion and inflicted a decisive defeat on the Zulu army at Ulundi on 4 July 1879. Cetewayo was captured on 27 August.

RESULT The Zulu kingdom was effectively destroyed. The British annexed Zulu territory in 1887 and absorbed it into the Cape Colony in 1897. The Zulu people attempted to resist the imposition of a poll tax in 1906 but were defeated at the battle of Mhome Gorge on 10 July 1906.

Abushiri's Rebellion 1880–90

MAIN EVENTS In September 1888, German attempts to collect trade revenues along the East African coastal belt (now Tanzania) led to armed resistance under Abushiri bin Salimu bin Abushiri al-Harthi and Heri. In the early stages, the rebels successfully repelled the German occupiers. The Germans countered with a large mercenary force of Turkish police, Nubian, Sudanese, Somalis and Zulus. By 1889 Abushiri was forced to retreat to the interior. In December 1889 Abushiri was captured and hanged when he was betrayed. Heri then fled to the interior where his forces continued a guerrilla campaign against the Germans.

RESULT Heri was eventually defeated in 1890 and forced to negotiate a settlement when his troops were reduced to starvation. He went into exile in Zanzibar where he died. Germany retained control over the area until its defeat in World War I.

First Mandinka War 1882–6

BACKGROUND In the late-nineteenth century French colonial expansion led to a collision with the expanding Mandinka empire in the Upper Niger region of West Africa (now Côte d'Ivoire). The empire, ruled by Samori Ture, controlled the trade routes to the interior. Having occupied the territory, the French began constructing a railway to secure French trading interests. In 1882 the French ordered Samori to leave Kenyeran, an important northern trading centre.

MAIN EVENTS The French attacked when Samori refused to obey their order to withdraw. The Mandinka army, one of the most powerful in the region, consisted of over 30,000 infantry and 3000 cavalry and was equipped with modern rifles. Samori repulsed the French attack but was unable to win a decisive victory and expel the invaders from the country because of his preoccupation with a conflict with the neighbouring Tukolor empire.

RESULT Samori signed a peace treaty with the French in 1886, giving up part of his territory on the left bank of the River Niger and agreeing to place the remainder under French protection.

Second Mandinka War 1891–8

BACKGROUND Under a treaty negotiated in 1886, the Mandinka empire had agreed to accept a French protectorate. The French broke the terms of the agreement by supplying weapons to the empire's external enemies and encouraging internal rebellion. The empire's leader, Samori Ture, withdrew from the agreement.

MAIN EVENTS In 1891 the French invaded Mandinka from the north. Samori's forces retreated east, destroying crops and villages, forcing the French to halt their advance. The Mandinka army, reduced to an elite numbering 2500, was forced to fight a renewed French invasion when its line of retreat was blocked by the British occupation of Asante. Samori was defeated and retreated again, intending to reconstruct the empire. Between 1895–8 he conquered the Abron kingdom and western Gonja but caught between French and British forces, he was defeated by the French and captured at Guelemou on 29 September 1898.

RESULT The power of the Mandinka empire was completely broken by French power and the area remained a French colony until 1960. Samori was exiled to Gabon where he died in 1900.

Asante 1895–6

BACKGROUND The Asante Asantehene, Prempeh I, reunited the Asante Confederacy following its collapse after the 1873–4 war with the British. This threatened British control of the Gold Coast (now Ghana).

MAIN EVENTS In 1895 Britain attempted to place Asante under its protection. Prempeh refused, rejected the treaty negotiated with the British in 1874 and sent a mission to London for discussion. The British government refused to meet the delegation. A British expeditionary force under Sir Francis Scott entered the Asante capital, Kumasi, without resistance on 17 January 1896.

RESULT Prempeh accepted that Asante would become a British protectorate but he, his mother and brother were arrested and deported to Sierra Leone and then to the Seychelles in 1900.

Hehe war *1891–8*

BACKGROUND In the late 1880s, the Hehe state under the leadership of Mkwawa came into conflict with German colonialism in East Africa (now Tanzania). The Germans objected to the levying of customs duties on trade caravans passing through Hehe territory. Mkwawa responded to a summons to meet the German colonial administrator by closing a trade route.

MAIN EVENTS In 1891, rejecting Mkwawa's offer of negotiations, the Germans sent a punitive expedition against the Hehe. Mkwawa ambushed the German force, killing 200 African troops, 100 porters and ten Europeans. The Hehe, armed with spears, lost 700 soldiers. The Hehe continued their resistance from a fortress at Kalanga in Uhehe province. When this was captured by a second German force in 1894, Mkwawa escaped and began a guerrilla war. German tactics of poisoning water supplies and burning homes and crops led to starvation and disease and forced Mkwawa's army to surrender in 1898. Mkwawa committed suicide to avoid capture.

RESULT The German colonial administration claimed that it had liberated the Hehe from a savage dictator but were careful in their relations with his successors. Germany retained control of the colony until its defeat in World War I.

Ndebele–Shona war of resistance (the First Chimurenga) *1896–1903*

BACKGROUND A British colonial expedition led by Cecil Rhodes occupied Mashonaland (now part of Zimbabwe) in 1890. The occupation was initially accepted by the Shona people as protection from the neighbouring Ndebele. However, the British proceeded to exploit Shona labour and impose both taxation and the racist 'Native laws' in force in South Africa.

MAIN EVENTS The Chimurenga began in Matabeleland on 20 March 1896 with the killing of an African police officer employed by the British South Africa Company (BSAC). Two days later seven Europeans were killed in Essexvale. The revolt spread rapidly through Matabeleland and Mashonaland and by the end of the month 100 Europeans were dead. The BSAC raised a Matabeleland Relief Force – with 2000 white and 600 African troops – and guerrilla war continued to December 1896, in which the British force destroyed African crops and cattle. Rhodes opened negotiations with the Ndebele which lasted from August 1897 to January 1898, when agreement was reached. Rhodes then turned to confronting the Shona resistance that had been raging since June 1896. Resistance was led by traditional priests, the custodians of Shona traditions, who urged the people to expel the Europeans. The death on 25 July of Mashayamombe, whose guerrillas had virtually paralysed communications between the main towns of Salisbury and Bulawayo, was a decisive blow. The capture and execution of two paramount chiefs in December 1897 and March 1898 further weakened

Shona resistance. Sporadic resistance continued until 1903.

RESULT In the course of the war of resistance, 8000 Africans died and 450 Europeans, 372 of whom were settlers (one-tenth of the white colonist population). The Second Chimurenga led to the liberation of Zimbabwe from white rule in 1980.

Sierra Leone *1898*

BACKGROUND The British declared Sierra Leone a protectorate in 1896. The British attempts to consolidate colonial control – the appointment of district commissioners, the abolition of slavery and the slave trade, the confiscation of unused land for settlement, and the undermining of traditional leaders – met with increased resistance. In 1898, the authorities attempted to levy a house tax. The Temne leaders' attempts to negotiate with the British were rejected.

MAIN EVENTS A British attempt in February 1898 to collect the tax at Port Loko, close to the area ruled by Bai Bureh, a leading Temne ruler, was taken as a provocation. Under Bai Bureh's leadership, the Temne opened an effective, skilful guerrilla war against the British forces, largely made up of the West India Regiment. The Mende people in the south of the country launched attacks on whites, Creoles and Africans who co-operated with the British authorities. In May 1898 Temne forces were within 30 miles of the capital, Freetown, and were pushed back by six companies of the West India Regiment despatched from Lagos. Further resistance was ended by British attacks on villages.

RESULT Bai Bureh escaped and was not captured until 1908. The British colonial authorities, although they retained control of Sierra Leone until independence in 1961,

recognized that the resistance represented a growing political consciousness.

Asante *1900*

MAIN EVENTS In April 1900 a group of Asante attempted to recapture the Golden Stool, the symbol of Asante royalty stolen by the British. The attempt was defeated but led to a general rising against the British in which Kumasi was besieged. A British force – consisting of the West India Regiment, the West African Frontier Force, the Central African Frontier Force and the West African Regiment – relieved Kumasi on 15 July after a battle in which it lost 122 dead and 733 wounded. Asante casualties are not known.

RESULT The British consolidated their hold on what became the Gold Coast colony (now Ghana).

Herero-Nama rising *1904-7*

BACKGROUND Germany took South West Africa (now Namibia) as a protectorate in 1884. The Herero people initially accepted this, although many Nama people resisted between 1890 and 1894. However, the Hereros resented the increasing loss of land to German settlers.

MAIN EVENTS The Herero people's rising against German colonialism began in January 1904 and met with early success – killing 100 Germans – with the element of surprise. The arrival of German reinforcements, bringing their strength up to 10,000 with machine guns, transformed the situation. The Hereros were forced back to the Waterberg Mountains and decisively defeated at the battle of Hamakar. Following the defeat, the Herero people attempted to flee through German lines, to the north to Ovamboland and to the east to British-controlled Bechuanaland. The proclamation of the German commander, General von Trotha, calling for the extermination of every

Herero opened a genocidal massacre. Of a population of 80,000, 65,000 Hereros died in the rising and in the massacre that followed. The Nama people had meanwhile risen in October 1907, too late to affect the Herero rising. Of a Nama population of 20,000, over half were killed by the Germans.

RESULT When the Germans realized they were destroying a source of cheap labour, the massacre ended. All Herero and Nama land and cattle were confiscated by the colonial authorities and the population were forced to work for white employers. African ethnic organizations and traditional religions were banned. The colony came under British control in 1915 and remained under martial law until 1921. An incidental effect was the inspiration the Herero rising gave to Ovambos living in Angola. In a short-lived rising in 1907, the Ovambo people ambushed a Portuguese military column, killing over 250 troops.

Maji Maji rising   *1905–7*

BACKGROUND In the early-twentieth century, there was popular resentment in the German colony in East Africa (now Tanzania) to the governor's attempt to force the establishment of cotton plantations, to the imposition of a hut tax, to the encouragement of the spread of Arab influence and to the abuses of German soldiers. Kinjikitile Nwagle, a leader of the Kolelo cult, preached resistance to German domination. In 1904 he began distributing a mixture of water and flour called maji to his followers, saying that it would protect them against German bullets.

MAIN EVENTS Resistance began in July 1905 in the south of the country with a spontaneous rebellion which spread over a wide area. German plantations, missions and the town of Samanga were destroyed. Taken by surprise, European planters and African

officials were killed. Nwagle, who had not been involved in the events, was captured and hanged in August 1905. The Ngoni people joined the rising in September but, facing superior weapons, the rebels suffered heavy casualties. The Ngoni then adopted guerrilla tactics but were weakened by the loss of their leader Chabruma. Resistance was finally crushed with the aid of Zulu, Sudanese and Somali mercenaries in 1907. The rebels lost 26,000 in battle and a further 50,000 died from starvation and disease brought on by the German scorched-earth policy.

RESULT The colonial administration abandoned attempts to enforce cotton production and allowed Africans to produce other cash crops. Forced labour for Europeans was also abolished. Traditional leaders were replaced by European-educated Africans.

Italian invasion of Ethiopia *1935–6*

BACKGROUND Following a border clash between Italian and Ethiopian forces at the Wal Wal Well in 1935, Italy demanded an apology, Ethiopia's recognition of Italian sovereignty in the area and payment of compensation. Emperor Haile Selassie refused and appealed to the League of Nations.

MAIN EVENTS Italian forces under General de Bono invaded Ethiopia on 3 October 1935 and, although the poorly armed Ethiopian army put up strong resistance, captured Adowa (the scene of an Italian defeat in 1896) on 6 October after an air and artillery bombardment. On 7 October, Italy was accused of aggression by the League of Nations. Following the capture of the fortress of Makalle on 8 November the Italian offensive slowed until its army was reorganized by Field Marshal Petro Badaglio in early 1936. In April and May 1936 the Italians used air bombing and poison gas against an Ethiopian counterattack. The capital Addis Ababa fell to the Italians on 5 May and Emperor Haile Selassie fled the country.

RESULT On 9 May Italy announced the annexation of Ethiopia and its amalgamation with Eritrea and Italian Somaliland to form Italian East Africa. Ethiopia remained under Italian occupation until 1941, when British forces restored Haile Selassie to his throne.

LIBERATION WARS

Haiti war of independence 1791–1804

BACKGROUND In 1790 the white rulers of the French Caribbean colony of Sainte Domingue (now Haiti), resisted a decision by the revolutionary French National Assembly to grant citizenship rights to the mulatto population and brutally crushed a mulatto rising. In 1791 French troops arriving in Port-au-Prince informed slaves that the National Assembly had abolished slavery.

MAIN EVENTS On 14 August 1791, delegates from over 100 plantations met under the leadership of Boukman and agreed on a slave rebellion. The rising opened in the Northern Province on 22 August and in the next two months 100,000 slaves destroyed over a thousand plantations and killed 2000 whites. Over 10,000 slaves died, among them Boukman. He was succeeded as leader in October 1791 by François Toussaint (L'Ouverture). Toussaint trained and equipped a guerrilla army which held the rural areas while the white colonists held the main towns. A civil war broke out between the whites following the execution of the French King Louis XVI in January 1793. In June 3000 slaves led by Macaya massacred 3000 whites in Le Cap, forcing 10,000 to flee as refugees to the USA. A weakened

French commissioner announced the abolition of slavery in August 1793 but a 60,000-strong British expeditionary force landed in the following month and began its restoration. In August 1797, Toussaint ordered the French commissioner to leave the colony and turned to deal with the British forts along the western seaboard. The British lost 40,000 men from disease and by February 1798, Toussaint's 16,000-strong army had captured the majority of the British-held towns. The British agreed to leave the island by treaty in June 1799. The rebels then faced a threat from a mulatto army which they pushed back in bloody fighting. On 26 January 1801 Toussaint had control of the colony. Of the 30,000 white population only 10,000 remained. A quarter of free blacks and mulattos had died, together with 100,000 slaves. Toussaint announced the abolition of slavery but, in a weakened economy, they were forced to remain on the plantations unless they had a permit to leave.

Toussaint introduced a constitution and proclaimed himself governor on 7 July 1801. In September Napoleon Bonaparte ordered the recapture of the colony and despatched an invasion force which landed in February 1802. Toussaint's guerrilla force inflicted heavy casualties on the French, already weakened by disease. Toussaint offered negotiations but was kidnapped at the first meeting on 7 June and taken to France. He died in a prison cell in April 1803. An African-born slave, Jean-Jacques Dessalines, took command of the army and drove the remaining French forces out in November 1803.

RESULT Sainte Domingue declared itself the independent state of Haiti on 1 January 1804. In October, Dessalines was crowned Emperor Jacques I. A constitution promulgated in May 1805 declared that slavery was illegal and that all Haitians, regardless of colour, were to be described as black.

Kenya – Mau Mau rising   *1952–60*

BACKGROUND   Britain declared a protectorate over what became Kenya in 1895 and encouraged European settlement. This faced African resistance from the beginning, particularly among the Kikuyu. In 1944 the Kenya African Union demanded black access to land in the 'White Highlands'. From this emerged the Mau Mau movement, building on long-standing squatter and peasant resistance. In addition, there were significant urban general strikes in Mombasa in 1947 and Nairobi in 1950.

MAIN EVENTS   Although Mau Mau was never effectively organized as a guerrilla army, and received little assistance from outside the country, its activity forced the British authorities to declare a State of Emergency on 20 October 1952. Mau Mau mounted sporadic action against white settlers, but attacks on Kikuyu who refused to give support demonstrated that the rising was as much a Kikuyu civil war as a confrontation with colonialism. Nevertheless, British forces in Kenya (including the King's African Rifles) were expanded to include the Royal Air Force and armoured cars. In 1953 leading Kikuyu allegedly involved with Mau Mau were arrested and in October, nationalist activist Jomo Kenyatta was imprisoned for seven years. At the battle of Aberdeen Forest on 15 June 1953, British forces killed 125 Mau Mau members, bringing the total killed since October 1952 to a thousand. The British instituted a 'villagization' policy to isolate Mau Mau and deported Kikuyu, Embu and Meru workers from the main towns. By the end of 1954 over 150,000 Africans were detained in brutal conditions. A 4000-strong Mau Mau force was broken up in the Mount Kenya and Aberdare Forest areas between February and June 1955 and, claiming that the guerrillas had been defeated, Britain began reducing its forces in September. The

British claimed that since 1952, 10,000 Mau Mau members had been killed and over a thousand had surrendered. However, the State of Emergency remained in force until 12 January 1960. Official estimates of Mau Mau deaths were 11,000. Security forces casualties were 534 Africans killed and 465 wounded, 63 Europeans killed and 102 wounded. Civilian deaths were 1817 Africans, 32 Europeans and 26 Asians.

RESULT   Whatever the military effectiveness of Mau Mau, the colonial authorities were compelled to make reforms. The Swynerton Plan of 1954 proposed changes in land-holding and the Lyttleton Constitution introduced elements of multi-racial representation. The Kenya African National Union won elections to the Legislative Council in 1961 but would not take office until Kenyatta was released. His release came on 14 August 1961 and Kenyatta took over as KANU leader. On 1 June 1963 he was appointed Prime Minister and Kenya became independent on 12 December 1963. In January 1964 Kenyatta requested British military assistance to suppress what he alleged was a 'Communist' rising.

Cameroon   *1955–62*

BACKGROUND   Germany established the Kamerun protectorate in 1884. After World War I the colony was divided between France and Britain as League of Nations mandated territories and following World War II as United Nations trust territories. In 1948, trade unions in the French section formed the radical national Union of the Cameroon Peoples (UPC), demanding reunification and independence.

MAIN EVENTS   In May 1955, following seven years of political repression by the colonial authorities, the UPC organized demonstrations in the main towns and cities of the French-controlled area. The UPC had organized 450 local committees throughout the country. The resulting riots were heavily suppressed by the French colonial authorities, leading to the deaths of hundreds of people and the banning of the UPC. The party's leader, Ruben Um Nyobé, retreated temporarily to the area under British control. Following the refusal of the colonial authorities to legalize the UPC to enable it to participate in the December 1956 elections, the party established a National Committee of Organisation (CNO) to carry out guerrilla warfare. The CNO concentrated on attacking political opponents, particularly chiefs and African members of the colonial administration, but avoided sabotage and attacks on Europeans. The movement faced ruthless French action and over 15,000 people were killed in Sanaga Maritime province, the scene of the heaviest conflict. In September 1958, Um Nyobé, who had begun to doubt the value of continuing armed struggle, was assassinated. The 3000 CNO guerrillas in Sanaga Maritime Province ended the conflict.

RESULT An internal wing of the UPC was legalized by the French authorities in return for a pledge to co-operate with the government. The external UPC gradually lost influence. A Federal Republic of Cameroon was established on 1 June 1961. The Bamileke people continued a separate rebellion which continued after independence and which was suppressed by 5000 French troops with air support.

South Africa   1961–94

BACKGROUND Following the election of the National Party government in 1948, racism became institutionalized in the apartheid system. The African National Congress (ANC) and the South African Indian Congress (SAIC) organized a defiance campaign of passive civil disobedience in 1952. In 1960 the Pan-Africanist Congress (PAC) mounted an anti-Pass Law campaign that culminated in the Sharpeville massacre in which 67 Africans were killed. Following this both the ANC and the PAC were outlawed. The ANC formed a guerrilla wing, Umkhonto we Sizwe, in 1961 and in 1962 the PAC established Poqo.

MAIN EVENTS Umkhonto we Sizwe (known as MK) tactics were aimed at achieving change through sabotage. The apartheid regime responded with repression, including indefinite detention of opponents, torture and murder. The leading ANC and MK activist, Nelson Mandela, was sentenced to life imprisonment in 1964. The collapse of Portuguese colonialism in Mozambique in 1974 made South Africa more vulnerable to guerrilla attack. Following the African township risings of 1976, most notably in Soweto, many young Africans left to join guerrilla forces operating from bases in neighbouring black states. MK guerrillas mounted sabotage missions on oil installations in the Orange Free State and the Transvaal in June 1980 and attacked a nuclear power station outside Cape Town in December 1982. The South African government responded with attacks on ANC bases in Mozambique and Lesotho. By the mid-1980s the apartheid regime was increasingly threatened internally by strikes and riots. In 1987 South African security forces assassinated ANC members in Swaziland, Botswana and Zambia. In 1988 tactical divisions appeared in the ANC leadership, with one section favouring terrorism and the other attacks on military and police targets combined with diplomacy. In response to attacks on civilian targets in June and July 1988, the South African government intensified its campaign against ANC bases in Zimbabwe, Mozambique and Botswana. With the release of Mandela and the legalization of opposition groups in 1990, the ANC suspended its military action. The PAC, which had continued attacks on civilians, ended its campaign on the eve of the country's first multi-racial elections in April 1994.

RESULT The dismantling of the legislative apparatus of apartheid began in 1990. The ANC gained an overwhelming majority in the 1994 elections and formed a Government of National Unity with the National Party.

Angola 1961–75

BACKGROUND There had been a Portuguese trading presence in the area that became Angola since the fifteenth century but the country did not come under Portuguese domination until the early-twentieth century. In 1951 the Portuguese government attempted to mask the colonial status of the territory by renaming it an 'overseas province'. There were, however, growing demands for independence and the Popular Movement for the Liberation of Angola (MPLA) was formed in December 1956.

MAIN EVENTS The war of independence opened on 3 February 1961 with an attempt by the MPLA to free political prisoners held in the capital, Lusaka. The attack failed but the Portuguese colonial authorities responded with heavy repression in 1961–2, killing thousands of Africans. Over 200 Portuguese soldiers were killed. A second nationalist movement, the National Liberation Front of Angola (FNLA) was established in March 1962 with largely Kongo and Zambo support. The FNLA was seen by the West as a counter to the Marxist–Leninist MPLA. In 1966, a breakaway faction from the FNLA formed the National Union for the Total Independence of Angola (UNITA) in Zambia. Support for the anti-Marxist UNITA was concentrated among the Ovimbundu people of southern

and central Angola. Guerrilla action against the Portuguese began in 1966 with attacks from Katanga province (now Shaba) in the neighbouring Congo (now Zaïre) and from western Zambia. Nationalist guerrillas gradually took control of large areas of eastern Angola, establishing 'liberated areas' which attempted to win popular support through the introduction of basic education and medical services. None of the three nationalist movements was initially able to dominate the independence struggle but in 1967 the MPLA gained Organization of African Unity (OAU) support and received the bulk of aid. In addition, the MPLA was assisted by the Soviet Union, China and the Scandinavian countries. The FNLA received support from China, Romania and Zaïre. The composition of the movements caused friction both between and within them. By 1974 Portuguese forces in the country amounted to 25,000 European and 38,000 African troops. There was a coup in Portugal in April 1974 but the new military government appeared determined to retain control over Angola. However, a new military leadership in September made moves towards negotiating independence. In January 1975, the MPLA, FNLA and UNITA declared an end to their mutual hostility as a preliminary to establishing a unified political programme for an independent Angola.

RESULT Negotiations with the Portuguese government led to the Alvor Agreement of January 1975. Angola was to achieve independence on 11 November 1975 and until then was to be under a transitional MPLA/FNLA/UNITA/Portuguese administration. Conflict between the nationalist movements continued and in July the MPLA, backed by the Soviet bloc and Cuba, drove the FNLA (now supported by South Africa and the USA) from the capital Lusaka. On 23 October a joint South

Africa–FNLA force invaded Angola but was forced back by the MPLA with Cuban weapons. On 5 November Cuba agreed to despatch troops. The MPLA, controlling the capital, declared Angola an independent Marxist–Leninist state on 11 November 1975 but the country faced civil war.

Guinea-Bissau *1963–74*

BACKGROUND Portugal had a trading presence in the area which became known as Guinea-Bissau since the fifteenth century but the country did not come under effective Portuguese domination until the early-twentieth century. There were, however, few European settlers in the country. In 1951 the Portuguese government attempted to mask the colonial status of the territory by renaming it an 'overseas province'. A revolutionary nationalist movement, the African Party for the Independence of Guinea and Cape Verde (PAIGC) was established in 1956 to achieve independence.

MAIN EVENTS In 1963 the PAIGC opened armed resistance against Portuguese occupation. Fighting took the form of raids across the border from Guinea and Senegal, both of which supported the PAIGC campaign. The guerrillas also received military assistance from the Soviet Union and Cuba. At the end of 1970 the Portuguese had 40,000 troops attempting to retain control but within four years the PAIGC forces held two-thirds of the country. Portuguese forces were confined to heavily fortified garrisons in the centre between Bissau and Bafata and were incapable of restoring their military dominance. However, Portuguese efforts to develop the economy created tensions between the movement's mulatto Cape Verdean leadership and African Guineans based in Conakry. This resulted in the assassination of the PAIGC leader, Amilcar Cabral, in January 1973, followed by the

execution of six PAIGC executive members. By 1973 Portugal had lost command of the air with the acquisition of ground-to-air missiles by the PAIGC guerrillas. The PAIGC built up a political infrastructure in its 'liberated zones' and won popular support through the provision of basic educational and medical services. In 1972 the PAIGC was able to hold elections to a national assembly in the area over which it exerted control. The assembly was mandated to make a declaration of independence. Portuguese casualties mounted in 1972 and 1973. Following the 25 April 1974 military coup in Portugal, negotiations were opened between Portuguese and PAIGC commanders. By the end of August Guinea-Bissau was clearly about to become an independent country. PAIGC casualties in the war were estimated at 2000 dead. A thousand members of the Portuguese forces were killed, while a further 30,000 were wounded or incapacitated by disease.

RESULT Guinea-Bissau became independent with the withdrawal of all Portuguese forces on 10 September 1974. Luis Cabral, brother of the founder of the PAIGC, Amilcar Cabral, became president and his government attempted to follow a non-aligned policy under the slogan 'national revolutionary democracy'. President Cabral was overthrown and replaced by João Vieira on 14 November 1980.

Eritrea *1963–91*

BACKGROUND Eritrea was an Italian colony from the nineteenth century until 1941 when it became a British protectorate. In 1952 Eritrea was federated with the Ethiopian empire, with a high degree of political autonomy. But in 1962, Haile Selassie's absorption of Eritrea into the Ethiopian empire as a province provoked resistance.

MAIN EVENTS The Eritrean Liberation Front (ELF) began guerrilla operations in 1963 with support from the Sudan. The movement had a number of successes and achieved international publicity through spectacular aircraft hijackings. But divisions within the independence movement erupted into near civil war in 1970 and in 1972 dissidents formed a breakaway Eritrean People's Liberation Front (EPLF). In 1971, Ethiopia declared martial law in Eritrea and began constructing fortified villages. Following the 1974 revolution in Ethiopia, the ELF and EPLF co-operated in a joint attack on the Eritrean capital, Asmara, almost capturing the city in February 1975. By 1977, with the EPLF advancing from the north and the ELF from the west, most Eritrean towns were in guerrilla hands. Those remaining under Ethiopian control were besieged. But, despite attempts at reunification, serious ethnic and religious divisions kept the two movements divided. This enabled a 100,000-strong Ethiopian army (with Cuban and Soviet support) to advance into Eritrea on 15 May 1978 and to recapture the majority of towns from the guerrillas. In 1980, the ELF split into three factions and, as its significance as a guerrilla force collapsed, the EPLF took on the brunt of the fighting.

Ethiopian forces suffered 30,000 casualties in a fruitless attempt to capture the town of Nacfa in 1982. An offer of negotiations to the EPLF collapsed because of Ethiopia's insistence that in any settlement Eritrea must remain part of Ethiopia. The EPLF launched a successful offensive in 1984, capturing Tessenai in January and destroying a 10,000-strong Ethiopian army in March. Ethiopian troops recaptured the town in August. Meanwhile, in Tigray province, Ethiopia was faced by a guerrilla force trained and armed by the EPLF, the Tigrean People's Liberation Army (TPLA). The EPLF began a new offensive in 1987 and this, allied with a successful TPLA attack, encouraged an attempted coup against Ethiopian President Mengistu in May 1989. He offered negotiations with both movements but by 1991 nothing had resulted from discussions. Faced by rising guerrilla successes, Mengistu fled the country on 21 May 1991. Addis Ababa and the Eritrean capital Asmara fell to the guerrillas.

RESULT Eritrea immediately declared its independence. This was confirmed almost overwhelmingly in a referendum held in the country on 25 April 1993. In February 1994, the EPLF transformed itself into a political party, the People's Front for Democracy and Justice.

Mozambique *1964–74*

BACKGROUND There had been a Portuguese trading presence in the area that became Mozambique since the fifteenth century but the country did not come under Portuguese domination until the early-twentieth century. In 1951 the Portuguese government attempted to mask the colonial status of the territory by renaming it an 'overseas province'. There were, however, growing demands for independence. The Mozambique Liberation Front (FRELIMO) was formed in 1962 and launched a war for independence in 1964.

MAIN EVENTS FRELIMO guerrillas launched their first attacks on the northern provinces of Cabo Delgado and Niassa and by the end of the decade had control over the rural areas. In 1968, guerrillas renewed an offensive against Portuguese garrisons in Tete province, overran them and advanced south against minimal effective resistance. FRELIMO instituted a strategy of creating liberated zones with a local political administration and the introduction of education and health services. In 1969, FRELIMO's president, Eduardo Mondlane, was assassinated by Portuguese agents. He was succeeded by Samora Machel.

By 1971 Portugal had 60,000 troops in Mozambique. When it became clear in 1974 that Mozambique would become independent, white settlers in the capital Lourenço Marques (now Maputo) and in Beira launched abortive risings to prevent the inevitable.

RESULT Following an army coup in Portugal in April 1974, FRELIMO and Portugal negotiated a transitional government. Mozambique became fully independent on 25 June 1975 under President Samora Machel. Almost immediately following independence, opponents of FRELIMO organized in the National Resistance Movement (RENAMO) began a civil war, supported first by the illegal white regime in Rhodesia (now Zimbabwe) and then by South Africa.

Zimbabwe (the Second Chimurenga) *1966–79*

BACKGROUND Southern Rhodesia became a self-governing colony under white control in 1923. On 11 November 1965, reluctant to work towards majority African rule, the white Rhodesian Front made an illegal declaration of independence. There were two major African nationalist groups, the Zimbabwe African People's Union (ZAPU), formed in September 1962, and the breakaway Zimbabwe African National Union (ZANU), formed in August 1963. In 1965 both were operating in exile.

MAIN EVENTS For the African population, the war against the white regime represented the Second Chimurenga ('war of independence'). The ZANU guerrilla campaign – mounted by its military wing, the Chinese-trained Zimbabwe African National Liberation Army (ZANLA) – opened with the 'Battle of Sinoia' in April 1966. ZAPU's military wing – the Soviet-trained Zimbabwe People's Revolutionary Army (ZIPRA) –

began operations in 1966. Both groups were based in neighbouring Zambia. Initial guerrilla operations across the Zambezi River were largely ineffective militarily but were intended to encourage an African spirit of resistance and to persuade Britain, as the colonial power, to intervene. From 1967–9, ZANLA restructured and retrained its forces. The support of members of the African National Congress (ANC) provided the South African apartheid regime with a pretext to assist the Rhodesian forces. In 1972, ZANLA moved its base to Mozambique and launched a well-prepared campaign in north-eastern Rhodesia in December. From 1972 to 1979 ZANLA undertook the bulk of fighting against Rhodesian forces. ZANLA's classical guerrilla tactics weakened the Rhodesian economy, discouraging further white immigration and forcing increased military expenditure. White repression of the African population, including the deportation of thousands into 'protected villages', encouraged further support and recruitment to ZANLA. By 1976 Robert Mugabe had emerged as the leading figure in ZANU while Joshua Nkomo continued to lead ZAPU. In October 1976 the two movements joined forces to form a Popular Front. In 1977 the 'front-line states' of Angola, Botswana, Mozambique, Tanzania and Zambia stepped up assistance to the guerrilla forces with Organization of African Unity (OAU) backing. The war intensified, forcing the white government to impose a curfew in all rural areas and to mount reprisal campaigns, including bombing of ZANU bases in neighbouring states. In June 1979 the country was renamed 'Zimbabwe-Rhodesia', with a transitional government headed by Bishop Abel Muzowera of the United African National Council (UNAC). As casualties and repression mounted, the British government agreed at the

DECOLONIZATION: DATES INDEPENDENCE REGAINED

Country	Colonial power	Independence regained
Angola	Portugal	11 November 1975
Antigua and Barbuda	Britain	1 November 1981
Bahamas	Britain	10 July 1973
Barbados	Britain	30 November 1966
Benin (Dahomey)	France	1 August 1960
Botswana	Britain	30 September 1966
Burkina Faso (Upper Volta)	France	5 August 1960
Burundi	Belgium (UN trusteeship)	1 July 1962
Cameroon	France (UN trusteeship)	1 January 1960
Cape Verde	Portugal	5 July 1975
Central African Republic	France	13 August 1960
Chad Republic	France	11 August 1960
Congo	France	15 August 1960
Côte d'Ivoire	France	7 August 1960
Dominica	Britain	3 November 1978
Equatorial Guinea	Spain	12 October 1968
Eritrea	Ethiopia	25 April 1993
Gabon	France	17 August 1960
The Gambia	Britain	18 February 1965
Ghana	Britain	6 March 1957
Grenada	Britain	7 February 1974
Guinea	France	2 October 1958
Guinea-Bissau	Portugal	10 September 1974
Haiti	France	1 January 1804
Jamaica	Britain	6 August 1962
Kenya	Britain	12 December 1963
Lesotho	Britain	4 October 1966
Liberia	(American Colonization League)	26 July 1847
Malawi	Britain	6 July 1964
Mali	France	20 June 1960

Country	Colonial power	Independence regained
Mozambique	Portugal	25 June 1975
Namibia	South Africa (UN trusteeship)	21 March 1990
Niger	France	3 August 1960
Nigeria	Britain	1 October 1960
Rwanda	Belgium (UN trusteeship)	1 July 1962
St Christopher and Nevis	Britain	19 September 1983
St Lucia	Britain	22 February 1979
St Vincent and the Grenadines	Britain	27 October 1979
São Tomé and Príncipe	Portugal	12 July 1975
Senegal	France	20 June 1960
Sierra Leone	Britain	27 April 1961
Somalia	Britain	1 July 1960
Swaziland	Britain	6 September 1968
Tanzania (Tanganyika)	Britain	9 December 1961
Togo	France	27 April 1960
Trinidad and Tobago	Britain	31 August 1962
Uganda	Britain	9 October 1962
Zaire (the Congo)	Belgium	30 June 1960
Zambia	Britain	24 October 1964
Zanzibar (now Tanzania)	Britain	10 December 1963
Zimbabwe	Britain	18 April 1980

Commonwealth Conference in Lusaka in August 1979 to convene a constitutional conference. An estimated 40,000 people died in the war, including 14,000 guerrillas and 1000 members of the government forces. Of a population of eight million, 1.5 million were displaced in the course of the war.

RESULT The constitutional conference met at Lancaster House in London from 10 September 1979 and negotiated a cease-fire. An agreement signed on 21 December 1979 provided for multi-racial elections to be followed by independence. The country became independent as the Republic of Zimbabwe on 18 April 1980, with Robert Mugabe as prime minister.

Namibia 1966–89

BACKGROUND South West Africa became a German colony in 1884. The territory was occupied by South African forces at the outbreak of World War I in 1914 and came under South African control as a League of Nations mandate in 1920. Despite a United Nations resolution terminating Namibia's trusteeship status, the country was effectively absorbed into South Africa in 1969. This was declared illegal by the United Nations in 1971. The leading nationalist movement, the South West Africa People's Organisation (SWAPO) was formed in 1960. In 1966 SWAPO announced the opening of an armed struggle against South African occupation.

MAIN EVENTS SWAPO's military wing, the People's Liberation Army of Namibia (PLAN), mounted its first action against South African forces in August 1968. South Africa responded by arresting 20 SWAPO leaders and sentencing them to life imprisonment for terrorism. Attempts at an internal settlement were thwarted in 1973 when SWAPO organized a boycott of South African-imposed elections to an Ovambo

legislature. PLAN intensified its military activity in 1975 from bases in Angola following the defeat of the Portuguese. South Africa increased its forces in Namibia to 45,000 and in 1978 killed 750 people in a raid on a SWAPO base at Kassinga in Angola. SWAPO nevertheless agreed to continue negotiations on a United Nations settlement proposal. However, South Africa attempted to impose elections to a national assembly. SWAPO once more mounted a successful boycott. Western mediators attempted in 1982 to encourage negotiations between South Africa and SWAPO but South Africa – using Namibia as a base for its involvement in the Angolan civil war – refused to comply unless Cuban troops were withdrawn from Angola. There were increasing criticisms internationally of human rights violations by South African forces. In 1985 South Africa claimed that PLAN activity was effectively over but by its own figures there were 656 clashes between PLAN and South African forces in 1985 and 476 in the following year. In 1987 PLAN intensified its attacks on areas of Namibia settled by Europeans while South Africa stepped up raids on bases in Angola. In May 1988 Angola, Cuba and South Africa reached agreement on the withdrawal of Cuban and South African troops from Angola and a transition to independence for Namibia. PLAN ended all military action in Namibia in April 1989.

RESULT SWAPO won a majority of seats in Constituent Assembly elections held in November 1989. SWAPO leader Sam Nujoma was elected president in February 1990 and Namibia became an independent state on 21 March 1990. SWAPO went on to a further sweeping victory on the first post-independence elections held in December 1994.

POST-INDEPENDENCE WARS

Congo civil war   *1960–7*

BACKGROUND   After having been the personal possession of King Léopold III, the Congo became a Belgian colony in 1906. Following nationalist demonstrations, Belgium agreed at the January 1960 Brussels Round Table Conference that the Congo would become independent on 30 June 1960. There were, however, disputes between the leading nationalist political groups over whether the independent Congo (now Zaïre) should be a unitary or a federal state.

MAIN EVENTS   Following independence in June 1960 the new state was confronted on 6 July by a military mutiny which succeeded in having Colonel Joseph-Désiré Mobutu appointed army chief of staff. Belgian civil servants and technicians began fleeing the country as the military insurrection spread, prompting the intervention of Belgian troops on 10 July. On 11 July the wealthy mineral-producing province of Katanga (now Shaba) seceded, declaring independence under Moïse Tshombe. Congo prime minister, Patrice Lumumba, appealed for Soviet and United Nations assistance on 14 July. The first UN troops arrived the following day. The government was forced to send troops in an attempt to quell a secessionist revolt in Kasai province on 24 August. As internal political dispute intensified, both President Joseph Kasavubu and Prime Minister Lumumba dismissed one another on 5 September. On 14 September, Colonel Mobutu seized power and ruled through a College of General Commissioners. Mobutu's troops arrested Lumumba and handed him over to the Katangese. Lumumba was murdered on 9 February 1961. In the north-east of the country, Lumumba's supporters claimed to be the legitimate government and formed an administration under Antoine Gizenga. There were then two years of fighting between Mobutu's government, Gizenga's forces and those of Tshombe's Katanga. A new central government was formed under Cyrille Adoula on 1 August 1961 and its forces, together with the UN peacekeeping force, defeated Gizenga in January 1962 and Tshombe in January 1963.

A new phase in the civil war opened with a rising in 1964 by the Mbunda people in Kwilu led by Pierre Mulele allied with Gizenga's Pende people. The effectively organized rising was not finally suppressed by government forces until 1966. Meanwhile, in April 1964 anti-government rebels in the east of the country in Kivu and northern Katanga seized control of a large area around Stanleyville. Moïse Tshombe became prime minister of the now renamed Democratic Republic of the Congo. The Congolese National Army (CNA) succeeded in suppressing the rebellion with the aid of mercenaries and former members of Katanga's army. On 24 November 1965 Colonel Mobutu seized power once more and ended a further rising with mercenary assistance. The mercenaries themselves then threatened the Congolese government but were forced to flee into neighbouring Rwanda.

RESULT   Colonel Mobutu retained power over a relatively united Congo and was elected president in November 1970. The country was renamed the Republic of Zaïre in October 1970. In January 1972 (under the policy of 'authenticity') Mobutu took the name Mobutu Sese Seko and ordered the changing of all European first names, surnames and place names to African names. In 1977 and 1978 Shaba province (formerly Katanga) was twice invaded by anti-Mobutu forces which were ejected with foreign aid.

Kenya v Somali Republic   *1963–7*

BACKGROUND Since independence in 1960, the Somali Republic had claimed the return of what it called its 'lost territories', areas populated by Somalis in Ethiopia, French Somaliland (later Djibouti) and an area of north-eastern Kenya.

MAIN EVENTS Somali and Kenyan troops clashed on the border in March 1963. Diplomatic relations between the two countries were broken in December. Fighting then took the form of a savage guerrilla war fought in north-eastern Kenya with Somali support until 1967.

RESULT Following mediation by President Kenneth Kaunda of Zambia, Somali prime minister, Muhammad Haji Ibrahim Egal signed the Declaration of Arusha on 28 October 1967 and agreed to seek a negotiated settlement of the conflict.

Rwandan civil war   *1963*

BACKGROUND Although they made up only a minority of the population the Tutsis had traditionally dominated Rwanda. In July 1959, King Mutara III died, to be succeeded by King Kigeri V. This triggered a Hutu rising in which half the Tutsi chiefs were dismissed from their posts and a large proportion of the Tutsi population fled to neighbouring Burundi and Uganda. In pre-independence elections held in 1961, the Party of the Movement of Hutu Emancipation (PARMEHUTU) won 77.4 per cent of the vote while the Tutsi National Union of Rwanda (UNAR) took only 16.8 per cent. Rwanda became independent on 1 July 1962 under the control of a Hutu government nominally committed to power sharing. However, Tutsi refugees based in Uganda attempted to regain power in the 'inyenzi' (cockroach) invasion.

MAIN EVENTS A force of over 2000 'inyenzi' crossed into Rwanda from Uganda in November 1963. The initial attack was unsuccessful but the Tutsis went on to capture a military base under construction at Gabo, seizing weapons and vehicles. The force was welcomed by Tutsi refugees encamped at Nyamata, a number of whom joined the invaders. The army advanced to within 12 miles of the capital Kigali but was defeated at the Kanzene bridge on the Nyabarongo River by the Belgian-led Rwandan National Gendarmerie.

RESULT Following the defeat an estimated 10–15,000 Tutsis were massacred, including prominent leaders who had previously been arrested, while thousands more fled the country. Rwanda came under complete Hutu control and PARMEHUTU candidates were elected unopposed in the 1965 and 1969 elections. Hutu–Tutsi conflict continued in Rwanda.

Ethiopia v Somali Republic   *1964*

BACKGROUND Since independence in 1960, the Somali Republic had claimed the return of what it called its 'lost territories', areas populated by Somalis in French Somaliland (later Djibouti), Kenya and Ethiopia. Somalia claimed that Ethiopia had taken territory in the Ogaden desert region as a colony during its nineteenth century expansion and demanded decolonization. Ethiopia saw the issue as one of a loosely delineated frontier which Somalia did not accept.

MAIN EVENTS Following border clashes and a state of intermittent undeclared war, Somali troops entered the Ogaden desert region of Ethiopia on 7 February 1964. The Organization of African Unity (OAU) called for an immediate end to hostilities.

RESULT A cease-fire negotiated by President Ibrahim Abboud of the Sudan came into effect with a withdrawal of forces to the existing border on 30 March 1964. The

Somali government continued to provide support to the Western Somali Liberation Front (WSLF) operating inside Ethiopia.

Chad civil war   *1965–90*

BACKGROUND   In January 1962 President Tombalbaye declared Chad a one-party state. This was accepted in the south of the country, which had filled the bulk of official positions since independence in 1960, but aroused protest in the predominantly Islamic north. In 1965 the Chad National Liberation Front (FROLINAT) was formed under the leadership of Hissène Habré together with a number of smaller separatist groupings.

MAIN EVENTS   The Chad government withstood the first phase of FROLINAT activity from April 1969 to August 1971 with French military assistance. In 1971 Libya began supplying weapons to FROLINAT, helping it become the largest and best-equipped guerrilla force in Africa. Libya signed a treaty of friendship with Chad in 1972 and cut off arms supplies to FROLINAT which, however, continued fighting. Libya occupied the Aozou Strip on Chad's northern border. By the mid-1970s FROLINAT had won control of over half of the country. President Tombalbaye was assassinated in April 1975 and replaced by General Felix Malloum who negotiated a cease-fire with the guerrilla movement. FROLINAT then broke into two factions, the Armed Forces of the North (FAN) under Habré and the Libyan-backed Popular Armed Forces (FAP) led by Goukouni Oueddei. FAP launched an offensive, capturing the northern capital of Faya-Largeau. Following a cease-fire the country was effectively divided between the government and FAP. FAP broke the cease-fire in April 1978 and its advance on the capital N'Djamena was halted only with the arrival of 2000 French legionnaires.

President Malloum appointed Habré prime minister on condition that his FAN forces were absorbed into the Chad army. However, in February 1979 FAN troops clashed with the army in the capital. As clashes between Muslims and Christians raged throughout the country, FAP once more advanced on the capital and fought alongside FAN troops. A number of attempts were made to form a Government of National Unity (GUNT) and the country was effectively divided between eleven separate factions. As fighting erupted once more in the capital and spread into central Chad, refugees began fleeing to neighbouring Cameroon and Nigeria. A treaty negotiated by President Malloum, without the agreement of the GUNT, in June 1980 allowed Libyan involvement in Chad's affairs. A FAN offensive opened on 7 October, while Libya attempted to halt them with bombing. In November FAN was forced from the capital with Libyan, East German and Soviet assistance. The deployment of an Inter-African peacekeeping force (with contingents from Nigeria, Zaïre and Senegal) failed to prevent Habré's forces recapturing the capital on 7 June 1982. FAP's leader, Goukouni Oueddei, fled to Algeria but his forces continued fighting, inflicting an almost decisive defeat on FAN in the north. In June 1983, FAP forces, with Libyan support, controlled the bulk of the Saharan region of Chad. France intervened in August to prevent an advance south. On 24 June, Habré launched a new grouping, the National Union for Independence (UNIR), with a policy of power-sharing in Chad. France and Libya agreed to withdraw their troops in September 1984, but Libyan forces remained in the north, supporting a FAP occupation which effectively divided the country into two. However, in 1986 – following a dispute with Libya – FAP forces changed sides. A united Chad attack in March 1987 forced Libya to withdraw.

RESULT Following the Libyan withdrawal, a new cease-fire between the main factions in Chad was negotiated by the Organization of African Unity (OAU) and signed on 13 September 1987. A government formed by Hissène Habré was overthrown by the Patriotic Salvation Movement under Idriss Deby in 1990. Political parties were legalized in 1991 and an election was scheduled for December 1996.

Nigerian civil war   *1967–70*

BACKGROUND Since independence in 1960, Nigerian politics was riven by ethnic divisions. Following the overthrow of the First Republic in the January 1966 military coup, Ibos living in the Northern Region were attacked by Hausas protesting at Ibo dominance in the military government. Northerners staged a counter-coup in July 1966 and there were massacres of Ibos throughout the country. Ibos began to return to the Eastern Region but in September and October 1966 a further 30,000 were murdered. These events led to increasing pressure for the Eastern Region to secede. On 26 May 1967 the Ibo consultative assembly voted for secession. The Eastern Region military governor, Lieutenant-Colonel Chuckwuemeka Odumegwu Ojukwu, announced the establishment of the Republic of Biafra on 30 May. This led to what Biafra described as 'The War of Biafran Independence' and what the Nigerian government called 'The War of National Unity'.

MAIN EVENTS On 7 July Nigeria mounted a naval blockade on the coast of Biafra while federal troops attacked the country from the north and west. Two days later Biafran troops passed through the Western Region in an attempt to encircle Lagos, the federal capital. Biafran forces met with early successes but by the end of 1967 the conflict had become a brutal war of attrition. Biafra's population was gradually worn down through starvation. Nigeria was supplied with equipment by Britain and the Soviet Union while Biafra received military supplies from France. By mid-1968 the federal forces had achieved a decisive superiority in numbers and equipment. The main towns and the non-Ibo areas of Biafra were overrun by federal troops. Port Harcourt fell on 20 May 1968. Biafra rallied briefly in advancing into the Western Region. But in December federal troops captured Owerri, bringing the airstrip that constituted Biafra's lifeline within artillery range. In January 1970 President Ojukwu fled to Côte d'Ivoire. The war ended on 12 January with a surrender by his deputy, Lieutenant-Colonel Philip Effiong. Military casualties were estimated at 100,000 dead. Unofficial figures put civilian dead at up to two million, the majority of them Ibos killed by starvation.

RESULT Following Biafra's surrender, a new federal structure announced in April 1968 came into force. The four regions were replaced by twelve states, with the Ibo area reabsorbed into Nigeria as the East Central State. Former Biafran military commanders were restored to their positions in the federal army. Ojukwu returned to Nigeria in 1982 following an amnesty.

Invasion of Uganda   *1972*

BACKGROUND President Milton Obote of Uganda was overthrown by Major-General Idi Amin on 25 January 1971. Obote supporters fled to neighbouring Tanzania. President Julius Nyerere accused Amin of racism and of violating human rights and provided support to Ugandan exiles organizing his overthrow.

MAIN EVENTS On 17 September approximately 1000 pro-Obote 'People's Army' guerrillas crossed into Uganda from Tanzania led by the former army chief of staff David Oyite-Ojok and Yoweri Museveni. The guerrillas, mainly former members of the Ugandan army and police, were quickly repulsed by Ugandan forces. The Ugandan air force retaliated by bombing the Tanzanian towns of Bukoba and Mwanza.

RESULT A cease-fire negotiated by President Siad Barre of Somalia came into effect under the Mogadishu Agreement of 5 October 1972. However, guerrilla war continued to the west of Lake Victoria. Libya began supplying troops and military equipment to Uganda and, in 1978, anti-Amin guerrillas invaded Uganda with substantial Tanzanian military support.

Burundian civil war 1972–3

BACKGROUND Burundi became independent from Belgium in 1962. The country was marked by tension between the two main ethnic groups, the Hutus and the minority (but politically dominant) Tutsis. Following an attempted coup in 1965, the Hutu political leadership was executed. In the following year the king, Ntare V, was deposed by his prime minister, Michel Micombero, who declared the country a republic.

MAIN EVENTS In April 1972, a Hutu guerrilla force invaded Burundi and killed over 10,000 Tutsis. During the attempted coup the deposed king Ntare V was executed. The Tutsi-controlled army, with assistance from neighbouring Zaïre, moved against the Hutus, killing over 100,000 and forcing many more to flee the country as refugees. Hutu guerrillas mounted a second attack, invading from Rwanda and Tanzania on 10 May 1973. Burundi responded by entering Tanzania on 29 June and killing a number of people.

RESULT President Mobutu of Zaïre negotiated an agreement between Burundi and Tanzania on 21 July 1973. On 1 November 1976, President Micombero was ousted by Jean-Baptiste Bagaza who himself was overthrown on 3 September 1987. In August 1988 violence broke out in the north of the country with Hutu attacks on the Tutsi minority. The Tutsi-dominated army responded with further massacres of the Hutu population, setting the scene for a civil war that was to erupt in 1994.

Angolan civil war 1975–94

BACKGROUND On 15 January 1975, following 14 years of the war of independence, the three liberation movements – the Popular Movement for the Liberation of Angola (MPLA), the National Union for the Total Independence of Angola (UNITA) and the National Front for the Liberation of Angola (FNLA) – signed an agreement ending Portuguese control over the country. But on 27 March fighting began between MPLA and FNLA forces in the capital Luanda. The MPLA was supported by the Soviet Union and Cuba, while UNITA (and the less significant FNLA) received aid from the USA and military assistance from South Africa.

MAIN EVENTS The MPLA secured control of Luanda in July 1975 and made a formal declaration of Angolan independence on 11 November. It was faced, however, by a rival UNITA/FNLA government in the country's second city, Huambo. MPLA troops captured Huambo on 8 February 1976, forcing the FNLA to withdraw into Zaïre. Three days later the Organization of African Unity (OAU) recognized the MPLA as the legitimate Angolan government. South Africa announced the withdrawal of its forces from the country in March. (In 1985 South Africa admitted that it continued to support

UNITA forces and would continue to do so until Cuban troops were withdrawn.) UNITA mounted a long and bloody guerrilla war against the MPLA government that was inextricably linked with the Cold War. In October 1987 an MPLA attack on the UNITA town of Mavinga was beaten off by South African forces. South Africa followed this up in January 1988 with an attack on Cuito Cuanavale to strengthen the UNITA position but suffered heavy casualties against a well-armed MPLA reinforced by Cuban troops. A formal cease-fire was negotiated on 8 August and by 1 September all South African forces had left Angola. In December 1988 agreement was reached at the United Nations for Soviet and Cuban disengagement.

Negotiations then opened between the MPLA government and UNITA and on 22 June 1989 President Eduardo dos Santos and UNITA leader Jonas Savimbi negotiated a cease-fire. This collapsed and fighting resumed. In April 1991 the MPLA formally abandoned Marxism–Leninism as the state ideology. Cuban troops were finally withdrawn and in May 1991 the MPLA and UNITA negotiated a cease-fire agreement, the Estoril Accord, in Lisbon. This too collapsed but, following a further cease-fire, presidential and legislative elections were held in Angola in September 1992. When it became clear that the MPLA had a significant lead, UNITA resumed fighting. By January 1993 there was full-scale civil war, with a thousand people a day being killed. In March UNITA captured Huambo following a 56-day battle. But UNITA's position was weakened when the USA formally recognized the MPLA government in May. Over 500,000 people were estimated to have been killed in the civil war.

RESULT President dos Santos and Jonas Savimbi signed a peace accord in Lusaka on 29 November 1994, although there were persistent violations of the cease-fire in the ensuing months. On 5 May 1995 Savimbi accepted the post of vice-president but in December negotiations continued to stall as UNITA announced a halt to the demobilization of its forces.

Mozambique civil war   1976–92

BACKGROUND Mozambique became independent from Portugal in 1975 and gave shelter and assistance to the Zimbabwe National Liberation Army in its struggle against the white Rhodesian regime. Rhodesia responded in 1976 by encouraging opponents of the Mozambique Liberation Front (FRELIMO) government to organize the National Resistance Movement (RENAMO).

MAIN EVENTS RENAMO forces guerrilla raids on communications and power links and attacks on development projects had a damaging effect on Mozambique's economy. When Rhodesia became independent as Zimbabwe in 1980, South Africa took over sponsorship of RENAMO and made use of it as a tool for destabilizing black states in the region. In 1982 Zimbabwe despatched troops to help protect road and rail links, together with an economically crucial oil pipeline, from RENAMO attack. On 16 March 1984 Mozambique and South Africa signed the Nkomati Accord by which Mozambique agreed to end support for the African National Congress (ANC) in return for South Africa's withdrawal of support from RENAMO. Mozambique adhered to the terms of the agreement but RENAMO, with the support of elements of the South African security forces, refused to end its attacks. In a major offensive against RENAMO launched in July 1985, government troops captured the rebel headquarters and a number of major bases. Tanzania sent troops to support the FRELIMO government in 1986. RENAMO began a temporary cease-fire in April 1989 to enable food supplies to reach areas affected by famine. In 1990 President Chissano announced FRELIMO's abandonment of Marxism, the end of the one-party state and proposed free elections in 1991. In July negotiations opened in Rome between FRELIMO and RENAMO. But in June 1991, RENAMO forces mounted attacks on the two main towns of Maputo and Beira. However, as the South African government made moves towards the creation of a multi-racial democracy, the support it provided for RENAMO declined. President Chissano and RENAMO leader Afonso Dhlakama reached agreement in August 1992 and signed a formal peace treaty on 4 October, although there were continuing arguments about a final political settlement. Over 800,000 people were estimated to have died in the civil war and 4 million forced to flee as refugees.

RESULT In multi-party elections held in Mozambique in October 1994, FRELIMO candidates took 44 per cent of the vote and RENAMO candidates 38 per cent. RENAMO had initially withdrawn on the eve of the elections but participated following international pressure. Disputes continued in 1995, however, over the allocation of provincial governorships by the FRELIMO government.

Somalia v Ethiopia 1977–8

BACKGROUND In a continuing dispute over Somalia's claim to the Ogaden region of south-east Ethiopia, the two countries had fought a short and indecisive war in 1964. Somalia continued to give support to Western Somali Liberation Front (WSLF) guerrillas. In the wake of the political confusion following the overthrow of Emperor Haile Selassie of Ethiopia in 1974, Somalia encouraged an intensification of WSLF activity.

MAIN EVENTS By early 1977 the WSLF had made significant gains in the Ogaden region. In July units of the Somali army entered Ethiopia to support the WSLF in a major offensive. Ethiopian forces were able to hold back an attack launched on the town of Harar on 23 November with Soviet-supplied tanks and aircraft. The arrival of 16,000 Cuban troops and pilots gave Ethiopia a decisive advantage and the Ethiopian army launched a counterattack on 7 February 1978. By early March Somali forces had retreated, although WSLF guerrilla action continued. An estimated 9000 people were killed during the fighting.

RESULT Guerrilla activity by the WSLF, and the smaller Somali Abo Liberation Front, gradually declined and by the mid-1980s the Cuban military presence was minimal. Ethiopia began providing military assistance to anti-Somali government forces organized in the Somali National Movement (SNM) and the Democratic Front for the Salvation of Somalia (DFSS). In July 1982, Ethiopian troops occupied two Somali villages in support of a DFSS offensive against government troops.

Invasion of Zaïre 1977–8

BACKGROUND Shaba province had, as Katanga, seceded from the Congo on independence in 1960. The population protested about continuing ill-treatment by the central government after reincorporation in 1963. Following the independence of Angola from Portugal in 1975 and improving relations with President Mobutu, President Neto agreed to return to Zaïre Katangese soldiers who had fled to the country following the collapse of the secessionist state in 1963.

MAIN EVENTS On 8 March 1977, a 2000-strong force calling itself the Congolese National Liberation Front (FNLC) under the leadership of General Nathaniel Mbumba crossed the Angolan border into the south-east of Shaba province. The FNLC took control of the railway carrying mineral exports from Shaba to the Angolan coast as a preliminary to attempting the overthrow of President Mobutu. The FNLC had the tacit support of the Angolan government and was allegedly supplied and trained by the USSR, the German Democratic Republic and Cuba. Much of the Shaba population welcomed the invasion and the FNLC pressure forced the virtual disintegration of the Zaïre forces. On 2 April, President Mobutu appealed for assistance and on 10 April French aircraft transported 1500 Moroccan troops who pushed the FNLC back into Angola. Zaïre government forces moved into Shaba and began a campaign of repression, directed particularly at the Lunda people who were accused of being FNLC supporters. On 11 May a second FNLC force invaded the province, capturing the major mining town of Kolwezi and the railway. France and Belgium provided paratroopers (ostensibly to protect civilians) and aided government forces to recapture Kolwezi on 19 May.

RESULT In June 1978 the Organization of African Unity (OAU) mounted a peace-keeping expedition to assist Zaïre in retaining control of Shaba and to help restructure the army. However, in November 1983 a small rebel force captured, and held, Moba in Shaba province before being dislodged by government troops.

Uganda v Tanzania *1978–9*

BACKGROUND There was long-standing antagonism between the Ugandan government and President Julius Nyerere of Tanzania since the January 1971 coup in which Major-General Idi Amin had seized power and ousted Milton Obote. Pro-Obote 'People's Army' guerrillas attacked Uganda in 1972 and Tanzania continued to shelter anti-Amin activists. Uganda deployed troops on the border in May 1978.

MAIN EVENTS On 9 October 1978 Ugandan troops entered Tanzania but quickly withdrew. The Ugandan air force bombed Bukoba on 28 October and invaded Tanzania the following day. Ugandan troops advanced as far as the Kagera River and the government announced the annexation of the 1840 square kilometre Kagera salient. Tanzanian forces counterattacked on 12 November leading, under Organization of African Unity (OAU) pressure, to a Ugandan withdrawal from occupied territory. In January 1979, 20,000 members of the Tanzanian People's Defence Force (TPDF) invaded Uganda. The TPDF was accompanied by 1200 anti-Amin Uganda National Liberation Army (UNLA) activists led by Lieutenant-Colonel David Oyite-Ojok and Yoweri Museveni. The force quickly gained control of the south of Uganda, capturing and partially destroying Mbarara and Masaka. In March 1979 Libya landed 1500 troops at Entebbe while Libyan aircraft bombed Mwanza in Tanzania. Tanzania retaliated with air attacks on Kampala, Jinja and Tororo. TPDF and UNLA forces continued their advance on Kampala, capturing the city on 11 April and killing most of the Libyan troops. The town of Jinja fell a week later and the West Nile area of Uganda was occupied by the TPDF in May 1979. Over 4000 people were killed in the course of the war.

RESULT President Amin fled to Libya and then to Saudi Arabia. A Ugandan National Liberation Front (UNLF) had been formed at the Moshi Conference in Tanzania in

March 1979 under the leadership of Yusufu Lule. Lule was sworn in as President of Uganda on 13 April 1979 but was dismissed on 19 June and replaced by Godfrey Binaisa. TPDF troops remained in Uganda until May 1980, when 10,000 were withdrawn. The remaining 10,000 left the country on the election of Milton Obote as President in December 1980. The UNLA divided into factions loyal respectively to David Oyite-Ojok and to Yoweri Museveni.

Somalian civil war   *1981* onwards

BACKGROUND Major-General Mohammed Siad Barre seized power in Somalia in 1969 and was elected president in 1980. The monopoly of political influence wielded by his Marehan clan excluded the northern Mijertyn and Isaaq clans. In October 1981 the Somali Salvation Democratic Front (SSDF), allied with the Somali National Movement (SNM), launched an invasion of Somalia with Ethiopian backing. The invasion failed but government forces were unable to expel the rebels.

MAIN EVENTS On 27 May 1988 an enlarged SNM army captured towns in the north of the country and by 1989 claimed to control 95 per cent of the area. Following rioting in the capital Mogadishu, fighting broke out between government forces and members of the Ogadeni clan organized in the Somali Patriotic Movement (SPM) in the south – supported by the United Somali Congress (USC) – and the Somali National Army (SNA) in central Somalia. President Siad Barre attempted to weaken the insurgents by offering government posts to opposition leaders. In March 1990, the government launched an offensive against the SNM and in August, despite the promise of democratic reforms, the SNM, SPM and the USC announced a co-ordination of their military effort to overthrow Siad Barre. In November

USC forces briefly held a town 100 kilometres north of the capital while the SPM captured Kismayu in the south. On 1 January 1991 the USC claimed control of the bulk of Mogadishu, forcing Siad Barre's flight on 27 January. USC leader Ali Mahdi Mohamed was appointed interim president, an appointment immediately rejected by the SNM and SPM. In the north, the SNM established an independent 'Republic of Somaliland'. Meanwhile, Siad Barre's supporters in the south formed the Somali National Front (SNF). In July the USC, SDM, SPM and SSDF allied against Siad Barre's SNF and Ali Mahdi was confirmed in office. However, military commander General Mohammed Farah Aidid led a faction out of the USC and by the end of December clashes between the two sections of the Hawiye clan had claimed over 4000 deaths in Mogadishu. As fighting continued between the competing groups throughout a devastated country, over 14,000 people (the majority of them civilians) had been killed by March 1992. On 3 March, President Ali Mahdi and General Aidid negotiated a cease-fire and in April Aidid's forces, now renamed the Somali Liberation Army (SLA), drove back an SNF attack on Mogadishu. Divisions were reopened when in August Aidid allied with the SPM and SDM to form the Somali National Alliance (SNA). Ali Mahdi's faction of the USC, the Somali Salvation Alliance (SSA), found allies in the SSDF and sections of the SPM and of Siad Barre's SNF.

The United Nations deployed a force to protect food supplies in December 1991. In December 1992, the UN agreed to a proposal from the USA to force a cease-fire. The first of a projected 30,000-strong force, headed by US Marines, landed on 9 December and immediately clashed with bandit groups and civilian demonstrators in Mogadishu. In January 1993 the 14 main political factions opened peace negotiations in the Ethiopian capital, Addis Ababa. But fighting continued throughout the country and in May there were clashes with UN troops in Mogadishu. A peace agreement reached between General Aidid and President Ali Mahdi in March 1994 broke down in June, with further heavy fighting in the capital. A reconciliation conference called by Aidid in November was boycotted by the president's supporters. In February 1995, as renewed clashes erupted between the factions, the UN announced a complete withdrawal of its troops, the final elements leaving on 1 March.

RESULT   General Aidid was ousted as leader of the Somali National Alliance on 12 June 1995. He responded by proclaiming himself president. Aidid extended his area of control when his forces captured Baidoa, south of Mogadishu, and in October he symbolized his confidence by announcing that his government would begin levying taxes throughout the country. General Aidid was killed in renewed fighting in August 1996.

Invasion of Grenada   *1983*

BACKGROUND   The People's Revolutionary Government (PRG) on the Caribbean island of Grenada which had seized power in 1979, feared an invasion from the USA in 1980 and 1981. This encouraged closer relations with the Soviet Union and Cuba. Grenada's Caribbean neighbour, Cuba, provided 40 per cent of the finance and several hundred workers to construct an international airport at Point Salines. The PRG leader, Maurice Bishop, attempted to conciliate the USA but was overthrown on 19 October 1983 by a Revolutionary Military Council led by General Hudson Austin and murdered. On 21 October, The Organisation of East Caribbean States called for intervention to restore democracy.

MAIN EVENTS   Operation 'Urgent Fury' began on 25 October 1983 with an invasion of Grenada by 1900 US Marines and airborne troops, accompanied by a token force of 150 Jamaicans and 250 soldiers from Antigua, Barbados, Dominica, St Lucia and St Vincent. The invasion ostensibly took place to rescue several hundred US medical students at the University of St George's and to counter a threat allegedly posed by 650 Cuban construction workers. The invading force took three days to take the island in an incompetently organized mission which finally involved 7000 US troops. There was little Grenadian resistance. The US forces lost 20 dead, a third of these in accidents. Grenadian casualties were 45 dead (including 18 accidentally killed in the bombing of a mental hospital). Cuban casualties were 24 dead.

RESULT   General Hudson Austin and the remainder of the Revolutionary Military Council were arrested. On 9 November 1983, the island's governor, Sir Paul Scoon, appointed a non-political interim council to administer Grenada until elections could be held. The majority of US troops were withdrawn in two months, a final 250 remaining on the island until June 1985.

Burkina Faso *v* Mali   *1985*

BACKGROUND   In September 1983, President Moussa Traoré of Mali and the Burkina Faso head of state, Captain Thomas Sankara, referred a long-standing border dispute over the Agacher strip to the International Court of Justice at The Hague. Despite progress in negotiations between the two states, tension increased when in 1985 Burkina Faso expelled the Malian secretary-general of the West African Economic Community (CEAO). In addition, Mali became increasingly concerned at the radicalism of Burkina Faso's political leadership.

MAIN EVENTS On 25 December 1985, Malian and Burkina Faso troops clashed in the disputed area. In fighting which continued until 31 December over 50 people were killed. Mali, with superior forces and equipment, inflicted heavy damage on Burkina Faso territory. The francophone West African Economic Community negotiated a cease-fire and deployed a peacekeeping force. President Traoré and Captain Sankara met in January 1986 and agreed to withdraw their troops from the disputed areas. Prisoners were exchanged in February.

RESULT In December 1986 the International Court of Justice ruled that the disputed Agacher strip should be divided between the two countries, with Mali receiving the western half and Burkina Faso taking the eastern district of Beli.

Kenya v Uganda *1987*

BACKGROUND The war broke out following growing tension between Uganda and Kenya, caused partly by the insecurity of the government of President Yoweri Museveni which had taken power in 1986 following the overthrow of President Milton Obote. Uganda accused Kenya of sheltering anti-Museveni rebels, while Kenya was concerned that Ugandan refugees were contributing to political instability. The growing crisis intensified when Uganda began transporting coffee exports by rail rather than road, causing a loss of $50 million revenue to Kenyan businesses. In March 1987, Kenya expelled Ugandan refugees and Uganda complained that Kenya had closed border-crossings at Busia and Malaba.

MAIN EVENTS In September 1987, Uganda alleged once again that Kenya was assisting anti-Museveni rebels and deployed troops on the border in October. Kenya warned that it would retaliate against Ugandan troops crossing the frontier in pursuit of rebels. In December Ugandan troops crossing the border were confronted by Kenyan forces and there were 15 deaths in fighting which lasted for several days.

RESULT Kenya expelled the Ugandan high commissioner following the clashes but President Daniel arap Moi of Kenya and President Museveni of Uganda met and agreed to co-operate on resolving cross-border issues. However, in July 1988 Uganda accused Kenya of allowing rebels to smuggle weapons into northern Uganda and sent troops across the frontier again, killing one civilian.

Liberian civil war *1989* onwards

BACKGROUND The seizure of power in a military coup by Master Sergeant Samuel Doe in April 1980 was seen as a revolt by the indigenous population of Liberia against the Americo-Liberian elite which had ruled the country. President Doe headed a brutal and increasingly unpopular regime. In November 1985, following his victory in a rigged election, Doe survived an unsuccessful coup attempt.

MAIN EVENTS On 24 December 1989, 150 members of the Libyan trained National Patriotic Front of Liberia (NPFL) crossed from Côte d'Ivoire into Nimba County in north-eastern Liberia. The NPLF, led by Charles Taylor, a former Liberian government official, included supporters from Sierra Leone and Burkina Faso. The brutal response of government forces in the area encouraged recruitment to the NPFL, particularly among the Mano and Gio peoples. In February Prince Yormi Johnson formed a breakaway Independent National Patriotic Front of Liberia (INPFL). On 1 July, the NPFL launched a two-pronged attack on the capital Monrovia, severing water and power supplies. The Economic

Community of West African States despatched a peacekeeping force (ECOMOG) on 24 to 25 August which was fired on by NPFL troops. Johnson's INPFL began negotiations with Doe in September, but on 10 September kidnapped and murdered the president. An Interim Government of National Unity formed in April 1991 under Amos Sawyer was weakened by the refusal of the NPFL, which controlled 90 per cent of Liberia, to participate. A peace conference at Yamassoukko chaired by President Félix Houphouët-Boigny of Côte d'Ivoire proposed disarming of the factions pending elections. Despite the reluctance of the NPFL to co-operate, there was an uneasy peace from March 1991 to October 1992.

However, a new faction, the United Liberian Movement for Democracy (ULIMO) was formed in Sierra Leone by Krahn and Mandingo refugees from NPFL ethnic violence. ULIMO invaded Liberia in 1992, seizing NPFL territory. On 15 October, the NPFL launched Operation Octopus against Monrovia, clashing with ECOMOG forces who bombed the ports of Buchanan and Greenville to disrupt the NPFL's supply routes. At negotiations between the factions in Geneva on 11 July 1993, Taylor withdrew his precondition that he should head the interim government pending elections. But the situation within Liberia was increasingly degenerating into violence between competing factions led by war-lords. There was, in addition, a clear link with the conflict in neighbouring Sierra Leone. A peace agreement was reached in August 1995, followed in September by the formation of a new transitional government. But in October there were clashes between the NPFL and a new faction, the Liberia Peace Council. In April 1996, the expulsion from the interim government of Roosevelt Johnson, leader of the breakaway ULIMO-J, led to further fighting. Attempts by the heads of state of nine West African governments to promote peace failed in May 1996.

RESULT Liberia faced continuing conflict between eight competing factions in a war which had destroyed the country's economy, caused the death of an estimated 150,000 people and forced 750,000 to flee as refugees. In August 1996 the main factions agreed on an ECOWAS peace plan.

Rwandan civil war *1990*

BACKGROUND Following the military coup of Major-General Juvénal Habyarimana in July 1973, the Hutus continued to dominate Rwanda, although some attempts were made towards establishing a political structure more reflective of the country's social composition.

MAIN EVENTS On 30 September 1990, a 2000 strong Tutsi force – led by Fred Rwigyema, formerly chief of staff of the National Resistance Army which overthrew President Obote of Uganda in 1986 – seized weapons from Ugandan army stores and advanced into Rwanda towards the capital Kigali. Belgium and France sent troops to Rwanda at the request of President Habyarimana on 4 October and these, together with forces from Zaïre defeated the invading force. Rwigyema was killed in the fighting.

RESULT A cease-fire was negotiated in October by Belgian Prime Minister Wilfred Martens. Paul Kagame, former head of military intelligence in the National Resistance Army, took command of the Tutsi forces and began guerrilla operations in northern Rwanda. The civil war resumed in January 1991 with invasion by the predominantly Tutsi Rwandan Patriotic Front (FPR).

Rwandan civil war   *1991 onwards*

BACKGROUND   Following the Tutsi invasion of September 1990, conflict between the Hutu and Tutsi population in Rwanda continued. The Tutsis, organized in the Rwandan Patriotic Front (FPR), mounted guerrilla operations in the north of the country from bases in Uganda.

MAIN EVENTS   In January 1991, 600 FPR members invaded Rwanda from Uganda. A cease-fire negotiated in March provided for the release of political prisoners by the Rwandan government and the formulation of a new multi-party constitution. But in March 1992, 300 Tutsis were assassinated and 15,000 forced to flee as refugees. Between 1990 and 1993, up to 15,000 Tutsis were killed by the Hutu militia. In January 1993, President Habyarimana withdrew from an agreement on power-sharing negotiated with the FPR by his prime minister, Dismas Nsengiyaremye. The agreement had also provided for the repatriation of Tutsi refugees from Uganda and Tanzania. The FPR launched a new offensive in February, capturing almost half the country and threatening the capital Kigali. On 6 April 1994, President Habyarimana and President Cyprien Ntaryamira of Burundi were killed when their aircraft was shot down by rocket fire following their attendance at a peace conference in Tanzania. Hutu militia and death squads began a systematic massacre of the Tutsi population, killing an estimated 500,000 within a month. Thousands more fled as refugees to Tanzania. As they advanced, the FPR troops (despite claims that 40 per cent of its members were members of the Twa and Hutu groups) massacred Hutus. On 4 July the FPR captured Kigali and on 7 August Faustin Twagiramungu, leader of the Democratic Republic Movement (MDR), accepted the FPR's request to form a government of national unity.

RESULT   In June 1994, France deployed a peacekeeping force and established a 'safe zone' for Hutus in the south west of the country. The withdrawal of French forces on 22 August 1994 was followed by the flight of 800,000 Hutu refugees into neighbouring Zaïre. The FPR forces were accused of attacking both Hutus and Tutsis. As conditions in the refugee camps in Zaïre and Tanzania worsened, thousands died. A United Nations-sponsored International Criminal Tribunal for Rwanda opened in Arusha, Tanzania, on 27 November 1995 to hear cases against individuals accused of participating in the 1994 massacres.

Sierra Leone civil war   *1991–6*

BACKGROUND   The All People's Congress (APC) ruled Sierra Leone as a one-party state since June 1978. In 1990, President Joseph Momoh announced the forthcoming restoration of multi-party democracy. However, the Revolutionary United Front (RUF), made up of Sierra Leonians who had fought with the National Patriotic Front of Liberia (NPFL) in the Liberian civil war, attempted to use popular disillusionment with the APC to overthrow the government.

MAIN EVENTS   On 23 March 1991 the Revolutionary United Front (RUF), assisted by mercenaries from Burkina Faso, crossed from NPFL territory in Liberia into eastern Sierra Leone. The RUF was led by Foday Sankoh, a former army corporal imprisoned in 1969 for alleged involvement in a coup against President Joseph Momoh. The RUF advanced in two columns, hoping to win support from potentially dissident populations in the border regions of Pujehun and Kailahun. The northern group reached Daru where it was held back by Sierra Leone troops with Guinean support. The southern group moved towards the capital, Freetown. The main objective was to capture Bo and Kenema, towns controlling the diamond-mining areas in the east and centre of the country. The RUF met with initial support following the brutality of the ruling All People's Congress militia. But the RUF made no attempt to organize civil admin-istration in the areas under its control. In addition, the brutality of mercenaries from Burkina Faso alienated the population. By the end of 1991, government forces – assisted by the United Liberian Movement for Democracy (ULIMO) – had driven the RUF towards the border from Pujehen in the south. In the north, the RUF was unable to advance against Guinean forces.

By early 1992 the RUF appeared to be on the verge of defeat. On 27 April, President Momoh was overthrown, ending 24 years of All People's Congress rule, and replaced by a civilian-military government under Captain Valentine Strasser. The RUF, which had fragmented into factions, continued hostil-ities against the new government. In November 1995, the RUF was driven from the diamond mining district of Mono by mercenaries recruited in South Africa.

RESULT The overthrow of Strasser by Brigadier Julius Madda Bio in January 1996 was followed by a seven-day cease-fire. But the factional warfare appeared to have degenerated into criminal attempts to secure control of Sierra Leone's mineral wealth. At the time of the cease-fire, an estimated 50,000 people had died.

Nigeria v Cameroon   1993–6

BACKGROUND A long-standing dispute between Nigeria and Cameroon over the Bakassi peninsula in the Gulf of Guinea appeared to have been settled when, in 1987, both announced the establishment of joint border controls. Nigeria's claim to the

territory was based on an agreement negotiated in 1913 by the colonial powers in the area, Britain and Germany. However, in 1991 Nigeria accused Cameroon of annexing a number of Nigerian fishing settlements.

MAIN EVENTS In 1993 Nigeria despatched 500 troops to the peninsula following the deaths of Nigerians at the hands of Cameroon security forces. Clashes between their forces were followed by negotiations in March 1994. But in May 1994 two Nigerian soldiers were killed in further clashes. Togo attempted to mediate between the two governments. In September Cameroon made further claims on Nigerian territory and ten Cameroon soldiers were killed in fighting. Hostilities resumed with further clashes on 3 and 4 February 1996. Negotiations were reopened following another confrontation on 20 February.

RESULT The dispute remained unresolved as negotiations continued.

Burundian civil war   1994 onwards

BACKGROUND Following clashes between Hutus and Tutsis in August 1988, President Buyoya announced proposals to end discrimination against Hutus and appointed Hutus to the majority of posts on the Council of Ministers, including that of prime minister. In free elections held in June 1993, Melchior Ndadaye was elected Burundi's first Hutu president. He was assassinated in a coup mounted by an extremist Tutsi faction in the army on 21 October 1993. His successor, Cyprien Ntaryamira, was killed when the aircraft in which he was travelling with Rwandan President Habyarimana was shot down on 6 April 1994.

MAIN EVENTS There were clashes between Hutu and Tutsi factions in February 1994. In March, the Tutsi-dominated army attacked Hutus in a search for illegal weapons. The Hutus were accused of attempting to establish an armed force strong enough to confront the Burundi army. Fighting continued between the army and Hutu rebels into April. Interim President Sylvestre Ntibantunganya ordered both Hutus and Tutsis to surrender illegal weapons and the armed forces shelled rebel bases in May 1994. The influx of 200,000 Hutu refugees from the civil war in neighbouring Rwanda intensified ethnic tensions in Burundi. Government forces attacked the Hutu suburbs of the capital Bujumbura, killing hundreds of civilians. In June human rights organizations reported that the Burundi army was co-operating with Tutsi extremists in attacks on Hutus. By the end of 1995 there were an estimated 150,000 civilian dead. Continuing conflict was marked by the flight of refugees to camps in Rwanda, Tanzania and Zaïre.

RESULT In June 1994, the Organization of African Unity (OAU) proposed intervention by peacekeeping forces to end the civil war and ethnic violence. Following negotiations with the leaders of other states in the region at Arusha in June 1996, Burundi's Tutsi prime minister, Antoine Nduwayo, and the Hutu president, Sylvestre Ntibantunganya, appeared willing to accept this. But extremist factions in Burundi threatened to fire on any foreign troops. As 100 people were dying every day and the country's economy was close to collapse, former president Julius Nyerere of Tanzania, threatened further pressure on 9 July 1996 to encourage acceptance of an East African peacekeeping force. On 25 July, President Ntibantunganya was overthrown by Pierre Buyoya.

Eritrea v Yemen *1995*

BACKGROUND Eritrea claimed three islands in the Red Sea Bab el Manded Strait occupied by the Yemen. Eritrea made this claim on the basis that they had formerly been controlled by the Ottoman empire, Britain, Italy and finally Ethiopia. In November 1995 an Eritrean naval patrol attempted to land on the islands following the construction of tourist facilities by the Yemen. Yemen responded with a military build-up. On 22 November, the Eritrean foreign minister visited the Yemen for negotiations. There were further discussions in Eritrea on 7 December.

MAIN EVENTS On 15 December Eritrea attacked the islands and captured the largest, Hanish al Kabir, following a three-day battle in which both sides used warships and aircraft. Six Eritrean and three Yemeni soldiers were killed in the fighting. On 18 December both sides agreed on a cease-fire which would be monitored by a four-strong committee of one Eritrean, one Yemeni and two US officials.

RESULT On 29 December United Nations Secretary-General, Boutros-Boutros Ghali, visited the Yemeni capital Sana'a to mediate in the dispute. On 31 December the Yemen agreed to withdraw its troops from the area and to abide by international mediation. However, on 27 January 1996, Eritrea expelled the Yemeni ambassador.

Zaïre civil war *1996 onwards*

BACKGROUND In October 1996 dissatisfaction with the 30-year regime of President Mobutu Sese Seko combined with regional conflict between Hutus and Tutsis. Following the 1994 Rwandan civil war, President Mobutu had given shelter to over a million Hutu refugees. Their camps were dominated by Hutu guerrillas and used as bases for attacks on Tutsi-controlled Rwanda. In 1981, the Zaïre government had revoked the citizenship of the Banyamulenge, Tutsis who had been living in the east of the territory for two centuries.

MAIN EVENTS On 19 October 1996, Zaïre accused the Tutsi-dominated Rwandan army of arming and organizing anti-Mobutu Banyamulenge guerrillas and, allied with the Hutu militia, launched an attack on the Banyamulenge, killing thousands. Fighting spread across eastern Zaïre as the Banyamulenge retaliated and Hutus began to flee the refugee camps. President Mobutu (convalescing in France after surgery) faced an Alliance of Democratic Forces for the Liberation of Congo–Zaïre led by Laurent Kabila, a long-term opponent of his government. On 22 October, Zaïre accused Rwanda of invading the country.

The United Nations appealed to Hutu refugees to return to Rwanda for their own safety. As Zaïrean troops fell back, the Alliance – supported by opposition groups seeking autonomy for Shaba and Kasai provinces – seized control of a 20,000-square-mile area on the Burundi and Rwanda borders. The spread of fighting into Burundi and exchanges of fire between Rwandan and Zaïrean troops on 29 October threatened to regionalize the conflict. Bukavu fell to the Alliance on 30 October. Zaïre rejected an Organization of African Unity (OAU) attempt to defuse the crisis, accusing Uganda of supporting the rebels. As Goma fell to Rwandan troops on 1 November, 700,000 Hutu refugees fled to Mugunga camp on the Zaïre–Rwanda border. There were calls – from France in particular – for the deployment of an international relief force. President Mobutu's announcement of his imminent return on 4 November prompted anti-government demonstrations in north-east Zaïre. On 15 November a combined Alliance and Rwandan army broke the Hutu militia defence of Mugunga camp.

Kabila's Alliance forces now turned to advance into Zaïre in an attempt to overthrow the government. By 2 December the rebels had made rapid progress, penetrating the northern regional capital of Kisangani. Zaïre accused Ugandan troops of supporting the Alliance when they attacked the border town of Beni. The Alliance captured the main military base of Kindo in central Zaïre on 4 December. Eight African leaders met in Nairobi on 16 December, in a fruitless attempt to prevent the spread of war across the Great Lakes region. President Mobutu landed in Zaïre the following day but returned to France in January 1997, leaving his army commanders, supported by white mercenaries, to defend the regime. By February 1997, President Mobutu having returned to his fortified base at Gbadolite, Kabila's troops were in control of eastern Zaïre, threatening the mineral-rich state of Shaba. Aircraft flown by foreign mercenaries bombed Alliance-controlled Bukavu on 18 February.

RESULT The United Nations Security Council unanimously endorsed a peace plan on 18 February, calling for an end to fighting and the withdrawal of all foreign forces, including mercenaries. At the end of the month, President Mandela attempted to mediate in the peace process as clashes continued.

COUNTRIES OF AFRICA AND THE AFRICAN DIASPORA

Angola
Antigua and Barbuda
Bahamas
Barbados
Benin
Botswana
Burkina Faso
Burundi
Cameroon
Cape Verde
Central African Republic
Chad
Congo
Côte d'Ivoire
Dominica
Equatorial Guinea
Eritrea
Ethiopia
Gabon
The Gambia
Ghana
Grenada
Guinea
Guinea-Bissau
Haiti
Jamaica

Kenya
Lesotho
Liberia
Malawi
Mali
Mozambique
Namibia
Niger
Nigeria
Rwanda
St Christopher and Nevis
St Lucia
St Vincent and the Grenadines
São Tomé and Príncipe
Senegal
Sierra Leone
Somalia
South Africa
Swaziland
Togo
Trinidad and Tobago
Uganda
United Republic of Tanzania
Zaïre
Zambia
Zimbabwe

In all lists, * indicates that no recent figures are available.

	Angola	**Antigua and Barbuda**
AREA	1,246,700 sq km/481,354 sq miles	Antigua 279 sq km/108 sq miles: Barbuda 160 sq km/62 sq miles
CAPITAL	Luanda	St John's
MAIN TOWNS	Huambo, Lobito, Lubango	Codrington
MAIN ETHNIC GROUPS	Ovimbundu, Mbundu, Kongo, Lunda-Chokwe, Ngangula	African descent
MAIN LANGUAGES	Portuguese (official), Kilongo, Umbundu, Kimbundu, Kioko	English
MAIN RELIGIONS	Christianity, traditional	Christianity
POPULATION	11,072,000 (1995 UN estimate)	65,962 (1991)
DENSITY/SQ KM	8	173
ANNUAL GROWTH	3.7% (1990–5)	*
URBAN	32%	35%
RURAL	68%	65%
FEMALES PER 100 MALES	103	*
INFANT MORTALITY (PER THOUSAND BIRTHS)	124	24
CALORIE INTAKE PER HEAD PER DAY	*	2178
HEALTH WORKERS (PER 10,000)	10.4	19.4
LIFE EXPECTANCY	Female 48, male 45	*
MAIN EMPLOYMENT SECTORS	Agriculture 20.5%, industry 23.9%	Tourism 66%
MAIN INDUSTRIES	Mining, farming, oil	Tourism and allied services, market gardening, fishing
MAIN EXPORTS	Oil, petroleum, diamonds, coffee, sisal, maize, palm oil, hardwoods	Rum, fish, cotton
MAIN DESTINATION OF EXPORTS	USA, Germany, Brazil	USA, UK, Germany
CURRENCY	New Kwanza (100 lwei)	East Caribbean dollar (100 cents)
GDP (IN $US MILLION)	5954	423
GDP PER HEAD (IN $US THOUSAND)	625	6404
RETAIL PRICE INDEX	733 (1990) (1980 = 100)	213 (1990) (1980 = 100)
MILITARY EXPENDITURE (% OF GDP)	23.9	*
MILITARY EXPENDITURE PER HEAD (IN $US)	173	*
ARMED FORCES PER 1000 POPULATION	17.3	*
EDUCATION EXPENDITURE AS % OF GDP	5.1	4
NUMBER IN POST-SECONDARY EDUCATION (PER 100,000)	62	*
LITERACY RATE AGE 15+	Female 19%, male 36%	*
MOTOR VEHICLES PER THOUSAND	18	299
TELEPHONE LINES PER HUNDRED	0.8	28.8
TELEVISIONS PER THOUSAND	6	355
NEWSPAPER CIRCULATION PER THOUSAND	13	92
NEWSPAPERS (D = DAILY, W = WEEKLY)	*Diário da Républica* (d), *O Jornal de Angola* (d), *Correio da Semana* (w)	*The Worker's Voice* (w), *The Outlet* (w), *The Nation* (w), *Antigua Today* (w)

	Bahamas	**Barbados**
AREA	13,935 sq km/5380 sq miles	430 sq km/166 sq miles
CAPITAL	Nassau	Bridgetown
MAIN TOWNS	Freeport	Hole Town, Speightstown, Oistins
MAIN ETHNIC GROUPS	African descent, mixed descent	African descent, mixed descent
MAIN LANGUAGES	English	English
MAIN RELIGIONS	Christianity	Christianity
POPULATION	277,000 (1995 UN estimate)	261,000 (1995 UN estimate)
DENSITY/SQ KM	12	593
ANNUAL GROWTH	1.7% (1990–5)	0.3% (1990–5)
URBAN	66%	48%
RURAL	34%	52%
FEMALES PER 100 MALES	101	109
INFANT MORTALITY (PER THOUSAND BIRTHS)	24	10
CALORIE INTAKE PER HEAD PER DAY	2680	3188
HEALTH WORKERS (PER 10,000)	61.5	52.2
LIFE EXPECTANCY	Female 76, male 69	Female 78, male 73
MAIN EMPLOYMENT SECTORS	Tourism 66%, agriculture 4.4%, industry 14.2%	Tourism 50%, agriculture 6.2%, industry 19.7%
MAIN INDUSTRIES	Tourism, agriculture, international banking, oil, fishing	Tourism, sugar, light manufacturing
MAIN EXPORTS	Rum, petroleum, fish	Sugar and by-products, chemicals, electrical equipment
MAIN DESTINATION OF EXPORTS	USA, Puerto Rico, Belgium	UK, USA, Trinidad and Tobago
CURRENCY	Bahamian dollar (100 cents)	Barbados dollar (100 cents)
GDP (IN $US MILLION)	3013	1687
GDP PER HEAD (IN $US THOUSAND)	11,588	6539
RETAIL PRICE INDEX	202 (1994) (1980 = 100)	200 (1994) (1980 = 100)
MILITARY EXPENDITURE (% OF GDP)	2.1	0.7
MILITARY EXPENDITURE PER HEAD (IN $US)	248	41
POPULATION	*	1.6
EDUCATION EXPENDITURE AS % OF GDP	4.4	5.4
NUMBER IN POST-SECONDARY EDUCATION (PER 100,000)	*	1665
LITERACY RATE AGE 15+	*	*
MOTOR VEHICLES PER THOUSAND	325	149
TELEPHONE LINES PER HUNDRED	23.8	30.2
TELEVISIONS PER THOUSAND	225	265
NEWSPAPER CIRCULATION PER THOUSAND	137	117
NEWSPAPERS (D = DAILY, W = WEEKLY)	*Freeport News* (d), *Nassau Daily Tribune* (d), *Nassau Guardian* (d)	*Barbados Advocate* (d), *The National* (d), *Sunday Advocate* (w), *Sunday Sun* (w)

	Benin	Botswana
AREA	122,622 sq km/43,484 sq miles	581,730 sq km/224,607 sq miles
CAPITAL	Porto Novo	Gaborone
MAIN TOWNS	Cotonou, Grand Popo, Ouidah, Abomey	Francistown, Selebi-Phikwe, Lobatse
MAIN ETHNIC GROUPS	Fon, Yoruba, Bariba, Somba	Batswana, San
MAIN LANGUAGES	French (official), Fon, Yoruba, Bariba, Dendi	English (official), Setswana
MAIN RELIGIONS	Christianity, Islam, traditional	Christianity, traditional
POPULATION	5,399,000 (1995 UN estimate)	1,433,000 (1995 UN estimate)
DENSITY/SQ KM	43	2
ANNUAL GROWTH	3.1% (1990–5)	2.9% (1990–5)
URBAN	42%	31%
RURAL	58%	69%
FEMALES PER 100 MALES	102	108
INFANT MORTALITY (PER THOUSAND BIRTHS)	87	60
CALORIE INTAKE PER HEAD PER DAY	2115	2251
HEALTH WORKERS (PER 10,000)	7.3	*
LIFE EXPECTANCY	Female 48, male 45	Female 64, male 58
MAIN EMPLOYMENT SECTORS	Agriculture 7.5%, industry 18.9%	Agriculture 2.6%, industry 30.6%
MAIN INDUSTRIES	Agriculture, animal husbandry, oil, cotton	Mining, livestock
MAIN EXPORTS	Cotton, coffee, palm oil, groundnuts	Copper-nickel, diamonds, beef and beef products
MAIN DESTINATION OF EXPORTS	Portugal, Italy, Thailand, Taiwan	European Union
CURRENCY	Franc CFA (100 centimes)	Pula (100 thebe)
GDP (IN $US MILLION)	1849	3467
GDP PER HEAD (IN $US THOUSAND)	388	2720
RETAIL PRICE INDEX	104 (1980 = 100)	393 (1994) (1980 = 100)
MILITARY EXPENDITURE (% OF GDP)	2.0	4.9
MILITARY EXPENDITURE PER HEAD (IN $US)	8	126.2
POPULATION	1.4	5.2
EDUCATION EXPENDITURE AS % OF GDP	4.0	6.7
NUMBER IN POST-SECONDARY EDUCATION (PER 100,000)	235	255
LITERACY RATE AGE 15+	*	*
MOTOR VEHICLES PER THOUSAND	7	58
TELEPHONE LINES PER HUNDRED	0.3	2.6
TELEVISIONS PER THOUSAND	5	16
NEWSPAPER CIRCULATION PER THOUSAND	3	15
NEWSPAPERS (D = DAILY, W = WEEKLY)	*Le Matin* (d), *Le Nation* (d), *Flash-Hebdo* (w), *Le Forum de la Semaine* (w)	*Dik Gang tsa Gompieno* (d), *Botswana Advertiser* (w), *Botswana Gazette* (w), *Botswana Guardian* (w), *Mmegi/The Reporter* (w)

	Burkina Faso	Burundi
AREA	274,200 sq km/105,869 sq miles	27,834 sq km/10,747 sq miles
CAPITAL	Ouagadougou	Bujumbura
MAIN TOWNS	Bobo-Dioulasso, Koudougou, Tambao	Kitega
MAIN ETHNIC GROUPS	Mossi, Fulani, Gourmantché, Bobo, Lobi, Senoufou	Hutu, Tutsi
MAIN LANGUAGES	French (official), More, Dyula, Gourmantché	French (official), Kirundi (official), Swahili
MAIN RELIGIONS	Traditional, Islam	Christianity, traditional
POPULATION	10,352,000 (1995 UN estimate)	6,343,000 (1995 UN estimate)
DENSITY/SQ KM	34	202
ANNUAL GROWTH	2.8% (1990–5)	2.9% (1990–5)
URBAN	20%	6%
RURAL	80%	94%
FEMALES PER 100 MALES	102	104
INFANT MORTALITY (PER THOUSAND BIRTHS)	118	106
CALORIE INTAKE PER HEAD PER DAY	2002	2320
HEALTH WORKERS (PER 10,000)	19.5	5.2
LIFE EXPECTANCY	Female 50, male 47	Female 50, male 46
MAIN EMPLOYMENT SECTORS	*	Industry 21.9%, agriculture 14.8%
MAIN INDUSTRIES	Agriculture and processing	Agriculture, mining
MAIN EXPORTS	Cattle, vegetables, sorghum, groundnuts	Coffee, cotton, minerals, tea
MAIN DESTINATION OF EXPORTS	Japan, France, Côte d'Ivoire	Germany, USA, Rwanda, UK
CURRENCY	Franc CFA (100 centimes)	Burundi franc (100 centimes)
GDP (IN $US MILLION)	2221	1170
GDP PER HEAD (IN $US THOUSAND)	240	207
RETAIL PRICE INDEX	137 (1994) (1980 = 100)	104 (1994) (1980 = 100)
MILITARY EXPENDITURE (% OF GDP)	2.7	2.4
MILITARY EXPENDITURE PER HEAD (IN $US)	11.0	4.7
POPULATION	1.1.	2.1
EDUCATION EXPENDITURE AS % OF GDP	2.0	4.0
NUMBER IN POST-SECONDARY EDUCATION (PER 100,000)	65	66
LITERACY RATE AGE 15+	*	Female 15%, male 38%
MOTOR VEHICLES PER THOUSAND	7	7
TELEPHONE LINES PER HUNDRED	0.2	0.2
TELEVISIONS PER THOUSAND	5	1
NEWSPAPER CIRCULATION PER THOUSAND	0.1	4
NEWSPAPERS (D = DAILY, W = WEEKLY)	*Observateur Paaiga* (d), *Le Pays* (d), *Sidwaya* (d), *Le Berger* (w), *Le Journal de Jeudi* (w)	*Le Renouveau du Burundi* (d), *Burundi chrétien* (w), *Ubumwe* (w)

	Cameroon	Cape Verde
AREA	475,422 sq km/183,569 sq miles	4033 sq km/1557 sq miles
CAPITAL	Yaoundé	Cidade de Praia
MAIN TOWNS	Douala	São Tiago, Santo Antão, Vicente
MAIN ETHNIC GROUPS	Sudanese Negroes, Foulbe, Choa	African-Portuguese descent
MAIN LANGUAGES	French (official), English (official), Beti, Ful, Arabic	Portuguese (official), Mandyak
MAIN RELIGIONS	Islam, Christianity, animist	Christianity
POPULATION	13,275,000 (1995 UN estimate)	419,000 (1995 UN estimate)
DENSITY/SQ KM	26	95
ANNUAL GROWTH	2.8 (1990–5)	2.9% (1990–5)
URBAN	45%	32%
RURAL	55%	68%
FEMALES PER 100 MALES	101	112
INFANT MORTALITY (PER THOUSAND BIRTHS)	63	40
CALORIE INTAKE PER HEAD PER DAY	2142	2500
HEALTH WORKERS (PER 10,000)	*	*
LIFE EXPECTANCY	Female 58, men 55	Female 69, male 57
MAIN EMPLOYMENT SECTORS	Agriculture 62%, industry 4.6%	Agriculture 42%, industry 4%
MAIN INDUSTRIES	Agriculture, mining, forestry, oil	Agriculture, fishing
MAIN EXPORTS	Coffee, cocoa, timber, bauxite	Bananas, coffee, fish, shellfish
MAIN DESTINATION OF EXPORTS	Netherlands, France, Italy	Portugal, Algeria, UK
CURRENCY	Franc CFA (100 centimes)	Escudo (100 centavos)
GDP (IN $US MILLION)	12,788 (1991)	341
GDP PER HEAD (IN $US THOUSAND)	1079 (1991)	913
RETAIL PRICE INDEX	181 (1985) (1980 = 100)	141 (1980 = 100)
MILITARY EXPENDITURE (% OF GDP)	1.6	12.1
MILITARY EXPENDITURE PER HEAD (IN $US)	13.7	43
POPULATION	2.0	2.6
EDUCATION EXPENDITURE AS % OF GDP	2.3	4.0
NUMBER IN POST-SECONDARY EDUCATION (PER 100,000)	242	*
LITERACY RATE AGE 15+	*	*
MOTOR VEHICLES PER THOUSAND	8	9
TELEPHONE LINES PER HUNDRED	0.3	2.3
TELEVISIONS PER THOUSAND	24	*
NEWSPAPER CIRCULATION PER THOUSAND	7	*
NEWSPAPERS (D = DAILY, W = WEEKLY)	*Cameroon Tribune* (d), *Cameroon Post* (w), *Le Combattant* (w), *Dikalo* (w)	*Novo Jornal Cabo Verde* (twice weekly), *A Semana* (w)

	Central African Republic	Chad
AREA	622,984 sq km/240,534 sq miles	1,284,000 sq km/495,755 sq miles
CAPITAL	Bangui	N'djaména
MAIN TOWNS	Bakouma, Berberati, Bossango	Doba, Bongor, Am Timan
MAIN ETHNIC GROUPS	Banda, Baya, Zande, Baka	Sara, Arab, Taureg
MAIN LANGUAGES	French, Sangho (official), Arabic, Swahili, Hausa	French (official), Arabic, others
MAIN RELIGIONS	Traditional, Christianity	Traditional, Islam, Christianity
POPULATION	3,429,000 (1995 UN estimate)	6,361,000 (1995 UN estimate)
DENSITY/SQ KM	5	5
ANNUAL GROWTH	2.6 (1990–5)	2.7% (1990–5)
URBAN	51%	37%
RURAL	49%	63%
FEMALES PER 100 MALES	106	103
INFANT MORTALITY (PER THOUSAND BIRTHS)	105	122
CALORIE INTAKE PER HEAD PER DAY	1965	*
HEALTH WORKERS (PER 10,000)	*	*
LIFE EXPECTANCY	Female 49, male 45	Female 49, male 46
MAIN EMPLOYMENT SECTORS	Agriculture 17.7%, industry 46.9%	Agriculture 11.2%, industry 52%
MAIN INDUSTRIES	Agriculture, mining, forestry	Agriculture, mining, fishing, forestry
MAIN EXPORTS	Cotton, coffee, diamonds, timber	Raw cotton, meat, dates
MAIN DESTINATION OF EXPORTS	Belgium, France, Sudan	Portugal, Germany, Japan, France
CURRENCY	Franc CFA (100 centimes)	Franc CFA (100 centimes)
GDP (IN $US MILLION)	1443	1290
GDP PER HEAD (IN $US THOUSAND)	467	227
RETAIL PRICE INDEX	138 (1980 = 100)	96 (1980 = 100)
MILITARY EXPENDITURE (% OF GDP)	2.2	5.2
MILITARY EXPENDITURE PER HEAD (IN $US)	8	13.0
POPULATION	1.3	9.7
EDUCATION EXPENDITURE AS % OF GDP	3.0	2.0
NUMBER IN POST-SECONDARY EDUCATION (PER 100,000)	118	34
LITERACY RATE AGE 15+	*	*
MOTOR VEHICLES PER THOUSAND	5	3
TELEPHONE LINES PER HUNDRED	0.2	0.1
TELEVISIONS PER THOUSAND	4	1
NEWSPAPER CIRCULATION PER THOUSAND	1	*
NEWSPAPERS (D = DAILY, W = WEEKLY)	E Le Songo (d), Tierre Africaine (w), Ta Tene (w), Renouveau Centrafricain (w)	Al Watan (w), Contact (monthly)

	Congo	**Côte d'Ivoire**
AREA	342,000 sq km/132,047 sq miles	322,463 sq km/124,503 sq miles
CAPITAL	Brazzaville	Abidjan
MAIN TOWNS	Pointe Noir	Yamoussouko, Bouaké, Dimbokor
MAIN ETHNIC GROUPS	Vili, Kongo, Teke, M'Bochi, Sanga	Agni, Baoulé
MAIN LANGUAGES	French (official), Kongo, Teke	French (official), Baoule Diole, Bete, Senufo, Dan
MAIN RELIGIONS	Traditional, Christianity	Traditional, Islam, Christianity
POPULATION	2,590,000 (1995 UN estimate)	14,401,000 (1995 UN estimate)
DENSITY/SQ KM	7	39
ANNUAL GROWTH	3% (1990–5)	3.7% (1990–5)
URBAN	43%	44%
RURAL	57%	56%
FEMALES PER 100 MALES	104	97
INFANT MORTALITY (PER THOUSAND BIRTHS)	82	91
CALORIE INTAKE PER HEAD PER DAY	2519	2405
HEALTH WORKERS (PER 10,000)	*	*
LIFE EXPECTANCY	Female 54, male 49	Female 53, male 50
MAIN EMPLOYMENT SECTORS	*	Agriculture 13.8%, industry 20.1%
MAIN INDUSTRIES	Agriculture, oil, forestry	Agriculture
MAIN EXPORTS	Petroleum, timber	Coffee
MAIN DESTINATION OF EXPORTS	USA, France, Belgium, Italy	France, Netherlands, Germany, Italy
CURRENCY	Franc CFA (100 centimes)	Franc CFA (100 centimes)
GDP (IN $US MILLION)	2909	12,360
GDP PER HEAD (IN $US THOUSAND)	1266	994
RETAIL PRICE INDEX	204 (1980 = 100)	165 (1980 = 100)
MILITARY EXPENDITURE (% OF GDP)	3.8	0.8
MILITARY EXPENDITURE PER HEAD (IN $US)	47	6.0
POPULATION	3.9	1.2
EDUCATION EXPENDITURE AS % OF GDP	6.0	6.0
NUMBER IN POST-SECONDARY EDUCATION (PER 100,000)	470	240
LITERACY RATE AGE 15+	*	Female 24%, male 45%
MOTOR VEHICLES PER THOUSAND	21	20
TELEPHONE LINES PER HUNDRED	0.7	0.6
TELEVISIONS PER THOUSAND	6	59
NEWSPAPER CIRCULATION PER THOUSAND	8	8
NEWSPAPERS (D = DAILY, W = WEEKLY)	*Aujourd'hui* (d), *L'Eveil de Pointe-Noire* (d), *Mweti* (d), *Etumba* (w), *Le Pays* (w), *La Semaine Africaine* (w)	*Fraternité-Matin* (d), *La Démocrate* (d), *Le Jour* (d), *Nouvelle République* (d)

	Dominica	Equatorial Guinea
AREA	748 sq km/289 sq miles	28,051 sq km/10,830 sq miles
CAPITAL	Roseau	Malabo
MAIN TOWNS	Portsmouth, Marigot	Bata, Mbini
MAIN ETHNIC GROUPS	African descent, Mixed race, Amerindian	Fang, Bubi, Duala
MAIN LANGUAGES	English	Spanish (official), Beti
MAIN RELIGIONS	Christianity	Traditional, Christianity
POPULATION	74,000 (1995 UN estimate)	400,000 (1995 UN estimate)
DENSITY/SQ KM	111	13
ANNUAL GROWTH	*	2.6% (1990–5)
URBAN	*	31%
RURAL	*	69%
FEMALES PER 100 MALES	101	103
INFANT MORTALITY (PER THOUSAND BIRTHS)	18	117
CALORIE INTAKE PER HEAD PER DAY	*	*
HEALTH WORKERS (PER 10,000)	32.5	*
LIFE EXPECTANCY	*	Female 50, male 46
MAIN EMPLOYMENT SECTORS	*	*
MAIN INDUSTRIES	Agriculture, tourism	Agriculture, forestry
MAIN EXPORTS	Bananas, coconut, citrus fruit, bay oil	Cocoa, coffee, timber
MAIN DESTINATION OF EXPORTS	UK, Jamaica, Italy, Taiwan	Cameroon, Spain, Nigeria
CURRENCY	East Caribbean dollar (100 cents)	Franc CFA (100 centimes)
GDP (IN $US MILLION)	177	165
GDP PER HEAD (IN $US THOUSAND)	2463	457
RETAIL PRICE INDEX	180 (1980 = 100)	* (1980 = 100)
MILITARY EXPENDITURE (% OF GDP)	*	1.8
MILITARY EXPENDITURE PER HEAD (IN $US)	*	9
POPULATION	*	2.6
EDUCATION EXPENDITURE AS % OF GDP	5.0	1.0
NUMBER IN POST-SECONDARY EDUCATION (PER 100,000)	*	*
LITERACY RATE AGE 15+	*	*
MOTOR VEHICLES PER THOUSAND	112	*
TELEPHONE LINES PER HUNDRED	19.4	0.4
TELEVISIONS PER THOUSAND	72	9
NEWSPAPER CIRCULATION PER THOUSAND	*	6
NEWSPAPERS (D = DAILY, W = WEEKLY)	*The New Chronicle* (w), *The Tropical Star* (w)	*El Sol* (w), *Hoja Parroquial* (w), *Le Verdad* (monthly)

	Eritrea	Ethiopia
AREA	118,500 sq km/45,745 sq miles	1,128,221 sq km/435,608 sq miles
CAPITAL	Asmara	Addis Ababa
MAIN TOWNS	Massawa, Assab	Dire Dawa, Aksum
MAIN ETHNIC GROUPS	Tigrinya, Tigre, Bilen, Afar, Saho, Kunama, Nara, Rashida	Amharas, Tigrayans, Oromos, Somalis, Afra
MAIN LANGUAGES	Amharic (official), English, Arabic, Tigre, Tigrinya, Afar, Bilen,	Amharic, Oromo, Tigrinya
MAIN RELIGIONS	Christianity, Islam	Christianity, Islam, animist, traditional
POPULATION	3,500,000 (1991 UN estimate)	58,039,000 (1995 UN estimate)
DENSITY/SQ KM	37	44
ANNUAL GROWTH	*	3% (1990–5)
URBAN	*	13%
RURAL	*	87%
FEMALES PER 100 MALES	*	100
INFANT MORTALITY (PER THOUSAND BIRTHS)	*	122
CALORIE INTAKE PER HEAD PER DAY	*	*
HEALTH WORKERS (PER 10,000)	*	*
LIFE EXPECTANCY	*	Female 49, male 45
MAIN EMPLOYMENT SECTORS	*	Agriculture 75.2%, industry 11%
MAIN INDUSTRIES	Agriculture, livestock	Agriculture, mining
MAIN EXPORTS	Minimal	Coffee, gold, copper, potash
MAIN DESTINATION OF EXPORTS	Ethiopia, Italy	Japan, Germany, Saudi Arabia
CURRENCY	Birr (100 cents)	Ethiopian birr (100 cents)
GDP (IN $US MILLION)	*	6592
GDP PER HEAD (IN $US THOUSAND)	*	137
RETAIL PRICE INDEX	* (1980 = 100)	256 (1980 = 100)
MILITARY EXPENDITURE (% OF GDP)	*	21.9
MILITARY EXPENDITURE PER HEAD (IN $US)	*	28
POPULATION	*	2.3
EDUCATION EXPENDITURE AS % OF GDP	*	4.0
NUMBER IN POST-SECONDARY EDUCATION (PER 100,000)	*	70
LITERACY RATE AGE 15+	*	*
MOTOR VEHICLES PER THOUSAND	*	1
TELEPHONE LINES PER HUNDRED	*	0.3
TELEVISIONS PER THOUSAND	*	3
NEWSPAPER CIRCULATION PER THOUSAND	*	1
NEWSPAPERS (D = DAILY, W = WEEKLY)	*Hadras Eritrea* (twice a week), *Eritrea Profile* (w)	*Addis Zemen* (d), *Ethiopia Herald* (d), *Addis Zimit* (w)

	Gabon	**The Gambia**
AREA	267,667 sq km/103,347 sq miles	11,295 sq km/4,361 sq miles
CAPITAL	Libreville	Banjul
MAIN TOWNS	Port Gentil, Franceville	Serekunda, Bakau, Georgetown
MAIN ETHNIC GROUPS	Fang, Eshira, Adonma	Mandingo, Fula, Wolof
MAIN LANGUAGES	French (official), Fang, Mpongwe	English (official), Mandingo, Fula, Wolof
MAIN RELIGIONS	Traditional, Christianity	Islam, Christianity
POPULATION	1,367,000 (1995 UN estimate)	980,000 (1995 UN estimate)
DENSITY/SQ KM	5	78
ANNUAL GROWTH	3.3% (1990–5)	2.6% (1990–5)
URBAN	50%	26%
RURAL	50%	74%
FEMALES PER 100 MALES	103	102
INFANT MORTALITY (PER THOUSAND BIRTHS)	94	132
CALORIE INTAKE PER HEAD PER DAY	*	2339
HEALTH WORKERS (PER 10,000)	32.2	*
LIFE EXPECTANCY	Female 55, male 52	Female 47, male 43
MAIN EMPLOYMENT SECTORS	Agriculture 65.6%	Agriculture 7.7%, industry 23.8%
MAIN INDUSTRIES	Agriculture, mining, oil	Agriculture, fishing, livestock, light industry, tourism
MAIN EXPORTS	Petroleum products, timber, manganese, uranium	Ground nuts, rice, maize, cotton
MAIN DESTINATION OF EXPORTS	France, USA, Netherlands	Belgium, Italy, Japan
CURRENCY	Franc CFA (100 centimes)	Dalasi (100 butut)
GDP (IN $US MILLION)	4438	306
GDP PER HEAD (IN $US THOUSAND)	3708	346
RETAIL PRICE INDEX	196 (1980 = 100)	627 (1980 = 100)
MILITARY EXPENDITURE (% OF GDP)	3.6	0.7
MILITARY EXPENDITURE PER HEAD (IN $US)	143	1
POPULATION	9.2	2.3
EDUCATION EXPENDITURE AS % OF GDP	5.0	3.0
NUMBER IN POST-SECONDARY EDUCATION (PER 100,000)	377	*
LITERACY RATE AGE 15+	*	Female 12%, male 29%
MOTOR VEHICLES PER THOUSAND	*	*
TELEPHONE LINES PER HUNDRED	1.8	1.6
TELEVISIONS PER THOUSAND	37	*
NEWSPAPER CIRCULATION PER THOUSAND	17	2
NEWSPAPERS (D = DAILY, W = WEEKLY)	*Gabon-Matin* (d), *L'Union* (d), *Sept Jours* (w), *Le Bûcheron* (w), *Gabon Libre* (w)	*Daily Observer* (d), *The Gambia Weekly* (w), *The Gambian Times* (twice a week), *Newsmonth* (monthly)

	Ghana	**Grenada**
AREA	238,537 sq km/92,100 sq miles	344 sq km/133 sq miles
CAPITAL	Accra	St George's
MAIN TOWNS	Kumasi, Sekondi-Takoradi, Tema, Cape Coast	Grenville, Hillsborough
MAIN ETHNIC GROUPS	Akan, Ga, Ewe, Guan, Moshi-Dagomba	African descent, mixed descent, East Indian, European
MAIN LANGUAGES	English (official), Twi, Fante, Ga, Ewa, Dagbeni, Hausa, Nzima	English
MAIN RELIGIONS	Traditional, Christianity, Islam	Christianity
POPULATION	17,453,000 (1995 UN estimate)	89,000 (1995 UN estimate)
DENSITY/SQ KM	65	244
ANNUAL GROWTH	3% (1990–5)	*
URBAN	36%	*
RURAL	64%	*
FEMALES PER 100 MALES	101	107
INFANT MORTALITY (PER THOUSAND BIRTHS)	81	15
CALORIE INTAKE PER HEAD PER DAY	2167	*
HEALTH WORKERS (PER 10,000)	*	*
LIFE EXPECTANCY	Female 58, male 54	*
MAIN EMPLOYMENT SECTORS	Agriculture 8.5%, industry 27.3%	*
MAIN INDUSTRIES	Agriculture, mining, fishing, light industry, forestry	Agriculture, tourism
MAIN EXPORTS	Cocoa, gold, industrial diamonds, manganese, timber	Cocoa, bananas, spices
MAIN DESTINATION OF EXPORTS	UK, USA, Netherlands	USA, UK, St Lucia
CURRENCY	Cedi (100 pesewas)	East Caribbean Dollar (100 cents)
GDP (IN $US MILLION)	7100	210
GDP PER HEAD (IN $US THOUSAND)	459	2309
RETAIL PRICE INDEX	7265 (1980 = 100)	127 (1980 = 100)
MILITARY EXPENDITURE (% OF GDP)	0.6	*
MILITARY EXPENDITURE PER HEAD (IN $US)	2.3	*
POPULATION	0.6	*
EDUCATION EXPENDITURE AS % OF GDP	3.0	5.0
NUMBER IN POST-SECONDARY EDUCATION (PER 100,000)	127	*
LITERACY RATE AGE 15+	*	*
MOTOR VEHICLES PER THOUSAND	8	*
TELEPHONE LINES PER HUNDRED	0.3	17.8
TELEVISIONS PER THOUSAND	15	330
NEWSPAPER CIRCULATION PER THOUSAND	13	*
NEWSPAPERS (D = DAILY, W = WEEKLY)	*Daily Graphic* (d), *The Ghanaian Times* (d), *Echo* (w), *Ghanaian Chronicle* (w), *The Ghanaian Voice* (w), *The Mirror* (w), *Weekly Spectator* (w)	*Grenada Guardian* (w), *The Grenada Times* (w), *The Informer* (w), *The Grenada Voice* (w)

	Guinea	**Guinea-Bissau**
AREA	245,857 sq km/94,926 sq miles	36,125 sq km/13,948 sq miles
CAPITAL	Conakry	Bissau
MAIN TOWNS	Mali, Kerouane, Kankan, Kindia, Labe, Nzérékoré	São Domingos
MAIN ETHNIC GROUPS	Susu, Tenda, Kissi, Malinke, Fula	Balante, Fula, Mandinka
MAIN LANGUAGES	French (official), Malinke, Fula, Susu	Portuguese (official), Crioulo, Mande
MAIN RELIGIONS	Islam, traditional, Christianity	Animism, Islam, Christianity
POPULATION	6,700,000 (1995 UN estimate)	1,073,000 (1995 UN estimate)
DENSITY/SQ KM	24	27
ANNUAL GROWTH	3% (1990–5)	2.1% (1990–5)
URBAN	30%	22%
RURAL	70%	78%
FEMALES PER 100 MALES	99	103
INFANT MORTALITY (PER THOUSAND BIRTHS)	134	140
CALORIE INTAKE PER HEAD PER DAY	2007	*
HEALTH WORKERS (PER 10,000)	*	11.6
LIFE EXPECTANCY	Female 45, male 44	Female 45, male 42
MAIN EMPLOYMENT SECTORS	Agriculture 74.9%	Agriculture 79.2%
MAIN INDUSTRIES	Agriculture, mining	Agriculture, forestry, mining
MAIN EXPORTS	Coffee, tobacco, bauxite	Cotton, ground nuts, timber, bauxite
MAIN DESTINATION OF EXPORTS	USA, France, Germany, Spain	Portugal, Spain, France, Japan
CURRENCY	Guinea franc (100 centimes)	Guinea-Bissau peso (100 centavos)
GDP (IN $US MILLION)	3016	251
GDP PER HEAD (IN $US THOUSAND)	508	255
RETAIL PRICE INDEX	272 (1980 = 100)	* (1980 = 100)
MILITARY EXPENDITURE (% OF GDP)	1.3	2.4
MILITARY EXPENDITURE PER HEAD (IN $US)	4.8	6
POPULATION	1.9	11.7
EDUCATION EXPENDITURE AS % OF GDP	3.3	3.0
NUMBER IN POST-SECONDARY EDUCATION (PER 100,000)	122	*
LITERACY RATE AGE 15+	*	*
MOTOR VEHICLES PER THOUSAND	16	8
TELEPHONE LINES PER HUNDRED	0.2	0.6
TELEVISIONS PER THOUSAND	7	*
NEWSPAPER CIRCULATION PER THOUSAND	*	6
NEWSPAPERS (D = DAILY, W = WEEKLY)	*L'Observateur* (w), *Horoya* (w), *Fonike* (w)	*Nô Pintcha* (d), *Banobero* (w), *Baguerra* (w)

	Haiti	**Jamaica**
AREA	27,750 sq km/10,714 sq miles	10,991 sq km/4244 sq miles
CAPITAL	Port-au-Prince	Kingston
MAIN TOWNS	Cap Haitien, Gonaives, Les Cayes	Mandeville, Montego Bay, Ocho Rios, Spanish Town
MAIN ETHNIC GROUPS	African descent, mulatto	African descent, mixed descent, Indian
MAIN LANGUAGES	Haitian creole (official), French (official)	English (official), Creole, Hindi, Spanish
MAIN RELIGIONS	Christianity, voodoo	Christianity
POPULATION	7,180,000 (1995 UN estimate)	2,547,000 (1995 UN estimate)
DENSITY/SQ KM	239	215
ANNUAL GROWTH	2% (1990–5)	1% (1990–5)
URBAN	32%	55%
RURAL	68%	45%
FEMALES PER 100 MALES	104	100
INFANT MORTALITY (PER THOUSAND BIRTHS)	86	14
CALORIE INTAKE PER HEAD PER DAY	1992	2579
HEALTH WORKERS (PER 10,000)	6.8	26.5
LIFE EXPECTANCY	Female 58, male 55	Female 76, male 71
MAIN EMPLOYMENT SECTORS	Agriculture 66.2%, industry 8.9%	Agriculture 54.9%, industry 14.1%
MAIN INDUSTRIES	Agriculture, light industry	Agriculture, mining, light industry, tourism
MAIN EXPORTS	Coffee, cocoa, sugar, textiles	Aluminium, bananas, sugar, bauxite, clothing
MAIN DESTINATION OF EXPORTS	USA, France, Italy	USA, UK, Canada, Norway
CURRENCY	Gourde (100 centimes)	Jamaican dollar (100 cents)
GDP (IN $US MILLION)	2951	3497
GDP PER HEAD (IN $US THOUSAND)	446	1431
RETAIL PRICE INDEX	333 (1980 = 100)	546 (1980 = 100)
MILITARY EXPENDITURE (% OF GDP)	2.0	0.7
MILITARY EXPENDITURE PER HEAD (IN $US)	8.3	9.9
POPULATION	1.3	1.2
EDUCATION EXPENDITURE AS % OF GDP	2.0	4.0
NUMBER IN POST-SECONDARY EDUCATION (PER 100,000)	107	515
LITERACY RATE AGE 15+	Female 32%, male 37%	*
MOTOR VEHICLES PER THOUSAND	6	44
TELEPHONE LINES PER HUNDRED	0.8	4.7
TELEVISIONS PER THOUSAND	5	131
NEWSPAPER CIRCULATION PER THOUSAND	7	64
NEWSPAPERS (D = DAILY, W = WEEKLY)	*Le Matin* (d), *Le Nouvelliste* (d), *L'Union* (d), *Haiti Observateur* (w), *Le Septenrion* (w), *Haiti Progrés* (w)	*Daily Gleaner* (d), *Daily Star* (d), *Jamaica Herald* (d), *Jamaica Observer* (d), *Weekend Star* (w), *Sunday Gleaner* (w)

	Kenya	**Lesotho**
AREA	582,646 sq km/224,961 sq miles	30,355 sq km/11,720 sq miles
CAPITAL	Nairobi	Maseru
MAIN TOWNS	Kisumu, Mombasa, Nakuru	Teyateyaneng, Mafeteng, Roma, Quthing
MAIN ETHNIC GROUPS	Kikuyu, Lihya, Luo, Kamba, Kalenjin, Masai	Basotho
MAIN LANGUAGES	Swahili (official), English (official)	Sesotho (official), English (official), Zulu, Xhosa
MAIN RELIGIONS	Christianity, Islam, traditional	Christianity, traditional
POPULATION	27,885,000 (1995 UN estimate)	1,977,000 (1995 UN estimate)
DENSITY/SQ KM	45	60
ANNUAL GROWTH	3.3% (1990–5)	2.5% (1990–5)
URBAN	28%	23%
RURAL	72%	77%
FEMALES PER 100 MALES	100	105
INFANT MORTALITY (PER THOUSAND BIRTHS)	66	79
CALORIE INTAKE PER HEAD PER DAY	2016	2275
HEALTH WORKERS (PER 10,000)	13.1	*
LIFE EXPECTANCY	Female 61, male 57	Female 63, male 58
MAIN EMPLOYMENT SECTORS	Agriculture 18.9%, industry 20%	Agriculture 80.4%
MAIN INDUSTRIES	Agriculture, oil refining, mining, light industry	Agriculture, livestock, light industry, tourism
MAIN EXPORTS	Coffee, tea, fruit	Fruit, wool
MAIN DESTINATION OF EXPORTS	UK, Uganda, Tanzania, Germany	South Africa, European Union
CURRENCY	Kenya shilling (100 cents)	Loti (100 lisente)
GDP (IN $US MILLION)	8261	596
GDP PER HEAD (IN $US THOUSAND)	339	333
RETAIL PRICE INDEX	305 (1980 = 100)	484 (1980 = 100)
MILITARY EXPENDITURE (% OF GDP)	2.8	3.8
MILITARY EXPENDITURE PER HEAD (IN $US)	8.6	33
POPULATION	0.8	1.1
EDUCATION EXPENDITURE AS % OF GDP	6.0	5.0
NUMBER IN POST-SECONDARY EDUCATION (PER 100,000)	135	333
LITERACY RATE AGE 15+	*	*
MOTOR VEHICLES PER THOUSAND	13	13
TELEPHONE LINES PER HUNDRED	0.8	0.6
TELEVISIONS PER THOUSAND	10	6
NEWSPAPER CIRCULATION PER THOUSAND	15	11
NEWSPAPERS (D = DAILY, W = WEEKLY)	*Kenya Leo* (d), *Kenya Times* (d), *The Standard* (d), *Taifo Leo* (w)	*Mphatlatsane* (d), *Lese Linyana la Lesotho* (twice weekly), *Lentsoe la Basotho* (monthly)

	Liberia	**Malawi**
AREA	111,369 sq km/43,000 sq miles	118,484 sq km/45,747 sq miles
CAPITAL	Monrovia	Lilongwe
MAIN TOWNS	Buchanan, Greeneville, Harper	Blantyre, Zomba
MAIN ETHNIC GROUPS	Kpelle, Bassa, Grebo, Gio, Kru, Mano	Maravi, Lomwe, Yao, Ngoni
MAIN LANGUAGES	English (official), Mande, West Atlantic, Kwa	English (official), Chichewa (official)
MAIN RELIGIONS	Christianity, Islam, traditional	Christianity, traditional, Islam
POPULATION	3,039,000 (1995 UN estimate)	11,304,000 (1995 UN estimate)
DENSITY/SQ KM	24	72
ANNUAL GROWTH	3.3% (1990–5)	3.3% (1990–5)
URBAN	51%	14%
RURAL	49%	86%
FEMALES PER 100 MALES	98	102
INFANT MORTALITY (PER THOUSAND BIRTHS)	126	142
CALORIE INTAKE PER HEAD PER DAY	2244	2057
HEALTH WORKERS (PER 10,000)	8.4	*
LIFE EXPECTANCY	Female 57, male 54	Female 45, male 44
MAIN EMPLOYMENT SECTORS	Agriculture 70.3%	Agriculture 40%, industry 21.5%
MAIN INDUSTRIES	Agriculture, mining, forestry	Agriculture, fishing, light industry
MAIN EXPORTS	Cocoa, coffee, timber, iron ore, diamonds	Tobacco, tea, sugar, ground nuts, cotton
MAIN DESTINATION OF EXPORTS	Germany, USA, France	UK, USA, Germany, South Africa
CURRENCY	Liberian dollar (100 cents)	Kwacha (100 tambala)
GDP (IN $US MILLION)	1037	2191
GDP PER HEAD (IN $US THOUSAND)	390	219
RETAIL PRICE INDEX	162 (1980 = 100)	201 (1980 = 100)
MILITARY EXPENDITURE (% OF GDP)	4.4	1.1
MILITARY EXPENDITURE PER HEAD (IN $US)	21	2.5
POPULATION	2.4	0.8
EDUCATION EXPENDITURE AS % OF GDP	5.0	2.0
NUMBER IN POST-SECONDARY EDUCATION (PER 100,000)	220	61
LITERACY RATE AGE 15+	*	*
MOTOR VEHICLES PER THOUSAND	14	5
TELEPHONE LINES PER HUNDRED	0.1	0.3
TELEVISIONS PER THOUSAND	18	*
NEWSPAPER CIRCULATION PER THOUSAND	14	3
NEWSPAPERS (D = DAILY, W = WEEKLY)	*Daily Observer* (d), *Sunday Express* (w), *Sunday People* (w), *The Inquirer* (w)	*Daily Times* (d), *Financial Post* (w), *News* (w), *Nation* (w), *New Express* (w)

	Mali	**Mozambique**
AREA	1,240,000 sq km/478,791 sq miles	801,590 sq km/309,495 sq miles
CAPITAL	Bamako	Maputo
MAIN TOWNS	Mopti, Timbuktu, Gao, Kayes	Nampula, Beira, Quelimane
MAIN ETHNIC GROUPS	Bambara, Fulani, Senufo, Sonike	Makua, Tsonga, Malawi, Shona, Yao, Swahili, Makonde
MAIN LANGUAGES	French (official), Bambara, Senufo, Sarakole	Portuguese (official), Bantu languages
MAIN RELIGIONS	Muslim, traditional	Traditional, Christianity, Islam
POPULATION	10,797,000 (1995 UN estimate)	16,359,000 (1995 UN estimate)
DENSITY/SQ KM	8	20
ANNUAL GROWTH	3.2% (1990–5)	2.8% (1990–5)
URBAN	27%	34%
RURAL	73%	66%
FEMALES PER 100 MALES	103	102
INFANT MORTALITY (PER THOUSAND BIRTHS)	159	147
CALORIE INTAKE PER HEAD PER DAY	2114	1604
HEALTH WORKERS (PER 10,000)	7.7	*
LIFE EXPECTANCY	Female 48, male 44	Female 48, male 45
MAIN EMPLOYMENT SECTORS	Agriculture 81.4%	Agriculture 8.4%, industry 72.6%
MAIN INDUSTRIES	Agriculture, mining	Agriculture, mining, light industry, fishing
MAIN EXPORTS	Gold, ground nuts, cotton, meat, dried fish	Seafood, cashew nuts, cotton, sugar, copra
MAIN DESTINATION OF EXPORTS	Russia, Algeria, Taiwan	Spain, USA, Japan, Portugal
CURRENCY	Franc CFA (100 centimes)	Metical (100 centavos)
GDP (IN $US MILLION)	2451	1275
GDP PER HEAD (IN $US THOUSAND)	258	84
RETAIL PRICE INDEX	119 (1980 = 100)	381 (1980 = 100)
MILITARY EXPENDITURE (% OF GDP)	2.0	13.0
MILITARY EXPENDITURE PER HEAD (IN $US)	5	9.6
POPULATION	1.5	4.4
EDUCATION EXPENDITURE AS % OF GDP	3.0	4.0
NUMBER IN POST-SECONDARY EDUCATION (PER 100,000)	73	16
LITERACY RATE AGE 15+	*	*
MOTOR VEHICLES PER THOUSAND	1	5
TELEPHONE LINES PER HUNDRED	0.1	0.4
TELEVISIONS PER THOUSAND	1	3
NEWSPAPER CIRCULATION PER THOUSAND	1	6
NEWSPAPERS (D = DAILY, W = WEEKLY)	L'Essor-La Voix du Peuple (d), La Républicain (w), Citoyen (w), L'Aurore (twice weekly)	Diário de Moçambique (d), Imparcial (d), Notícias (d), Domingo (w)

	Namibia	**Niger**
AREA	824,292 sq km/318,261 sq miles	1,267,080 sq km/489,191 sq miles
CAPITAL	Windhoek	Niamey
MAIN TOWNS	Walvis Bay, Ondangwa	Zinder
MAIN ETHNIC GROUPS	Ovambo, Kavango, Herero, Damara, Coloureds, Europeans	Hausa, Zerma, Kanuri, Fulani, Tuareg, Songhi, Djerma, Beriberi-Manga
MAIN LANGUAGES	English (official), Afrikaans	French (official), Hausa
MAIN RELIGIONS	Christianity, traditional	Islam, Animism
POPULATION	1,688,000 (1995 UN estimate)	9,102,000 (1995 UN estimate)
DENSITY/SQ KM	2	6
ANNUAL GROWTH	3.2% (1990–5)	3.3% (1990–5)
URBAN	31%	23%
RURAL	69%	77%
FEMALES PER 100 MALES	99	102
INFANT MORTALITY (PER THOUSAND BIRTHS)	70	124
CALORIE INTAKE PER HEAD PER DAY	*	2321
HEALTH WORKERS (PER 10,000)	*	23.6
LIFE EXPECTANCY	Female 60, male 58	Female 48, male 45
MAIN EMPLOYMENT SECTORS	Agriculture 35.8%	Agriculture 7.9%, industry 48.5%
MAIN INDUSTRIES	Agriculture, mining, fishing	Agriculture, livestock, mining
MAIN EXPORTS	Diamonds, uranium, base metals, livestock products, fish	Ground nuts, cattle, hides, uranium
MAIN DESTINATION OF EXPORTS	USA, South Africa, Japan	France, Nigeria, USA
CURRENCY	Rand (100 cents)	Franc CFA (100 centimes)
GDP (IN $US MILLION)	2421	2464
GDP PER HEAD (IN $US THOUSAND)	1629	309
RETAIL PRICE INDEX	142 (1980 = 100)	95 (1980 = 100)
MILITARY EXPENDITURE (% OF GDP)	*	1.0
MILITARY EXPENDITURE PER HEAD (IN $US)	*	3.8
POPULATION	*	0.6
EDUCATION EXPENDITURE AS % OF GDP	4.0	3.0
NUMBER IN POST-SECONDARY EDUCATION (PER 100,000)	280	60
LITERACY RATE AGE 15+	*	*
MOTOR VEHICLES PER THOUSAND	*	7
TELEPHONE LINES PER HUNDRED	3.8	0.1
TELEVISIONS PER THOUSAND	21	5
NEWSPAPER CIRCULATION PER THOUSAND	153	1
NEWSPAPERS (D = DAILY, W = WEEKLY)	*The Namibian* (d), *The Windhoek Advertiser* (d), *Namib Times* (twice weekly), *Nambia Today* (twice weekly), *New Era* (w), *Aloe* (monthly)	*Le Sahel* (d), *Le Sahel Dimanche* (w), *Le Républicain* (w), *Haske* (w)

	Nigeria	Rwanda
AREA	923,768 sq km/356,669 sq miles	26,338 sq km/10,169 sq miles
CAPITAL	Abuja	Kigali
MAIN TOWNS	Lagos, Ibadan, Kaduna, Kano, Benin City, Port Harcourt	Butari, Ruhengeri
MAIN ETHNIC GROUPS	Hausa, Fulani, Yoruba, Ibo	Hutu, Tutsi, Twa
MAIN LANGUAGES	English (official), Hausa, Ibo, Yoruba	French (official), Kinyarwanda, Kiswahili
MAIN RELIGIONS	Islam, Christianity, traditional	Christianity, Islam, traditional
POPULATION	126,929,000 (1995 UN estimate)	8,330,000 (1995 UN estimate)
DENSITY/SQ KM	121	294
ANNUAL GROWTH	3.1% (1990–5)	3.4% (1990–5)
URBAN	39%	6%
RURAL	61%	94%
FEMALES PER 100 MALES	102	102
INFANT MORTALITY (PER THOUSAND BIRTHS)	96	110
CALORIE INTAKE PER HEAD PER DAY	2083	1817
HEALTH WORKERS (PER 10,000)	12.2	3
LIFE EXPECTANCY	Female 54, male 51	Female 48, male 45
MAIN EMPLOYMENT SECTORS	Agriculture 65.1%	Agriculture 91.4%
MAIN INDUSTRIES	Agriculture, oil, mining, forestry	Agriculture, mining, livestock
MAIN EXPORTS	Oil, ground nuts, palm oil, tin, cocoa, rubber, timber	Coffee, tin, hides
MAIN DESTINATION OF EXPORTS	USA, Spain, Germany	Germany, Netherlands, Belgium, UK
CURRENCY	Naira (100 kobo)	Rwanda franc (100 centimes)
GDP (IN $US MILLION)	32,788	1701
GDP PER HEAD (IN $US THOUSAND)	292	234
RETAIL PRICE INDEX	800 (1980 = 100)	216 (1980 = 100)
MILITARY EXPENDITURE (% OF GDP)	0.8	7.5
MILITARY EXPENDITURE PER HEAD (IN $US)	2.0	14.8
POPULATION	0.8	3.8
EDUCATION EXPENDITURE AS % OF GDP	1.0	4.0
NUMBER IN POST-SECONDARY EDUCATION (PER 100,000)	320	48
LITERACY RATE AGE 15+	*	*
MOTOR VEHICLES PER THOUSAND	3	2
TELEPHONE LINES PER HUNDRED	0.2	0.2
TELEVISIONS PER THOUSAND	33	*
NEWSPAPER CIRCULATION PER THOUSAND	16	*
NEWSPAPERS (D = DAILY, W = WEEKLY)	Daily Sketch (d), Daily Times (d), The Democrat (d), Nigeria Observer (d), Nigeria Standard (d), Nigeria Tribune (d), Sunday Chronicle (w), Sunday Observer (w), Sunday Times (w)	Imvaho (w), La Rèleve (monthly), Umuhinzi-Mworozi (monthly)

	St Christopher and Nevis	St Lucia
AREA	261 sq km/101 sq miles	616 sq km/238 sq miles
CAPITAL	Basseterre	Castries
MAIN TOWNS	Charlestown (Nevis)	Soufriere, Vieux-Fort
MAIN ETHNIC GROUPS	African descent, mixed descent	African descent, mixed descent
MAIN LANGUAGES	English	English, French patois
MAIN RELIGIONS	Christianity	Christianity
POPULATION	44,000 (1995 UN estimate)	148,000 (1995 UN estimate)
DENSITY/SQ KM	169	246
ANNUAL GROWTH	0.3% (1990–5)	1.2% (1990–5)
URBAN	53%	46%
RURAL	47%	54%
FEMALES PER 100 MALES	95	106
INFANT MORTALITY (PER THOUSAND BIRTHS)	24	18
CALORIE INTAKE PER HEAD PER DAY	2822	2760
HEALTH WORKERS (PER 10,000)	32.4	22.1
LIFE EXPECTANCY	Female 71, male 66	Female 75, male 68
MAIN EMPLOYMENT SECTORS	*	*
MAIN INDUSTRIES	Sugar, tourism, light industry	Agriculture, light industry, tourism
MAIN EXPORTS	Sugar	Bananas, coconut products, textiles
MAIN DESTINATION OF EXPORTS	USA, UK, Trinidad and Tobago	UK, USA, Dominica
CURRENCY	East Caribbean dollar (100 cents)	East Caribbean dollar (100 cents)
GDP (IN $US MILLION)	121	275
GDP PER HEAD (IN $US THOUSAND)	2880	2037
RETAIL PRICE INDEX	150 (1980 = 100)	140 (1980 = 100)
MILITARY EXPENDITURE (% OF GDP)	*	*
MILITARY EXPENDITURE PER HEAD (IN $US)	*	*
POPULATION	*	*
EDUCATION EXPENDITURE AS % OF GDP	3.0	5.0
NUMBER IN POST-SECONDARY EDUCATION (PER 100,000)	*	*
LITERACY RATE AGE 15+	*	*
MOTOR VEHICLES PER THOUSAND	133	58
TELEPHONE LINES PER HUNDRED	*	12.7
TELEVISIONS PER THOUSAND	205	189
NEWSPAPER CIRCULATION PER THOUSAND	*	*
NEWSPAPERS (D = DAILY, W = WEEKLY)	*The Democrat* (w), *The Labour Spokesman* (twice weekly)	*The Voice of St Lucia* (three times a week), *The Crusader* (w), *The Mirror* (w), *The Vanguard* (fortnightly)

	St Vincent and the Grenadines	São Tomé and Príncipe
AREA	388 sq km/150 sq miles	964 sq km/372 sq miles
CAPITAL	Kingstown	São Tomé
MAIN TOWNS	Georgetown, Chateaubelair	Santo Antonio, Santa Cruz
MAIN ETHNIC GROUPS	African descent, mixed descent	African-European mixed descent
MAIN LANGUAGES	English, French patois	Portuguese (official), Fang
MAIN RELIGIONS	Christianity	Christianity, animist
POPULATION	98,000 (1995 UN estimate)	97,000 (1995 UN estimate)
DENSITY/SQ KM	302	129
ANNUAL GROWTH	*	*
URBAN	22%	47%
RURAL	78%	53%
FEMALES PER 100 MALES	106	101
INFANT MORTALITY (PER THOUSAND BIRTHS)	22	72
CALORIE INTAKE PER HEAD PER DAY	2764	*
HEALTH WORKERS (PER 10,000)	35.6	44.3
LIFE EXPECTANCY	*	*
MAIN EMPLOYMENT SECTORS	*	Agriculture 53.9%
MAIN INDUSTRIES	Agriculture, light manufacturing, tourism	Agriculture
MAIN EXPORTS	Bananas, cocoa, spices	Cacao
MAIN DESTINATION OF EXPORTS	UK, Trinidad and Tobago, St Lucia, USA	Germany, Netherlands
CURRENCY	East Caribbean dollar (100 cents)	Dobra (100 centavos)
GDP (IN $US MILLION)	178	45
GDP PER HEAD (IN $US THOUSAND)	1648	373
RETAIL PRICE INDEX	130 (1980 = 100)	* (1980 = 100)
MILITARY EXPENDITURE (% OF GDP)	*	1.6
MILITARY EXPENDITURE PER HEAD (IN $US)	*	6
POPULATION	*	7.8
EDUCATION EXPENDITURE AS % OF GDP	5.0	*
NUMBER IN POST-SECONDARY EDUCATION (PER 100,000)	*	*
LITERACY RATE AGE 15+	*	*
MOTOR VEHICLES PER THOUSAND	70	*
TELEPHONE LINES PER HUNDRED	13.9	1.8
TELEVISIONS PER THOUSAND	144	*
NEWSPAPER CIRCULATION PER THOUSAND	*	*
NEWSPAPERS (D = DAILY, W = WEEKLY)	*The Independent Weekly* (w), *The Vincentian* (weekly), *Justice* (weekly), *The New Times* (w), *The Star* (fortnightly)	*O Independente* (d), *O Parvo* (d), *O Páis Hoje* (d), *Nova Républica* (d)

226

	Senegal	**Sierra Leone**
AREA	196,192 sq km/75,750 sq miles	71,740 sq km/27,699 sq miles
CAPITAL	Dakar	Freetown
MAIN TOWNS	Thiés, Kaolack, St Louis, Zinguinchor	Koidu, Bo, Kenema, Makeni
MAIN ETHNIC GROUPS	Wolf, Sere, Tukulor, Fulani, Dioula, Malinke	Temne, Mende, Lokko, Sherbo, Limba, Creole
MAIN LANGUAGES	French (official)	Temne, Mende, Krio
MAIN RELIGIONS	Islam, Christianity, traditional	Traditional, Christianity, Islam
POPULATION	8,387,000 (1995 UN estimate)	4,740,000 (1995 UN estimate)
DENSITY/SQ KM	38	59
ANNUAL GROWTH	2.7% (1990–5)	2.7% (1990–5)
URBAN	42%	36%
RURAL	58%	64%
FEMALES PER 100 MALES	100	103
INFANT MORTALITY (PER THOUSAND BIRTHS)	80	143
CALORIE INTAKE PER HEAD PER DAY	2162	1813
HEALTH WORKERS (PER 10,000)	6	9.9
LIFE EXPECTANCY	Female 50, male 48	Female 45, male 41
MAIN EMPLOYMENT SECTORS	Agriculture 78.7%	Agriculture 10.4%, industry 38.8%
MAIN INDUSTRIES	Agriculture, mining, tourism	Agriculture, mining
MAIN EXPORTS	Ground nuts, phosphates	Diamonds, iron ore, bauxite, cocoa, coffee, palm kernels
MAIN DESTINATION OF EXPORTS	France, India, Mali, Italy	USA, UK, Germany
CURRENCY	Franc CFA (100 centimes)	Leone (100 cents)
GDP (IN $US MILLION)	5608	508
GDP PER HEAD (IN $US THOUSAND)	745	119
RETAIL PRICE INDEX	173 (1980 = 100)	58,824 (1980 = 100)
MILITARY EXPENDITURE (% OF GDP)	2.1	2.3
MILITARY EXPENDITURE PER HEAD (IN $US)	16	2.7
POPULATION	2.3	1.1
EDUCATION EXPENDITURE AS % OF GDP	4.0	1.0
NUMBER IN POST-SECONDARY EDUCATION (PER 100,000)	253	125
LITERACY RATE AGE 15+	*	*
MOTOR VEHICLES PER THOUSAND	*	*
TELEPHONE LINES PER HUNDRED	0.6	0.4
TELEVISIONS PER THOUSAND	36	10
NEWSPAPER CIRCULATION PER THOUSAND	7	2
NEWSPAPERS (D = DAILY, W = WEEKLY)	*Réveil de L'Afrique Noire* (d), *Le Soleil* (d), *Wal Fadjiri* (d), *Sud au Quotidian* (d)	*Daily Mail* (d), *Weekend Spark* (w), *Progress* (w), *The New Globe* (w)

	Somalia	**South Africa**
AREA	637,657 sq km/246,201 sq miles	1,221,031 sq km/471,445 sq miles
CAPITAL	Mogadishu	Pretoria/Cape Town
MAIN TOWNS	Boroma, Kismayu, Hargeisa	Johannesburg, Durban, Port Elizabeth, Pietermaritzburg, East London
MAIN ETHNIC GROUPS	Somalis	African, European, Coloured, Indian
MAIN LANGUAGES	Somali, Italian, English	Afrikaans (official), English (official), Bantu, Xhosa
MAIN RELIGIONS	Islam	Christianity, Hindu, Islam
POPULATION	10,173,000 (1995 UN estimate)	42,741,000 (1995 UN estimate)
DENSITY/SQ KM	12	30
ANNUAL GROWTH	3.2% (1990–5)	2.4% (1990–5)
URBAN	26%	51%
RURAL	74%	49%
FEMALES PER 100 MALES	102	101
INFANT MORTALITY (PER THOUSAND BIRTHS)	122	53
CALORIE INTAKE PER HEAD PER DAY	1781	2963
HEALTH WORKERS (PER 10,000)	6.9	*
LIFE EXPECTANCY	Female 49, male 45	Female 66, male 60
MAIN EMPLOYMENT SECTORS	Agriculture 71.5%	Agriculture 14.1%, industry 48.1%
MAIN INDUSTRIES	Agriculture, livestock	Agriculture, mining, forestry, fishing
MAIN EXPORTS	Skins, hides, bananas	Gold, diamonds, chemicals, base metals, fruit, machinery
MAIN DESTINATION OF EXPORTS	Italy, Saudi Arabia, Yemen	Italy, Germany, Japan, USA, UK
CURRENCY	Somali shilling (100 cents)	Rand (100 cents)
GDP (IN $US MILLION)	1253	108,076
GDP PER HEAD (IN $US THOUSAND)	141	2780
RETAIL PRICE INDEX	640 (1980 = 100)	627 (1980 = 100)
MILITARY EXPENDITURE (% OF GDP)	3.2	3.7
MILITARY EXPENDITURE PER HEAD (IN $US)	6	99
POPULATION	*	2.0
EDUCATION EXPENDITURE AS % OF GDP	*	*
NUMBER IN POST-SECONDARY EDUCATION (PER 100,000)	195	*
LITERACY RATE AGE 15+	*	*
MOTOR VEHICLES PER THOUSAND	*	137
TELEPHONE LINES PER HUNDRED	0.2	8.8
TELEVISIONS PER THOUSAND	12	98
NEWSPAPER CIRCULATION PER THOUSAND	1	35
NEWSPAPERS (D = DAILY, W = WEEKLY)	*The Country* (d), *Xiddigta* (d), *Dalka* (w), *Heegan* (w)	*The Argus* (d), *Die Burger* (d), *Cape Times* (d), *Daily Dispatch* (d), *The Daily News* (d), *Natal Mercury* (d), *Beeld* (d), *The Citizen* (d), *Sowetan* (d)

	Swaziland	**Togo**
AREA	17,363 sq km/6,704 sq miles	56,785 sq km/21,925 sq miles
CAPITAL	Mbabane	Lomé
MAIN TOWNS	Manzini, Big Bend, Mhlambanyati, Mhlume	Atakmae, Kpalime, Sokode
MAIN ETHNIC GROUPS	Swazi, Zulu	Ewe, Kabre
MAIN LANGUAGES	Siswati (official), English (official)	French (official), Ewe, Kabre, English
MAIN RELIGIONS	Christianity, traditional	Christianity, Islam, traditional
POPULATION	859,000 (1995 UN estimate)	4,138,000 (1995 UN estimate)
DENSITY/SQ KM	47	64
ANNUAL GROWTH	2.7% (1990–5)	3.2% (1990–5)
URBAN	31%	31%
RURAL	69%	69%
FEMALES PER 100 MALES	103	102
INFANT MORTALITY (PER THOUSAND BIRTHS)	73	85
CALORIE INTAKE PER HEAD PER DAY	2554	2110
HEALTH WORKERS (PER 10,000)	11.0	10.9
LIFE EXPECTANCY	Female 60, male 56	Female 57, male 53
MAIN EMPLOYMENT SECTORS	Agriculture 30.2%, industry 26.2%	Agriculture 8.9%, industry 24.1%
MAIN INDUSTRIES	Agriculture, light industry	Agriculture, mining
MAIN EXPORTS	Pineapples, sugar	Phosphates, palm kernels, copra
MAIN DESTINATION OF EXPORTS	South Africa, USA, UK	Africa, France, Russia, Germany
CURRENCY	Lilangeni (100 cents)	Franc CFA (100 centimes)
GDP (IN $US MILLION)	615	1847
GDP PER HEAD (IN $US THOUSAND)	797	507
RETAIL PRICE INDEX	157 (1980 = 100)	144 (1980 = 100)
MILITARY EXPENDITURE (% OF GDP)	1.7	3.0
MILITARY EXPENDITURE PER HEAD (IN $US)	13	12.4
POPULATION	3.4	2.1
EDUCATION EXPENDITURE AS % OF GDP	6.0	5.0
NUMBER IN POST-SECONDARY EDUCATION (PER 100,000)	418	226
LITERACY RATE AGE 15+	*	Female 18%, male 47%
MOTOR VEHICLES PER THOUSAND	71	*
TELEPHONE LINES PER HUNDRED	1.9	0.3
TELEVISIONS PER THOUSAND	19	6
NEWSPAPER CIRCULATION PER THOUSAND	13	3
NEWSPAPERS (D = DAILY, W = WEEKLY)	*Swaziland Observer* (d), *The Times of Swaziland* (d), *The Swaziland News* (w)	*Togo-Presse* (d), *Forum Hebdo* (w), *Togo-Images* (monthly)

	Trinidad and Tobago	Uganda
AREA	5,130 sq km/1,981 sq miles	236,036 sq km/91,259 sq miles
CAPITAL	Port of Spain	Kampala
MAIN TOWNS	San Fernando, Scarborough (Tobago)	Jinja, M'bale, Entebbe, Masaka
MAIN ETHNIC GROUPS	African descent, Indian	Baganda, Basoga, Banyankole
MAIN LANGUAGES	English	English (official), Swahili, Luganda
MAIN RELIGIONS	Christianity, Hinduism, Islam	Christianity, Islam, traditional
POPULATION	1,305,000 (1995 UN estimate)	20,405,000 (1995 UN estimate)
DENSITY/SQ KM	244	83
ANNUAL GROWTH	1.1% (1990–5)	3% (1990–5)
URBAN	67%	13%
RURAL	33%	87%
FEMALES PER 100 MALES	102	101
INFANT MORTALITY (PER THOUSAND BIRTHS)	18	104
CALORIE INTAKE PER HEAD PER DAY	2983	2034
HEALTH WORKERS (PER 10,000)	52.2	*
LIFE EXPECTANCY	Female 74, male 69	Female 43, male 41
MAIN EMPLOYMENT SECTORS	Agriculture 11.6%, industry 26.9%	Agriculture 81.4%
MAIN INDUSTRIES	Agriculture, oil, natural gas, light industry, chemicals	Agriculture
MAIN EXPORTS	Oil, fertilizers, natural gas	Coffee, cotton, tea
MAIN DESTINATION OF EXPORTS	USA, Barbados, Guyana	Netherlands, France, USA, Spain, Germany
CURRENCY	Trinidad & Tobago dollar (100 cents)	Uganda shilling (100 cents)
GDP (IN $US MILLION)	5275	3051
GDP PER HEAD (IN $US THOUSAND)	4217	168
RETAIL PRICE INDEX	385 (1980 = 100)	288 (1980 = 100)
MILITARY EXPENDITURE (% OF GDP)	0.6	2.6
MILITARY EXPENDITURE PER HEAD (IN $US)	22.6	4.1
POPULATION	1.6	3.2
EDUCATION EXPENDITURE AS % OF GDP	4.0	3.0
NUMBER IN POST-SECONDARY EDUCATION (PER 100,000)	563	82
LITERACY RATE AGE 15+	Female 93%, male 97%	Female 40%, male 65%
MOTOR VEHICLES PER THOUSAND	165	2
TELEPHONE LINES PER HUNDRED	14.1	0.2
TELEVISIONS PER THOUSAND	315	10
NEWSPAPER CIRCULATION PER THOUSAND	77	2
NEWSPAPERS (D = DAILY, W = WEEKLY)	*Newsday* (d), *Trinidad Guardian* (d), *Trinidad and Tobago Express* (d)	*New Vision* (d), *Munno* (d), *Taifa Uganda Empya* (d), *Focus* (four times a week), *The Monitor* (three times a week), *The People* (w)

	United Republic of Tanzania	Zaïre
AREA	945,087 sq km/364,900 sq miles	2,345,409 sq km/905,567 sq miles
CAPITAL	Dodoma	Kinshasa
MAIN TOWNS	Dar es Salaam, Mwanza, Tanga	Kananga, Lumbumbashi, Kisangani,
MAIN ETHNIC GROUPS	Bantu groups, Shirazi, Arab	Bantu groups
MAIN LANGUAGES	Swahili (official), English (official)	French (official), Swahili, Tshiluba, Lingala, Kikongo
MAIN RELIGIONS	Islam, Christianity	Christianity, Islam, traditional
POPULATION	30,742,000 (1995 UN estimate)	43,814,000 (1995 UN estimate)
DENSITY/SQ KM	30	16
ANNUAL GROWTH	3.4% (1990–5)	3.2% (1990–5)
URBAN	24%	29%
RURAL	76%	71%
FEMALES PER 100 MALES	102	102
INFANT MORTALITY (PER THOUSAND BIRTHS)	102	93
CALORIE INTAKE PER HEAD PER DAY	2186	2079
HEALTH WORKERS (PER 10,000)	*	*
LIFE EXPECTANCY	Female 52, male 49	Female 53, male 50
MAIN EMPLOYMENT SECTORS	Agriculture 13.9%, industry 25.6%	Agriculture 66.3%
MAIN INDUSTRIES	Agriculture, mining, light industry	Agriculture, mining, light industry, oil
MAIN EXPORTS	Coffee, cotton, tobacco, tea, hides, skins, diamonds	Coffee, rubber, copper, timber, crude oil, industrial diamonds, cobalt, zinc
MAIN DESTINATION OF EXPORTS	Germany, UK, Netherlands, Singapore	Belgium, USA, Germany, Italy, Japan
CURRENCY	Tanzanian shilling (100 cents)	Zaïre (100 makuta)
GDP (IN $US MILLION)	3150	3594
GDP PER HEAD (IN $US THOUSAND)	117	93
RETAIL PRICE INDEX	2547 (1980 = 100)	* (1980 = 100)
MILITARY EXPENDITURE (% OF GDP)	5.3	2.6
MILITARY EXPENDITURE PER HEAD (IN $US)	5	8
POPULATION	1.5	1.6
EDUCATION EXPENDITURE AS % OF GDP	5.0	1%
NUMBER IN POST-SECONDARY EDUCATION (PER 100,000)	25	184
LITERACY RATE AGE 15+	*	Female 37%, male 74%
MOTOR VEHICLES PER THOUSAND	4	5
TELEPHONE LINES PER HUNDRED	0.3	0.1
TELEVISIONS PER THOUSAND	2	1
NEWSPAPER CIRCULATION PER THOUSAND	8	2
NEWSPAPERS (D = DAILY, W = WEEKLY)	Daily News (d), Kipanga (d), Uhuru (d), The Express (w), Mzalendo (w), Sunday News (w)	L'Analyste (d), Boyoma (d), Mjumbe (d), Beto na Beto (w), Le Courrier du Zaïre (w)

	Zambia	**Zimbabwe**
AREA	752,614 sq km/290,586 sq miles	390,580 sq km/150,804 sq miles
CAPITAL	Lusaka	Harare
MAIN TOWNS	Kitwe, Livingstone, Kabwe, Ndole, Chingola	Bulawayo, Gweru, Kwekwe, Mutare, Hwange
MAIN ETHNIC GROUPS	Memba, Nyanja, Tonga, Lozi	Shona, Ndebele, Europeans
MAIN LANGUAGES	English (official), Bemba, Nyaja, Tonga, Lozi	English (official), Shona, Ndebele
MAIN RELIGIONS	Christianity, Islam, traditional, animist	Christianity, traditional, animist, Hindu, Islam
POPULATION	9,381,000 (1995 UN estimate)	11,536,000 (1995 UN estimate)
DENSITY/SQ KM	12	34
ANNUAL GROWTH	3.8% (1990–5)	3% (1990–5)
URBAN	13%	32%
RURAL	87%	68%
FEMALES PER 100 MALES	102	102
INFANT MORTALITY (PER THOUSAND BIRTHS)	84	59
CALORIE INTAKE PER HEAD PER DAY	2028	2193
HEALTH WORKERS (PER 10,000)	15.0	*
LIFE EXPECTANCY	Female 45, male 43	Female 57, male 54
MAIN EMPLOYMENT SECTORS	Agriculture 10.3%, industry 37.4%	Agriculture 23.9%, industry 28.7%
MAIN INDUSTRIES	Agriculture, mining	Agriculture, mining, light industry
MAIN EXPORTS	Copper, cobalt, zinc, lead, emeralds, ground nuts, livestock	Tobacco, beef, gold, cotton, asbestos, silver, copper
MAIN DESTINATION OF EXPORTS	Japan, France, Thailand, India	South Africa, UK, Germany, USA, Japan
CURRENCY	Kwacha (100 ngwee)	Zimbabwe dollar (100 cents)
GDP (IN $US MILLION)	3799	6194
GDP PER HEAD (IN $US THOUSAND)	453	603
RETAIL PRICE INDEX	38,929 (1980 = 100)	368 (1980 = 100)
MILITARY EXPENDITURE (% OF GDP)	2.7	5.5
MILITARY EXPENDITURE PER HEAD (IN $US)	10	29.5
POPULATION	1.9	4.2
EDUCATION EXPENDITURE AS % OF GDP	3.0	8.0
NUMBER IN POST-SECONDARY EDUCATION (PER 100,000)	178	585
LITERACY RATE AGE 15+	Female 53%, male 75%	Female 61%, male 76%
MOTOR VEHICLES PER THOUSAND	16	39
TELEPHONE LINES PER HUNDRED	0.8	1.2
TELEVISIONS PER THOUSAND	26	26
NEWSPAPER CIRCULATION PER THOUSAND	12	21
NEWSPAPERS (D = DAILY, W = WEEKLY)	*The Times of Zambia* (d), *Zambia Daily Mail* (d), *National Mirror* (w), *Sunday Express* (w), *Sunday Times of Zambia* (w)	*The Chronicle* (d), *The Herald* (d), *Sunday Mail* (w), *Sunday News* (w), *Makonde Star* (w)

POLITICAL PARTIES AND LEADERS

ANGOLA

Heads of State

Presidents

Agostinho Antonio Neto   (1975–9)
José Eduardo dos Santos   (1979–)

Prime Minister

Marcolino José Carlos Moco   (1990–)

People's Movement for the Liberation of Angola (Movimento Popular de Libertação de Angola – MPLA)

Founded as a coalition of nationalist political groups in December 1956 by Ilido Machado, Mario Coelto Pinto de Andrade, Antonio Agostinho Neto and Amilcar Cabral (from Guinea-Bissau). Neto emerged as the eventual leader. The bulk of MPLA support is urban. In 1977 the MPLA restructured and declared itself a Marxist–Leninist vanguard party – People's Movement for the Liberation of Angola-Workers' Party (Movimento Popular de Libertação de Angola-Partido do Trabalho MPLA-PT). José Eduardo dos Santos became the leader on the death of Neto in 1979. In December 1990 the party abandoned Marxism for democratic socialism. In multi-party elections in 1992, MPLA-PT won an overwhelming victory taking 54 per cent of the vote. The dos Santos government made a power-sharing agreement with the rival UNITA in 1993.

Union of the People of Angola (União das Populações de Angola – UPA).

Nationalist organization formed in 1958 by Holden Roberto. UPA membership largely consisted of the northern Angola Kongo people. The UPA received US funding to counter the Soviet-sponsored MPLA. The UPA initiated resistance against the Portuguese in the north of the country in 1961. In 1962, UPA merged with other northern groupings to form the FNLA.

National Front for the Liberation of Angola (Frente Nacional de Libertação de Angola – FNLA)

Founded in March 1962 by Holden Roberto through a merger of the predominantly Kongo Union of Angolan Peoples (UPA) and the predominantly Zambo Angolan Democratic Party (PDA). By 1963 the FNLA was recognized by the Organization of African Unity as the official Angolan liberation movement. A split in the FNLA in December 1964 led to the formation of UNITA. Although a member of the transitional government in 1974, by March 1976 FNLA had all but ceased to exist following the end of US aid.

Front for the Liberation of Cabinda Enclave (Frente de Libertação do Enclave de Cabinda – FLEC)

Formed in 1963 by Henriques Tiago Nzita to remove the oil-rich province of Cabinda from Portuguese control. FLEC mounted an armed struggle against Portugal from 1975 and continued guerrilla actions against the government after independence. FLEC suspended its activity in 1985 but reformed in 1995 as Front for the Liberation of Cabinda Enclave-Renewal (Frente de Libertação do Enclave de Cabinda-Renovada – FLEC-Renewal).

National Union for the Total Independence of Angola (União Nacional para a Independência Total de Angola – UNITA).

Founded in March 1966 by Jonas Malheiro Savimbi as a breakaway from the FNLA with an anti-Marxist, pro-capitalist policy. Its main support came from the Ovambos. Initially a member of the transitional government in 1974, UNITA then fought the MPLA government with aid from South Africa and the USA until an agreement on elections was reached in 1992. Fighting was renewed when UNITA took only 30 per cent of the vote. An end to aid from the USA in 1993 and waning support from South Africa led to UNITA agreeing to sign a peace accord in November 1994.

Among other parties in Angola are the Angolan Democratic Forum (FDA) led by Jorge Rebelo Pinto Chicoti, the Democratic Renewal Party (PRD) led by Luís dos Passos and the Angolan Youth Worker Peasant Alliance (PAJOCA) led by Miguel João Sebastião.

ANTIGUA AND BARBUDA

Head of State
Queen Elizabeth II

Prime Ministers
Vere C. Bird   (1976–94)
Lester B. Bird   (1994–)

Antigua Labour Party (ALP)
Founded by Vere C. Bird in 1951 and based on the Antigua Trade and Labour Union (ATLU). The ALP was unopposed in elections in 1951 and 1956 and won all seats on the Legislative Council. It went on to win elections in 1961 and 1965. After a split in the ATLU in 1967, the ALP was defeated by the PLM in the 1971 elections. The ALP was returned to power in 1976 and remained undefeated in elections in 1980, 1984, 1989 and 1994.

Progressive Labour Movement (PLM)
Opposition political party founded by George Walter, leader of the Antigua Workers' Union in 1967 as a breakaway from the ALP. The PLM won power in the 1971 elections but lost it in 1976. Walter was imprisoned for corruption in 1979 but released on appeal in 1980. PLM merged with the United Democratic Party in 1989.

Antigua Caribbean Liberation Movement (ACLM)
Founded in 1968 as the Afro-Caribbean Liberation Movement, the party changed its name in 1973 and attempted to form a united opposition movement with the PLM to contest the 1980 elections.

United People's Movement (UPM)
Founded in 1982 by George Walter, the party won no seats in the 1984 elections. In 1986 the UPM merged with the smaller National Democratic Party (formed in 1985) to form the United National Democratic Party.

United National Democratic Party (UNDP)
Formed in 1986 through a merger of the United People's Movement and the National Democratic Party under the leadership of the NDP leader Ivor Heath.

Barbuda People's Movement (BPM)
Founded in 1979 to campaign for independence for Barbuda. The party won all the seats on the Barbuda Council in 1989 but took only one seat in the 1994 elections.

Among other parties are the United Progressive Party (UPP), which took five seats in the 1994 elections and the Barbuda Independence Movement (BIM).

THE BAHAMAS

Head of State
Queen Elizabeth II

Prime Ministers
Lynden O. Pindling   (1967–92)
Hubert A. Ingraham   (1992–)

Progressive Liberal Party (PLP)
Founded in 1953 to oppose the racist white élite 'Bay Street Boys'. The PLP won seats in the 1956 general election and its leader Lynden Pindling became chief minister in

1967 when the PLP, with independent support, formed the first black majority government. A breakaway group left to form the Free National Movement in 1971 but the PLP went on to success in the 1972, 1977, 1982 and 1987 elections. The PLP was defeated in elections in 1992.

United Bahamian Party (UBP)

A white-dominated party founded in 1958. The UBP was defeated in the 1967 elections and in 1971 its remaining members joined forces with defectors from the PLP to form the FNM.

Free National Movement (FNM)

Conservative party founded by Cecil Wallace-Whitfield in 1971. The party was made up of defectors from the PLP, members of the UBP and opponents of Bahamian independence. Under the leadership of Hubert Ingraham, the FNM won a majority in the 1992 elections.

Bahamas Democratic Party (BDP)

Formed in 1975 by Henry Bostwick when he lost the leadership of the FNM. The BDP reunited with the FNM in 1981.

Vanguard Nationalist and Socialist Party (VNSP)

Formed as a black power party in 1971. The VNSP, led by John McCarthy and then by Lionel Carey, met with no success in the 1977 and 1982 elections.

BARBADOS

Head of State

Queen Elizabeth II

Prime Ministers

L. Erskine Sandiford   (1987–94)
Owen Arthur   (1994–)

Barbados Labour Party (BLP)

Founded in 1938 as the Barbados Progressive League, the first modern political party in the British Caribbean. Grantley Adams was elected leader in 1939 and the party was renamed the BLP in 1944. Following the 1946 elections the BLP formed a coalition with the Congress Party and was successful in the elections in 1948, 1951 and 1956. Adams resigned to take up the position of prime minister of the West Indies Federation and was succeeded by Hugh Cummins. The BLP was unsuccessful in the 1961, 1966 and 1971 elections but went on to win 1976 and 1981 elections. Defeated in 1986, the BLP had a victory in 1994.

Democratic Labour Party (DLP)

Formed in 1955 by Errol Barrow as a breakaway from the BLP. The DLP won only four seats in the 1956 general elections and none in the 1958 West Indies Federation elections. It won a majority in the 1961, 1966 and 1971 general elections but lost in 1976 and 1981. The DLP was returned to power in 1986. Erskine Sandiford became leader of the party after Barrow's death, won the 1991 election but was defeated in 1994.

National Democratic Party (NDP)

Founded in 1989 by former DLP finance minister Richie Haynes. The NDP won four seats in the 1989 elections.

BENIN (FORMERLY DAHOMEY)

Heads of State and Government

Presidents

Hubert Coutoucou Maga   (1960–3)
Colonel Christophe Soglo   (1963–4)
Sourou-Migan Apithy   (1964–5)
Tahirou Congacou   (1965 November–December)
General Christophe Soglo   (1965–7)
Lieutenant-Colonel Alphonse Alley   (1967–8)
Emile Derlin Zinsou   (1968–9)
Lieutenant-Colonel Paul Emile de Souza   (1969–70)

Hubert Coutoucou Maga (1970–2)
Justin T. Ahomadegbé (1972
  May–October)

Head of Military Council
Major (later Brigadier-General) Mathieu
  Kérékou (1972–80)

Presidents
Mathieu Kérékou (1980–91)
Nicéphore Soglo (1991–6)
Mathieu Kérékou (1996–)

United Party of Dahomey (Parti Dahoméen de l'Unité – PDU)

Coalition party formed in 1960 by Hubert Maga. He was elected president of Dahomey in 1961.

Popular Revolutionary Party of Benin (Parti de la Révolution Populaire du Bénin – PRPB)

Formed as a Marxist–Leninist party by the military ruler Lieutenant-Colonel Mathieu Kérékou in 1975. On the restoration of civilian rule, Kérékou became president in 1980. The PRPB abandoned Marxism–Leninism in 1989.

Union of Progressive Forces (Union des forces du progrès – UFP)

Founded in 1990 as a coalition of three official parties, the UFP replaced the PRPB as the official party of Benin.

Benin Renaissance Party (Parti de la renaissance du Bénin – PRB)

Formed in 1992 by Rosine Soglo. President Nicéphore Soglo assumed leadership of the PRB in 1994. The party went on to win the 1995 elections and formed a coalition government. Soglo was defeated in presidential elections held in March 1996.

Among 34 parties formed when political activity was legalized in 1991 were the Party of Democratic Renewal (Parti du renouveau démocratique – PRD); the African Assembly for Progress and Solidarity (Rassemblement Africain pour le progrès et la solidarité – RAP), a coalition formed in 1993 to support former President Kérékou; Alafia Action Front for Renewal and Development (Front d'action pour le renouveau et le développement-Alafia – FARD), northern-based supporters of former President Kérékou.

BOTSWANA

Heads of State and Government

Presidents
Sir Seretse Khama (1966–80)
Sir Quett Ketumile Masire (1980–)

Botswana Democratic Party (BDP)

Founded in 1962 as the multi-racial Bechuanaland Democratic Party by Seretse Khama and Quett Ketumile Masire. The BDP has remained the ruling party since independence in 1966. Co-founder Masire became leader on Seretse Khama's death in 1980. The party was returned to office in 1994 with a reduced majority.

Botswana People's Party (BPP)

Founded in 1960 by Kgaleman Motetse as a radical opposition party campaigning for independence along Pan-Africanist lines. The BPP won only three seats in the 1965 elections. It has remained a minority party with its main support in the north-east of the country. The BPP was led by P. P. G. Matante until his death in 1981. He was succeeded by K. M. Mkhwa.

Botswana Independence Party (BIP)

Formed in 1962 by Motsamai Mpho, left-wing former secretary-general of the BPP, following his expulsion. The BIP is a minority party active in the north-west among the Bayei people.

Botswana National Front (BNF)

Founded in 1965 by Kenneth Koma as a Marxist minority opposition party with support among the urban working-class. The BNF formed the main opposition to the ruling BDP following the 1994 election.

Botswana Labour Party (BLP)

Formed in 1989 under the leadership of former members of the BNP. The party described itself as non-aligned, taking neither a capitalist nor a socialist position.

Botswana People's Progressive Front (BPPF)

Founded in 1991 as an alliance of the BPP, BNF, the Botswana Progressive Union, the Botswana Political Union and the Independent Freedom Party.

BURKINA FASO (FORMERLY UPPER VOLTA)

Heads of State

Presidents

Maurice Yaméogo (1960–6)
Lieutenant-Colonel (later General) Sangoulé Lamizana (1966–80)
Colonel Saye Zerbo (1980–2)
Major-General Jean-Baptiste Ouédraogo (1982–3)

Head of the National Council of the Revolution

Captain Thomas Sankara (1983–7)

Chairman of the Popular Front

Captain Blaise Compaoré (1987–91)

President

Blaise Compaoré (1991–)

Prime Ministers

Youssouf Ouédraogo (1991–4)
Roch Christian Kaboré (1994–6)
Kadre Desire Ouédraogo (1996–)

Democratic Voltaic Union (Union Démocratique Voltaïque/ Rassemblement Démocratique Africain (UDV/RDA))

The UDV, (a branch of the trans-territorial RDA) was founded in 1957 by Maurice Yaméogo as a coalition of northern ethnic groups opposed to French colonial government. Following independence in 1960, the UDV instituted a one-party state.

Patriotic Development League (Ligue patriotique pour le développement – LIPAD)

Marxist party founded in 1973 and which operated underground from 1980 to 1982. LIPAD joined the Sankara government in 1983.

Movement for National Renewal (Mouvement national pour le renouveau – MNR)

Formed in 1976 by Colonel Sangoulé Lamizana as a party of national unity. He won elections in 1977 with 56 per cent of the votes cast but was deposed in a bloodless coup in 1980 by Colonel Saye Zerbo.

National Union for the Defence of Democracy (Union Nationale pour la Defense de la Démocratie – UNDD)

Established in 1977 by supporters of deposed president Yaméogo under the leadership of Macaire Ouédraogo following a split in the UDV.

Refusal Front (Frente de refus – (FR)

Opposition party formed by Youssouf Ouédraogo following a split with the UDV when he opposed Lamizana as a presidential candidate. Its main support was in the capital and among the labour unions.

Organisation for Popular Democracy-Labour Movement (Organisation pour la démocratie populaire-Mouvement du travail – ODP-MT)

A broad-based coalition formed in 1989 by Blaise Compaoré. The coalition included the Popular Front (Front Populaire – FP), founded by Compaoré in 1987. The ODP-MT became the ruling party following elections in 1992, bringing an end to military rule. In 1994, Compaoré was succeeded as ODP-MT leader by Roch Christian Kaboré.

Congress for Democracy and Progress (Congrès pour la Démocratie et le Progrès – CDP)

Coalition formed in 1996 by the merger of the ODP-MT and ten other groups supporting President Compaoré under the leadership of Roch Christian Kaboré. The CDP's programme was intended to strengthen and revitalize economic development in Burkina Faso

BURUNDI

Heads of State
Mwami Mwambutsa IV   (1962–6)
Mwami Ntare V   (1966 July–November)
A Republic was declared in 1966.

Presidents
Colonel (later Lieutenant-General) Michel
  Micombero   (1966–76)
Lieutenant-Colonel Jean-Baptiste
  Bagaza   (1976–87)
Major Pierre Buyoya   (1987–93)
Melchior Ndadaye   (1993 July–October)

Head of the National Committee for Public Salvation
François Ngeze   (1993 October)

President
Giles Bimazubute (acting)   (1993–4)
Cyprien Ntaryamira   (1994
  February–April)

Sylvestre Ntibantunganya   (1994–6)
Pierre Buyoya   (1996–)

Prime Ministers
Adrien Sibomana   (1988–93)
Sylvie Kinigi   (1993–4)
Anatole Kanyenkiko   (1994–5)
Antoine Nduwayo   (1995–6)
Pascal-Firmin Ndimira   (1996–)

Union for National Progress (Union pour le progrès national – UPRONA)

Formed in 1958 under the leadership of Prince Louis Rwagasore. Initially supported by both the Tutsi and Hutu sections of the population, ethnic divisions grew following Prince Rwagasore's assassination in 1961 and the Hutus were expelled from the party. UPRONA became the sole legal political party following the overthrow of the monarchy in 1966. Amendments to the 1981 Constitution restricted candidature to the National Assembly to UPRONA members. President Micombero was deposed in a military coup in 1973 led by Colonel Jean-Baptiste Bagaza who was elected president in 1984. The party was suspended following the 1987 coup led by Major Pierre Buyoya. After the introduction of multi-party elections in 1993, UPRONA became the leading opposition party.

Democratic Front of Burundi (Front pour la démocratie au Burundi – FRODEBU)

Founded in 1992 under the leadership of Melchior Ndadaye following the legalization of political parties. He became Burundi's first Hutu president in 1993. FRODEBU took power with 71 per cent of the vote in the 1993 elections. Cyprien Ntaryamira succeeded to the presidency on Ndadaye's death. Ntaryamira was killed in April 1994 and was succeeded by President Sylvestre Ntibantunganya who was deposed in a bloodless coup in July 1996 led by Pierre Buyoya.

Among other parties, until all political activity was banned by Pierre Buyoya in July 1996, were the Rally of the people of Burundi (Rassemblement du peuple Burundien – RPB) and the Rally for democracy and economic and social development (Rassemblement pour le démocratie et le développement économique et social – RADDES).

CAMEROON

Heads of State

President and Commander-in-Chief of the Armed Forces
Ahmadou Ahidjo   (1960–82)
Paul Biya   (1982–)

Prime Minister
Simon Achidi Achue   (1990–)

Union of the Cameroon Populations (Union des Populations Camerounaises – UPC)

Formed in 1948 by nationalists based in the trade-union movement as the Cameroon section of the African Democratic Rally (Rassemblement Démocratique Africain – RDA). Led by Ruben Um Nyobé, the UPC demanded the unification of the British- and French-ruled areas of Cameroon and independence. The UPC was banned in 1952 and operated as an underground organization in exile from the British section carrying out guerrilla operations. In 1960 the section of the UPC remaining in the French area was legalized after agreeing to co-operate with the French government. The external UPC gradually lost influence following the death of Ruben Um Nyobé.

Cameroon National Union (Union Nationale Camerounais – UNC)

Formed by the merger of six parties in eastern and western Cameroon in 1966 under the leadership of Ahmadou Ahidjo on the platform of Pan-Africanism and a mixed economy. Ahidjo was the country's first president on independence in 1960 and remained in office until 1982. The UNC was Cameroon's sole legal party from 1972 until 1990.

Democratic Assembly of the People of Cameroon (Rassemblement Démocratique du Peuple Camerounais – RDPC)

The successor party to the UNC, the RDPC won 88 of 180 National Assembly seats in the March 1992 legislative elections. The party's victory in the October 1992 presidential elections with 39 per cent of the vote prompted opposition claims of fraud. The RDPC retained office following elections in 1996 at the head of a coalition government.

Movement for the Defence of the Republic (Mouvement pour la Défense de la République – MDR)

An opposition party founded in 1991 by Dakole Daissala which entered into a coalition government with the RDPC following the 1996 elections.

National Union for Democracy and Progress (Union Nationale pour la Démocratie et le Progrès – UNDP)

An opposition party founded in 1991 by Bello Bouba Maigari which entered into a coalition government with the RDPC following the 1996 elections.

CAPE VERDE

Heads of State

Presidents
Aristides Maria Pereira   (1975–91)
António Mascarenhas Monteiro   (1991–)

Prime Ministers
Pedro Verona Rodrigues Rires
  (1975–92)

Carlos Alberto Wahnon de Carvalho Veiga (1992–)

African Party for the Independence of Guinea and Cape Verde (Partido Africano da Independência da Guinê e Cabo Verde – PAIGC)

Nationalist party founded in 1956 by Amilcar Cabral and Aristides Pereira who became the country's first president on independence in 1975. From 1975–80 the PAIGC ruled the Cape Verde archipelago and Guinea as the sole legal party. A split in the party led to abandonment of plans for unification and in 1981 the Cape Verde wing of the party was renamed the African Party for the Independence of Cape Verde.

African Party for the Independence of Cape Verde (Partido Africano da Independência da Cabo Verde – PAICV)

Formed in 1981 by Aristides Pereira following a split in the ruling PAIGC. The PAICV remained the ruling party until its defeat in the 1991 elections.

Movement for Democracy (Movimento para a Democracia – MPD)

Social-democratic party formed in 1990 to contest the country's first multi-party elections in 1991. Under the leadership of António Mascarenhas Monteiro, the MPD defeated the PAICV government and Monteiro became president.

CENTRAL AFRICAN REPUBLIC

Heads of State

President

David Dacko (1960–6)
Lieutenant-Colonel Jean-Bédel Bokassa (1966–79)
(President for Life, 1972; Emperor of Central African Empire, 1977)
David Dacko (1979–81)

President and General of the Armed Forces

General André Kolingba (1981–93)
Ange-Félix Patassé (1993–)

Prime Ministers

Edouard Franck (1991)
Timothée Malendoma (1992–93)
Enoch Durant Lakoué (1993)
Jean-Luc Mandaba (1993–5)
Gabriel Koyambounou (1995–)

Movement for the Social Evolution of Black Africa (Mouvement de Évolution sociale de l'Afrique Noire – MESAN)

Nationalist party founded in 1949 by Barthelemy Boganda, the country's first prime minister in 1957, aimed at forming a 'United States of Latin Africa'. On Boganda's death in 1959 he was succeeded as leader by his cousin David Dacko, the Republic's first president on independence in 1960. In 1966, Dacko was deposed in a coup led by Colonel Jean-Bédel Bokassa and the party was outlawed.

Movement for the Social Evolution of Central Africa (Mouvement de l'Évolution sociale de l'Afrique Centrale – MEDAC)

Founded in 1960 by former minister, Dr Abel Goumba, following disputes in MESAN. The party was dissolved in 1960 and Goumba was exiled.

Central African People's Liberation Party (Mouvement pour la libération du peuple Centrafricain – MLPC)

Party opposing the regime of President Bokassa founded in Paris in 1979 by former prime minister, Ange-Félix Patassé. Following the institution of multi-party democracy in 1991, the MLPC contested the 1993 legislative elections, emerging at the head of a coalition government as the largest single party in the National Assembly with 34 of the 85 seats. Patassé was elected president.

Ubanguian Patriotic Front-Workers' Party (Front Patriotique Oubanguin-Parti du Travail – FPO-PT)

Party opposing the regime of President Bokassa formed in exile in the Congo in 1977 under the leadership of Abel Goumba, leader of the outlawed MEDAC. The party contested the 1981 elections.

Among parties formed following the legalization of political activity in 1991 were the Liberal Democratic Party, the Alliance for Democracy and Progress, the David Dacko Movement and the Consultative Group of Democratic Forces.

CHAD

Heads of State

Presidents
François Ngarta Tombalbaye   (1960–75)
Major-General Felix Malloum   (1975–9)
Colonel Wadal Abdelkader Kamouge
    (1979 March–April)
Goukouni Oueddei   (1979–82)
Hissène Habré   (1982–90)
Idriss Déby   (1990–)

Prime Ministers
Jean Bawoyeu   (1991–2)
Joseph Yodoyman   (1992–3)
Fidèle Moungar   (1993)
Delwa Kassire   (1993–4)
Djimasta Koibla   (1994–)

Chad Progressive Party (Parti Progressiste Tchadien – PPT)

Founded in 1946 by Gabriel Lisette, a West Indian who had served in the country's French administration, as the Chad section of the African Democratic Rally (Rassemblement Démocratique Africain – RDA). The PPT's main support lay in the south among the Sara people and its monopoly on political power provoked a civil war. Lisette was forced to resign the leadership in 1959 and was replaced by François Tombalbaye who went on to became the country's first president on independence. The PPT became the sole political party in 1962. Tombalbaye was killed in a coup in 1975.

Chad National Liberation Front (Front de Libération Nationale du Tchad – FROLINAT)

Guerrilla grouping formed to resist the PPT government in June 1966. In the course of the civil war FROLINAT exerted increasing control over the country but fragmented into competing factions, the Armed Forces of the North (FAN) under Hissène Habré and the Libyan-backed Popular Armed Forces (FAP). Habré's faction joined a government of national unity in the early 1980s. Following the 1987 cease-fire, FROLINAT remained as an ineffective exile group.

Patriotic Salvation Movement (Mouvement patriotique du salut – MPS)

A coalition of opposition movements – including Action for 1 April and the Movement for Chad National Salvation – formed in 1990 under the leadership of Idriss Déby. The MPS launched an offensive against the government of Hissène Habré in November 1990 and took power in December.

Following the legalization of political activity after the introduction of a Transitional Charter in 1991, over 50 political organizations were established to compete in elections planned for December 1996. Among these were the Alliance of Political Parties for Democracy (Alliance des partis politiques pour la démocratie – APD), a grouping of eight organizations; Collective of Parties for Change (Collectif des partis pour le changement – COPAC), an alliance of eight opposition parties; Union for Renewal and Democracy (Union pour le renouveau et la démocratie – URD).

CONGO

Heads of State

Presidents

Abbé Fulbert Youlou   (1960–3)
Alphonse Massamba-Débat   (1963–8)
Captain (later Major) Marien N'gouabi   (1968–77)
Colonel Jacques-Joachim Yhombi-Opango   (1977–9)
Colonel (later General) Denis Sassou-Nguesso   (1979–92)
Pascal Lissouba   (1992–)

Prime Ministers

Alphonse Poaty-Souchalaty   (1989–90)
General Goma   (1991)
André Milongo   (1991)
Maurice-Stéphane Bongho-Nouarra
Claude Antoine Dacosta   (1992–3)
General Jacques-Joachim Yhombi-Opango   (1993–7)
Charles David Ganao   (1997–)

Democratic Union for the Defence of African Interests (Union démocratique pour la défense des intérets africains-UDDIA)

Founded in 1956 by Fulbert Youlou. The UDDIA was the ruling party before and after independence from 1957–63. Youlou became president of the Congo Republic in 1960 at independence until forced to resign in 1963, accused of neo-colonialism because of his pro-Western policies.

National Movement of the Revolution (Mouvement national de la révolution – MNR)

Founded in 1964 by Alphonse Massamba-Débat. Marxist–Leninist party whose radical youth wing challenged the leadership and whose paramilitary activities led to a coup instigated by Major Marien Ngouabi. The MNR was dissolved in 1968.

Congolese Labour Party (Parti congolais du travail – PCT)

Founded as a Marxist–Leninist party by President Marien Ngouabi in 1969. The chairman of the party's central committee held the office of President of the Congo. The PCT was the sole legal political party from 1970–90 and renamed the country the People's Republic of the Congo in 1970. President Ngouabi was assassinated in 1977. The PCT was controlled from 1978–9 by a military council led by Denis Sassou-Nguesso. The PCT abandoned its former socialist ideology in 1990, moved towards a greater emphasis on a market economy and abandoned its monopoly on political activity.

Union for Congolese Democracy (Union pour la Démocratie Congolaise – UDC)

Formed in 1989 and led by Félix Makosso, the UDC was officially registered in 1990 when the one-party state was abandoned. The UDC advocated liberal economic policies.

National Union for Democracy and Progress (Union Nationale pour la Démocratie et le Progrès – UNDP)

Formed in 1990; led by Pierre Ndze when the one-party state was abandoned in the Congo.

Pan-African Union of Social Democracy (Union panafricaine pour la démocratie sociale – UPADS)

Party led by Pascal Lissouba. UPADS defeated the PCT in elections held in 1992 following a period of transitional government and formed a coalition government. Lissouba became president. UPADS was defeated by the PCT later that year after failing to gain a majority in the National Assembly. UPADS was successful in elections held in 1993 but President

Lissouba was forced to hold further elections following charges of irregularities.

Congolese Movement for Democracy and Development (Mouvement congolais pour la démocratie et le developpement intégral – MCDDI)

Formed in 1990 by Bernard Kolelas to contest the 1993 general election. The party won 28 seats in the National Assembly.

Union of Democratic Renewal (Union pour le renouveau démocratique – URD)

Alliance of seven political parties formed in 1992 by Bernard Kolelas. It includes MCDDI and the Rally for Democracy and Social Progress (Rassemblement pour la démocratie et le progrès social – RDPS). The URD formed a coalition with the PCT.

Union of Democratic Forces (Forces démocratiques unies – FDU)

Alliance of six political parties formed in 1994 under Itahi Osseteoumba with the support of former president and PCT leader Denis Sassou-Nguesso.

CÔTE D'IVOIRE

Heads of State

Presidents
Félix Houphouet-Boigny   (1960–93)
Henri Konan Bédié   (1993–)

Prime Ministers
Alassane Dramane Ouattara   (1990–3)
Daniel Kablan Duncan   (1993–)

Ivory Coast Democratic Party (Parti Démocratique de la Côte d'Ivoire – PDCI).

Founded in 1946 by Félix Houphouet-Boigny as part of the territorial African Democratic Rally (Rassemblement Démocratique Africain – RDA) which he had established in 1944. The PDCI was the first political group in the Ivory Coast and the first territorial branch of the RDA. Houphouet-Boigny became president on independence in 1960. The PDCI remained the only official party until 1990. Henri Konan Bédié became president in 1993 following Houphouet-Boigny's death and was re-elected in 1995.

Opposition parties (formed when political activity was legalized in 1990) which won seats in the National Assembly were the Assembly of Republicans (Rassemblement des Républicains – RDR) founded by former members of the PDCI and led by Djény Kobina, and the Ivoirian Popular Front (Front populaire ivoirien – FPI), led by Laurent Koudou Gbagbo. Among other parties are the Ivoirian Labour Party (Parti Ivoirien des Travailleurs – PIT), led by Francis Wodié and the Ivoirian Socialist Party (Parti Socialiste Ivoirien – PSI).

DOMINICA

Heads of State

Presidents
Frederick Degazon   (1978–80)
Sir Clarence Seignoret   (1980–93)
Crispin A. Sorhaindo   (1993–)

Prime Ministers
Patrick John   (1978–9)
Committee of National Salvation   (1979 May–July)
Oliver Seraphim (interim)   (1979–80)
Dame (Mary) Eugenia Charles   (1980–95)
Edison James   (1995–)

Dominica Labour Party (DLP)

Established in 1955 by E. C. Loblack as a socialist party with a programme of land reform and improved working conditions. Under the leadership of Edward LeBlanc, the DLP became the ruling party in 1961. LeBlanc was chief minister until he was succeeded by Patrick John in 1975.

Dominica Freedom Party (DFP)

Formed in 1968 as a party representing the middle class and landowners, the DFP attracted support from dissident DLP members. Under the leadership of Eugenia Charles, the DFP met with minor successes in the 1970 and 1975 general elections but won landslide victories in 1980 and 1985. The party was returned to power with a narrow majority in 1990. Charles resigned in 1995 when the DFP suffered electoral defeat and was succeeded as leader by Brian Alleyne.

Dominica United Workers Party (DUWP)

Founded as a centre-left party in 1988, the DUWP, under the leadership of Edison James, replaced the DLP as the main opposition party. The party's victory in the 1995 elections ended 15 years of DFP rule.

EQUATORIAL GUINEA

Heads of State

President
Francisco Macías Nguema   (1968–79)

President of the Supreme Military Council
Lieutenant-Colonel (later General)
    Teodoro Obiang Nguema Mbasogo
    (1979–)

Prime Ministers
Cristino Seriche Bioko   (1989–92)
Silvestre Siale Bileka   (1992–6)
Angel Serafin Seriche Dougan   (1996–)

Traditional Workers' Party (Partido Unico Nacional Trabajadores – PUNT)

Founded in 1969 by Macías Nguema, PUNT was the only legal party until 1979 when President Nguema was executed following a coup led by his nephew Lieutenant-Colonel Obiang Mbasogo. All political parties were outlawed until 1987 and PUNT was dissolved.

Democratic Party of Equatorial Guinea (Partido Democrático de Guinea Ecuatorial – PDGE)

A government party founded by President Obiang Nguema Mbasogo. Was the sole legal party from 1987 to 1992. At the first multi-party elections held in 1993, the PDGE took 68 of the 80 National Assembly seats.

Among opposition parties formed following the legalization of political organizations in 1991 were Convergence for Social Democracy (Convención Socialdemocrática Popular – CSDP), which gained six seats in the 1993 as part of a Joint Opposition Platform led by Plácido Mikó; and the Union for Democratic and Social Development in Equatorial Guinea (Union Democrática y Social de Guinea Ecuatorial – UDDS).

ERITREA

Head of State and Government

(President, Chairman of the National Assembly, Chairman of the State Council)
Issaias Afewerki   (1993–)

People's Front for Democracy and Justice (PFDJ)

Party formed following independence from the Eritrean People's Liberation Front (EPLF). The EPLF was founded in 1970 following a split in the Eritrean Liberation Front (ELF). After the collapse of the Ethiopian government, against which the EPLF had fought a guerrilla war of independence, the EPLF formed a provisional government in 1991 under Issaias Afewerki. The EPLF transformed itself into a political party in 1993.

Eritrea National Pact Alliance (ENPA)

Founded in 1992 by remnants of the Eritrean Liberation Front (ELF), together with the Eritrean Democratic Liberation Movement, to oppose the EPLF.

ETHIOPIA

Emperors
Menelik II   (1889–1913)
Iyasu V   (1913–16)
(Empress) Zauditu   (1916–28)
Zanditu was overthrown by Ras Tafari Makonnen, who was crowned Emperor as Haile Selassie in 1930.
Haile Selassie I   (1930–74)
Asfa Wossen (in exile)   (1974–75)

Prime Ministers
Aklilou Habte Wold   (1960–74)
Lij Endalkatchew Makonnen   (1974 February–July)
Lij Mithail Imru Haile Selassie   (1974 (July–September)

Heads of Military Council (following military coup)
General Aman Mikhail Andom   (1974 September–November)
General Teferi Banti   (1974)

Heads of State (following declaration of a Republic)
Teferi Benti   (1974–7)
Lieutenant-Colonel Haile Mariam Mengistu   (1977–9)

Presidents
Haile Mariam Mengistu   (1977–91)
Meles Zenawi   (1991–95)
Negasso Gidada   (1995–)

Prime Ministers
Tamrat Layne   (1991–5)
Meles Zenawi   (1995–)

Ethiopian Worker's Party (WPE)
Government party founded by President Haile Mariam Mengistu in 1984 with a socialist programme. The party was restructured in 1990, abandoned Marxism–Leninism and was renamed the Ethiopian Democratic Unity Party. President Mengistu fled the country following military defeat.

The party remained in existence and contested the May 1995 parliamentary elections.

Ethiopian People's Revolutionary Democratic Front (EPRDF)
A coalition of the opposition Ethiopian People's Democratic Movement (EPDM), the Oromo People's Democratic Organisation (OPDO) and the Tigre People's Liberation Front (TPLF), formed in 1989 under the leadership of Meles Zenawi. The EPRDF formed a transitional government with Zenawi as interim president after taking the capital, Addis Ababa, in 1991. In elections held to the Federal Parliamentary Assembly in May 1995, the EPRDF took 483 seats and Meles Zenawi was elected prime minister by the council.

Among other parties are the Coalition of Alternative Forces for Peace and Democracy in Ethiopia (CAFPDE), the Ethiopian Somali Democratic League (ESDL), the Southern Ethiopian People's Democratic Union (SEPDU) and the Ethiopian National Democratic Party (ENDP).

GABON

Heads of State

Presidents
Léon M'Ba   (1960–7)
Albert-Bernard (later Omar) Bongo   (1967–)

Prime Ministers
Casimir Oye Mba   (1990–4)
Paulin Obame-Nguema   (1994–)

Democratic Party of Gabon (Bloc Démocratique Gabonaise – BDG)
Founded in 1946 under the leadership of Léon M'ba as the territorial branch of the African Democratic Rally RDA (Rassemblement Démocratique Africain – RDA). M'Ba became president on independence in 1960

and the BDG was the sole legal party until his death in 1967.

Gabon Democratic Party (Parti Démocratique Gabonais – PDG)

Founded in 1968 under the leadership of President Omar Bongo, the PDG was the only legal party until 1990. The party's motto, 'Dialogue, Tolerance, Peace', symbolized its attempt to surmount ethnic divisions. Despite allegations of malpractice, the PDG won an overall majority in the 1990 elections. Bongo was re-elected president in 1993.

National Re-orientation Movement (Mouvement de Redressement National – MORENA)

Founded in 1981 under the leadership of Max Anicet Kouma Mbadinga. MORENA demanded the re-introduction of multi-party democracy and formed a government in exile in Paris in 1985. The party refused to participate in the 1990 elections.

National Rally of Woodcutters (Rassemblement National des Bûcherons – RNB)

Founded in 1991 under the leadership of Fr Paul M'Ba Abessole. In 1994 the RNB became the main opposition party.

Among other parties formed following the legalization of political organizations were the Democratic Opposition Co-ordination (Coordination de l'opposition démocratique – COD), the Gabonese Progressive Party (Parti Gabonais du Progrès – PGP); and the Circle for Renewal (Cercle des Libéraux Réformateurs – CLR), formed by former PDG ministers.

THE GAMBIA

Head of State
Queen Elizabeth II (1965–70)

Prime Minister
Dawda Kairaba Jawara (1965–70)
A Republic was declared in 1970.

Head of State and Government

President
Sir Dawda Kairaba Jawara (1970–94)

Chairman of the Provisional Ruling Council of Patriotic Forces
Lieutenant Yahya A. J. J. Jammeh (1994–)

Progressive People's Party (PPP)

Founded in 1960 by Dawda Kairaba Jawara. The PPP advocated unity among the various ethnic groups and found the bulk of its support in the rural districts. The party won pre-independence elections in 1961 and following independence in 1965 declared a multi-party republic with Jawara as the first president. The PPP government held power from 1961–94 when it was overthrown in a coup.

National Convention Party (NCP)

Founded in 1975 by Sheriff Mustapha Dibba following his expulsion from the PPP. The NCP's base was mainly among farmers in rural areas.

Gambian People's Party (GPP)

Reformist party founded by former members of the PPP in 1986 under the leadership of Assan Mussa Camara to contest the 1987 elections.

Movement for Justice in Africa (MOJA)

Marxist group led by Ousman Manjang and Hamidou Drammeh. The MOJA was banned in 1981 following an attempted coup. The ban was lifted in 1992.

GHANA

Head of State
Queen Elizabeth II (1957–60)

Prime Minister
Kwame Nkrumah   (1957–60)
A Republic was declared in 1960.

Heads of State and Government

President
Kwame Nkrumah   (1960–6)

Chairman of National Liberation Council
Lieutenant-General Joseph Ankrah
   (1966–9)
Brigadier-General Akwasi Afrifa   (1969
   April–August)
(Three-man presidential Commission)
   (1969–70)

Prime Minister
Kofi Busia   (1969–72)

Chairman of National Redemption Council
Colonel (later General) Ignatius Kutu
   Acheampong   (1972–5)

Chairman of Supreme Military Council
Ignatius Kutu Acheampong   (1975–8)
Lieutenant-General Frederick W. K.
   Akuffo   (1978–9)

Head of Armed Forces Revolutionary Council
Flight-Lieutenant Jerry John Rawlings
   (1979 June–September)

President
Hilla Limann   (1979–81)

Chairman of Provisional National Defence Council
Jerry John Rawlings   (1981–92)

President
Jerry John Rawlings   (1992–)

Convention People's Party (CPP)

Ghanaian political party active from 1949–66. The CPP was founded in 1949 by Kwame Nkrumah and his supporters as a radical breakaway from the moderate United Gold Coast Convention. The CPP's pro-gramme called for immediate independence, democratic socialism and international anti-imperialism. The party formed the government under British rule from 1951–7, winning elections in 1951, 1954 and 1956, and led Ghana to independence in 1957. It became the sole legal political organization when Ghana was declared a one-party state in 1963 but was increasingly criticized for the corruption of some of its members. The CPP was banned following the military coup of 1966 led by General Joseph Ankrah.

Progress Party (PP)

Founded in 1951 in opposition to the CPP. Led by Kofi Busia; was supported by capitalist and middle-class interests and sought to delay independence. The party was banned in 1957. Busia won an overwhelming victory in the 1969 presidential elections but was overthrown in a military coup in 1972. The party was banned by the military-dominated National Redemption Council.

People's National Party (PNP)

Founded under the leadership of Hilla Limann on the restoration of civilian rule in 1979. The PNP included supporters of former President Nkrumah and was successful in the 1979 elections, Limann becoming president. The PNP was dissolved following a military coup led by Flight-Lieutenant Jerry Rawlings in 1981.

New Democratic Party (NDP)

Formed in 1990 by President Jerry Rawlings as a vehicle for his support in the 1992 elections which followed the approval of multi-party democracy. Rawlings was elected president and the party took 189 of the 200 seats in the legislature.

New Patriotic Party (NPP)

Formed in 1992 when political parties were legalized, the NPP candidate in the 1992 presidential elections, Albert Adu Boahen, won 30.2 per cent. The party refused to contest elections to the legislature held in December 1992.

Movement for Freedom and Justice (MFJ)

Formed on the legalization of political parties in 1990, the MFJ advocated the return to civilian rule and a multi-party system.

GRENADA

Head of State
Queen Elizabeth II

Prime Minister
Sir Eric Gairy   (1974–9)

People's Revolutionary Government

Prime Minister
Maurice Bishop   (1979–83)
Revolutionary Military Council   (1983 October)
Interim Advisory Council   (1983–4)

Prime Ministers
Herbert Blaize   (1984–9)
Ben Jones   (1989–90)
Nicholas Braithwaite   (1990–5)
Keith Mitchell   (1995–)

Grenada United Labour Party (GULP)

Founded by Eric Gairy in 1950 as the Grenada People's Party with a base in the trade-union movement. GULP won successive elections to the legislature from 1951 but was defeated by the Grenada National Party (GNP) in 1962. GULP was returned to power in 1967, 1972 and 1976 but Gairy's government was overthrown in a coup in 1979. The party has remained in opposition.

Grenada National Party (GNP)

Founded in 1955 under the leadership of Herbert Blaize. Blaize was chief minister until 1961 following the GNP's victory in the 1955 elections. The party was returned to power in 1962 but returned to opposition when Blaize left politics.

New Jewel Movement (NJM)

Formed in 1973 through the merger of the Movement for Assemblies of the People and Joint Endeavour for Welfare, Education and Liberation (JEWEL) under the leadership of Maurice Bishop. NJM combined Marxist and black power elements. In 1976 the NJM formed a People's Alliance with the GNP and Bishop became opposition leader following elections. The NJM developed into a rigid Leninist vanguard party and seized power in March 1979, forming a radical reforming People's Revolutionary Government. Following internal divisions, Bishop was murdered in October 1983. This precipitated an invasion led by the USA.

New National Party (NNP)

A conservative coalition formed in 1984 under Herbert Blaize through the merger of the Grenada Democratic Movement, Grenada National Party, and the National Democratic Party, with financial support from the USA The NNP won the 1984 elections but lost its majority following internal divisions. Blaize was replaced as leader by Keith Mitchell in 1988. The party won two seats at the 1990 elections and became the ruling party following the 1995 elections.

The National Party (TNP)

Founded in 1989 as a coalition party by Herbert Blaize following disputes in the NNP. Blaize died two days after he was elected as leader and was succeeded by Ben Jones.

Maurice Bishop Patriotic Movement (MBPM)

Founded in 1984 by Kendrick Radix and George Louison, former ministers in the Bishop government. The party achieved no electoral success.

GUINEA

Heads of State and Government

Presidents
Ahmed Sekou Touré   (1958–84)
General Lansana Conté   (1984–)

Prime Minister
Sidia Toure   (1996–)

Guinea Democratic Party (Parti Démocratique de Guinée – PDG)

Founded in 1947 by Ahmed Sekou Touré with its base in the labour unions. The PDG was declared a 'State Party' in 1978 and remained the sole legal party until the death of President Touré in 1984. The PDG was dissolved following a military coup in 1984.

Following a period of military rule, a Transitional Committee of National Recovery was formed in 1991. Political parties were legalized in 1992 in preparation for multi-party elections promised for 1993.

Party of Unity and Progress (Parti de l'unité et du progrès – PUP)

Founded in 1993 by President Lansana Conté to fight the first multi-party elections. PUP won a majority in the 1993 elections but the results were challenged by opposition parties. In further elections held in June 1994, the PUP took 71 of the 114 parliamentary seats. The results were again challenged by opposition parties who boycotted parliament in protest.

Among the other parties formed to contest the 1993 elections were the Union for the New Republic (Union pour la Nouvelle République – UNR) led by Mamadou Boye Bâ which won nine seats; Rally of the Guinean People (Rassemblement populaire Guinéen – RPG) led by Alpha Condé; the Party of Renewal and Progress (Parti pour le renouveau et le progrès – PRP); and the Movement for Renewal in Guinea (Mouvement pour le Renouveau en Guinée – MRG).

GUINEA-BISSAU

Heads of State

Presidents
Luis de Almeida Cabral   (1974–80)
Major João Bernardo Nino Vieira
   (1980–)

Prime Ministers
Carlos Correia   (1992–4)
Manuel Saturnino da Costa   (1994–)

African Party for the Independence of Guinea and Cape Verde (Partido Africano da Independência da Guiné e Cabo Verde – PAIGC)

Founded in 1956 by Amilcar Cabral, the PAIGC conducted a war for the independence of Guinea-Bissau and Cape Verde against Portugal. Portugal withdrew in 1974 and Luis Cabral, brother of the movement's founder, became president. The PAIGC was the sole legal party. Cabral was overthrown in a coup by João Bernardo Vieira in 1980 following accusations that preference was given to Cape Verdeans in official appointments. The Cape Verde section withdrew from the party after the coup. The party abandoned Marxism–Leninism in 1991 and moved towards the introduction of a multi-party system. The PAIGC won the July 1994 general election with 64 of the 100 parliamentary seats and Vieira was elected president in August 1994.

Guinea-Bissau Resistance Movement (Resisténcia da Guiné-Bissau-Movimento Bah-Fatah – RGB-MB)

Formed in exile in Portugal in 1986, led by Domingos Fernandes Gomes, the party was registered in 1991. The RGB-MB took 19 seats in the 1994 general election.

Union for Change (Uniäo para a Mudança – UM)

Opposition coalition originally formed to contest the 1994 elections. Led by Joâo da

Costa, the coalition was re-established in 1995. Its members include the Movement for Unity and Democracy (Movimento para a Unidade e a Democracia – MUDE), led by Filinto Vaz Martins; the Democratic Social Front (Frente Democrática Sociale – FDS), led by Rafael Barbosa; the Democratic Front (Frente Democrática – FD), led by Canjura Injai; and the Democratic Party for Progress (Partido Democrático do Progresso – PDP), led by Michel Saad.

HAITI

Heads of State

Presidents
Dumarsais Estimé   (1946–50)
Paul Magloire   (1950–56)
François Duvalier   (1957–71) (President for Life, 1964)
Jean Claude Duvalier   (1971–86)

Head of the National Council of Government
General Henri Namphy   (1986–8)

Presidents
Leslie Manigat   (1988 February–June)
General Henry Namphy   (1988 June–September)
Brigadier-General Prosper Avril (1988–90)
Ertha Pascal-Trouillot   (1990–1)
Father Jean-Bertrand Aristide (forced into exile following a coup)   (1991 February–September)
Joseph Nerette   (1991–2)
Presidency was left vacant 1992–4.
Emile Jonassaint (provisional)   (1994 May–October)
Father Jean-Bertrand Aristide   (1994–6)
René Préval   (1996–)

Prime Ministers
René Préval   (1991)
Marc Bazin (provisional)   (1991–3)

Robert Malval   (1993–4)
Michel Smarck   (1994–5)
Claudette Werleigh   (1995–6)
Rosny Smarth   (1996–)

National Unity Party (PUN)
Founded in 1956 by François 'Papa Doc' Duvalier as a party of national unity, PUN's main support was among black intellectuals. By 1964, Duvalier had destroyed all opposition and declared himself president for life. On his death in 1971 he was succeeded by his son Jean Claude 'Baby Doc' Duvalier who was overthrown in a coup and went into exile in France in 1986.

National Agricultural and Industrial Party (PAIN)
Christian democratic party founded in 1956 by Louis Déjoie. The party was reformed in 1981 by his son Louis Déjoie II.

Rally of National Progressive Democrats (RDNP)
Centre-left party founded in exile in Venezuela in 1979 by Leslie Manigat who returned to Haiti in 1986 and contested elections in 1988.

National Committee of Democratic Movements (KONAKOM)
Centre-left political party formed in January 1987 at a congress attended by over 300 organizations, led by Victor Benoit. KONAKOM called for economic and political reforms and for an acknowledgement of the centrality of Creole and voodoo as components of Haitian culture. KONAKOM was at the centre of the Group of 57 which led anti-government protests in 1987 and was officially recognized as a political party in 1989.

National Front for Change and Democracy (FNCD)
Coalition grouping founded in 1990 under the leadership of Fr Jean-Bertrand Aristide

with its main support among the urban poor. FNCD won 67 per cent of votes cast in the first free presidential elections in December 1990. Aristide was prevented from taking office until February 1991 and was then ousted in a coup until October 1994.

Haitian Progressive Revolutionary Party (Panpra)

A social democratic party founded in 1986 under the leadership of Serge Gilles.

JAMAICA

Head of State
Queen Elizabeth II

Prime Ministers
Sir Alexander Bustamente   (1962–7)
Hugh Shearer   (1967–72)
Michael Manley   (1972–80)
Edward Seaga   (1980–9)
Michael Manley   (1989–92)
Percival J. Patterson   (1992–)

People's National Party (PNP)

Socialist party founded by Norman Manley in 1938. Following electoral defeats in 1944 and 1952, the PNP dropped its left-wing emphasis and went on to success in the 1955 and 1959 general elections. The party lost in 1962 and 1967 and Manley was replaced as leader by his son Michael in 1969. He took the party further left and won the 1976 election, but opposition from business interests (supported by the USA) led to defeat in 1980. Manley moderated his policies, severed links with the Workers' Party of Jamaica and, after boycotting the 1983 election, went on to victory in 1989. Following his resignation in 1992 he was succeeded by P. J. Patterson and the PNP went on to win a landslide victory in elections in 1993.

Jamaican Labour Party (JLP)

A conservative party founded in 1943 by Alexander Bustamente as a wing of the Bustamente Industrial Trade Union. The JLP won elections to the Legislative Council in 1944 and 1949 but was defeated by the People's National Party in 1955 and 1959. The JLP won the general election of 1962 and led Jamaica to independence and Bustamente became Jamaica's first prime minister. The party won the 1967 general election and Bustamente resigned in favour of Donald Sangster who died the following month. He was succeeded by Hugh Shearer as prime minister. The JLP was defeated in the 1972 elections and Shearer was replaced by Edward Seaga in 1974. The party was again defeated in elections in 1976. Success came eventually in 1980 with US support and in 1983 when the PNP boycotted the poll. The JLP was defeated in 1989 and again in 1993.

Workers' Party of Jamaica (WPJ)

Marxist–Leninist party founded by Trevor Munroe in 1978, initially a supporter of the Norman Manley government. Manley's PNP severed links in 1981. The WPJ was weakened by Munroe's support for the radicals who killed Maurice Bishop in Grenada in 1983, and further weakened by the resignation of the deputy leader and five central committee members in 1988. Munroe agreed on greater inner-party democracy and to make WPJ policies more relevant to the Jamaican situation. The party has a trade union wing, the University and Allied Workers' Union.

African Comprehensive Party (ACP)

Founded in 1988 as the political section of the Rastafarian movement attached to the Royal Ethiopian Judah Coptic church. Led by Abuna Stedwick Whyte. The ACP is opposed to the domination of foreign capital and advocates the legalization of cannabis for religious purposes.

National Democratic Movement (NDM)

Founded in 1995 by Bruce Goldin, a former member of JLP to campaign for constitutional reform, private enterprise and a market economy. The NDM is supported by former JLP and PNP members.

KENYA

Head of State

Queen Elizabeth II   (1963–5)

Prime Minister

Jomo Kenyatta   (1963–5)
A Republic was declared in 1965.

Head of State and Government

Presidents

Jomo Kenyatta   (1965–78)
Daniel Torotitch arap Moi   (1978–)

Kenya African Union (KAU)

The first mass African nationalist movement in Kenya, established in 1944 as the Kenya African Study Union and renamed in 1946. The KAU was created to defend Kikuyu interests and its support was concentrated in central Kenya. By 1952 it claimed 100,000 members. Jomo Kenyatta became KAU president in 1947. In 1960 it was superseded by the Kenya African National Union.

Kenya African National Union (KANU)

Founded in 1960 by Kenyatta, who was elected party president while in prison. KANU was a coalition of the various local parties, the only form of political organization allowed by the colonial government following the Mau Mau rebellion. With the ban on mass political parties lifted, KANU represented the major tribal groups, the Luo, Kikuyu and Kamba and had its base in urban

areas. In 1961, KANU won 19 of the 30 seats on the legislative council but refused to form a government until Kenyatta was released from detention. From 1964, KANU opposed attempts to form opposition parties and in June 1982 became the sole legal party until 1991 when President Moi approved constitutional changes to institute a multi-party democracy.

Kenya African Democratic Union (KADU)

Founded in 1960 by Ronald Ngala, KADU had its base among the groups who saw KANU as a Kikuyu- and Luo-dominated organization. KADU formed a coalition government with KANU in the run up to independence in December 1963 but left the coalition when its preference for a federal constitution was rejected. KADU was absorbed into KANU in December 1964.

Kenya People's Union (KPU)

Opposition party founded in 1966 by KANU member Oginga Odinga when he was forced to resign as Vice-President of Kenya. Support for the KPU came mainly from the Luo people and represented dissatisfaction with the increasing conservatism of KANU. The party was banned in 1969.

Forum for the Restoration of Democracy (FORD)

Founded in 1991 by Oginga Odinga. Originally a political lobby group supported by lawyers, trade unions, clergy and politicians, FORD became the main opposition grouping. The party split on 13 October 1992 to form two parties, FORD-Asili led by Kenneth Matiba and FORD-Kenya. In 1993 FORD-Kenya united with the Democratic Party to oppose President Moi. Michael Wamalwa Kijana was appointed acting chair of FORD-Kenya in 1994. Two more factions broke away during 1996.

Safina (Noah's Ark)

Founded in 1995 by Richard Leakey and Paul Muite of the banned Mwangaza Trust, to combat corruption and human rights abuses. The party advocated proportional representation. President Moi refused to allow the registration of Safina on the grounds that as a white man Leakey could not be involved in Kenyan politics.

Among other parties are the Moral Alliance for Peace (MAP) and the Democratic Party (PD), led by Mwai Kibaki.

LESOTHO

Heads of State

King Moshoeshoe II   (1966–90 deposed)
Letsie III   (1990–5 abdicated)
King Moshoeshoe II   (1995–6)
Letsie III   (1996–)

Prime Ministers

Chief Leabua Jonathan   (1966–86)
Ntsu Mokhehle   (1992–)

Chairman of the Military Council

Major-General Justin Lekhanya
    (1986–91)
Major-General Elias Phitsoane
    Ramaema   (1991–)

Basotho Congress Party (BCP)

Founded in 1952 as the Basutoland African Congress by Ntsu Mokhehle, the country's first prime minister. The party was renamed the BCP in 1966 and took on an increasingly nationalist stance with links to the African National Congress (ANC) and Pan-Africanist Congress (PAC). The BCP victory in the 1970 elections was overturned in a bloodless coup mounted by Leabua Jonathan. Following the arrest and exile of Mokhehle, the BSP's armed wing – the Lesotho Liberation Army – undertook armed resistance against the BNP government. The BCP won an overwhelming victory in elections held in 1993, taking all 65 National Assembly seats. The BCP government survived two attempted military coups in 1994.

Basotho National Party (BNP)

A conservative party founded in 1958 by Leabua Jonathan, a minor chief of the Basuto people. The BNP attracted support from traditional rulers, their followers and the Catholic Church. It advocated co-operation with South Africa while rejecting apartheid. The BNP won office in the 1965 elections but, following its defeat by the BCP in 1970, Leabua Jonathan mounted a coup and appointed himself prime minister. The BNP government was overthrown in a military coup in January 1986 and the party was banned.

Marema-Tlou Party (MP)

Monarchist party founded in 1957 by Chief Matete, supported by King Moshoeshoe II of Lesotho and traditional rulers. MP merged with the Basutoland Freedom Party in 1963.

Basutoland Freedom Party (BFP)

A moderate party formed by B. Khaketla in 1961 as a breakaway from the BCP following his resignation as BCP deputy leader. The BFP merged with the Marema-Tlou Party in 1963.

Marema-Tlou Freedom Party (MFP)

Formed by a merger of the Marema-Tlou Party and the Basutoland Freedom Party in 1963 under the leadership of Seth Makotoko. The MFP won four seats in pre-independence elections held in 1965. The party was banned in 1986.

Lesotho Communist Party (LCP)

Founded in 1962 and led by Mokhafisi Jacob Kena, the LCP drew the bulk of its support from migrant workers employed in South Africa. The party was outlawed between 1970 and 1991.

LIBERIA

Heads of State and Government

Presidents

Joseph J. Roberts   (1848–56)
Stephen A. Benson   (1856–64)
Daniel B. Warner   (1864–8)
James S. Payne   (1868–70)
Edward J. Roye   (1870–1)
James S. Smith   (1871–2)
Joseph J. Roberts   (1872–6)
James S. Payne   (1876–8)
Anthony W. Gardiner   (1878–83)
Alfred F. Russell   (1883–4)
Hilary R. W. Johnson   (1884–92)
Joseph J. Cheeseman   (1892–6)
William D. Coleman   (1896–1900)
Garretson W. Gibson   (1900–4)
Arthur Barclay   (1904–12)
Daniel E. Howard   (1912–20)
Charles D. B. King   (1920–30)
Edwin Barclay   (1930–44)
William V. S. Tubman   (1944–71)
William R. Tolbert   (1971–80)
Samuel K. Doe   (1980–90)
Amos Sawyer (interim)   (1990–94)
Ruth Sands Perry (interim)   (1996–)

Chairman of the Council of State

David Kpomakpor   (1994–5)
Wilton Sankawulo   (1995–)

True Whig Party

Liberian political party established in 1868. The party, which represented the interests of the Americo-Liberian elite, ruled Liberia continuously until 1980 when President Tolbert was killed in a coup led by Master Sergeant Samuel Doe who became leader of a People's Redemption Council. The party was abolished.

People's Party

Established in 1922 by former president, Daniel B. Howard, in opposition to the True Whig Party, the People's Party was unable to overturn the governing party's dominance of Liberian politics.

United People's Party (UPP)

Left-wing party led by Gabriel Bacchus Matthews. The party was the leading opposition party before the 1980 coup. The UPP was prohibited from taking part in the 1985 elections on the grounds that as a socialist party it did not conform to Liberia's political tradition.

National Democratic Party of Liberia (NDPL)

Formed in 1984 by President Doe to campaign in forthcoming elections. Doe was elected president in October 1985, and NDPL candidates won 51 of the 64 House of Representatives seats and 22 of the 26 places in the Senate.

Liberia Unification Party (LUP)

Established by William Gabriel Kpolleh to contest the 1985 elections following the lifting of the ban on political parties in 1984. The LUP advocated a market economy and freedom of the press, speech and religion. Kpolleh took 11.1 per cent of the vote in the presidential elections. LUP became part of an opposition Liberia Grand Coalition (LGC) formed in 1986.

Liberia People's Party (LPP)

Left-wing opposition party led by Amos Sawyer composed of former members of the Movement for Justice in Africa (MOJA), a group active before the 1980 coup. The LPP was banned in 1985 because of its socialist policies. Following Doe's assassination in 1990, Sawyer led an Interim Government of National Unity formed in April 1991 but factional fighting led to all-out civil war.

Progressive People's Party (PPP)

Originally founded as the Progressive Alliance of Liberia (PAL). After its renaming in 1979, the PPP registered as a political party in 1980. It was banned by President Tolbert. Following the 1980 coup, Matthews was appointed to a post in the Doe government but was dismissed in 1981.

Following the assassination of President Doe in 1990 and the spread of civil war in Liberia, factions competed for power. These included the National Patriotic Front of Liberia (NPFL), a rebel movement led by Charles Taylor. A split in the movement in 1990 led to the formation of the Independent Patriotic Front of Liberia (INPFL) under Prince Johnson. In 1991, supporters of the late President Doe formed the United Liberation Movement of Liberia for Democracy (ULIMO). This fragmented in 1992. One faction under Alhaji Kromah was supported by Islamic groups and the Libyan government. The other, led by Raleigh Seekie, operated from Sierra Leone and carried out attacks on the NPFL.

MALAWI

Head of State

Queen Elizabeth II   (1964–6)

Prime Minister

Hastings Kamuzu Banda   (1964–6)
A Republic was declared in 1966.

Head of State and Government

Presidents

Hastings Kamuzu Banda   (1966–94)
(Three-man Presidential Council)   (1993
    October–December)
Bakili Muluzi   (1994–)

Malawi Congress Party (MCP)

Founded in 1959 (after the banning by the British colonial authorities of the Nyasaland African Congress) as a conservative multi-racial party led by Orton Chirwa between 1959–60 while Hastings Banda was in detention. Banda led the MCP to victory in the 1961 election. The MCP became the sole legal political party in 1966 and in 1974 all adult Malawians were ordered to become members. In elections in 1994, following the institution of a multi-party system, the MCP lost power, gaining 55 of 176 National Assembly seats.

Malawi Freedom Movement (MAFREMO)

Formed in 1977 by left-wing exiles in Tanzania, MAFREMO had some support from Mozambique, Tanzania and Zimbabwe. Led by Orton and Vera Chirwa, MAFREMO aimed at the overthrow of President Banda and the establishment of a socialist state. Leadership passed to Dr Edward Yapwantha after the arrest and imprisonment of the Chirwas in 1981. MAFREMO was dissolved in 1993.

United Democratic Front (UDF)

Founded in 1992 to contest the 1994 elections, under the leadership of Bakili Muluzi, a former MCP minister. The UDF took 84 of the 176 National Assembly seats in the 1994 elections and formed a coalition government with AFORD, MNDP and UFMD.

Alliance for Democracy (AFORD)

Pro-democracy group founded in 1992, led by Chakufwa Chihana. AFORD included members of the former Malawi Freedom Movement and became a member of the coalition government formed after the 1994 elections.

Among other parties formed following the legalization of political organizations are the Malawi Democratic Party, the Malawi Socialist Labour Party, the United Front for Multi-party Democracy, the Congress for the Second Republic and the Christian-Islamic Alliance for Democracy.

MALI

Heads of State

President
Modibo Keita (1960–8)

President and Commander-in-Chief of Armed Forces
Lieutenant (later General) Moussa
  Traoré (1968–91)
Lieutenant-Colonel Amadou Toumani
  Touré (1991–2)

President
Alpha Oumar Konare (1992–)

Prime Ministers
Younoussi Touré (1992–3)
Abdoulaye Sekou Sow (1993–4)
Ibrahim Boubacar Keita (1994–)

Sudanese Union-African Democratic Rally (Union Soudanaise-Rassemblement démocratique africain – US-RDA)

Founded in 1960 by Modibo Keita as the territorial section of the RDA. Keita became Mali's first president on independence in 1960. The US-RDA was the sole legal political party from 1960 until Keita was deposed in a coup led by Lieutenant Moussa Traoré in 1968. The party was dissolved.

Mali People's Democratic Union (Union démocratique du peuple Malien – UDPM)

Official party founded by President Moussa Traoré in 1979. The UDPM remained the only legal political party until it was dissolved in 1991 following Traoré's overthrow.

Alliance for Democracy in Mali (Alliance pour la démocratie au Mali – ADEMA)

Formed in 1990 by Alpha Oumar Konaré at the head of a group of prominent Mali citizens In 1992 Konare was elected as President in the first multi-party elections since 1960.

National Committee for Democratic Initiative (Congrès national d'initiative démocratique – CNID)

Opposition party formed by lawyers under the leadership of Amida Diabaté in 1990 to campaign for a multi-party system.

Sudanese Union-African Democratic Group (Union Soudanaise-Rassemblement démocratique africain – US-RDA)

Opposition party based on the 1960 Sudanese Union formed in 1991 by Mamadou Konate.

Among other parties formed following the legalization of political activity were the Rally for Democracy and Progress (Rassemblement pour la démocratie et le progrès – RDP), the Movement for Independence, Rebirth and African Integration (Mouvement pour l'indépendance, le renaissance et le intégration africaines – MIRIA), and the Patriotic Renewal Movement (Mouvement patriotique pour le renouveau – MPR).

MOZAMBIQUE

Heads of State

Presidents
Samora Moises Machel (1975–86)
Joaquim Alberto Chissano (1986–)

Prime Ministers
Mario da Graça Machungo (1986–94)
Pascoal Mocumbi (1994–)

Front for the Liberation of Mozambique (Frente de Libertação de Moçambique – FRELIMO)

Formed in Tanzania in1962 by Eduardo Mondlane as a coalition of anti-Portuguese groups. FRELIMO carried out its first armed action against Portugal in 1964. Following

Mondlane's assassination in 1969, Samora Machel became leader and in 1970 FRELIMO was declared to be a Marxist–Leninist party. FRELIMO became the sole party on independence in 1974. In 1986 Machel was killed in an aircrash and was succeeded by Joaquim Chissano and the party abandoned socialism in 1989. A constitution introduced in 1990 instituted a multi-party democracy. Following the 1994 elections FRELIMO remained the ruling party, having won 129 of the 250 seats in the legislature.

Mozambican National Resistance (Resistência Nacional Moçambicana – RENAMO)

Founded in 1976 and supported by the white minority Rhodesian regime. RENAMO waged a civil war against the FRELIMO government until 1992, when a multi-party system was introduced. RENAMO registered as a political party in August 1994 under the leadership of Afonso Macacho Marceta Dhlakama and took 112 seats in the legislative elections

Democratic Union (União Democrática – UD)

A coalition formed in 1994 under the leadership of António Palange. UD won nine seats in the 1994 legislative elections.

Among other parties are the Mozambique Democratic Party (Partido Democrático de Moçambique – PADEMO), the Democratic Union of Mozambique (União Democrática de Moçambique – UDEMO) and the Mozambique Communist Party (PACOMO).

NAMIBIA

Heads of State

President
Sam Nujoma   (1990–)

Prime Minister
Hage Geingob   (1990–)

South West Africa People's Organisation (SWAPO)

Formed in 1960, under the leadership of Sam Nujoma as president. SWAPO emerged from the Ovamboland People's Party, established in 1957 by Toivo ja Toiva to campaign against the contract labour system. SWAPO established its headquarters in Dar es Salaam in 1961 and opened an armed struggle against South African occupation in 1966. In 1968 it changed its name to SWAPO of Namibia. SWAPO successfully organized boycotts of South African controlled elections in the 1980s. In November 1989, SWAPO candidates won 44 of the 72 seats in the Constituent Assembly election and Nujoma became the country's president. SWAPO abandoned Marxism, accepting multi-party democracy in a mixed economy. The party retained its position as the ruling party following the 1994 elections.

South West African National Union (SWANU)

Militant nationalist movement formed in exile in 1959 by Jariretunda Kozonguisi. Its main support was among the Herero people. Support for SWANU lessened after 1966. Following a split in SWANU in 1985 the majority of the members joined SWAPO.

South West Africa People's Organisation – Democrats (SWAPO-D)

Formed in 1978 by a breakaway group from SWAPO led by Andreas Shipanga. SWAPO-D participated in the 1985–9 Transitional Government of National Unity, a South African puppet government which gained little support in Namibia because it was a clear attempt to prevent SWAPO taking power.

Democratic Turnhalle Alliance (DTA)

Opposition coalition party founded in 1977 with South African backing at the Turnhalle Conference. The DTA is a moderate, multi-ethnic grouping led by Dirk Mudge, a white politician. In pre-independence elections organized in 1978 by the South African administration (and boycotted by SWAPO), the DTA won 41 of the 50 Constituent Assembly seats. The DTA went on to form a government with little black or white support and in 1983 the administration was dissolved. The party was defeated by SWAPO when it contested the 1994 elections.

NIGER

Heads of State

President
Hamani Diori   (1960–74)

President of the Supreme Military Council
Lieutenant-Colonel Seyni Kountché
   (1974–87)
Brigadier Ali Saïbou   (1987–91)

Head of transitional government
Amadou Cheiffou   (1991–3)

President
Mahamane Ousmane   (1993–6)

Chairman of the Niger National Salvation Council
General Ibrahim Barre Mainassara
   (1996–)

Prime Ministers
Aliou Mahamidou   (1989–91)
Amadou Cheiffou   (1991–3)
Mahamadou Issoufou   (1993–4)
Souley Abdoulaye   (1994–5)
Hama Amadou   (1995–6)
Boukary Adji   (1996–)

Niger Progressive Party (Parti Progressiste Nigérien – PPN)

Founded in 1957 by Hamani Diori. The PPN developed out of the territorial section of the African Democratic Rally (Rassemblement Démocratique Africain – RDA), established in 1946. The PPN became the sole legal party in 1958. The party was banned in 1974 when President Diori was deposed in a military coup.

Sawaba (Freedom) Party

Left-wing group which split from the PPN in 1951 under Djibo Bakary. Sawaba formed the first African government in Niger but only held power for a few months following the 1957 elections. The party unsuccessfully recommended a vote against continuing association with France in a 1958 referendum. Sawaba was banned in 1959 but continued its opposition activities in exile in Ghana.

National Movement for a Society of Development (Mouvement National pour une société de Développement – MNSD)

Founded in August 1988 when Brigadier Ali Saïbou became interim president following the death of Niger's military leader, Seyni Kountché. The MNSD was the sole legal party until the introduction of a multi-party system in December 1990. The MNSD failed to retain its position as the ruling party in 1993 but was elected to office under Hama Amadou in 1995 following defections from the AFC.

Alliance of Forces for Change (AFC)

Opposition alliance led by Mahamane Ousmane. The AFC took office after winning 50 seats in the 1993 election but lost support in 1995 through defections in one of the alliance parties. Ousmane was deposed in 1996 following a military takeover by Ibrahim Barre Mainassara.

Among other parties formed in 1990 when the registration of political parties was authorized were the Niger Progressive Party – African Democratic Rally (Parti Progressiste Nigérien-Rassemblement Démocratique Africain – PPN-RDA), and the Niger Progressive Party-African Democratic Rally (Union des Forces populaires pour la démocratie et le progrès – UDPF).

NIGERIA

Head of State
Queen Elizabeth II   (1960–3)

Prime Minister
Tafawa Balewa   (1960–6)
A Republic was declared in 1963.

Head of State and Government

President
Nnamdi Azikiwe   (1963–6)

Heads of Supreme Military Council
Major-General J. T. U. Aguiyi-Ironsi
   (1966 January–July)
Lieutenant-Colonel (later General) Y.
   Gowon   (1966–75)

Heads of State
Brigadier Murtala Muhammed   (1975–6)
Lieutenant-General Olusegun Obasanjo
   (1976–9)

President
Shehu Shagari   (1979–83)

Head of State and military government
Major-General Mohammadu Buhari
   (1983–5)

President and Commander-in-Chief
Major-General Ibrahim Babangida
   (1985–93)

Head of interim government
Ernest Shonekan   (1993
   August–November)

Chairman of the Provisional Ruling Council
General Sani Abacha   (1993–)

National Party of Nigeria (NPN)
Founded in 1978 in the run-up to the return to civilian rule. The NPN was a conservative party with an emphasis on law and order and a free market. Its candidate Shagari won the presidency in 1979, while the NPN also took seven of the 19 state governorships and won up to 40 per cent of the vote in election to the Senate, House of Representatives and state assemblies. The NPN spent heavily to win the 1983 election but was discredited by the open corruption involved. The party was banned with all other parties following the January 1986 military coup.

Nigerian National Democratic Party (NNDP)
Formed in western Nigeria in 1964 by Herbert Macaulay and which served in a coalition federal government as a junior partner to the Northern People's Congress. Disorder following allegations of fraud in the NNDP's victory in the 1965 Western Region election helped provoke the January 1966 military coup following which all political parties were banned.

Nigerian People's Party (NPP)
Founded in 1978 in the run-up to the return to civilian rule. The NPP's conservative and traditional policies attracted support from the owners of small businesses. In the 1979 election the NPP presidential candidate, Nnamdi Azikiwe, came third but the party won three state governorships and a majority in three state assemblies. Allied with the ruling National Party of Nigeria from 1979–81, the NPP then supported the main opposition party, the Unity Party of Nigeria. The NPP was banned with all other parties following the January 1966 military coup.

261

Northern People's Congress (NPC)

A party with strong Muslim support formed by Ahmadu Bello in 1951 from a northern Nigerian cultural organization founded two years previously which found its strongest support among the Hausa people. The NPC advocated regional autonomy, fearing southern domination of Nigeria after independence. The NPC deputy leader, Abubakar Tafawa Balewa, became federal prime minister in 1957 and led Nigeria to independence in 1960. The NPC was the senior party in coalition governments until all parties were banned following the military coup in January 1966.

Action Group

Opposition party founded by Obafemi Awolowo in 1951. The ruling party in the West Region, the Action Group found its support among the Yoruba people and was a reaction against fears of Ibo domination. The party was banned in 1966.

National Convention of Nigerian Citizens (NCNC)

Formed in 1944 as the National Council of Nigeria and the Cameroons, renamed in 1961 when the Southern Cameroons reversed its policy of joining Nigeria. With mainly Ibo support in eastern Nigeria, the NCNC campaigned for independence under the leadership of Nnamdi Azikiwe. The party formed the Eastern Region government from 1954 to 1966 and Azikiwe was regional premier in 1954–9. A junior partner with the Northern People's Congress in the coalition federal government from 1959 to 1964, the NCNC was banned with all other political parties following the military coup of January 1966.

National Republican Convention (NRC)

Right-of-centre party created in 1989 with government finance in preparation for the restoration of civilian rule. The NRC was defeated in the 1992 legislative elections and its presidential candidate came second with 41.6 per cent of the vote in the annulled 1993 presidential election.

Social Democratic Party (SDP)

Left-of-centre party created in 1989 with government finance in preparation for the restoration of civilian rule. The SDP won a majority of seats in the 1992 National Assembly and House of Representatives elections. The party's presidential candidate, Moshood Abiola, won 58.4 per cent in elections held in 1993 but was barred from office following an annulment of the elections.

RWANDA

Heads of State

Grégoire Kayibanda (1962–73)
Major-General Juvénal Habyarimana (1973–94)
Theodore Sindkubgabo (1994 April–July)

President

Pasteur Bizimungu (1994–)

Prime Ministers

Dismas Nsengiyaremye (1992–3)
Agathe Uwilingiyimana (1993–4)
Faustin Twagiramungu (1994–5)
Pierre-Célestin Rwigyema (1995–)

Party for Hutu Emancipation (Parti de l'émancipation du peuple Hutu – Parmehutu)

Founded in 1958 by Grégoire Kayibanda, the country's first president on independence in 1962. Parmehutu derived from the Hutu Democratic Republican Movement, formed in 1959, and became the sole legal political party in 1965. It was suspended following the 1973 military coup.

National Republican Movement for Development (Mouvement République pour la National Developpement – MRND)

Founded in 1975 as the National Revolutionary Movement for Development, the sole political party between 1976–90. The party was led by Juvénal Habyarimana, president after seizing power in 1973, and was intended to be a party of national unity.

Committee for the Defence of the Republic (Comité pour la Defense de la République – CDR)

Extremist Bahutu party which emerged from the MRND.

ST CHRISTOPHER & NEVIS

Head of State
Queen Elizabeth II

Prime Ministers
Kennedy A. Simmonds   (1980–95)
Denzil Douglas   (1995–)

People's Action Movement (PAM)

Conservative party founded in 1965. PAM was unsuccessful in the 1966, 1971 and 1975 general elections but in 1980 ended 28 years of Labour rule when Kennedy Simmonds became premier in coalition with the Nevis Reformation Party. PAM went on to win the 1984 and 1989 elections.

St Kitts-Nevis Labour Party (SKNLP)

Founded in 1946, based on the Workers' League and the St Kitts Trades and Labour Union. The party won Legislative Council elections in 1952 and 1957, going on to win the general elections of 1966, 1971 and 1975. Internal divisions opened up following the death in 1978 of the party's founder, Robert Bradshaw. The SKNLP lost power in 1980 and performed badly in the 1984 and 1989 general election. Under the leadership of Denzil Douglas the party took part in inconclusive elections in 1990 but went on to win in 1995, ending fifteen years of PAM government.

Nevis Reformation Party (NRP)

Separatist movement founded in 1970 by Simeon Daniel. The NRP advocated self-rule for Nevis. A referendum in which 99 per cent of the population voted to secede from St Kitts was followed by a demand for the island to be made a British Dependency. The request was denied but the island was given its own Assembly in 1993.

ST LUCIA

Head of State
Queen Elizabeth II

Prime Ministers
John G. M. Compton   (1982–96)
Vaughan Lewis   (1996–)

St Lucia Labour Party (SLP)

Founded in 1950 by George Charles with its base in the St Lucia Workers Union. The SLP won the 1951, 1954 and 1957 general elections but was defeated in the 1964, 1969 and 1974 general elections by the United Workers' Party, a party made up partly of breakaway members of the SLP. Successful in the 1979 general election under the leadership of Allan Louisy, the SLP returned to office but lost power in 1982 following internal divisions. Julian Hunte became party leader in 1996.

United Workers' Party (UWP)

Conservative party, formed in 1964 by breakaway section of the St Lucia Labour Party (SLP) in alliance with the People's Progressive Party. Led by John Compton, who became the first prime minister on independence, the UWP successfully contested the 1964, 1969 and 1974 general elections, was defeated by the SLP in 1979, but went on to victory in 1982, twice in 1987 and in 1992. The present leader is Neville Cenac.

Progressive Labour Party (PLP)

Founded by George Odlum in 1981 after a dispute in the SLP. The PLP's leftist stance lost it support after the collapse of the Grenada revolution in 1983.

ST VINCENT AND THE GRENADINES

Head of State
Queen Elizabeth II

Prime Ministers
Milton Cato   (1979–84)
James Mitchell   (1984–)

St Vincent Labour Party (SVLP)

Conservative party founded in 1955 by Milton Cato. Its main support was among the middle class. The party's first success was in the 1967 elections. It lost the 1972 elections to the PPP but was returned to power in 1974 in a coalition with the PPP and again in 1979. In 1989 the party lost every seat. The party formed an alliance with the Movement for National Unity and the United People's Movement to fight the 1994 election.

New Democratic Party (NDP)

Centrist party founded in 1975 by James Mitchell, a former premier and member of the SVLP who had contributed to the party's defeat in 1972 when he resigned as a SVLP MP. The NDP won seats in the 1979 general election and took power as the ruling party with Mitchell as prime minister following the 1984 election. The party remained in power following the 1989 and 1994 elections.

United People's Movement (UPM)

Formed in 1979 initially as a left-wing electoral coalition by Adrian Saunders. The UPM comprised the Youlou Liberation Movement, Arwee and the People's Demo-cratic Movement and took 14 per cent in the 1979 election. The coalition broke up after the election, and the UPM retained an increasingly weak existence as an organization, taking 3 per cent of the vote in the 1984 election and 1 per cent in 1989.

Movement for National Unity (MNU)

Formed in 1982 by Ralph Gonsalves, following his resignation as leader of the UPM. He objected to what he described as 'Marxist tendencies' in the UPM.

United Labour Party (ULP)

Electoral alliance formed in 1994 by a merger between the SVLP and the MNU as a moderate social democratic party under Vincent Beache. The ULP is the main opposition party

SÃO TOMÉ AND PRÍNCIPE

Heads of State

Presidents
Manuel Pinto da Costa   (1975–91)
Miguel Trovoada   (1991–)

Prime Ministers
Miguel Trovoada   (1975–9)
Celestino Rocha da Costa   (1988–91)
Daniel Lima dos Santos Daio   (1991–4)
Carlos Alberto Monteiro Dias da Graça   (1994–)

Movement for the Liberation of São Tomé and Principe-Social Democratic Party (Movimento de Libertação de São Tomé e Príncipe-Parti do Social Democrata – MLSTP-PSD)

Formed in exile in 1972 by Manuel Pinto da Costa to lead the independence struggle. Following independence in 1975, the MLSTP was the sole legal party until multi-party elections were allowed in 1991. The party lost power to Miguel Trovoada, a former MLSTP prime minister standing as an independent.

Democratic Convergence Party-Reflection Group (Partido de Convergência Democrática-Grupo de Reflexão – PCD-GR)

Opposition party founded in 1987 by former MLSTP minister Daniel Lima dos Santos Daio. The party supported the candidacy of Miguel Trovoada as an independent in the 1991 elections.

Democratic Opposition Coalition (Partido Democrática da Oposição – CODO)

Opposition party which took one seat in the 1991 elections.

SENEGAL

Heads of State

Presidents
Léopold Sédar Senghor   (1960–80)
Abdou Diouf   (1981–)

Prime Minister
Habib Thiam   (1991–)

Socialist Party (Parti socialiste – PS)

Founded in 1958 as the Union Progressiste Sénégalaise by Léopold Senghor. The party assumed its present name in 1978. Abdou Diouf became the leader in 1980 and was re-elected as president in 1983, 1988 and 1993. The PS formed a coalition government with the PDS in 1995.

Senegalese Democratic Bloc (Bloc Démocratique Sénégalais – BDS)

Founded in 1948 by Léopold Senghor when he left the PS. The BDS won the 1951 elections and Senghor continued to dominate political life until his retirement in 1980.

Senegalese Democratic Party (Parti Démocratique Sénégalais – PDS)

Founded in 1974 led by Abdoulaye Wade. The PDS was the most significant of the opposition parties and won 25 per cent of the vote in the 1988 election.

African Independence Party (Parti Africain de l'Indépendance – PAI)

Marxist–Leninist independence party founded in 1957 by Mahjmout Diop. The PAI was banned in 1960 and operated underground until it was legalized in 1976.

African And-Jéf Party for Democracy and Socialism (And Jéf-Parti africain pour la démocratie et le socialisme – AJ-PADS)

Pro-communist movement founded in 1991 by a merger of three parties advocating progressive reforms.

A multi-party political system was introduced in 1981. Among the parties formed were the Democratic League-Labour Movement Party (Ligue démocratique-Mouvement pour le parti du travail – LD-MPT), Party of Independence and Labour (Parti de l'indépendance et du travail – PIT), National Democratic Rally (Rassemblement national démocratique – RND), and the People's Liberation Party (Parti pour la libération du peuple – PLP).

SIERRA LEONE

Head of State
Queen Elizabeth II   (1961–71)

Prime Ministers
Sir Milton Margai   (1961–4)
Sir Albert Margai   (1964–7)

Head of National Reformation Council
Brigadier-General David Lansana
    (1967–8)
Brigadier-General Andrew Juxon-Smith
    (1968–71)

Prime Minister
Siaka Stevens   (1968–71)

A Republic was declared in 1971.

Heads of State and Government

Presidents
Siaka Stevens   (1971–85)
Major-General Joseph Saidu Momoh
  (1985–92)
Valentine Strasser   (1992–6)

Chairman of the National Provisional Ruling Council
Brigadier-General Julius Maada Bio
  (1996 January–March)

President
Ahmad Tejan Kabbah   (1996–)

Sierra Leone People's Party (SLPP)
Founded in 1951 and led by Sir Milton Margai, the SLPP formed the country's government before and after independence in 1961. He died in office in 1964 and was succeeded by his brother Sir Albert Margai. Defeated in the 1967 general election, the party refused to relinquish office and the military seized power. On the restoration of civilian rule in 1968, the SLPP went into opposition. The party won the 1977 elections but was dissolved when Sierra Leone became a one-party state in 1978. The SLPP was returned to power in 1996 in elections which brought an end to 19 years of one-party and military rule.

All People's Congress (APC)
Founded in 1960 by Siaka Stevens as the main opponent of the SLPP. The APC narrowly won the 1967 election but the SLPP's refusal to give up office led to military intervention. The APC formed a government under Stevens in 1968, after his return from exile in Guinea, and went on to win in 1973. In 1978 Sierra Leone was declared a one-party state with the APC as the sole official party. Stevens was succeeded on his retirement by Major-General Momoh in 1985. Momoh was overthrown in a coup in 1992.

A number of opposition parties and movements operated in exile between 1992 and the restoration of civilian rule. Among these were the Sierra Leone Alliance Movement (SLAM); the Sierra Leone Democratic Party (SLDP), the National Action Party (NAP); and the Revolutionary United Front (RUF), engaged in armed struggle against the government. Among parties contesting the 1996 elections were the United National People's Party (UNPP) led by John-Karifa Smart; and the People's Democratic Party (PDP).

SOMALIA

Heads of State

Presidents
Aden Abdulle Osman   (1960–7)
Abdi Rashid Ali Shirmarke   (1967–9)
Major-General Mohamed Siad Barre
  (1969–91)
Ali Mahdi Mohamed (interim)   (1991–)

Prime Ministers
Lieutenant-General Ali Samatar
  (1989–90)
Umar Arteh Qalib   (1991–)

Somali Revolutionary Socialist Party (SRSP)
Formed in 1976 by Siad Barre when he dissolved the military council which had seized control in 1960. The SRSP was the sole legal party until Barre was deposed in 1991. The SRSP now operates as a guerrilla group in the Gedo region on the Kenyan border.

United Somali Congress (USC)
Opposition movement founded in 1989 by Ali Mahdi Mohamed with its main support among the Hawiye clan. The USC deposed Siad Barre and established an interim administration with Mahdi as resident.

Somali National Alliance

Coalition founded in 1992 by General Mohamed Farah Aidid, leader of the military wing of the USC. The coalition included the Southern Somali National Movement (SSNM) (withdrew in 1993), factions of the United Somali Congress, the Somali Democratic Movement and the Somali Patriotic Movement.

Somali Salvation Democratic Front (SSDF)

Founded in 1981 as the Democratic Front for the Salvation of Somalia, an alliance of three parties with its main support in central Somalia.

Political activity in Somalia became fragmented in 1991 following the overthrow of President Siad Barre. A number of factions representing clans were formed. These include the Somali Democratic Alliance formed in 1989 and representing the Gadabursi people of north-west Somalia; the Islamic Union Party (Ittihad) based in northern Somalia which advocates an Islamic union of ethnic Somalis from Somalia, Djibouti and Kenya; the United Somali Front, founded in 1989 and representing Issas in north-west Somalia; the Somali Salvation Alliance (SSA), formed in 1993 as an alliance of twelve groups in opposition to General Aidid; and the Somali National Front (SNF), a Darod clan guerrilla movement founded in 1991 and operating in southern Somalia.

SOUTH AFRICA

Head of State and Government

President
Nelson Mandela   (1994–)

African National Congress (ANC)

Founded in Bloemfontein, South Africa, in 1912 by Zulu Methodist minister J. W. Dube as the South African Native National Congress to organize peaceful protest against the discrimination inherent in the 1910 Act of Union which gave the country dominion status within the British empire. The ANC's constitutional stance made little progress against white discrimination through the 1920s and 1930s. In 1939 the ANC supported South Africa's participation in the war against Germany and participated in the government-organized 'Native Representative Councils'. Radicals opposed to the ANC's passive line – including Oliver Tambo and Walter Sisulu – formed the Congress Youth League in 1944, seeking a more activist stance. When apartheid was introduced in 1948 the ANC organized mass protests and passive resistance and in 1952 its older leaders were ousted. Nelson Mandela was elected to the national executive and the Defiance Campaign of mass disobedience was launched. However, the ANC continued to denounce violent protest. In 1955, as links were developed with the South African Communist Party, the ANC launched its Freedom Charter setting out the movement's goals of national independence and black majority rule. This was followed by the formation of the Congress Alliance with the South African Indian Congress, the South African Coloured People's Organisation, the white Congress of Democrats, and later the South African Congress of Trade Unions. A section of the ANC which opposed co-operation with whites broke away in 1959 to form the Pan-Africanist Congress (PAC). Following the Sharpeville massacre in March 1960 the ANC was banned, its leaders who were not arrested going into exile or underground. The ANC adopted a strategy of violence in 1961 and set up an armed wing Umkhonto we Sizwe (Xhosa for Spear of the Nation) under Mandela's leadership. Acts of economic sabotage were mounted until 1963. Mandela and other ANC leaders were arrested; Mandela was sentenced to life imprisonment at the Rivonia Trial, and the movement did not recover from intense government repression until the mid-1970s. ANC was reorganized in exile under Tambo. The ANC was strengthened in the wake of the June 1976 Soweto uprising by an influx of youth to its training camps in Angola, Mozambique and Tanzania and in 1978 resumed its armed campaign. As repression within South Africa increased, ANC support mounted. In the 1980s the ANC's role in internal conflict was limited, the movement concentrating its efforts on securing international diplomatic pressure on the white government. In 1987, ANC leaders held talks with leading white businessmen on the basis of the demands set out in the Freedom Charter. Mandela was released in February 1990 and assumed the post of ANC vice-president but was in effect the movement's national leader. The ANC presented itself as an alternative government and campaigned for one-person one-vote and an end to apartheid. In 1990 the ANC renounced violence. In the first multi-racial elections in South Africa in 1994, 12.5 million votes went to the ANC representing 62.65 per cent of the total vote.

Azanian People's Liberation Organization (AZAPO)

Founded in South Africa in May 1978 to continue the work of the black consciousness movement following the murder by police of Steve Biko. AZAPO rejected co-operation with whites in the overthrow of apartheid and was prominent in the 1985 uprising and the disruption of US Senator Edward Kennedy's visit to the country. AZAPO members clashed with supporters of the United Democratic Front (UDF) in the 1980s. By the late 1980s AZAPO had an estimated 86 branches and 110,000 members and was developing links with socialist organizations. AZAPO rejected the willingness of the ANC and other groups to enter into negotiations with the white government in 1990.

Inkatha Peace and Freedom Party

Originally the Inkatha ye Nkululeko ye Sizwe, a Zulu cultural and political organization founded by Chief Buthelezi in 1974. It descended from Inkatha ka Zula, a cultural organization founded in 1928. Based in the homeland of KwaZulu, Inkatha's opposition to sanctions against the apartheid regime and support for capitalist development led to serious clashes with ANC and Democratic Forum activists in the 1980s and 1990s. The organization was relaunched as the Inkatha Peace and Freedom Party, a multi-racial political party to contest the 1994 election and went on to take 2 million votes representing 10.5 per cent of the total. The party became a participant in the Government of National Unity.

Pan-Africanist Congress (PAC)

Formed in South Africa in 1959 by a breakaway section from the ANC which opposed the ANC's multi-racialism and its co-operation with whites. Robert Sobukwe was elected president. The PAC won support among workers in the south Transvaal and migrant workers in the Cape through its anti-pass laws campaign and organized the March 1960 Sharpeville rally at which 67 black people were shot. In the aftermath, the PAC was banned and Sobuke arrested. PAC members fled to Lesotho and Botswana. A military wing, Poqo (Xhosa for 'pure') was formed. The PAC was supported by China and recognized by the Organization of African Unity (OAU) and the United Nations but was weakened by internal divisions and was virtually destroyed by the police in 1965. Some members went on to help form the Black People's Convention in 1972. With the South African thaw, many of its leaders were released in 1990. The PAC continued its armed actions against whites with the slogan, 'One settler, one bullet' but in January 1994 suspended the armed struggle and agreed to participate in the April election. The PAC appeared close to collapse in 1996.

SWAZILAND

Heads of State
King Sobhuza II   (1967–82)
Queen Mother Indlovukazi Dzeliwe (1982)
Queen Regent Indlovukazi Ntombi (1983–6)
King Mswati III   (1986–)

Prime Ministers
Makhosini Dlamini   (1967–76)
In 1976 the King took all political power.
Obed Dlamini   (1989–93)
Prince Jameson Mbilini Dlamini (1993–6)
Sibusis Barnabas Dlamini   (1996–)

Swaziland Progressive Party (SPP)
Founded in 1960 by John Nquku to campaign for self-government and eventual independence. Internal disputes caused a split in the party in 1961.

Ngwane National Liberatory Congress (NNLC)
Nationalist party founded in 1962 by A. P. Zwane following a split in the SPP. Influenced by Pan-African ideas, the NNLC called for democratic reform, universal suffrage and resistance to incorporation in South Africa. The party had strong support in urban areas. It was banned in 1978.

Imbokodvo National Movement (INM)
Founded in 1964 as a traditionalist party supported by King Sobhuza II to contest pre-independence elections in 1964. The party advocated social reform and supported free enterprise. The INM was banned in 1978.

Confederation for Full Democracy in Swaziland (CFDS)
Founded in 1992 as an alliance of organizations advocating democratic reform.

People's United Democratic Movement (PUDEMO)
Established in 1983 by Elmond Shongwe. PUDEMO is a member of the CFDS and seeks constitutional reform. It became the official opposition party in 1992.

TANGANYIKA
See United Republic of Tanzania.

TOGO

Heads of State

Presidents
Sylvanus Olympio   (1960–3)
Nicolas Grunitzky   (1963–7)
Lieutenant-Colonel (later General) Etienne Gnassingbe Eyadéma   (1967–)

Prime Ministers
Joseph Kokou Koffigoh   (1991–4)
Edem Kodjo   (1994–6)
Kwasi Klutse   (1996–)

Committee for Togolese Unity (Comité de l'unité Togolaise – CUT)
Nationalist party founded in 1946 by Sylvanus Olympio who became President at independence. CUT was the ruling party from 1958–63 when Olympio was killed in a military coup led by Gnassingbe Eyadéma.

Togolese United Party (Parti de l'unité Togolaise – PUT)
Formed in 1946 by Nicolas Grunitzky with French support. PUT lost power to CUT in pre-independence elections in 1958 and Grunitzky went into exile. He returned to Togo in 1963 at the invitation of Eyadéma and assumed the presidency. Grunitzky was deposed in a bloodless coup in 1967 and

went into exile. PUT, and all other parties, were banned from 1967–9.

Rally of the Togolese People (Rassemblement du peuple togolais – RPT)

Founded in 1969 by Gnassingbe Eyadéma, the RPT was the sole legal party until 1991. The RPT was re-established in 1992 following several attempted coups. Presidential elections were held in 1993 in which Eyadéma retained his position. The RPT took 35 of 81 National Assembly seats in the 1994 legislative elections, losing its position as the ruling party.

Action Committee for Renewal (Comité d'action pour le renouveau – CAR)

Founded by Me Yao Agboyibo in 1991 when political parties were legalized. CAR became the main party after winning 36 of the 81 National Assembly seats in the 1994 elections. CAR and the UTD united in a coalition government under Edem Kodjo.

Togolese Democratic Union (Union Togolaise pour la démocratie – UTD)

Founded in 1991 by Edem Kodjo, the UTD won seven seats in the 1994 elections and went on to form a coalition government with CAR.

Union for Justice and Democracy (Union pour la justice et la démocratie – UJD)

Pro-Eyadéma party led by Lal Taxpandjan. The UJD won two seats in the 1994 elections.

National Co-ordination of New Forces (CFN) Coordination nationale des forces nouvelles

Pro-Eyadéma party formed in 1993 and led by Joseph Kokou Koffigoh. The CFN won one seat in the 1994 elections.

Alliance of Togolese Democrats (Alliance des Démocrats Togolais – ATD)

Formed in 1991 as the first recognized opposition party in Togo for 24 years.

TRINIDAD AND TOBAGO

Head of State
Queen Elizabeth II   (1962–76)

A Republic was declared in 1976.

Presidents
Ellis Clarke   (1976–86)
Noor Mohammed Hassanali   (1987–97)
Arthur Robinson   (1997–)

Prime Ministers
Eric Williams   (1962–81)
George Chambers   (1981–6)
Arthur Robinson   (1986–91)
Patrick Manning   (1991–5)
Badeo Panday   (1995–)

British Empire Workers' and Citizens' Home Rule Party

Also known as the Butler Party, founded in Trinidad in 1936 by Tubal Uriah Butler, following his expulsion from the Trinidad Labour Party.

People's National Movement (PNM)

Founded in 1956 by Eric Williams as a party of national unity. The PNM had its main support among Afro-Trinidadians and held power from 1956 until Williams' death in 1981. The PNM resumed office in 1991 under Patrick Manning. Following the 1995 general election a coalition agreement was reached when the PNM and UNC both gained 17 seats in the 36 member House of Representatives.

National Alliance for Reconstruction (NAR)

Founded by Arthur Robinson in 1985 from a merger of four opposition parties. The NAR won office in elections in 1986, ending

30 years of PAM government, lost power in 1991 and took only two seats in 1995.

United National Congress (UNC)
Formed in 1989 by Basdeo Panday with former members of the NAR. Its main support is among Indo-Trinidadians. Panday became head of a PNM-UNC coalition following the 1995 elections.

Among other parties are the Movement for Unity and Progress (MUP), founded by Hulsie Bhaggan in 1994, and the National Development Party (NDP), formed by Carson Charles.

UGANDA

Head of State
Queen Elizabeth II   (1962–63)

Prime Minister
Milton Obote   (1962–3)
A Republic was declared in 1963.

Heads of State

Presidents
Milton Obote   (1966–71)
Major-General (later Field Marshal) Idi Oumee Amin Dada   (1971–9)
Yusufu Lule   (1979 April–June)
Godfrey Binaisa   (1979–80)

Chairman of the Military Commission of the Uganda National Liberation Front
Paulo Muwanga   (1980 May–December)

President
Milton Obote   (1980–85)

Head of the Military Council
General Tito Okello   (1985–6)

President
Lieutenant-General Yoweri Kaguta Museveni   (1986–)

Prime Ministers
Samson Kisekka   (1989–91)

George Kosmas Adyebo   (1991–4)
Kintu Musoke   (1994–)

Uganda National Congress (UNC)
Founded in 1952 by Enoch Malira, the UNC was the country's first national party. The UNC's main support came from Uganda's largest ethnic group, the Protestant Baganda people of Buganda.

Democratic Party (DP)
Founded in 1954, the DP's main support came from Catholics opposed to Protestant leadership of Buganda. The urban-based DP became the ruling party in 1961 but lost to the UPC in the first elections after independence in 1962. Banned in 1970, the DP renewed activity on the legalization of parties in 1980.

Uganda People's Congress (UPC)
Founded in 1960 under the leadership of Milton Obote, the UPC was supported by Protestants in the north of the country. The UPC was the main party on independence in 1962. In 1969 Obote moved the UPC to the left and banned all other parties. Following Amin's seizure of power in January 1971, the UPC operated in exile in Tanzania. The party returned in 1979 and, despite allegations of malpractice, won the 1980 election. Obote became Uganda's president but was deposed in 1985. Some UPC members participated in the 1985–6 military government while others supported the later Museveni government which took power in 1986.

Kabaka Yekka (King Only) (KY)
Founded in 1961 as a royalist party supporting the King of Buganda, to retain political control and privileges for the elite. The KY formed an alliance with the UPC to fight the 1962 election The party was dissolved in 1966 when the Ugandan troops occupied the kingdom of Buganda.

Ugandan National Liberation Front (UNLF)

Coalition of the opponents of President Amin founded at the Moshi Conference in March 1979. Lule was elected compromise leader. UNFL forces, supported by Tanzania, overthrew Amin in April 1979 and formed a caretaker government. Lule was ousted by the National Consultative Council in June. The Front collapsed in 1980 when members who had refused to support Milton Obote were dismissed following his election as Uganda's president.

National Resistance Movement (NRM)

Founded in 1980. Led by Yoweri Museveni in opposition to the UPC government and to Obote. The NRM took power after the civil war in 1986 and established a ruling National Resistance Council. Museveni was returned to power in multi-party elections held in 1996.

Among other parties are the Uganda Patriotic Movement (UPM) formed in 1980; Nationalist Liberal Party formed in 1984 by a faction of the DP; the Federal Democratic Movement (FEDEMO); the Forum for Multi-Party Democracy; the Uganda Democratic Alliance; the Uganda Democratic Freedom Movement; the Uganda People's Democratic Movement; and the Movement for New Democracy in Uganda (MNDU), which operates from Zambia.

UNITED REPUBLIC OF TANZANIA

Tanganyika became independent from Britain in 1961. Zanzibar became independent in 1963. The two amalgamated as the United Republic of Tanzania in 1964.

TANGANYIKA

Head of State

Queen Elizabeth II   (1961–2)

Prime Minister

Julius Nyerere   (1961–2)

A Republic was declared in 1962.

Heads of State

President

Julius Nyerere   (1962–4)

Prime Minister

R. Kawawa   (1962–4)

ZANZIBAR

Head of State

Sultan Seyyid Jamshid bin-Abdullah bin-Khalifah   (1963–4)

Prime Minister

Muhammed Shamte Hamadi   (1963–4)

UNITED REPUBLIC OF TANZANIA

Presidents

Julius Nyerere   (1964–85)
Ali Hassan Mwinyi   (1985–95)
Benjamin Mkapa   (1995–)

Prime Ministers (post reintroduced 1972)

R. Kawawa   (1972–7)
E. Sokoine   (1977–80)
C. D. Msuya   (1980–3)
E. Sokoine   (1983–4)
S. A. Salim   (1984–5)
J. Warioba   (1985–90)
John Malecela   (1990–3)
Cleopa David Msuya   (1993–5)
Frederick Sumaye   (1995–)

Tanganyika African National Union (TANU)

The leading nationalist movement in Tanganyika (now Tanzania), formed by Julius Nyerere in 1954 from the Tanganyika African Association. TANU won widespread popular support in the 1958–60 election, going on to form the government on independence in 1961. Nyerere resigned shortly after as prime minister to develop the party's African socialist programme. Following the army rebellions of 1964, TANU became Tanzania's only legal political party and in 1967 adopted the Arusha Declaration, a programme of self-reliance and egalitarianism. TANU amalgamated in 1977 with the Afro-Shirazi Party (Zanzibar's sole party) to form Chama Cha Mapinduzi.

Afro-Shirazi Party

Zanzibar political party formed in 1957 with African and Arab membership. Following independence, the party merged with Umma in 1964 and took power in Zanzibar. In 1977 it merged with the Tanganyika African National Union to form Chama Cha Mapinduzu, as Tanzania's sole legal political party.

Chama Cha Mapinduzi (CCM)

Tanzanian 'Party of the Revolution', formed in 1977 by the merger of the TANU and the Afro-Shirazi Party under the chairmanship of President Nyerere. Nyerere remained party chairman when he resigned the Tanzanian presidency in 1985. Ali Hassan Mwinyi, the CCM's sole candidate, was elected as president. He was re-elected in elections in 1990. The CCM remained the sole legal political party until 1992 when the introduction of multi-party politics was authorized.

Civic United Front (CUF)

Founded in 1992 through a merger of Kamahuru (Zanzibar opposition party) and Chama Cha Wananchi (mainland opposition party). The party's main support lay in Zanzibar and Pemba.

Among other parties operating since the introduction of a multi-party system are the Movement for Democratic Alternative (MDA) which seeks a review of the terms of the 1964 union of Tanzania with Zanzibar; the National Convention for Construction and Reform (NCCR–Mageuzi); the National League for Democracy; the National Reconstruction Alliance (NRA); the Popular National Party (PONA); the Tanzania Democratic Alliance Party (TADEA); the Tanzania People's Party (TPP); the United People's Democratic Party (UPDP); the Union for Multi-Party Democracy of Tanzania (UMD).

ZAÏRE

Heads of State

Presidents

Joseph Kasavubu (1960–5)
Joseph-Désiré Mobutu (later Mobutu Sese Seko Kuku Ngbendu Wa Za Banga) (1965–)

Prime Ministers

Patrice Lumumba (1960 July–September)
Joseph Ileo (1960 September)
(Role performed by College of Commissioners) (1960–1)
Joseph Ileo (1961 February–August)
Cyrille Adoula (1961–4)
Moïse Tshombe (1964–5)
Evariste Kimba (1965 October–November)
Léonard Mulamba (1965–6)
Joseph-Désiré Mobutu (1966–7)
(Post abolished until 1977)
Bo-Boliko Lokonga (1977–9)
Nguza Kari-i-Bond (1980–1)
N'Singa Udjuu (1981–2)
(Post abolished until 1990)
Lunda Bululu (1990–1)
Mulumba Lukesi (1991 March–September)
Etienne Tshisekedi (1991 September)
Bernardin Mungul Diaka (1991 September–November)
The political situation became increasingly complex with rival holders of the post

appointed over the next three years by President Mobutu and by the opposition.

Etienne Tshiskedi (opposition
   appointee) (1991–2)
Jean Nguza Kari-i-Bond (President
   Mobutu appointee) (1991–2)
Etienne Tshisekedi (National Conference
   appointee) (1992–4)
Faustin Birindwa (President Mobutu
   appointee) (1993–4)
Léon Kengo Wa Dondo (appointee of the
   transitional legislature; the High
   Council of the Republic) (1994–)
Etienne Tshiskedi (April 1997)
General Likulia Bolongo (1997–)

ABAKO Alliance des Ba-Kongo

Founded in 1951 as a cultural organization supported by the Bakongo people. In 1957 ABAKO emerged as a nationalist political movement under Joseph Kasavubu who became the country's first president. The coalition he headed suffered internal conflicts and was threatened by military coups and civil war.

Congolese National Movement (Mouvement National Congolais – MNC)

Founded in 1958 by Patrice Lumumba as the first nation-wide political party. The MNC advocated a unitary state although its main support came from the people of Orientale, Lumumba's home province. The MNC was a significant force in the struggle for independence from Belgian rule. The MNC emerged as the largest single party in elections held in May 1960 and Lumumba headed a coalition government. Four months later he was dismissed by President Kasavubu and formed a rival government in Léopoldville. He was captured by Congolese troops and murdered.

Katanga Tribal Federation (Confédération des Associations Tribales du Katanga – CONAKAT)

Founded by Moïse Tshombe in 1958 with Belgian aid. The party's main support came from the Lunda people of the Katanga region. CONAKAT favoured a federal structure for the Congo Republic. Following the end of Belgian rule in 1960, Tshombe declared Katanga an independent republic. The country was reunited in 1963. Tshombe became prime minister of the Congo Republic in 1964 but was forced to flee the country in 1965.

Congolese National Movement – Kalondji (Mouvement National Congolais – Kalondji – MNC-Kalondji)

Founded in 1959 by Albert Kalondji as a breakaway from the MNC. The party had a federalist programme and was composed of a group of dissidents from the Luba people. In 1960 the party formed an alliance with ABAKO.

Popular Movement of the Revolution (Mouvement Populaire de la Révolution – MPR)

Zaïre's only legal political party from 1967–91. Formed in April 1967 and led by President Mobutu; all Zaïre citizens were members from birth. In 1970 the MPR Political Bureau was given total control over central and local government, the judiciary and the National Legislative Council.

A multi-party system was introduced in November 1990 and elections were promised for 1995 and then 1997. President Mobutu established over 400 state-financed 'pseudo-parties', allegedly to cause popular confusion. Mobutu's opponents formed a Sacred Union of Radical Opposition (Union sacrée de l'opposition radicale – USOR) in 1991, made up of over 100 parties and factions. Among the many opposition parties formed since 1990 are the Federation of Zaïre Liberals (Fédération des libéraux du Zaïre – FLZ), the National Democratic and Social Christian Party (Partie démocrate et social chrétien national – PDSCN), the Union for Democracy and Social Progress (Union pour la démocratie et le progrès social – UDPS), the Lumumba Front for Unity and Peace in Africa (Front Lumumba pour l'unité et la paix en Afrique – FLUPA).

ZAMBIA

Heads of State and Government

Presidents
Kenneth D. Kaunda   (1964–91)
Frederick T. Chiluba   (1991–)

African National Congress (ANC) (Zambia)

Founded in 1951 by Harry Nkumbula. Campaigned unsuccessfully against racial discrimination and the formation of the Central African Federation. In 1958 the leadership divided over a decision to participate in federation elections and Kenneth Kaunda led a breakaway radical section to form the Zambia African National Congress. This became the United National Independence Party (UNIP) which from 1962–4 led a coalition government with the ANC-Z as a junior partner. ANC-Z became the main opposition party after independence in 1964 but was dissolved when Zambia became a one-party state in 1972.

United National Independence Party (UNIP)

Founded in 1958 as the Northern Rhodesia National Congress, the party organized civil disobedience against the imposition of the Central African Federation. UNIP was the leading partner in Northern Rhodesia's period of internal self-rule from 1962–4 and following independence as Zambia in 1964.

In 1972 the constitution was amended to make UNIP Zambia's sole legal party until 1990. The first multi-party elections were held in 1991 and UNIP was defeated by MMD. Kaunda was placed under house arrest in 1994 after attempting to re-enter politics.

United People's Party (UPP)

Formed in 1971 because of public discontent over rising prices and urban unemployment. The UPP claimed that the benefits of independence were not spread widely enough. Its main support was among skilled workers in urban areas but the party also attempted to build support along ethnic and regional lines. The party was banned in 1972.

Movement for Multi-Party Democracy (MMD)

Founded in 1990 by trade-union leader Frederick Chiluba. Pressure from the MMP and other opposition parties led to multi-party elections in 1991. The MMP became the ruling party when it took 125 of the 150 legislature seats.

Among other parties are the Democratic Party (DP), formed in 1991 by Emmanuel Mwamba; the Movement for Democratic Process (MDP), founded in 1991 by Chama Chakomboka; the National Democratic Alliance (NADA), a moderate centrist party founded in 1991 by Yonam Phiri; the United Democratic Congress Party (UDCP), established in 1992, led by Daniel Lisulo; the United Democratic Party (UDP), formed in 1992 by Enoch Kavindele with support from dissenting members of UNIP; and the Zambia Opposition Front (ZOFRO), an opposition alliance founded in 1994 under Mike Kaira.

ZIMBABWE

Head of State

President
Canaan Banana (1980–7)

Head of State and Government

President
Robert Mugabe (1987–)

Prime Minister
Robert Mugabe (1980–7)

African National Congress (ANC) (Southern Rhodesia)

A socialist party formed in Southern Rhodesia (now Zimbabwe) in 1934 to protest against racial discrimination. Allied with other groups in 1957 to form a new ANC led by Joshua Nkomo. The new party was banned and its leaders arrested in 1959. The ANC was succeeded by the more militant National Democratic Party (NDP) in 1960.

African National Council (ANC)

Formed in 1971 by Bishop Muzowera, the first African party allowed by the white regime since 1964. The council successfully led opposition to a proposed British settlement with the rebel white government in 1971. The council co-operated with the white regime to set up a transitional government in 1978 and won a majority of seats in elections held in 1979. But the resulting government was not recognized in or outside 'Zimbabwe-Rhodesia'. The council won only three seats in the 1980 pre-independence elections and none in 1985.

National Democratic Party (NDP)

Zimbabwean nationalist party founded in 1960 by Joshua Nkomo following the banning of the African National Congress. An active opponent of white rule in Southern Rhodesia, the NDP was outlawed in 1961.

Zimbabwe African People's Union (ZAPU)

Political party formed by Joshua Nkomo in 1962. A breakaway section left ZAPU in 1963 to form the Zimbabwe African National Union. Following the declaration of independence by the white minority government in 1965, ZAPU formed a military wing, the Zimbabwe People's Revolutionary Army. In 1976, ZAPU combined with the Zimbabwe African National Union to form the Popular Front (PF) against white rule. ZAPU fought the 1980 pre-independence general election as the Popular Front, won 20 seats and joined a coalition government. The ZANU ministers were dismissed from the government in 1982 and ZAPU agreed to merge as a party with the ruling ZANU (PF) in 1987.

Zimbabwe African National Union (ZANU)

Formed in 1963 under Revd Ndabaningi Sithole, ZANU was joined by a breakaway section of the Zimbabwe African People's Union which included Robert Mugabe. ZANU was immediately banned by the white Rhodesian government and formed a military wing, the Zimbabwe African National Liberation Army. ZANU combined with the Zimbabwe African People's Union to form the Popular Front (PF) against white rule in 1976. Mugabe replaced Sithole as leader the following year. ZANU contested and won the pre-independence 1980 general election as ZANU-PF. The party went on to win the 1985, 1990 and 1995 general elections.

Zimbabwe African National Union – Ndonga (ZANU-Ndonga)

Right-wing opposition party founded in 1977 as a breakaway faction of ZANU. Led by the Revd Ndabaningi Sithole, the party won two seats in the 1995 general elections in a contest widely boycotted by parties which opposed President Mugabe's ZANU. Revd Sithole was arrested on a charge of plotting to assassinate President Mugabe in October 1995.

Zimbabwe Unity Movement (ZUM)

Political party formed by Edgar Tekere in 1989 in opposition to the ruling ZANU-PF. ZUM favoured a market economy and criticized government corruption and mismanagement. In the 1990 general election ZUM was endorsed by the white Conservative Alliance of Zimbabwe and won two parliamentary seats. Tekere took a fifth of the popular vote in presidential elections held at the same time.

Forum Party of Zimbabwe (FPZ)

A conservative party formed by Enoch Dumbutshena in 1993. FPZ merged with the Forum for Democratic Reform, a pressure group formed in 1992, to oppose the ZANU-PF government.

Among other parties are the Front for Popular Democracy (FPD), an opposition party founded by Austin Chakawodza in 1994, and the Zimbabwe Congress Party (ZCP), formed in 1994 as a traditionalist party, under the leadership of James Chilkerema.

INTER-
GOVERNMENTAL
ORGANIZATIONS
AND TREATIES

ORGANIZATIONS

The following are the major organizations of which African states or states of the African diaspora are members. The lists of members set out only the membership of African states or states of the African diaspora.

African, Caribbean and Pacific States (ACP)

HEADQUARTERS   Brussels, Belgium

FOUNDATION   The African, Caribbean and Pacific States (ACP) became part of a co-operative framework with the European Community (now the European Union) through the first Lomé Convention (Lomé I) signed in Lomé, Togo, in February 1975 and which came into effect on 1 April 1976. The convention succeeded the Yaoundé Convention and Arusha Agreement which had allowed trade concessions in the European market to former British and French colonies. The Convention has been developed by Lomé II (1981), Lomé III (1985) and Lomé IV (1990).

ORGANIZATION   Joint ACP and European Union (EU) institutions are a Council of Ministers, made up of one minister from each ACP and EU member state, which meets annually. A Committee of Ministers from each state has a minimum of two meetings a year. There is also a Joint Assembly made up of delegates from each APC state together with an equal number of members of the European Parliament. The ACP itself has a Council of Ministers and a Committee of Ambassadors, each comprising a delegate from each member state.

OBJECTIVES   The ACP works with the EU on a co-operative framework to reflect the needs of member states of the ACP for aid, investment and trade. Lomé I in 1976 provided for 99 per cent of ACP exports to enter the European Community free of all duty. These concessions have been developed in succeeding Conventions.

MEMBERS   There are 70 members of the ACP. African states and states of the African diaspora which are members are Angola, Antigua and Barbuda, Bahamas, Barbados, Benin, Botswana, Burkina Faso, Burundi, Cameroon, Cape Verde, Central African Republic, Chad, Congo, Côte d'Ivoire, Equatorial Guinea, Eritrea, Ethiopia, Gabon, The Gambia, Ghana, Grenada, Guinea, Guinea-Bissau, Haiti, Jamaica, Kenya, Lesotho, Liberia, Malawi, Mali, Mozambique, Namibia, Niger, Nigeria, Rwanda, St Christopher and Nevis, St Lucia, St Vincent and the Grenadines, São Tomé and Príncipe, Senegal, Sierra Leone, Somalia, Swaziland, Tanzania, Togo, Trinidad and Tobago, Uganda, Zaïre, Zambia, Zimbabwe.

African Development Bank (ADB)

HEADQUARTERS   Abidjan, Côte d'Ivoire. Regional offices in Cameroon, Ethiopia, Guinea, Kenya, Morocco, Nigeria, Zimbabwe

FOUNDATION   Established in August 1963; began functioning in July 1966.

ORGANIZATION   The central policy-making body is the Board of Governors. This is made up of one representative, usually a finance and economic affairs minister, from each member state. The Board meets once a year and elects the ADB President and a Board of Directors. The 18-strong (6 from non-African states) Board of Directors is elected for a three-year term and oversees the general functioning of the ADB. It meets twice a month. The president is responsible for day-to-day operations and is elected for a five-year term. He is assisted by five vice-presidents elected for a three-year term. The ADB group includes the African Development Fund (ADF), which began operations in 1973, and the Nigeria Trust Fund (NTF), which was formed by the ADB and the Nigerian government and began its functions in 1976. Among associated institutions are the Africa Reinsurance Corporation, the African Export-Import Bank, the Association of African Development Finance Institutions, *Shelter-Afrique* and the *Société internationale financière pour les investissements et le développement en Afrique.*

OBJECTIVES   The ADB's primary objective is to finance African economic and social development. The ADB makes loans at a variable rate of annual interest. The African Development Fund provides interest-free loans with a repayment period of up to 50 years for development projects. The Nigeria Trust Fund grants loans for up to 25 years and has a data-base of international financial institutions willing to finance African trade.

MEMBERS   There are 75 members of the ADB. Sub-Saharan Africa members are Angola, Benin, Botswana, Burkina Faso, Burundi, Cameroon, Cape Verde, Central African Republic, Chad, Congo, Côte d'Ivoire, Equatorial Guinea, Eritrea, Ethiopia, Gabon, The Gambia, Guinea, Guinea-Bissau, Kenya, Lesotho, Liberia, Malawi, Mali, Mozambique, Namibia, Niger, Nigeria, Rwanda, São Tomé and Príncipe, Senegal, Sierra Leone, Somalia, Swaziland, Tanzania, Uganda, Zaïre, Zambia, Zimbabwe.

The Commonwealth

HEADQUARTERS   London, England

FOUNDATION   Established on 31 December 1931 by the Statute of Westminster. Membership was redefined in 1949 to provide for states which had achieved independence from Britain to become Republics within the Commonwealth.

ORGANIZATION   All members recognize Queen Elizabeth as Head of the Commonwealth. There is no formal structure. All members agree to subscribe to a number of declarations, including the 1971 Declaration of Commonwealth Principles and the 1979 Lusaka Declaration on Racism and Racial Prejudice. Commonwealth Heads of Government meetings are held every two years and foreign ministers meetings are held annually. There are also meetings of ministers of a range of specific subjects including international finance, women, education and health. A Commonwealth Secretariat was set up in 1966 to co-ordinate consultation and meetings and to provide specialized assistance to members. The Secretariat is headed by a Secretary-General.

OBJECTIVES   Part of the 1971 Declaration of Commonwealth Principles states, 'The Commonwealth of Nations is a voluntary association of independent sovereign states, each responsible for its own policies, consulting and co-operating in the common interests of their peoples and in the promotion of international understanding and world peace.' Part of the 1979 Declaration on Racism and Racial Prejudice states, 'We reject as inhuman and intolerable all policies designed to perpetuate apartheid, racial segregation or other policies based on theories that racial groups are or may be inherently superior or inferior.'

MEMBERS   African states and states of the African diaspora which are members, with their dates of joining, are: Antigua and Barbuda 1981, Bahamas 1973, Barbados 1966, Botswana 1966, Dominica 1978, The Gambia 1965, Ghana 1957, Grenada 1974, Jamaica 1962, Kenya 1963, Lesotho 1966, Malawi 1964, Mozambique 1996, Namibia 1990, Nigeria, 1960 (membership suspended 1995), St Christopher and Nevis 1983, St Lucia 1979, St Vincent and the

Grenadines 1979, Sierra Leone 1961, South Africa (left 1961, rejoined 1994), Swaziland 1968, Tanzania 1961, Trinidad and Tobago 1962, Uganda 1962, Zambia 1964, Zimbabwe 1980.

Economic Community of West African States (ECOWAS)

HEADQUARTERS Abuja, Nigeria

FOUNDATION Established by the Treaty of Lagos in May 1975, ratified in 1976. A revised treaty was signed by member states in 1993 to accelerate economic integration and increase political co-operation.

ORGANIZATION ECOWAS has a Council of Ministers made up of two members from each member state which meets twice a year. A Community Tribunal interprets the treaty and deals with disputes between members. Administration of ECOWAS is dealt with by an Executive-Secretariat headed by an executive-secretary elected for a four-year term. There are also six specialized commissions on 1) Trade, Customs, Immigration, Monetary and Payments; 2) Industry, Agriculture and Natural Resources; 3) Transport, Communications and Energy; 4) Social and Cultural Affairs; 5) Administration and Finance; 6) Information. A Standing Mediation Committee was established in 1990 to mediate in disputes between member states. The Committee deployed troops in Liberia as part of a Monitoring Group in 1990.

OBJECTIVES ECOWAS exists to promote economic, social and cultural co-operation and development between member states. It aims to abolish all obstacles to the free movement of people, services and capital, to harmonize agricultural policies, to eliminate tariffs between member states and to establish a common external tariff. The revised 1993 treaty set the goal of achieving a common market and single currency and the establishment of a West African Parliament.

MEMBERS Benin, Burkina Faso, Cape Verde, Côte d'Ivoire, The Gambia, Ghana, Guinea, Guinea-Bissau, Liberia, Mali, Mauritania, Niger, Nigeria, Senegal, Sierra Leone, Togo.

Inter-American Development Board (IDB)

HEADQUARTERS Washington, DC, USA

FOUNDATION The IDB was founded in 1959.

ORGANIZATION The central policy making body is a Board of Governors made up of one representative from each member state, generally a finance minister or president of the central bank. This meets annually. A twelve-strong Board of Executive Directors is elected by groups of two or more member countries. There are eight specialist departments dealing with operations, finance, economic and social development, project analysis, legal affairs, planning, administration, and secretarial organization.

OBJECTIVES The IDB exists to provide loans and grants to public bodies and private institutions for economic and social development projects. Between 1961 and 1993 the Bahamas borrowed $124.1 million, Barbados $149.4 million, Haiti $277.2 million, Jamaica $839.7 million, Trinidad and Tobago $15.7 million.

MEMBERS The IDB has 46 members. States of the African diaspora which are members are Bahamas, Barbados, Haiti, Jamaica, Trinidad and Tobago.

International Organisation for Migration (IOM)

HEADQUARTERS Geneva, Switzerland

FOUNDATION The IOM was founded as the Intergovernmental Committee for Migration

(ICM) in 1951 and changed its name to the International Organisation for Migration in 1989.

ORGANIZATION The IOM governing body is the council, made up of one representative from each member state. A ten-strong Executive Committee elected by the Council makes recommendations on projects.

OBJECTIVES The IOM was formed as a non-political and humanitarian organization to assist migrants and refugees. At the request of member states, the IOM organizes the movement of refugees, co-ordinates relief activities and medical services. The IOM also arranges the recruitment and placement of technical and professional workers to assist in economic development projects in member states.

MEMBERS The IOM has 55 members. African states and states of the African diaspora which are members are Angola, Kenya, Senegal, Zambia. The following have observer status: Cape Verde, Ghana, Guinea-Bissau, Liberia, Mozambique, Namibia, Rwanda, São Tomé and Príncipe, Somalia, Zimbabwe.

Islamic Development Bank

HEADQUARTERS Jeddah, Saudi Arabia

FOUNDATION The Islamic Development Bank was established in October 1975.

ORGANIZATION The governing body is a Board of Governors which meets annually. The Board is made up of a representative from each member state, generally the finance minister. The bank's operations are directed by an eleven-strong Board of Executive Directors, five of whom are appointed by the five main subscribers, and each of whom serves a three-year term.

OBJECTIVES The Bank was formed to encourage economic and social development in member states and in Islamic communities in non-member states in accordance with Sharia (Islamic sacred law). The Bank provides interest-free loans (with a service charge) for agricultural, industrial, transport and communications projects and for social services provision. It also provides emergency aid and assistance.

MEMBERS The Islamic Development Bank has 51 members. African states which are members are Burkina Faso, Cameroon, Chad, Gabon, The Gambia, Guinea, Guinea-Bissau, Mali, Niger, Senegal, Sierra Leone, Somalia.

Organization of African Unity (OAU)

HEADQUARTERS Addis Ababa, Ethiopia

FOUNDATION The OAU was founded in 1963 following a conference at which 30 Heads of State signed a Charter.

ORGANIZATION The Assembly of Heads of State, which meets annually, co-ordinates overall policy. To become effective, a resolution presented to the Assembly must secure a two-thirds majority. A chairman is elected annually by member states. A Council of Ministers meets twice a year to act as a preparatory body for the Assembly. The OAU is administered by a Secretariat headed by a General Secretary who is elected by the Assembly for a four-year term. The Secretariat has a number of specialist departments including political, finance, education, science and cultural affairs, economic development and co-operation, administration. In addition there are a number of specialized agencies which are part of the OAU. These include the African Bureau for Educational Sciences, the African Civil Aviation Commission, the African Commission on Human and People's Rights, the Organization of African Trade Unions, the Special Health Fund for Africa, the Union of African Railways. A Co-ordinating Committee for the Liberation of Africa was terminated in August 1994.

OBJECTIVES   The aims of the OAU are to promote African unity and solidarity; to co-ordinate efforts to improve living standards across the continent; to defend the independence, sovereignty and territorial integrity of member states; to eradicate colonialism from Africa; to promote international co-operation.

MEMBERS   The OAU has 53 members on the continent of Africa and offshore islands. These are Algeria, Angola, Benin, Botswana, Burkina Faso, Burundi, Cameroon, Cape Verde, Central African Republic, Chad, The Comoros, Congo, Côte d'Ivoire, Djibouti, Egypt, Equatorial Guinea, Eritrea, Ethiopia, Gabon, The Gambia, Ghana, Guinea, Guinea-Bissau, Kenya, Lesotho, Liberia, Libya, Madagascar, Malawi, Mali, Mauritania, Mozambique, Namibia, Niger, Nigeria, Rwanda, São Tomé and Príncipe, Senegal, Seychelles, Sierra Leone, Somalia, South Africa, Sudan, Swaziland, Tanzania, Togo, Tunisia, Uganda, Zaïre, Zambia, Zimbabwe.

Organization of American States (OAS)

HEADQUARTERS   Washington, DC, USA

FOUNDATION   Established by a treaty signed on 30 April 1948 which came into force on 13 December 1951. The OAS was a successor organization to the International Union of American Republics, founded in 1890.

ORGANIZATION   The OAS has a General Assembly which meets annually and supervises the general policy and activity of the organization. A Permanent Council made up of one member from each state meets at the OAS headquarters, supervises and oversees the organization's work and liaises with other international bodies. A

Meeting of Consultation of Ministers of Foreign Affairs can be called by any member to discuss urgent issues. The OAS is administered by the General Secretariat. There are also four specialized councils: the Inter-American Economic and Social Council, the Inter-American Council for Education, Science and Culture; the Inter-American Juridical Committee and the Inter-American Commission on Human Rights.

OBJECTIVES   To achieve peace and justice, solidarity of the American continent, co-operation among member states and the defence of their independence and sovereignty.

MEMBERS   The OAS has 35 members. States of the African diaspora which are members, with their date of joining, are Antigua and Barbuda 1981, Bahamas 1982, Barbados 1967, Dominica 1979, Grenada 1975, Jamaica 1969, St Christopher and Nevis 1984, St Lucia 1979, St Vincent and the Grenadines 1981, Trinidad and Tobago 1967. Angola and Equatorial Guinea have observer status.

Organisation of the Islamic Conference (OIC)

HEADQUARTERS   Jeddah, Saudi Arabia

FOUNDATION   Established in May 1971. An official charter was adopted in 1972.

ORGANIZATION   The OIC holds a Heads of State conference every three years and an annual conference of foreign ministers from each member state. The annual conference is responsible for the implementation of OIC policy. In addition, the OIC has six standing committees dealing with economic and commercial co-operation; economic, cultural and social affairs; information; and finance.

OBJECTIVES   To promote Islamic solidarity; to encourage cultural, economic, social, scientific and other co-operation; to eradicate racial discrimination, segregation and colonialism; to protect the Islamic holy places and to work for Palestinian liberation.

MEMBERS   There are 53 members of the OIC. African states which are members are: Benin, Burkina Faso, Cameroon, Chad, Eritrea, Gabon, The Gambia, Guinea, Guinea-Bissau, Mali, Mozambique (observer), Niger, Nigeria (withdrew 1991), Senegal, Sierra Leone, Somalia, Uganda, Zanzibar (withdrew 1993).

Southern African Development Community (SADC)

HEADQUARTERS   Gaborone, Botswana

FOUNDATION   Founded by treaty signed in 1992, ratified by member states in 1993. The South African Development Community is a successor organization to the South African Development Co-ordination Conference which had been set up in 1979 to reduce the region's economic dependence on the apartheid regime in South Africa.

ORGANIZATION   The SADC's supreme policy-making body is the Heads of State and Government meeting which is held annually. A Council of Ministers, made up of ministers representing each member state, has a minimum of two meetings a year, with special meetings called to discuss specific areas of interest. A Secretariat is responsible for administration. There are, in addition, co-ordinating offices to oversee specific areas of work including agriculture, culture and information, economic affairs, mining, transport and communications, tourism, and trade and industry. There has been a proposal to create a regional peacekeeping organization, the Association of Southern African States (ASAS).

OBJECTIVES   To promote the creation of a regional common market. To encourage and facilitate economic co-operation and development, the free movement of capital and labour, respect for human rights and the rule of law, popular participation in the democratic process, regional solidarity, peace and security.

MEMBERS   Angola, Botswana, Lesotho, Malawi, Mozambique, Namibia, South Africa, Swaziland, Tanzania, Zambia, Zimbabwe.

United Nations

HEADQUARTERS   New York City, USA

FOUNDATION   Founded by a Charter signed on 26 June 1945, UNO came officially into existence on 24 October 1945.

ORGANIZATION   The central forum of the United Nations is the General Assembly which consists of five delegates (one of whom has voting rights) from each member state. The General Assembly meets regularly for three months of the year, with provision for special sessions on request and with the agreement of a majority of members. Decisions made by the General Assembly require a two-thirds majority. There are seven main committees on which each member state is represented: Disarmament; Special Political; Economic and Financial; Social, Humanitarian and Cultural; Decolonization; Administration and Budgeting; Legal. A Security Council has responsibility for maintaining international peace and security. The Council consists of five permanent members and ten members elected for a two-year period. A Secretariat operates under the Secretary-General who is elected for a five-year term. An International Court of Justice consists of 15 independent judges elected by the General Assembly and Security Council. There are also a number of regional commissions which initiate and co-ordinate measures for economic development within their particular area. Among these are the Economic Commission for Latin America and the Caribbean (established 1948) and the Economic Commission for Africa (established 1958).

OBJECTIVES   The objectives of the UN are set out in a Charter of 111 Articles. Section 1 of Article I sets the organization's central objective as:

'To maintain international peace and security, and to that end: to take effective collective measures for the prevention and removal of threats to peace, and for the suppression of acts of aggression or other breaches of the peace, and to bring about by peaceful means, and in conformity with the principles of justice and international law, adjustment or settlement of international disputes or situations which might lead to a breach of the peace.'

Article I also sets the objectives of developing friendly relations between states and assisting in solving economic, cultural, social and humanitarian problems.

MEMBERS   Sub-Saharan African states and states of the African diaspora which are members, with their dates of joining, are: Angola (1 December 1976), Antigua and Barbuda (11 November 1981), Bahamas (18 September 1983), Barbados (9 December 1966), Benin (20 September 1960), Botswana (17 October 1966), Burkina Faso (20 September 1960), Burundi (18 September 1962), Cameroon (20 September 1960), Cape Verde (16 September 1975), Central African Republic (20 September 1960), Chad (20 September 1960), Congo (20 September 1960), Côte d'Ivoire (20 September 1960), Dominica (18 December 1978), Equatorial Guinea (12 November 1968), Eritrea (28 May 1993), Ethiopia (13 November 1945), Gabon (20 September 1960), The Gambia (21 September 1965), Ghana (8 March 1957), Grenada (17 September 1974), Guinea (12 December 1958), Guinea-Bissau (17 September 1974), Haiti (24 October 1945), Jamaica (18 September 1962), Kenya (16 December 1963), Lesotho (17 October 1966), Liberia (2 November 1945), Malawi (1 September 1964), Mali (28 September 1960), Mozambique (16 September 1975), Namibia (23 April 1990), Niger (20 September 1960), Nigeria (7 October 1960), Rwanda (18 September 1962), St Kitts and Nevis (23 September 1983), St Lucia (18 September 1979), St Vincent and the Grenadines (16 September 1980), São Tomé and Príncipe (16 September 1975), Senegal (20 September 1960), Sierra Leone (27 September 1961), Somalia (20 September 1960), South Africa (7 November 1945), Swaziland (24 September 1968), United Republic of Tanzania (14 December 1964), Togo (20 September 1960), Trinidad and Tobago (18 September 1962), Uganda (25 October 1962), Zaïre (20 September 1960), Zambia (1 December 1964), Zimbabwe (18 April 1980).

PARTICIPATION IN UNITED NATIONS PEACEKEEPING FORCES

United Nations Operation in the Congo (UNCO)

LOCATION   Republic of Congo (now Zaïre)

PURPOSE   To oversee the withdrawal of Belgian forces and to assist the government in maintaining order. To maintain the Congo's territorial integrity and political independence, to prevent civil war and to ensure the removal of all foreign military personnel, including mercenaries.

DATES   15 July 1960 to 30 June 1964

MEMBERS   Thirty states were represented in UNCO, including eight from Africa. The force was commanded by Lieutenant-General Kebbede Guebre (Ethiopia) from April 1962 to July 1963 and by Major-General Aguiyu Ironsi (Nigeria) from January to June 1964.

ETHIOPIA troops and staff personnel from July 1960 to June 1964.

GHANA troops, staff personnel and civilian police from July 1960 to September 1963.

GUINEA troops from July 1960 to January 1961.

LIBERIA troops and staff personnel from July 1960 to May 1963.

FEDERATION OF MALI (now Mali and Senegal) troops from August to November 1960.

NIGERIA troops, staff personnel and civilian police from November 1960 to June 1964.

REPUBLIC OF THE CONGO (now Zaïre) troops from February 1963 to June 1964.

SIERRA LEONE troops from January 1962 to March 1963.

United Nations Security Force in West New Guinea (West Irian) (UNSF)

LOCATION West New Guinea (West Irian)

PURPOSE To maintain peace until sovereignty over the territory passed from the Netherlands to Indonesia.

DATES 3 October 1962 to 30 April 1963

MEMBERS Nine states were represented in UNSF, including one from Africa.

NIGERIA military observers from August to September 1962.

United Nations Yemen Observation Mission (UNYOM)

LOCATION Yemen

PURPOSE To supervise the disengagement agreement in the Yemen between Saudi Arabia and the United Arab Republic.

DATES 4 July 1963 to 4 September 1964.

MEMBERS Eleven states were represented in UNYOM, including one from Africa.

GHANA military observers from July 1963 to September 1964.

United Nations India-Pakistan Observation Mission (UNIPOM)

LOCATION The border between India and Pakistan between Kashmir and the Arabian Sea

PURPOSE To supervise the cease-fire between India and Pakistan and to oversee the withdrawal of Indian and Pakistani troops to positions held before the outbreak of fighting on 5 August 1965.

DATES 23 September 1965 to 22 March 1966

MEMBERS Ten states were represented in UNIPOM, including two from Africa.

Ethiopia and Nigeria contributed observers from September 1965 to March 1966.

United Nations Emergency Force (UNEF)

LOCATION The Suez Canal sector and the Sinai peninsula

PURPOSE To supervise the cease-fire between Egypt and Israel, to oversee the redeployment of Egyptian and Israeli forces and to control the buffer zones between them.

DATES 25 October 1973 to 24 July 1979

MEMBERS Thirteen states were represented in UNEF, including two from Africa.

GHANA troops from January 1974 to July 1979.

SENEGAL troops from January 1974 to June 1976.

United Nations Interim Force in Lebanon (UNIFIL)

LOCATION Southern Lebanon

PURPOSE To confirm the withdrawal of Israeli troops from southern Lebanon, to restore peace and to help restore the authority of the Lebanese government in the area.

DATES   19 March 1978 to the present

MEMBERS   Fourteen states have been represented in UNIFIL, including three from Africa. From March 1978 to February 1981, the force was commanded by Lieutenant-General Emmanuel A. Erskine from Ghana.

GHANA   troops from September 1979 onwards.

NIGERIA   troops from May 1978 to February 1983.

SENEGAL   troops from April 1978 to November 1984.

United Nations Good Offices Mission in Afghanistan and Pakistan (UNGOMAP)

LOCATION   Afghanistan and Pakistan

PURPOSE   To supervise implementation and to investigate violations of agreements on resolving the civil war in Afghanistan.

DATES   15 May 1988 to 5 March 1990

MEMBERS   Ten states were represented in UNGOMAP, including one from Africa.

GHANA   military observers from May 1988 to March 1990.

United Nations Iran–Iraq Military Observers' Group (UNIIMOG)

LOCATION   The Iran–Iraq border

PURPOSE   To supervise the cease-fire in the 1980–8 war between Iran and Iraq and to ensure the withdrawal of armed forces beyond internationally recognized borders.

DATES   20 August 1988 to February 1991

MEMBERS   Twenty-six states were represented in UNIIMOG, including five from Africa.

Ghana, Kenya, Nigeria, Senegal and Zambia contributed military observers from August 1988 to February 1991.

United Nations Angola Verification Mission I (UNAVEM I)

LOCATION   Angola

PURPOSE   To supervise the phased withdrawal of Cuban troops from Angola in accordance with the agreed timetable.

DATES   3 January 1989 to May 1991

MEMBERS   Ten states were represented in UNAVEM I, one from Africa.

CONGO   military observers from January 1989 to May 1991.

United Nations Transition Assistance Group in Namibia (UNTAG)

LOCATION   Namibia

PURPOSE   To ensure the independence of Namibia (formerly South West Africa) from South Africa and to supervise free and fair elections.

DATES   1 April 1989 to 21 March 1990

MEMBERS   Fifty states were represented in UNTAG, including five from Africa and three from the Caribbean.

BARBADOS   police monitors from April 1989 to March 1990.

CONGO   electoral supervisors from April 1989 to March 1990.

GHANA   police monitors and electoral supervisors from April 1989 to March 1990.

JAMAICA   electoral supervisors from April 1989 to March 1990.

KENYA   military observers, police monitors and electoral supervisors from April 1989 to March 1990.

NIGERIA   electoral supervisors and police monitors from April 1989 to March 1990.

TOGO   military observers from April 1989 to March 1990.

TRINIDAD AND TOBAGO   electoral supervisors from April 1989 to March 1990.

United Nations Iraq–Kuwait Observation Mission (UNIKOM)

LOCATION   The demilitarized zone on the border between Kuwait and Iraq.

PURPOSE   To monitor the demilitarized zone, to deter violations and to observe any aggressive action mounted by either state following the recapture of Kuwait from Iraq in the Gulf War. UNIKOM was strengthened in February 1993 when unarmed observers were replaced by armed troops.

DATES   April 1991 to the present

MEMBERS   Thirty-two states have participated in UNIKOM, including four from Africa.

GHANA, KENYA, NIGERIA, SENEGAL   observers from April 1991.

United Nations Angola Verification Mission II (UNAVEM II)

LOCATION   Angola

PURPOSE   To verify implementation of the Peace Accord of 1 May 1991 between the Angolan government and UNITA and to supervise the activities of the Angolan police. UNAVEM II was later extended to provide assistance in preparing for and observing elections and then to assist in establishing a cease-fire when fighting was renewed after the 1992 elections.

DATES   June 1991 to the present

MEMBERS   Sixteen states have participated in UNAVEM II, including four from Africa.

CONGO   military observers from June 1991.

GUINEA-BISSAU   military observers from June 1991.

NIGERIA   military observers from June 1991.

ZIMBABWE   civilian police and military observers from June 1991.

United Nations Mission for the Referendum in Western Sahara (MINURSO)

LOCATION   Western Sahara

PURPOSE   To verify the withdrawal to designated areas of Moroccan and Polisario Front troops following the cease-fire between them, to oversee the exchange of prisoners, and to supervise a referendum on independence for the territory.

DATES   September 1991 to the present

MEMBERS   Twenty-seven states have participated in MINURSO, including four from Africa.

GHANA   troops and observers from September 1991.

KENYA   observers from September 1991.

NIGERIA   civilian police and observers from September 1991.

TOGO   civilian police from September 1991.

United Nations Protection Force (UNPROFOR)

LOCATION   Bosnia and Herzegovina, Croatia, the Federal Republic of Yugoslavia (Serbia and Montenegro) and the former Yugoslav Republic of Macedonia.

PURPOSE   To ensure the demilitarization of the United Nations Protected Areas, to protect their populations from armed attack and to assist in the return of refugees from the areas.

DATES   March 1992 to the present

MEMBERS   Thirty-seven states have participated in UNPROFOR, including three from Africa.

GHANA   observers from March 1992.

KENYA   civilian police, troops and observers from March 1992.

NIGERIA   civilian police and observers from March 1992.

United Nations Operation in Mozambique (ONUMOZ)

LOCATION   Mozambique

PURPOSE   To monitor the 4 October 1992 cease-fire between the Mozambique government and the forces of the Mozambique National Resistance (RENAMO), to oversee the disbanding of military forces and the withdrawal of foreign forces, to monitor elections, to assist in the return of refugees and to ensure provision of relief supplies.

DATES   December 1992 to the present

MEMBERS   Thirty-five states have participated in ONUMOZ, including seven from Africa.

BOTSWANA   civilian police and troops from December 1992.

CAPE VERDE   observers from December 1992.

GHANA   civilian police from December 1992.

GUINEA-BISSAU   civilian police and observers from December 1992.

NIGERIA   civilian police from December 1992.

TOGO   civilian police from December 1992.

ZAMBIA   civilian police and troops from December 1992.

United Nations Operation in Somalia (UNOSOM)

LOCATION   Somalia

PURPOSE   To monitor a cease-fire negotiated by the warring factions in Somalia in February 1992, to arrange for and to escort relief supplies to the population and to assist in convening a conference on national reconciliation and unity. UNOSOM was withdrawn when it became clear that the factions had little intention of making peace.

DATES   April 1992 to March 1995

MEMBERS   Twenty-nine states participated in UNOSOM, including five from Africa.

BOTSWANA   civilian police and troops.

NIGERIA   civilian police and troops.

ZIMBABWE   civilian police and troops.

GHANA   civilian police.

ZAMBIA   civilian police.

United Nations Observer Mission in Liberia (UNOMIL)

LOCATION   Liberia

PURPOSE   UNOMIL was established in co-operation with the peacekeeping mission established by the Economic Community of West African States (ECOWAS). Its purpose was to monitor and ensure compliance with a cease-fire negotiated on 1 August 1993, to supervise the embargo on weapons supplies and the demobilization of combatants, and to co-ordinate relief activities.

DATES   From September 1993 to the present

MEMBERS   Eleven states have participated in UNOMIL, including two from Africa.

GUINEA-BISSAU   observers.

KENYA   observers.

United Nations Assistance Mission for Rwanda (UNAMIR)

LOCATION   Rwanda

PURPOSE   There was a cease-fire in fighting between the Armed Forces of the Government of Rwanda and the Rwanda Patriotic Front in October 1990. Clashes resumed in February 1993 but a further cease-fire was negotiated in March. UNAMIR's task was to monitor the cease-fire, to ensure the security of the capital, Kigali, to establish a demilitarized zone, to supervise the preparation of elections and to assist with mine clearance. When this was interrupted by further fighting, UNAMIR's role was to act as an intermediary and to attempt to negotiate a renewal of the cease-fire.

DATES From October 1993 to the present

MEMBERS Twenty-seven states have participated in UNAMIR, including fourteen from Africa.

CHAD troops from October 1993.

CONGO civilian police from October 1993.

ETHIOPIA troops from October 1993.

GHANA troops, civilian police and observers from October 1993.

GUINEA observers from October 1993.

GUINEA-BISSAU troops and civilian police from October 1993.

MALAWI troops and observers from October 1993.

MALI troops, civilian police and observers from October 1993.

NIGER troops, civilian police and observers from October 1993.

NIGERIA troops, police and observers from October 1993.

SENEGAL troops from October 1993.

TOGO troops and civilian police from October 1993.

ZAMBIA troops, civilian police and observers from October 1993.

ZIMBABWE observers from October 1993.

SPECIALIST ORGANIZATIONS

There are also a number of organizations devoted to specialist areas of inter-state interest. The most important are listed below.

African Timber Organization

HEADQUARTERS Libreville, Gabon

OBJECTIVES The organization was established in 1976 to co-ordinate the utilization and conservation of forests and their resources in the member states.

MEMBERS Angola, Cameroon, Central African Republic, Congo, Côte d'Ivoire, Equatorial Guinea, Gabon, Ghana, Liberia, Nigeria, São Tomé and Príncipe, Tanzania, Zaïre.

Caribbean Food and Nutritional Institute

HEADQUARTERS Kingston, Jamaica

OBJECTIVES The institute was established in 1967 to conduct research into food and nutrition issues in the region and to provide a training and advice service to member states.

MEMBERS Antigua and Barbuda, Bahamas, Barbados, Belize, Dominica, Grenada, Guyana, Jamaica, Montserrat, St Christopher and Nevis, St Lucia, St Vincent, Trinidad and Tobago.

Desert Locust Control Organization for Eastern Africa

HEADQUARTERS Nairobi, Kenya

OBJECTIVES The organization was established in 1962 to undertake research and analysis to assist in the control of the desert locust problem in the region and to monitor and co-ordinate the control of other pests.

MEMBERS Djibouti, Ethiopia, Kenya, Somalia, Sudan, Tanzania, Uganda.

The Franc Zone

HEADQUARTERS Paris, France

OBJECTIVES To link the currencies of former French colonies to the French franc, to maintain members' currency reserves, and to provide machinery for French budgetary support, aid and technical assistance to member states. The common currency is the franc Communauté Financière Africaine (CFA).

MEMBERS As well as France itself, the members of the Franc Zone are Benin, Burkina Faso, Cameroon, Central African Republic, Chad, the Comoros, Congo, Côte d'Ivoire, Equatorial Guinea, Gabon, Niger, Senegal, Togo.

There are a number of regional organizations within the Franc Zone. These are divided between Central and West Africa.

West Africa The West African States Central Bank (BCEAO) was established in 1962 with its headquarters in Dakar, Senegal, to manage the CFA in West Africa. The West African Development Bank (BOAD) was established in 1973 with its headquarters in Lomé, Togo, to facilitate economic development and integration. The West African Economic and Monetary Union (UEMOA) was established in 1994 by Benin, Burkina Faso, Côte d'Ivoire, Mali, Niger, Senegal and Togo to facilitate the free movement of capital and labour between member states.

Central Africa The Central African Customs and Economic Union (UDEAC) was established in 1966 by Cameroon, Central African Republic, Chad, Congo, Equatorial Guinea and Gabon to establish a customs union, to facilitate free trade between member states and to establish a common tariff on imports. In 1988 member states established a regional common market in meat and entered into agreement on the construction of regional highways. Its headquarters are in Bangui, Central African Republic. A Central African States Bank (BEAC) was established in 1973 with its headquarters in Yaoundé, Cameroon. A Central African States Development Bank (BDEAC) was established in 1974 with its headquarters in Brazzaville, Congo.

Joint Organization for Control of Desert Locust and Bird Pests

HEADQUARTERS Dakar, Senegal

OBJECTIVES The organization was established in 1965 to undertake research in, and to assist in the eradication of, the desert locust and bird pests which threaten agriculture in the member states.

MEMBERS Benin, Burkina Faso, Cameroon, Chad, Côte d'Ivoire, The Gambia, Mali, Mauritania, Niger, Senegal.

African Groundnut Council

HEADQUARTERS Lagos, Nigeria

OBJECTIVES The council was established in 1964 to assist the economies of member states through the provision of marketing information on groundnuts.

MEMBERS The Gambia, Mali, Niger, Nigeria, Senegal, Sudan.

African Oil Palm Development Association

HEADQUARTERS Abidjan, Côte d'Ivoire

OBJECTIVES The association was established in 1985 to assist member states in developing the production and marketing of palm oil.

MEMBERS Benin, Cameroon, Côte d'Ivoire, Ghana, Guinea, Nigeria, Togo, Zaïre.

African Petroleum Producers' Association

HEADQUARTERS Brazzaville, Congo

OBJECTIVES The association was established in 1987 to encourage co-operation between member states to assist their economies by preserving the stability of oil prices.

MEMBERS Algeria, Angola, Benin, Cameroon, Congo, Côte d'Ivoire, Egypt, Gabon, Libya, Nigeria, Zaïre.

Agency for the Prohibition of Nuclear Weapons in Latin America and the Caribbean

HEADQUARTERS   Mexico City, Mexico

OBJECTIVES   The agency was formed in 1969 to ensure compliance with the 1967 Treaty of Tlatelolco. Member states agreed to prevent deployment of nuclear weapons in the area covered by the treaty, to contribute to nuclear non-proliferation, and to promote general and complete disarmament. The agency holds a general conference twice a year.

MEMBERS   The agency has 28 members. Caribbean states of the African diaspora which are members are Antigua and Barbuda, Bahamas, Barbados, Grenada, Haiti, Jamaica, St Vincent and the Grenadines, Suriname, Trinidad and Tobago.

Cocoa Producers' Alliance

HEADQUARTERS   Lagos, Nigeria

OBJECTIVES   The alliance was established in 1962 to encourage the production and consumption of cocoa and to disseminate technical information and advice to member states.

MEMBERS   There are 13 members internationally. Members in the African continent or in states of the African diaspora are Cameroon, Côte d'Ivoire, Gabon, Ghana, Nigeria, São Tomé and Príncipe, Togo, Trinidad and Tobago.

Economic Community of Central African States

HEADQUARTERS   Libreville, Gabon

OBJECTIVES   The community was formed in 1985 to promote progress towards abolishing trade restrictions between member states, establishing a common external tariff, encouraging co-operation between commercial banks, establishing a development fund, promoting regional security. The community also planned to combat drug abuse.

MEMBERS   Burundi, Cameroon, Central African Republic, Chad, Congo, Equatorial Guinea, Gabon, Rwanda, São Tomé and Príncipe, Zaïre.

Economic Community of the Great Lakes Countries

HEADQUARTERS   Gisenyi, Rwanda

OBJECTIVES   The community was formed in 1976 to encourage agricultural, industrial and energy projects in the area. It has four specialized component agencies: a development bank at Goma, Zaïre; an energy centre at Bujumbura, Burundi; an Institute of Agronomy and Zootechnical Research at Kitega, Burundi; a regional electricity company at Bukavu, Zaïre. The community holds an annual conference of heads of state.

MEMBERS   Burundi, Rwanda, Zaïre.

International Tea Promotion Association

HEADQUARTERS   Nairobi, Kenya

OBJECTIVES   The association was established in 1979 to encourage the production and consumption of tea.

MEMBERS   There are eight members internationally. Members in the African continent are Kenya, Malawi, Mozambique, Tanzania and Uganda.

Liptako-Gourma Integrated Development Authority

HEADQUARTERS   Ouagadougou, Burkina Faso

OBJECTIVES   The authority was formed in 1972 to promote co-operation in the use of the water resources in the Niger river basin for hydro-electricity and irrigation, in telecommunications and in the construction of transportation facilities.

MEMBERS   Burkina Faso, Mali, Niger.

Organization for the Management and Development of the Kagera River Basin

HEADQUARTERS   Kigali, Rwanda

OBJECTIVES   The organization was formed in 1978 to encourage the joint management and development of the river basin's resources. This included plans for the construction of a hydro-electric dam between Rwanda and Tanzania together with road and railway construction.

MEMBERS   Burundi, Rwanda, Tanzania, Uganda.

Common Market for Eastern and Southern Africa – COMESA

HEADQUARTERS   Lusaka, Zambia

OBJECTIVES   The Common Market was established in 1994, as a successor to the Preferential Trade Area for Eastern and Southern African States (founded in 1981). Its aim was to encourage economic and commercial co-operation between member states, to facilitate trade, develop basic and strategic industries, and to promote agricultural development and improved transportation networks. In 1984 the Reserve Bank of Zimbabwe was designated the Area's clearing house to enable member states to conduct multi-lateral trade. In 1986 an Eastern and Southern African Trade and Development Bank was established in Bujumbura, Rwanda. In November 1993, 15 members signed a treaty to establish a Common Market for Eastern and Southern Africa (COMESA) by the year 2000. Zimbabwe has not yet ratified this treaty.

MEMBERS   Angola, Burundi, the Comoros, Djibouti, Eritrea, Ethiopia, Kenya, Lesotho, Madagascar, Malawi, Mauritius, Mozambique, Namibia, Rwanda, Seychelles, Somalia, Sudan, Swaziland, Tanzania, Uganda, Zambia, Zimbabwe.

West Africa Rice Development Association

HEADQUARTERS   Bouaké, Côte d'Ivoire

OBJECTIVES   The association was established in 1971 to undertake research into rice production in the region and to provide training for personnel from member states.

MEMBERS   Benin, Burkina Faso, Chad, Côte d'Ivoire, The Gambia, Ghana, Guinea, Guinea-Bissau, Liberia, Mali, Mauritania, Niger, Nigeria, Senegal, Sierra Leone, Togo.

Gambia River Basin Development Organization

HEADQUARTERS   Dakar, Senegal

OBJECTIVES   The organization was established in 1978 to encourage co-operative development of the resources of the Gambia River basin in agriculture, the generation of electrical power and to assist in the construction of a bridge spanning the river.

MEMBERS   The Gambia, Guinea, Guinea-Bissau, Senegal.

Inter-governmental Authority on Drought and Development

HEADQUARTERS   Djibouti

OBJECTIVES   The authority was established in 1986 to encourage co-ordination of efforts to combat drought and desertification affecting the economies of member states and to undertake research on agricultural methods, water supplies and food provision.

MEMBERS   Djibouti, Eritrea, Ethiopia, Kenya, Somalia, Sudan, Uganda.

Lake Chad Basin Commission

HEADQUARTERS   N'Djamena, Chad

OBJECTIVES   The commission was established in 1964 to assist in co-operation to develop the resources of Lake Chad and to encourage investment and the provision of technical aid, the prevention of desertification, and to improve land communications between member states.

MEMBERS   Cameroon, Central African Republic, Chad, Niger, Nigeria.

Niger Basin Authority

HEADQUARTERS   Niamey, Niger

OBJECTIVES   The authority was established in 1964 to co-ordinate and plan member states' activities in the River Niger Basin, and to provide assistance in projects directed towards infrastructural and agricultural development.

MEMBERS   Benin, Burkina Faso, Cameroon, Chad, Côte d'Ivoire, Guinea, Mali, Niger, Nigeria.

Permanent Inter-State Committee on Drought Control in the Sahel

HEADQUARTERS   Ouagadougou, Burkina Faso

OBJECTIVES   The committee was established in 1973 to work, in co-operation with the United Nations, to counter the effect of drought in the Sahel region through irrigation, anti-deforestation measures, and the maintenance of food reserves.

MEMBERS   Burkina Faso, Cape Verde, Chad, The Gambia, Guinea-Bissau, Mali, Mauritania, Niger, Senegal.

MULTI-LATERAL AGREEMENTS ON WEAPONS CONTROL

There have been a number of treaties and conventions which attempt to limit the production, testing or use of particular types of weapons. The lists of members set out only the membership of African states or states of the African diaspora. Where the year is in brackets, the agreement has been signed by the state in question but not yet ratified.

Geneva Protocol 1928

DATE   The Geneva Protocol was signed on 17 June 1925 and came into force on 8 February 1928.

PURPOSE   States adhering to the protocol agree that they will not use asphyxiating, poisonous or other gases or bacteriological weapons in warfare.

SIGNATORIES   Angola 1990, Antigua and Barbuda 1990, Barbados 1976, Benin 1976, Burkina Faso 1971, Cameroon 1989, Central African Republic 1970, Côte d'Ivoire 1970, Equatorial Guinea 1989, Ethiopia 1935, The Gambia 1966, Grenada 1989, Guinea-Bissau 1989, Jamaica 1970, Kenya 1970, Lesotho 1972, Liberia 1927, Malawi 1970, Niger 1967, Nigeria 1968, Rwanda 1964, St Lucia 1988, Senegal 1977, Sierra Leone 1967, South Africa 1930, Swaziland 1991, Tanzania 1964, Togo 1971, Trinidad and Tobago 1970, Uganda 1965.

Partial Test Ban Treaty 1963

DATE   The Partial Test Ban Treaty was signed on 5 August 1963 and came into force on 10 October 1963.

PURPOSE   States adhering to the treaty agree that they will not test nuclear weapons in the atmosphere, under water or in outer space.

SIGNATORIES   Bahamas 1976, Benin 1964, Botswana 1968, Burkina Faso (1963), Burundi (1963), Cape Verde 1979, Central African Republic 1964, Chad 1965, Côte d'Ivoire 1965, Equatorial Guinea 1989, Ethiopia (1963), Gabon 1964, The Gambia 1965, Guinea-Bissau 1976, Jamaica (1963),

Kenya 1965, Liberia 1964, Malawi 1964, Mali (1963), Niger 1964, Nigeria 1967, Rwanda 1963, Saint Vincent and the Grenadines 1964, Senegal 1964, Sierra Leone 1964, Somalia (1963), South Africa 1963, Swaziland 1969, Tanzania 1964, Trinidad and Tobago 1964, Uganda 1964, Zaïre 1965, Zambia 1965.

Outer Space Treaty 1967

DATE   The Outer Space Treaty was signed on 27 January 1967 and came into force on 10 October 1967.

PURPOSE   States adhering to the treaty agree not to place objects in space carrying weapons of mass destruction.

SIGNATORIES   Bahamas 1976, Barbados 1968, Benin 1986, Botswana (1967), Burkina Faso 1968, Burundi (1967), Cameroon (1967), Central African Republic (1967), Equatorial Guinea 1989, Ethiopia (1967), The Gambia (1967), Guinea-Bissau 1976, Jamaica 1970, Lesotho (1967), Mali 1968, Niger 1967, Nigeria 1967, Rwanda (1967), St Vincent and the Grenadines 1968, Sierra Leone 1967, Somalia (1967), South Africa 1968, Togo 1989, Trinidad and Tobago (1967), Uganda 1968, Zaïre (1967), Zambia 1973.

Treaty of Tlatelolco 1968

DATE   The Treaty of Tlatelolco was signed on 14 February 1967 and came into force on 22 April 1968.

PURPOSE   States adhering to the treaty agree to prohibit nuclear weapons in Latin America.

SIGNATORIES   Bahamas 1977, Barbados 1969, Grenada 1975, Jamaica 1969, Trinidad and Tobago 1970.

Non-Proliferation Treaty 1970

DATE   The Non-Proliferation Treaty was signed on 1 July 1968 and came into force on 5 March 1970.

PURPOSE   Non-nuclear states adhering to the treaty agree not to acquire or manufacture nuclear weapons.

SIGNATORIES   Bahamas 1976, Benin 1976, Botswana 1969, Burkina Faso 1970, Burundi 1971, Cameroon 1969, Cape Verde 1979, Central African Republic 1970, Chad 1971, Congo 1978, Côte d'Ivoire 1973, Dominica 1984, Equatorial Guinea 1984, Ethiopia 1970, Gabon 1974, The Gambia 1975, Grenada 1975, Guinea 1985, Guinea-Bissau 1976, Jamaica 1970, Kenya 1970, Lesotho 1970, Liberia 1970, Malawi 1986, Mali 1970, Nigeria 1968, Rwanda 1975, St Lucia 1979, St Vincent and the Grenadines 1984, São Tomé and Príncipe 1983, Senegal 1970, Sierra Leone 1975, Somalia 1970, South Africa 1991, Swaziland 1969, Togo 1970, Trinidad and Tobago (1968), Uganda 1982, Zaïre 1970, Zambia 1991, Zimbabwe 1991.

Sea-Bed Treaty 1972

DATE   The Sea-Bed Treaty was signed on 11 February 1971 and came into force on 18 May 1972.

PURPOSE   States adhering to the treaty agree not to place weapons of mass destruction on the sea-bed.

SIGNATORIES   Bahamas 1989, Benin 1986, Botswana 1972, Burundi (1971), Cameroon (1971), Cape Verde 1979, Central African Republic 1981, Congo 1978, Côte d'Ivoire 1972, Equatorial Guinea (1971), Ethiopia 1977, The Gambia (1971), Guinea (1971), Guinea-Bissau 1976, Jamaica (1971), Lesotho 1973, Liberia (1971), Mali (1971), Niger 1971, Rwanda 1975, São Tomé and Príncipe 1979, Senegal (1971), Sierra Leone

1985, South Africa 1973, Swaziland 1971, Tanzania (1971), Togo 1971, Zambia 1972.

Biological Weapons Convention 1975

DATE The Biological Weapons Convention was signed on 10 April 1972 and came into force on 26 March 1975.

PURPOSE States adhering to the convention agree not to develop, produce or stockpile biological or toxin weapons and to destroy any in their possession.

SIGNATORIES Bahamas 1986, Barbados 1973, Benin 1975, Botswana 1991, Burkina Faso 1991, Burundi (1972), Cape Verde 1977, Central African Republic (1972), Congo 1978, Côte d'Ivoire (1972), Equatorial Guinea 1989, Ethiopia 1975, Gabon (1972), The Gambia (1972), Grenada 1986, Guinea-Bissau 1976, Jamaica 1975, Kenya 1976, Lesotho 1977, Liberia (1972), Malawi (1972), Mali (1972), Niger 1972, Nigeria 1973, Rwanda 1975, Saint Vincent and the Grenadines 1975, São Tomé and Príncipe 1979, Senegal 1975, Sierra Leone 1976, Somalia 1972, South Africa 1975, Tanzania (1972), Togo 1976, Zaïre 1977, Zimbabwe 1990.

Environmental Modification Convention 1978

DATE The Environmental Modification Convention was signed on 18 May 1977 and came into force on 5 October 1978.

PURPOSE States adhering to the convention agree not to undertake any hostile use of environmental modification techniques.

SIGNATORIES Benin 1986, Cape Verde 1979, Ethiopia (1977), Liberia (1977), Malawi

1978, São Tomé and Príncipe 1979, Sierra Leone (1978), Uganda (1977).

Inhumane Weapons Convention 1983

DATE The Inhumane Weapons Convention was signed on 10 April 1981 and came into force on 2 December 1983.

PURPOSE States adhering to the convention agree not to use conventional weapons which have an excessive or indiscriminate effect, such as incendiaries or mines.

SIGNATORIES Benin 1989, Nigeria (1982).

Treaty of Pelindaba 1996

DATE The Treaty of Pelindaba was signed on 11 April 1996.

PURPOSE States adhering to the treaty agree neither to possess nor allow the deployment of nuclear weapons on the African continent or the islands surrounding it. There is a prohibition on importing radioactive waste into the continent. The states also agree to establish an African Commission on Nuclear Energy (AFCONE) in South Africa to work for co-operation between African states on the peaceful use of nuclear energy.

SIGNATORIES Sub-Saharan African states which have signed the treaty are: Angola, Benin, Botswana, Burkina Faso, Burundi, Cameroon, Cape Verde, Central African Republic, Chad, Congo, Côte d'Ivoire, Equatorial Guinea, Eritrea, Ethiopia, Gabon, The Gambia, Ghana, Guinea, Guinea-Bissau, Kenya, Lesotho, Liberia, Malawi, Mali, Mozambique, Namibia, Niger, Nigeria, Rwanda, São Tomé and Príncipe, Senegal, Sierra Leone, Somalia, South Africa, Swaziland, Tanzania, Togo, Uganda, Zaïre, Zambia, Zimbabwe.

REBELLION, EMANCIPATION AND CIVIL RIGHTS IN THE USA

Slave-risings in colonial America and the USA

NEW YORK RISING

A slave rebellion in the British North American colony of New York which had a dramatic impact on attitudes towards slavery. When the rising began on 6 April 1712, the slave population of New York City was 1000 and the white colonist population 5000. The rebels were protesting against persistent ill treatment by their owners. Nine whites were killed and many injured in a rising that was finally put down by the militia. Over 20 slaves were executed in the aftermath. Fear of a repetition encouraged the northern colonies to attempt to prevent a growth in the slave population. In August 1712 the colony of Pennsylvania placed a high duty on the import of slaves and in 1713 Massachusetts imposed a total ban.

ST JOHN'S PARISH RISING

A plan by slaves in the British North American colony of South Carolina in 1730, to attack the town of Charleston and spread slave rebellion throughout plantations in the area. The rebels gathered on the pretext of organizing a dance in Charleston and prepared to seize weapons. A black servant betrayed the plan and the meeting was attacked by the militia. The majority of slaves involved were killed during the attack.

STONO RISING

A rebellion by slaves in Stono, a town in the British North American colony of Carolina. On 9 September 1739, 30 Angolans led by Jemmy killed two whites, seized weapons and made their way south towards Georgia. Their ultimate objective was to reach the Spanish colony of Florida. The Spanish colonial administration encouraged slaves to escape in the hope of weakening British control. As the party moved south it burned buildings, killed a further 18 whites and gathered more support among slaves until the rebels were up to a hundred in strength. Confronted by the white militia, 14 slaves were killed and a further 21 died in the pursuit that followed.

NEW YORK 'NEGRO CONSPIRACY'

In March 1741, Fort George in New York City was destroyed by fire. This incident was attributed by the townspeople to blacks and a connection was made with a spate of robberies the previous month which were also blamed on black residents of the city. Mary Burton, a European servant, went to the authorities with a story of a black conspiracy involving large-scale organized theft by blacks who frequented a drink shop. Its owner, she alleged, was a receiver of stolen goods. A panic ensued and hundreds of whites fled the city fearing a black uprising. The militia was called out and a number of blacks were put to death: 15 were burned alive, 8 hanged (as well as the white owner of the shop and his wife) and 71 blacks were transported. Six committed suicide. Following a trial the prosecutor admitted that there was no evidence of a plot.

PROSSER REBELLION

A revolt in 1800 led by Gabriel Prosser (*c.* 1775–1800), a slave who worked as a coachman in Henrico County, Virginia. At the time of the rising 32,000 slaves and 8000 whites lived in the area. Prosser's plan (organized with his wife Nanny, his brothers Solomon and Martin, and Jack Bowler), was to kill all whites except Quakers (because of their involvement in the abolitionist movement), children and old women. The slaves would then march on Richmond, the state capital, and seize the armoury, prison and the governor's residence. The 300,000 slaves in the state would then be called to join the rebellion. The conspirators manufactured firearms and bullets and Prosser learnt the layout of Richmond. But the rising, due to take place on 30 August 1800, was betrayed by two house slaves, Tom and Pharaoh, to their owner. A thousand rebels nevertheless gathered at Old Brook Swamp. More had been prevented from reaching the meeting place by torrential rain. State governor James Madison declared martial law and despatched 650 men from Richmond to disperse and then hunt down the rebels. Prosser and 30 others who were captured were hanged.

LOUISIANA RISING

On 8 January 1811, 400 slaves led by Charles Deslondes, a free mulatto from San Domingo (now Haiti), rebelled on plantations in the parishes of St Charles and St John the Baptist in Louisiana. The rebels destroyed plantations and killed two whites, forcing many others in the area to flee to New Orleans. The revolt spread and the slaves, now in possession of captured weapons, prepared to march on New Orleans. The group was intercepted by 400 militia and 260 troops outside the city and 66 slaves were killed and 17 captured in a pitched battle. Troops pursued the survivors. Sixteen of the rising's leaders were executed and their heads were displayed on poles outside New Orleans. There were further slave risings in the state in September and October 1840. In Iberville, 400 slaves rebelled and of these 20 were hanged. In Avoyelles and Rapides a conspiracy to escape was betrayed and many of the slaves involved were lynched by whites.

DENMARK VESEY CONSPIRACY

Denmark Vesey (1767–1822) worked as an artisan in Charleston, South Carolina, after buying his freedom following a lottery win in 1800. He was an admirer of the 1791–1804 Haitian Revolution, the only successful slave rebellion in the New World. From 1817, Vesey, with four others – Gullah Jack, an Angolan slave, Mingo Harth, Peter Poyas and Rolla, a slave belonging to the state governor) – planned a rising to take place on 14 July 1822. As the conspiracy developed, Vesey gathered 9000 supporters in an 80-mile radius and began to manufacture weapons. He wrote to the Haitian government seeking assistance. But a domestic slave revealed the plot and Harth and Poyas were arrested. Although they were released, Vesey decided to move the planned rising forward to 16 June. The authorities were informed once more by another domestic slave, Monday Gell, and mobilized the state militia which arrested 135 suspected slaves. Of these, 35, including Vesey and Gullah Jack, were hanged and 45 were transported.

NAT TURNER REVOLT

Nat Turner (1800–31), a slave in Southampton County, Virginia, began planning a rising with four others, in February 1831, initially to take place on 4 July – Independence Day – but moved to 22 August because of Turner's illness. On 14 August Turner preached at religious meetings at which conspirators wore red bandannas to show their support. Turner declared that it was necessary to 'take up Christ's struggle for the liberation of the oppressed'. On 22 August, Turner and eight comrades killed Turner's owner and his family, seizing horses and firearms. Over the course of the next 24 hours they attacked isolated houses, killing a further 60 whites and collecting weapons and supporters. The rebels, now 70 strong, then moved towards the county seat, Jerusalem, where they intended to seize weapons from the town armoury. They were intercepted by the state militia and vigilantes three miles from the town. The rebels fled from their better-armed opponents but 16 slaves and three free blacks were hanged immediately. Turner escaped, hiding alone in Dismal Swamp until his capture on 30 October. He was hanged on 11 November 1831. Turner's body was then skinned and used to manufacture grease. A total of 60 whites died in the rising, 55 slaves were executed and a further 200 killed by white vigilantes. The revolt caused panic throughout the slave-owning southern states. Potentially rebellious slaves were arrested and executed throughout the south. Religious meetings addressed by blacks were immediately outlawed for fear they were a means of organizing conspiracies.

CHARLESTON FIRE

As well as direct rebellion, slaves also resisted through sabotage and arson. The Charleston, Virginia, fire of December 1861, in which 600 buildings were destroyed and an estimated $7 million damage was caused, was the largest of many fires attributed to slaves. Other notable fires were those in Augusta, Georgia, in 1829, and in New Orleans in January 1830. An estimated $300,000 damage was caused in the New Orleans fire.

PLANTER INCIDENT

The escape of black American slaves by ship from Charleston, South Carolina, in 1862. Robert Smalls was forced to join the crew of a Confederate transport steamer, the *Planter*, when the American Civil War began in 1861. After learning to navigate, Smalls smuggled his wife and two children on to the *Planter* and took the steamer with its crew of twelve fellow slaves past Confederate guns. They then surrendered to Union ships surrounding the harbour. The crew were welcomed as heroes by the Union. Smalls became a US navy pilot and was given command of the *Planter* until it was taken out of commission in 1866.

BOONE COUNTY ESCAPE

A mass escape of slaves from Boone County, Missouri, during the 1861–5 American Civil War led by Robert T. Hickman. Almost 200 slaves escaped by raft up the Mississippi to St Paul, Minnesota. Calling themselves 'the pilgrims', some of the escapees remained in St Paul and founded the Pilgrim Baptist Church with Hickman as minister.

Civil rights and legislation

PROCLAMATION ENDING SLAVERY, 1862

President Abraham Lincoln (Republican) made his proclamation ending slavery in the Confederate States, which were in rebellion against the United States, on 22 September 1862. Slavery became illegal in those states from 1 January 1863. Black Americans were also to be allowed to serve in the US army and navy. The proclamation did not apply to the over 800,000 slaves in the United States and areas occupied by Union forces. The main points of the proclamation were:

That on the first day of January, in the year of our Lord one thousand eight hundred and sixty-three, all persons held as slaves within any state or designated part of a state, the people whereof shall then be in rebellion against the United States, shall be then, thenceforward, and forever, free; and the Executive government of the United States, including the military and naval authority thereof, will recognize and maintain the freedom of such persons, and will do no act or acts to repress such persons, or any of them, in any efforts they may make for their actual freedom . . .

Now, therefore, I, Abraham Lincoln, President of the United States . . . order and designate as the states and parts of states wherein the people thereof, respectively, are this day in rebellion against the United States, the following, to wit:

Arkansas, Texas, Louisiana (except the parishes of St Bernard, Plaquemines, Jefferson, St. John, St. Charles, St. James,

Ascension, Assumption, Terre Bonne, Lafourche, St. Mary, St. Martin, and Orleans, including the city of New Orleans), Mississippi, Alabama, Florida, Georgia, South Carolina, North Carolina, and Virginia (except the forty-eight counties designated as West Virginia, and also the counties of Berkeley, Accomac, Northampton, Elizabeth City, York, Princess Abb, and Norfolk, including the cities of Norfolk and Portsmouth) and which excepted parts are for the present left precisely as if this proclamation were not issued.

And by virtue of the power and for the purpose aforesaid, I do order and declare that all persons held as slaves within said designated states and parts of states are, and henceforward shall be, free . . .

And I hereby enjoin upon the people so declared to be free to abstain from all violence, unless in necessary self-defence; and I recommend to them that, in all cases when allowed, they labor faithfully for reasonable wages.

And I further declare and make known that such persons, of suitable condition, will be received into the armed service of the United States to garrison forts, positions, stations, and other places, and to man vessels of all sorts in said service . . .

AMENDMENTS TO THE US CONSTITUTION

Thirteenth Amendment, 1865

The Thirteenth Amendment was ratified on 18 December 1865 under President Andrew Johnson (Republican) and abolished slavery in the USA. Its provisions were:

Section 1.   Neither slavery nor involuntary servitude, except as a punishment for crime whereof the party shall have been duly convicted, shall exist within the United States, or any place subject to their jurisdiction.

Section 2.   Congress shall have power to enforce this article by appropriate legislation.

Fourteenth Amendment, 1868

The Fourteenth Amendment was ratified on 28 July 1868 under President Andrew Johnson (Republican) and affirmed the rights of citizenship to black people in the USA. Its provisions were:

Section 1.   All persons born or naturalised in the United States and subject to the jurisdiction thereof, are citizens of the United States and of the State wherein they reside. No State shall make or enforce any law which shall abridge the privileges or immunities of citizens of the United States; nor shall any State deprive any person of life, liberty, or property, without due process of law; nor deny to any person without jurisdiction the equal protection of the law; nor deny to any person within its jurisdiction the equal protection of the laws.

Section 2.   Representatives shall be apportioned among the several States according to their respective numbers, counting the whole number of persons in each State, excluding Indians not taxed. But when the right to vote at any election for the choice of electors for President and Vice President of the United States, Representatives in Congress, the Executive and Judicial officers of a State, or the members of the Legislature thereof, is denied to any of the male inhabitants of such State, being twenty-one years of age, and citizens of the United States, or in any way abridged, except for participation in rebellion, or other crime, the basis of representation therein shall be reduced in the proportion which the number of such male citizens shall bear to the whole number of male citizens twenty-one years of age in such State.

Section 4. ... neither the United States nor any state shall assume or pay ... any claim for the loss or emancipation of any slave ...

Fifteenth Amendment, 1870

The Fifteenth Amendment was ratified on 30 March 1870 under President Ulysses S. Grant (Republican) and made illegal any interference with the right to vote on the grounds of race, colour or having previously been a slave. Its provisions were:

Section 1. The right of citizens of the USA to vote shall not be denied or abridged by the United States or by any State on account of race, colour or previous condition of servitude.

Section 2. The Congress shall have power to enforce this article by appropriate legislation.

Twenty-Fourth Amendment, 1964

The Twenty-Fourth Amendment was ratified on 4 February 1964 under President Lyndon B. Johnson (Democrat) and abolished enforcement of the payment of poll tax as a condition for voting in federal elections. The poll tax had been used to obstruct access to voting by black Americans. The Amendment was originally proposed in 1962. Most states had already discontinued the poll tax, with the exception of Alabama, Arkansas, Mississippi, Texas and Virginia. The Amendment's main provisions were:

Section 1. The right of citizens of the United States to vote in any primary or other election for President or Vice President, for electors for President or Vice President, or for Senator or Representative in Congress, shall not be denied or abridged by the United States or any State by reason of failure to pay any poll tax or other tax.

Section 2. The Congress shall have power to enforce this article by appropriate legislation.

LEGISLATION ON SLAVERY AND CIVIL RIGHTS

Fugitives Act, 12 February 1793

The Fugitives Act of 1793 was enacted under President George Washington (Federalist) and allowed for the arrest of any fugitive slave or fugitive from justice in the States and territories of the USA. Anyone harbouring an escaped slave could be ordered to pay $500 to the owner. The main provision applying to escaping slaves was:

Section 3. That when a person held to labour in any of the United States, or in either of the territories on the north-west or south of the river Ohio, under the laws thereof, shall escape into any other of the said states or territory, the person to whom such labour or service may be due, his agent or attorney, is hereby empowered to seize or arrest such fugitive from labour, and to take him or her before any judge of the circuit or district courts of the United States, residing or being within the state, or before any magistrate of a county, city or town corporate, wherein such seizure or arrest shall be made, and upon proof to the satisfaction of such judge or magistrate ... that the person so seized or arrested, doth, under the laws of the state or territory from which he or she fled, owe service or labour to the person claiming him or her, it shall be the duty of such judge or magistrate to give a certificate thereof to such claimant, his agent or attorney, which shall be sufficient warrant for removing the said fugitive from labour, to the state or territory from which he or she fled.

Prohibition on Importation of Slaves Act, 2 March 1807

The Prohibition on Importation of Slaves Act of 1807 was enacted under President Thomas Jefferson (Republican). The Act was in ten sections and subjected anyone convicted of preparing a ship to import slaves 'from any of the coasts or kingdoms of Africa, or from any other foreign kingdom, place, or country' to forfeiture of the vessel and to a $20,000 fine. Anyone responsible for importing a slave into the USA could be imprisoned for between five and ten years and fined between $5000 and $1000. There was, in addition, punishment proscribed for the commanders of vessels found to be carrying slaves into the USA. US navy vessels were empowered to intercept and board ships suspected of carrying slaves to the USA. The sale of slaves who were already in the USA remained legal. The main provision of the Act was:

Section 1.   That from and after the first day of January, one thousand eight hundred and eight, it shall not be lawful to import or bring into the United States or the territories thereof from any foreign kingdom, place, or country, any negro, mulatto, or person of colour, as a slave, or to be held to service or labour.

Suppression of the Slave Trade in the District of Columbia Act, 20 September 1850

The Suppression of the Slave Trade in the District of Columbia Act of 1850 was enacted under President Millard Fillmore

(Whig) and outlawed trade in slaves in the area of the US capital, Washington. The Act was part of the Compromise of 1850 on the question of slavery. In return for California being admitted to the Union as a free state, slavery was authorized in New Mexico and Utah but the slave trade was forbidden in the District of Columbia. In addition, further legislation was passed strengthening the power of slaveholders to recover fugitive slaves. The main provisions of the Act were:

Section 1.   That from and after the first day of January, eighteen hundred and fifty-one, it shall not be lawful to bring into the District of Columbia any slave whatever, for the purpose of being sold, or for the purpose of being placed in depot to be subsequently transferred to any other State or place to be sold as merchandize. And if any slave shall be brought into the said District by its owner, or by the authority or consent of its owner, contrary to the provisions of this act, such slave shall thereupon become liberated and free.

Section 2.   That it shall and may be lawful for each of the corporations of the cities of Washington and Georgetown, from time to time, and as often as may be necessary, to abate, break up, and abolish any depot or place of confinement of slaves brought into the said District as merchandize, contrary to the provisions of this act, by such appropriate means as may appear to either the said corporation expedient and proper . . .

Fugitives Act, 18 September 1850

The Fugitives Act was enacted under President Millard Fillmore (Whig) and strengthened the rights of slaveholders in pursuing escaped slaves under the Fugitives Act of 1793. The Act was part of the Compromise of 1850 on the question of slavery. In return for California being admitted to the Union as a free state, slavery was authorized in New Mexico and Utah but the slave trade was forbidden in the District of Columbia. Anyone convicted of harbouring an escaped slave could be ordered to pay up to $1000 to the slave holder in civil damages. The main provision of the Act which applied to fugitive slaves was:

> Section 6. That when a person held to service or labor in any State or Territory of the United States, has heretofore or shall hereafter escape into another State or Territory of the United States, the person or persons to whom such service or labour may be due . . . may pursue and reclaim such fugitive from service or labor, either by procuring a warrant from one of the courts, judges or commissioners . . . or by seizing and arresting such fugitive, where the same can be done without process . . . In no trial or hearing under this act shall the testimony of such alleged fugitive be admitted in evidence . . .

Mails Act, 3 March 1865

The Mails Act of 1865 was enacted under President Abraham Lincoln (Republican) and was the first US legislation removing bars on federal employment from black Americans. The Act repealed previous legislation allowing for such discrimination. The main provision of the Act was:

> That from and after the passage of this act no person, by reason of color, shall be disqualified from employment in carrying the mails, and all acts and parts of acts establishing such disqualification, including especially the seventh section of the act of March third, eighteen hundred and twenty-five, are hereby repealed.

Freedmen's Bureau Act, 3 March 1865

The Act to Establish a Bureau for the Relief of Freedmen and Refugees of 1865 was enacted under President Abraham Lincoln (Republican) and initially established the Freedmen's Bureau for one year. The bureau was intended to provide assistance to freed slaves and to refugees of the 1861–5 American Civil War. The Act's main provisions were:

> Section 1. That there is hereby established in the War Department, to continue during the present war of rebellion, and for one year thereafter a bureau of refugees, freedmen, and abandoned lands, to which shall be committed, as hereinafter provided, the supervision and management of all abandoned lands, and the control of all subjects relating to refugees and freedmen from rebel states, or from any district of country within the territory embraced in the operations of the army, under such rules as may be prescribed by the head of the bureau and approved by the President. The said bureau shall be under the management and control of a commissioner . . .

> Section 2. That the Secretary of War may direct such issues of provisions, clothing, and fuel, as he may deem needful for the immediate and temporary shelter and supply of destitute and suffering refugees and freedmen and their wives and children, under such rules and regulations as he may direct.

> Section 4. That the commissioner, under the direction of the President, shall have authority to set apart, for the use of loyal refugees and freedmen, such tracts of land within the insurrectionary states as shall have been abandoned, or to which the United States shall have acquired title

by confiscation or sale, or otherwise, and to every male citizen, whether refugee or freedman, as aforesaid, shall be assigned not more than forty acres of such land, and the person to whom it was so assigned shall be protected in the use and enjoyment of the land for the term of three years at an annual rent of not exceeding six per centum of the value of such land . . . At the end of said term, the occupants of any parcels so assigned may purchase the land . . .

Civil Rights Act, 9 April 1866

The Civil Rights Act of 1866 was enacted in defiance of a veto by President Andrew Johnson (Republican) and was based on the Thirteenth Amendment to the US Constitution. The Act set out the rights of US citizens and was intended to stress inclusion of black Americans (and the exclusion of most Native Americans) and the means by which rights were to be protected. The Act was particularly aimed against Black Codes being enacted by former slave states intended to set limits to the rights and liberties of former slaves. The Act was in ten sections and its main provisions were:

Section 1.   That all persons born in the United States and not subject to any foreign power, excluding Indians not taxed, are hereby declared citizens of the United States; and such citizens, of every race and color, without regard to any previous condition of slavery or involuntary servitude, except as punishment for crime whereof the party shall have been duly convicted, shall have every right to make and enforce contracts, to sue, be parties, and give evidence, to inherit, purchase, lease, sell, hold, and convey real and personal property, and to full and equal benefit of all laws and proceedings for the security of person and property, as is enjoyed by white citizens, and shall be subject to like punishment, pains, and penalties, and to none other, any law, statute, ordinance, regulation, or custom, to the contrary notwithstanding.

Section 2.   That any person who . . . shall subject, or cause to be subjected, any inhabitant of any State or Territory to the deprivation of any right secured or protected by this act, or to different punishment, pains, or penalties on account of such person having at any time been held in a condition of slavery . . . shall be deemed guilty of a misdemeanor . . .

Section 3.   That the district courts of the United States, within their respective districts, shall have, exclusively of the courts of the several States, cognizance of all crimes and offences committed against the provisions of this act . . .

Section 9.   That it shall be lawful for the President of the United States, or such person as he may empower for that purpose, to employ such part of the land or naval forces of the United States or of the militia, as shall be necessary to prevent the violation and enforce the due execution of this act.

Prevention and Punishment of Kidnapping Act, 21 May 1866

The Prevention and Punishment of Kidnapping Act of 1866 was enacted under President Andrew Johnson (Republican) and was intended to prevent any attempt at a return to slavery. The Act's main provisions were:

Section 1.   That if any person shall kidnap or carry away any other person, whether negro, mulatto, or otherwise, with the intent that such other person shall be sold or carried into involuntary servitude, or held as a slave; or if any person shall entice, persuade, or knowingly induce any other person to go on board any vessel to any other place, with the intent that he or she shall be made or held as a slave, or sent out of the country to be made or held, or shall in any way knowingly aid in causing any other person to be held, sold, or carried away, to be held or sold as a slave, he or she shall be punished, on conviction thereof, by a fine of not less than five hundred nor more than five thousand dollars, or by imprisonment not exceeding five years, or by both of said punishments.

Section 2. That if the master or owners, or person having charge of any vessel, shall receive on board any other person, whether negro, mulatto, or otherwise, with the knowledge or intent that such person shall be carried from any State, Territory, or district of the United States, to a foreign country, state, or place, to be held as a slave . . . shall be punished by a fine not exceeding five thousand nor less than five hundred dollars, or by imprisonment not exceeding five years, or by both said punishments . . .

Enforcement Act, 31 May 1870

The Enforcement Act of 1870 was enacted under President Ulysses S. Grant (Republican) and guaranteed the right of black Americans to vote and imposed penalties on anyone who tried to obstruct this right. Part of the legislation was directed against Ku-Klux-Klan intimidation of black citizens. The main provisions were:

Section 1. That all citizens of the United States who are or shall be otherwise qualified to vote by law to vote at any election by the people in any State, Territory, district, county, city, parish, township, school district, municipality, or other territorial sub-division, shall be entitled to vote at all such elections, without distinction of race, color, or previous condition of servitude; any constitution, law, custom, usage, or regulation of any State or Territory, or by or under its authority, to the contrary notwithstanding.

Section 4. That if any person, by force, bribery, threats, intimidation, or other unlawful means, shall hinder, delay, prevent, or obstruct . . . any citizen from doing any act required to be done to qualify him to vote or from voting at any election as aforesaid, such person shall for every such offence forfeit and pay the sum of five hundred dollars to the person aggrieved thereby . . .

Section 6. That if any two or more persons shall band or conspire together, or go in disguise upon the public highway, or upon the premises of another, with intent to violate any provision of this act, or to injure, oppress, threaten, or intimidate any citizen with intent to prevent or hinder his free exercise and enjoyment of any right or privilege granted or secured to him by the Constitution or laws of the United States, or because of his having exercised the same, such persons shall be guilty of a felony, and, on conviction thereof, shall be fined or imprisoned, or both . . .

Section 13. That it shall be lawful for the President of the United States to employ such part of the land or naval forces of the United States, or of the militia, as shall be necessary to aid in the execution of judicial process issued under this act.

Section 16. That all persons within the jurisdiction of the United States shall have the same right in every State and Territory in the United States to make and enforce contracts, to sue, be parties, give evidence, and to the full and equal benefit of all laws and proceedings for the security of person and property as is enjoyed by white citizens, and shall be subject to like punishment, pains, penalties, taxes, licences, and exactions of every kind, and none other . . .

Civil Rights Act, 1 March 1875

The Civil Rights Act of 1875 was enacted under President Ulysses S. Grant (Republican). It was the last piece of civil rights legislation passed in the USA until 1957. The Act's main provisions were:

Whereas, it is essential to just government we recognize the equality of all men before the law, and hold that it is the duty of government in the dealings with the people to mete out equal and exact justice to all, of whatever nativity, race, color, or persuasion, religious or political; and it being the appropriate object of legislation to enact great fundamental principles into law: Therefore:

Section 1. Be it enacted . . . that all persons within the jurisdiction of the United States shall be entitled to the full and equal enjoyment of the accommodations, advantages, facilities, and privileges of inns, public conveyances, on land or water, theaters, and other places of public amusement; subject only to the conditions and limitations established by law, and applicable alike to citizens of every race and color, regardless of any previous condition of servitude.

Section 2. That any person who shall violate the foregoing section . . . shall be deemed guilty of a misdemeanor . . .

Section 4. That no citizen possessing all other qualifications which are or may be prescribed by law shall be disqualified for service as grand or petit juror in any court of the United States, or of any State, on account of race, color, or previous condition of servitude; and any officer or other person charged with any duty in the selection or summoning of jurors who shall exclude or fail to summon any citizen for the cause aforesaid shall . . . be deemed guilty of a misdemeanor . . .

LEGISLATION IN INDIVIDUAL STATES

During the period of Reconstruction which followed the Civil War, some southern states enacted legislation to protect black civil rights. But as Reconstruction came to an end in 1877, many reintroduced discrimination through legislation. Examples of this included unequal punishment for the same crime, exclusion from the right to jury service, separate schools and public facilities, and the prohibition of marriage between the races.

In the early twentieth century some states enacted legislation which attempted to protect black civil rights. For example, in Illinois in 1919 and California in 1925, laws were passed forbidding open racist verbal abuse or the publication of materials intended to encourage racial hatred. In 1911, Pennsylvania prohibited the establishment of racially segregated schools. A number of northern and southern states passed legislation to prevent lynching and vigilante activity. There were also some attempts at banning discrimination in employment.

However, few cases were mounted under the terms of civil rights legislation and the legislation remained ineffective because of the underlying weakness of enforcement provisions. States circumvented the intention of legislation on suffrage by, for example, imposing white primaries, poll taxes and literacy or comprehension tests on voting.

Following the end of World War I in 1918 growing Ku-Klux-Klan activity was supplemented by the 'Red Scare' of 1919 which discouraged any moves towards strengthening civil rights.

Until the passing of the Civil Rights Act of 1957, attempts to develop civil rights came through Executive Orders of the US president, which had the force of law.

Executive Order No 8802, 1941

Executive Order No 8802 was signed by President Franklin D. Roosevelt (Democrat) following the threat of a March on Washington by black labour organizer and civil rights activist A. Philip Randolph. Its main provisions were:

All government departments, agencies and federal contracting agencies were to ensure that there was no discrimination in any activity connected with national defence on the basis of race, creed, colour or national origins.

A Fair Employment Practices Committee was established to investigate complaints about discrimination and to redress grievances. Although the commission had no enforcement powers, it dealt with approximately 10,000 complaints during its five years existence.

Executive Order No 9808, 1946

Executive Order 9808 was signed by President Harry S. Truman (Democrat) and established a Committee on Civil Rights to study, report and recommend measures for the protection of civil rights in the USA. The committee produced a document entitled *To Secure These Rights* and recommended enactment of 27 separate pieces of civil rights legislation. In 1948, President Truman presented a programme of civil rights legislation to Congress based on the committee's recommendations but this met with strong opposition in the Senate and was withdrawn.

Executive Order No 9981, 1948

Executive Order No 9981 was signed by President Harry S. Truman (Democrat). The Order provided for integration in the US armed forces and established the Fahy Committee on Equality of Treatment and Opportunity. The action was taken following the threat of a militant civil disobedience campaign which called on black Americans to refuse to serve in segregated forces. Pressure for change had also come from the Civil Rights Committee which opposed segregation in the military.

Executive Order No 10308, 1951

Executive Order No 10308 was signed by President Harry S. Truman (Democrat). It was a development of the 1941 Executive Order No 8802 and created a Committee on Contract Compliance to deal with complaints about failure to comply with anti-discrimination provisions in government contracts.

Executive Order No 10730, 1957

Executive Order No 10730 was signed by President Dwight D. Eisenhower (Republican). It arose out of the mobilization by Arkansas Governor, Orval Faubus, of the state National Guard to prevent the entry of black students into the Central High School in Little Rock. President Eisenhower ordered an end to this obstruction and authorized the deployment of the National Guard and the Air National Guard to assist in desegregation in Little Rock.

Executive Order No 11053, 1962

Executive Order No 11053 was signed by President John F. Kennedy (Democrat). It was introduced following riots at the University of Mississippi campus when Governor Ross Barnett attempted to prevent James H. Meredith becoming a student. It ordered Governor Barnett and other officials to end their obstruction and authorized the use of federal troops to restore order.

Executive Order No 11246, 1965

Executive Order No 11246 was signed by President Lyndon B. Johnson (Democrat). It prohibited discrimination in government employment and government contracting and ordered the head of each executive department and agency to establish and maintain an equal employment opportunity programme to prevent discrimination on grounds of race, creed, color or national origin.

Civil Rights Act, 9 September 1957

The 1957 Civil Rights Act, the first federal legislation in this area since 1875, was enacted under President Dwight D. Eisenhower (Republican) and created a Commission on Civil Rights. It also provided for the appointment of an additional Assistant-Attorney-General to concentrate on civil rights issues. The Act's main provisions were:

Part I – Section 104 (a) The Commission shall -

(1) investigate allegations in writing under oath or affirmation that certain citizens of the United States are being deprived of their right to vote and have that vote counted by reason of their color, race, religion, or national origin . . .

(2) study and collect information concerning legal developments constitu-ting a denial of equal protection of the laws under the Constitution . . .

Part IV – Section 131 (b) No person, whether acting under color of law or otherwise, shall intimidate, threaten, coerce, or attempt to intimidate, threaten, or coerce any other person for the purpose of interfering with the right of such other person to vote or to vote as he may choose, or of causing such other person to vote for, or not to vote for, any candidate . . .

Civil Rights Act, 1960

The 1960 Civil Rights act was enacted under President Dwight D. Eisenhower (Republican) and attempted to remedy continuing interference with the right of black Americans to vote. Registrars in southern states resigned to avoid legal action being taken against them for contravening previous legislation or refused to make registration and voting records available for inspection. The Act's main provisions were:

Title III, Federal election records, Section 301. Every officer of election shall retain and preserve, for a period of twenty-one months of any general, special, or primary election of which candidates for the office of President, Vice President, presidential elector, Member of the Senate, Member of the House of Representatives . . . are voted for, all records and papers which come into his possession relating to any application, registration, payment of poll tax, or other act requisite to voting in such elections . . . Any officer of election or custodian who wilfully fails to comply with this section shall be fined not more than $1,000 or imprisoned not more than one year, or both.

Section 302. Any person, whether or not an officer of election or custodian, who wilfully steals, destroys, conceals, mutilates or alters any record or paper required by section 301 to be retained and preserved shall be fined not more than $1,000 or imprisoned not more than one year, or both.

Section 303. Any record or paper required by section 301 to be retained or preserved shall, upon demand in writing by the Attorney General or his representative . . . be made available for inspection . . .

Title IV, Extension of the powers of the Civil Rights Commission. Section 401. . . . each member of the Commission shall have the power and authority to administer oaths or take statements of witnesses under affirmation.

Title VI, amendment to the 1957 Civil Rights Act. Section 601 . . . . in the event the court finds that any person has been deprived on account of race or color of any right or privilege . . . the court . . . shall make a finding whether such deprivation was or is pursuant to a pattern or practice. If the court finds such pattern or practice, any person of such race or color resident within the affected area shall, for one year and thereafter until the court subsequently finds that such pattern or practice has ceased, be entitled . . . to an order qualifying him to vote . . . Such order shall be effective as to any election held within the longest period for which such applicant could have been registered or otherwise qualified under State law . . . The court may appoint one or more persons who are qualified voters in the judicial district, to be known as voting referees . . . The court, or at its direction the voting referee, shall issue to each applicant so declared qualified a certificate identifying the holder thereof as a person so qualified.

The 1960 Act failed to establish effective enforcement measures. Continuing violence and brutality – for example, when James Meredith was admitted to the University of Mississippi, the murder of Medgar Evans and the Birmingham church bombing of 1963 – created a climate in which the need for further legislation was undeniable. A new Civil Rights Bill was before Congress in 1963 when President John F. Kennedy was assassinated. Against a background of national grief, President Lyndon B. Johnson was able to win significant support for the Bill's passage.

Civil Rights Act, 1964

The 1964 Civil Rights Act was enacted under President Lyndon B. Johnson (Democrat) and each of its sections was intended to strengthen the provisions of previous Civil Rights Acts. It represented the most extensive civil rights legislation since the nineteenth century. Among its main provisions were:

Title I, Voting Rights, Section 101 – (a)(2) No person acting under color of law shall –

(A) in determining whether any individual is qualified under State law or laws to vote in any Federal election, apply any standard, practice or procedure different from the standards, practices, or procedures applied under such law or laws to other individuals . . .

(B) deny the right of any individual to vote in any Federal election because of an error or omission on any record or paper relating to any application . . . if such error or omission is not material in determining whether such individual is qualified under State law to vote . . .

(C) employ any literacy test as a qualification for voting in any Federal election unless (i) such test is administered to each individual and is conducted wholly in writing . . .

Title II, Injunctive Relief against discrimination in places of public accommodation, Section 201 –

(a) All persons shall be entitled to the full and equal enjoyment of the goods, services, facilities, privileges, advantages, and accommodations of any place of public accommodation, as defined in this section, without discrimination or segregation on the ground of race, color, religion or national origin.

(b) Each of the following establishments which services the public is a place of public accommodation . . . (1) any inn, hotel, motel, or other establishment which provides lodging to transient guests . . . (2) any restaurant, cafeteria, lunchroom, lunch counter, soda fountain, or other facility principally engaged in selling food for consumption on the premises . . . (3) any motion picture house, theater, concert hall, sports arena, stadium or other place of exhibition or entertainment . . .

Title III, Desegregation of Public Facilities, Section 301. (a) Whenever the Attorney General receives a complaint in writing signed by an individual to the effect that he is being deprived of or threatened with the loss of his right to equal protection of the laws, on account or his race, color, religion, or national origin, by being denied equal utilization of any public facility which is owned, operated, or managed by or on behalf of any State or subdivision thereof . . . the Attorney General is authorized to institute for or in the name of the United States a civil action against such parties and for such relief as may be appropriate . . .

Title IV, Desegregation of Public Education, Section 402. The Commissioner of Education shall conduct a survey and make a report to the President and the Congress, within two years of the enactment of this title, concerning the lack of availability of equal educational opportunities for individuals by reasons of race, color, religion or national origin in public educational institutions at all levels . . .

Section 403. The Commissioner is authorized . . . to render technical assistance . . . in the preparation, adoption, and implementation of plans for the desegregation of public schools.

Section 407. Whenever the Attorney General receives a complaint in writing – (1) signed by a parent or group of parents to the effect that his or their minor children . . . are being deprived by a school board of the equal protection of the laws, or (2) signed by an individual, or his parent, to the effect that he has been denied admission to or not permitted to continue in attendance at a public college by reason of race, color, religion, or national origin . . . the Attorney General is authorized . . . to institute for and in the name of the United States a civil action against such parties and for such relief as may be appropriate . . .

Title V, Commission on Civil Rights, Section 104. The Commission shall – (1) investigate allegation in writing under oath or affirmation that certain citizens of the United States are being deprived of their right to vote and have that vote counted by reason of their color, race, religion or national origin . . . (2) study and collect information concerning legal developments constituting a denial of equal protection of the laws . . .

(3) appraise the laws and policies of the Federal Government with respect to denials of equal protection of the laws . . . (4) serve as a national clearinghouse for information in respect to denials of equal protection of the laws because of race, color, religion, or national origin, including but not limited to the fields of voting, education, housing, employment, the use of public facilities, and transportation, or in the administration of justice . . .

Title VI, Nondiscrimination in Federally assisted programmes, Section 601. No person in the United States shall, on the ground of race, color, or national origin, be excluded from participation in, be denied the benefits of, or be subjected to discrimination under any program or activity receiving Federal financial assistance.

Title VII, Equal employment opportunity, Section 703. (a) It shall be an unlawful employment practice for an employer – (1) to fail or refuse to hire or to discharge any individual, or otherwise to discriminate against any individual with respect to his compensation, terms, conditions, or privileges of employment, because of such individual's race, color, religion, sex, or national origin; or (2) to limit, segregate, or classify his employees in any way which would deprive or tend to deprive any individual of employment opportunities or otherwise affect his status as an employee . . . (c) It shall be an unlawful employment practice for a labor organization – (1) to exclude or to expel from its membership, or otherwise to discriminate against, any individual because of his race, color, religion, sex, or national, origin . . .

Voting Rights Act, 2 July 1964

The 1964 Voting Rights Act was enacted under President Lyndon B. Johnson (Democrat). It was intended to strengthen voting rights guaranteed in the 1957 and 1960 Civil Rights Act. Among the main provisions of the Act was:

Title I, Voting Rights. Section 101. No person acting under color of law shall – (A) in determining whether any individual is qualified to vote under State law or laws to vote in any Federal election, apply any standard, practice, or procedure different from standards, practices, or procedures applied under such law or laws to other individuals . . . (B) deny the right of any individual to vote in any Federal election because of an error or omission on any record or paper relating to any application . . . if such error or omission is not material . . . (C) employ any literacy test as a qualification for voting in any Federal election unless (i) such test is administered to each individual and is conducted wholly in writing . . .

Voting Rights Act, 6 August 1965

The 1965 Voting Rights Act was enacted under President Lyndon B. Johnson (Democrat). There had been no significant increase in black registration or voting following the passage of the 1964 Voting Rights Act. Voter-registration workers in the southern states were attacked and civil rights activists murdered. Among the main provisions of the Act were:

Section 2 No voting qualification or prerequisite to voting, or standard, practice, or procedure shall be imposed by any State or political subdivision to deny or abridge the right of any citizen of the United States to vote on account of race or color.

Section 3(b) If in a proceeding instituted by the Attorney General under any statute to enforce the guarantees of the fifteenth amendment in any State or political subdivision the court finds that a test or device has been used for the purpose or with the effect of denying or abridging the right of any citizens of the United States to vote on account of race or color, it shall suspend the use of tests and devices in such State or political subdivisions as the court shall determine is appropriate and for such period as it deems necessary.

Section 4(c) The phrase 'test or device' shall mean any requirement that a person as a prerequisite for voting or registration for voting (1) demonstrate the ability to read, write, understand, or interpret any matter, (2) demonstrate any educational achievement or his knowledge of any particular subject, (3) possess good moral character, or (4) prove his qualifications by the voucher of registered voters or members of any other class.

Section 10(a) The Congress finds that the requirement of the payment of a poll tax as a precondition to voting (i) precludes persons of limited means from voting or imposes unreasonable financial hardship upon such persons as precondition to their exercise of the franchise, (ii) does not bear a reasonable relationship to any legitimate State interest in the conduct of elections, and (iii) in some areas has the purpose or effect of denying persons the right to vote because of race or color. Upon the basis of these findings, Congress declares that the constitutional right of citizens to vote is denied or abridged in some areas by the requirement of the payment of a poll tax as a precondition to voting.

Section 11(a) No person acting under color of law shall fail or refuse to permit any person to vote who is entitled to vote under any provision of this Act or is otherwise qualified to vote, or wilfully fail or refuse to tabulate, count, and report such person's vote.

(b) No person, whether acting under color of law or otherwise, shall intimidate, threaten, or coerce, or attempt to intimidate, threaten, or coerce any person for voting or attempting to vote, or intimidate, threaten, or coerce, or attempt to intimidate, threaten, or coerce any person for urging or aiding any person to vote or attempt to vote . . .

By 1968 over 50 per cent of black Americans of voting age were registered in every southern state. The proportion registered rose from 19 per cent to 52 per cent in Alabama, 27 per cent to 53 per cent in Georgia and from 7 per cent to 60 per cent in Mississippi, following passage of the 1965 Act.

Fair Housing Act, 1968

The 1968 Fair Housing Act (also known as the Civil Rights Act) was enacted under President Lyndon B. Johnson (Democrat). Following the passage of the 1964 Civil Rights Act there had been a growing white and Congressional shift against further legislation. A Civil Rights Bill in 1966 designed to provide protection to civil rights workers passed through the House of Representatives but was defeated in the Senate. A Civil Rights Bill in 1967 passed through the House of Representatives and an open-housing provision was added in the Senate. The Bill appeared likely to fall until the assassination of Martin Luther King on 4 April 1968. Among the main provisions of the 1968 Act were:

Title VIII, Section 804. It shall be unlawful – (a) to refuse to sell or rent after the making of a bona fide offer, or to refuse to negotiate for the sale or rental of, or otherwise make unavailable or deny, a dwelling to any person because of race, color, religion, or national origin.

Title IX, Section 901. Anyone was committing an offence, who . . . by force or threat of force wilfully injures, intimidates or interferes with, or attempts to injure, intimidate or interfere with – (a) any person because of his race, color, religion or national origin and because he is or has been selling, purchasing, renting, financing, occupying, or contracting or negotiating for the sale, purchase, rental, financing or occupation of any dwelling . . .

The 1968 Civil Rights Act represented the end of an era of civil rights legislation. Black American agitation ended as the possibility of what could be achieved through legislation appeared exhausted. The remaining issue was that of enforcement by the US Supreme Court and the executive.

Civil Rights Act, 21 November 1991

The 1991 Civil Rights Act was enacted under President George Bush (Republican). President Bush had initially vetoed the Bill on 22 October 1990 on the grounds that it employed 'a maze of highly legalistic language to introduce the destructive force of quotas into our Nation's employment system'. The Act was intended to strengthen provisions of the 1964 Civil Rights Act and to provide for damages in cases of intentional employment discrimination and for investigation of artificial barriers to promotion for minorities and women. Among the main provisions of the 1991 Act were:

Title I, Federal Civil Rights remedies, Section 102 – A complaining party may recover punitive damages under this section against a respondent (other than a government, government agency or political subdivision) if the complaining party demonstrates that the respondent engaged in a discriminatory practice or discriminatory practices with malice or with reckless indifference to the federally protected rights of an aggrieved individual.

Section 106 – It shall be an unlawful employment practice for a respondent, in connection with the selection or referral of applicants or candidates for employment or promotion, to adjust the scores of, use different cutoff scores for, or otherwise alter the results of, employment related tests on the basis of race, color, religion, sex, or national origin.

Section 107 – . . . an unlawful employment practice is established when the complaining party demonstrates that race, color, religion, sex, or national origin was a motivating factor for any employment practice, even though other factors also motivated the practice.

Section 112 – For the purposes of this section, an unlawful employment practice occurs, with respect to a seniority system that has been adopted for an intentionally discriminatory purpose in violation of this title (whether or not that discriminatory practice is apparent on the face of the seniority provision), when the seniority system is adopted, when an individual becomes subject to the seniority system, or when a person aggrieved is injured by the application of the seniority system or provision of the system.

Title II, Glass Ceiling, Section 203 – There is established a Glass Ceiling Commission . . . to conduct a study and prepare recommendations concerning (1) eliminating artificial barriers to the advancement of women and minorities; and (2) increasing the opportunities and developmental experiences of women and minorities to foster advancement of women and minorities to management and decisionmaking positions in business.

Section 204 – The Commission shall conduct a study of opportunities for, and artificial barriers to, the advancement of women and minorities to management and decisionmaking positions in business.

Title III, Government employee rights, Section 301 – The purpose of this title is to provide procedures to protect the right of Senate and other government employees, with respect to their public employment, to be free of discrimination on the basis of race, color, religion, sex, national origin, age, or disability.

US SUPREME COURT CASES

DRED SCOTT V SANDFORD, 1857

A slave, Dred Scott, sued for his freedom because he had lived in a state (Illinois) and a territory (Wisconsin) in which slavery was illegal after being taken there by his owner. Supreme Court Justice Roger Brook Taney rejected his claim on the grounds that slaves were not US citizens and therefore had no standing in court. He added that black people in the USA had 'no rights which any white man was bound to respect'. The Missouri Compromise, which had barred slavery in the northern territories, was ruled unconstitutional. The decision was greeted with outrage in the anti-slavery northern states, welcomed by the south, and helped encourage the atmosphere that brought the Civil War closer.

SLAUGHTERHOUSE CASES, 1873

This collection of cases, which involved white butchers in Louisiana, seriously undermined the intention of the Fourteenth Amendment to the US Constitution. The butchers had attempted to use the Fourteenth Amendment to assert their right to trade against a Louisiana statute which had granted a monopoly to a private corporation. The Supreme Court rejected the claim on the grounds that state and national citizenship were separate and that the state court's decision could not be interfered with. As the majority of civil rights infringements suffered by black Americans were imposed by state rather than federal government, this undermined the protection the Fourteenth Amendment had intended to provide.

USA V REESE, 1876

This decision ruled sections of the Enforcement Act of 1870 unconstitutional. The Act, building on the Fifteenth Amendment to the Constitution, imposed penalties on individuals who prevented US citizens from voting. The Supreme Court ruled that the Fifteenth Amendment prohibited the federal government and state governments from disenfranchising individuals on the grounds of race, colour or previous servitude but did not guarantee the right to vote.

USA V CRUIKSHANK, 1876

A white American was charged with conspiring to prevent black Americans from voting by force and intimidation when he broke up a meeting they were holding. The Supreme Court ruled that interference in this way by a private individual could only be a federal crime if the meeting had a purpose that was connected with federal citizenship. Both this decision, and that of USA v Reese in the same year, weakened the effectiveness of the Fourteenth and Fifteenth Amendments and the Enforcement Acts in protecting black voting rights.

HALL V DE CUIR, 1878

The plaintiff, a black woman, was attempting to assert her right to a cabin on a steamboat operating between the states of Louisiana and Mississippi under a Louisiana statute passed during the Reconstruction period guaranteeing equal rights and privileges. The Supreme Court ruled that the statute was an unconstitutional interference with the power of the US Congress to regulate commerce.

STRAUDER *V* WEST VIRGINIA, 1880

The Supreme Court ruled a West Virginia state statute limiting the franchise to white males to be unconstitutional. On the same day, in the case *ex parte* Virginia, the court ruled against a judge who was contesting his arrest for having kept black Americans from juries appearing before him. The equal protection clauses Fourteenth Amendment to the Constitution made it a requirement that black Americans should have access to juries. A petition for the judge's release was rejected.

VIRGINIA *V* RIVES, 1880

The Supreme Court ruled in this case that the absence of black Americans from juries in the state of Virginia was not a valid obstacle to conviction of black defendants. In order to prove discrimination, a complainant would have to demonstrate that there had been active discrimination by state officials preventing black people from serving as jurors. This, naturally, was difficult to prove.

PACE *V* ALABAMA, 1883

An Alabama state statute provided for harsher punishment for adultery and fornication between a black and white couple than between a couple of the same race. A mixed-race couple claimed that this violated the equal protection clauses of the Fourteenth Amendment to the Constitution. The Supreme Court rejected this argument on the grounds that both had been equally punished for the same offence.

CIVIL RIGHTS CASES, 1883

In a series of linked cases, (USA *v* Singleton, USA *v* Stanley, USA *v* Nichols, USA *v* Ryan, USA *v* Hamilton, and Robinson *v* Memphis and Charleston Railroad), the Supreme Court further weakened the Fourteenth Amendment to the Constitution. Following the Fourteenth Amendment, the 1872 Civil Rights Act had provided for equal accommodations in public places for black Americans. The Supreme Court ruled that this was unconstitutional on the grounds that the Amendment had intended to prohibit discriminatory action by the state. The Civil Rights Act was unconstitutional in attempting to punish the private actions of an individual who had refused admission to black Americans to a public place. A series of similar cases taken to the Supreme Court made the equal protection clause of the Fourteenth Amendment effectively valueless.

PLESSY *V* FERGUSON, 1896

The Supreme Court's landmark decision in this case gave sanction to racial segregation until the passing of the 1964 Civil Rights Act. The case tested the constitutionality of the state of Louisiana's Jim Crow laws. A black American, Homer Adolph Plessy, who had refused to ride in a designated black railway carriage in Louisiana, was charged with violating state law which required 'equal but separate' accommodations for blacks and whites. He appeared before Judge Ferguson. The Supreme Court ruled that the Louisiana law was in accord with the equal protection terms of the Fourteenth Amendment to the Constitution. The Amendment, the court declared, required only that separate accommodations should be equal.

CARTER *V* TEXAS, 1900

The plaintiff in this case was able to demonstrate to the Supreme Court that the systematic exclusion of black Americans from juries on racial grounds violated the equal protection clause of the Fourteenth Amendment to the Constitution. However, it consistently remained difficult to prove that systematic exclusion was taking place even in areas where there were no black jurors or even black members of the pool from which jurors were selected.

MCCABE V ATCHISON, TOPEKA AND SANTA FE RAILWAY COMPANY, 1914

The Supreme Court ruled that under the 'separate but equal' decision (Plessy v Ferguson, 1896) the provision for black passengers on a railway must include, for example, carriages, sleeping and dining cars.

GUINN V UNITED STATES, 1915

In this case, the Supreme Court declared 'grandfather clauses' to be unconstitutional. These clauses had been inserted in the legislation of individual states as a means of disenfranchising black Americans. They generally stated that a person could vote, regardless of any other qualification, if his ancestors had been eligible before the abolition of slavery. The timing of the decision came when, with the passing of time, the clauses were having less effect on preserving an exclusive franchise.

BUCHANAN V WARLEY, 1917

A Louisiana ordinance forbad a person of one race moving into an area occupied predominantly by people of another race, thus in effect enforcing segregation in housing. The Supreme Court – more concerned with property rights than with the segregationist impact – ruled the ordinance unconstitutional on the grounds that it 'destroyed the right of the individual to acquire, enjoy, and dispose of his property'.

CUTIS V BUCKLEY, 1926

Overturning the decision in the Buchanan v Warley case of 1917 on enforced segregation of housing, the Supreme Court ruled that any such ordinance was not unconstitutional under the equal protection clause of the Fourteenth Amendment to the Constitution. However, in Harmon v Tyle in the same year, the court ruled that a city order preventing black Americans from moving into white areas without the written consent of the majority of the white population was unconstitutional. Once again, this was not based on the rights of black Americans to live where they chose but on the rights of white property owners to dispose of their own property as they wished.

ALDRIDGE V USA, 1931

In this case, the Supreme Court ruled that judges in the District of Columbia had acted wrongly in denying the request of a black defendant accused of murder that prospective jurors should be questioned on their racial attitudes.

NORRIS V ALABAMA, 1935

This was taken to the Supreme Court as a consequence of the Scottsboro case in which nine black youths were accused of the rape of two white girls. The Supreme Court found there had been a systematic exclusion of blacks from the jury and restated the Carter v Texas decision of 1900. The court said there were clearly sufficient qualified black citizens in the area to participate in the pool from which jurors were selected.

MISSOURI EX REL GAINES V CANADA, 1938

In this case, Lloyd Lionel Gaines had been refused admission to the all-white University of Missouri Law School. Under the equal protection clause of the Fourteenth Amendment, the Supreme Court ordered the state either to admit Gaines or to provide equal facilities in the state. The state complied by establishing a temporary law school at the black Lincoln University. Gaines did not take his place.

SWEATT *V* PAINTER, 1950

Hermann Sweatt was refused a place at the all-white University of Texas Law School in 1946. A court in Texas instructed the university to establish a separate law school for black students within six months. The Supreme Court overturned this and ordered the university to admit Sweatt. Other similar cases, for example, Sipuel *v* Board of Regents of the University of Oklahoma in 1948 and McLaurin *v* Oklahoma State Regents in 1950, confirmed that segregated educational facilities were not equal.

BROWN *V* BOARD OF EDUCATION OF TOPEKA, 1954

This was one of a linked series of cases in which the Supreme Court overturned the 'separate but equal' doctrine set out in 1896 in Plessy *v* Ferguson. The other cases were Gebhart *v* Belton, Bolling *v* Sharpe, Briggs *v* Ellitt and Davis *v* County School Board of Prince Edward County. The Supreme Court ruled that 'in the field of public education the doctrine of "separate but equal" has no place': segregated facilities were 'inherently unequal'. The court issued enforcement decrees in 1955 ordering compliance with its ruling 'with all deliberate speed'.

ALEXANDER *V* HOLMES COUNTY BOARD OF EDUCATION, 1969

Following the Supreme Court's 1954 ruling in Brown *v* Board of Education of Topeka, some southern states had admitted to evading its spirit by, for example, establishing private white schools with public funds. The Supreme Court moved on from its enforcement decrees of 1955 and declared that educational desegregation should be undertaken 'at once' rather than 'with all deliberate speed'.

SWANN *V* CHARLOTTE-MECKLENBURG BOARD OF EDUCATION, 1971

By the nature of the arrangement of neighbourhoods, *de facto* segregated education remained. Attempts were made to surmount this by 'bussing' students into different areas but this aroused resistance. The Supreme Court ruled that bussing could constitute an essential means of establishing racial balance in schools. This did not, however, resolve what remained a contentious issue.

UNIVERSITY OF CALIFORNIA *V* BAKKE, 1978

Bakke, a white student, was denied admission to the University of California Medical School because places were reserved for black students under a quota system. The Supreme Court ruled that the university should admit Bakke but did not reject race as a factor in admissions policies.

RICHMOND *V* J. A. CROSON CO., 1989

The City of Richmond had instituted a policy of allocating 30 per cent of contracting work to minority owned businesses as part of an affirmative action programme. A company claimed that this represented a violation of an individual's right to equal treatment. The Supreme Court ruled that any such policy should be subject to as rigorous scrutiny when challenged constitutionally as any other race-based classification.

ADARAND CONSTRUCTORS INC. *V* FEDERICO PENA, SECRETARY OF TRANSPORTATION *ET AL.*, 1995

In this case, the Supreme Court ruled on the Federal Government practice of giving contractors on government contracts a financial incentive to hire sub-contractors controlled by 'socially and economically disadvantaged individuals.' The court declared that 'any person, of whatever race, has the right to demand that any governmental actor subject to the Constitution justify any racial classification subjecting that person to unequal treatment under the strictest scrutiny.' The effect of the ruling was to weaken affirmative action programmes.

CHRONOLOGY OF AFRICA AND THE AFRICAN DIASPORA

1494

Pope Nicholas V authorized King of Portugal to 'invade, conquer and submit to perpetual slavery the people of Africa'.

1522

27 December   Slave rebellion on the estate owned by Columbus's son in Hispaniola (now Haiti).

1596

11 August   First decision to deport black people from England recorded in the Acts of the Privy Council.

1619

August   Twenty Africans, the first to arrive in English North America, landed at Jamestown, in the colony of Virginia, as indentured servants.

1624

The first black child born in the English colonies in North America, William, christened at Jamestown, Virginia.

1639

Slave rebellion in St Christopher.

1641

Massachusetts became the first English colony in North America to legalize slavery.

1644

Eleven black slaves' petition for freedom accepted in Dutch North American colony of New Netherlands (later New York) on grounds that they had been promised their liberty.

1649

First slave revolt in Barbados.

1650

English North American colony of Connecticut legalized slavery.

1652

English North American colony of Rhode Island outlawed slavery.

1651

One of the earliest free black settlers, Anthony Johnson, granted 250 acres in Northampton County, Virginia.

1660

Blacks made up 2920 of the British North American colonies' population of 75,058.

1661

English North American colony of Virginia legalized slavery.

1662

English King Charles II granted monopoly to the Royal African Company to transport African slaves to the West Indies.

1663

English North American colony of Maryland legalized slavery.

1664

English North American colonies of New Jersey and New York legalized slavery.

20 September English North American colony of Maryland banned marriage between black men and English women.

1673

Slave rebellion in Saint Ann's Parish, Jamaica.

1678

Slave rebellion in Saint Catherine's Parish, Jamaica.

1680

Blacks made up 6971 of the English North American colonies' population of 151,507.

1682

English North American colony of South Carolina legalized slavery.

1685

France introduced *Code Noire* to administer slavery in its colonies.

July Slave rebellion in Guanaboa Vale, Jamaica.

1690

Slave rebellion in Clarendon, Jamaica.

1691

English North American colony of Virginia banned marriage between black men and English women.

1700

Blacks made up 27,817 of the English North American colonies' population of 250,888.

English North American colonies of Pennsylvania and Rhode Island legalized slavery.

1701

Slave rebellion in Antigua.

1705

English North American colony of Massachusetts banned marriage between black men and English women.

1708

Two black slaves and an Indian slave hanged following revolt in which seven whites were killed on Long Island (in the English North American colony of New York).

1712

7 April Slave revolt in New York City (in the English North American colony of New York) in which nine whites were killed and 20 slaves executed.

1715

English North American colony of North Carolina legalized slavery and banned marriage between black men and English women.

1717

English North American colony of South Carolina banned marriage between black men and English women.

1721

English North American colony of Delaware banned marriage between black men and English women.

1725

English North American colony of Pennsylvania banned marriage between black men and English women.

1733

Slaves captured and held the Caribbean island of St John during a rebellion.

1734

First Maroon War in Jamaica.

1739

9 September   Slave revolt led by Jemmy in Stono in the English North American colony of Carolina in which 20 whites died and 35 slaves were killed.

1741

March   Twenty-three slaves and free blacks in New York killed by the militia after whites fled the city fearing a 'Negro Conspiracy'.

1746

6 November   Absalom Jones, the first black priest of the Episcopal Church in America and a founder of the African Methodist Episcopal Church, born a slave in the English North American colony of Delaware.

1750

English North American colony of Georgia legalized slavery.

30 September   Crispus Attucks, a black hero of the American Revolution, escaped from slavery in the English North American colony of Massachusetts.

1755

First school for black children in the English North American colonies opened in Philadelphia.

1759

17 January   Paul Cuffe, trader and advocate of black American emigration to Africa, born in English North American colony of Massachusetts.

1760

14 February   Richard Allen, founding bishop of the African Methodist Episcopal Church, born a slave in the English North American colony of Pennsylvania.

8 April   Slave rebellion in Saint Mary Parish, Jamaica, led by Tacky.

1765
Slave rebellions in Saint Mary Parish, Jamaica, and in Grenada.

1766
Slave rebellion in Westmoreland, Jamaica.

1770
Slave rebellion in Courland Bay, Tobago.

5 March   Crispus Attucks killed in clash with British troops at the Boston Massacre, becoming one of the first to die in the American Revolution.

1771
Slave rebellion in Bloody Bay, Tobago.

1772
Chief Justice Mansfield declared slavery illegal in England.

1773
6 January   Slaves in English North American colony of Massachusetts petitioned the legislature for their freedom.

1774
Slave rebellion in Queen's Bay, Tobago.

1775
19 April   Black American soldiers fought the British alongside whites at Concord and Lexington.

23 October   Free blacks and slaves banned from serving in the Continental army against the British by Congress.

31 December   George Washington reversed ban on free blacks serving in Continental army following a British offer to free slaves who joined the British army.

1776
Slave rebellion on the Caribbean island of Montserrat.

1777
Vermont became the first British North American colony to abolish slavery.

1778
Enlistment of slaves into the army approved by the Rhode Island General Assembly.

1780
Slaves granted gradual freedom in Pennsylvania.

1781
4 September   Los Angeles, California, founded by 44 people, at least 25 of whom were of African descent.

1783
Slavery prohibited in Massachusetts and New Hampshire.

1784

Slavery prohibited in Connecticut and Rhode Island.

1785

Slavery prohibited in the state of New York.

1786

Slavery prohibited in New Jersey.

1787

12 April   Free African Society organized in Philadelphia, Pennsylvania, by Richard Allen and Absalom Jones.

13 July   Slavery outlawed in the Northwest Territory by the US Congress.

17 September   US Constitution containing three clauses supporting slavery approved by the Philadelphia Convention.

17 October   Blacks in Boston, Massachusetts presented petition seeking equal education.

1790

Census recorded black population of 757,208 (19.3 per cent) in USA, 697,000 of whom were slaves.

1791

January   Slave rebellion in Dominica.

22 August   Haitian Revolution opened with a slave revolt in the northern province led by Boukman.

1793

12 February   Fugitive slave law making it an offence to harbour a fugitive slave enacted by US Congress.

1795

Slave-risings in Curaçao, Dominica and Grenada.

July–December   Second Maroon War in Jamaica.

1797

30 January   US Congress refused to accept the first petition from American blacks. Sojourner Truth, anti-slavery and women's rights activist, born a slave in New York State.

1799

Slaves granted gradual freedom in New York.

1800

Census recorded black population of 1,377,808 (19 per cent) in USA. Nat Turner, preacher and leader of a slave revolt in 1831, born in Virginia.

30 August   Slave-rising in Virginia led by Gabriel Prosser in which 30 slaves were killed.

1802

8th Battalion West India Regiment mutinied in Dominica.

7 June   Haitian revolutionary leader Toussaint L'Ouverture kidnapped by French.

July   Napoleon Bonaparte banned the entry of black people into France.

1803
7 April   Haitian revolutionary leader Toussaint L'Ouverture found dead in his prison cell in Fort-de-Joux, France.

1804
1 January   The French Caribbean colony of Sainte Domingue became independent as Haiti.

1806
Asante under King Osei Bonsu began conquest of the Gold Coast (now Ghana).

17 October   Emperor Jacques I (Jean-Jacques Dessalines) of Haiti assassinated by mulatto officers.

1807
Dingiswayo began eight-year reign over the Zulu people. Slaves marched on Government House during rebellion in the British Caribbean colony of Tobago.

1808
Two white officers killed in mutiny by 50 members of the 2nd Battalion West India Regiment in Fort Augusta, Jamaica.

1 January   Importing of slaves into the USA made illegal by Congress.

1811
Eight-year war began between the Xhosa people and the British and Boers in South Africa.

8–10 January   Slave-rising in Louisiana in which two whites died and over 100 slaves were killed.

1815
Ibo-led plan to rise and kill slave-masters discovered in Saint Elizabeth, Jamaica.

1816
14 April   Slave rebellion in the British Caribbean colony of Barbados led by Bussa.

27 July   Fugitive slaves and Indians holding Fort Blount in Florida attacked by US troops following a siege.

1817
January   Black protest meetings against plans of American Colonisation Society to remove American blacks to Africa held in Philadelphia, Pennsylvania.

February   Frederick Douglass, anti-slavery activist, reformer and women's rights supporter, born a slave in Tuckahoe, Maryland.

9 September   Paul Cuffe, US emigrationist and trader, died in Massachusetts aged 58.

1818
Year-long civil war began among Zulus.

13 February   Absalom Jones died in Philadelphia aged 71.

1819

Dingiswayo, ruler of Zulu people, killed. Nine-year reign of Shaka began.

3 March   US emigrationist, Alexander Crummell, born in New York City.

1820

Census recorded black population of 1,771,656 (18.4 per cent) in USA.

6 February   86 black Americans sailed from New York City on the *Mayflower of Liberia*, arriving in Sierra Leone on 9 March.

3 March   Missouri Compromise prohibited slavery in the USA north of the southern border of Missouri.

1822

16 June   Planned revolt involving thousands of slaves in Charleston, South Carolina, organized by Denmark Vesey, betrayed. Over 30 slaves, including Vesey, were hanged and 45 transported.

27 September   Hiram R. Revels, the first black US Senator, born.

1823

Free blacks granted full citizenship rights in the British Caribbean colony of Grenada.

1824

First war began between the Asante and the British and lasted until 1831.

1827

16 March   Publication in New York of *Freedom's Journal*, the first black newspaper in the USA.

4 July   Slavery prohibited in New York State.

1828

23 September   Shaka, ruler of the Zulu people, murdered by his half-brothers. Succeeded by Dingaan.

1829

10 August   Over a thousand blacks fled to Canada following a race riot in Cincinnati, Ohio.

1830

Census recorded black population of 2,328,642 (18.1 per cent) in USA.

Widespread slave rebellion in British Caribbean colony of Antigua.

20 September   First national black convention in USA attended by 38 delegates from eight states at Bethel African Methodist Episcopal Church, Philadelphia.

1831

Anti-missionary riots in Barbados and Jamaica. Free blacks granted full citizenship rights in Barbados, Jamaica and the French Antilles. Extensive slave rebellion in Antigua.

6–11 June   Second national black convention with 15 delegates from five states met in Philadelphia.

21–23 August   Slave revolt in Southampton County, Virginia, led by Nat Turner resulted in the death of 60 whites and over 250 slaves.

11 November   Nat Turner hanged for his part in the Southampton County slave revolt.

1832

4–13 June   Third national black convention with 29 delegates from eight states held in Philadelphia.

1833

3–13 June   Fourth national black convention with 62 delegates from eight states met in Philadelphia.

1834

Frontier war between Bantu people and Boers in South Africa.

2–13 June   Fifth national black convention with 50 delegates from eight states met in New York.

1 August   Slavery abolished in the British Empire.

1835

1–5 June   Sixth national black convention with 35 delegates from six states and the District of Columbia met in Philadelphia.

1837

1st Battalion West India Regiment mutinied in Trinidad.

1838

Underground Railroad established in the USA to assist slaves escape to the north.

February   Zulus defeated Boer force in Durban.

16 December   Boers defeated Zulus at the battle of Blood River, enabling the Boers to set up the Republic of Natal.

1839

July   *Amistad* incident, in which slaves led by Joseph Cinque, seized the slave ship intending to return to Africa, but were captured off Long Island on 26 August.

13 November   The first anti-slavery party, the Liberty Party, formed in Warsaw, New York.

1840

January   Zulu ruler Dingaan overthrown by alliance of his brother Mpande and Boers.

1841

1 March   Blanche Kelso Bruce, the first black to serve a full term in the US Senate, born a slave in Virginia.

9 March   Joseph Cinque and the *Amistad* mutineers freed by the US Supreme Court following a long campaign in their support.

September   First black American magazine, the *African Methodist Church Episcopal Magazine*, published in Brooklyn.

7 November   Slaves seized control of the *Creole*, sailing from New Orleans to Virginia, taking the ship to the Bahamas where they were given asylum and their freedom.

25 November   Thirty-five of the *Amistad* rebels of July 1839 sailed for Africa.

1842

US Supreme Court declared a Pennsylvania state law forbidding the capture of fugitive slaves unconstitutional.

1843

15 August   National black convention with 70 delegates from twelve states met in Buffalo, New York. Henry Highland Garnet called for a general strike of slaves.

1845

October   William A. Leidesdorff became the first black US diplomat when he was appointed sub-consul in the Mexican territory of Yerba Buena.

1846

Slavery abolished in Swedish Caribbean colony of St Barthélmy.

1847

26 July   Liberia declared an independent republic by President Joseph Jenkins Roberts.

6–9 October   National black convention with 60 delegates from nine states met in Troy, New York.

3 December   First issue of the *North Star* published by Frederick Douglass.

1848

15 February   The first school integration suit filed in the US by Benjamin Roberts when his daughter, Sarah, was refused admission to a school in Boston, Massachusetts.

9–10 August   Black abolitionists participated in the national convention of the Free Soil Party in Buffalo, New York.

22 September   Slavery abolished in Danish Caribbean colonies.

1849

Town of Libreville established in Gabon, the first freed slave settlement, by the French.

1850

Census recorded black population of 3,638,808 (15.7 per cent) in USA.

March   Massachusetts Supreme Court rejected school integration and proclaimed the concept of 'separate but equal' education for black Americans.

18 September   Fugitive Slave Act passed by the US Congress.

1851

First major work on black American history, *Services of Colored Americans in the Wars of 1776 and 1812*, published by abolitionist William C. Nell.

15 February   Black anti-slavery activists rescued a fugitive slave from a Boston courtroom.

11 September   Blacks clashed with whites pursuing fugitive slaves in Pennsylvania, killing one and wounding another.

1 October   Black and white anti-slavery activists rescued a fugitive slave from a courtroom in Syracuse, New York.

1852

First major publication setting out the black nationalist position, *The Condition, Elevation, Emigration and Destiny of the Colored People of the United States*, published by Martin R. Delany.

1853

Clotel, the first novel by a black American, Williams Wells Brown, published.

6–8 July National black convention with 140 delegates from nine states met in Rochester, New York.

1854

Zulus began 23-year campaign to attempt to prevent further Boer incursions into their territory.

30 May Kansas-Nebraska Act repealed the Missouri Compromise of 1820, allowing slavery in the Northern territory.

24–26 August National Emigration Convention, a black organization advocating the emigration of black Americans to Africa, met in Cleveland with 100 delegates.

1855

Theodore II crowned Emperor of Ethiopia.

16–19 October National black convention with over a hundred delegates from six states met in Philadelphia.

1856

5 April Booker Taliaferro Washington, activist and educationist, born a slave in Virginia.

December Civil war in Zululand ended in the victory of Cetewayo, over his brother Mbulazi, at the battle of the Tugela River.

1857

6 March US Supreme Court decision in the *Dred Scott v. Sandford* case legalized slavery in the Northern territory and denied citizenship rights to black people.

1858

Basutos under Moshoeshoe began ten-year struggle to prevent further Boer annexation of territory.

1859

February Legislation in the state of Arkansas gave free blacks the choice of leaving the state or becoming slaves.

December The final landing of slaves in the USA was made by the *Clothilde* in Alabama.

1860

Census recorded black population of 4,441,830 (14.1 per cent) in USA.

1861

11 March Confederate Congress prohibited any law which banned slavery.

15 April US President Abraham Lincoln called for 75,000 soldiers to combat the Confederate rebellion but refused to recruit black troops.

25 September   US navy accepted the recruitment of slaves.

1862

6 March   President Lincoln recommended gradual freeing of slaves with compensation for their owners.

16 April   US Congress prohibited slavery in Washington, DC.

9 May   Unofficial black regiment, 1st South Carolina Volunteers, raised by David Hunter.

August   1st Kansas Colored Volunteers raised by Jim Lane. Ben Butler issued a recruitment call to blacks in New Orleans.

13 May   *Planter* incident, in which Robert Smalls, a black pilot, seized a Confederate steamer from Charleston harbour, taking the ship into Union waters.

17 July   USA approved the recruitment of black soldiers.

14 August   President Lincoln called on American blacks to emigrate to Central America and Africa at his first official meeting with a black delegation.

22 September   President Lincoln warned Confederate states that he would free slaves held by rebels on 1 January 1863.

27 September   1st Louisiana Colored Volunteers, made up of free blacks from New Orleans, became the first black regiment to be officially recognized by the USA.

28 October   1st Kansas Colored Volunteers became the first black regiment to go into action against Confederate forces.

1863

1 January   President Lincoln's Emancipation Proclamation freed slaves in the Confederate states in all but a number of areas in Louisiana, West Virginia and Virginia.

1 May   Confederate Congress declared Northern black troops criminals, threatening almost certain death or enslavement if captured.

22 May   US War Department set up Bureau of Colored Troops to encourage recruitment to Union forces.

1 July   Slavery abolished in Dutch Caribbean colonies.

13–17 July   New York riots against conscription into the Union army turned into race riots in which blacks were attacked and murdered.

18 July   Sergeant William H. Carney became the first black American soldier to be awarded the Congressional Medal of Honor.

1864

15 June   US Congress passed legislation giving equal arms, pay and medical treatment to black soldiers.

4 October   First black daily newspaper, the *New Orleans Tribune*, published by Louis C. Roudanez.

4–7 October   National black convention held in Syracuse, New York.

1865

31 January   Slavery abolished in the USA by the Thirteenth Amendment to the Constitution by 121 to 24 votes.

3 March   Freedmen's Bureau (the Bureau of Refugees, Freedmen and Abandoned Lands) established by the US Congress to assist freed slaves and white refugees.

11 April   President Lincoln recommended granting of the vote to black war veterans and 'very intelligent' blacks.

11 May   First of a series of meetings by blacks in Virginia, Mississippi, Tennessee and North Carolina calling for votes and equal rights.

7 October   Morant Bay rebellion began in Saint Thomas Parish, Jamaica.

25 November   Mississippi legislature introduced Black Code restricting the rights of freed slaves. This imposition was followed by other southern states.

18 December   Thirteenth Amendment to the US Constitution abolishing slavery ratified by Congress.

1866

5 February   Proposal to distribute land to freed slaves through the Freedmen's Bureau defeated in the US House of Representatives by 126 votes to 37.

7 February   US President Andrew Johnson declared his opposition to black suffrage to delegation led by Frederick Douglass.

2 March   Alexandria, Virginia, became the first southern city to allow black Americans to vote.

1–3 May   Forty-six blacks and two white supporters killed and over 70 injured in attack by white Democrats and police on freedmen in Memphis, Tennessee.

July   Race riots in New Orleans in which 48 blacks were killed.

1867

British began war against Ethiopia following killing of diplomatic representatives.

8 January   Blacks granted vote in the District of Columbia despite opposition of President Johnson.

2 March   First of a series of Reconstruction Acts passed by US Congress, placing the southern states under military control, and enfranchising freed slaves.

27 March   Blacks mount sit-in on streetcars in Charleston, forcing the owners to allow them to use them equally with whites.

1 May   Registration of black voters began in the southern states. By October 700,000 had registered, forming a black majority in Alabama, Florida, Louisiana, Mississippi and South Carolina.

1 August   Tennessee blacks voted for first time in a state election in the south, giving the Republican Party a majority.

October   Monroe Baker elected mayor of St Martin, Louisiana, becoming the first black town mayor.

1868

23 February   W. E. B. Du Bois, US writer and Pan-African activist, born in Massachusetts.

10 April   British defeated Ethiopians at the battle of Arogee leading to the suicide of Emperor Theodore II. Civil war in Ethiopia followed.

16 April   Francis L. Cardozo elected South Carolina secretary of state, the first black cabinet member.

17 April   Oscar J. Dunn elected Louisiana lieutenant-governor and Antoine Dubuclet state treasurer.

20–21 May   Blacks participate in the Republican Party National Convention for the first time.

June   States of Alabama, Arkansas, Florida, Georgia, Louisiana, North Carolina and South Carolina allowed to rejoin the USA on condition that blacks retained the franchise.

28 July   Fourteenth Amendment to the US Constitution ratified, guaranteeing equal citizenship and protection of the law.

28 September   Over two hundred blacks killed by white terrorists in massacre in Louisiana.

3 November   John W. Menard elected from Louisiana as the first black member of the US Congress by 5107 votes to his white opponent's 2833. Black voters gave Ulysses S. Grant the majority that elected him as president.

1869

13 January   National Convention of Colored Men formed in Washington, DC, with Frederick Douglass as president.

27 February   US Congress refused to allow John W. Menard to become a member, despite his election victory, on the grounds that 'it was too early to admit a Negro'.

6 December   First black US union, the Colored National Labor Convention, met in Washington, DC.

1870

Census recorded black population of 4,880,009 (12.7 per cent) in USA.

20 January   Hiram R. Revels elected to the US Senate as the first black senator.

26 January   Virginia allowed to rejoin the USA on condition that blacks retained the franchise.

1 February   Jonathan Jasper Wright elected to the South Carolina Supreme Court.

17 February   Mississippi allowed to rejoin the USA on condition that blacks retained the franchise.

23 February   Hiram R. Revels took his seat as the first black US senator.

30 March   Fifteenth Amendment to the United Constitution ratified guaranteeing the right to vote.

31 May   USA passed Enforcement Act to guarantee civil rights and suffrage, authorizing the use of the army to protect black rights.

19 October   Robert B. Elliott, Robert C. DeLarge and Joseph H. Rainey elected as first black members of the US House of Representatives.

1871

1 March   J. Milton Turner appointed minister to Liberia, the first black American to be accredited as a diplomat to an African country.

27 February   Charlotte E. Ray became the first black American woman to qualify as a lawyer.

1872

Cetewayo became ruler of the Zulu people.

10–14 April   National black convention met in New Orleans under presidency of Frederick Douglass.

30 June   Freedmen's Bureau closed down.

21 September   John Henry Conyers became first black American to be admitted to Annapolis Naval Academy.

9 December   Pinckney Stewart Pinchback sworn in as first black governor of Louisiana following impeachment of his predecessor.

1873

Asante armies attacked the Gold Coast (now Ghana) in an unsuccessful attempt to force the British out.

13 January   Pinckney Stewart Pinchback elected to the US Senate.

22 March   Slavery abolished in Spanish Caribbean colony of Puerto Rico.

13 April   Over 60 blacks murdered in the Colfax Massacre in Louisiana.

1874

4 February   Asante defeated in what is now Ghana by British forces at the battle of Kumasi.

3 November   James Theodore Holly, a black American, elected Roman Catholic Bishop of Haiti.

1875

1 March   US President Ulysses S. Grant signed Civil Rights Act guaranteeing black Americans equal treatment in inns and theatres and on public transport.

5 March   Blanche Kelso Bruce sworn in as US senator, becoming the first black American to be elected to a full term.

10 July   Mary McLeod Bethune, educationalist and civil rights activist, born in South Carolina.

4–6 September   Over 30 blacks killed in the Clinton Massacre in Louisiana as whites attempt to prevent them voting. Federal troops were deployed at the governor's request to protect black voters.

6 December   One black senator and seven black congressmen elected to the US Congress.

1876

8 March   US Senate refused to allow Pinckney Stewart Pinchback to take his seat.

27 March   US Supreme Court ruled in *USA v .Cruikshank* that the Fourteenth Amendment protected blacks against violation of their rights by states but not individuals.

26 October   Federal troops deployed in South Carolina following a race riot in which one black and five whites were killed.

November   Edward A. Bouchet became the first black American to be awarded the PhD degree. The doctorate, in physics, was awarded by Yale University.

1877

18 March   Frederick Douglass appointed marshal of the District of Columbia by US President Rutherford B. Hayes.

15 June   Henry O. Flipper became first black American graduate from West Point Military Academy.

September   The Exodusters, blacks from the southern USA, began moving to Kansas to escape discrimination.

1878

Slavery abolished in Spanish Caribbean colony of Cuba.

21 April   Over 200 black emigrants to Liberia sailed from Charleston on the *Azor*.

11 December   Cetewayo rejected British demands for right to impose a protectorate on Zululand.

1879

11 January   British began invasion of Zululand.

22 January   Zulu army inflicted a decisive defeat on British forces at the battle of Isandhlwana. British forces survived an attack at Rorke's Drift.

February   Beginning of the 'Exodus' in which blacks from the southern USA fled to escape increasing attacks on their liberty and rights.

29 March   British army survived Zulu attack at the battle of Kambula.

4 July   Zulus under Cetewayo suffered overwhelming defeat by British forces at the battle of Ulundi.

1880

Census recorded black population of 6,580,793 (13.1 per cent) in USA.

Basutos began an unsuccessful year long resistance to British attempts to disarm them.

1881

Systematic segregation of black people began in Tennessee.

The Tuskegee Institute, a black college, founded by Booker T. Washington.

30 June   Henry Highland Garnet appointed US minister to Liberia.

24–31 December   5000 black Americans leave South Carolina for Arkansas following persistent violence against them.

1882

13 February   Death of Henry Highland Garnet in Liberia.

1883

Year-long Zulu civil war. Cetewayo was overthrown by Zibelu who was then ousted by Cetewayo's son, Dinizulu.

24 September　National black convention met in Louisville, Kentucky.

15 October　US Supreme Court declared 1875 Civil Rights Act unconstitutional.

26 November　Death of Sojourner Truth.

1884

First protest against pass laws in South Africa mounted by the Native Education Association.

15 November　Opening of Berlin Congress which organized the sharing out between the European colonial powers of the remaining unoccupied parts of Africa.

22 November　First publication of the *New York Freeman* (later the *New York Age*) by T. Thomas Fortune and the *Philadelphia Tribune* by Christopher J. Perry.

1885

Ivory Coast Mandinga people under Samori began unsuccessful year-long resistance against French.

Four-year religious war between Catholic Christians under Mwanga and Muslims began in Uganda.

24 January　Death of black US political activist Martin R. Delany.

1 July　Congo Free State under the personal sovereignty of King Leopold II of Belgium proclaimed.

1886

British annexed Zululand following the discovery of gold in the Witwatersrand.

17 March　Twenty black Americans killed in Carrollton Massacre in Mississippi.

1887

Systematic segregation of black people began in Florida.

26 January　Ethiopians defeated Italian force at battle of Dogali.

12 May　Ahmadu, ruler of the West African Tukuloor, accepted French imposition of a protectorate under the treaty of Gori.

June–August　Unsuccessful Zulu campaign against British annexation.

1888

Systematic segregation of black people began in Mississippi.

17 October　The first black American bank, the Capital Savings Bank of Washington, DC, opened.

1889

Twenty-year reign of Menelik began in Ethiopia.

Systematic segregation of black people began in Texas.

February　French captured the main fortress of the West African Tukuloor empire at Kundian.

15 April   US civil rights and union activist, Asa Philip Randolph, born in Florida.

1890

People of Dahomey defeated by the French who established a protectorate following a year-long resistance.

Census recorded black population of 7,488,676 (11.9 per cent) in USA.

Systematic segregation of black people began in Louisiana.

25 January   National Afro-American League founded in Chicago under the presidency of Joseph C. Price.

20 March   Bill to provide federal funds to combat illiteracy among freedmen defeated in the US Senate by 37 votes to 31.

12 August   Mississippi began process of excluding black voters by literacy tests.

1891

The Hehe War, an unsuccessful two-year resistance to German occupation of East Africa, began. Systematic segregation of black people began in Alabama, Arkansas, Georgia and Kentucky.

23 January   First training school for black American nurses opened at Provident Hospital, Chicago.

September   Black Texas cotton pickers organized a union and struck for increased pay.

1892

Further resistance by Dahomey people against French occupation defeated.

April   Black longshoremen in St Louis, Missouri, went on strike for increased pay.

23 July   Haile Selassie, Emperor of Ethiopia, born.

1893

1 July   Civil rights leader Walter Francis Wright born in Atlanta, Georgia.

March–October   Matabele people under Lobengula began resistance to British attempt at occupation of territory.

July–November   Matabele people attempted to take Mashona territory.

23 October   British victory over Lobengula's army at the battle of Bulawayo weakened resistance against the occupation of Matabeleland.

1894

Mandinga people under Samori re-opened resistance to French imposition of a protectorate.

January   Capture of Lobengula by the British ended resistance against the occupation of Matabeleland.

1895

20 February   American black activist leader, Frederick Douglass, died aged 78.

18 March   Two hundred blacks from Savannah, Georgia, sailed for Liberia.

4 December   South Carolina adopted an 'understanding clause' in its constitution to exclude black voters.

1896

Asantes under Prempeh forced to accept a British protectorate following defeat in war.

28 January   Strikes and riots for higher wages began in St Christopher and Nevis and lasted until the end of February.

1 March   Ethiopian army inflicted a decisive defeat on the Italians at the battle of Adowa. Three hundred black American immigrants arrived in Liberia in an expedition organized by Bishop Henry McNeal Turner.

18 May   US Supreme Court decision in *Plessy v. Ferguson* approved the principal of 'separate but equal' facilities for blacks and whites.

21 July   National Association of Colored Women formed by the merger of the National Federation of Afro-American Women and the Colored Women's League under the presidency of Mary Church Terrell.

26 October   Italy forced to sign the Treaty of Addis Ababa recognizing Ethiopian independence.

1897

24 September   African Association formed in London by Henry Sylvester Williams.

1898

Systematic segregation of black people began in South Carolina.

9 April   Paul Robeson, black American actor and civil rights activist, born in Princeton, New Jersey.

12 May   Louisiana introduced a 'grandfather clause' to its constitution to exclude black voters.

24 June   Black American 10th Cavalry in action against Spanish forces in Cuba. Sixteen black regiments were raised during the Spanish–American war.

August   Black longshoremen in Galveston, Texas, struck for increased pay and improved conditions.

10 September   US emigrationist Alexander Crummell died in New York at the age of 69.

15 September   National Afro-American Council formed in New York under the presidency of Bishop Alexander Walters.

29 September   French captured Samori and finally defeated the Mandinga people.

1899

Systematic segregation of black people began in North Carolina.

2 June   National Afro-American Council called a day of fasting to protest against lynchings.

1900

Batetela people defeated by Belgian forces in the Congo (now Zaïre) after three years of resistance.

Census recorded black population of 8,833,994 (11.6 per cent) in USA.

Systematic segregation of black people began in Virginia. North Carolina began excluding black voters by literacy tests.

22 April   French conquered Chad after long resistance.

23–25 July   First Pan-African Congress met in London.

24–27 July   Rioting in New Orleans, Louisiana. Black homes and schools destroyed.

23–24 August   National Negro Business League formed in Boston, Massachusetts, under presidency of Booker T. Washington.

1901

Virginia began excluding black voters by literacy tests.

16 January   Hiram R. Revels died in Mississippi aged 73.

October   Militant black newspaper, the *Boston Guardian*, founded by civil rights activist William Monroe Trotter. First issue of *The Pan African*, organ of the Pan African Association produced in London.

11 November   Alabama adopted 'grandfather clause' in its constitution to exclude black voters.

1902

All Africans in Rhodesia over the age of 14 forced to carry passes.

1903

27 April   US Supreme Court upheld Alabama's 'grandfather clause' which denied black voting rights in the state.

1904

Systematic segregation of black people began in Maryland.

January   Herero rising against German occupation of South West Africa (Namibia) began.

October   Nama rising against German occupation of South West Africa (Namibia) began.

16 November   Nigerian politician Nnamdi Benjamin ('Zik') Azikiwe born in Zungeru.

1905

5 May   The *Chicago Defender* began publication.

14 May   Hastings Kamuzu Banda, President of Malawi from 1966–94, born.

11–13 July   The Niagara Movement organized by black American activists and intellectuals at a meeting attended by representatives from 14 states.

1906

13 August   Brownsville Incident when black soldiers were accused of attacking the Texas town following persistent racial harassment.

22–24 September   Eighteen blacks and three whites killed in race riot in Atlanta, Georgia.

1907

Systematic segregation of black people began in Oklahoma.

29 December   Robert Weaver, first black US Cabinet member, born.

1908

Riots in the British Caribbean colony of St Lucia.

Georgia began using literacy tests to exclude black voters.

14–19 August Race riot in Springfield, Illinois, in which troops were deployed.

1909

12 February National Association for the Advancement of Colored People (NAACP) founded by six black Americans and 47 whites on the 100th anniversary of Abraham Lincoln's birth.

31 May–1 June First conference of the NAACP held in New York City, attended by 300 black and white Americans.

21 September Kwame Nkrumah, Ghanaian politician, born in Ankroful, Gold Coast.

4 December New York Amsterdam News began publishing.

9 December Vere C. Bird, Antiguan politician, born.

1910

Census recorded black population of 9,827,763 (10.7 per cent) in USA.

Oklahoma began using literacy tests to exclude black voters.

25 March Commission appointed by President Roosevelt following disturbances in Liberia recommended increased aid.

April National Urban League founded to assist black Americans moving from southern to northern states.

12–14 May Second NAACP conference held in New York City.

1 November W. E. B. Du Bois began publishing *The Crisis* as the official organ of the NAACP.

19 December Baltimore City Council introduced the first legislation in the USA segregating black and white residential areas.

1911

Universal Negro Improvement Association (UNIA) formed in Jamaica by Marcus Garvey.

26 March William H. Lewis, a former black college football player, appointed US Assistant-Attorney-General.

1912

8 January South African National Native Congress (later the African National Congress) formed in Bloemfontein.

Riots in Kingston, capital of the British Caribbean colony of Jamaica.

1913

13 March Black rights activist, Harriet Tubman, died in New York aged 80.

11 April US cabinet discussions on race relations culminated in the introduction by President Wilson of segregation of black workers in government departments.

26 June Aimé Césaire, writer and political activist, born in French Caribbean colony of Martinique.

December Death of Menelik II, Emperor of Ethiopia.

1914

27 June Ethiopia signed a commercial treaty with the USA.

July Blaise Diagne elected from Senegal as the first African member of the French Chamber of Deputies.

1915

The 'Great Migration' (in which over two million black Americans from the southern states moved to industrial areas in the north) began.

21 June US Supreme Court ruled in *Guinn v. United States* that 'grandfather clauses' in the state constitutions of Maryland and Oklahoma excluding black voters violated the Fifteenth Amendment.

18 July US marines landed in Haiti, making the country a *de facto* American protectorate until 1934.

14 November Booker T. Washington, activist and educationalist, died in Alabama, aged 59. NAACP led protests in USA against the film *Birth of a Nation*.

1917

17 January Sovereignty over the Virgin Islands passed from Denmark to the USA.

February USA forced Haiti to allow whites to own property in the country for the first time since 1805.

19–26 March Strikes by oil field workers in Trinidad defeated by troops.

1–3 July Race riot in East St Louis, Illinois, in which over 40 black Americans were killed.

28 July NAACP organized 10,000-strong silent march along Fifth Avenue, New York, against racial discrimination.

23 August Clashes in Houston, Texas, between soldiers of black 24th Infantry Regiment and white civilians in which two black soldiers and 17 whites were killed.

5 November US Supreme Court ruled in *Buchanan v. Warley* against residential segregation laws introduced in Louisville, Kentucky.

11 December Thirteen black soldiers hanged for their alleged involvement in the August Houston riot. A further five were hanged in September 1918.

1918

21 February Sixty delegates attended the First Pan-African Congress in Paris under the presidency of W. E. B. Du Bois, held to coincide with the Paris Peace Conference.

1 July Fifteen thousand striking miners in South Africa forced back to work by armed police.

18 July Nelson Mandela, politician and liberation leader, born in Umtata, South Africa.

25–29 July Three blacks and two whites killed in riot in Chester, Pennsylvania.

26–29 July One black and three whites killed in riot in Philadelphia.

11 November End of World War I in which 370,000 black soldiers and 1400 black officers served in the American forces, half of them in Europe.

6 December Mutiny of British West Indies Regiment troops in Taranto, Italy, over racism.

1919

Rhodesian Native National Congress formed.

19–21 February Second Pan-African Congress met in Paris with 57 representatives from sixteen countries, 14 of them from Africa and 16 from the USA. Blaise Diagne of Senegal was elected president and W. E. B. Du Bois of the USA, secretary.

11–29 March First conference of the National Congress of British West Africa (NCBWA) held in Accra, Gold Coast (now Ghana).

10 May Race riot in Charleston, South Carolina, begins the 'Red Summer' in which 26 riots occurred with many black deaths.

10–11 June Race riots in Cardiff, South Wales.

July Attacks on British sailors in Port of Spain, Trinidad, following reports of anti-black riots in Britain.

1920

Census recorded black population of 10,463,131 (9.9 per cent) in USA.

12 January James Farmer, founder of the Congress of Racial Equality (CORE), born.

February Over 70,000 stopped work in the largest black strike in South Africa.

1–2 August Marcus Garvey proclaimed a 'Back to Africa' message at the Universal Negro Improvement Association (UNIA) national convention in Harlem.

6 November NAACP appointed James Weldon Johnson as its first black executive secretary.

1921

1 June Sixty blacks and 21 whites killed in race riot in Oklahoma.

1 July East African Association established in Nairobi, Kenya, by Harry Thuku, Jesse Kariuki, Job Muchuchu and Abdullah Tarrara.

14 September Simon Kimbangu, anti-colonialist religious leader in the Belgian Congo (now Zaïre), deported by colonial authorities.

21 December Pinckney Stewart Pinchback died in Washington, DC, aged 84.

1922

26 January A bill against lynching was passed in the US House of Representatives by 230 votes to 119 but fell in the Senate following a filibuster.

18 February Eric Gairy, Grenadian politician, born.

16 March Police killed 21 people in demonstrations in Nairobi, Kenya, against the arrest of East African Association leader Harry Thuku.

May Over 100 killed in Bondelswart rising in South West Africa (now Namibia) against tax increases.

21 June Marcus Garvey sentenced to five years imprisonment in the USA for alleged mail fraud.

17 September   Antonio Agostinho Neto, leader of the Popular Movement for the Liberation of Angola (MPLA) born in Ikolu-in-Bengu, Angola.

7–8 November   Third Pan-African Congress held its first session in London, holding the second in Lisbon.

1923

Nigerian National Democratic Party formed under Herbert Macaulay.

January–February   Second conference of the National Congress of British West Africa (NCBWA) held in Freetown, Sierra Leone.

18 May   Hugh Shearer, Jamaican politician, born.

23 September   Ethiopia admitted to the League of Nations.

1924

Ligue Universelle pour la Défense de la Race Noire (Universal League for the Defence of the Black Race) founded in Paris by Dahomean Prince Kojo Tovalou Houéon.

12 September   Amilcar Lopes Cabral, leader of the African Party for the Independence of Guinea and Cape Verde (PAIGC), born in Bafata, Guinea-Bissau.

10 December   Michael Manley, Jamaican politician, born.

1925

February   Black student demonstration at Fisk University against the policies of the white faculty and administration, forcing the president's resignation.

19 May   Malcolm X (Malcolm Little) born in Nebraska.

2 July   Patrice Lumumba, Prime Minister of the former Belgian Congo (now Zaïre) on independence, born in Kasai Province.

7 August   West African Students' Union founded in London.

25 August   Brotherhood of Sleeping Car Porters established in Harlem under the leadership of A. Philip Randolph.

December   Third conference of the National Congress of British West Africa (NCBWA).

1926

11 March   Ralph D. Abernathy, US civil rights activist, born.

1 May   John Compton, St Lucian politician, born.

1927

7 March   US Supreme Court in *Nixon v. Herndon* ruled against a Texas state law excluding black voters from Democratic primary elections.

21–24 August   Fourth Pan-African Congress held in New York City.

December   Marcus Garvey released from prison and deported from the USA to Jamaica.

1929

15 January   Martin Luther King, Jr born in Atlanta, Georgia.

December   'Don't Buy Where You Can't Work' campaign began in Chicago and spread throughout black areas of the USA.

1930

Census recorded black population of 11,891,143 (9.7 per cent) in USA.

28 May   Edward Seaga, Jamaican politician, born.

7 June   *New York Times* announced it would in future spell 'Negro' with a capital N to respect black American wishes.

2 November   Ras Tafari crowned Emperor Haile Selassie I of Ethiopia.

1931

6 April   First trial of nine black youths (the 'Scottsboro Boys') accused of rape began in Scottsboro, Alabama. The case became a notorious example of racist justice.

7 October   Desmond Tutu, South African clergyman and anti-apartheid activist, born.

1933

15 March   NAACP opened a concerted campaign against discrimination and segregation by filing a suit against the University of North Carolina.

1935

January   Riots in St Christopher and Nevis following refusal of sugar cane employers to increase wages.

22 May   First mass organized black strike by miners in Northern Rhodesia (now Zambia). Over 25 killed and wounded by troops.

3 October   Italian invasion of Ethiopia.

21 October   A week of riots began in St Vincent against price rises.

5 December   National Council of Negro Women founded in USA with Mary McLeod Bethune as president.

1936

14–16 February   National Negro Congress formed in USA with 817 delegates representing over 500 organizations, under the presidency of A. Philip Randolph.

6 May   Italian forces occupied the Ethiopian capital Addis Ababa.

24 June   Mary McLeod Bethune became the first black American woman to be given a federal post when she was appointed Division of Negro Affairs director in the National Youth Administration.

3 July   Black American athlete, Jesse Owens, won four gold medals at the Olympic Games in Berlin, angering Nazi dictator, Adolf Hitler.

8 December   NAACP opened campaign in the state of Maryland to secure equal pay for black teachers.

1937

Trade unions legalized in French West African colonies.

26 March   William H. Hastie became the first black American federal judge when he was appointed to the Virgin Islands District Court.

October   Massacre of 20,000 Haitian migrants by Dominican troops.

1 October   The Brotherhood of Sleeping Car Porters was recognized by the Pullman Company in the USA.

1938

8 November   Crystal Bird Fauset became the first black American woman elected politician when she was elected to the Pennsylvania legislature.

12 December   US Supreme Court ruled in *Missouri ex rel Gaines* that states were obliged to provide equal educational facilities for black students.

1939

22 July   Jane Matilda Bolin became the first black American woman judge when she was appointed in New York City.

1940

Census recorded black population of 12,865,518 (9.8 per cent) in USA. Trade unions legalized in British colony of Nigeria.

10 June   Marcus Garvey, Pan-African leader and founder of the Universal Negro Improvement Association, died in London aged 53.

27 September   Black leaders condemned race discrimination in the US armed forces and industry in a meeting with President Roosevelt.

9 October   The US government declared that it was not American policy to allow integration in the armed forces.

16 October   Benjamin Oliver Davis, Sr became the first black American general.

25 October   US President Roosevelt met a delegation from the Committee on the Participation of Negroes in the National Defense Program.

1941

16 January   The setting up of the first black Army Air Squadron in the USA was announced.

18 April   New York City bus companies began employing black drivers and mechanics following a month-long boycott.

28 April   US Supreme Court ruled that separate railroad facilities provided for black people should be equal to those of whites.

1 May   A. Philip Randolph announced a 100,000-strong black march on Washington, DC, to demonstrate against race discrimination in industry and the armed forces.

5 May   Emperor Haile Selassie of Ethiopia returned to the capital Addis Ababa following a five-year exile.

18 June   President Roosevelt's appeal for the march on Washington to be abandoned, was rejected by Randolph and other black leaders.

25 June   President Roosevelt announced Executive Order 8802 banning race and religious discrimination in American war industries, government industries and on government training schemes.

19 July   Fair Employment Practices Committee appointed in USA by President Roosevelt.

6 August   Racial clashes between soldiers and civilians in North Carolina.

8 October Jesse Jackson, American politician and civil rights activist, born.

1942

Trade unions legalized in British colony of Uganda.

7 March First cadets graduated from the black US Army Air Corps academy at Tuskegee, Alabama.

18 June Hugh Mulzac became first black captain of an American merchant ship when the *Booker T. Washington* was launched.

20 October 'Durham Manifesto' issued in Durham, North Carolina, by 60 southern black leaders demanding major changes in race relations in the USA.

November Congress of Racial Equality (CORE) formed in Chicago by black and white American activists.

1943

5 January William H. Hastie resigned as a black aide to the US secretary of war in protest against segregation in the armed forces.

2 June Black American 99th Pursuit Squadron in action for the first time in Italy.

20–22 June Thirty-five black people killed and over 500 injured in a race riot in Detroit, Illinois.

1–2 August Race riot in Harlem, New York.

1944

Universal adult suffrage granted in British Caribbean colony of Jamaica.

3 April US Supreme Court ruled in *Smith v. Allwright* that primary elections that excluded black voters were illegal.

29 May Maurice Bishop, Grenadian radical politician, born.

1 August Adam Clayton Powell elected as the first black American member of the House of Representatives from an eastern state.

1945

21 June Colonel Benjamin Oliver Davis, Jr, became the first black American to command an Army Air Force base.

July–August Successful 37-day general strike by government employees in Nigeria over demands for increase in minimum wage and cost of living allowances.

15–21 October Fifth Pan-African Congress met in Manchester, England, with W. E. B. Du Bois as president.

1 November John H. Johnson began publishing *Ebony* magazine in the USA.

1946

Trade unions legalized in Belgian Congo (now Zaïre). Universal adult suffrage granted in British Caribbean colony of Trinidad.

African National Congress formed an alliance with the South African Indian Congress to campaign against white domination.

January   Student demonstrations, strikes and rioting forced resignation of President Elie Lescot of Haiti.

26 February   Two killed and ten injured in a race riot in Columbia, Tennessee.

March   Constitution published making the Gold Coast (now Ghana) the first British African colony with a black majority Legislative Council.

7 May   William H. Hastie became first American black governor of the Virgin Islands.

3 June   US Supreme Court ruled segregation in interstate bus travel illegal in *Morgan v. Virginia*.

August   Dumarsais Estimé elected as first black president of Haiti since 1915.

5 December   US President Harry S. Truman issued Executive Order 9808 establishing a Committee on Civil Rights, with two black members, Sadie M. Alexander and Channing H. Tobias.

1947

New Nigerian Constitution gave a black majority on the Legislative Council.

9 April   Freedom Riders despatched through the southern USA by CORE and the Fellowship of Reconciliation to test effectiveness of the Supreme Court's decision on 3 June 1946.

16 August   Carol Moseley Brown, first black American woman US senator, born.

23 October   NAACP petition against racism presented to the United Nations.

29 October   Committee on Civil Rights report 'To Secure These Rights' attacked racial discrimination in the USA.

1948

12 January   US Supreme Court ruled in *Sipuel v. Oklahoma State Board of Regents* that black students should have equal rights in legal studies.

February   Twenty-nine people killed in anti-British riots in Accra, Gold Coast (now Ghana).

2 February   President Truman called on the US Congress to adopt legislation to prevent lynching, discrimination in voting, and to establish a Fair Employment Practices Commission.

3 May   US Supreme Court declared the illegality of restrictive covenants barring the right of black Americans to own or occupy property.

31 March   A. Philip Randolph demanded an end to segregation and discrimination in the armed forces before the US Senate Armed Services Committee.

26 July   President Truman issued Executive Order 9981 outlawing racial discrimination in the armed forces and federal employment.

1 October   Supreme Court of California declared a state law against inter-racial marriage unconstitutional.

1949

Trade unions legalized in the British colony of Nyasaland (now Malawi)

18 January   Congressman William L. Dawson elected as the first black chair of an American Congressional standing committee, the House Expenditure Committee.

3 June   Wesley A. Brown became the first black American to graduate from the Annapolis Naval Academy.

3 October   The first black-owned radio station in the United States, WERD, opened in Atlanta, Georgia.

November   CORE intensified sit-in campaign in St Louis to end segregation in public facilities.

1950

Census recorded black population of 15,042,286 (10 per cent) in USA. Universal adult suffrage granted in British Caribbean colony of Barbados.

May   President Dumarsais Estimé of Haiti overthrown in a military coup.

5 June   US Supreme Court ruled in *Sweatt v. Painter* that educational equality demanded more than equal facilities; and in *McLaurin v. Oklahoma State Board of Regents* that no educational distinctions should be made on racial grounds.

21 July   Black American 24th Infantry Regiment won first US success in Korean War by capturing Yechon.

24 August   Edith Sampson appointed the first black American representative at the United Nations.

22 September   Ralph J. Bunche awarded Nobel Peace Prize for his role as mediator in Palestine.

1951

Universal adult suffrage granted in the British Caribbean colonies of the Leeward and Windward Islands.

16 February   New York City Council declared racial discrimination in city-aided housing projects illegal.

10 May   Washington, DC, Municipal Appeals Court declared racial segregation in restaurants illegal.

12 July   Rioting in Cicero, Illinois, when over 3000 whites attempted to prevent a black family from moving in.

1 October   The final all-black American army unit, the 24th Infantry Regiment – formed in 1866 – disbanded in Korea.

25 December   NAACP official, Harry T. Moore, killed by bomb in Mims, Florida.

1952

12 January   First black American student admitted to University of Tennessee.

20 October   State of Emergency declared in Kenya by the British authorities following Mau Mau rebellion. Nationalist leader Jomo Kenyatta arrested.

8–9 November   Rioting in South Africa suppressed by security forces.

15 November   Former Italian colony of Eritrea federated with Ethiopia.

7 December   Civil rights body reported increasing racist bombing incidents in the USA.

30 December   Tuskegee Institute, Alabama, reported that 1952 was the first year in which no lynchings took place in the USA since records were first kept in 1881.

1953

8 June   US Supreme Court outlawed racial segregation in restaurants in Washington, DC.

4 June   Rioting in Chicago when black families attempted to move into a housing project.

15 June   Over 100 Mau Mau fighters killed by British forces in the Aberdare Forest, Kenya.

19 June   Black bus boycott against discrimination began in Baton Rouge, Louisiana.

13 August   Government Contract Compliance Committee established by President Eisenhower to ensure adherence to anti-discrimination regulations.

20 October   Kenyan independence leader, Jomo Kenyatta, sentenced to seven years imprisonment by British authorities.

1954

17 May   US Supreme Court ruled unanimously in *Brown v. Board of Education of Topeka, Kansas,* that racial segregation in public schools was unconstitutional.

27 October   Benjamin Oliver Davis, Jr was appointed the first black general in the United States Air Force.

30 October   US Defense Department announced the abolition of all segregated regiments in the armed forces.

1955

18 April   Bandung Conference of leaders of African Asian nations opened in Indonesia.

18 May   Mary McLeod Bethune, US educationalist and activist, died in Florida at the age of 80.

31 May   US Supreme Court ordered integration in education 'with all deliberate speed'.

26 June   Freedom Charter adopted by the anti-apartheid Congress Alliance in South Africa.

28 August   Murder of Emmett Till in Mississippi drew media attention to the treatment of black Americans in the southern states.

25 November   US Interstate Commerce Commission outlawed racial segregation in buses and waiting rooms.

1 December   Rosa Parks arrested after refusing to give up her seat on a bus in Montgomery, Alabama, to a white man.

5 December   Black boycott of buses began in Montgomery, Alabama. Asa Philip Randolph and Willard S. Townsend elected vice-presidents of the American Federation of Labor-Congress of Industrial Organizations.

1956

Bus boycott by Africans in Rhodesia.

30 January   Bombing at home of Martin Luther King, Jr, the leader of the Montgomery bus boycott.

11 April   Black American singer, Nat King Cole, attacked in Birmingham, Alabama.

30 May   Black boycott of buses began in Tallahassee, Florida.

2 August   British parliament passed Act setting up the Federation of the West Indies.

19–22 September   International conference of black artists and writers opened at the Sorbonne in Paris.

13 November   US Supreme Court upheld ban on segregation of buses in Montgomery.

21 December   Integration introduced on buses in Montgomery. The boycott ended.

26 December   Black protests began against segregation on buses in Birmingham, Alabama, following the bombing of a civil rights activist's home.

27 December   Buses desegregated in Tallahassee, Florida, following six months black boycott.

1957

13–14 February   Southern Christian Leadership Conference (SCLC) organized at a conference in New Orleans, Louisiana, under the presidency of Martin Luther King, Jr.

6 March   The Gold Coast became independent as Ghana.

17 May   The largest US civil rights demonstration to date, the Prayer Pilgrimage, was held in Washington, DC.

June   Black boycott of stores started in Tuskegee, Alabama, in protest against discrimination in voting rights.

29 August   1957 Voting Rights Act passed by the US Congress set up a Civil Rights Commission and a Justice Department civil rights division.

September   François 'Papa Doc' Duvalier elected President of Haiti.

25 September   US President Eisenhower despatched federal troops to Little Rock, Arkansas, to enforce school integration.

5 December   State of New York introduced Fair Housing Practices law against racial and religious discrimination in housing.

1958

March   First issue of the *West Indies Gazette and Afro-Asian Caribbean News* published in London.

22 April   First meeting of the Federation of the West Indies parliament.

12–13 May   National Negro Leaders meeting called for intensified campaign against discrimination and segregation in the USA.

29 June   Bomb exploded at the church of a Baptist minister involved in civil rights activities in Birmingham, Alabama.

July   Attempted coup against President Duvalier of Haiti.

19 August   NAACP Youth Council began campaign of black sit-ins in Oklahoma City lunch counters.

23 August   Clashes between blacks and whites in Nottingham, England. A week of race riots began in Notting Hill area of London.

20 September   Martin Luther King, Jr, stabbed in Harlem, New York.

2 October   Guinea became independent.

25 October   Ten thousand students participated in a Youth March for Integrated Schools in Washington, DC.

1959

5 January   Fifty killed and 300 wounded in anti-colonial demonstrations in the Belgian Congo (now Zaïre) capital of Léopoldville (now Kinshasa) organized by the Alliance des Ba-Kongo (ABAKO).

3 March   Dr Hastings Banda and 200 supporters arrested in Nyasaland (now Malawi), following anti-British riots in which over 50 people were killed.

April   Ovamboland People's Organisation (renamed South West Africa People's Organisation) founded.

August   Student demonstration against President Duvalier of Haiti supported by Roman Catholic Church hierarchy.

1960

Census recorded black population of 18,871,831 (10.5 per cent) in USA.

January   Belgium agreed at the Brussels Round Table Conference to grant independence to the Belgian Congo (now Zaïre) on 30 June.

1 January   Cameroon became independent.

1 February   Sit-in campaign at segregated lunch counter mounted by four students at Greensboro, North Carolina, which spread to 15 cities in five southern states.

23 February   Race riot followed a civil rights sit-in protest in Chattanooga, Tennessee.

3 March   Roman Catholic Bishop Laurian Rugambwa appointed the first black cardinal in modern times by Pope John XXIII.

21 March   South African police killed 67 National Anti-Pass Law Campaign demonstrators in Sharpeville Massacre.

15–17 April   Student Non-violent Co-ordinating Committee (SNCC) formed in Raleigh, North Carolina.

19 April   South West Africa People's Organisation (SWAPO) formed.

27 April   Togo became independent.

6 May   US President Eisenhower signed Voting Rights Act appointing 'voting referees' to assist black voter registration. The Act was invoked for the first time on 9 May.

20 June   Mali and Senegal became independent.

30 June   Belgian Congo (now Zaïre) became independent.

1 July   Somalia (formerly British Somaliland and Italian Somaliland) became independent.

6 July   Army mutiny in the newly independent Congo.

11 July   Katanga province declared independence from former Belgian Congo under Moïshe Tshombe.

31 July   Nation of Islam leader, Elijah Muhammad, advocated the formation of a separate black state in America.

1 August   Dahomey (later Benin) became independent.

3 August   Niger became independent.

5 August   Upper Volta (later Burkina Faso) became independent.

7 August   Black and white students began kneel-in protests in Atlanta churches.

8 August   Côte d'Ivoire became independent.

11 August   Chad Republic became independent.

12 August   United Nations troops deployed in Katanga to end secession from the newly independent Congo.

14 August   Border clashes between Ethiopian and Somali troops over disputed Ogaden desert region.

13 August   Central African Republic became independent.

15 August   Congo Brazzaville (later the Congo Republic) became independent.

17 August   Gabon became independent.

24 August   Revolt against Congo's central government in Kasai province.

27 August   Fifty people were injured in a race riot in Jacksonville, Florida, following sit-in protests.

14 September   Prime Minister Patrice Lumumba overthrown by Colonel Joseph-Désiré Mobutu in former Belgian Congo (now Zaïre).

22 September   Mali became independent.

1 October   Nigeria became independent.

28 November   Mauritania became independent.

15 December   African and Malagasy Organisation for Economic Co-operation established by ten French-speaking African states in Brazzaville.

17 December   Emperor Haile Selassie survived a military coup mounted by Brigadier-General Mengistu Neway in which his son Afa-Wossen was temporarily installed as ruler.

1961

3 January   Adam Clayton Powell elected chairman of the US House of Representatives Education and Labor Committee.

3 February   Angolan independence struggle against Portugal began with an attack on a Lusaka prison.

9 February   Patrice Lumumba, Congolese prime minister, murdered.

11–12 February   Southern Cameroons voted in referendum to join Republic of Cameroon and North Cameroons voted to join the Northern Region of Nigeria.

12 March   New Congo Federation declared by President Kasavubu and Prime Minister Ileo.

15 March   Resistance struggle against Portugal began in northern Angola.

27 April   Sierra Leone became independent.

4 May   Freedom Riders sponsored by CORE began testing anti-discrimination laws on buses in the southern USA.

14 May   Freedom Riders attacked by white segregationists in Alabama.

26 May   Freedom Ride Co-ordinating Committee formed in Atlanta, Georgia.

31 May   South Africa, under the apartheid regime, became a Republic and left the Commonwealth.

14 August   Kenyan independence leader, Jomo Kenyatta, released by British colonial authorities.

13–21 September   United Nations forces unsuccessfully attempted to capture the capital of secessionist Katanga.

19 September   Referendum in Jamaica went against continued participation in the Federation of the West Indies.

22 September   US Interstate Commerce Commission banned racial segregation on interstate buses and at terminals.

1 October   Former British territory of the Southern Cameroons joined the Republic of Cameroon following a plebiscite.

9 December   Tanganyika (now Tanzania) became independent.

12 December   Over 700 black demonstrators arrested in anti-segregation protests in Albany, Georgia.

1962

21 January   Unsuccessful attempt to assassinate President Sylvanus Olympio of Togo.

31 January   First black American naval officer given command of a warship when Lieutenant-Commander Samuel Lee Gravely took over the USS *Falgout*.

12 February   Black boycott of buses began in Macon, Georgia.

23 May   Federation of the West Indies terminated.

1 July   Burundi and Rwanda became independent.

21 July   Over 160 demonstrators were imprisoned following anti-desegregation protests in Albany, Georgia.

1 August   Unsuccessful attempt to assassinate President Kwame Nkrumah of Ghana.

6 August   Jamaica became independent.

31 August   Trinidad and Tobago became independent.

9 September   Two black churches were burnt down in Georgia.

10 September   US Supreme Court ordered the University of Mississippi to admit Air Force veteran James H. Meredith as a student.

17 September   Four black churches were burnt down in Georgia.

20 September   James H. Meredith was personally refused admission to the University of Mississippi by the state governor.

30 September   James H. Meredith registered at the University of Mississippi, escorted by federal marshals.

9 October   Uganda became independent.

20 November   President Kennedy issued an Executive Order outlawing racial discrimination in federal-funded housing.

17 December   Prime Minister Mamadou Dia of Senegal arrested following unsuccessful coup attempt against President Senghor.

1963

13 January   President Sylvanus Olympio of Togo assassinated in a military coup led by Sergeant Etienne Gnassingbe Eyadéma and replaced by Nicolas Grunitzky.

15 January   United Nations troops captured Katanga, forcing Tshombe into exile.

March   Border clashes between Kenyan and Somali troops opened a four-year war.

18 March   War of independence launched against Portugal in Guinea-Bissau.

3 April   Anti-segregation demonstrations began in Montgomery, Alabama, under leadership of Martin Luther King, Jr.

10 May   Agreement on limited integration in Montgomery, Alabama, ended a campaign in which over 2000 demonstrators were arrested.

25 May   Heads of 30 African states signed the Charter of the Organisation of African Unity (OAU) in Addis Ababa, Ethiopia.

1 June   Jomo Kenyatta became prime minister of Kenya.

13 June   NAACP Mississippi field secretary Medgar W. Evers murdered in Jackson, allegedly by a white segregationist.

18 June   Boycott of schools in Boston by 3000 black students protesting against segregated education.

15 August   President Fulbert Youlou of the Congo Republic replaced by Alphonse Massemba-Débat following a military coup.

27 August   W. E. B. Du Bois, writer, Pan-African activist and founder of the NAACP, died in Accra, Ghana, aged 95.

28 August   Over 250,000 people participated in the March on Washington for Jobs and Freedom. Martin Luther King, Jr delivered his 'I have a dream' speech.

15 September   Four black girls were killed in the bombing of the 16th Street Baptist Church in Birmingham, Alabama.

1 October   Nigeria became a Republic within the Commonwealth.

9 October   Uganda became a Republic within the Commonwealth.

22 October   Boycott of schools in Chicago by over 200,000 black students protesting against segregated education.

23 October   Colonel Christophe Soglo overthrew President Maga in a military coup in Dahomey (now Benin).

10 December   Zanzibar (now part of Tanzania) became independent.

12 December   Kenya became independent.

17 December   President Christophe Soglo overthrown in a military coup in Dahomey (now Benin).

31 December   Central African Federation dissolved.

1964

2 January   Unsuccessful attempt to assassinate President Kwame Nkrumah of Ghana.

12 January   Zanzibar government overthrown by African nationalists.

20 January   Army mutiny in Tanganyika over pay put down with British assistance.

23 January   Army mutinies in Kenya and Uganda put down with British assistance.

4 February   Twenty-fourth Amendment to the US Constitution ended imposition of poll tax as a requirement for voting in federal elections.

3 February   Boycott of schools in New York City by over 460,000 black and Puerto Rican students in protests against segregated education.

7 February   Somali troops invaded Ethiopia to assert claim to Ogaden desert area.

18 February   President Leon M'ba restored to power in Gabon by French troops, following an attempted coup led by Jean-Hilaire Aubume.

12 March   Malcolm X severed links with the Nation of Islam.

26 April   Zanzibar amalgamated with Tanganyika to form the United Republic of Tanzania.

12 June   Nelson Mandela sentenced to life imprisonment.

28 June   Malcolm X founded Organisation for Afro-American Unity in New York.

30 June   United Nations forces leave the Congo.

2 July   1964 Civil Rights Act signed by US President Johnson in the presence of Martin Luther King, Jr, and other black American leaders.

6 July   Malawi became independent.

18–22 July   Rioting in Harlem, spreading to the Bedford-Stuyvesant section of Brooklyn.

25 July   Rioting in Rochester, New York.

2 August   Rioting in Jersey City, New Jersey.

4 August   Bodies of three murdered civil rights workers, two black and one white, found near Philadelphia, Mississippi.

11–12 August   Rioting in Paterson, New Jersey.

12–13 August   Rioting in Elizabeth, New Jersey.

28–30 August   Rioting in Philadelphia, Pennsylvania.

10 September   African Development Bank established.

24 October   Zambia became independent.

10 December   Martin Luther King, Jr, presented with the Nobel Peace Prize.

December   US Congress passed the Economic Opportunity Act.

1965

2 January   Martin Luther King, Jr, opened voter registration campaign in Selma, Alabama.

1 February   Over 700 demonstrators arrested in Selma, Alabama.

16 February   Attempt by the Black Liberation Movement to bomb the Statue of Liberty and the Washington Memorial foiled.

18 February   The Gambia became independent.

21 February   Malcolm X assassinated at a rally in New York City.

23 February   Black Muslim headquarters in New York and San Francisco burnt down.

7 March   Selma to Montgomery civil rights march attacked by Alabama state troopers with clubs and tear gas.

25 March   Fifty thousand civil rights marchers rally in Montgomery.

19 May   Patricia R. Harris became the first black American woman ambassador when she was appointed to Luxembourg.

16 June   Civil war began in Chad.

6 August   US President Johnson signed Voting Rights Act suspending literacy tests for voting.

11–16 August   Six days of rioting began in Watts section of Los Angeles. Thirty-four people died, 900 were injured and over 3500 arrested. Thurgood Marshall confirmed by the US Senate as the first black US Solicitor-General.

12–14 August   Rioting in the West Side of Chicago.

13–15 August   General strike and demonstrations forced resignation of President Fulbert Youlou of the Congo Republic.

18 October   Burundi prime minister, Léopold Biha, wounded in attack on the King's palace by army mutineers.

20 October   Martial law declared in Burundi.

11 November   Whites in Southern Rhodesia declared illegal unilateral independence.

24 November   General Joseph-Désiré Mobutu ousted President Kasavubu in his second military coup in the Congo (now Zaïre).

29 November   Military coup in Dahomey (now Benin) led by Colonel Christophe Soglo.

22 December   Second military coup in Dahomey led by Colonel Christophe Soglo.

1966

1 January   President David Dacko of the Central African Republic ousted in a military coup by army commander Jean-Bédel Bokassa.

4 January   President Maurice Yaméogo of Burkina Faso deposed in a military coup by Lieutenant-Colonel Sangoulé Lamizana.

13 January   Robert C. Weaver became the first black American cabinet member when he was appointed Secretary of Housing and Urban Development.

15 January   Prime Minister Sir Abubakar Tafawa Balewa killed in Nigeria's first military coup and replaced by Major-General Johnson Aguiyi-Ironsi.

24 February   President Kwame Nkrumah overthrown in Ghana's first military coup while visiting China.

13 April   Martin Luther King, Jr, attacked American involvement in the Vietnam War.

28 April   Seven guerrillas killed in Rhodesia (now Zimbabwe) at Sinoia in first engagement of the armed struggle against white rule.

16 May   Stokely Carmichael appointed chairman of the Student Non-violent Co-ordinating Committee (SNCC).

24 May   New Nigerian Constitution replaced federation with a unitary state. The Kabaka of Buganda expelled from Uganda.

29 May   Rioting between Hausas and Ibos in northern Nigeria.

30 May   Unsuccessful coup attempt against General Mobutu in the Congo (now Zaïre).

5 June   James Meredith began a lone civil rights march from Memphis, Tennessee to Jackson, Mississippi.

7–26 June   Expression 'Black power' first used by Stokely Carmichael and others on the 'march against fear' from Memphis, Tennessee to Jackson, Mississippi.

3–5 July   Rioting in Omaha, Nebraska.

12–15 July   Rioting in Chicago in which two blacks died.

18–23 July   Rioting in Cleveland, Ohio, in which five died and 50 were injured.

29 July   Second military coup in Nigeria by northern army officers. Ibo head of military government Major-General Johnson Aguiyi-Ironsi assassinated and replaced by Lieutenant-Colonel Yakuba Gowon.

20 August   Constance Baker Motley appointed first black woman American federal judge.

26 August   South West Africa People's Organisation began armed struggle against South African occupation of Namibia.

27 August   Rioting in Waukegan, Illinois.

30 August   Burundi, Rwanda and Zaïre signed a mutual security pact.

1–2 September   Rioting in Dayton, Ohio.

6 September   Rioting in Atlanta, Georgia.

30 September   Botswana became independent.

October   Black Panther Party founded in Oakland, California by Huey P. Newton and Bobby Seale.

4 October   Lesotho became independent.

8 November   Edward W. Brooke elected as the first black US senator since the Reconstruction period.

26 November   Burundi proclaimed a republic following the overthrow of King Ntare V by Michel Micombero.

30 November   Barbados became independent.

16 December   United Nations Security Council called for international sanctions against the white regime in Rhodesia (Zimbabwe).

1967

4–5 January   Conference at Aburi, Ghana, failed to prevent the secession of Biafra from Nigeria and the ensuing civil war.

13 January   President Nicolas Grunitzky of Togo ousted in a military coup led by Lieutenant-Colonel Etienne Gnassingbe Eyadéma.

16 January   First black government took office in the Bahamas.

5 February   President Nyerere of Tanzania made his Arusha Declaration on African socialism.

8 February   Unsuccessful military coup in Sierra Leone.

23 March   Sir Albert Margai overthrown in military coup in Sierra Leone led by Brigadier-General Andrew Juxon-Smith.

4 April   Martin Luther King, Jr, called for an end to American involvement in Vietnam.

14 April   Lieutenant-Colonel Gnassingbe Eyadéma seized power in Togo.

17 April   Unsuccessful military coup in Ghana. The leaders were publicly executed on 9 May.

28 April   Muhammad Ali stripped of world heavyweight boxing championship by World Boxing Association following his refusal to join the US armed forces.

27 May   Military ruler, General Yakubu Gowon, declared a state of emergency and divided Nigeria into twelve states.

30 May   Biafra declared independence from Nigeria; recognized by Gabon, Haiti, Ivory Coast, Tanzania and Zambia. Anguilla seceded from St Kitts.

2–5 June   Rioting in Boston, Massachusetts.

11–13 June   Rioting in Tampa, Florida.

12 June   US Supreme Court declared Virginia state law against inter-racial marriage unconstitutional.

12–15 June   Rioting in Cincinnati, Ohio.

20 June   Muhammad Ali fined $10,000 and sentenced to five years imprisonment for refusing to serve in US armed forces.

27–30 June   Rioting in Buffalo, New York.

July   Black power activist, Michael X, became the first person to be prosecuted in Britain under the 1965 Race Relations Act for incitement to racial hatred.

5 July   Mutiny by European mercenaries in the Congo (now Zaïre) put down by Congolese National Army troops.

6 July   Nigerian troops attacked Biafra, opening a three-year civil war.

12–17 July   Rioting in Newark, New Jersey. Twenty-six people killed and over 1500 injured.

17–19 July   Rioting in Cairo, Illinois.

19–20 July   Rioting in Durham, North Carolina.

20 July   Rioting in Memphis, Tennessee.

20–23 July   First Black Power Conference in Newark, New Jersey, attended by over 1000 people.

23–30 July   Rioting in Detroit, Illinois. Forty-three people killed and over 2000 injured.

24–26 July   Rioting in Cambridge, Maryland.

30 July   Rioting in Milwaukee, Wisconsin.

17 August   Stokely Carmichael called on American blacks to launch an insurrection.

18 September   New Ugandan Constitution abolished traditional kingdoms.

2 October   Thurgood Marshall sworn in as the first black justice in the US Supreme Court.

28 October   Kenya and Somalia signed Arusha Declaration ending border war.

13 November   Carl B. Stokes became first black mayor of a major American city when he was sworn in as mayor of Cleveland, Ohio.

1 December   East African Community (established by treaty 6 June) came into existence.

17 December   Military coup in Dahomey (now Benin) led by Major Maurice Kouandété.

1968

8 February   Three black students demonstrating against segregation killed at South Carolina State College.

29 February   National Commission on Civil Disorders report blamed white racism for black riots in American cities.

19–21 March   Students occupied administration building at Howard University, Washington, DC, in demonstration for a curriculum relevant to black needs.

28 March   Rally in support of striking sanitation workers led by Martin Luther King, Jr, in Memphis, Tennessee, attacked by whites.

4 April   Martin Luther King, Jr, assassinated in Memphis, Tennessee. Forty-six people were killed in rioting which followed in 125 towns and cities.

18 April   Sierra Leone military government of Brigadier-General Andrew Juxon-Smith overthrown in a coup by army non-commissioned officers.

11 April   US President Johnson signed the 1968 Civil Rights Act (Fair Housing Act).

23–24 April   Black and white students at Columbia University occupied five buildings.

24 April   Black students at Boston University seized administration building in demonstration for Afro-American history courses.

26 April   Students at Ohio State University occupied administration building.

1 May   Caribbean Free Trade Association (CARIFTA) established.

11 May   Poor People's Campaign, a coalition representing blacks, Native Americans, Spanish-Americans and poor whites, arrived in Washington, DC, erecting Resurrection City.

18 June   US Supreme Court outlawed racial discrimination in renting and sale of housing.

19 June   Poor People's Campaign Solidarity Day March attracted 50,000 supporters in Washington, DC.

24 June   Over a hundred people arrested after refusing to close Resurrection City.

23–24 July   Eleven people died in rioting in Cleveland, Ohio.

27–28 July   Rioting in Gary, Indiana.

7 August   Three killed and hundreds injured in race riot in Miami.

26 August   Mutiny in Chad put down by French troops after appeal for assistance from President Tombalbaye.

4 September   President Massemba-Débat overthrown in a military coup in Congo.

6 September   Swaziland became independent.

October   Black power Rodney riots in Kingston, Jamaica.

12 October   Equatorial Guinea became independent.

16 October   US athletes John Carlos and Tommie Smith staged demonstration against racism in America at the Olympic Games in Mexico City.

5 November   Shirley Chisholm became the first black woman American Congressional representative.

19 November   President Modibo Keita of Mali replaced by a National Liberation Committee following a military coup led by Lieutenant Moussa Traoré.

14 December   Black Student Union and Third World Liberation Front demonstrations disrupt San Francisco State University classes.

1969

6 February   Anguilla declared independence from St Kitts following a referendum.

5 March   Equatorial Guinea foreign minister, Atanasio Ndongo, unsuccessfully attempted to seize power.

10 March   Unsuccessful coup attempt against President Sekou Touré of Guinea.

19 March   Invasion of Anguilla by British troops and police in 'Operation Sheepskin'.

19 April   A hundred armed black students occupied the Cornell University student union building in an anti-racism demonstration.

26 April   Black Manifesto demanding $500 million compensation for slavery issued in the USA by the Black Economic Development Conference.

5 June   Rioting in Hartford, Connecticut.

5 July   Kenyan Minister for Economic Planning and Development, Tom Mboya, assassinated in Nairobi.

19 July   Rioting in Cairo, Illinois.

31 July   Rioting in Baton Rouge, Louisiana.

30 August   Rioting in Fort Lauderdale, Florida.

1–5 September   Rioting in Hartford, Connecticut.

1 October   Restoration of civilian rule in Ghana.

8 October   Shooting between armed black youths and police in the West Side of Chicago.

14–18 October   Rioting in Springfield, Massachusetts.

15 October   President Abdirashid Ali Shirmake of Somalia assassinated in a coup by military and police officers.

21 October   Major-General Mohamed Siad Barre seized power in Somalia following assassination of President Abdirashid Ali Shirmake and renamed the country the Somali Democratic Republic.

29 October   US Supreme Court declared in *Alexander v. Holmes* that segregation in schools should end 'at once'.

31 October   Rioting in Jacksonville, Florida.

15 November   Tanzania and Zambia signed an agreement with China on the construction of the Tan-Zam Railway.

4 December   Chicago police killed two Black Panther leaders, Mark Clark and Fred Hampton.

10 December   President Zinsou of Dahomey (now Benin) overthrown in a military coup led by Colonel Maurice Kouandété.

19 December   President Milton Obote of Uganda wounded in an assassination attempt.

23 December   Popular Revolutionary Movement (MNR) declared the sole legal party in the Republic of Congo (now Zaïre).

1970
Census recorded black population of 22,600,000 (11.1 per cent) in USA.

2 January   FBI director J. Edgar Hoover reported that seven police officers had been killed and 120 injured in attacks by black activists over the past six months.

12 January   End of three-year civil war in Nigeria with the surrender of Biafra.

24 January   US army report said that the forces had 'a race problem because our country has a race problem'.

20 March   Successful student strike at the University of Michigan in support of increased numbers of black students.

21 April   Army mutiny in Trinidad as part of black power uprising.

24 April   The Gambia became a Republic within the Commonwealth.

12 May   Six blacks killed by police in rioting in Augusta, Georgia.

14 May   Two black students killed by police in demonstrations at Jackson State University, Mississippi.

21 May   Black and white students demonstrate at Ohio State University for more places for black students and against military training.

9 June   Ethiopia and Kenya signed a border agreement.

16 June   Rioting in Miami, Florida.

22 June   US President Nixon extended the 1965 Voting Rights Act to 1975.

4–8 July   Over 40 people shot during rioting in Asbury Park, New Jersey.

29 July   Rioting in Hartford, Connecticut.

3–7 August   Conference of African Peoples Congress in Atlanta, Georgia, attended by over 2000 representatives.

29–31 August   Armed clash between Black Panthers and police in Philadelphia, Pennsylvania. One police officer was killed and six injured.

5–7 September   Black Panther Party, Women's and Gay Liberation organizations hold Revolutionary People's Constitutional Convention in Philadelphia, Pennsylvania.

14–15 September   Armed clash between black militants and police in New Orleans. One black youth was killed.

5 November   Rioting over segregated education in Henderson, North Carolina.

7–9 November   Rioting in Daytona Beach, Florida.

26 November   Benjamin Oliver Davis, Sr, the first black American general, died in Chicago aged 93.

1971

François 'Papa Doc' Duvalier, Haitian politician, died.

4 January   US Congressional Black Caucus formed.

21 January   Twelve black US Congressmen boycotted President Nixon's State of the Union speech in protest against his attitude to black Americans.

25 January   Major-General Idi Amin ousted President Milton Obote of Uganda in military coup.

6–9 February   Rioting during black school boycott in Wilmington, North Carolina. Two people were killed.

8 March   US Supreme Court ruled against employment tests that effectively discriminated against black applicants.

22 March   Unsuccessful military coup against Prime Minister Siaka Stevens in Sierra Leone.

20 April   US Supreme Court declared bussing to achieve school integration constitutional.

28 April   Samuel Lee Gravely, Jr appointed first black US navy admiral.

5 May   Rioting in Brownsville, New York City, in protest against cuts in welfare and education spending.

18 May   US President rejected demands of Congressional Black Caucus for reforms to aid black Americans.

21–26 May   Rioting in Chattanooga, Tennessee.

13 June   Fighting between black and white American servicemen at Sheppard Air Force Base, Texas.

14 June   US Supreme Court declared that it was not discriminatory to close swimming pools and other public facilities to avoid desegregation.

16–20 June   Rioting in Jacksonville, Florida.

19–23 June   Rioting in Columbus, Georgia.

28 June   US Supreme Court quashed conviction of Muhammad Ali for refusing to serve in armed forces.

5 July   Unsuccessful coup attempt in Burundi.

6 July   Hastings Banda inaugurated as President for Life of Malawi.

11 July   Unsuccessful attempt to overthrow President Amin of Uganda by troops in the north east of the country.

26 July   US report showed that black Americans continued to lag behind whites in income and educational advance.

18 August   Police raid on Republic of New Africa headquarters in Jackson, Mississippi. One police officer was killed.

21 August   George Jackson shot in the back and killed in San Quentin Prison, California.

23 August   US House of Representatives Internal Security Committee reported that the Black Panthers were not capable of overthrowing the government by violence.

13 September   Forty-three prisoners, the majority of them black, killed in the storming of Attica State Prison, New York, following a five-day occupation and strike.

14–23 October   Rioting in Memphis, Tennessee.

27 October   Republic of Congo renamed Zaïre.

16 November   US President Nixon criticized by the Commission on Civil Rights for inadequate enforcement of civil rights laws.

18 December   People United to Save Humanity (PUSH) formed in Chicago by Revd Jesse Jackson.

1972

10–12 January   Rioting in Baton Rouge, Louisiana. Two black youths and two white deputy sheriffs were killed.

13 January   President Kofi Busia of Ghana deposed in military coup led by Lieutenant-Colonel Ignatius Kutu Acheampong.

25 January   Shirley Chisholm began campaigning for the US presidency.

4 April   Adam Clayton Powell, Jr, US House of Representatives member for Harlem from 1945–69, died.

7 April   Tanzanian vice-president, Sheikh Karume, assassinated.

19 April   Major-General Frederic E. Davidson became the first black American to command an army division when he was appointed head of the Eighth Infantry Division.

27 April   Kwame Nkrumah, former president of Ghana, died in exile in Guinea aged 62.

29 April   Hutu guerrillas in Burundi killed over 10,000 of the majority Tutsis in an attempted coup.

19 May   US National Education Association reported that over 30,000 black teachers had lost their jobs since 1954 as a result of school desegregation.

2 June   Former SNCC leader, H. Rap Brown, sentenced to five years imprisonment for a weapons offence.

4 June   Angela Davis acquitted of murder, kidnapping and conspiracy.

8 June   Bussing to achieve school integration in the USA postponed for 18 months.

29 June   US Supreme Court declared that the death penalty was a cruel and unusual punishment and so unconstitutional. Of the 600 awaiting execution, 329 were black.

17 September   One thousand supporters of deposed president, Milton Obote, invaded Uganda from Tanzania.

28 September   US Secretary of the Army rescinded dishonourable discharge imposed on 167 black American soldiers following the Brownsville Raid in 1906.

5 October   Tanzania and Uganda signed a peace treaty.

12–13 October   Clashes between black and white sailors on the US aircraft carrier *Kitty Hawk* off Vietnam.

26 October   Marxist–Leninist government under Lieutenant-Colonel Mathieu Kérékou seized power in Dahomey (later Benin).

16 November   Two black students killed at Baton Rouge, Louisiana, in clashes with police.

17 November   Andrew Young became the first black American elected to the US Congress from the Deep South since the Reconstruction period.

11 December   Chad and Nigeria signed treaty of co-operation and mutual assistance.

1973

20 January   Amilcar Lopes Cabral, leader of the African Party for the Independence of Guinea and Cape Verde (PAIGC), assassinated in Conakry.

3 March   Mali and Nigeria signed treaty of co-operation and mutual assistance.

29 May   Thomas Bradley elected mayor of Los Angeles, California.

5 July   President Kayibanda of Rwanda overthrown in military coup by Major-General Habyarimana.

10 July   Bahamas became independent.

15 August   National Black Feminist Organisation founded in New York City.

16 October   Maynard Jackson elected mayor of Atlanta, Georgia, the first black mayor of a major city in the southern USA.

6 November   Coleman Young elected mayor of Detroit, Michigan.

2 December   US District Court in San Francisco, California, ordered city authorities to introduce employment quota systems for minorities in the police and fire department.

1974

7 January   Unsuccessful military coup in Lesotho.

17 January   US Department of Health, Education and Welfare reported that race discrimination continued in Topeka, Kansas, schools 20 years after the landmark Supreme Court *Brown v. Board of Education* decision.

7 February   Grenada became independent.

26 February   Government of Emperor Haile Selassie of Ethiopia resigned following capture of Asmara by dissident troops.

24 March   Unsuccessful military coup against President Amin of Uganda.

15 April   President Hamani Diori of Niger overthrown in a military coup led by Lieutenant-Colonel Seyni Kountché.

19–27 May   Sixth Pan-African Congress held in Dar es Salaam, Tanzania.

10 September   Guinea-Bissau became independent.

12 September   Emperor Haile Selassie overthrown by a military coup in Ethiopia.

30 November   Dahomey (now Benin) declared a Marxist–Leninist state.

1975

25 February   Elijah Muhammad, leader of the Nation of Islam, died in Chicago aged 77.

28 February   Lomé Convention establishing economic co-operation between African states and the European Community signed in Togo.

13 April   President Ngarta Tombalbaye of the Chad Republic killed in a military coup and replaced by General Felix Malloum.

28 May   Treaty establishing the Economic Community of West African States signed.

25 June   Mozambique became independent.

5 July   Cape Verde became independent.

12 July   São Tomé and Príncipe became independent.

28 July   US House of Representatives voted to extend the 1965 Voting Rights Act a further seven years.

29 August   General Yakubu Gowon overthrown in Nigeria's third, bloodless, military coup and replaced by Brigadier Murtala Ramat Muhammed.

1 September   Daniel 'Chappie' James appointed first black American four-star general as Commander-in-Chief of the North American Air Defense Command.

29 September   First black American television station, WGPR–TV, opened in Detroit, Illinois.

11 November   Angola became independent.

30 November   The African state of Dahomey renamed the People's Republic of Benin.

1976

23 January   Paul Robeson, black American actor and civil rights activist, died in Philadelphia, Pennsylvania, at the age of 77.

13 February   Nigerian head of state, General Murtala Muhammed, assassinated in abortive military coup and replaced by Lieutenant Olusegun Obasanjo.

15 March   Unsuccessful military coup in Niger.

11 June   Unsuccessful attempt to assassinate President Amin of Uganda.

25 June   US Supreme Court ruled against right of private schools to exclude students on racial grounds.

28 August   Haile Selassie, former Emperor of Ethiopia, died in Addis Ababa at the age of 83.

9 October   Patriotic Front against white rule formed in Rhodesia (now Zimbabwe) by ZAPU and ZANU.

25 October   Pardon granted to Clarence Norris, the last of the Scottsboro Boys convicted of rape in 1931, by Governor George Wallace of Alabama.

1 November   President Michel Micombero of Burundi overthrown by Colonel Jean-Baptiste Bagaza in bloodless coup.

20 November   Angola, Mozambique, Tanzania and Zambia signed an agreement on regional defence co-operation.

4 December   President Bokassa of the Central African Republic proclaimed himself Emperor of the Central African Empire.

16 December   Andrew Young appointed US ambassador at the United Nations.

21 December   Patricia R. Harris became the first black woman US cabinet member when she was appointed Secretary of Housing and Urban Development.

1977

16 January   Mercenaries mounted an unsuccessful military coup in Benin.

3 February   Ethiopian military ruler Brigadier-General Teferi Benti killed and replaced by Lieutenant-Colonel Haile Mariam Mengistu.

11 February   Clifford Alexander, Jr appointed first black American Secretary of the Army.

8 March   Two thousand members of the Congolese National Liberation Front (FNLC) invaded Zaïre's Shaba Province from Angola.

18 March   President Marien Ngouabi of the Congo assassinated in a military coup and replaced by Colonel Yhombi-Opango.

1 April   Unsuccessful military coup in Chad.

14 April   William H. Hastie, the first black American to sit on the US Court of Appeals, died in Philadelphia, Pennsylvania, at the age of 71.

27 May   Unsuccessful pro-Soviet coup mounted in Angola by Nito Alves.

27 June   Djibouti became independent.

12 September   South African black consciousness leader, Steve Biko, died in police custody.

4 November   United Nations imposed mandatory embargo on arms trade with South Africa.

23 November   Forces of the illegal white Rhodesian regime attacked nationalist guerrilla bases at Tembue and Chimoio in Mozambique, killing over a thousand people.

1978

1 May   South African black consciousness Azanian People's Organisation (AZAPO) formed.

3 May   Three thousand members of the Congolese National Liberation Front (FNLC) invaded Zaïre's Shaba Province from Angola.

4 May   South African forces attacked South West African People's Organisation refugee camp in Angola.

9 May   President Kenneth Kaunda of Zambia awarded the Martin Luther King, Jr Non-Violent Peace Prize.

3 July   US Supreme Court upheld right of the Bell Telephone System to use quotas to end race and sex discrimination in employment.

6 August   Eleven died and 76 injured in a bomb explosion in a store in Salisbury (now Harare) the capital of Rhodesia (now Zimbabwe).

22 August   Jomo Kenyatta, President of Kenya, died aged 82.

18 October   Forces of the illegal white Rhodesian regime attacked nationalist guerrilla base in Mozambique, killing over 200 people.

27 October   Ugandan troops invaded Tanzania, occupying the Kagera salient.

3 November   Dominica became independent.

1979

January   Tanzanian forces and Ugandan political exiles invaded Uganda.

30 January   Frank E. Peterson, Jr appointed first black general in the US Marine Corps.

31 January   Ethiopia and Kenya signed treaty of co-operation and friendship.

13 February   Civil Rights Commission reported that 25 years after segregation was ruled illegal, 46 per cent of black American children were still attending racially segregated schools.

22 February   St Lucia became independent.

13 March   Grenadian government overthrown by the New Jewel Movement which formed a People's Revolutionary Government.

11 April   President Amin fled from Uganda following the fall of the capital Kampala.

15 May   Flight-Lieutenant Jerry Rawlings arrested following an unsuccessful coup attempt by junior and non-commissioned officers in Ghana.

16 May   Civil rights and trade-union activist Asa Philip Randolph died in New York aged 90.

1 June   Bishop Abel Muzowera became prime minister of 'Zimbabwe-Rhodesia' following elections in which the Popular Front refused to participate.

4 June   Flight-Lieutenant Jerry Rawlings seized power in a military coup in Ghana.

27 June   US Supreme Court declared in *Weber v. Kaiser Aluminium & Chemical Corporation* that unions and employers could set up programmes to assist minorities in work.

14 July   Demonstrations in Liberian capital, Monrovia, against increase in rice prices led by opposition Progressive Alliance of Liberia.

3 August   President Macías Nguema of Equatorial Guinea overthrown in a military coup by Colonel Teodoro Obiang Nguema Mbasogo.

10 September   President Agostinho Neto of Angola died and was succeeded by José Eduardo dos Santos. Lancaster House Conference on independence for 'Zimbabwe-Rhodesia' opened and continued until 15 December.

20 September   Emperor Bokassa of the Central African Empire overthrown by David Dacko in bloodless coup with French assistance.

24 September   Civilian rule restored in Ghana.

29 September   Ex-president Macías Nguema executed following his overthrow on 3 August.

1 October   Civilian rule restored in Nigeria.

12 October   Angola, Zaïre and Zambia signed a non-aggression pact.

27 October   St Vincent and the Grenadines became independent.

28 December   Cease-fire in Zimbabwe.

1980

Census recorded black population of 26,500,000 (11.7 per cent) in USA.

20 January   Rioting in Idabell, Oklahoma. Two people were killed.

4 March   ZANU–PF under Robert Mugabe won the first free elections in Zimbabwe.

2 April   Rioting in the St Paul's area of Bristol, England.

8 April   Rioting in Wrightsville, Georgia.

12 April   William R. Tolbert, Jr, president of Liberia, killed in non-commissioned officers' coup led by Master Sergeant Samuel K. Doe.

18 April   Zimbabwe became independent.

17–19 May   Rioting in Miami, Florida, following the acquittal of four white police who had killed a black man. Sixteen people were killed and over 300 injured.

23 May   Mozambique and Zimbabwe signed an agreement on military co-operation.

5–17 July   Rioting in Miami, Florida.

13 July   Botswana politician, Sir Seretse Khama, died aged 59.

14 November   President Luis Cabral of Guinea-Bissau overthrown in a coup led by prime minister João Vieira.

15 December   Milton Obote inaugurated as President of Uganda.

1981

2 March   Ten thousand-strong march in London organized by the New Cross Massacre Action Committee following death of 13 black youths in a house fire.

29 March   Eric Williams, historian and prime minister of Trinidad and Tobago, died in Port of Spain aged 69.

10–11 April   Rioting in Brixton, South London, following police anti-street crime Operation Swamp.

5 June   Niger and Somalia signed an agreement on co-operation.

29 June   Kenya and Somalia signed an agreement on co-operation.

3–7 July   Rioting in Toxteth, Liverpool, following alleged police harassment.

10 August   Following a national boycott organized by PUSH, Coca-Cola promised $34 million aid to American black businesses.

1 September   Central African Republic president, David Dacko, overthrown by General André Kolingba in a bloodless coup.

8 September   Roy Wilkins, executive director of NAACP, died in New York aged 80.

27 October   Andrew Young, former UN ambassador, elected mayor of Atlanta, Georgia.

1 November   Antigua and Barbuda became independent.

2 December   Kenya and Somalia signed a border agreement.

18 December   Robert Mugabe and ZANU Central Committee survived assassination attempt in bombing of party headquarters in Harare.

31 December   Flight-Lieutenant Jerry Rawlings seized power in Ghana in a military coup.

1982

February   The Gambia and Senegal united as Senegambia.

15 February   Mozambique and Tanzania signed agreement on economic and military co-operation.

5 July   US Supreme Court declared non-violent boycotts to achieve constitutional rights were protected by the free speech First Amendment to the Constitution.

1 August   Kenyan Air Force disbanded following attempted coup by non-commissioned officers in which 159 died.

6 November   Paul Biya succeeded to office of President of Cameroon.

7 November   Jean-Baptiste Ouédraogo appointed head of state following non-commissioned officers coup in Burkina Faso.

28–29 December   Rioting in Miami, Florida, after the shooting of an alleged black looter by police. Two people were killed and 27 injured.

1983

12 April   Harold Washington elected Mayor of Chicago, the first black mayor of a major US city.

20 May   Eighteen dead in a car bomb explosion in Pretoria, South Africa.

22 June   Louisiana repealed the last US racial classification laws under which anyone who had over a thirty-secondth 'Negro blood' was categorized as black.

4 August   Captain Thomas Sankara seized power in a military coup in Burkina Faso.

20 August   South African anti-apartheid umbrella organization, United Democratic Front, launched in Mitchells Plain, Cape Town.

19 September   St Christopher and Nevis became independent.

19 October   Maurice Bishop, Grenadian radical politician, executed.

25 October   Invasion of Grenada by USA, Jamaica and troops from five other Caribbean islands.

2 November   US President Ronald Reagan signed a bill establishing a federal holiday in honour of Martin Luther King, Jr.

31 December   Nigerian civilian government of President Shehu Shagari overthrown in fourth, bloodless, military coup led by Major-General Muhammadu Buhari.

1984

2 January   Major-General Muhammadu Buhari declared military Head of State in Nigeria.

14 January   Paul Biya elected as President of Cameroon.

16 March   Mozambique and South Africa signed Nkomati Accord on mutual non-aggression.

26 March   President Sekou Touré of Guinea died under surgery at the age of 62. Military Committee for National Recovery led by Colonel Lansana Conté and Colonel Diarra Traoré seized power.

6 April   Elite republican guard mounted an unsuccessful coup against President Paul Biya of Cameroon.

17 July   US study reported that the gap between average black and white American incomes was as wide as in 1960.

23 October   Malawi and Mozambique signed agreement on defence co-operation.

10 December   Benin, Ghana, Nigeria and Togo signed a co-operation agreement.

1985

7 January   US Supreme Court ruled that affirmative action for minorities to assist employment was lawful.

9 July   Chad and Zaïre signed an agreement on military co-operation.

27 July   President Obote of Uganda overthrown and replaced by a military council under General Tito Okello.

27 August   Major General Muhammadu Buhari ousted in military coup in Nigeria led by Major-General Ibrahim Babangida.

29 September   Rioting in Brixton, South London, following the shooting by police of Cherry Groce.

5 October   Rioting in Broadwater Farm, North London, following the death of Cynthia Jarrett during a police raid.

17 October   Attempted military coup in Guinea-Bissau.

November   Death of four children in demonstration against food shortages provoked a revolt that ousted President Jean Claude 'Baby Doc' Duvalier of Haiti in February 1986.

12 November   Over 600 killed in Liberia in unsuccessful military coup against President Samuel Doe led by former Brigadier-General Thomas Quiwonkpa.

25 December   Six-day war began between Mali and Algeria over the disputed Agacher strip.

1986

10 January   Military ruler General Babangida announced that civilian rule would be restored in Nigeria in October 1990.

20 January   Bishop Desmond Tutu awarded the Martin Luther King, Jr Non-Violent Peace Prize for his anti-apartheid activity. Chief Leabua Jonathan of Lesotho deposed in military coup led by Major-General Justin Lekhanya.

29 January   Yoweri Museveni inaugurated as President of Uganda on capture of the capital, Kampala, by National Resistance Army forces.

February   President Jean Claude Duvalier of Haiti fled to Europe following demonstrations against him.

25 April   Mswati III became King of Swaziland.

2 July   US Supreme Court declared affirmative action in employment constitutional.

30 September   Edward Perkins appointed the first black American ambassador to South Africa.

19 October   President Samora Machel of Mozambique killed in an air crash in South Africa and replaced by Joaquim Chissano.

November   Referendum in the Central African Republic approved the establishment of a one-party state.

1987

January   Ugandan government forces killed 350 Uganda People's Front opponents in the battle of Corner Kilak.

24 January   Over 20,000 black and white demonstrators marched against racism in Georgia, the largest such event since the 1960s.

19 February   Rioting in Tampa, Florida, following the killing of a black man by police.

26 February   Edgar Daniel Nixon, black American civil rights activist, died in Montgomery, Alabama, aged 87.

June   Zimbabwean government announced end of separate white representation in the House of Assembly.

11 June   Diane Abbott, Paul Boateng and Bernie Grant elected first British Members of Parliament of African descent.

11 July   Nigerian military government postponed restoration of civilian rule from October 1990 to 1992.

30 July   Sixty-eight injured in an alleged African National Congress bomb explosion near a military barracks in Johannesburg, South Africa. Police admitted they were responsible in July 1996.

24 August   Bayard Rustin, black American civil rights activist and organizer of the 1963 March on Washington, died in New York City aged 75.

15 October   Thomas Sankara, Head of the Military Council of the Revolution, assassinated in a military coup and replaced by Captain Blaise Compaoré in Burkina Faso.

25 November   Harold Washington, the first black mayor of Chicago, Illinois (elected in 1983 and 1987), died.

1 December   James Baldwin, black American writer and civil rights activist, died in France aged 63.

15 December   Septima Pointsetta Clark, black American civil rights activist, died in South Carolina aged 89.

31 December   Robert Mugabe succeeded Canaan Banana and became Zimbabwe's first executive president.

1988

19 February   Black students demonstrated against racism at the University of Massachusetts. Fourteen died in bomb explosion in Nairobi, Kenya.

15 March   Eugene Antonio Marino appointed Archbishop of Atlanta, Georgia, the first black American Roman Catholic archbishop.

16 March   US President Reagan vetoed a Civil Rights Restoration Bill.

22 March President Reagan's vetoing of the Civil Rights Restoration Bill overturned by US Congress.

7 April Protest riots in Nigeria against fuel price increases.

24 April Paul Biya re-elected as president of Cameroon.

19 June President Leslie Manigat of Haiti overthrown by General Henri Namphy.

20 July Jesse Jackson came second in the Democratic nomination for US president with 1218.5 delegates.

27 August Over 50,000 marched in Washington, DC, to celebrate the 25th anniversary of the 1963 March on Washington.

18 September General Henri Namphy replaced as head of military government in Haiti by Lieutenant-General Avril Prosper.

1989

23 January US Supreme Court declared setting aside contracts for minority owned businesses unconstitutional.

10 February Ronald Brown became the first black American to head a major political party when he was elected chairman of the Democratic National Committee.

6 March US Supreme Court declared against affirmative action policies in Florida and Michigan.

9 March Vere Bird elected as prime minister of Antigua and Barbuda for fourth successive term.

30 April Opposition Zimbabwe Unity Movement formed by Edgar Tekere.

3 May Ban on political activity lifted in Nigeria.

16 May Governing New Democratic Party won all 15 House of Assembly seats in St Vincent elections.

10 August General Colin L. Powell became the first black American to be appointed chairman of the Joint Chiefs of Staff.

22 August Huey P. Newton, co-founder of the Black Panther Party, shot dead in Oakland, California, aged 47.

26 August Over 25,000 people re-enacted the 1917 NAACP march in Washington, DC, to protest against the US Supreme Court's undermining of affirmative action.

28 August Rioting in Vineland, New Jersey, following the killing of a black man by police.

31 August Demonstrations in Brooklyn, New York, following the death of a black 16 year old.

September Attempted military coup in Ghana.

3 September Violent clashes between black students and police in Virginia Beach, Virginia.

7 October Two government-sponsored political parties – the Social Democratic Party and the National Republican Convention - formed in Nigeria.

1 November Elections held for the Namibia Constituent Assembly.

5 November   Monument to the martyrs of the Civil Rights Movement dedicated in Montgomery, Alabama.

7 November   David Dinkins elected as the first black American mayor of New York City. Lawrence Douglas Wilder elected the first black American governor of Virginia.

December   The People's Republic of Benin renounced Marxism–Leninism as a state ideology.

24 December   Invasion of Liberia by rebel National Patriotic Front forces began a civil war. Ernest Nathan Morial, the first black American mayor of New Orleans, died aged 60.

31 December   Senegambia (formed in 1981) dissolved into separate states of The Gambia and Senegal.

1990

Census recorded black population of 26,500,000 (11.7 per cent) in USA.

10 January   Marcelite J. Harris appointed the first black woman American general in the US Air Force.

2 February   Ban lifted on over 60 opposition organizations in South Africa including the African National Congress, the Pan-Africanist Congress and the Communist Party.

10 February   Sam Nujoma elected president of South West Africa (Namibia).

11 February   Nelson Mandela released from prison after serving 27 years with other leading anti-apartheid activists.

March   Robert Mugabe re-elected president of Zimbabwe with 78 per cent of the vote.

10 March   President Prosper of Haiti replaced by Ertha Pascal-Trouillot and a Council of State.

21 March   Namibia became independent.

26 March   Negotiations between the African National Congress and the South African government threatened by police killing of eleven black demonstrators in Sebokeng.

17 April   Ralph D. Abernathy, civil rights leader, died in Atlanta, Georgia, aged 64.

22 April   Attempted military coup in Nigeria.

24 April   President Mobutu of Zaïre announced gradual transition to multi-party democracy.

23 May   Rioting in Gabon following assassination of opposition leader, Joseph Randjambe.

24 May   Over 100 killed in demonstrations against Babangida regime in Nigeria.

25 June   Student pro-democracy demonstrations in Lusaka, Zambia.

30 June   Attempted military coup in Zambia.

July   The ruling Congolese Parti Congolais du Travail abandoned Marxism–Leninism and its monopoly of power.

7 July   Twenty killed in rioting following police attack on pro-democracy rally in Nairobi, Kenya.

27 July   Thirty killed in attempted coup by Black Muslim militants in Trinidad and Tobago.

22 August   Referendum in São Tomé and Príncipe voted 71.9 per cent in favour of multi-party democracy.

24 August   Four thousand-strong ECOWAS peacekeeping force (Ghana, Guinea, The Gambia, Nigeria, Sierra Leone) deployed in Liberia.

3 September   Civil war began in Rwanda.

11 September   President Samuel Doe of Liberia killed by rebels.

16 September   First multi-party elections in Gabon since 1964.

1 October   Tutsi Rwandan Patriotic Front launched an invasion of Rwanda from Uganda.

5 October   Four killed in demonstrations for an end to one-party rule in Lomé, Togo.

22 October   US president, George Bush, vetoed the Civil Rights Bill supporting employment quotas.

28 October   Ali Hassan Mwinyi re-elected president of Tanzania. First multi-party presidential elections in Côte d'Ivoire since independence in 1960.

November   King Moshoeshoe III of Lesotho deposed by his son Letsie III.

14 November   South West Africa People's Organisation candidates won 41 of 72 seats in the pre-independence Constituent Assembly.

15 November   President Ali Saibou of Niger announced legalization of political parties following a five-day general strike.

30 November   Mozambique adopted multi-party democracy and the free market under a new constitution.

1 December   President Habré of Chad overthrown by the Patriotic Salvation Front (MPS) under Colonel Idriss Deby.

4 December   Multi-party system instituted in Zambia for the first time since 1973.

16 December   Father Jean-Bertrand Aristide elected president of Haiti.

1991

29 January   A study reported that a majority of black Americans preferred the term black rather than African American.

13 February   Opposition National Democratic Party formed in Kenya by Oginga Odinga.

March   President Traoré of Mali overthrown in a military coup by Lieutenant-Colonel Touré.

4 April   Nicéphore Soglo inaugurated as president of Benin.

30 April   Major-General Justin Lekhanya overthrown by Colonel Elias Ramaema in a military coup in Lesotho.

April   Over 200 killed in rioting between Christians and Muslims in northern Nigeria.

Ruling Popular Movement for the Liberation of Angola (MPLA) abandoned Marxism–Leninism and became a social democratic party.

May   Independent Republic of Somaliland declared independence from Somalia.

31 May　Estoril Accord ended 16-year civil war in Angola.

June　Ruling Zimbabwe African National Union formally abandoned Marxism–Leninism and removed references to 'scientific socialism' from the party constitution.

5 June　Repeal of Land and Group Areas Act began the end of apartheid in South Africa.

7 July　Oliver Tambo replaced as president of the African National Congress by Nelson Mandela.

August　Forum for the Restoration of Democracy (FORD) formed by opposition groupings in Kenya.

7 August　African National Congress announced end of 30-year armed struggle against the South African apartheid regime.

30 September　President Aristide of Haiti overthrown in military coup.

November　President Kaunda replaced by Frederick Chilumba in the first multi-party elections in Malawi for 23 years.

December　President Compaoré of Burkina Faso returned in elections boycotted by opposition parties.

20 December　Convention on a Democratic South Africa (CODESA) representing 19 parties began meeting in Johannesburg.

1992

18 January　Opposition Democratic Party formed in Kenya by former minister, Mwai Kibanki.

8 March　Seven Roman Catholic prelates arrested in Malawi after criticizing corruption and human rights violations of President Banda.

2 April　General strike in Kenya called by the Forum for the Restoration of Democracy (FORD) demanding release of political prisoners and multi-party elections.

28 April　Ghanaians voted for multi-party democracy in a referendum. Alpha Oumar Konaré elected president of Mali.

29 April　Rioting began in Los Angeles when four police officers videoed beating a black man were acquitted. Federal troops deployed after 52 people died and over 500 buildings were destroyed. Sierra Leone government overthrown by Captain Valentine Strasser in a military coup.

6–7 May　Hundreds arrested during protest demonstrations in Blantyre and Lilongwe against the regime of President Banda of Malawi.

13 May　Two-day general strike began in Lagos against the rule of Nigerian President Babangida.

16 June　African National Congress began a 'mass action' campaign to remove President de Klerk from power.

17 June　Forty people killed in South African township of Boipatong by Inkatha Freedom Party supporters.

4 July　National Assembly elections in Nigeria won by the government-sponsored Social Democratic Party against the government-sponsored National Republican Convention.

3 August   Four million black workers supported two-day general strike against the white government called by the Congress of South African Trade Unions.

7 August   Truce called in Mozambique civil war between the government and National Resistance Movement (RENAMO) forces.

16 August   Pascal Lissouba elected president of the Congo Republic.

19 August   Free National Movement won elections in the Bahamas ending 19 years of Progressive Liberal Party rule.

29 September   Elections in Angola. Results announced on 17 October.

10 October   Paul Biya re-elected president of Cameroon.

13 October   Kenyan opposition party Forum for the Restoration of Democracy (FORD) split into FORD-Asili and FORD-Kenya.

17 October   President dos Santos re-elected in Angola with 49.8 per cent of the vote. His opponent, Jonas Savimbi took 40.1 per cent.

20 October   Constitutional Amendment Act opened way for entry of black South Africans to the cabinet. West African peacekeeping force bombarded rebel forces in Buchanan, Liberia.

30 October   A thousand killed in fighting between the MPLA government and opposition UNITA forces in Angola following disputed election results.

3 November   Carol Moseley Braun elected the first black woman American senator.

4 November   Flight-Lieutenant Jerry Rawlings elected president of Ghana with 58.5 per cent of the vote. Rioting by opposition supporters.

9 December   US Marines landed in Somalia to protect UN airlift of food aid to population in civil war.

29 December   President Daniel arap Moi returned to office in first multi-party elections in Kenya for 26 years with 1.9 million votes against a divided opposition total of 3.3 million.

1993

1 January   President Banda of Malawi promised to hold a referendum on an end to one-party rule.

4 January   Nigerian Transitional Council under Ernest Shonekan sworn in. Kenyan opposition parties Forum for the Restoration of Democracy (FORD), FORD-Asili, FORD-Kenya and the Democratic Party formed a united front.

14 January   High Council of the Republic in Zaïre declared President Mobutu guilty of treason for dissolving cabinet.

20 February   First black members of South African cabinet appointed by President de Klerk.

21 February   Abdou Diouf re-elected president of Senegal.

3 March   Mahamane Ousmane elected president of Niger. Miguel Trovoada elected president of São Tomé and Príncipe.

4 March   President Chiluba declared State of Emergency in Zambia following alleged plot by opposition United National Independence Party to seize power.

30 March   People's National Party returned to power in Jamaican elections in which 13 people were killed.

10 April   Chris Hani, South African Communist Party leader and ANC executive member, assassinated.

22 May   Issaias Afewerki elected president of Eritrea.

24 May   Eritrea became independent from Ethiopia following a referendum on 24 April.

25 May   State of Emergency imposed on 4 March in Zambia lifted.

1 June   Melchior Ndadaye elected president of Burundi.

12 June   Election for civilian president in Nigeria won by Chief Moshood Abiola of the Social Democratic Party but the military government refused to announce result.

16 June   Malawi electorate voted in referendum for end to one-party state.

23 June   Nigerian military government declared presidential elections invalid.

25 August   Demonstrations in Lagos demanding end to military rule in Nigeria.

26 August   Nigerian military ruler, Major-General Ibrahim Babangida, handed power to interim president, Ernest Shonekan.

8 September   Nineteen dead and 22 injured in a shooting at the Wadeville industrial area, Johannesburg, South Africa.

22 September   Thirty-one killed in a 'Day of Terror' as South African Parliament began discussing establishing a Transitional Council.

25 October   Nigeria Airways plane hijacked by the Movement for the Advancement of Democracy.

17 November   Nigerian interim president, Ernest Shonekan, replaced by General Sani Abacha. Political parties banned. Restoration of civilian rule delayed until August 1993.

3 December   President Félix Houphouet-Boigny of Côte d'Ivoire died at the age of 88.

1994
3 January   Five hundred Nigerian troops occupied Diamond Island and Djabane, Cameroonian islands in the Gulf of Guinea. Negotiations led to joint military patrols from 6 January.

5 January   Forty were killed in an unsuccessful assassination attempt on President Gnassingbe Eyadéma of Togo in the capital, Lomé.

10 January   Ugandan rebel Lord's Resistance Army offered to surrender in return for resettlement aid.

14 January   Fighting between rival political factions in the Royal Lesotho Defence Force.

16 January   Pan-Africanist Congress announced the end of its armed struggle in South Africa.

20 January   Veteran Kenyan politician, Oginga Odinga, died in Kisumu at the age of 82.

3 February   A thousand people died and 150,000 were displaced in a week of clashes in northern Ghana between the Konkomba and Namumba ethnic groups.

22–25 February   Ten killed in clashes between security forces and opposition demonstrators in Libreville, Gabon.

10 March   President Mangope forced to resign in the South African 'homeland' of Bophuthatswana.

25 March   Attempted assassination of President Gnassingbe Eyadéma of Togo.

6 April   Presidents Juvénal Habyarimana of Rwanda and Cyprien Ntaryamira of Burundi killed in an air crash at Kigali airport.

26 April   State of Emergency declared in Dominica following anti-government strikes and protests.

26–29 April   South Africa's first multi-racial elections ended over 350 years of white domination.

10 May   Nelson Mandela inaugurated as president of South Africa with Thabo Mbeki as first deputy-president.

11 May   First multi-racial cabinet appointed in South Africa.

17 May   President Hastings Banda of Malawi was defeated in elections which ended 30 years of one-party rule. National Democratic Coalition formed in Nigeria.

23 June   Moshod Abiola, reputed winner of the 1993 Nigerian presidential elections, arrested for treason after calling for an uprising.

4 July   Three months oil workers' strike against the Abacha regime began in Nigeria.

23 July   President Sir Dawda Kairaba Jawara of The Gambia overthrown in a bloodless coup and replaced by Lieutenant Yahya Jammeh.

5 October   Anti-government demonstrations in the Equatorial Guinea capital of Malabo.

15 October   Jean-Bertrand Aristide restored to power as president of Haiti, three years after a military coup.

28 October   Joaquim Chissano re-elected president of Mozambique.

10 November   Unsuccessful coup in The Gambia against the new Provisional Ruling Council of Patriotic Armed Forces.

16 November   Peace accord signed between MPLA government in Angola and opposition UNITA forces.

17 November   Bomb exploded at Lagos International Airport, Nigeria.

December   South West Africa People's Organisation won overwhelming victory in Namibia's first post-independence elections.

5 December   Eritrea alleged that Sudan was training anti-government guerrillas and broke diplomatic relations.

8 December   Ethiopia adopted a new federal constitution guaranteeing the right of any area to secede.

11 December   Trial began of former Ethiopian president Mengistu and 72 other Dergue members on charges of crimes against humanity.

1995

25 January　President Chiluba of Zambia ordered all ministers to declare their assets and liabilities in an anti-corruption drive.

20 February　Former President Kenneth Kaunda arrested for holding an illegal political meeting.

March　President Moi of Kenya accused Uganda of attempting to destabilize the country by supporting the dissident February 18 Popular Resistance Army.

18 March　US lobbying organization TransAfrica criticized Nigerian military regime for human rights abuses.

5 April　Ethiopia and Eritrea signed agreement to establish an economic and customs union.

25 April　Restoration of civilian rule in Nigeria delayed indefinitely by military ruler, General Sani Abacha.

May　Ethiopian People's Revolutionary Democratic Front (EPRDF) won majority of seats in elections to the Council of People's Representatives.

7 May　A new opposition party, Safina, was formed in Kenya.

11 May　Five people killed in protests in Accra, Ghana, against increases in taxes.

12 June　US Supreme Court ruling in *Adarand Constructors Inc. v. Federico Peno, Secretary of Transportation et al.* weakened affirmative action employment programmes.

28 June　Former president, Kenneth Kaunda, of Zambia elected president of the opposition United National Independence Party (UNIP).

1 July　People's Action Movement lost elections to the Labour Party in St Christopher and Nevis after 15 years in office.

30 July　Opposition Zambia Democratic Congress (ZDC) formed.

17 August　British Caribbean colony of Bermuda voted in a referendum to remain a Crown dependency by 73.7 per cent to 25.6 per cent.

19 August　Abuja Accord brought temporary cessation in Liberian civil war.

22 August　Republic of Ethiopia formally proclaimed.

15 September　Herero demonstration outside the German Embassy in Windhoek, Namibia, demanding compensation for massacres carried out by German colonial forces from 1896–1905.

2 October　Leading Kenyan opposition figure, Koigi wa Wamwere, imprisoned for allegedly attempting to steal weapons.

8 October　Three members of the armed dissident group, Chimwenje, were arrested for plotting the assassination of President Mugabe of Zimbabwe.

15 October　Zimbabwean opposition leader, Revd Ndabaningi Sithole, arrested in connection with a plot to assassinate President Mugabe.

16 October　Million Man March on Washington, DC, organized by the Nation of Islam. Estimates of numbers participating ranged from 400,000 to over a million.

1 November   African National Congress (ANC) candidates took two-thirds of the votes in South African local elections.

7 November   People's National Movement and United National Congress tied in Trinidad and Tobago elections, giving the National Alliance for Reconstruction the balance of power.

30 November   Opponents of President Moi of Kenya announced the formation of an Opposition Alliance.

5 December   Mozambique admitted to the Commonwealth.

14 December   Rioting in Brixton, South London, following death of Wayne Douglas in police custody.

17 December   Eritrean and Yemeni forces clashed in dispute over the Red Sea island of Greater Hanish.

1996

16 January   President Valentine Strasser of Sierra Leone overthrown in a military coup and replaced by Brigadier-General Julius Maada Bio.

20 January   President Mahamane Ousmane of Niger overthrown in a military coup and replaced by Colonel Ibrahim Barre Mainassara.

22 January   Week-long general strike for democracy led by the Federation of Trade Unions began in Swaziland.

28 January   Rioting in Jerusalem by Ethiopian immigrants following reports that Israeli health authorities routinely destroyed blood donated by Ethiopians.

2 February   Unsuccessful military coup in Guinea against President Lansana Conté.

3–4 February   Clashes between Cameroonian and Nigerian soldiers in the disputed Bakassi peninsula.

14–19 February   Five civilians killed by soldiers mutinying over unpaid wages in the Congo capital, Brazzaville.

16 February   South African Supreme Court ordered the predominantly white Potgietersrus Primary School to admit black pupils in a landmark post-apartheid ruling. King Mswati III of Swaziland promised new constitution following January general strike.

20 February   Further clashes between Cameroonian and Nigerian soldiers in the disputed Bakassi peninsula following a cease-fire.

25 February   President Teodoro Obiang Nguema of Equatorial Guinea re-elected with 99 per cent of the vote after five opposition candidates withdrew from the election.

March   Lord's Resistance Army guerrillas killed over 200 people in attacks in northern Uganda.

17 March   Ahmad Kabbah elected as first civilian president of Sierra Leone for 30 years with 59 per cent of the vote.

18 March   Robert Mugabe re-elected as president of Zimbabwe following withdrawal of opposition candidates Bishop Abel Muzowera and Revd Ndabaningi Sithole.

21 March   Mathieu Kérékou and Nicéphore Soglo both claimed to have been elected president of Benin.

29 March   Sierra Leone returned to civilian rule under President Ahmad Tejan Kabbah.

11 April   Treaty of Pelindaba making Africa a nuclear-free zone signed by all African states.

14 April   Former Nigerian president, Nnamdi Benjamin ('Zik') Azikiwe, died at the age of 91.

18–20 April   Twelve killed in Central African Republic during army mutiny over unpaid wages.

9 May   President Yoweri Museveni of Uganda overwhelmingly re-elected. White National Party withdrew from South African Government of National Unity with the African National Congress (ANC).

19 May   Army uprising in Central African Republic put down in six days with the assistance of French troops.

3 June   Major-General Tito Lutwa Okello, chairman of the military council in Uganda from 1985–6, died at the age of 82.

4 June   Kudirat Olayinka Abiola, wife of the imprisoned victor in the 1993 Nigerian presidential elections Chief Moshood Abiola, murdered.

10 July   Rioting in Niger capital, Niamey, following election victory of General Ibrahim Barre Mainassara after placing opposition candidates under house arrest.

12–13 July   Lord's Resistance Army guerrillas massacred 91 Sudanese at refugee camps in northern Uganda.

25 July   President Sylvestre Ntibantunganya of Burundi overthrown by Pierre Buyoya (president from 1987–93) who banned political parties.

1 August   Somali National Alliance leader Mohammed Farah Aidid killed in renewed fighting in Mogadishu.

16 August   ECOWAS peace plan accepted by main faction leaders in Liberia.

17 September   Soufriere Hill volcano erupted on Caribbean island of Montserrat, forcing evacuation of the south.

26 September   Civil rule restored in the Gambia following election of Yahya Jammeh as president.

19 October   Zaïrean army and Hutu militia attack on Banyamulenge Tutsis opened civil war in east of the country.

3 November   Former Central African Republic president Jean-Bedel Bokassa died.

7 December   President Jerry Rawlings of Ghana re-elected with 57.2 per cent of the vote.

10 December   President Nelson Mandela signed the new South African Constitution in Sharpeville.

1997

1 January   Kofi Annan installed as first black African United Nations Secretary-General.

13 January   US President Clinton awarded the Congressional Medal of Honor for bravery in World War II to seven black servicemen, only one of whom – Vernon Baker – was still alive.

≡ INDEX ≡

For reasons of space, many leaders and parties do not have individual entries in this index. They can be found under the appropriate country in the Political Parties and Leaders section.

NATIONAL UNIVERSITY
LIBRARY SACRAMENTO

7740